UNEASY ALLIANCE

Recent Titles in
Contributions to the Study of World History

Prophecy of Berchán: Irish and Scottish High-Kings of the Early Middle Ages
Benjamin T. Hudson

Assimilation and Acculturation in Seventeenth-Century Europe: Roussillon and France,
1659–1715
David Stewart

Town Origins and Development in Early England, c.400–950 A.D.
Daniel G. Russo

The Identity of Geneva: The Christian Commonwealth, 1564–1864
John B. Roney and Martin I. Klauber, editors

Losing a Continent: France's North American Policy, 1753–1763
Frank W. Brecher

"Gone Native" in Polynesia: Captivity Narratives and Experiences from the South Pacific
I. C. Campbell

The Jacobean Union: A Reconsideration of British Civil Policies under the Early Stuarts
Andrew D. Nicholls

Ireland's Children: Quality of Life, Stress, and Child Development in the Famine Era
Thomas E. Jordan

In Search of Woodrow Wilson: Beliefs and Behavior
Robert M. Saunders

Opposition Beyond the Water's Edge: Liberal Internationalists, Pacifists and Containment,
1945–1953
E. Timothy Smith

Ethnic Cleansing in the USSR, 1937–1949
J. Otto Pohl

Populist Nationalism: Republican Insurgency and American Foreign Policy Making,
1918–1925
Karen A. J. Miller

UNEASY ALLIANCE
Relations Between Russia and Kazakhstan in the Post-Soviet Era, 1992–1997

Mikhail Alexandrov

Contributions to the Study of World History, Number 66

GREENWOOD PRESS
Westport, Connecticut • London

Library of Congress Cataloging-in-Publication Data

Alexandrov, Mikhail, 1960–
    Uneasy alliance : relations between Russia and Kazakhstan in
the post-Soviet era, 1992–1997 / Mikhail Alexandrov.
      p. cm.—(Contributions to the study of world history, ISSN
0885–9159 ; no. 66)
    Includes bibliographical references and index.
    ISBN 0–313–30965–5 (alk. paper)
    1. Russia (Federation)—Relations—Kazakhstan. 2.
Kazakhstan—Relations—Russia (Federation) I. Title. II. Series.
DK68.7.K3 A44   1999
303.48′24705845—dc21   98–45028

British Library Cataloguing in Publication Data is available.

Library of Congress Catalog Card Number: 98–45028
ISBN: 0–313–30965–5
ISSN: 0885–9159

First published in 1999

Greenwood Press, 88 Post Road West, Westport, CT 06881
An imprint of Greenwood Publishing Group, Inc.
www.greenwood.com

Printed in the United States of America

The paper used in this book complies with the
Permanent Paper Standard issued by the National
Information Standards Organization (Z39.48–1984).

10 9 8 7 6 5 4 3 2 1

Contents

Tables and Maps   vii

Introduction   ix

Chapter 1   Emergence of Independent Kazakhstan   1

Chapter 2   Formulation of Russian Policy Towards   57
                 Kazakhstan

Chapter 3   Problem of Ethnic Russians in Kazakhstan   99

Chapter 4   Russian and Kazakh Approaches to CIS   155
                 Integration

Chapter 5   Relations Between Russia and Kazakhstan in   203
                 the Military and Strategic Spheres

Chapter 6   Russia and International Competition for   259
                 Kazakhstan's Energy Resources

Appendix   309

Index   321

Tables and Maps

TABLES

Table 1.1	Population of Kazakhstan by Nationality (1989 census)	24
Table 2.1	Reserves and Production of Strategic Minerals in USSR (1991)	66
Table 3.1	Number of Kazakh and Russian Language Secondary Schools in Kazakhstan (1989–1996)	103
Table 3.2	Distribution of Pupils in Secondary Schools in Kazakhstan as per Language of Study (1991–1996)	104
Table 3.3	Regions of Kazakhstan with Russian Majority or Plurality (1995)	111
Table 3.4	Reasons for Emigration from Kazakhstan	114
Table 3.5	Reasons for Emigration from Kazakhstan	114
Table 3.6	Reasons for Emigration from Kazakhstan	115
Table 6.1	Gas Production in Kazakhstan (1991–1996)	294
Table 6.2	Oil Production in Kazakhstan (1991–1996)	295
Table A.1	Population of Kazakhstan by Nationality (1897–1989)	310
Table A.2	Agricultural Development of Kazakhstan (1906–1985)	311
Table A.3	Production of Some Industrial Commodities in Kazakhstan (1913–1985)	312

Table A.4   Education in Kazakhstan (1914–1985)   313

Table A.5   Medical Care in Kazakhstan (1914–1985)   313

Table A.6   Agricultural Development of Kazakhstan (1985–1995)   314

Table A.7   Production of Major Industrial Commodities in   315
             Kazakhstan (1985–1995)

MAPS

Map A.1   Kazakhstan on the Verge of Accession to the Russian   316
           State

Map A.2   Administrative Borders of Kazakhstan at the End of   317
           the Nineteenth Century

Map A.3   Kazakhstan: Ethnic-Geographical Division   318

Map A.4   Cosmodrome Baykonur   319

Map A.5   Kazakhstan: Major Military Objects Rented by Russia   320

Introduction

The collapse of the Soviet Union created a new geopolitical reality on the vast spaces of Eurasia. Instead of one superpower, fifteen new independent states emerged, each with its own national identity, problems and policies. Kazakhstan was the second largest republic of the former Union of Soviet Socialist Republic (USSR) and consequently the second largest new independent state, after the Russian Federation, to appear in the wake of the USSR's collapse. The economic and geostrategic importance of this new player on the international scene can hardly be exaggerated. Possessing huge valuable mineral resources, including large deposits of oil and gas, Kazakhstan is the focal point of a major diplomatic struggle between world powers that includes the United States, Russia, the European Union and China, and important regional countries such as Iran and Turkey.

Kazakhstan's relations with Russia, the former imperial power that controlled various regions of Kazakhstan for more than two centuries, is of interest both academically and politically. Undoubtedly, Russian-Kazakh relations are of exceptional importance for Kazakhstan's development as a new independent state and for the geostrategic situation in Eurasia in the twenty-first century. In other words, maintaining existing geopolitical equilibrium on the Eurasian mainland depends to a large degree on Russian-Kazakh relations and whether Kazakhstan survives as an independent state.

Western and Russian books on postindependence Central Asia have tended to concentrate on broad, regional issues such as Russian policy on Central Asia or the Commonwealth of Independent States (CIS) as a whole, or the political and economic development of the Central Asian States, touching only briefly on specific issues such as Russian-Kazakh relations. Research on that issue is rare and consists mainly of articles, reports and essays published in journals or collective works. Some of these publications have substantial academic value, but they usually address narrow issues of Russian-Kazakh relations, cover short time frames, and do not depict or draw conclusions about the relationship as a whole. So far, only one book (by T. Mansurov, Kazakhstan's ambassador to Moscow[1]) has been devoted entirely to post-independence Russian-Kazakh relations. It is an academic representation of Kazakhstan's official position and is valuable mainly for its collection of factual material, which is useful to other scholars.

This book discusses Russian-Kazakh relations after the collapse of the USSR, primarily the period 1992–1997. Chapter 1 provides the background of the relationship. It examines the period 1985–1991, the last years of the USSR, known as Gorbachev's perestroika. During the Gorbachev period, certain processes in Russian-Kazakh relations were initiated that developed a new stage after independence and will influence the nature of the relationship for many years to come.

Chapter 2 examines the evolution of Russian political thinking on issues of relations with Kazakhstan and Central Asia in the first year after the break up of the USSR. It shows how new geopolitical concepts provided a source for the formulation of Russia's post-Soviet policy towards Kazakhstan. The remaining four chapters analyse four major problems in Russian-Kazakh relations.

Chapter 3 looks at the status of the Russian community in Kazakhstan. It analyses such issues as the Kazakh leadership's policy of nation-state building and its effects on Kazakhstan's Russian population and on relations between the two countries. While exploring this problem the term "Russian" is used in an extended fashion, to include not only ethnic Russians, but people who associate themselves with the Russian cultural heritage. An accepted term in Russia for this group is "Russian-speaking", but the term is not entirely accurate, because many Kazakhs, especially in the political elite, are Russian-speakers. Generally, this group includes other Slavs — Ukrainians and Belorussians — as well as some ethnic Germans.

Chapter 4 compares Kazakh and Russian attitudes towards economic and political integration of the post-Soviet space. This issue is important for two reasons. First, it indicates the extent of cooperation and the level of trust between the two countries. Second, as the two major players among post-Soviet states, Russia and Kazakhstan have a decisive role in determining the future geopolitical architecture of the Eurasian mainland: will it develop along an integrative path leading to the formation of a new supranational entity, or will it move towards greater separation and consolidation of nation-states?

Chapter 5 examines a set of military and strategic issues in Russian-Kazakh relations. Russia's past substantial military and strategic interests in Kazakhstan did not disappear with the USSR's collapse. Moreover, they are even more acute. Kazakhstan has the longest common border with Russia and serves as a buffer state between Russia and the turbulent Muslim world. Some military and other defence-related installations in Kazakhstan are still important to Russia's defence capabilities. Hence Russia's long-standing interest in keeping Kazakhstan within the sphere of its military and strategic influence. The issues examined in the chapter are Kazakhstan's nuclear disarmament, the problem of the Baykonur cosmodrome, Kazakhstan's participation in the CIS collective security system, and bilateral relations in the military sphere.

Chapter 6 addresses Russia's energy policy towards Kazakhstan. After independence, Kazakhstan, a country with large deposits of oil and gas, attracted the attention of major international oil companies, which provoked a diplomatic struggle for access to and control of the republic's energy resources. Russia has a very important stake in the game — the ability to keep Kazakhstan and the Caspian basin within the sphere of its economic and political influence. The outcome of this struggle will to a large degree determine Russia's future role on the Eurasian mainland. The chapter examines such questions as the Caspian Pipeline Consortium, Tengiz and Karachaganak energy projects and the Kazakhstan and Russian positions on the legal status of the Caspian Sea.

In preparing this book, I relied on a wide range of new, often unique sources from both Russia and Kazakhstan. One such source is a collection of Russian-Kazakh treaties and agreements published by the Kazakhstan Embassy in Moscow.[2] Another valuable source was a set of documents prepared for the Russian State Duma Committee on CIS Affairs and Ties with Compatriots hearings on Russian-Kazakh relations held in April 1995. Besides several significant agreements between Russia and Kazakhstan not included in the Kazakhstan Embassy publication, the collection contained official reports by Russian government agencies on the status of relations with Kazakhstan in their respective fields, documents prepared by Russian community organisations in Kazakhstan, and several analytical reports prepared by the Duma's own experts. Of special interest were the minutes of the hearings themselves.[3] They included testimony by high-ranking Russian officials from various government departments, such as Foreign Affairs, Defence, Russian Space Agency, Federal Migration Service and Presidential Administration. The opinions voiced by them helped to form an impression of the Russian government's real attitude to relations with Kazakhstan. The hearings were also attended by Kazakhstan Ambassador Mansurov and representatives from Russian community organisations in Kazakhstan and from several Russian research institutions.

The author also made use of documents published in various Russian and Kazakhstan official bulletins and periodicals, such as the *Diplomaticheskiy vestnik* of the Russian and *Diplomaticheskiy kurier* of the Kazakhstan Ministry of Foreign Affairs, the *Bulleten' mezhdunarodnykh dogovorov* of the Russian Presidential Administration and *Informatsionnyy bulleten'* of the CIS Parliamentary Assembly, as well as documents published in Russian and Kazakhstan official newspapers such as *Rossiyskaya gazeta, Rossiyskie vesti* and *Kazakhstanskaya pravda*. A valuable source for the Gorbachev period was a collection of documents on the nationalities question in the USSR, prepared by Ch. F. Furtado and A. Chandler.[4] Official materials such as publications, statements and interviews by Presidents Yeltsin and Nazarbayev, the prime ministers and foreign ministers of the two countries, or other ministers and high-ranking officials were used, as were official materials such as statements, resolutions and publications by various government agencies.

With regard to facts and developments in Russian-Kazakh relations, I made extensive use of reports by information agencies, especially Routers, ITAR-TASS, Radio Liberty, USIA and publications in the Russian, Kazakhstan and sometimes Western periodical press. The BBC Summary of World Broadcasts, particularly, contained very valuable material on events in Kazakhstan. Also of great utility was the monthly bulletin of the Russian Institute for Scientific Information on Social Sciences *Russia and the Muslim World*, which publishes summaries of almost all articles pertaining to post-Soviet Central Asia that appear in the Russian press.

Another group of sources comprised memoirs, books, brochures and academic journal articles. The memoirs provided insight into some events that took place behind the scenes. I drew extensively on the memoirs of Kunayev, Nazarbayev and Gorbachev, and to a lesser extent on those of Boldin, Pavlov and Ligachev. A biographical publication on Nazarbayev, by D. Valovoy, and an essay by a Russian journalist, N. Kuzmin, were also informative. As memoirs are very subjective, the reminiscences of each memorialist were checked against those of others wherever possible.

Among academic sources in Russia the only major publication on post-Soviet Kazakhstan was a collective work by the Russian Institute of Strategic Studies (RISI),[5] covering Kazakhstan's economic situation (G. D. Bessarabov), stages of economic development (Yu. I. Puzanov), prospects for economic union with Russia (E. M. Ivanov), the oil and gas industry (A. N. Loginov), military issues (G. G. Tishchenko, A. G. Onopko, A. A. Makunin, A. T. Volkov), political parties (A. A. Kurtov), the ethnic and political situation (M. N. Guboglo) and some other problems. It contained many interesting facts and some valuable assessments. The institute, though not formally affiliated with any government agency, is closely linked to the Russian defence and security establishment.

Russia's relations with Central Asian states, including Kazakhstan, found reflection in brochures and articles by M. Khroustalev, A. Zagorsky, D. Trofimov and S. Solodovnik, produced by the Centre for International Studies at Moscow State Institute of International Relations (MGIMO). Since MGIMO is a subdivision of the Russian Foreign Ministry, it is not surprising that their views reflect the attitudes prevalent among Russian diplomats. Another Moscow academic who specialises in Kazakhstan is Professor Bagramov, chief editor of the journal *Eurasia*, which is subsidised by the Kazakhstan government. The number of Russian academic publications both on Russian-Kazakh relations and on Kazakhstan is insignificant. Serious research and production of quality academic material is hampered by the unavailability of funds and the government's refusal to increase budget allocations for scholarship.

Far more publications on Russian-Kazakh relations are issued in Kazakhstan. There are two think tanks producing literature on issues of foreign policy, defence and security: Kazakhstan Institute of Strategic Studies (KISI) and the Institute for Development of Kazakhstan (IRK). Both are closely linked to the government. KISI is a subdivision of the presidential administration, and

IRK was founded by the cabinet of ministers. KISI publishes one journal, *Kazakhstan i mirovoe soobschestvo*, and IRK publishes two journals, *Politika (Sayasat)* and *Evraziyskoe soobschestvo: ekonomika, politika, bezopasnost'*. Both institutions also regularly publish brochures and reports.

The major expert on Russian-Kazakh relations, KISI's director, U. T. Kasenov, has published more on the subject than any other Kazakh scholar. Other KISI researchers who contribute to the study of the subject are B. B. Abdigaliev, A. K. Sultangalieva, M. Laumulin, Sh. E. Zhaksibekova and M. Zaslavskaya. IRK's has published academic works by its president, E. M. Arinov, director R. K. Zhulamanov and researcher M. U. Spanov, and by outside experts such as L. Bakaev, head of a branch in the Division of International Security of the Kazakhstan Foreign Ministry, and B. T. Ayaganov, A. U. Kuvandikov and S. Z. Baimagambetov, senior Kazakhstan government officials. Valuable information was contained in a publication by M. Arenov and S. Kalmikov. Naturally, the views and concepts expressed by all these authors conform to the official ideology of Nazarbayev's regime. But they also have the advantage of expressing the government's position more bluntly, without excessive regard for intergovernmental civilities. In other words, Kasenov can say publicly what Nazarbayev cannot, which gives a clear hint of what Kazakhstan's president and government are thinking.

Academics of the Kazakhstan National University, such as Doctor of Political Science R. M. Kaliyeva, express their views more independently. The university also harbours scholars steadfastly opposed to Nazarbayev's regime, such as professors N. E. Masanov and N. Amerkulov. But such academics are rare; Masanov, for example, has had difficulties in publishing his works in Kazakhstan and has had to approach Russian and Western publishers.

Due to limitations, I have chosen not to include an explicit bibliography, but all sources used to prepare the text are listed in the Notes at the end of each chapter.

NOTES

1. Mansurov, T., *Kazakhstan—Rossiya: suverenizatsiya, integratsiya, opit strategicheskogo partnerstva 1991–1995*, Moscow, 1996.

2. Sbornik dokumentov i materialov, Moscow: Posol'stvo Respubliki Kazakhstan v Rossiyskoy Federatsii, 1995. (a Collection of documents and materials, Moscow: Embassy of the Republic of Kazakhstan in the Russian Federation, 1995).

3. Gosudarstvennaya Duma Federal'nogo Sobraniya Rossiyskoy Federatsii, Stenogramma parlamentskikh slushaniy Komiteta po delam Sodruzhestva Nezavisimykh Gosudarstv i svyazyam s sootechestvennikami "O rossiysko-kazakhstanskikh otnosheniyakh", Moscow [No publisher], 18.04.95. (State Duma of the Federal Assembly of the Russian Federation, Committee on Matters of the Commonwealth of Independent States and Ties with Compatriots. Minutes of hearings on Russian-Kazakhs relations, Moscow, 18 April 1995).

4.   Furtado, Ch. F., Chandler, A., eds., *Perestroika in the Soviet Republics, Documents on the National Questions*, Boulder and Oxford: Westview Press, 1992.

5.   Kozhokin, E. M., ed., *Kazakhstan: realii i perspektivy nezavisimogo razvitiya*, Moscow: RISI, 1995.

Emergence of Independent Kazakhstan

Gorbachev's reforms had a most significant impact on Russian-Kazakh relations in the post-Soviet era, and not simply because independent Kazakhstan emerged only as a result of USSR's collapse. Gorbachev's policy towards Kazakhstan and especially its consequences have very directly influenced the current attitudes of Russians and Kazakhs towards each other. When Gorbachev came into office in March 1985 he had no clear vision of future reforms, only a general idea that the Soviet system should be made more viable and effective.[1] He approached this problem in traditional Soviet style by applying traditional administrative mechanisms. Hence the concept of "acceleration", accompanied by measures such as an anti-alcohol campaign and struggles against protectionism in public service and against corruption. These measures all entailed more centralisation and control and had nothing to do with democratisation of political or economic life.

At the centre of Gorbachev's effort was a personnel policy directed at cardinal renovation of the state and party apparatus. At the Politburo meeting on 1 December 1985, he said that the main reason for stagnation was "ossification of leading personnel", and "that [i]f we want to improve the situation we should change personnel, personnel policy". On another occasion, referring to personnel policy, he noted that moving ahead was impossible without a "small revolution in the party". He advocated tough personnel measures because he was convinced that his policies were being "directly sabotaged". There was, however, another important reason for Gorbachev's personnel policy. He feared removal from office and strove to consolidate his power base by getting rid of Brezhnev's associates, who could oust him as they had ousted Khrushchev. Gorbachev openly referred to this danger in his memoirs.[2]

Gorbachev's personnel policy boiled down to a large-scale purge of the state and party apparatus, very reminiscent of all his predecessors. During his first year in power, 1985, Gorbachev managed to oust three influential Politburo members — G. Romanov (July), Prime Minister Tikhonov (September) and Moscow Party Chief V. Grishin (December). Moreover, 45% of USSR government ministers and 30% of the powerful regional Party First Secretaries were replaced. By March 1986 42.7% of voting members of the Central Committee of the Communist Party of Soviet Union (SPSU) were new.[3] The only problem Gorbachev faced was how to politically legitimise this massive purge. He found two major issues on which to consolidate his power, economic mismanagement and corruption. Both were very popular with the public, who were annoyed by shortages of some consumer goods and irritated by the arrogant behaviour of bureaucrats in the state and party apparatus.

A massive campaign against corruption began early in the summer of 1985, after A. Yakovlev was appointed as head of the Communist Party of the Soviet Union (CPSU) Central Committee Department for Propaganda. Central Asian republics figured very highly in the campaign, probably because they were considered soft targets. Gorbachev had solid reasons to expect morale among Central Asian leaders to be low, following Andropov's large-scale crackdown on corruption in Uzbekistan in 1983.[4] His expectations soon proved mostly justified. By the end of 1985 he had smoothly removed three leaders of Central Asian republics — Kyrgyzia (T. Usubaliev), Turkmenistan (M. Gapurov) and Tajikistan (R. Nabiev). Uzbek Communist Party First Secretary I. Usmankhodzhaev survived simply because he had been appointed after the corruption case in Uzbekistan had ended.

The charges against Usubaliev, Gapurov and Nabiev were almost identical. An impression of them can be gleaned from the report A. Masaliev, the new leader of Kyrgyzia, delivered at the 18th Congress of the Kyrgyz Communist Party in January 1986, in which said:

Leninist principles of personnel policy were seriously violated. Many officials were chosen on grounds of personal loyalty, kinship or common origin. . . . [Usubaliev] essentially decided personnel and other matters by himself, did not permit objections, tolerated no opinion that did not agree with his own, and did not hesitate to persecute those who were recalcitrant . . . to justify his mistaken decisions he forced officials to be insincere or even fiddle with facts. . . . [C]riticism and self-criticism were lacking while servility, sycophancy and flattery spread. . . . [T]here were groundless promotions and receipt of academic titles, degrees and awards.[5]

Masaliev's remarks are important because they reflected Moscow's position and thus revealed Gorbachev's views on what should be done in Central Asia. Gorbachev failed to comprehend the importance of clan attitudes and clan politics in Central Asian societies. What Masaliev singled out as unacceptable behaviour had in fact been characteristic of the life of Central Asian peoples for centuries. To attack it was to attack their traditions, values and culture. Thus

Gorbachev's personnel policy had one significant fault, which proved fateful. It was based on the concept of uniformity, which did not take into account the complexity and diversity of Soviet society. It also ignored the fact that personnel policy in ethnic republics was always an inalienable part of Soviet nationality policy, and Gorbachev's personal policy should have been subordinate to it. It soon became obvious that Gorbachev's leadership lacked a coherent nationality policy.

Though Gorbachev denies this in his memoirs, his experience in nationality affairs was very limited and much weaker than that of Stalin, Khrushchev and Brezhnev.[6] Gorbachev came from Stavropol region, a territory of Russia proper, where interethnic relations were not a problem. The region was not ethnically homogeneous, having a small autonomous province inhabited by two minor nationalities — Karachai and Cherkess — besides a Russian majority. But the status of autonomous provinces was very low, in no way comparable to a union republic with its own government, state symbols and other attributes of statehood. Autonomous provinces were subordinate to regional administrations, and their elites intermingled with those of the region. Throughout his career in Stavropol Gorbachev apparently never experienced any problems with the Karachai or Cherkess minorities.

Gorbachev did not accept, or more precisely did not understand, the essence of Brezhnev's nationalities policy, which was based on social concord with the republics' national elites. He wrote in his memoirs, "Brezhnev could not be unaware of abuses, which were taking place in Uzbekistan, malfeasances in other republics and Russian provinces, but he preferred not to raise Cain and not to foul his own nest. He went no farther than talking privately like a Dutch uncle to a miscreant leader, and in the last resort sending him somewhere as an ambassador".[7] Gorbachev understood Brezhnev's behaviour not as a wellconceived policy (sometimes referred to as the "stability of cadres") but as a major deviation from the basic principles of Communist doctrine which he, Gorbachev, was destined to correct.

Gorbachev's approach to nationalities policy was rooted in his close association with Marxist theory. As distinct from Stalin and Brezhnev, who applied Marxism in a politically expedient way to suit their domestic and foreign policy objectives, Gorbachev's adherence to Marxism was genuine. In this he stood much closer to leaders such as Lenin, Trotsky, Zinoviev, Bukharin and later Khrushchev. Not surprisingly, Gorbachev's 'purification' campaign was accompanied by vocal claims of the necessity to revive the true spirit of Marxism-Leninism. As witnessed by Gorbachev's chief of staff, Boldin, in 1986 and 1987 Gorbachev "was strongly under the influence of Lenin's writings. . . . It was my impression that he was anxious to propose some concept that might continue Lenin's thinking and perhaps shake the world as powerfully as anything the Soviet Union's founding father had done".[8]

But what was the Marxist theory of nationalities relations? In fact, there was very little of relevance. Marxist theory was based on the illusory postulate that class is a more powerful factor than nation and deduced from this an erroneous doctrine of proletarian internationalism. Neither Stalin nor Brezhnev took it seriously, but for propaganda purposes both stopped short of denouncing it. Gorbachev had a different vision. He surrounded himself with people bogged down in dogmas of Marxist theory, and this was the second factor that led to the failure of his nationality policy. The leading figure among them was Alexander Yakovlev, long known for his fierce opposition to nationalism, particularly Russian nationalism.[9] Gorbachev's other principal advisors – A. Chernyaev, V. Zagladin, G. Shakhnazarov and I. Frolov – held views close to Yakovlev's. This team's combined efforts produced a strange but logically interrelated mixture of Marxism (international communism) and liberalism. According to Boldin, "the notion of perestroika, together with all its basic components, was mainly Yakovlev's work".[10]

Like anything else emanating from Marxism the doctrine of "new political thinking" was globalist. At its core lay the assumption that growing economic interdependence of the world's peoples and nations, would lead to interdependence in all other spheres. Therefore the role of national states in world politics would progressively diminish, and that of supranational structures (United Nations [UN], European Economic Community [EEC], Organisation for Security and Cooperation in Europe [OSCE], etc.) increase. New transnational organisations would appear, some with Soviet participation, such as the Common European Home advocated by Gorbachev. The trend to interdependence would inevitably lead to universalisation of life in general and specifically to the emergence of universal *values*. International contradictions would become less acute, and conflict potential of the world system would abate, creating a basis for relinquishing power politics, achieving balance of interests among nations and prevalence of the rule of law in international conduct.

The problem of nationalism was very inconvenient in the context of new political thinking. Nationalism contravened the doctrine's basic postulate, the growth of interdependence, by demonstrating diversity and contradictions among nations. Accentuating issues of nationality relations could place the whole of Gorbachev's scheme in jeopardy and with it his own political standing, hence, Gorbachev tried to avoid addressing the topic of nationalism and evaded searching for real solutions by sticking to traditional Soviet formulas and clichés. For example, his statements on the nationality question at the 27th CPSU Congress were entirely routine, and no new ideas found their way into the new party program. At the January 1987 Central Committee plenum he admitted the existence of problems in nationality relations but blamed them on former leaders' mistakes.[11]

Meanwhile, by alienating national elites Gorbachev ruined Brezhnev's mechanism for running Soviet nationality affairs without substituting a mechanism of his own. Into opposition, elites moved to the union centre, and Gorbachev began losing control over the republics. Apparently, he sincerely believed that the trend to interdependence would overwhelm nationalist sentiments and that the best policy was to wait while the objective laws of history did their work.

The Kazakh national elite was the first to pose a direct and open challenge. Initially, this appeared as a personal clash between Gorbachev and Kunayev. Gorbachev was interested in Kunayev's speedy removal for several reasons. First, Kunayev was a very close associate of Brezhnev from the mid-1950s, and Gorbachev's strategy for building his own popularity consisted of denigrating Brezhnev's heritage. Besides, Kunayev belonged to the so-called war generation of Soviet leaders, which obviously made his vision of the world very different from Gorbachev's.[12] Kunayev also headed the territorially second largest republic of the USSR and was a full member of the ruling Politburo. All this made his position in the party especially strong. Gorbachev had little doubt which side Kunayev would take in the event of a showdown with the conservatives on the Central Committee.

Gorbachev had been general secretary for just three months when he delivered his first attack. The victim was A. Askarov, first secretary of Shymkent province party committee and a distant relative of Kunayev. He was removed from office on 10 July 1985.[13] There was an interesting discrepancy in comments on the event by Kazakh and Moscow media. The former criticised the provincial party organisation under Askarov's leadership for not succeeding completely "in reconstructing its style and methods of work in directing the economy". This criticism did not beyond very general and vague hints of economic mismanagement, not unusual even in Brezhnev's time.[14] But a *Pravda* article three days later, not only identified economic failures but also mentioned mismanagement and corruption that had been ignored by local party officials. Without accusing Askarov himself of corruption, the article gave the impression that he had somehow benefited by spreading corruption around himself.[15] The striking difference between the two accounts clearly indicated that Moscow was trying to embarrass the Kazakh authorities, above all Kunayev.

Kunayev, however, did not lose his nerve. He had nothing to fear; subsequent investigations proved beyond doubt that he was not involved in any corruption. Moreover, he himself telephoned the USSR Attorney-General in Moscow and asked him to send an experienced investigator to Kazakhstan, to look into with corruption there. The investigator, sent without delay, was V. Kalinichenko, a member of the group that cracked down on corruption in Uzbekistan.[16]

Kunayev's political positions inside the republic were exceptionally strong. He was not just another first secretary, he was a leader of a national elite he himself had helped create, and whose allegiance to him was very strong. Besides, in Kunayev's years Kazakhstan had made notable economic and social progress, and the living standard of ordinary citizens had improved, not as much as desirable but to a level well above that of the mid-1950s, when he first came to office. This won Kunayev the respect not only of the national elite but also of the rank-and-file party members. Interethnic relations in Kazakhstan under Kunayev were quite stable. Like any other first secretary in a union republic, Kunayev had control of his own propaganda machine. He skillfully used it to tone down Moscow's criticisms in the local, especially Kazakh language, mass media, but stopped short of anything which would enable Gorbachev to accuse him of deviation from the general party line. Thus it was very difficult for Gorbachev to remove Kunayev by democratic means.

Gorbachev chose to undermine Kunayev's position from within the republic, first, by discrediting him in the eyes of public opinion and, second, by destroying his power base. To this end, subversive rumours against Kunayev were spread through unofficial channels.[17] At the official level, Gorbachev attacked Kazakhstan's economic performance. In September 1985 he visited Tselinograd, capital of the Kazakhstan Virgin Lands region, to address an interprovincial conference of Party and business executives on agriculture. In his speech he specifically singled out Kazakhstan for not meeting agricultural production targets.[18]

Leading up to the 16th Congress of the Communist Party of Kazakhstan (CPK) Moscow arranged three important personnel changes. On 5 December 1985, A. Koichumanov, first secretary of the Alma-Ata city party committee was dismissed and a week later lost his Party membership "for falsification of autobiographical data, immodesty and abuse of office". He was succeeded by his deputy, G. Shulico, a Slav.[19] It was later reported that Koichumanov was under investigation for corruption.[20] On 9 January 1986 Russian V. Miroshnik replaced Kazakh Z. Kamaledenov as Chairman of the Kazakhstan KGB. Kamaledenov was transferred to the more prestigious but less powerful position of CPK Central Committee Secretary for Ideology.[21] Finally, on 5 February G. Knyazev became Kazakhstan's new minister of internal affairs, succeeding A. Platayev, who retired on pension.[22] Nobody knew then that these appointments would play an important role in the political showdown in December 1986.

Gorbachev also sought allies against Kunayev among high-ranking members of the Kazakh elite. He found at least two, Premier N. Nazarbayev and First Secretary of the Kzyl Orda Province Party Committee E. Auyelbekov. Both were young and ambitious, looking to succeed Kunayev, and Gorbachev exploited their vanity. Nazarbayev admitted in his memoirs that Gorbachev supported him against Kunayev because "he needed allies in the struggle with the old generation of the Politburo members".[23]

Nazarbayev attracted Moscow's attention by ardently supporting of all sorts of economic experiments in Kazakhstan, but Kunayev objected to his initiatives, and their relationship deteriorated.[24] Indicatively, Kunayev wrote in his memoirs that Nazarbayev's work in the republic's Council of Ministers "does not always go smoothly", and that it had been necessary "to correct him and point out his shortcomings".[25]

Although it was Kunayev who had promoted Nazarbayev from the low-ranking position of party secretary at the Karaganda metallurgic combine to the second highest post in Kazakhstan, the new Premier displayed only transient loyalty to his patron. By late 1985 he was already discussing anti-Kunayev strategy in Moscow with *Pravda* Deputy Chief Editor Valovoy. Nazarbayev advised Valovoy that he would have a final talk with Kunayev on "improving the situation in the economy", and if they failed to agree he would voice his criticisms at the forthcoming 16th CPK Congress.

In his report to the congress on 8 February 1986, Nazarbayev delivered veiled criticism of Kunayev. He said that "highlighting of successes and unfounded praise for leaders, which had been imposed from above for years led to fading criticism and self-criticism, weakening of ties with the masses", and that "[f]aulted methods of administration are not nipped, which does tremendous damage to the economy". But the major criticism was a personal attack against Kunayev's younger brother, Askar Kunayev, President of the Kazakh Academy of Sciences, who, he said, "has opted out of work and does not even attend meetings of the Council of Ministers". It was obvious to all that this was an indirect attack on Kunayev. In his autobiography Kunayev described Nazarbayev's criticism of his brother as not "objective".

Interestingly, Nazarbayev promptly passed the text of his report to Valovoy, who had come to Alma-Ata to observe the Congress's proceedings. Valovoy used the report as a basis for an article, "Time Demands", very critical of Kazakhstan's realities. He claimed that after Nazarbayev's speech a smear campaign against him started to unfold in Kazakhstan. Within a month fifty complaints were arranged, alleging that Nazarbayev was a power seeker whose major aim was to unseat Kunayev and take his place.[26]

Auyelbekov also criticised Kunayev at the 16th CPK Congress. During discussion of Kunayev's report, Auyelbekov referred to instances of corruption, window dressing, "highlighting of successes and hushing up of shortcomings", of promotion of officials on the basis of personal loyalty, kinship and geographical origin in his province under its previous leadership. He said that the situation had existed for years and implied that the republic's leadership knew this but took no corrective measures.[27] However, neither Nazarbayev nor Auyelbekov could muster any significant opposition to Kunayev.

Kunayev made only token sacrifices for his critics' benefit. Neither his brother nor Chairman of the Republic State Planning Committee Mukhamed-Rakhimov, also criticised, was re-elected to the CPK Central Committee.[28] But Kunayev was re-elected unopposed as Kazakhstan's first secretary and in this capacity led its delegation to the 27th CPSU Congress, in Moscow on 25 February 1986.[29]

In Moscow Kunayev again became subject to criticism, this time from Gorbachev himself. Kazakhstan was one of only a few regions specifically mentioned in the Central Committee report as failing to pay enough attention to "raising production efficiency" and producing "national income per unit of fixed capital one-third lower than on average in the economy". That Gorbachev used such an abstract indicator suggests that he had difficulties finding anything incriminating to use against Kunayev. The general economic slowdown affected every region, and Kazakhstan was not conspicuously less successful than other republics. Gorbachev coupled his criticism of Kazakhstan with that of Turkmenistan, where the party first secretary had recently been dismissed, a clear hint to the delegates that Kunayev must follow suit. In the subsequent discussion Kunayev partially accepted the criticism, while at the same time pointing to some achievements. He also attacked central government ministries responsible for managing a substantial part of Kazakhstan's economy, a clear hint to Gorbachev that Moscow must share the responsibility.[30] At that time Gorbachev refrained from sacking Kunayev, obviously, unsure of who should succeed the head of this large and important republic.

Media attacks against Kunayev continued after the Congress. In July 1996 *Pravda* published two very critical articles, one citing instances of corruption among senior Kazakh officials, the other using Kazakhstan party officials to exemplify undesirable work styles.[31] Kunayev was deeply offended by the Moscow press's concentration on Kazakhstan's shortcomings and exclusion of positive social and economic achievements. Later he wrote that this "conspiracy of silence" was one factor that forced his retirement.[32] Meanwhile, in Kazakhstan career-minded party leaders and government officials began betraying their leader to save their jobs. In his memoirs Kunayev referred to "double-dealing members" of the republic's Central Committee who sent false information about him to Moscow.[33] Gorbachev also noted in his book that he had been visited more than once by province party committee secretaries and later by a group of secretaries of the CPK Central Committee led by Second Secretary Miroshkhin. They advised him that "things were not going well in the republic".[34]

Among such "dishonest" people and "time-servers" Kunayev named only Miroshkhin, Mukashev, Kamaledenov and Mendibayev. He did not mention Nazarbayev, but it was no secret that Kunayev actively tried to get rid of Nazarbayev. More than once he raised the question of removing him from the premiership, but the CPSU Central Committee rejected the proposition. This is substantiated by Gorbachev, who explained Kunayev's enmity to Nazarbayev as a reaction to Nazarbayev's exposure of some irregularities in the allocation of funds.[35] Nazarbayev's speech at the 8th CPK Central Committee plenum in March 1987 also confirms that he actively worked to undermine Kunayev's position. To show that he was not Kunayev's man, Nazarbayev artfully turned to his account compromising anonymous letters about himself sent to Kunayev by his loyalists. In revealing this, Nazarbayev implied that he had covertly acted against Kunayev and had been systematically reported as so doing.[36] If Nazarbayev was not allied with Gorbachev against Kunayev he surely would have lost the premiership after Kunayev's retirement.

Why did Kunayev choose not to mention Nazarbayev's intrigues? The answer is that when Kunayev's memoirs were being published, Nazarbayev was already Kazakhstan's president. Very likely in that situation Kunayev had several reasons not to write negatively about Nazarbayev. The latter acknowledged this restraint; he wrote that in his last years Kunayev "behaved himself responsibly, wisely, supported the difficult work conducted in the republic. . . . Today in Almaty there is a street named after D. Kunayev. . . . His name is awarded to the enterprise institute where he worked. Today the Kunayev Foundation is functioning, his book of reminiscences is published and re-published. We kept a monument to him in the city centre."[37] This may be called a tactical compromise between the old and new leaders. Nazarbayev received carte blanche to create an image of himself as Kunayev's worthy successor, and Kunayev ensured posthumous status for himself as a great leader of Kazakhstan.

In August 1986 the CPSU Central Committee passed a highly critical resolution on the state of Kazakhstan's agriculture. It stated inter alia: "extensive methods for development of livestock production had taken root . . . gross output was growing at an extremely slow rate . . . cattle and sheep are delivered for processing before they are adequately fattened . . . a great deal of low-quality milk is purchased . . . quality of wool and karakul has declined . . . plans for meat and milk deliveries to all-Union stock are not being met".[38] Not all this criticism was fair. The extensive method of livestock breeding was traditional in Kazakhstan, and there was nothing unusual about its having taken root. To change to intensive methods, huge investments were necessary and obviously lacking.

Moscow's demand for sharp increases in meat, milk and wool deliveries coupled with a rise in product quality defied economic logic, as both could not be achieved simultaneously. But the important thing was that gross output was growing, not declining. Gorbachev, however, was not interested in objective assessment. The resolution blamed all the alleged failures on Kazakhstan's leadership.[39]

Kunayev understood that pressure for his resignation was building. Indications of this were everywhere. He was conspicuously not invited to the Politburo meeting held in early November to discuss the economic development plan for 1987, though existing practice was for all Politburo members to participate in these meetings. Moreover, the report delivered by Ligachev on the 69th anniversary of the October revolution did not even mention Kazakhstan as a major contributor to Soviet grain output, except for a reference to Kustanay and Kokchetav provinces, which Gorbachev had visited, as fulfilling the economic plan.

In late November Kunayev came to Moscow for the USSR Supreme Soviet session, and had a long meeting with Gorbachev, during which he gave his views on various political matters and expressed his dissatisfaction with some aspects of Gorbachev's policy. "As I was leaving him I reached the final decision to retire", he recalled.[40] According to Gorbachev, Kunayev requested the meeting, and tried to convince Gorbachev that the complicated situation in the CPK Central Committee Bureau was the result of "intrigues" by Nazarbayev, who was "yearning for power", spoke very negatively of Nazarbayev and kept repeating "This is a dangerous man. He must be stopped".

Finally he asked Gorbachev to transfer Nazarbayev to Moscow or send him abroad as a foreign ministry representative. But Gorbachev refused. After all, he had masterminded the intrigues against Kunayev. He told Kunayev that he disagreed on the reasons for the current situation, accused him of serious errors in personnel policy (i.e., encouraging kinship or common origin ties, protecting embezzlers and persecuting internal dissidents) and suggested they continue the discussion at a joint meeting of the Politburo and CPK Central Committee bureau. Kunayev then offered his resignation, to be formally submitted after Gorbachev's return from India.[41]

In early December 1986 Kunayev visited Gorbachev for the last time. He claimed that when he asked who would replace him, Gorbachev replied, "Leave the decision on this matter to us. A good Communist will be recommended and sent to the republic".[42] Gorbachev gave a completely different account, in which he asked Kunayev whom he would recommend. According to Gorbachev, Kunayev replied, "nobody, especially among local Kazakhs", and advised that "in this difficult situation the position of first secretary must be held by a Russian".[43] Which of the two was more truthful can never be established, but Gorbachev's credibility is more dubious. His ousting of Kunayev provoked rioting in Kazakhstan, and his replacement proved a bad choice, so he had incentive to shift some of the blame for poor decision making.

Kunayev's retirement was formally approved at the Politburo meeting on 11 December 1986, to which Kunayev was not invited, though formally still a member, and though the meeting appointed his successor. Gorbachev selected Gennadiy Kolbin, who was not an ethnic Kazakh and had no ties with Kazakhstan,[44] a circumstance which proved crucial for subsequent events. Only Gaydar Aliyev, Azerbaijan's First Secretary, expressed doubts about Kolbin's appointment; Gorbachev ignored them, and Kolbin's candidature was approved.[45] Later Gorbachev admitted that Kolbin's appointment was a mistake. "We were at the start of perestroika, and acted in a certain degree by old methods", he wrote.[46]

On 16 December 1986 a plenum of the CPK Central Committee took place. It was attended by Secretary of the CPSU Central Committee for Organisational Matters Razumovsky. The plenum was extraordinary short — eighteen minutes.[47] Razumovsky announced the Politburo decision on Kunayev's retirement and recommended Kolbin as new first secretary. Nobody objected and Kolbin was unanimously elected. After that Razumovsky visited Palace of Pioneers, Palace of Lenin, the economic exhibition and at 1 P.M. left for Moscow. Nothing foreshadowed trouble. It was like thunder on a clear day when on 18 December TASS reported that "a group of students, incited by nationalistic elements ... took to the streets of Alma-Ata expressing disapproval of the recent plenum of the Kazakhstan's Communist Party Central Committee. . . . Hooligans, parasites and other anti-social persons utilised this situation and resorted to unlawful actions against representatives of law and order".[48]

According to later revelations, the riots in Alma-Ata were not spontaneous. Turmoil started in student dormitories on 17 December. Student activists ran from one room to another and shouted, "All to the square! Let's save Kunayev!" Those who refused to go were called traitors and beaten up. Standing near dormitories were snow-white Volga cars, the type available only in the Kazakhstan Council of Ministers' garage. The cars were full of cases of vodka, which was freely available to students who rushed out to the streets.[49] At that time Gorbachev's anti-alcohol campaign was in full swing, and vodka was very difficult to get. Thus large amounts of vodka could be obtained only by people in positions of authority. The sudden availability of free vodka was a real boon for the students.

Soon a large crowd arrived to the Central Committee building in the centre of Alma-Ata. Those in the building locked themselves up. At 11 A.M. Miroshkhin telephoned Kunayev and said that a group of young people has gathered on the central square. "They requested [an explanation for] the decisions of the Central Committee plenum held yesterday. It would be good for you to speak to them and explain the gist of the matter", he said. When Kunayev arrived to the Central Committee he went straight to Kolbin's office, where all members of the bureau were present. They discussed what measures to take, and Kolbin suggested that Nazarbayev and Kamaledenov speak to the protesters. Kunayev was not invited to speak. After a conversation with Moscow, Kolbin advised Kunayev to go home. "We will take measures ourselves and establish order", he said. At the CPSU Central Committee plenum in June 1987, Miroshkhin confirmed that Kunayev had not been allowed to speak to the protesters. At 1 P.M. Gorbachev telephoned Kunayev at home and asked what provoked demonstration. He was also interested in who organised the event. Kunayev replied that he did not know the organisers and referred Gorbachev to the republic's leadership for any other information.[50]

Meanwhile, the protesters, besieging the Central Committee building, became annoyed with the lack of response to their demonstration. Some of the protesters moved to the republican television broadcasting centre. Their plan obviously was to break the news to the rest of the republic and raise similar demonstrations in other provinces. Such attempts were in fact made by distributing leaflets and making appeals in twelve of Kazakhstan's provincial centres, but they were unsuccessful.[51] The crowd burst into the television centre, knocked out the police officer who guarded the entrance and disarmed him. Protesters were stopped at the door to the studio by engineer Savitskiy, a Russian by nationality, who blocked their way. He was beaten to death. The protesters did not have the expertise to use the equipment and failed to make broadcast. The disarmed policeman managed to telephone a police station and report what was happening at the TV centre.[52] After that the events started to unfold with increasing speed.

Moscow newspapers reported that protesters "set fire to a food store and private cars" and committed "insulting actions against citizens of the city".[53] They had allegedly carried banners with nationalistic slogans and later were joined by "hooligans, drunkards and other anti-social individuals ... armed with metal rods, sticks and stones" who "beat up and insulted citizens, overturned cars and set them on fire, and broke windows in stores, dormitories and other public buildings".[54] One report said that the protestors had been "excited by alcohol and narcotics" and throwing "pieces of marble at unarmed volunteer police aides and policemen".[55]

Leaders of party committees in the Alma-Ata districts populated by ethnic Russians formed self-defence units of Russian workers who were armed with metal bars, lengths of cable and sticks. Active role in organising such detachments was played by First Secretary of the Alma-Ata City Party Committee G. Shuliko, Head of Department in the same committee A. Khmyzov, First Secretary of Moskovskiy District Party Committee Yu. Yeshkov, First Secretary of the Oktyabrskiy District Party Committee Yu. Meshcheryakov, and Chairman of Frunzenskiy District Soviet V. Dolzhenkov played an active role in organising the workers. Soon clashes between the protesters and the Russian volunteer detachments and local police were raging throughout Alma-Ata. The report of the Kazakhstan parliamentary commission of inquiry into Alma-Ata events (released on 28 September, 1990) stated that "behaviour of some of the demonstrators was frequently outside the law. ... In disobeying the forces of order they insulted them, skirmished and fought with them, [sic] stoned them and caused them bodily harm. There were irresponsible and provocative calls for illegal actions. Cars were set alight and buildings damaged". Late on 17 December troops of the Ministry of Interior entered the city and started suppression of the riots. The sanction for the operation, assigned a code name "Metel" (Snowstorm)-86, was given by Moscow on the request of Kazakhstan's leadership, obviously, Kolbin in the first instance. The troops did not employ firearms, but used sticks, sappers' shovels and dogs. According to official figures 2,212–2,401 participants in the riots were detained. The Kazakhstan parliamentary commission of inquiry reported 8,500. The latter figure included those who were taken outside the city and detained for a period of several hours. Figures ranging from 763 to 1,137 were given for the number of injured. In the commission's assessment over 1,700 people sustained bodily harm, however, the commission did not elaborate on how many of those were Russians and how many were Kazakhs. Three Kazakhs died in the riots — M. Spatayev, a student at Alma-Ata Institute of Power Engineering, S. Mukhamedzhanova, a student at Ust-Kamenogorsk Pedagogical Institute, and L. Asanova, a student at Alma-Ata Academy of Music.[56]

In the wake of the Alma-Ata events ninety nine people were convicted. One of them, K.Ryskulbekov, a student at Alma-Ata Architectural College, was sentenced to death for murdering Savitskiy.[57] Others tried and convicted with Ryskulbekov were T. Tashenov, as an accessory, and another student, Zh. Taidzhumaev, for arson and attempted murder. They received long prison sentences. K. Kuzembaev, a welder, was given fourteen years for seriously injuring Police Major I. Zimulkin, and E. Kopesbaev was sentenced to four years for beating up Police Sergeant A. Almabekov.[58] The nonpolitical nature of these cases is attested by the relatively long duration of the investigations. The situation was different in the trials of the so-called instigators of the riots, which were held in January 1987. Zh. Sabitova, a school teacher, was sentenced to five-years' imprisonment for having prepared "a poster and leaflets of provocative content with the aid of which she attempted to stir up enmity between nationalities and tried to persuade young people to commit unlawful actions".[59] K. Rakhmetov, student and Young Communist League leader from Kazakhstan State University, received a seven-year sentence for "inciting students to flagrantly violate public order".[60] And M. Asylbaev, unemployed, was sentenced to ten years for "inciting" young people "to violate public order, refuse to obey representatives of the bodies of power and assault policemen, servicemen and volunteer police aides".[61] These were clearly political convictions. By September 1990, forty six convicted persons were rehabilitated and some of those not rehabilitated had their sentences reduced.[62]

The Alma-Ata events were a serious setback for Gorbachev. For the first time, his political judgment and handling of nationality affairs was questioned. The Moscow leadership was destabilised, which was clearly indicated by the abrupt postponement of the CPSU Central Committee plenum on personnel issues.[63] Kolbin admitted to the gravity of the situation in his speech at the 19th CPSU Conference "The situation that arose in Kazakhstan 18 months ago caused serious concern. In that time a real threat emerged to the intended perestroika reforms".[64] Gorbachev feared that events in Alma-Ata might turn the majority of the Central Committee against him. He needed time to prepare the plenum and formulate a version of the events that suited him.

On 25 December the Politburo reached its verdict and proclaimed inter alia that "working people are vigorously condemning the manifestations of nationalism that occurred in Alma-Ata and demanding that their instigators be punished".[65] The reference to manifestations of nationalism was the first formal political assessment of the Alma-Ata events. The Politburo version was soon upheld by the semi-official Moscow media, which started to muse on the subject of Kazakh nationalism.[66]

Gorbachev used the time preceding the plenum to "persuade" other members of the Central Committee that despite the Alma-Ata events his policy was correct.[67] The plenum, held on 27 January 1987, resulted in Kunayev's losing his Politburo membership; the reason given for his removal "retirement on pension", and for the time being he retained his CPSU Central Committee seat. Plenum documents contained no criticism of him.[68] It was not until early June that the Politburo condemned Kunayev for "violations of Leninist principles of nationality policy that occurred in Kazakhstan".[69]

At the CPSU Central Committee plenum on 25 June 1987, Kunayev was openly attacked for his policy in the field of nationality affairs. The attack was led by Kolbin, who, according to Kunayev, presented "unchecked, unfounded data and sometimes blatant lies". Kamaledenov, Mukashev and Mendibayev helped Kolbin in prepare the report. Kunayev wrote that the report portrayed him as one of the principal organisers of the Alma-Ata riots, though he had had absolutely no connection to it. Nevertheless, this accusation served as cause for dismissal from the CPSU Central Committee and, a month later, the CPK Central Committee.[70] This time the official position for dismissal was "for serious failures committed in leading the republican party organisation".[71]

Kunayev definitely was not responsible for organising the protests in Alma-Ata. Kunayev had nothing to gain from these events. He had retired honourably, and instigating trouble in the republic would only damage his reputation. He understood very well that under no circumstances would he get his job back; moreover, he no longer wanted to stay in office because of old age. Of course, it is possible that Kunayev could be motivated to take revenge on Gorbachev, but the Alma-Ata events were clearly out of proportion with settling personal scores. If Kunayev had organised the demonstrations, nothing could prevent his openly announcing it after Kazakhstan had become an independent state, but he did not do so; moreover, he continued to deny it.

If not Kunayev, who was the major player behind the scenes? In his memoirs Kunayev asserted that he did not speak at the plenum, but eyewitness accounts atlest otherwise. The minutes of the CPSU Central Committee plenum on 25 June 1987 (which are still unavailable to the public) he indicated that he did take the floor, disagreed with the accusations levied against him and said that Nazarbayev had masterminded the Alma-Ata riots. Though Gorbachev stopped Kunayev from finishing his speech, its effect on Nazarbayev was so strong that he was taken to a hospital immediately after the plenum.[72]

The fact that Nazarbayev was making a bid for the top job in Kazakhstan indicates that he could have organised the events. One can only imagine Nazarbayev's frustration when someone from outside Kazakhstan received the job, which he had considered his own. Nazarbayev certainly received support from influential members of the Kazakh elite who were afraid that an outsider might initiate a massive purge, as occured in other Central Asian republics. There were only two persons in Kazakhstan's leadership who had both the reason and resources for organising the Alma-Ata events, Nazarbayev and Kamaledenov, both contenders for Kunayev's position.[73] The latter was not, however, mentioned by Kunayev, despite all the negative attitude to him. Kunayev described Kamaledenov as an active participant of the investigations of the Alma-Ata events and the purge that followed them. Moreover, after the collapse of the USSR there were nothing to prevent Kamaledenov from revealing his role in organising the events, if it had been the case, and this portray himself as a national hero.

The June plenum resulted in CPSU Central Committee resolution On Work of Kazakh Republic Party Organisation in Internationalist and Patriotic Upbringing of Working People, which confirmed that the Alma-Ata events were a "manifestation of Kazakh nationalism". The resolution was very critical of Kunayev's record in the field of nationality affairs. The charges of nationalism were as follows. First, Moscow was dissatisfied with Kazakhstan's contribution to the common all-union economic complex, claiming that it "increasingly failed to correspond" to the republic's "growing economic and scientific potential".[74] While being formally true, this charge can hardly be applicable to the case of nationalism. In the former USSR, it was an open secret that every republic or territory, disregarding its national composition, tried to keep as much economic resources as possible to themselves, and contributed as little as possible to the common economic complex.

The second set of accusations dealt with personnel policy. Kunayev was charged with creating preferential conditions for Kazakh young people in admission to tertiary educational institutions.[75] This was definitely true, but it is was hardly the result of Kunayev's purposeful actions. It is more likely that this situation developed in a de facto manner. The growing number of Kazakh intelligentsia who staffed major colleges and universities facilitated admission to tertiary education of their relatives, friends, acquaintances and persons giving bribes, in accordance with Eastern tradition.

Another charge was that the republic's leadership "kept aloof from the purposeful formation of national cadres of the working class — the basic transmitter of the ideas of internationalism. The percentage of Kazakhs among industrial workers, especially in the coal and metallurgical branches, decreased. Few people of the Kazakh nationality entered vocational-technical schools and specialised secondary educational institutions that train personnel for the main branches of industry".[76] Though this charge was true (Russians comprised 79% of those employed in industry in Kazakhstan[77]), it was a classic example of Gorbachev's attempt to explain Kazakhstan's realities in terms of Marxist dogma. The Kazakhs, with their nomadic-pastoral background, were disinclined to work in industry.

The next fault cited in the resolution was the most serious one: "Proper representation of the nations and nationalities living in the republic was not ensured at all levels of the public and political structure. National-group distortion occurred in the formation of the Party and state apparatus, law enforcement agencies and scientific and cultural institutions . . . in admission to the Party, and in submitting names for state awards".[78] If true, this accusation alone would be enough to justify Kunayev's removal. The principle of proportional representation in Party and state apparatus was the foundation on which the whole edifice of Kazakhstan statehood had been built. For decades it had maintained stability and ethnic peace in Kazakhstan. But this allegation was not deserved. True, Kunayev increased Kazakh participation in the leadership of both party and state apparatus, but he simply corrected distortions made under Krushchev. Under Kunayev the balance of Russians and Kazakhs in the leadership reflected the balance of these two nationalities in Kazakhstan's population.

The above might not have been true for scientific and cultural institutions, but that was a different matter. While Kazakhstan was part of the USSR, Russian intellectuals residing in Kazakhstan could join unions in Russia or in the USSR as a whole. Many preferred to do so, since it was more prestigious and because they represented Russian, not Kazakh, culture. For Kazakhs it was more logical to join unions in Kazakhstan and this was the major reason for the disproportion. Where admission to the party was concerned, the preferential treatment of national minorities had been a long-term CPSU policy since the 1920s, designed to draw into the party more national cadres, who were initially more reluctant than Slavs to join. In time this policy became outdated, but it stood unchanged up to Gorbachev's period. It was, of course, not Kunayev's creation, and accusing him of initiating it was inappropriate. The argument of preferential treatment of Kazakhs in submitting names for state awards was probably true, though no statistics are available. In any case, this allegation was of minor importance.

The third group of charges brought against Kunayev concerned ideology. The resolution blamed the CPK Central Committee and lower level party committees for failing "to examine questions of internationalist education for years". It noted particularly that the CPK Central Committee "did not give an incisive political assessment of the nationalistic actions that took place in Tselinograd in 1979". The faults depicted in the resolution were as follows:

1. In historical research, literature and art, the Kazakh people's past was "frequently idealised", and attempts were made to rehabilitate "bourgeois nationalists".
2. The revolutionary past of the people of Kazakhstan and their struggle to establish Soviet power and socialism were "essentially passed over in silence".
3. The struggle against "feudal-bey" and "patriarchal-tribal" customs was allowed to slacken.
4. No effective measures were taken "to expose the reactionary essence of Islam and its attempts to preserve outmoded traditions and ideas and reinforce national aloofness." In many areas religious activity and clerical influence increased. Party organisations took a benign attitude to officials and members participating in religious ceremonies, citing specific local conditions.

There was a certain amount of idealisation of the Kazakh people's past in historical research. This practice is not uncommon in most nations, including Russia. Under the practices of a totalitarian society, to which Gorbachev adhered, no free polemics on historical issues, including that of Kazakhstan, had been allowed.[79] In all, the resolution made a controversial impression. It contained a number of observations that were certainly true but presented them through a prism of Marxist dogmatism, creating a distorted picture of a socially complex phenomenon. The document was strongly influenced by Gorbachev's vendetta against Kunayev, which had become personal and deterred fair analysis of the facts. The resolution had a clear political purpose — making Kunayev a scapegoat would shield Gorbachev and his lieutenants from criticism for the outbreak of the Alma-Ata riots.

Moscow's official assessment of the Alma-Ata events caused hidden and later open resistance of the Kazakh elite. At the 8th CPK Central Committee plenum in March 1987 no Kazakh leader used the term "nationalism" to characterise the situation in the republic. Chairman of the Presidium of the Kazakhstan Supreme Soviet Mukashev attributed the riots to "Comrade

Kunayev's personality cult" and described the protesters as "inexperienced, politically immature young people". Trofimov, First Secretary of Aktyubinsk province Party Committee, an ethnic Russian but a native of Kazakhstan, preferred to avoid the topic altogether. Only Kzyl-Orda province Party Committee First Secretary Auyelbekov referred to nationalism, but in a casual, incidental manner, not attributing it to Kazakhs as such. He cited "propagating nationalism" as a fault of Kunayev.[80]

Kolbin clearly sensed this mood and could not ignore it. Yet he had to advance the official line. Hence his statement:

Extremist-minded nationalistic elements are few in number and do not constitute any sort of organisation. They whispered, agitated, worked up and sordidly excited the thoughts of young people, and some of those with whom they conducted active work succumbed to the provocation. . . . The people have correctly understood and condemned what happened. And we can not, we have no right to, pin a label of nationalism on the Kazakh people as a whole.[81]

The plenum consequently adopted the resolution "that D. Kunayev must be held . . . accountable to the party for flagrant violations of the norms of party life, creation of a personality cult, distortion of personnel policy and manifestation of an 'anything goes' attitude which led to the development . . . of favouritism, abuse of office, bribe-taking and to nationalistic and other negative manifestations".[82] The submergence of nationalistic manifestations among other faults and its equivalence with other negative manifestations was a victory for the Kazakh elite; nationalism was not the major issue.

Not surprisingly the CPSU Central Committee resolution's accusation of Kazakh nationalism was received very negatively by the Kazakh elite, thereafter various Kazakh politicians, officials and intellectuals insisted on its revocation. According to Gorbachev, Nazarbayev lobbied actively in Moscow for this purpose. Finally, Gorbachev agreed and the accusation of Kazakh nationalism was partially acknowledged as mistaken. The new resduction said that there were demonstrations by young people, provoked by extremist and nationalist elements. Thus the charge was mitigated but remained essentially unaltered. Moreover, the Politburo's decision to revoke the previous resolution was published only in the restricted-circulation CPSU Central Committee bulletin *Izvestiya CK KPSS*, while the original resolution had been published in central Moscow newspapers with circulations in the tens of millions. This prompted sharp criticism from the Commission of Inquiry into the Alma-Ata events established by the Kazakhstan Supreme Soviet Presidium. It said that the decision "does not contain so much as a hint that the authorities even partially admit their guilt". In the commission's assessment the Alma-Ata events "were not nationalist. . . . They were a first attempt to exercise the right freely to express a civic and political position, a right guaranteed by the Constitution and proclaimed by perestroika". Gorbachev, however, was unmoved by the commission's findings. He remains convinced that the initial definition of the events was corrected. "A word is not a sparrow, history cannot be corrected", he concluded in his memoirs.[83]

The official Kazakh interpretation of the nature of the Alma-Ata events is indeed problematic. They maintain that the events were not nationalist, but it is difficult to deny what every citizen of Alma-Ata who saw them knows. The crowd carried banners that said "Kazakhstan for Kazakhs!" and "Russians, Go Home!". The crowd attacked and insulted only Russians, overturned and burned a car driven by a Russian,[84] and killed a Russian television engineer. After independence, the Kazakh authorities attached nationalist overtones to the Alma-Ata riots. Kazakhstan's independence was proclaimed symbolically on 16 December, the anniversary of the day the riots began, and the day has become Kazakhstan's national holiday, with the riots commemorated in that context. Controversially, on 9 December 1996, just before the tenth anniversary of the events, Nazarbayev conferred Kazakhstan's highest award posthumously on Ryskulbekov, who was executed for killing the Russian television engineer.[85] Referring to the riots in his memoirs, he asserted that they showed "to what extent the self-awareness of Kazakh youth has grown. . . . The youth, on behalf of the people, openly stated that it will no longer tolerate trampling on the national pride characteristic of any nationality".[86] In a tenth-anniversary commemorative article, Kazakhstan's State Secretary A. Kekilbaev went even further, characterising the riots as a popular "national-liberation" and "anti-colonial" uprising: "The Alma-Ata events became the first in a chain of national demonstrations in union republics . . . serving as the first quake in the process of disintegration of the 'Red empire'".[87] It seems the Kazakh authorities want to have it both ways, not wanting to admit the presence of nationalism in the riots, while portraying them as a major milestone on the way to independence.

Following the riots, Kolbin faced the difficult task of creating order in what proved to be an unstable republic. He approached the problem with the vigour typical of a myopic bureaucrat. He directed an intense campaign against "parasitic"[88] elements and alcohol abuse, similar to those staged elsewhere in the USSR. The campaign's primary purpose was to remove potential troublemakers, primarily Kazakh youths, from major cities, to forestall a repetition of the Alma-Ata riots.

However, his main effort concentrated on intimidating the Kazakh national elite. Kazakhstan's party and state apparatuses were substantially purged. Among those expelled from the party were D. Bekezhanov, Kunayev's former personal assistant;[89] Statenin, former head of the Administrative Department of the CPK Central Committee; Kadyrbaev, former chairman of the Council of Trade Unions; and Akkoziev, former president of Dzhambul Province Soviet Executive Committee. The former head of the CPK Central Committee Department of Science and Educational Institutions lost his post and then received a strict reprimand through party channels.[90] In all, 1,836 members of party committees and bureaus and 450 secretaries of primary party organisations were removed from office.[91] Even Kunayev's brother, who had been retired for almost a year, was not spared. He received a Party reprimand for serious shortcomings in organising the work of the Kazakh Republic Academy of Sciences, which he had headed for twelve years. The charges against him were unoriginal — favouritism, nepotism, preference by geographic origin, abandonment of collective leadership and even abuse of alcoholic beverages.[92]

The purge strongly affected Kazakhstan's tertiary education system, which seemed reasonable to Kolbin, since most of the demonstrators were students. The Minister of Higher and Specialised Secondary Education K. Naribayev, tried to resign, but was not allowed to go honourably. The CPK Central Committee Bureau alleged that he "failed to provide the necessary level of leadership of the tertiary education system" and that under his rule "favouritism, preference shown to home-town friends, nepotism and associated covering for each other, bribe-taking and other abuses . . . continued and increased".[93] Naribaev's deputy, Ikenov, and two directors of departments, Mergaliev and Boesanbekov, shared his fate. The rector of Kazakhstan State University, Dzholdasbekov, and rectors of three other Alma-Ata colleges, Amirov, Babilov and Mamyrov, were dismissed, and 271 students were expelled.[94]

The purge could not, of course, bypass the Kazakhstan Young Communist League (YCL), because the rioters were mostly young. Kolbin attributed this to poor ideological work by the League's organisers. On 14 February 1987 a YCL Central Committee plenum removed First Secretary S. Abrakhmanov, and in his stead elected S. Kordybaev, then second secretary of the Ilyich District Party Committee. Kolbin attended the session to prevent any surprises from "undisciplined" young people.[95] In the purge that followed some, 787 persons were expelled from the League, and 1,138 received lesser penalties.[96]

Kolbin did his best to obtain compromising material against Kunayev to facilitate his conviction on criminal charges and to destroy his image as a great Kazakh leader once and for all. Moscow was prepared to go to great lengths to achieve this goal. According to Kunayev, during Askarov's trial[97] in Bishkek, Kalinichenko and his group used unlawful methods of interrogation, beating the detainees, denying them water, putting them in cells with criminals, and exposing them to "other methods of physical pressure". Despite this, they obtained no evidence incriminating Kunayev.[98] Although substantial, the purge in Kazakhstan never acquired the dimensions of those in Uzbekistan or other Central Asian republics. In 1989 Kalinichenko admitted ruefully that they had failed to create a case in Kazakhstan similar to that in Uzbekistan.[99]

Another feature of Kolbin's policy was populism. He began taking steps aimed at producing an immediate positive impact on public opinion, while indirectly decrying Kunayev's record as a leader. He transferred several rural villas used for vacations by high party and government bureaucrats to public health agencies and children's institutions. A total of 247 small hotels, 84 cottages, 414 guest apartments, 22 hunting lodges and 6 spare apartments were converted into hospitals, clinics and surgeries, rehabilitation centres, a children's holiday home and children's summer camps, and 365 large families, families of veterans and the disabled received apartments.[100] Similarly, move Kolbin banned the sale of meat products by an autonomous distribution network which serviced various offices, institutions, ministries and departments, and transferred it to the public network.[101] His next populist step was to promise a swift solution to the housing problem, launching a highly publicised program, "Housing 91", to provide accommodation by the year 1991 for some 520,000 families then on waiting lists.[102] To appeal to Kazakh national sentiments, Kolbin issued a decree On Improving Study of the Kazakh Language, which did little to improve knowledge of Kazakh in the republic.[103] Kolbin announced that he himself was taking Kazakh language lessons, and eighteen months later claimed to have delivered part of his speech to the CPK Central Committee in Kazakh.[104] According to Kunayev, this never happened.[105]

These superficial measures had no effect on the economic situation in Kazakhstan; they engendered increasing hatred of Moscow among the Kazakh elite, and did nothing to improve the lot of ordinary people. Substantial long-term policies were needed, but were not forthcoming. The only progress, and that very modest, was in housing construction, which went up 20% in one year.[106] But from a base too small to make any significant impact on the enormous waiting lists. In other areas Kazakhstan's performance fell short of what was expected or promised. The livestock breeding situation did not improve, and bad weather plagued the 1987 grain harvest. Republican industry registered no successes either and continued to experience serious difficulties in meeting its targets. In the 1987–1988 economic year, Kazakhstan failed to attain the national income growth rates set by the five-year plan.[107]

Kazakhstan's unimpressive economic performance and the emergence of nationalist movements elsewhere in the USSR created a favourable atmosphere for the revival of anti-Russian opposition in the republic. But intimidated by the brutal suppression of the Alma-Ata riots and subsequent purges, it acted with exceptional caution, most of its resistance taking passive forms. On 4 February 1988 *Kazakhstanskaya Pravda* reported that S. Adenov, a lecturer in Marxism-Leninism, wrote a manuscript on the nationality question and distributed it in many cities of Kazakhstan. Adenov skillfully used Lenin's criticism of Russian great-power chauvinism to condemn Gorbachev's nationality policy in general and in Kazakhstan particularly, where, he claimed the Alma-Ata riots were its direct consequence.[108] In December 1988 the Akikat historical and educational club came into being. Its aim was revival of Kazakh folk customs and learning of Kazakh history, with a view to restoring the truth about the genocide against Kazakhs in the 1920s–30s and the fate of Kazakh national organisations.

On 3 November 1988 activists from ecological organisations Green Front, Initiative and Referendum proclaimed the establishment of a political organisation, the Alma-Ata People's Front. But it did little, and on 30 April

1989 it disbanded. Probably the most serious organisation representing Kazakh national sentiments in that period was the Nevada-Semipalatinsk antinuclear movement, created on the initiative of Kazakh poet Olzhas Suleimenov. It staged public meetings, demonstrations and congresses, and adopted resolutions addressed to the authorities. Its proclaimed goals were the elimination of nuclear weapons and social and economic rehabilitation of regions adversely affected by nuclear tests. Its main goal, termination of nuclear testing at the Semipalatinsk test site, reflected opposition to Moscow's administrative control of Kazakhstan.[109]

Influential Kazakh literary personalities started a campaign for the rehabilitation of Kazakh poets and writers who had been branded "bourgeois nationalists" in Stalin's years. In late February 1988, Kazakh writer A. Nurpeisov called for the rehabilitation of Quadayberdiev, an outstanding early twentieth-century Kazakh poet.[110] At the USSR Writers' Union Board plenum on 1–2 March, Kazakh writer M. Shakhanov called for "objective critical assessment" of the works of several Kazakh literary figures — Quadayberdiev, Aymautov, Baytursynov and Zhumabayev.[111] The last three had been active Alash Orda members, and Baytursynov had been one of the Alash Orda government's leaders during the Civil War. Another Alash Orda leader to become a focus of public attention was Tinishbayev, the subject of a full-length film entitled *Turksib* (Turkestan-Siberia Railway, a major construction project of the late 1920s). The Kazakh press enthusiastically praised the film and acclaimed Tinishbayev as the first Kazakh railway engineer.[112] At the CPK Central Committee plenum on 4 June 1988, Kazakh Writers' Union President Suleimenov proposed establishing a commission to study the works of writers and scholars exiled in the 1930s.[113] In April 1989, Adilet, a society for the rehabilitation of victims of political repression, was formed. Its aims included rehabilitation of participants in the Alma-Ata riots.[114]

Nationality policy issues were discussed at the 19th CPSU Conference in June 1988. The conference adopted a resolution on interethnic relations which, inter alia, provided for "expansion of the rights of union republics and autonomous formations through demarcation of the areas of competence of the USSR and Soviet Republics, decentralisation, transfer of a number of managerial functions to localities, and strengthening of self-government and responsibility in the spheres of the economy, social and cultural development, and environmental protection". It also stated a need to convene a special CPSU plenum to draft a specific program on nationality policy.[115] This was a sign that Gorbachev was losing status vis-à-vis the Union Republics and had to seek a compromise with them. He tried to postpone formalising this compromise as long as possible, but finally had to give in.

A notable indication of the Kazakh national elite's growing assertiveness was a statement by Kazakhstan foreign minister M. Isinaliev delivered at the 19th CPSU Conference in June 1988, warning against tampering with the republic's territory, a move provoked by renewed speculation on the desirability of creating a German autonomous province in Kazakhstan: "I stress

territorial integrity, since recently people have on occasion appeared who wish
to cut it into a patch-work quilt along nationality lines", he said.[116] Gorbachev,
who had had enough trouble with Kazakhstan, hastened to provide assurances
that "nobody casts doubt on the integrity of the Kazakh Republic".[117]

The primary objective pursued by the Kazakh national elite in that period
was Kolbin's removal. Attacks against him started at the CPK Central
Committee plenum in late January 1988, when some Kazakh party officials,
portraying themselves as supporters of Gorbachev's reforms, accused Kolbin of
issuing too many directives, holding too many conferences, and monitoring too
closely the work of agencies and party committees. Several speakers claimed
that his administrative techniques shackled Party bodies and robbed them of
autonomy.[118] Kolbin's critics artfully used Gorbachev's initiatives, some of
which implied limiting bureaucratic procedures. What lay behind these attacks
was the local bureaucrats' desire to distance themselves from the Republic's
Central Committee, thus shielding themselves and the structures they
controlled from Kolbin's policies.

An opportunity for Kolbin's removal arose in mid-1989, sparked by events
in Tbilisi on 9 April, when sixteen people were killed and over two hundred
injured in clashes with army troops. The events, very reminiscent of the
December 1986 Alma-Ata riots, were reported in Moscow's liberal press, while
Gorbachev denied responsibility for what had happened. Soon after, on 25
May, the First Congress of USSR Peoples' Deputies, the new highest body of
power created by the political reform, convened in a politically tense
atmosphere. Opposition deputies demanded proper investigation of the Tbilisi
events, and on 31 May the congress voted to create a commission of inquiry.
The Kazakhstan delegation was represented on the commission by Nazarbayev
and Miroshnik.[119]

This gave the Kazakhs their chance, and they did not let it slip. On 6 June
Kazakh writer M. Shakhanov, speaking on behalf of nineteen deputies from
Kazakhstan, requested establishment of a commission to investigate the Alma-
Ata events.[120] Gorbachev, already on the defensive over Tbilisi, was eager to
avoid the embarrassment establishment of a second commission would bring.
The Kazakh delegation's price for dropping the issue was Kolbin's removal.
On the next day, 7 June, Gorbachev successfully proposed Kolbin's election as
chairman of the People's Control Committee, which meant transferring him to
Moscow. The next important issue was who would be Kazakhstan's new
leader? The Kazakh elite did not want another outsider appointed as first
secretary. No one knew precisely what Gorbachev had in mind, so pressure had
to be applied. Events in the town of Novy Uzen, like Tselinograd in 1979 and
Alma-Ata in 1986, served that purpose.

On the night of 16–17 June, disturbances were sparked by a dance-floor
fight between Kazakh youths and Azerbaijani, Lezgin and other migrant
oilfield workers in Novy Uzen. The police suppressed it and made several
arrests. A group of Kazakh youths armed with sticks, iron rods and stones tried
to break into the police station but fled after warning shots were fired.[121] This

incident may have been spontaneous, but what happened next implies the presence of an organisation. The next morning a rally was held in the central square of Novy Uzen. Protesters voiced complaints about poor conditions and high prices, and the demonstrators, 5,000–7,000 strong, demanded release of those arrested, expulsion of migrant contract workers and jobs for all unemployed Kazakhs. Groups of Kazakhs then began attacking market stalls and homes and setting cars on fire. Altogether 51 facilities were damaged, 5 vehicles burned, 5 people killed, 20 people hospitalised, and 3,516 people fled to the Caucasus. According to Kazakhstan Internal Affairs Minister Knyazev, the rioters' actions were well organised.[122] Interior Ministry troops and police reinforcements were dispatched to Novy Uzen and a curfew was imposed.

The disturbances began spreading to nearby areas, and tension increased throughout Kazakhstan. Rallies and demonstrations were held in Munaishy, Dzetybai, Yeraliev, Mangyshlak Station, Kulsary, Shepke and Fort Shevchenko.[123] Alarming reports on the mood of people came from other parts of Kazakhstan: rumours inciting inter-ethnic discord were being disseminated in Tselinograd, Semipalatinsk, Kokchetav, Pavlodar, Kustanay and Shymkent provinces. In Kzyl-Orda, some thirty taxi drivers drove around the city trying to assemble people for a rally, but this was suppressed. In Dzhambul province and several other areas leaflets calling for disturbances were scattered.[124]

Under circumstances, selection of Nazarbayev as Kazakhstan's leader was inevitable. The events in Novy Uzen had backed Gorbachev into a corner; appointing an outsider was now out of the question, and even appointing a Russian from Kazakhstan was problematic. The message to Gorbachev was clear: if he wanted the interethnic tension to subside, he must select a Kazakh capable of controlling the indigenous nationality. What better choice than Nazarbayev, who had helped Gorbachev to remove Kunayev and had ardently supported Gorbachev's reforms? On 22 June 1989 Nazarbayev was elected first secretary of the CPK Central Committee, and the disturbances in Kazakhstan immediately ceased.[125]

After his election Nazarbayev took steps to boost his popularity by appealing to Kazakh national sentiments. On 26 June 1989 the Presidium of Kazakhstan's Supreme Soviet established a commission of inquiry into the Alma-Ata events. Eight of its fourteen members were Kazakhs, including all three co-chairmen, with only four ethnic Russians and two from other nationalities. Thus Kazakhs were in a position to reach whatever findings they saw fit, with little more than token Russian input.[126]

Nationalist overtones were perceptible in Kazakhstan's Law on Languages, enacted by the Supreme Soviet on 29 August 1989. Article 1 stated: "The state language of the Kazakh SSR is the Kazakh language. The Kazakh SSR officially protects the Kazakh language and guarantees its active use in state institutions and social organisations, bodies of public education, culture, science, mass media and others". Russian was assigned secondary status as the "language of interethnic communication".[127] This was probably Nazarbayev's first move that contributed to the growth of interethnic tensions, as Kazakhs were not a majority of Kazakhstan's population. Table 1.1 shows ethnic composition of the republic's population (1989 census).

Table 1.1
Population of Kazakhstan by Nationality (1989 census)

Nationality	Kazakh	Russian	Ukrainian	Belorussian	Tatar	Uzbek	German	Others
Number of people	6,534,600	6,227,500	896,200	182,600	328,000	332,000	957,500	840,700
As % to the total	39.7	37.8	5.4	1.1	2.0	2.0	5.8	6.2

Source: Brown, B., "Kazakhs Now Largest National Group in Kazakhstan", *Radio Liberty Report on the USSR*, Vol. 2, No. 18, May 4, 1990, p. 19.

Table 1.1 shows that Kazakhstan was a typical multinational state, in which Kazakhs were the largest ethnic group but not a majority. Moreover they were numerically inferior to the combined Slavic population, who generally identified themselves as Russian speakers. Naturally, that group was unimpressed by the Law on Languages, which did not assign Russian equal status with Kazakh. According to Supreme Soviet Deputy Dokuchaeva protests against the law "poured in from north and east Kazakhstan". Dokuchaeva said that 98% of the letters sent to the Supreme Soviet and *Kazakhstanskaya pravda* from Russians and other non-Kazakhs expressed the need for two state languages, Kazakh and Russian, while the same percentage of letters from Kazakhs favoured a single state language. A small group of Russian deputies in the Supreme Soviet protested, and the Ust-Kamenogorsk City Soviet passed a special resolution on the need for two state languages. But all that was ignored.[128]

Nazarbayev's ascendancy also opened the way for nationalist parties and movements to emerge. In June 1989 Kazakhs who had taken part in the Alma-Ata riots formed the *Zheltoksan* (December) political society. Its initial aim was to achieve the rehabilitation of those convicted following the riots. A year later Zheltoksan conducted a founding congress at which it renamed itself the National Democratic Party Zheltoksan. Members advocated excluding Russian from official use, even for interethnic communication, banning Russian immigration to Kazakhstan, and adopting of legislation to create Kazakhstan citizenship.[129]

In April 1990 the founding congress of the Alash party took place. Its political agenda was based on Muslim solidarity and pan-Turkism and envisioned the creation of a Greater Turkestan (Land of Turks), which would include Kazakhstan, Central Asia, Azerbaijan and ultimately Turkic republics within the Russian Federation. Among its more immediate goals the party named state regulation of migration, assisting Kazakhs residing in other states to immigrate to Kazakhstan, and encouraging non-Kazakhs, especially Russians, to leave. Though the party proclaimed itself successor to Alash Orda, its aims were different. Alash Orda's leaders were European-educated Kazakhs, many of them members of the Russian State Duma and of the Constitutional Democratic Party, which espoused Western liberal ideas. Their agenda advocated Kazakh autonomy within the empire, not secession from it. Pan-Turkism was alien to them, and not even mentioned in their program.[130]

In May 1990 another political movement, *Azat* (Freedom), came into being. It proclaimed slogans such as freedom, equality and fraternity of all citizens of Kazakhstan, creation of civil society in the republic, but its primary aim was to achieve Kazakhstan sovereignty, that is, independence. Azat leaders vehemently denied that their movement was nationalist and tried to prove its democratic nature, but some offensive actions and statements by its leaders to and about ethnic Russians indicated otherwise.[131]

Nazarbayev encouraged the Nevada-Semipalatinsk movement's activities, either out of sympathy with its objectives or through unwillingness to risk losing the political initiative to Suleimenov, another prominent personality in Kazakh politics. Nevertheless, Kazakhstan's official position on nuclear testing was only slightly less radical than that of Nevada-Semipalatinsk. In early June 1990 the 17th CPK Congress and in early August 1991 the CPK Politburo adopted resolutions demanding closure of the Semipalatinsk test site,[132] despite Gorbachev's personal appeals to Kazakh leadership to postpone the closure and an offer of compensation amounting to 4.5–5 billion roubles.[133] Nazarbayev closed the test site by decree on 29 August 1991, as soon as the changed political situation in Moscow undermined the USSR Government.

The creation of various Kazakh nationalist parties and movements promoted similar actions by Kazakhstan's Russian population. On 29 August 1990 the founding conference of the Edinstvo (Unity) movement took place in Alma-Ata. It united mostly Russian industrial workers and established branches in several provinces, mostly among workers in defence industries. Its leaders claimed over forty enterprises in the military-industrial complex as collective members. Edinstvo proclaimed its major goals to be promotion of the principles of the Universal Declaration of Human Rights and prevention of interethnic violence, but also warned that it would fight "aggressive manifestations of chauvinism and nationalism" with strikes, rallies and civil disobedience. Edinstvo insisted that both Russian and Kazakh should be recognised as state languages and protested some of the government's nationalist actions, such as compiling a list of occupations in which knowledge of Kazakh would be obligatory.[134]

The year 1990 also saw the emergence of first the Cossack political organisations in Kazakhstan. They started to register in provincial centres as national and cultural associations, but their activities were clearly political. In the summer of 1990 in the northern provinces the *Gorkaya Liniya* (Sorrow Line)[135] Cossacks formed an organisation and elected V. Achkasov as *ataman* (leader). At about the same time the *Vozrozhdeniye* (Rebirth) Cossack committee was established in Uralsk. At every meeting it voted for a demand "to acknowledge as illegal and revoke all decrees on the basis of which territory of the Ural Cossacks was taken from Russia and included in Kazakhstan".[136] In an article in *Moskovskiye novosti* in June 1991, Vozrozhdeniye's ataman, Alexander Galagan, proclaimed northern Kazakhstan and Alma-Ata province zones of Cossack interests and ancient Russian lands erroneously allotted to Kazakhstan.[137] In early 1991 the Union of Semirechye Cossacks came into being. For some time it was headed by V. Ovsyannikov, a former Airborne Forces officer, but he was replaced by N. Gunkin.[138] The Cossacks were the most dynamic and best organised among the Russian groups in Kazakhstan. From the outset they established firm links with their counterparts in Russia. For example, representatives of the Ural Cossacks took part in the founding congress of the Union of Cossacks of Russia held in Moscow on 28 June 1990, which united all the former Cossack Forces that had existed in tsarist Russia.[139]

The Cossacks were not alone in expressing separatist views. Non-Cossack representatives of the Russian community voiced similar sentiments. For example, in September 1989 the East Kazakhstan province newspaper *Rudnyi Altai* published an article by USSR People's Deputy S. Vasilyeva, who argued that the lands along the right bank of the Irtysh River were allocated wrongly to Kazakhstan in 1920, as their indigenous population was Russian. This article received an indignant response from the Kazakhstan Communist Party newspaper, *Kazakhstanskaya Pravda*.[140] In September 1990 Kazakh nationalist organisations held a massive rally in Alma-Ata condemning Russian separatists. Growth of separatist attitudes among ethnic Russians became a major problem for Nazarbayev's leadership. At a press conference on 24 September 1990, CPK Central Committee Second Secretary Anufriyev said "special alarm" was caused by "separatist tendencies" and "irresponsible appeals made by some groups, which are aimed at division of the republic's territory, thereby exacerbating interethnic relations".[141]

The first serious confrontation between Cossacks and Kazakhs took place on 14–15 September 1991 in Uralsk, where Vozrozhdeniye arranged festivities to celebrate the four-hundred-years anniversary of the Ural Cossack Force, attended by the Ataman of the Union of Cossacks of Russia A. Martinov; one of his deputies, V. Naumov; and Cossack representatives from the Don, Kuban, North Caucasus, Southern Urals and Siberia. During the celebrations the tricolour flag of the Russian Empire was unfurled. At the same time members of Azat, Zheltoksan and Nevada-Semipalatinsk came to Uralsk from Alma-Ata, Shymkent, Aktyubinsk and a number of other towns in Kazakhstan. The situation had the potential to develop into a serious interethnic conflict, but the law enforcement agencies managed to confine the hostilities to a few minor clashes.[142]

Events in Uralsk prompted Nazarbayev to protest to Yeltsin that the "provocative actions staged by Cossacks on 15 September this year on the territory of Kazakhstan under the Russian flag were perceived by people and public movements of the republic as a political act demonstrating open disregard for the state sovereignty of Kazakhstan" and to stress that the events created a serious threat "to civic accord and socio-political stability in the republic". Nazarbayev also said that if the Russian leadership had properly assessed the seriousness of the Cossack movement's unfounded claims, which ran contrary to previous agreements, the Kazakh leaders would not have been faced with such reckless actions.[143] The Kazakhstan Supreme Soviet Presidium described the Uralsk celebrations as an "attempt to artificially import interethnic conflicts".[144] There was no public response from Yeltsin.

Another conflict between Cossacks and Kazakhs occurred on 29 September 1991, when Cossacks in Tselinograd attempted to hold an assembly. The city authorities declared it illegal, and a large crowd of belligerent Kazakhs turned up at the intended venue. Given the risk of serious interethnic conflict, representatives of the city "dissuaded" the Cossacks from proceeding with the event.[145] But on 5 November the Union of Cossacks was registered as a public organisation at the justice directorate of the province executive committee. (The directorate at that stage was obviously controlled by ethnic Russians.) This provoked another Kazakh rally in Tselinograd, at which speakers demanded an immediate halt to the Cossack organisation's activities. The provincial procurator later demanded cancellation of its registration, and the justice directorate complied.[146] Since then confrontations between the Cossacks and the Kazakh authorities and Kazakh nationalist parties have become a constant feature of Kazakhstan's political reality.

The growth of ethnic nationalism did not leave the Russian Federation untouched. The reasons for this were basically the same as in other union republics, though the process had some specific features. Ethnic nationalism was a concept relatively new to Russians because the Russian elite traditionally perceived the country as a multi-ethnic state, first as an empire and later as the USSR, though Russians ascribed the role of leading nation to themselves. But Russian ethnic nationalism meant something other than recognition of the leading role of Russians in a multinational community. Its primary goal was national self-identification of ethnic Russians within the Soviet Union. The first public organisation to openly proclaim its adherence to Russian nationalist ideology was the national-patriotic movement Pamyat. This organisation was formed within the All-Russian Society for Preservation of Historical and Cultural Monuments in the mid-1970s for the purpose of renovating and restoring old buildings of historical or cultural value, primarily churches. Soon, however, Pamyat found itself involved in politics.

In late May 1987 Pamyat conducted its first rally in Manezh Square in the centre of Moscow. The demonstrators carried banners saying Save Our Monuments and demanded official registration of their organisation. Surprisingly, representatives of Pamyat were received by Boris Yeltsin, then first secretary of the Moscow City Party Committee and a candidate (nonvoting) member of the Politburo. In those days, this was an unprecedented

and courageous move. According to reports Yeltsin and the Pamyat deputation
engage in a heated discussion that lasted for two hours. Yeltsin allegedly
agreed with the members of the deputation on a number of issues, and
disagreed on others;[147] unfortunately, the reports do not specify the issues on
which they agreed or disagreed. However, it seems likely that the meeting,
Yeltsin's first encounter with a political process outside the official Party
bureaucracy, influenced the evolution of his political views.

In the manifesto of 12 January 1989, Pamyat unveiled its political program,
which among other things demanded that the Russian people should "have
rights equal to those of other peoples in our country". The manifesto called for
establishment of a Russian Academy of Sciences and Conservatory of Music,
an Institute for Russian History, Centre for Russian Culture, Russian Theatre,
Russian Film Industry and publication of a Russian encyclopaedia. It also
demanded "proportional national representation in the governing apparatus,
and also in art, science, and education". The manifesto did not call for
dissolution of the Soviet Union but argued for providing all Union republics
with "true autonomy", putting special emphasis on "economic autonomy".[148]
This implied economic autonomy for Russia, virtually a call for economic
separation.

The idea of Russia's political separation from the USSR, though
hypothetical, was soon in the air, openly voiced by prominent Russian writer
Valentin Rasputin at the Congress of People's Deputies in June 1989.[149] His
high public profile immediately gave the idea a touch of political respectability.
In December 1989 twelve public organisations sharing the concept of Russian
ethnic nationalism formed the Bloc of Russian Public-Patriotic Movements to
contest the Russian Soviet Federated Socialist Republic (RSFSR) Supreme
Soviet elections scheduled for 4 March 1990.[150] The bloc's program included
creating a Russian Communist Party; providing for Russia's equal and
proportional representation in the Union's administrative bodies; achieving
greater autonomy from the USSR government; giving Russia full control over
its natural resources; eliminating economic subsidies to other republics; and, in
the event of the USSR's disintegration, Russia's taking control of territory
populated by ethnic Russians in other republics.[151]

In 1990 the concept of Russian ethnic nationalism received a powerful new
boost from the well-known Russian émigré writer, Alexander Solzhenitsyn. His
pamphlet *Rebuilding Russia* was published in September by two Moscow
newspapers with a total circulation of 25 million copies. Solzhenitsyn argued
for Russia to secede from the USSR and for three Slavic republics – Russia,
Ukraine and Belorussia – to form a common statehood. With regard to
Kazakhstan, Solzhenitsyn offered two options, total annexation by Russia or
partition into an independent Kazakh south and a Russian north incorporated
into the Russian state. [152] The ideas of Solzhenitsyn, who represented a
conservative trend in Russian ethnic nationalism, could not fail to influence
wide sectors of Russian public opinion and even received qualified support
from liberal politicians in Yeltsin's entourage, such as Y. Karyakin,

G. Yakunin, G. Starovoitova and others. Yeltsin himself embraced Solzhenitsyn's vision of Russia's future and was so impressed by the pamphlet that he ordered it to the photocopied and distributed to all members of the Russian Parliament. The article, he asserted, contained "a lot of interesting thoughts". In November 1990, Yeltsin told the RSFSR Supreme Soviet that he was "intrigued by the idea of a union of the three Slavic republics", a central point in Solzhenitsyn's program.[153]

The difference between conservative and liberal Russian ethnic nationalists was that the liberals had no interest in achieving objectives such as a Slavic Union or unification with Russian communities in other republics. They were prepared to see the new Russia simply as the Russian Federation detached from the union. Nor did they share the goal of preserving Russian cultural uniqueness. On the contrary, their major aim was prompt implementation of Western-style political and economic reforms, and they regarded the rest of the Soviet Union as ballast which hampered progressive development of the Russian state and which should be got rid of as soon as possible. But liberals obviously saw that they could use conservative Russian nationalists to attack Gorbachev and the Union government.

At that time real opposition to ethnic nationalists could come from only one ideology, based on the strong Russian imperial tradition, which can be identified as Russian neo-Eurasianism. As a philosophical school, Eurasianism emerged in 1920s in the left wing of the Russian postrevolutionary emigration.[154] Eurasianists perceived the USSR as a continuation of the empire and regarded ethnic nationalism, including Russian ethnic nationalism, as extremely dangerous to the future integrity of the common state. As an alternative, they advocated a concept of "common Eurasian nationalism".[155] The main theoretician of Russian neo-Eurasianism was a popular novelist, A. Prokhanov.[156] Another prominent contemporary ideologist of Russian neo-Eurasianism was Vladimir Zhirinovskiy, now chairman of the Liberal Democratic Party of Russia (LDPR).[157] The first neo-Eurasianist organisation, the United Council of Russia, was launched in mid-September 1989, with the objective of preserving the USSR.[158] The ideology of neo-Eurasianism was clearly present in the activities of the *Soyuz* (Union) faction in the USSR Supreme Soviet. After its creation in mid-1990, the Communist Party of the Russian Federation also supported ideas of neo-Eurasianism, though its leaders' close links to Gorbachev deprived them of political credibility.

The Kazakh elite closely watched the political debate in Russia on relations with Kazakhstan and could not fail to be concerned at the proposals for partition voiced by Russian ethnic nationalists. Discussions on the territorial issue started as early as autumn of 1989. Moscow Mayor G. Popov was among the first to raise it, arguing that provinces of Kazakhstan where the population is predominantly Russian should not have been included in the Kazakh republic when it was created in 1920. In early 1990 the Moscow journal *Istoriya SSSR* published an article by historian and ethnographer V. I. Kozlov, who maintained that northwest Kazakhstan and the Semirechye region in the southeast should have remained part of the RSFSR. These claims prompted the June 1990 publication of an article in the Kazakh-language official newspaper *Sotsialistik Kazakhstan* which argued that the lands in question were traditionally Kazakh. Russian territorial claims were rejected a couple of days later by Nazarbayev in his speech to the republican Party congress.[159] But the greatest indignation in Kazakhstan was provoked by Solzhenitsyn's article. He was vehemently condemned by speakers at a rally held in September 1990 in the centre of Alma-Ata,[160] and a series of articles attacking him appeared simultaneously in the Kazakhstan and Moscow press.[161] However, the Kazakh elite had no liking for Russian neo-Eurasianism either, since it supported preservation of the USSR as a single state and Moscow's firm control over the republics.

On 20 September 1989 a long-awaited plenum on nationality affairs was finally held. It adopted a CPSU platform on nationality policy which called for a "renewed federation filled with real political and economic content, to ensure the satisfaction of the diverse requirements of all Soviet nations" and advocated "optimal correlation between the rights of the union republics and the USSR as a whole" by clearly defining "the jurisdiction and mutual obligations of the Union and the republics". Most important among its suggested innovations were economic self-reliance for the republics, increased autonomy for republican Communist Parties and a new Union Treaty.[162] At the plenum Nazarbayev revealed his political objective of achieving maximum independence from Moscow. He claimed that the Soviet Union in its present form was not a federation but a unitary state. To turn it into a real federation the republics' rights must be expanded, especially in ownership and administration of land, minerals and other resources. He advocated transferring ownership of basic industries from union to republican ministries and argued strongly for granting republics the right to enter into international economic agreements. On the other hand he advocated that Moscow retain ownership of defence industries and means of communication.[163]

In his speech at the Second Congress of USSR People's Deputies in December 1989 Nazarbayev emphasised that "republics need complete economic independence in the framework of a federation and right of ownership of their territory, and they need guaranteed freedom in relations with the Centre, ministries and foreign partners."[164] Thus Nazarbayev's initial concept was a political and military union with full economic independence for the republics, including external economic relations. In this he was simply following the Baltic nationalist leaders, who had been the first to advance economic sovereignty. Nazarbayev still supported preservation of the Soviet Union and did not advocate full political independence for the republics, but it is quite possible that he already had in mind the goal of full independence. In his memoirs he wrote, "From the beginning of 1990 I started to think that Kazakhstan would have to get out of the post-perestroika impasse independently. Already nobody believed in the power of the Centre".[165]

Nazarbayev saw a real chance for Kazakhstan's full independence in mid-1990, after the newly elected RSFSR Supreme Soviet adopted a declaration of sovereignty. The declaration among other things proclaimed that the RSFSR "recognises and respects the sovereign rights of the union republics and the USSR".[166] According to Nazarbayev, from the "formal" point of view, the Russian declaration of sovereignty meant "inability of the USSR to exist further in its previous quality".[167] Kazakhstan's own declaration was adopted by the Republic's Supreme Soviet on 25 October 1990. Much of it repeated provisions contained in the Russian declaration. Kazakhstan proclaimed itself a "sovereign state which voluntarily associates with other republics in a Union of Sovereign Republics and builds relations with them on a treaty basis". It said that "citizens of the republic of all nationalities constitute the people of Kazakhstan, and they are the sole exponent of sovereignty and the source of state power in the Kazakh SSR". The declaration established the supremacy of the constitution and Kazakhstan's laws in its territory "except for matters which it voluntarily delegates to the union." Kazakhstan reserved the right to freely secede from the union.[168]

There were, however, substantial distinctions between the Russian and Kazakh declarations, which reflected different policies with regard to the future of the USSR and the individual development of these two republics. While the Russian declaration claimed the right to have RSFSR "plenipotentiary representation in other union republics and foreign countries", Kazakhstan's went much further, proclaiming its right "to act as an independent subject of international relations, determine foreign policy in its own interests, exchange diplomatic and consular missions, and participate in the activity of international organisations." It also claimed the right to have its own troops, bodies of state security and internal affairs and a national bank, not subordinate to Moscow. Thus Kazakhstan's concept of sovereignty was much broader than Russia's.

The Kazakh declaration also differed on the issue of nationality relations. In several places it emphasised the special role of the Kazakh nation. Thus the preamble mentioned "responsibility for the fate of the Kazakh nation". Section 2 specified the necessity for "revival and development of the distinctive culture, traditions, and language and strengthening of the national dignity of the Kazakh nation". The Russian declaration contained no mention of the Russian nation and used the phrase "citizens of the RSFSR". The Kazakh declaration contained other singular provisions. It said, for example, that Kazakhstan "regulates migration within the republic and between the republic and other republics." It also warned of legal persecution of those who would make public appeals for violation of the republic's territorial integrity and "inciting national discord." The latter provision was clearly directed against those Russian organisations and individuals who advocated annexing the Russian-populated northern regions of Kazakhstan to the RSFSR. The Kazakh declaration contained obvious nationalist overtones, despite several references to the multinational nature of Kazakhstan as a state. Implementation of all of its provisions would mean that the republic de facto became an independent state.

With the declaration adopted, Kazakhstan's government proceeded to consolidate the republic's sovereignty. In late October it introduced customs controls, including on trade with other republics of the USSR, to prevent export from the republic of all sorts of goods.[169] In January 1991 it made its first claims on the Baykonur cosmodrome. During his visit to Baykonur on 14 January, Nazarbayev said that "the cosmodrome's scientific and technical potential will work directly towards resolving some of Kazakhstan's problems, such as space communications, space television, study of natural resources, weather monitoring". In early February he met in Alma-Ata with representatives of the Defence Ministry and other ministries and departments, scientific institutions and enterprises connected with space activities, and stressed at the meeting that union ministries and departments should pay more attention to the social sphere. Leaders of the space programs and the government of Kazakhstan signed a number of documents which constituted a plan to set up a warning system for contingencies such as earthquakes, mudslides, and other natural calamities. The space research institute of the Kazakh Academy of Sciences would be transferred to a centre for space studies, scientists could take a more active part in the solution of ecological problems, earth studies and prospecting for natural resources in outer space.[170]

On 9 April 1991 the Kazakhstan Supreme Soviet Presidium passed a resolution transferring oil and gas deposits in Kazakhstan to the republic's jurisdiction, and instructing the Committee for Administering State Property to conclude agreements to that effect with the USSR Ministry of the Oil and Gas Industry.[171] The decision was taken just before the start of the first drilling operations in the Tengiz oilfield, an enterprise expected to be a joint venture between Kazakhstan and the U.S. Chevron Corporation, and was eventually to yield 30–35 million tons of oil a year plus natural gas.[172] On 25 March Nazarbayev met with heads of enterprises subordinate to all-Union ministries to discuss how they fitted into Kazakhstan's economic reform program, particularly how powers should be redefined and relations changed between Moscow, Alma-Ata and the enterprises themselves.[173]

In early May 1991 Kazakhstan's Supreme Soviet prepared a draft citizenship law, which contemplated granting citizenship only to those who had lived in the republic for at least ten years and had a command of the state language.[174] Soon after that the Kazakh authorities began repatriating Kazakhs from Mongolia; the first group of 170 arrived in July 1991.[175]

Besides such straightforward measures, Nazarbayev began a devious game aimed at creating a legal basis for inter-republican relations bypassing the USSR government. He initiated a process of conclusion of multiple inter-republic agreements which undermined the power of the Union's centre. The first such agreement was concluded less than a fortnight after the RSFSR declared its sovereignty. On 23 June 1990 Nazarbayev invited the leaders of Uzbekistan, Kyrgyzstan, Tajikistan and Turkmenistan to Alma-Ata, where they signed the Agreement on Economic, Scientific-Technological and Cultural Cooperation, covering the period up to the year 1996. The agreement's preamble stated the principle of "state and economic sovereignty of republics" and proclaimed as a major objective "coordination of actions in attaining economic self-sufficiency of the republics, realisation of effective economic strategy and tactics with respect for mutual interests, and acceleration of social progress of the multinational population of the republics". The agreement envisaged a permanent Coordinating Council with its secretariat in Alma-Ata. The council would consist of representatives of each republic's State Planning Committee and would meet not less than twice a year, in each capital in rotation. Its propose was "to guarantee the coordination of general economic, scientific-technological, and cultural-political directions, and fulfilment of the conditions of this Agreement".[176]

It was typical of Nazarbayev's political style to describe the meeting as an "event to strengthen our Union, our Federation as a whole",[177] whereas in reality the meeting and the agreement signed there served the opposite purpose of involving the other Central Asian leaders in a process of fragmenting the union, artfully capitalising on their natural anxiety about the Russian declaration of sovereignty's potential consequences for Central Asia. In a way it was a collective reply to Yeltsin, but in practice the agreement had a far-reaching ulterior motive, that is, to undermine the central government's power by establishing alternative mechanisms for political and economic management of inter-republican relations.

Later, Nazarbayev made similar deals with other republics, all accompanied by vocal declarations that they were being concluded for the Union's sake, to lay foundations for the new union treaty. In a speech on 17 August 1991 Nazarbayev actually took credit for Kazakhstan's being the first to conclude agreements establishing "horizontal ties" with the other republics of Central Asia. "At that, frankly speaking, crucial point, a lot depended on the other republics understanding our aims. And we are grateful to Russia, Ukraine and Belorussia for not only supporting us, but also agreeing to conclude similar treaties with us", he said.[178]

On 5 October 1990 Kazakhstan and Belorussia signed an agreement on economic, scientific, technical and cultural cooperation. It emphasised that direct ties could become a reliable base for drafting a new union treaty and established a coordinating council to regulate business contacts.[179] In late November 1990 Kazakhstan signed an agreement with Ukraine on economic and cultural cooperation, which provided for setting up a permanent coordinating council for business cooperation, consisting of representatives of economic and management bodies, and to complete the drafting of treaties on various issues, including diplomatic and foreign relations, within two months.[180]

On 21 November 1990 in Moscow Yeltsin and Nazarbayev signed a treaty between the Kazakh SSR and RSFSR, which was a more comprehensive document than the previous inter-republican agreements. The treaty proclaimed policies of equality; noninterference in internal affairs; denunciation of pressure, coercion and blackmail in mutual relations; and guarantees of the rights and freedoms of Russians in Kazakhstan and Kazakhs in Russia. They also signed an economic agreement containing obligations on mutual supplies, identifying strategic directions for moving towards a market economy, and of cooperation in television, other means of communication, including via space, and transportation, including transcontinental transportation. At the joint press conference that followed the signing, Yeltsin made an important statement designed to allay Nazarbayev's fears about future Russian policy towards Kazakhstan and to draw him to his side in his struggle with Gorbachev. Yeltsin said that Russia had abandoned once and for all the policy of supremacy, or of putting pressure on the republics, particularly on Kazakhstan.[181] But later events showed that Nazarbayev had no intention of taking sides; he played for one side only, his own.

The treaty with Russia set an important precedent, and thus similar treaties soon followed. On 18 February 1991 Nazarbayev and President Akayev of Kyrgyzstan signed a treaty of friendship and cooperation. Nazarbayev told a news conference that it opened up "vast opportunities for the republics to develop cooperation by recognising their sovereignty".[182] On 20 February 1991 Nazarbayev and Kravchuk concluded a bilateral treaty between Kazakhstan and Ukraine, which provided for mutual recognition of sovereignty of the republics, respect for their territorial integrity, and equal rights for all irrespective of nationality, religion or other differences. It was again stressed that such agreements would be the basis of a new union treaty.[183]

In addition to undermining the USSR government's power through bilateral agreements with other republics, Nazarbayev made similar attempts in the sphere of international relations. In 1990–1991 he toured the United States, Canada, South Korea and China, seeking to establish independent economic relations with them. But in that domain his efforts were less successful; he failed to induce any foreign state to bypass Moscow and establish direct relations with Kazakhstan.

A major element in Nazarbayev's political tactics in that period was exploitation of the rivalry between Yeltsin and Gorbachev. This became evident at the at the 28th CPSU Congress in July 1990. In his speech there Nazarbayev confirmed his stand in favour of the Union: "Our position, which the Communists and the majority of toilers in Kazakhstan share, is for a renewed strong Union of Soviet Socialist Republics and a unified CPSU", he said.[184] But another passage contained a warning to Gorbachev: "How can Kazakhstan be helped, if 90% of its industry is under Moscow's industrial control?.... Our repeated proposals and demands concerning economic and foreign trade independence for enterprises remain a voice in the wilderness", and the speech ended with a clear overture to Yeltsin: "We are sincerely happy at the goodwill shown by the new leadership of the Russian Federation, which is also striving to strengthen horizontal inter-republic ties. We believe that agreements of this sort will create the foundation for a new Union Treaty".[185]

Thus Nazarbayev used the Yeltsin factor to put pressure on the USSR government and to demand more concessions from it in the matter of putting

Kazakhstan's economy under Alma-Ata's jurisdiction. If these demands were not met, Kazakhstan would establish direct economic ties with the RSFSR. Such ties were in fact already established when Nazarbayev saw his warning fall on deaf ears in the Kremlin. From November 1990 Nazarbayev steadily moved towards a coalition with Yeltsin against Gorbachev. The peak of this process was reached in January 1991.

Early in 1991 Gorbachev, feeling political power slipping from his hands, took a series of steps to reverse the situation in what the media later called the conservative offensive. The use of military force in Vilnius on 12 January sent an unpleasant message to national leaders in other republics. On 14 January, after returning from his tour of the Baltic states, Yeltsin threatened Gorbachev with the possibility of a comprehensive quadripartite treaty between Russia, Ukraine, Belorussia and Kazakhstan without waiting for the a new Union treaty.[186] On 16 January Gorbachev made a countermove, decreeing a referendum on the future of the USSR to be held on 17 March. Gorbachev calculated correctly that most of the Soviet population would support maintaining its integrity, and this would legitimise his efforts to keep the union intact. This prospect was fraught with obvious dangers for the republican national elites, whose long-awaited goal of independence could become unattainable.

This worried Nazarbayev. On 4 February 1991 he met with the leaders of Russia, Ukraine and Belorussia behind Gorbachev's back. They discussed accelerating the conclusion of the new union treaty and signed an agreement on direct relations, bypassing the central government. As later revealed by Shushkevich, former chairman of the Belorussian Supreme Soviet, in February they drafted the treaty which became the basis of the Belovezhskaya agreement.[187] Commenting on the results of the meeting, Nazarbayev said, "The central government itself directed us towards developing horizontal links; we concluded an economic treaty, and we have a political declaration between these republics". Nazarbayev explained that the meeting's purpose was to create a common front against the USSR government. "When it is a question of preserving, so to speak, of winning, or, perhaps, of winning back, the declaration adopted by the Supreme Soviets of the republics on the sovereignty of the republics, we have to fight together.... We will stand up together against the dictate of the central departments, against return to the past, or against elements of the administrative and command system again — yes, we will resist".[188] Thus Nazarbayev's position was no different from that of the other three republican leaders, who later became the initiators of the Belovezhskaya Pushcha accords, which dissolved the Soviet Union.

On 11 February 1991, at an extraordinary session of Kazakhstan's Supreme Soviet, Nazarbayev strongly advocated speeding up the process of negotiating the new union treaty, on the grounds that the "exacerbated political situation" in the USSR made it impossible to wait for all republics to determine their attitude to it. The Supreme Soviet therefore passed a resolution declaring that [a] dialogue must be started urgently with those who advocate preservation of the country's unity, leaving the remaining republics the right to join it whenever they have made their final choice".[189] Nazarbayev's formula was not as simple as it appeared. He wanted to keep Gorbachev involved as deeply as possible in the new treaty negotiations to prevent his going over completely to the hardliners' side n the Soviet leadership, who advocated introducing a union-wide state of emergency and crushing separatist tendencies by force.

The last part of Nazarbayev's formula cited above actually facilitated the Baltic republics' quest for independence. While formally speaking for preserving the USSR's integrity, he in fact proposed permitting all those who did not want to be part of the new Union to opt out of the negotiating process. With the existing union already considered inadequate by all the republics and the Kremlin, this call was tantamount to allowing secession. If the USSR government had done as he suggested, it would have legitimised those republics' independence and facilitated further moves by Kazakhstan in the same direction. Thus Nazarbayev was actually furthering the USSR's disintegration while verbally stating his allegiance to its preservation.

Soon, however, Nazarbayev turned, from opposing Gorbachev to defending him against Yeltsin. This was prompted by Yeltsin's speech on Russian television on 19 February 1991, in which he demanded that Gorbachev resign and hand over all political power to the Federation Council. On the next day, at a joint press conference with Ukrainian leader Kravchuk in Alma-Ata, Nazarbayev described Yeltsin's proposition as "simply unacceptable. . . . There will not be a leader of the state, on the whole there will be no centre. What he is proposing is that all republics again become part of the Great Russian Empire. This is also unacceptable for the republics . . . what he said was not constructive and this proposal cannot be supported in Kazakhstan".[190]

Nazarbayev definitely feared Yeltsin and wanted to retain Gorbachev as a counterbalance. When asked in an interview which of the two he preferred, Nazarbayev said, "An important quality in every politician is predictability of his actions. I believe that M. S. Gorbachev has this quality. Therefore I am very much afraid of drastic changes in the top echelon of power, which today could lead to loss of even the rather small democratic gains that perestroika has given us".[191] Nazarbayev's implied criticism of Yeltsin as unpredictable showed that he was unsure which way Yeltsin's policy would turn once all restraints on his power were removed. In this Nazarbayev took into account Yeltsin's unconcealed fascination with Solzhenitsyn's concept of rearranging Russia, including the annexation of much or all of Kazakhstan to the Russian state.

Nazarbayev's support for Gorbachev was only a tactical move, and soon he was again opposing him. Kazakhstan was the only republic in the USSR to change the wording of the referendum question on its future. In the question Do you consider it necessary to preserve the USSR as a union of equal sovereign republics? the word "republics" was replaced by "states".[192] According to Nazarbayev, this change was made to bring it into line with the formulation contained in Kazakhstan's declaration of sovereignty.[193] The tactic he applied was very ingenious. He could not refuse to hold the referendum, as some other republics did, because a number of the Russian-populated regions would hold it anyway, and this could lead to a de facto split of Kazakhstan. But the change in the wording could achieve the same goal by permitting him to claim in future negotiations with Moscow that the voters had supported his concept of a much looser Union.

Gorbachev, obviously, understood what lay behind Nazarbayev's move and tried to apply pressure. According to Nazarbayev, he received daily phone calls from Gorbachev or his aides, demanding that the union question be put in some Russian-populated areas first. "They tried to intimidate us: 'We won't count the results'. I told them, it is important for us to know ourselves the opinion of citizens of Kazakhstan. . . . Passions became inflamed, and on the eve of the referendum I had to appear on television and say: 'Dear citizens of Kazakhstan! I consider the referendum a vote of confidence in myself as President".[194] And Nazarbayev managed to get away with his manoeuvre, although the change of wording caused resentment in some Russian-populated areas (e.g, in Ust-Kamenogorsk, Uralsk) where the local authorities insisted that the USSR Supreme Soviet's wording be retained.[195] But in the overwhelming majority of Kazakhstan's provinces, it was Nazarbayev's question that was put to the vote.

The results of the referendum in Kazakhstan were significant: 88.2% of the electorate voted, and 94.1% of them voted Yes, the fourth highest among the union republics. The USSR average was 80% voting and 76.4% of those voting Yes; in Russia, 75.4% and 71.3%, respectively.[196] Despite the controversy surrounding Kazakhstan's position on the referendum, Nazarbayev artfully used it to his benefit, killing three birds with one stone. First, over Moscow's objections he pushed through wording that suited him, which created a wide field for him to manoeuvre vis-à-vis Gorbachev. Second, he did so without antagonising Gorbachev to the point of enmity. Third, he exploited the public's strong pro-union mood to consolidate his position. He could later portray his linkage between the Yes vote and vote of confidence in himself as almost the main reason why the people of Kazakhstan had so strongly supported the Union.

The results of the referendum strengthened Gorbachev's position vis-à-vis national elites and allowed him to press for preservation of the union. On 23 April 1991 Gorbachev met the leaders of the nine republics that had participated in the referendum. The meeting adopted a joint statement which inter alia provided for speedy conclusion of a new union treaty "taking into account the results of the all-Union referendum". Gorbachev made substantial concessions, agreeing to recognise Union Republics as "sovereign states", promising "fundamental enhancement" of their powers and committing himself to early elections after signing a new Union Treaty.[197] During negotiations for the new draft Union treaty Gorbachev tried to enlist Nazarbayev as an ally against Yeltsin. He, obviously, failed to grasp the essence of Nazarbayev's policy and fell for his multiple declarations in favour of the new union treaty.

On 28 May Gorbachev went to Kazakhstan on a public relations visit designed to boost his political standing in the final stages of the new union treaty negotiations. Nazarbayev used Gorbachev's visit to maximum benefit for himself. He reiterated Kazakhstan's commitment to the renewed union and extracted important new concessions from the USSR government. He lobbied Gorbachev to transfer industrial enterprises located in Kazakhstan but run by USSR ministries to the republic's jurisdiction. At a meeting with Gorbachev and members of Kazakhstan's political and industrial establishment on 30 May 1991, Nazarbayev voiced assurances that when the enterprises were transferred, the republic's leadership would display maximum balance and circumspection to maintain the coordination and management of production in the country as a whole".[198] To please Nazarbayev, Gorbachev gave way on this issue.

On 14–15 June 1991, at a meeting between Nazarbayev and M. Shadov, USSR minister of the coal industry, O. Soskovets, USSR minister of metallurgy and V. Shimko, USSR minister of radio industry, it was agreed to transfer these enterprises to Kazakhstan's jurisdiction.[199] This was an important victory for Nazarbayev. Neither he nor anybody else at that time could predict that the USSR would disintegrate before the end of the year, and assuming control of the major industrial enterprises in the republic was a breakthrough towards full economic sovereignty.

Nazarbayev also tried to use Gorbachev to block Yeltsin's plans to revive Cossack structures. At a meeting on 30 May, Nazarbayev expressed concern about forming separate Cossack army units. "One wonders whom they are preparing to defend? Perhaps they want to remind the national minorities of the former Tsarist empire of the period of colonisation of unarmed nomads?", he said.[200] After Nazarbayev spoke Kazakh writer A. Nurpeisov took the floor and delivered a major anti-Cossack speech.[201] It is not known whether Gorbachev promised anything on the Cossack issue, but after his departure Nazarbayev's position hardened. In mid-June he appeared on television and threatened legal reprisals against Russian separatists, condemned the creation of Cossack organisations, describing them as military units, and warned the Urals Cossacks against celebrating the 400th anniversary of their service of the Russian tsar.[202]

In mid-June a draft union treaty was sent to the republican parliaments for consideration. The Kazakhstan Supreme Soviet approved it on 24 June, though Nazarbayev voiced some reservations, particularly on the principle of joint property on the territory of the republics and the proposed federal taxation mechanism. The Supreme Soviet approved the draft on the whole and nominated a delegation headed by Nazarbayev to oversee final amendments.[203] By the end of June the Supreme Soviets of eight of the nine Union republics willing to sign the treaty had approved the draft and nominated their delegations, the Ukrainian Supreme Soviet postponing its decision until mid-September.[204] On 12 July the draft was also approved in general by the USSR Supreme Soviet. The ceremony for signing the treaty was set for 20 August, and the first republics to do so would be Russia, Kazakhstan and Uzbekistan.[205]

On 16–17 August an important meeting between Yeltsin and Nazarbayev took place in Alma-Ata. Formally it was devoted to exchanging instruments of ratification of the bilateral treaty signed a year before, but its political purpose was to project both republics' self-proclaimed image as sovereign states on the eve of signing the new union treaty. But Nazarbayev used the occasion to extract major concessions from Yeltsin on the territorial issue. Besides signing a protocol on ratification, Yeltsin and Nazarbayev adopted a joint declaration, On Guarantees of Stability of the Union of Sovereign States. It said that "preservation of the territorial integrity of Kazakhstan and the Russian Federation is the most important guarantee for preventing disintegration of the country and its component states". The declaration especially emphasised that, in making the new union Russia was acting as a founding state "together with republics within the RSFSR".[206]

Nazarbayev chose the right moment for extracting from Yeltsin unequivocal obligations with regard to Kazakhstan's territorial integrity. Yeltsin was faced with growing separatism inside the RSFSR. Following its declaration of sovereignty, autonomous entities within RSFSR were one after another proclaiming their sovereignty, too. This was encouraged by Gorbachev, who was trying to undermine Yeltsin's grip on power within the RSFSR and play the autonomous republics against Yeltsin, just as Yeltsin had played the union republics against him. Some Russian autonomies even suggested signing the union treaty independently of Russia, thereby effectively assigning themselves the status of union republics, and Yeltsin wanted to prevent this. At the conclusion of the talks with Nazarbayev, he said that the joint declaration concerned "the integral nature of our two states. . . . We believe the unity of Russia is quite crucial to the future of the union, since 16 republics within Russia have declared their sovereignty". In Yeltsin's words, Nazarbayev "firmly upheld" the position that neither Tatarstan, nor any other autonomous republic should be a party to the union treaty.[207]

For the first time Yeltsin publicly condemned Russian separatism in Kazakhstan, saying that revival of the Cossack movement "must not be allowed to grow into some sort of territorial claims", and that "[t]here can be no question of our tolerating the seizing of any territory of Kazakhstan in favour of Russia".[208] Nazarbayev also drew Yeltsin into signing a declaration, On Common Economic Space, which invited all republics of the Soviet Union to meet to discuss formation of a common market space and principles of creation of an inter-republican economic committee.[209] The declaration represented Nazarbayev's line of establishing maximum direct ties between republics, bypassing the union government, and committed the RSFSR leadership to further actions to undermine the integrity of the union after signing the new union treaty, even though Yeltsin was still committed to preservation of the union state, though in a form less burdensome for Russia. The new union treaty obviously suited him, but the proposed declaration showed that it did not suit Nazarbayev. After signing the treaty, he intended to proceed to his ultimate goal — full independence for Kazakhstan.

On 19 August 1991 the USSR's gradual political evolution was interrupted. At 8 A.M. Moscow television and radio stations announced the introduction of a six-month state of emergency in some parts of the country and the formation of a State Committee for the State of Emergency (SCSE). The notorious abortive coup d'état had begun. On 19 August nobody, Nazarbayev included, knew what the coup was about, or that it would fail. Nazarbayev confirmed his reputation for caution by refraining from sudden moves or taking sides. Undoubtedly, Nazarbayev was personally opposed to the coup, because its leaders wanted to preserve the USSR as a strong federation, keeping republics subordinate to Moscow.

In his statement on the evening of 19 August, Nazarbayev offered no assessment whatsoever of the events but urged citizens to remain calm and show restraint. By midday on 20 August he knew that the Airborne Forces had gone over to Yeltsin, so he issued another statement, now criticising the SCSE as "not provided for by the USSR constitution". Only on the evening of 20 August, when the scales had definitely tipped against the SCSE, did Nazarbayev appear on television for the second time to make his position quite clear: "The Committee that has been created in the country without participation of the USSR Supreme Soviet and the republics is knowingly producing illegal documents that, apart from everything else, flout the republics' declarations of sovereignty".[210]

Nazarbayev was among those republican leaders who saw the collapse of the USSR Government as an opportunity to opt for full independence. Gorbachev had lost real power and could do little to stop them. On 24 August the Ukrainian and on 25 August the Belorussian Supreme Soviets declared independence. Nazarbayev refrained from doing so, but at the USSR Supreme Soviet session on 26 August 1991 he stated that "the renewed union can no longer be a federation" and a new "confederative treaty" should be concluded, adding that the new union should have neither a union government nor a union parliament. He also said that the treaty must be signed not only by union republics, but also by autonomous republics, which "have declared, and will want to declare themselves sovereign", advocated giving those that decided to leave the union the opportunity to do so, and called "for immediate solution to the question of giving full freedom to the Baltic republics, Moldavia and Georgia, and all who expressed their aspiration for independence and autonomy".[211]

This was a program for dismantling the union, a stance similar to that of national leaders in other union republics. But at that moment it contradicted the positions of both Gorbachev and Yeltsin. On the previous day Yeltsin had stated that the new union must be a federation, and Gorbachev proposed at the session to sign the union treaty and create central bodies to administer the union until a new constitution took effect.[212] Moreover, Nazarbayev had clearly backtracked on his promise to Yeltsin, made only nine days before, not to support independence for autonomous republics, clearly aiming to undercut the unprecedented power Yeltsin had acquired after the coup and damp down his possible imperial ambitions.

Not surprisingly, the Russian government's statement opposing uncontrolled disintegration of the union was not well received by Nazarbayev. The statement was published on 27 August in *Rossiyskaya gazeta,* signed by Yeltsin's press secretary, Voshchanov. It said: "In the past few days a number of union republics have proclaimed state independence and announced their secession from the USSR.... The Russian Federation does not question the constitutional right of every state and people to self-determination. However, there is a problem of borders, a problem that can and may remain unsettled only given the existence of relations of union, codified in an appropriate treaty. If these relations are broken off, the RSFSR reserves the right to raise the question of reviewing its borders. This applies to all adjacent republics with the exception of the three Baltic republics (Latvia, Lithuania and Estonia), whose state independence Russia has already recognised."[213]

On 29 August Nazarbayev sent a telegram to Yeltsin, expressing concern that Russia had not yet clearly repudiated territorial claims on Kazakhstan's borders and claiming that public protest, gathering force in Kazakhstan, could have unforeseeable consequences. He requested dispatch of an official representative of the RSFSR to Alma-Ata to sign an "appropriate communiqué".[214] On the same day Dzhanibekov, a USSR Supreme Soviet deputy from Kazakhstan, also criticised the statement.[215] A Russian delegation headed by Vice-President Rutskoy did in fact arrive in Alma-Ata on 29 August. It was met by angry demonstrators from the Nevada-Semipalatinsk movement, who paraded in the capital's centre with banners declaring "Boris, you're wrong! Kazakh land is indivisible!, The borders of Kazakhstan are unalterable!, No to federation! Yes to confederation!, and demanded that leaders of the Cossack movement and "instigators" of territorial division of Kazakhstan be prosecuted.[216] Despite this cold reception, the negotiations between Rutskoy and Nazarbayev were quite fruitful. They resulted in a joint communiqué which provided for joint measures "to prevent uncontrolled disintegration of the union state", confirmed mutual obligations "on the issues of human rights and territorial integrity of the sides", and contained a provision declaring unlawful actions by "public associations and movements, directed at violating interethnic accord". These were the obligations Nazarbayev had wanted Russia to confirm.

On the other hand Nazarbayev had to agree to certain demands made by the Russian delegation. One provision of the communiqué stipulated that during the transitional period "temporary inter-governmental structures of administration" must be established, while another called for speedy formation of a "system of collective security" stipulated that decisions on military and strategic questions, space research and communications might be taken only on the basis of "inter-governmental consultations and coordination", and provided that units of the USSR armed forces stationed in republics would have "dual subordination" to prevent their use for unconstitutional purposes. Another important undertaking was that both sides confirmed their acceptance of the former USSR's international obligations. This was to put Kazakhstan's future actions in international relations within a certain legal framework, which as later events showed played an essential role.[217]

Thus Yeltsin's political demarche played its part. The common statement by
the president of the USSR and leaders of ten union republics prepared on the
eve of an extraordinary Congress of People's Deputies (2–5 September 1991)
repeated the major provisions of the Russian-Kazakh declaration. Announced
at the Congress by Nazarbayev, the statement provided for concluding a
collective security treaty for the purposes of maintaining joint armed forces and
a single military-strategic space; adopting a declaration guaranteeing citizens'
rights and freedoms, conducting basic reforms in the army, KGB, Ministry of
Interior, USSR Procurator's Office, and taking the republics' sovereignty into
account. The republics undertook to observe the USSR's international
obligations, including arms control and foreign economic relations.

At the same time the statement reflected a total lack of prospects for the
union state. It said that all republics which so wished so could "prepare and
sign" a union treaty and that each republic could "independently determine the
form of its participation in the union". This was tantamount to Gorbachev's
consent to dissolution of the USSR, because it allowed republics either not to
join or to join but undertake only insignificant obligations. Moreover, the
statement abolished central union government, proposing to replace it with an
Inter-Republican Economic Committee on a parity principle to coordinate only
economic management. The Congress itself was to disband and be replaced by
a State Council, comprising Gorbachev and the republics' presidents as the
supreme authority in the reformed USSR. Nazarbayev also inserted in the
statement his proposal for an inter-republican economic treaty to be joined by
all republics, whatever their proclaimed status. The statement also asked the
Congress to support the republics for membership in the UN and for
recognition as subjects of international law.[218] Thus the program contained in
the statement was one of gradual abolition of the union state and its
replacement by a sort of international organisation with functions resembling
those of a combined North Atlantic Treaty Organisation (NATO) and European
Union.

After the Congress, Nazarbayev proceeded to consolidate Kazakhstan's
sovereignty. On 13 September 1991 he issued a decree on conscription for
military service, giving Kazakhstan's military commissariat the status of a
republican body, thus putting it under the control of Kazakhstan's leadership.
The decree also provided that as of autumn 1991, Kazakhstan's Interior
Ministry forces would be manned "by citizens called up for actual military
service from the territory of the republic". This would guarantee that Moscow
could not use them in any internal conflict in Kazakhstan without his consent.
The decree prohibited sending conscripts to military construction detachments
and Interior Forces units outside Kazakhstan.[219] In October, Nazarbayev
explained that the Interior Forces constitute the backbone of the future National
Guard, to be established "as an important link in strengthening the republic's
security", a necessity caused "by the tragic events of last August".[220]
Nazarbayev needed a National Guard to counter any acts of force initiated by
Moscow.

In early September, Nazarbayev took a number of steps to assume full control of the economy. He issued decrees transferring union-subordinated enterprises and organisations in Kazakhstan to the republic's jurisdiction, providing for independent foreign trade and creating Kazakhstan's own reserves of precious metals and diamonds.[221] Supreme Soviet Chairman Asanbayev said in an interview that it would be wrong for the "centre" to control all gold and hard currency reserves, that central reserves should be created from contributions by the union's member-states and should not consist of all the gold extracted in the republics, and added that the republics themselves must control the credit resources formed on their territory.[222] On Nazarbayev's instructions, Kazakhstan set up customs posts on the border with Russia's Chelyabinsk province to stem the outflow of food and consumer goods.[223]

In an interview with *Hokkaido Shimbun*, published by *Kazakhstanskaya pravda* on 2 October 1991, Nazarbayev explained that he saw the new union "as a community of sovereign states united in resolving similar economic, political, social and other problems . . . with each republic deciding for itself how it is to join and the conditions for its membership of the new organisation". Use of such terms as "community" and "association" was not accidental. They meant that Nazarbayev had made a firm choice for dissolution of the single union state and envisioned in its place an organisation similar to the European Union. Nazarbayev also indicated that relations between Kazakhstan and Russia would be based on the treaty they signed, thus denying central government any future role in regulating them.[224]

In October, Nazarbayev attempted to put the Soviet military infrastructure in Kazakhstan under his control. In a speech on Republic Day, he revealed his plan "to build our relations with the troops stationed on the territory of Kazakhstan on a very strict legal basis, with the requirement that they be jointly subordinate to the republic's President".[225] To this end on 25 October he issued a decree establishing the State Defence Committee of Kazakhstan. The decree specifically stressed that it was created to guarantee the independence, territorial integrity, defence and other vitally important interests of Kazakhstan.[226] Lieutenant-General S. Nurmagambetov was appointed chairman. He said in an interview that a sovereign state such as Kazakhstan must have all the attributes of statehood, including those concerned with defence, and that Kazakhstan was not about to set up its own armed forces, but that the State Defence Committee would cover all the republic's military infrastructure and take all forces in Kazakhstan under its control.[227]

At a meeting with voters in mid-November 1991 Nazarbayev said that civil defence troops and military commissariats with all their property and weapons would come under the control of the republic's State Defence Committee. A certain contingent of troops subordinate to the central authorities in Moscow would remain in Kazakhstan, but their number would be determined by a special treaty with the union centre.[228] On November 7 Kazakhstan also declared its intention to take control of Baykonur cosmodrome through an announcement by a spokesman for the Kazakhstan Space Research Agency. The spokesman said that Baykonur would become a joint-stock company called International Spaceport, which would compete with U.S., European and Chinese aerospace firms to launch commercial payloads with Soviet rockets.[229]

On 30 September, Nazarbayev hosted a conference of leaders of twelve union republics in Alma-Ata. Formally, its purpose was to prepare the text of an economic treaty. Nazarbayev later said that members of the State Council were dissatisfied that Gorbachev's presiding at the council's meetings. "Therefore, proposals began to be heard to assemble without the president of the USSR and, if required, to elect a chairman of the State Council". This was not, of course, the result of mere dislike of Gorbachev. His presiding over the meetings was a manifestation, though a token one, that a single union state still existed. Nazarbayev decided to further undermine the authority of the union centre by inviting all State Council members except Gorbachev to meet in Alma-Ata[230] to show that Gorbachev's authority was null and void.

The Alma-Ata conference coincided with a major shift in the RSFSR leadership's position on the union treaty. A group of influential politicians and advisers in Yeltsin's entourage, aware of what was happening in the other republics, concluded that preservation of the union was no longer possible. They prepared a confidential report, Russia's Strategy in the Transitional Period, and presented it to Yeltsin while he was on vacation in Sochi. The report indicated that the other republics' interest in the union treaty was purely tactical, because during the period of transition they needed to preserve the existing system of flows of material and financial resources, which was advantageous to them but disadvantageous to Russia. "Having established control over the property on their territories, they are trying through union bodies to redistribute Russian property and resources for their benefit", the report said. This would, it alleged, enable the republics to reconstruct their economies at Russia's expense, while Russia's own chances for economic revival would decrease. After that the republics could easily secede, leaving Russia out in the cold. The report recommended that Russia "refrain from entering into long-term, firm and comprehensive economic unions", "be uninterested in creation of permanent super-republican bodies of economic administration", "categorically object to introduction of tax payments to the union budget", and "have its own customs service".[231]

This was why many influential Russian politicians fiercely objected to the conclusion of the economic treaty in Alma-Ata. Though the Russian delegation pledged to sign the treaty not later than 15 October 1991[232], their promise was strongly criticised by several members of the Russian government. According to press reports, the RSFSR government in effect disavowed Deputy Premier E. Saburov's signature, and he and State Secretary Burbulis flew to Sochi to see Yeltsin, who would have the final say on the matter.[233] RSFSR Justice Minister N. Fedorov said on television on 5 October that the treaty was unacceptable since it attempted to reanimate former union structures. On 7 October Saburov went on TV to defend his actions. He said that Russia had managed to delete most of the articles it did not like, argued that Russia needed the treaty, and said it had been approved in the main by Yeltsin.[234] However, on the next day Vice President Rutskoy publicly rejected the Alma-Ata agreement, alleging it would make Russia a "milch cow" for the republics and accusing Saburov of negotiating it without a proper mandate from his government. Saburov then resigned from his post. New acting RSFSR Premier O. Lobov stressed that the Alma-Ata agreement "smacked of a new attempt to restore the domination of the centre" and that its proposed mechanism for intra-community relations infringed upon Russian interests. Yeltsin yielded to the anti-unionist pressure, obviously concluding that preservation of the single state by previous totalitarian methods was unacceptable, but its rearrangement on new democratic lines unrealistic and unfeasible.

Gorbachev, on the other hand, was keen to preserve any super-republican structures which allowed him to maintain the semblance of a union state. He was quick to intervene in the dispute and announced that the State Council would convene on 11 October to discuss conclusion of a union treaty and creation of an economic community in the USSR. This was meant to put pressure on Yeltsin to comply with the economic treaty signed in Alma-Ata.[235] At the State Council meeting Yeltsin reluctantly agreed to sign the economic treaty, provided that all seventeen supplementary documents were ready and that financing of economic bodies not provided for in the treaty was stopped.[236] The treaty was finally signed on 18 October. But it soon became clear that this was only a political manoeuvre on Yeltsin's part and that he had no intention of observing the treaty. This fully revealed itself on 28 October, when in a speech to the Russian Congress of People's Deputies Yeltsin proposed radical economic reform, including price liberalisation, privatisation, land reform, tightening of credit policy and possible introduction of a new currency.[237] These proposals were made without consulting the other republics and without regard to Russia's obligations under the economic treaty.

Now it was mainly Yeltsin's position that deadlocked the negotiations for a new union treaty. Very little progress was achieved at the State Council meetings on 4 and 14 November with Yeltsin insisting that the term "union state" be substituted by "union of states". At the State Council meeting on 25 November Yeltsin refused to initial the draft union treaty until its examination by the Russian parliament. This was a delaying tactic. Gorbachev still thought the treaty could be signed in late December and scheduled a meeting with Yeltsin, Nazarbayev, Kravchuk and Shushkevich for 9 December, to find a way out of the deadlock. But everybody else was waiting for the results of the referendum in Ukraine.

On 1 December Ukrainians voted overwhelmingly for independence. This opened the way to implement the plan to dissolve the USSR. Yeltsin telephoned Nazarbayev and said that he would go to Belorussia to consult with Kravchuk and Shushkevich on presenting a joint position on the union treaty to Gorbachev. Yeltsin did not invite Nazarbayev to the meeting. However, when late on 8 December Nazarbayev arrived at Moscow airport, he was met by

Yeltsin's representative, who connected him by telephone to Yeltsin. The Russian president invited Nazarbayev to Belorussia to sign "important documents", which had been already agreed to by the three leaders. Nazarbayev, clearly offended by such treatment, declined to go, saying he was not prepared to sign important documents without "consultations and advice".[238] At a press conference held the next day he said, "Such questions should be resolved in a coordinated way, not without consulting other republics. They did not even know about them. I can only regret that it happened this way."[239] Gorbachev asserted in his memoirs that Nazarbayev consulted him before deciding not to go.[240]

The decisions taken by the leaders of the three Slavic republics at Belovezhskaya Pushcha proclaimed formation of a new political entity – the Commonwealth of Independent States (CIS) – and declared that the USSR "as a subject of international law and geopolitical reality ceases its existence".[241] The CIS was formed not as a state, nor even a confederation, but as an international organisation. It provided no post of president of the commonwealth, and that meant the end of Gorbachev's political career.

The fact that Nazarbayev took offence in the lack of consultation with him did not mean that he objected to the substance of the Belovezhskaya accords. As soon as the Supreme Soviets of Belorussia, Ukraine and Russia ratified the Minsk agreement, Kazakhstan's Supreme Soviet proclaimed independence. This happened on a very symbolic date, 16 December, the fifth anniversary of the Alma-Ata riots. Nazarbayev also played a central role in organising the 21 December Alma-Ata conference of eleven union republics, which endorsed the Belovezhskaya accords and signed a number of documents effectively abolishing the common union state. On 25 December 1991 Gorbachev relinquished the presidency, the Soviet union ceased to exist, and Kazakhstan emerged as a new independent state.

NOTES

1. Gorbachev, M., *Zhizn' i reformy*, Kniga 1–2, Moscow: Novosti, 1995, p. 293.
2. Ibid., pp. 297–298, 305, 307.
3. Kaiser, R., *Why Gorbachev Happened: His Triumph and His Failure*, New York: Simon & Schuster, 1991, p. 115.
4. The corruption case in Uzbekistan was real, not a propaganda ploy. First Secretary of the Uzbek *Communist* Party S. Rashidov, candidate member of the Politburo since 1961, falsified figures of cotton production by some 4 million tons and distributed 2 billion extra roubles among his relatives and associates. The swindle was discovered accidentally by means of satellite measurements, when an experiment to count stacks of harvest cotton was conducted. The results of the survey did not tally with the quantity according to the declared accounts. When confronted with the evidence and the charges, Rashidov committed suicide. He was buried with full state honours, and no revelations about his crimes were made until the beginning of Gorbachev's anti-corruption campaign. *See* Murarka, D., *Gorbachev: The Limits of Power*, London: Hutchinson Ltd., 1988, pp. 253–254.

5. Brown, B., "Eighteenth Congress of the *Communist* Party of Kirgiziya: An Attack on the Past", *Radio Liberty Research Bulletin,* RL 88/86, February 20, 1986, pp. 1–2.

6. Gorbachev, M., *Zhizn' i reformy*, p. 492.

7. Ibid., p. 283.

8. Boldin, V., *Ten Years That Shook the World*, New York: Basic Books, 1994, p. 96.

9. In November 1972, while heading the CPSU Central Committee Propaganda Department, Yakovlev wrote a long article in *ILiteraturnaya gazeta* attacking as anti-Leninist Russophile tendencies in literature, journalism and historical writings. He also criticised the "extra-class and extra-social approach" of the nationalists to history, and censured any dabbling with religion, such as excessive admiration for old icons and churches. Yakovlev's article caused much controversy among the Soviet leadership, and a few months after its appearance he disappeared into honourable exile as Soviet Ambassador to Canada. Sheehy, A., "Gorbachev's New Propaganda Chief a Critic of Russian Nationalists", *Radio Liberty Research Bulletin,* RL 357/85, October 31, 1985, pp. 2, 5].

10. Boldin, V., *Ten Years That Shook the World*, p. 113.

11. *Kommunist*, No. 3, 1987, p. 29.

12. The generation that lived through the Second World War. Kunayev was born on 12 January 1912.

13. *Pravda*, 11.07.85.

14. *Kazakhstanskaya pravda*, 14.07.85.

15. *Pravda*, 14.07.85.

16. Kuzmin, N., "Nochnyye besedy", *Molodaya Gvardiya*, No. 2, 1997, pp. 312, 318.

17. A characteristic example may be "unofficial" Marxist historian R. Medvedev, who had been expelled from the CPSU in 1979 and since then regarded as a dissident. Said Medvedev: "Through Kunayev's personal connections, the corruption even spread to Moscow, even inside the Brezhnev clan. . . . Kunayev would go to Moscow bearing expensive gifts for Brezhnev and his family, and for many other government leaders. These gifts frequently came in the form of hard cash." Medvedev, R., & Chiesa, G., *Time of Change: An Insider's View of Russia's Transformation*, New York: Pantheon Books, 1989, p. 55.

18. *Pravda*, 11.09.85.

19. *Kazakhstanskaya pravda*, 05.12.85, 11.12.85.

20. Medvedev, R., & Chiesa, G., *Time of Change*, p. 88.

21. *Kazakhstanskaya pravda*, 10.01.86.

22. *Kazakhstanskaya pravda*, 06.0286.

23. Nazarbayev, N., *Na poroge XXI veka*, Almaty: Oner, 1996, p. 54.

24. Valovoy, D., *Kremlevskiy tupik i Nazarbayev*, Moscow: Molodaya gvardiya, 1993, p. 70.

25. Kunayev, D., *Ot Stalina do Gorbacheva (V aspekte istorii Kazakhstana)*, Almaty: Sanat, 1994, pp. 277, 284, 289, 293, 305.

26. Valovoy, D., *Kremlevskiy tupik i Nazarbayev*, pp. 71–74, 77.

27. *Kazakhstanskaya pravda*, 08.02.86.

28. In April Askar Kunayev was removed from the position of president of the Academy of Sciences, and in March Mukhamed-Rakhimov lost his post as chairman of the Kazakhstan State Planning Committee. *Kazakhstanskaya pravda*, 22.04.86, *Pravda*, 27.06.86.

29. *Kazakhstanskaya pravda*, 9.02.86.

30. XVII S'ezd Kommunisticheskoy Partii Sovetskogo Soyuza, Stenograficheskiy otchet, t.1, Moscow: Politizdat, 1986, pp. 59, 159–161.

31. *Pravda*, 7.07.86, 22.07.86.

32. Kunayev, D., *Ot Stalina do Gorbacheva*, pp. 287–288.

33. Ibid., p. 289.

34. Gorbachev, M., *Zhizn' i reformy*, p. 497.

35. Kunayev, D., *Ot Stalina do Gorbacheva*, pp. 284, 293–294; Valovoy, D., *Kremlevskiy tupik i Nazarbayev*, p. 78; Gorbachev, M., *Zhizn' i reformy*, pp. 497–498.

36. *Kazakhstanskaya pravda*, 17.03.87.

37. Nazarbayev, N., *Na poroge XXI veka*, pp. 50–51.

38. *Pravda*, 28.08.86.

39. Ibid.

40. Kunayev, D., *Ot Stalina do Gorbacheva*, pp. 287–288.

41. Gorbachev, M., *Zhizn' i reformy*, pp. 497–498.

42. Kunayev, D., *Ot Stalina do Gorbacheva*, pp. 9–10.

43. Gorbachev, M., *Zhizn' i reformy*, pp. 497–498.

44. Gennady Kolbin, ethnic Chuvash, engineer by profession, started his party career in 1959 in Sverdlovsk. In 1975 he was appointed second party secretary in Georgia. In this capacity he worked closely with E. Shevardnadze, Gorbachev's foreign minister, who headed Georgia in those days. In December 1983 he was appointed first secretary in the Uliyanovsk province, the post he held until the transfer to Kazakhstan.

45. Kunayev, D., *Ot Stalina do Gorbacheva*, pp. 272, 290.

46. Gorbachev, M., *Zhizn' i reformy*, p. 498.

47. *Pravda*, 21.09.89.

48. Sheehy, A., "Earlier Instances of Nationality Unrest in the USSR", *Radio Liberty Research Bulletin*, RL 475/86, December 19, 1986, p. 1.

49. Kuzmin, N.,"Nochnyye besedy", *Molodaya Gvardiya*, No. 2, 1997, p. 249.

50. Kunayev, D., *Ot Stalina do Gorbacheva*, pp. 291–292.

51. *Izvestiya*, 07.06.88.

52. Kuzmin, N., "Nochnyye besedy", p. 323.

53. *Pravda*, 19.12.86.

54. *Literaturnaya gazeta*, 01.01.87.

55. *Komsomolskaya pravda*, 10.01.87.

56. "Conclusions and Proposals of the Kazakh SSR Supreme Soviet Presidium Commission for Final Appraisal of the Circumstances Linked to the Events in the City of Alma-Ata on 17th and 18th December 1986", *BBC Monitoring Service*, Part 1, The USSR, Third Series, 26.10.90.

57. Ryskulbekov's sentence was later commuted to a long-term imprisonment, obviously to avoid further inflaming interethnic enmity. Following that he suddenly died in a supposed suicide. Brown, B., "Alma-Ata Commission of Inquiry Publishes Report", *Radio Liberty, Report on the USSR*, Vol. 2, No. 42, October 19, 1990, p. 20. It is quite possible that he was simply eliminated by Interior Ministry personnel who wanted to avenge the death of a Russian.

58. *Izvestiya*, 27.07.87.

59. *Kazakhstanskaya pravda*, 07.01.87.

60. *Kazakhstanskaya pravda*, 11.07.87.

61. *Kazakhstanskaya pravda*, 04.02.87.

62. "Conclusions and Proposals of the Kazakh SSR Supreme Soviet Presidium Commission for Final Appraisal of the Circumstances Linked to the Events in the City

of Alma-Ata on 17th and 18th December 1986", *BBC Monitoring Service*, Part 1, The USSR, Third Series, 26.10.90.

63. *Pravda*, 24.12.86.

64. XIX Vsesoyuznaya konferentsiya Kommunisticheskoy Partii Sovetskogo Soyuza, Stenograficheskiy otchet, t.1, Moscow: Politizdat, 1988, p. 104.

65. *Pravda*, 26.12.86.

66. See: *Komsomolskaya pravda*, 10.01.87; *Literaturnaya gazeta*, 14.01.87; *Izvestiya*, 24.01.87; *Pravda*, 11.02.87.

67. For more information on this see: Kaiser, R., *Why Gorbachev Happened*, pp. 151–152.

68. *Kommunist*, No. 7, 1987, p. 4.

69. *Pravda*, 12.06.87.

70. Kunayev, D., *Ot Stalina do Gorbacheva*, pp. 294–295; *Pravda*, 28.07.87.

71. *Kommunist*, No.10, 1987, p. 4.

72. Kunayev, D., *Ot Stalina do Gorbacheva*, p. 294; Valovoy, D., *Kremlevskiy tupik i Nazarbayev*, p. 80.

73. For example, Auyelbekov, who was another contender for Kunayev's job, was based in Kzyl Orda and could not very much influence the situation in the capital.

74. *Pravda*, 16.07.87.

75. Articles in official Moscow media substantiated this accusation. One article claimed that the number of Kazakhs in the Alma-Ata Architectural Institute was 78%; Institute of National Economy, 73.7%; Kazakhstan State University, 75.8%; Agricultural Institute, 79.6%, and Veterinary Institute, 90.4%. *Izvestiya*, 24.01.87

76. *Pravda*, 16.07.87.

77. Harris, Ch., "Novie russkie menshinstva: statisticheskoe obozrenie [perevod s angliyskogo]", *Evraziyskoye soobshchestvo: ekonomika, politika, bezopasnost'*, No. 2, 1995, p. 53.

78. *Pravda*, 16.07.87.

79. Ibid.

80. *Kazakhstanskaya pravda*, 15.03.87.

81. Ibid.

82. *Pravda*, 16.03.87.

83. "Conclusions and Proposals of the Kazakh SSR Supreme Soviet Presidium Commission for Final Appraisal of the Circumstances Linked to the Events in the City of Alma-Ata on 17th and 18th December 1986", *BBC Monitoring Service*, Part 1, The USSR, Third Series, 26.10.90; Gorbachev, M., *Zhizn' i reformy*, pp. 498–499.

84. Kuzmin, N., "Nochnyye besedy", pp. 249–250.

85. *Kazakhstanskaya pravda*, 11.12.96.

86. Nazarbayev, N., *Na poroge XXI veka*, p. 37.

87. *Kazakhstanskaya pravda*, 12.11.96.

88. By "parasities" officials meant people refusing to work. In Kazakhstan this term applied to a large number of young, poorly educated Kazakhs from auls, who flocked to large cities but were unable to find jobs and formed a sort of urban "underclass".

89. In April 1988 Bekezhanov was sentenced to eight years of imprisonment for "bribe-taking, misappropriation of property, misuse of foreign currency funds and protectionism", *Kazakhstanskaya pravda*, 02.04.88.

90. *Kazakhstanskaya pravda*, 22.02.87; *Pravda*, 09.03.87.

91. *Pravda*, 24.04.87.

92. *Pravda*, 14.02.87.

93. *Kazakhstanskaya pravda*, 15.02.87.

94. *Pravda*, 7.01.87; *Komsomolskaya pravda*, 18.07.82.

95. *Kazakhstanskaya pravda*, 15.02.87.

96. *Komsomolskaya pravda*, 18.07.82.

97. In May 1991 Askarov was sentenced to eleven years for receiving bribes to the tune of 112,000 roubles. Six of his associates were tried with him and given prison sentences of various lengths. Former First Secretary of Kazakhstan Oblast Given 11 Years in Prison, *BBC Monitoring Service*, Part 1, The USSR, 07.06.91.

98. Kunayev, D., *Ot Stalina do Gorbacheva*, pp. 301–302.

99. *Literaturnaya gazeta*, 12.04.89.

100. *Izvestiya*, 15.03.87.

101. *Kazakhstanskaya pravda*, 11.01.87.

102. Brown, B., "New First Secretary in Kazakhstan Notes Some Successes", *Radio Liberty Research Bulletin,* RL 258/87, July 2, 1987, p. 1–2.

103. *Kazakhstanskaya pravda*, 05.03.87.

104. Doder, D. and Branson, L., *Gorbachev: Heretic in the Kremlin*, New York: Viking, 1990, p. 178.

105. Kunayev, D., *Ot Stalina do Gorbacheva*, p. 304.

106. XIX Vsesoyuznaya konferentsiya Kommunisticheskoy Partii Sovetskogo Soyuza, Stenograficheskiy otchet, t.1, Moscow: Politizdat, 1988, p. 105.

107. *Izvestiya*, 28.10.95.

108. Sheehy, A., "Kazakh Lecturer Disseminates Unorthodox Views on Nationality Question", *Radio Liberty Research Bulletin,* RL 81/88, February 18, 1988, p. 2.

109. Zaslavskaya, M., *Politicheskie partii i obshchestvenyye ob'edineniya Kazakhstana na sovremennom etape razvitiya*, Almaty: KISI, 1994, pp. 7, 9–10, 16–17.

110. Sheehy, A., "Renewed Appeal for Rehabilitation of Kazakh Poet", *Radio Liberty Research Bulletin,* RL 107/88, March, 10, 1988, p. 1–2.

111. *Literaturnaya gazeta*, No. 10, 1988.

112. Sheehy, A., "Kazakh Party Scholar Condemns Rehabilitation of Muhametjan Tinishbayev", *Radio Liberty Research Bulletin,* RL 266/88, June 16, 1988, p. 2.

113. In mid-December 1988 a brief formal announcement from the attorney-general stated that the Kazakhstan Supreme Court had annulled the convictions of Zhumabayev, Baytursynov and Aymautov on grounds of lack of evidence. *Kazakhstanskaya pravda*, 08.07.88

114. Zaslavskaya, M., *Politicheskie partii i obshchestvenyye ob'edineniya Kazakhstana*, p. 12.

115. Hazan, B. A., ed., *Gorbachev's Gamble: The 19th All-Union Party Conference*, Boulder and London: Westview Press, 1990, pp. 390, 393.

116. Sheehy, A., "Kazakh Minister Defends Territorial Integrity of Kazakhstan", *Radio Liberty Research Bulletin,* RL 264/88, June 15, 1988, pp. 1–2.

117. XIX Vsesoyuznaya konferentsiya Kommunisticheskoy Partii Sovetskogo Soyuza, Stenograficheskiy otchet, t.1, Moscow: Politizdat, 1988 p. 68.

118. *Pravda*, 4.02.87.

119. *Pravda*, 01.06.89.

120. *Izvestiya*, 08.06.89.

121. *Pravda*, 20.06.89; *Izvestiya*, 20.06.89.

122. *Izvestiya*, 21.06.89; *Kazakhstanskaya pravda*, 27.12.89; *Pravda*, 23.06.89.

123. *Izvestiya*, 23.06.89, *Pravda*, 25.06.89.

124. *Izvestiya*, 24.06.89.

125. *Pravda*, 23.06.89.

126. "Conclusions and Proposals of the Kazakh SSR Supreme Soviet Presidium Commission for Final Appraisal of the Circumstances Linked to the Events in the City of Alma-Ata on 17th and 18th December 1986", *BBC Monitoring Service*, Part 1, The USSR, Third Series, 26.10.90.

127. Furtado, Ch. F, and Chandler, A., eds., "Law of the Kazakh Soviet Socialist Republic on Languages, 22 August 1989", *Perestroika in the Soviet Republics: Documents on the National Questions*, Boulder and Oxford: Westview Press, 1992, p. 479.

128. *Rossiyskaya gazeta*, 05.06.93.

129. "Azat Leader on Need for Unified Democratic Movement in Kazakhstan", *BBC Monitoring Service*, Part 1, The USSR, Third Series, 04.12.91; Zaslavskaya, M., *Politicheskie partii i obshchestvenyye ob'edineniya Kazakhstana*, p. 12.

130. For more information on this issue *see*: Martinenko, N., ed., *Alash Orda: Sbornik dokumentov*, Alma-Ata: Aykap, 1992; Amanzholova, D. A., *Kazakhskiy avtonomizm i Rossiya: istoriya dvizheniya Alash*, Moscow: Rossiya Molodaya, 1994.

131. Zaslavskaya, M., *Politicheskie partii i obshchestvenyye ob'edineniya Kazakhstana*, pp. 13–15.

132. "CP of Kazakhstan Congress: Independent Platform Adopted", *BBC Monitoring Service*, Part 1, The USSR, Third Series, 18.06.90.

133. "Gorbachev to Address Kazakh Supreme Soviet on Two More Nuclear Explosions", *BBC Monitoring Service*, Part 1, The USSR, 07.06.91; "Semipalatinsk Residents Offered R5bn to Accept Nuclear Testing", *BBC Monitoring Service*, Part 1, The USSR, 10.08.91.

134. Zaslavskaya, M., *Politicheskie partii i obshchestvenyye ob'edineniya Kazakhstana*, pp. 15–16; *Rabochaya tribuna*, 27.04.91; "Azat Chairman Attacks Lack of Kazakh Sovereignity", *BBC Summary of World Broadcasts*, Part 1, The USSR, Second Series, 18.01.91.

135. Sorrow Line was the name of the line of Russian fortresses from Kurgan to Petropavlovsk, which separated Russian territory from the Steppe.

136. "Possibility of Interethnic Conflict in Kazakhstan Viewed", *BBC Summary of World Broadcasts*, Part 1, The USSR, Second Series, 29.09.90.

137. "Kazakh Writer Appeals to Gorbachev over Cossack Territorial Claims", *BBC Summary of World Broadcasts*, Part 1, The USSR, Second Series, 06.07.91.

138. Kozhokin, E. M, ed., *Kazakhstan: realii i perspektivi nezavisimogo razvitiya*, Moscow: RISI, 1995, pp. 208–209.

139. Abdirov, M., Abdirova, B., "Kazachestvo v kontekste sovremennykh kazakhstansko-rossiyskikh otnosheniy" *Kazakhstan i mirovoe soobshchestvo*, No. 2(3), 1995, p. 58.

140. Carlson, Ch., "Kazakhs Refute Russian Territorial Claims", *Radio Liberty Report on the USSR*, Vol. 2, No. 32, August 10, 1990, pp. 18–19.

141. "Possibility of Interethnic Conflict in Kazakhstan Viewed", *BBC Summary of World Broadcasts*, Part 1, The USSR, Second Series, 29.09.90.

142. "Clashes prevented between Cossacks and Kazakhs in Uralsk", *BBC Monitoring Service*, Part 1, The USSR, 18.09.91; Abdirov, M., Abdirova, B., "Kazachestvo v kontekste sovremennykh kazakhstansko-rossiyskikh otnosheniy", *Kazakhstan i mirovoe soobshchestvo*, No 2(3), 1995, p. 57; Kurtov, A., "Politicheskie partii i dvizheniya Kazakhstana", *Novaya Evrasiya*, No. 2, 1994, p. 53.

143. "Nazarbayev Protests to Yeltsin over Cossack Celebrations in Uralsk", *BBC Monitoring Service*, Part 1, The USSR, 20.09.91.

144. Abdirov, M., Abdirova, B., "Kazachestvo v kontekste sovremennykh kazakhstansko-rossiyskikh otnosheniy", p. 58.

145. "Interethnic Conflict in Tselinograd 'Defused'", *BBC Monitoring Service*, Part 1, The USSR, 30.10.91.

146. "Cossack Union Suspended in Kazakhstan", *BBC Monitoring Service*, Part 1, The USSR, 30.11.91.

147. "Yeltsin's Meeting with Memory Association Example of 'Glasnost'", BBC Summary of World Broadcasts, Part 1, The USSR, Second Series, 26.05.87.

148. Furtado, Ch. F, and Chandler, A., eds., "Manifesto of the National-Patriotic Front 'Pamyat'", *Perestroika in the Soviet Republics: Documents on the National Question*, Boulder and Oxford: Westview Press, 1992, pp. 314–316.

149. Brzezinski, Z., "Post-Communist Nationalism", *Foreign Affairs*, Vol. 68, No. 5, winter 1989–1990, p. 15.

150. It included the All-Russian Society for the Preservation of Historical and Cultural Monuments, the Unity Association of Lovers of Russian Literature and Art, the All-Russian Culture Fund, the Russian Section of the International Foundation for Slavic Literatures and Slavic Cultures, the Fund to Restore the Church of Christ the Savior, the Association of Russian Artists, the Public Committee to Save the Volga and some others.

151. *Sovetskaya Rossiya*, 23.07.91.

152. Solzhenitsyn, A., *Rebuilding Russia*, New York: Farrar, Straus and Giroux, 1991, pp. 9–12.

153. Dunlop, J. B., "Russian Reactions to Solzhenitsyn's Brochure", *Radio Liberty, Report on the USSR*, Vol. 2, No. 50, December 14, 1990, pp. 4–6.

154. Among most prominent Eurasianists one can name geographer and economist P. N. Savitsky, philosopher and historian L. P. Karsavin, ethnologist and linguist N. S. Trubetskoy, historian G. V. Vernadsky, art researcher P. P. Suvchinskiy, religious philosophers G. V. Florovskiy and V. N. Iliin, literary researcher D. P. Sviatopolk-Mirskiy, law scientist N. N. Alekseev, economist Y. D. Sadovskiy. The group manifested itself for the first time by publication of a collection of articles, "Exodus to the East", which appeared in Sofia, Bulgaria, in 1921.

155. Trubetskoy, N., "Obscheevraziyskiy natsionalism", *Etnopoliticheskiy vestnik*, No. 4, 1995, pp. 218–221.

156. Prokhanov, A., "Tragediya tsentralisma", *Literaturnaya Rossiya*, No. 1, 1990.

157. The party was created on 31 March 1990, and its program spoke for "preserving the unity and the territorial integrity of the great power". It recommended to return to it the historical name of Russia. It also proclaimed that the RSFSR should become a unitary state and that the union republics should join it, creating a "union entity . . . on the basis of federation or confederation (that is with lesser or larger amount of powers)" (Liberalno-Demokraticheskaya Partiya Sovetskogo Soyuza, Dokumenty i materialy, Moscow [No publisher], 1991, pp. 39–41).

158. Members of the association included United Workers' Fronts of Moscow and Leningrad, the Union of Patriotic Organizations of the Urals and Siberia, Internationalist Fronts from Latvia, Estonia, Lithuania and Moldova. *Sovetskaya Rossiya*, 14.09.89.

159. Carlson, Ch., "Kazakhs Refute Russian Territorial Claims", *Radio Liberty, Report on the USSR*, Vol. 2, No. 32, August 10, 1990, pp. 18–19.

160. *Izvestiya*, 24.09.90.

161. *See*, for example, Nupreisov, A., "Svoya i chuzhaya bol", *Izvestiya*, 31.09.90.

162. *Pravda*, 17.08.90.

163. *Pravda*, 21.09.89.

164. *Izvestiya*, 15.12.89.

165. Nazarbayev, N., *Na poroge XXI veka*, p. 86.

166. Furtado, Ch. F. and Chandler, A., eds., "Declaration on the State Sovereignty of the RSFSR Adopted by the First Congress of RSFSR People's Deputies, 12 June 1990", *Perestroika in the Soviet Republics*, p. 325.

167. Nazarbayev, N., *Na poroge XXI veka*, p. 43.

168. Furtado, Ch. F. and Chandler, A., eds., "Declaration of State Sovereignity of the Kazakh SSR, 25 October 1990", *Perestroika in the Soviet Republics*, pp. 485–488.

169. *Izvestiya*, 29.10.90.

170. "Kazakhstan Signs Space Programme Agreement", *BBC Monitoring Service*, Part 1, The USSR, 13.02.91.

171. "Kazakh Resolution on Oil and Gas Deposits", *BBC Monitoring Service*, Part 1, The USSR, 15.04.91.

172. *Radio Free Europe/ Radio Liberty (RFE/RL) Daily Report*, No. 83, 30.04.91.

173. *RFE/RL Daily Report*, No. 60, 26.03.91.

174. "Kazakh Draft Law on Citizenship", *BBC Monitoring Service*, Part 1, The USSR, 09.05.91.

175. *RFE/RL Daily Report*, No.142, 29.07.91.

176. Furtado, Ch. F. and Chandler, A., eds., "Agreement on Economic, Scientific-Technical and Cultural Cooperation of the Uzbek, Kazakh, Kyrgyz, Tajik and Turkmen SSRs, 23 June 1990", *Perestroika in the Soviet Republics*, pp. 481–483.

177. "Central Asian Leaders Meeting in Alma-Ata", *BBC Monitoring Service*, Part 1, The USSR, Third Series, 27.06.90.

178. "Nazarbayev's Speech at Document Signing Ceremony", *BBC Monitoring Service*, Part 1, The USSR, 20.08.91.

179. "Belorussia-Kazakhstan Cooperation Agreement", *BBC Monitoring Service*, Part 1, The USSR, 09.10.90.

180. "Ukraine-Kazakhstan Agreement Signed", *BBC Monitoring Service*, Part 1, The USSR, Third Series, 01.12.90.

181. *Izvestiya*, 22.11.90.

182. "Kazakhstan and Kyrgyzia sign agreement", *BBC Monitoring Service*, Part 1, The USSR, 20.02.91.

183. "Kazakhstan and Ukraine: Leaders Conclude Treaty and Criticise Yeltsin", *BBC Monitoring Service*, Part 1, The USSR, 22.02.91.

184. *Pravda*, 6.07.90.

185. *Pravda*, 6.07.90.

186. *Izvestiya*, 15.01.91.

187. Gorbachev, M., *Zhizn' i reformy*, p. 516

188. "Kazakh President Answers Television Viewers' Questions", *BBC Monitoring Service*, Part 1, The USSR, 05.03.91.

189. "Kazakh President Urges Signing of Union Treaty: Supreme Soviet Appeal", *BBC Monitoring Service*, Part 1, The USSR, 13.02.91.

190. "Kazakhstan and Ukraine: Leaders Conclude Treaty and Criticise Yeltsin", *BBC Monitoring Service*, Part 1, The USSR, 22.02.91.

191. *Komsomolskaya pravda*, 13.04.91

192. "Kazakhstan Changes Wording of Referendum Question", *BBC Monitoring Service*, Part 1, The USSR, 14.03.91.

193. "Kazakh President Answers Television Viewers' Questions", *BBC Monitoring Service*, Part 1, The USSR, 05.03.91.

194. *Komsomolskaya pravda*, 13.04.91.

195. "Some Kazakh Towns Disagree with Wording of the Referendum", *BBC Monitoring Service*, Part 1, The USSR, 16.03.91.

196. *Izvestiya*, 27.03.91.

197. *Izvestiya*, 24.04.91.

198. "Nazarbayev Speaks to Alma-Ata Activists", *BBC Monitoring Service*, Part 1, The USSR, 03.06.91.

199. "Communique on Meeting between Nazarbayev and USSR Ministers", *BBC Monitoring Service*, Part 1, The USSR, 11.07.91.

200. "Nazarbayev Speaks to Alma-Ata Activists", *BBC Monitoring Service*, Part 1, The USSR, 03.06.91.

201. "Kazakh Writer Appeals to Gorbachev over Cossack Territorial Claims", *BBC Monitoring Service*, Part 1, The USSR, 06.07.91.

202. "Nazarbayev: the Future Lies with the Union Treaty", *BBC Monitoring Service*, Part 1, The USSR, 06.07.91.

203. *RFE/RL Daily Report*, No. 120, 25.06.91.

204. Sheehy, A., "A Progress Report on the Union Treaty", *Radio Liberty Report on the USSR*, Vol. 3, No. 28, July 12, 1991, p. 18.

205. *Izvestiya*, 3.08.91.

206. "O garantiyakh stabil'nosti Soyuza Suverennikh Gosudarstv (sovmestnoe zayavlenie Prezidenta Kazakhstana i Prezidenta Rossiyskoy Federatsii) 17 avgusta 1991", *Kazakhstansko-Rossiyskie otnosheniya, 1991–1995 gody, Sbornik dokumentov i materialov*, Moscow: Posol'stvo Respubliki Kazakhstan v Rossiyskoy Federatsii, 1995, p. 81.

207. "Yeltsin on Joint Documents to Be Signed with Kazakhstan", *BBC Monitoring Service*, Part 1, The USSR, 20.08.91; "Nazarbayev's Speech at Document Signing Ceremony", *BBC Monitoring Service*, Part 1, The USSR, 20.08.91.

208. *Kazakhstanskaya pravda*, 21.08.91.

209. "O edinom ekonomicheskom prostranstve (sovmestnoe zayavlenie Prezidenta Kazakhstana i Prezidenta Rossiyskoy Federatsii) 17 avgusta 1991", *Kazakhstansko-Rossiyskie otnosheniya, 1991–1995 gody*, p. 80.

210. *Nezavisimaya gazaeta*, 22.08.91; 27.08.91.

211. "Speech by Nazarbayev", *BBC Monitoring Service*, Part 1, The USSR, 26.08.91.

212. *RFE/RL Daily Report*, No. 161, 26.08.91; *Nezavisimaya gazeta*, 27.08.91.

213. *Rossiyskaya gazeta*, 27.08.1991.

214. "Nazarbayev Warns of the Dangers of Border Claims", *BBC Monitoring Service*, Part 1, The USSR, 31.08.91.

215. "Kazakh Deputy Asks for Intercession over Borders with RSFSR", *BBC Monitoring Service*, Part 1, The USSR, 31.08.91.

216. *Nezavisimaya gazeta*, 31.08.91.

217. "Kommyunike ob itogakh peregovorov mezhdu delegatsiyami Kazakhskoy Sovetskoy Sotsialisticheskoy Respubliki i Rossiyskoy Sovetskoy Federativnoy Sotsialisticheskoy Respubliki, 30 avgusta 1991 goda", *Kazakhstansko-Rossiyskie otnosheniya, 1991–1995 gody*, pp. 82–83.

218. Gorbachev, M., *Zhizn' i reformy*, pp. 585–586.

219. "Nazarbayev Decree on Military Service: No Conscription Outside Republic", *BBC Monitoring Service*, Part 1, The USSR, 18.09.91; "Nazarbayev Decree on Call-up in Kazakhstan", *BBC Monitoring Service*, Part 1, The USSR, 27.09.91.

220. *Krasnaya zvezda*, 12.10.91.

221. *Izvestiya*, 02.09.91.

222. "Kazakh Supreme Soviet Chairman Says Economic Treaty Must Be Signed", *BBC Monitoring Service*, Part 1, The USSR, 10.10.91.

223. "Kazakhstan Sets up Customs Posts to Stem Food Drain to Chelyabinsk Oblast", *BBC Monitoring Service*, Part 1, The USSR, 03.10.91.

224. "Nazarbayev on the Future of Kazakhstan", *BBC Monitoring Service*, Part 1, The USSR, 18.10.91.

225. *Krasnaya zvezda*, 12.10.91.

226. "Kazakhstan Sets up State Defence Committee", *BBC Monitoring Service*, Part 1, The USSR, 30.10.91.

227. "Kazakhstan to Set up National Guard", *BBC Monitoring Service*, Part 1, The USSR, 22.11.91.

228. "Nazarbayev: Internal Troops to Form Future Kazakh National Guard", *BBC Monitoring Service*, Part 1, The USSR, 04.12.91.

229. *RFE/RL Daily Report*, No. 212, 07.11.91.

230. "Nazarbayev on the CIS, Kazakhstan, the Future", *BBC Monitoring Service*: Former USSR, 06.05.92.

231. Gorbachev, M., *Zhizn' i reformy*, pp. 589–590.

232. Three republics Kazakhstan, Belorussia and Uzbekistan signed the treaty immediately. Five others Russia, Ukraine, Kyrgyzstan, Tajikistan and Turkmenistan promised to do it before 15 October 1991. *Izvestiya*, 02.10.91.

233. *RFE/RL Daily Report* No. 190, 07.10.91.

234. *RFE/RL Daily Report* No. 191, 08.10.91.

235. *RFE/RL Daily Report* No. 192, 09.10.91; No. 193, 10.10.91.

236. *RFE/RL Daily Report* No. 195, 14.10.91.

237. *RFE/RL Daily Report* No. 206, 29.10.91

238. Valovoy, D., *Kremlevskiy tupik i Nazarbayev*, pp. 147–148.

239. *Izvestiya*, 10.12.91.

240. Gorbachev, M., *Zhizn' i reformy*, pp. 598–599.

241. "Soglashenie o sozdanii Sodruzhestva Nezavisimykh Gosudarstv", *Kazakhstansko-Rossiyskie otnosheniya, 1991–1995 gody*, p. 319.

Formulation of Russian Policy Towards Kazakhstan

Official Russian policy towards Kazakhstan developed within the framework of Moscow's broader strategy towards the post-Soviet states. It was a long and painful process to adjust abstract ideological perceptions, dogmas and prejudices to the harsh political realities of the Eurasian continent. After the dissolution of the USSR, the Russian government found that it had to make foreign policy decisions regarding areas which had recently been part of one country. Russia could build its foreign policy with the rest of the world upon the former USSR's diplomatic and conceptual apparatus, but it had no diplomatic experience or appropriate mechanisms for conducting relations with the new independent states. First Deputy Foreign Minister Shelov-Kovedyaev, given charge of CIS affairs, was not a professional diplomat; he had neither knowledge of international issues nor diplomatic experience. Foreign Minister Kozyrev's adviser and media liaison officer G. Sidorova had to admit as late as the end of March 1992 that Russia's foreign ministry had not developed a foreign policy toward the CIS.[1] This resulted in Yeltsin's leadership being forced to act on the spur of the moment, reacting to events instead of anticipating and channeling them in a desirable direction.

Crystalisation of Russian policy regarding Central Asia and Kazakhstan was helped by the public debate about future relations with this region that was unfolding in Russia. After the collapse of the USSR, liberals among Russian ethnic nationalists continued to push for Russia to disengage from Central Asia and join the club of Western nations. "We have no other way to go, but integrating ourselves into European civilisation", Kozyrev stated in one of his first post-Soviet interviews.[2] In another interview in March he reiterated that the gist of Russian foreign policy doctrine was Russia's "joining the club of the most dynamically developing democratic states".[3]

Simultaneously, a scaremongering campaign about the Central Asian republics was developing, based on an alleged threat of Islamic and Turkic expan-
sionism. In an article for the Swiss daily *Le Nouveau Quotidien* of 22 January
1992, V. Fedorovsky, press secretary of the Movement for Democratic Reform's Political Council, warned of the possible breakup of the Russian Federation. He floated the possibility of a Pan-Turkic union, combining Central
Asia, Tatarstan and Bashkiriya.[4] Kozyrev himself warned of the danger of the
Central Asian republics embracing Islamic fundamentalism.[5] In March 1991 he
wrote an article for *Izvestiya* denying that Russia had any specific interests in
Asia aside from questions of national security, and these, he said, must be addressed in close coordination with Russia's Western partners.[6] In the view of
KISI's Director U. Kasenov, "Kozyrev in his initial period of activity as head
of Russian foreign policy . . . clearly demonstrated a one-sided orientation toward the West, a desire to integrate Russia into the North American–European
community and depreciation of Asia in general and the former Asian Soviet
republics in particular. They were regarded as nothing more than an object of
lust for Islamic fundamentalism".[7]

The campaign was eagerly echoed by the official Moscow media. In a typical example, an article, "The Demographic Wave Will Soon Cover Us All",
published in January 1992 by *Rossiyskie vesti*, an official Russian government
newspaper. The authors, A. Avdeev and A. Sagradov of Moscow State University's Centre for Demographic Studies, examined population trends in Central
Asia and their potential consequences for Russia. They claimed that the Central
Asian republics were undergoing a "demographic explosion" which would lead
to massive unemployment sometime in the 1990s, spurring uncontrolled Muslim migration to the European republics of the CIS. The article stated that "in
1994 Russians will already cease to be the majority of the CIS' population, by
2040 the Turkic population on the former USSR's territory will numerically
exceed the Russian, and in the next 10 years the Commonwealth's population
will cease to be mainly Slavic".[8]

A similar article, "Islamic Extremism: New Challenge for Russia?", was
published by the Ministry of Defence daily, *Krasnaya zvezda*. It claimed that
Islamic radicals were trying to exploit Central Asia's "cultural and historical
association with the Muslim world" and that "already in the immediate future
Islamic extremism can take advantage of the situation that a substantial number
of Muslims live in Russia. . . . This could become a contributory factor in the
emergence of fierce inter-ethnic and territorial conflicts, disintegration and re-
gionalisation of Russia along ethno-confessional lines".[9] Another official Russian newspaper, *Rossiyskaya gazeta,* argued that the Muslim republics of Central Asia could become a base for "a challenge to Russia's national interests
and security", that "it would be a mistake to underestimate the undesirable consequences for Russian foreign policy of Islamic fundamentalism's gaining in
strength". It went on to say that if Islamic fundamentalists gained an upper
hand in the CIS Muslim republics "Russia's geopolitical position would change
dramatically, and it would most probably no longer be regarded as a natural

ally. Then would come the time for politicised Islam to challenge Russia".[10] The purposes of the campaign were clear — to induce suspicion and mistrust of Central Asia in ordinary Russians and to portray it as a turbulent, dangerous region capable of causing Russia all sorts of troubles and misfortunes, a region it would be wiser to shun as far as possible.

The liberal camp's views found reflection in an analytical report on prospects for the CIS, prepared in September 1992 by the MGIMO's Centre for International Studies. Assessing basic trends in the CIS, the report singled out a group of states, namely Russia, Kazakhstan, Kyrgyzstan, Uzbekistan and Tajikistan, that "appeared to be establishing a network of special relations" which might allow them "to become the core of a Commonwealth marked by close cooperation and partnership". The report concluded that this trend ran "contrary to Russia's interests" on the grounds that "the idea of transforming the CIS into a more cohesive community of states proceeding along the path of integration is illusory. . . . The European member states will proceed with their present policy of trying to overcome their one-sided dependence on Russia and the Eurasian area. The possible consolidation of an emerging core group within CIS will not entice them back, but will result in transformation of CIS into a Russian-Central Asian union".[11]

The authors explained that they did not oppose cooperation with Kazakhstan and Central Asia in principle, but wanted to distinguish between different forms of cooperation — "it should not lead to development of regional integration and creation of institutions that are likely to limit Russia's freedom of manoeuvre in areas crucial for economic and political reform", and went on to say that "incompatibility between the economic policies" of Russia and the Central Asian states might "cause the postponement, if not collapse, of market reforms in Russia", with a "danger of degeneration of the 'reform union' into an anti-reformist bloc, with conservative elites remaining in power."[12]

The second danger mentioned in the report was that integration with Central Asian states could involve Russia in various regional conflicts. "Signing bilateral mutual assistance accords means that Russia commits itself to guaranteeing not only national security but domestic peace in these states as well. . . . Thus mechanisms are lacking to avoid dragging Russia automatically into a military conflict". The report suggested that Russia should "withdraw all its troops completely from non-Russian territories as soon as possible. . . . The former Soviet military infrastructure should also be dismantled, except for sites operating within the framework of strategic forces agreements (early warning systems, satellite communications and the like), which should remain on a bilaterally agreed legal basis".[13]

The report clearly followed the line of thought typical of Russian liberal ethnic nationalists. It saw Kazakhstan and Central Asia not as a valuable partner but as a burden, an obstacle to Russia's progressive development to be gotten rid of as soon as possible. This was only to be expected. MGIMO is a subdivision of the Ministry of Foreign Affairs and bound to reflect the attitudes of the ministry's top leadership, which at that stage was definitely pro-liberal.

The report's authors made no secret of this association; they thanked the CIS Department of the Ministry for its assistance in drafting the report.

When in Moscow to commemorate the fifth anniversary of the CIS, Nazarbayev commented regretfully that in the first post-Soviet years "Russia's leadership lost the chance to become the centre, the nucleus, the natural axis of the Commonwealth" and explained this by the attitude of the Russian government: "Their approach to integration was based on one sole postulate — Russia should get rid of the 'ballast'. By 'ballast' they meant most of the other former republics of the USSR".[14] Though Nazarbayev did not specify which former republics, it was clear that he was speaking primarily about Kazakhstan and the other Central Asian states.

The liberals' position on relations with Central Asia came under attack from Eurasianist-controlled media. In one such critique, A. Frolov charged "Yeltsin's closest advisers" with failing "to evaluate the new alignment of forces and Kazakhstan's place in it correctly". In his view the former USSR had become two zones, a Slavic-Christian zone and a Turkic-Muslim zone, and this was "potentially detrimental to Russia, which has long bestrode the border between the Christian and Islamic worlds. A one-sided orientation, even if motivated by something as dear to the Russian heart as Slavic unity, is not in Russia's national interests". The article characterised Yeltsin's behaviour as "incomprehensible" for not taking into account Russia's 5000-km-long border with Kazakhstan. The author cited three major factors necessitating Russia's interest in increased cooperation with Kazakhstan: (1) Kazakhstan's leadership potential in the Muslim world "as the first Muslim nuclear and space power", (2) growing interdependence due to Kazakh influence on Russia's Muslims and Russian influence on Kazakhstan's Slavs, (3) a moral imperative to devise truly universal human values of East and West as opposed to the values of Western capitalist civilisation. Frolov argued that Russia and Kazakhstan "by virtue of their intermediate position between Eastern and Western cultures, and their unique historical experience, can set an example of the new kind of cooperation humanity needs", and that to follow Solzhenitsyn's line of thinking, particularly getting involved in a territorial dispute with Kazakhstan, would be "demonstrating political blindness and ineptitude". He also attacked the liberals' foreign policy orientation, claiming that "the West needs Russia not as an industrial centre and competitor in high technology, but as a new Third World region — a source of raw materials and cheap labour and a dump-site for industrial wastes. Our Central Asian neighbours, on the other hand, have an objective economic interest in a strong Russia". In conclusion, he called for increased cooperation with Central Asia.[15]

In a similar article, "The Eastern Question for Russia", A. Bogaturov and M. Kozhokin discussed alternatives for Russian foreign policy and sharply criticised the supporters of the "European choice". They argued that "the Ukrainian-Russian-Belorussian triad is only one of the probable (and increasingly less probable) options for the foundation of a very shaky CIS. . . . Not all interests of Moscow, Kiev and Minsk coincide. There are also interests that bring Russia closer to the East. . . . Russia is an enormous Eurasian power, while Belarus and Ukraine have historically developed in the context of a European orientation". They asserted that most important among Russian foreign policy priorities was "preserving a potential field of integration" and warned that while "appeasing Kiev" Moscow could lose the trust of its Asian neighbours and alienate Kazakhstan, "the main stabilising force of the entire CIS".[16]

The Eurasianists' Central Asian strategy was not yet comprehensively formulated, but the general trends could already be discerned in publications emanating from the opposition camp. An article by Sh. Sultanov, "The Spirit of an Eurasianist", published in July 1992 in *Nash sovremennik*. He stated that historically and geopolitically Russia should be defined within the boundaries of the former Soviet Union. The Russian Federation was not the historical Russia. Russia's revival would depend on a strategic approach to the problem of securing the historical Slavic-Turkic alliance: "Russia needs Central Asia no less than Central Asia needs Russia. . . . Both are in a geopolitical encirclement which in the final analysis respects only strength. In the absence of such strength, today's friends could become tomorrow's mortal enemies. Economically both Russia and Central Asia are still unable to do without each other. . . . If the separation between them grows, the negative consequences will be felt more in the Central Asian republics in the next 2–3 years, but in 5–7 years will already affect the Russian Federation to a greater extent".[17] Thus Sultanov identified two major factors — defence and security on the one hand, economic on the other — as reasons for increased Russian association with Central Asia and possible reincorporation as one state.

While Sultanov did not elaborate on particulars, other Eurasianist ideologists later did so. S. Platonov, in his article "Russian interests in Central Asia", published in October 1992, accused Yeltsin's administration of pursuing policies on Central Asia contrary to Russia's traditional national interests, for which it was paramount to keep Central Asia in Moscow's sphere of influence. He argued that Russia's disengagement from Central Asia would undermine its security in the middle and long term:

1. Russia's withdrawal would prompt political destabilisation in Central Asia and a thousand-kilometer arc of instability from Ust-Kamenogorsk to Krasnodar would appear, along which various areas of conflict would emerge.
2. Central Asia's post-Soviet borders with Iran, Afghanistan and China should be regarded as Russia's southern borders. Billions of roubles were spent to strengthen these borders. Transferring the border northwards would increase its length, causing an inconceivable waste of material resources and sharply decreasing the effectiveness of Russia's border security, already endangered by the infiltration of weapons from Afghanistan via Central Asia.
3. Disengaging from Central Asia would disrupt Russia's relations with Kazakhstan since it would lead to a massive movement for reunification with Russia in several parts of Kazakhstan. Alma-Ata's possession of nuclear weapons would give it pow-

erful leverage in this matter. The Kazakh leadership could also opt to shift into the Chinese sphere of influence.

4. Russian withdrawal would automatically confer on Central Asia increased influence on Moscow's geopolitical rivals. The major competition would be between Ankara, Teheran, Kabul and Beijing.

5. A Russian retreat would symbolise further decline of state power and have a strong negative influence on the integrity of the Russian Federation. It would manifest first as increased centrifugal tendencies among Turkic peoples and as growth of separatism among Russian Siberian territories.

6. There are twelve million Slavs in Central Asia. Political instability there would cause an influx of refugees into Russia, and this would cause a humanitarian catastrophe, given the poor state of Russia's economy and its inability to take care of refugees.

7. Left alone, Central Asia would become a security risk through drug traffic. An influx of Central Asian drugs into Russia could be expected.

8. Central Asia's industrial and agricultural potential remains an important element of the former Soviet integrated economic complex. It is a traditional supplier of many of raw materials (cotton, leather, wool) for Russian light industry, and a traditional and relatively large market for Russian industrial exports.[18]

Criticism of official liberal policy on Central Asia came not only from the Eurasianist opposition, but also from some elements within Yeltsin's administration. This was inevitable, since Russia's post-Soviet leadership included a diverse coalition of forces united by Russian ethnic nationalism, but divided on almost everything else. The USSR's dissolution and Gorbachev's ousting removed a common purpose and was followed by growing fragmentation and an internal struggle in Yeltsin's entourage. The first symptoms of this appeared as early as late January 1992, when Vice-President Rutskoy made several public statements at odds with the Foreign Ministry's official line. On 30 January Rutskoy wrote in the pro-Communist newspaper *Pravda* that "[t]he historical consciousness of Russians will not allow anyone to equate the borders of Russia mechanically with those of the Russian Federation, and to take away what constituted glorious pages of Russian history", and the CIS "should be regarded as no more than a transitional form between the former union and a new state to be created by the former Union republics".[19]

On 26 June 1992 Rutskoy's principal aide, V. Lipitsky, publicised a wide range of disagreements with the Foreign Ministry in an article. He criticised its pro-Western orientation and expressed dissatisfaction with its performance in Central Asia, where, he said, "the Foreign Ministry contemplates with a certain sense of doom the peaceful expansion of Iran, Turkey and Afghanistan—an expansion that encompasses the lands that are closest to Russia, as well as their leaders. Commentaries like 'West is West and East is East' are viewed only as an admission of the ministry's own impotence".[20] On 16 July 1992 Rutskoy himself openly attacked Kozyrev and demanded his resignation.[21] But at that time Kozyrev had the support of still powerful State Secretary Burbulis and survived.

Another centre of opposition to the Foreign Ministry formed in the Supreme Soviet (Russian parliament). In June, E. Ambartsumov, chairman of its Committee on International Affairs joined Rutskoy in questioning the validity of post-Soviet borders. Ambartsumov said that changing the borders of CIS states could be justified by both human rights considerations and "Russia's general geopolitical interests".[22] The Supreme Soviet refused to endorse the concept of Russian foreign policy submitted by the ministry in February, criticised it harshly, and in early July returned it to the ministry for revision.[23] In August the parliamentary Committee on International Affairs prepared a secret set of recommendations for the Ministry of Foreign Affairs, calling for development of a Russian foreign policy concept similar to the Monroe Doctrine. Ambartsumov allegedly wrote in the report that Russia, "as internationally recognised legal successor to the USSR", should base its foreign policy "on a doctrine that proclaims the former Union's entire geopolitical space a sphere of its vital interests".[24]

To undermine the Foreign Ministry's influence the Supreme Soviet's leadership proposed creation of a separate Ministry for CIS Affairs.[25] The proposal was rejected, but Kozyrev's opponents scored an important victory when on 7 July Yeltsin signed a decree creating the Security Council, a powerful structure in the presidential administration designed to coordinate the activities of various ministries and departments on foreign and security policy. Y. Skokov, a former business executive with links to the military-industrial complex, was appointed secretary of the council. Creation of the council effectively reduced Kozyrev's role in foreign policy-making. Yeltsin did not publicly commit himself to any side. His pronouncements on the subject were vague. In one of his rare interviews he characterised Russia's major foreign policy interest as "seeing the world truly stable and in affirming the norms of civilised life and strengthening mutually advantageous cooperation in the world community".[26] Yeltsin, an experienced bureaucrat, followed the well-established tactic of balancing the different centres of power.

Political debate on Russia's relations with Central Asia vividly reflected the crystallisation of two major opposing schools of thought on foreign policy. In March 1992 Professor A. Vasiliev, president of the Russian Centre for Arab, African and Islamic Studies, wrote a spectacular article, "Russia and the Muslim World: Partners or Adversaries", in which he outlined the differences between the two schools. He called the first group "Atlantists", because they allegedly favoured "the earliest possible maximum rapprochement with the West and establishment of allied relations with the USA". In his opinion Atlantists had antipathy to Iran as a focus of Islamic fundamentalism. The second major group, to which he obviously attached himself, believed it was a mistake to fully equate Russia's interests with those of the West. Vasiliev argued that while during the Cold War the line of global confrontation had lain between NATO and the Warsaw Pact (West and East), it had now shifted to the North-South axis (i.e., between the West and primarily the Muslim world), and that it was in Russia's interests to avoid being drawn into this confrontation because of all European countries Russia had the longest border (several thousand kilometres long) with the Muslim world. Meanwhile Russia's treatment of the former USSR's Muslim republics was "becoming a touchstone for its future relations with the entire Muslim world". Vasiliev admitted that the collapse of the USSR and the concurrent process of "self-identification of the Turkic peoples and legitimisation of their political elites" had "certain anti-Russian overtones", pushed Russians and Central Asians apart and "put a certain distance between them at state level". He suggested that Russians should react to this "without hysteria", as it was only natural "if the new states moved three or four steps away from Russia". Central Asian nationalism, "even with Islamic overtones", could have "a long-term anti-Russian orientation only if artificially incited". To prove his point Vasiliev cited the historical background: the Eurasian space traditionally had been a zone of cohabitation and interaction between the Slavic (primarily Russian) and Turkic ethnoses, between Orthodox Christians and Muslims. It was in the interests of both to use all conceivable means to convert inevitable conflicts between them into non-violent forms and work to resolve them. "If conflicts turn into bloody civil strife, this would mean the self-destruction of both Russia and the Turkic Muslim people".[27]

Vasiliev decisively discarded the notion that the Muslim republics could unite into a single anti-Russian bloc on the basis of Muslim fundamentalism or pan-Turkism. He pointed out that in the rest of the world nationalism had proved stronger than religion and that "nowhere had Islam become a basis for stable political alliances". As for pan-Turkism, Vasiliev demonstrated that the Turkic peoples living on former Soviet territory were noted for manifestations of disunity rather than of integration and expressed serious doubts about the viability of Central Asian economic reorientation towards other Muslim states. "Just building roads to Turkey and Iran will take billions, and who is going to finance them?", he asked rhetorically. He pointed out that the Central Asian republics' economic ties were oriented towards the North (i.e., Russia) and their economic structures were competitive, not complementary to Iran, Turkey and most other Muslim countries. Naturally enough, Vasiliev singled out economic necessity as the first among three major factors that "would force Russia and the new Muslim states to take two or three steps toward each other". He identified the russified Central Asian intellectual elites, who would maintain "traditional ties with Russian centres of science and education", as a second factor. As the third factor, Vasiliev named "the inhabitants of various republics who found themselves outside the borders of their national states. . . . Any confrontation between Russia and Kazakhstan, where half the population is Russian, or Kyrgyzstan, where Russians make up almost a third, could lead to destructive civil wars. . . . The Russian-speaking population will obviously urge the new states to cooperate with Russia".[28]

Political debate in Russia on relations with Central Asia and Kazakhstan generated new ideas, some of which were later fully or partially incorporated into official foreign policy. Yet, the existence of two competing schools of foreign policy thought, particularly inside the government apparatus, engendered an inconsistent approach to the region in Russia's first post-Soviet months. Policy towards Kazakhstan represented a mixture of uncoordinated and often conflicting efforts by different economic interests, government departments, public organisations and individual politicians. But the necessity to solve important outstanding issues inherited from the Soviet past soon prevailed over ideological considerations and led to the emergence of a coherent Russian policy toward Kazakhstan.

The most immediate problems were a wide range of economic, financial and trade issues, to which the new situation added a diplomatic dimension. With the USSR gone, economic interrelations between post-Soviet states found themselves in a legalistic vacuum. The system of Union ministries which had regulated the economic currents had been destroyed, without a new interstate system of cooperation to replace it. The founding documents of the CIS contained no detailed provisions for regulating economic relations between the new independent states. The lack of explicit economic provisions was a major shortcoming of the accords and from the outset had a negative effect on economic relations between members of the CIS.

When Nazarbayev saw that multilateral economic agreements within the CIS were difficult to achieve, he began to initiate bilateral solutions. Following the CIS summit in Moscow on 16 January 1992, Russia and Kazakhstan signed a bilateral agreement, On Removing Constraints in Economic Activity, which provided for unhindered acquisition and movement of goods, services, labour and finances between them and gave Russian and Kazakh companies the right to freely establish branches in each other's territories. Almaty recognised the Russian rouble as the only legal tender in Kazakhstan. Both agreed not to levy extra duties on goods transiting each other's territory (including in pipelines), to coordinate export and import policies for items crucial to their bilateral trade, and not to adopt legislation restricting free development of market relations.[29]

Kazakhstan's turning to Russia in the hope of solving its outstanding economic problems was no accident. Russia was its main supplier of many essential commodities, including all its imports of timber; 90%–95% of construction materials; 94% of microbiological products; 95% of alcohol; 90% of synthetic rubber, synthetic resins and plastics; 84% of fish, marine products and medical equipment; 80% of tyres, cellulose and paper goods; 70% of chemicals; and 60% of enamels paints, machines and industrial equipment. In the 1980s Kazakhstan's import from Russia exceeded in 1.5 times its exports to Russia, and in 1990 this figure rose to 1.8 times.[30]

One of the most important elements in Russian-Kazakh economic relations was Kazakhstan's geographical position as a landlocked country. The major transport routes to world markets ran through Russia, making Kazakhstan's foreign trade wholly dependent on Russia's transport infrastructure. A World Bank report on Kazakhstan's economic prospects, prepared in the first half of 1992, emphasised that Russian oil and gas pipelines and railroads were vital for Kazakhstan's main exports: "In the energy sector, the first priority should be to establish the legal and economic basis needed to maintain existing trade links".[31] World Bank and International Monetary Fund (IMF) analyses of Kazakhstan's economy pinpointed the oil and gas sector as its most important current source of hard-currency earnings, and these were the principal means by which Nazarbayev intended to spur his country's economic modernisation.

Kazakhstan's heavy economic dependence on Russia revealed itself in several ways in the first few months of independent existence, the most obvious being Russia's role in Kazakhstan's price increases. The first post-Soviet Russian government tried to implement radical economic reforms as quickly as possible. It had no intention of allowing its reformist endeavours to be retarded by endless negotiations with other republics and began raising prices, introducing new exchange rates and changing interest rates without prior consultations with other CIS states. Kazakhstan had no alternative but to follow Russia's price increases. In the first nine months of 1992 prices rose in 17.1 times in Russia, and twenty-fold in Kazakhstan.[32] Kazakh experts later complained that their country's heavy economic dependence on Russia negatively affected the course of its economic reforms. In the opinion of researchers at the Centre for Strategic Studies in Almaty, Kazakhstan was forced "to follow Russia in implementation of reforms which were not always acceptable to the republic, since they caused difficulties, augmented by local characteristics".[33]

Russia's dependence on Kazakhstan's economy was miniscule compared to Kazakhstan's dependence on Russia's economy. Indeed, Kazakhstan accounted for barely 3% of the former USSR's economy, and its gross domestic product (GDP) in the last Soviet years was a mere 6%–7% of Russia's.[34] Only some of its mineral resources, particularly nonferrous and rare metals, were of real value to Russia's economy. Table 2.1 shows Kazakhstan's and Russia's shares of the reserves and production of some strategic minerals in the USSR in 1991.

Table 2.1
Reserves and Production of Strategic Minerals in USSR (1991) (%)

Mineral	Kazakhstan		Russia	
	Reserves	Output	Reserves	Output
Silver	26	49	36	42
Chrome	96	95	3	5
Lead	38	61	34	25
Zinc	36	55	48	38
Barium	82	83	-	-
Phosphates	65	65	-	-

Source: Kozhokin, E. M., ed., *Kazakhstan: realii i perspektivy nezavisimogo razvitiya*, Moscow: RISI, 1995, pp. 10–12.

Meanwhile 85% of Kazakhstan's exports of nonferrous metals went to Russia. But the most important consideration was that Russia had vital interests in Kazakhstan, military and strategic, and in a Russian diaspora. Moscow understood that satisfactory resolution of these issues would be impossible if Kazakhstan lost too many of the economic opportunities it previously enjoyed in Russia.

Another reason for Russian interest in Kazakhstan's economy was the peculiarities of disposition of industries inherited from the Soviet period. Strange as it may seem, Kazakhstan exported to Russia a number of commodities that it also imported from Russia. In Soviet times the economies of both developed within a single economic complex, and industrial enterprises were deployed on the basis of an economic rationale. Given the size of both countries, it was sometimes more rational to supply neighbouring areas of Russia from adjacent areas of Kazakhstan, and vice versa, rather than from more distant areas within each country.

For example, Russian electrical power stations in the Urals and Siberia were traditionally fueled by coal from Kazakhstan, while Magnitogorsk and Chelyabinsk metallurgical combines and two giant vehicle producers, KAMAZ and VAZ, were major Russian consumers of Kazakhstan's ferrous metal ores. Hence Russia wished to continue receiving from Kazakhstan commodities such as oil, coal, ferrous metals, agricultural machines, some chemical products, alumina, tyres, polyester, synthetic rubber, as well as grain, wool and leather.[35] In principle Russia could obtain what it needed elsewhere, but at extra cost which would make the prices of its goods less competitive.

After the CIS Kiev summit of March 1992 failed to produce solutions to major economic problems, Kazakhstan and Russia held a separate governmental-level meeting in Uralsk on 23 March, mainly devoted to resolving monetary and credit issues and related economic problems. They declared that they intended to "persistently contribute . . . to development of integration processes within the single economic space of both states". They called on leaders of other CIS states to reach an agreement to strengthen economic integration, and to consider at the next CIS summit a draft CIS charter which would contain provisions on supremacy of interstate agreements over national legislation. They also confirmed their intention to facilitate "forming an Interbank union for the purposes of "joint regulation of credit and monetary circulation, financial stabilisation and struggle against inflation". Kazakhstan reiterated its commitment to using the Russian rouble as its sole currency and promised to take "all necessary measures" to maintain its value.

Both agreed to work to unify the rules governing foreign trade, including "establishment of joint tariff rates for export and import of goods from their territory, a common regime of non-tariff regulation of foreign economic activities". They also announced their intention to coordinate export and import and customs policies in relation to nonmembers of the customs union and to conclude a special agreement on coordination in regulating foreign economic activities within a month.[36]

They also undertook to settle trade imbalances either through bilateral trade or through covering disparities by state bonds. This issue was of particular importance for Russia, because the bilateral agreement on removing constraints in economic activity was not being fulfilled. Kazakhstan repeatedly failed to meet its obligations to supply goods to Russia in exchange for Russian products and blocked free acquisition of such goods by Russian companies. As a result Kazakhstan's debt to Russia was growing rapidly. In Uralsk it was decided to conclude a special agreement on procedures for removing disparities in the bilateral trade balance within a month. One way of facilitating bilateral trade was seen in creation of joint-stock companies with Russian and Kazakh capital. They decided to form an expert working group to select specific facilities, conditions and amounts to be invested. This provision opened the way for Russian enterprises to buy Kazakhstan firms which supplied strategic resources to Russia.[37]

Kazakhstan also secured important concessions from Russia, mainly in connection with interstate transportation. The relevant agreement, signed on 23 March 1992 by Burbulis and Kazakhstan's Prime Minister Tereshchenko, established that both countries would "create favourable conditions for the functioning of all types of transport" of passengers and cargoes. The agreement established that "means of transport conducting such transportation are exempt from taxes and state charges connected with use and maintenance of roads, possession and use of means of transport, as well as taxes and charges on profits received through transportation".[38]

It was also in Uralsk that Russia and Kazakhstan agreed to prepare a comprehensive treaty to cover major issues of bilateral relations — economic, political and military.[39] This treaty was signed by Yeltsin and Nazarbayev in Moscow on 25 May 1992. It was the first such treaty between post-Soviet Russia and another former Soviet republic, and is in effect for ten years with automatic prolongation for another ten. It is very comprehensive, dealing with issues from common security to economic cooperation to human rights.[40] Its economic provisions represent a compromise, Russia undertaking a number of unilateral obligations to compensate Almaty for concessions in other fields. Article 16 stipulated that the contracting parties agree "to refrain from unilateral actions destabilising the other's economic position". They also promised "to interact in various international economic, financial and other organisations and institutions, assisting each other in participation and entrance into international organisations, of which one party is a member". Because Kazakhstan was economically much weaker than Russia it could do nothing that would destabilise the economic situation in Russia, and Russia, not Kazakhstan had membership in various international organisations, so the these points addressed mostly Kazakh concerns.

Another economic provision of importance to Kazakhstan was in Article 20. It said that the sides would strictly observe the agreement on principles of cooperation in the field of transport, providing "unhampered and duty-free transit by all means of transport of passengers and cargoes". The inclusion of provisions on transportation in such a fundamental document gave them special status and linked them to obligations undertaken by Kazakhstan in other spheres. Article 21 said the contracting parties would "interact on an equal basis in the matter of . . . use and exports of oil and natural gas". Kazakhstan could not export these items without Moscow's co-operation because all the pipelines connecting it to major world markets passed through Russian territory.

Article 13 dealt with border crossing and migration. It stipulated that the contracting parties, "adhering to the principle of open borders between them, recognise the necessity to devise and implement a coordinated complex of measures for regulation of migratory processes, including mutual guarantees for free movement of people of both states and a common regime for entry and exit of citizens of the Parties to third countries". Closely linked to the above provision was one in Article 16, which said that both sides should "secure unhampered movement of goods, capitals and services between them". For Kazakhstan freedom of movement across Russia's border was of primary importance, because most of its surface communication lines to the rest of the world ran through Russia. Besides, Almaty wanted to ensure that Russia would not create barriers to emigration of Kazakhstan's Slav population.

The bilateral economic agreements reached in the first half of 1992 could have ensured a positive turnaround in Russian-Kazakh economic relations, but did not do so because neither side had the will or desire to fulfill its part of the bargain. As a result, Russia's positive trade balance with Kazakhstan, and therefore Kazakhstan's debt to Russia, skyrocketed, reaching 247.6 billion roubles by the end of 1992.[41] Although in 1992 Russia remained Kazakhstan's main trading partner (60% of trade), total trade shrank to 21.5 billion roubles, almost one-third less than in 1991.[42] This decline marked the beginning of a partial reorientation of Russia's and Kazakhstan's economies away from each other.

The other set of important issues that post-Soviet Russian diplomacy had to tackle was the future of the vast military complex spread throughout all former Soviet republics. The agreement to create the CIS provided for preserving "[t]he common military and strategic space under joint command, including joint control over nuclear armaments, to be regulated by a special agreement".[43] By decision of the Alma-Ata summit, command of the former USSR armed forces was entrusted to Marshal E. Shaposhnikov. But plans to maintain a unified command of the CIS Joint Armed Forces failed, because some of the new independent states (e.g., Ukraine, Moldova, Azerbaijan) were unwilling to have constraints of centralised control imposed on their military activities. At the CIS summit in Minsk on 30 December 1991, all other member states agreed to keep conventional forces under unified command, but also decided that each could establish its own armed forces if it so desired.[44]

Among all CIS leaders, the most ardent supporter of joint armed forces was Nazarbayev. His position, of course, rested not on sentimental adherence to unity of the former Soviet republics but on pragmatic considerations. He had no illusions about what sort of army independent Kazakhstan could create. In an interview he admitted that "in order to organise normal defence or armed forces, and to draw up a doctrine, a state like Kazakhstan, at least, needs time".[45] And continued existence of the joint armed forces would allow Kazakhstan to participate in decisions regarding their use and to prevent their employment against Kazakhstan's interests.

Yeltsin, on the other hand, had two options. Separate armed forces would suit Russia's leadership, but there were some major complications. First, Yeltsin had promised the Russian military leaders that the CIS would have joint armed forces. Secondly, he did not want to take the initiative in breaking up the remnants of the joint military structure, because he was already under fierce attack at home for breaking up the USSR. Finally, there were enormous technical difficulties in dividing the single military complex, and it could not be done quickly or without a transitional period. This, however, did not preclude Yeltsin from exploring the issue of separate Russian armed forces immediatly after the collapse of the USSR. The first sign of this was Yeltsin's decree on the text of the military oath of allegiance to the Russian Federation issued on 5 January 1992, which required all military personnel, including those stationed in other republics, to swear allegiance solely to the Russian Federation and its people.[46]

In mid-January the Russian leadership began preparing a draft presidential decree, on the armed forces of the Russian Federation and on collective security of the member-states of the Commonwealth of Independent States. The document provided for Russia to proclaim itself the USSR's legal successor in military matters and to assume the former USSR's rights and duties with regard to armed forces, including those deployed outside Russian territory.[47]

These developments seriously concerned Nazarbayev. He criticised Yeltsin's decree and said that service personnel should maintain their previous oath to the USSR.[48] At the republic's Security Council meeting in mid-January he reaffirmed his conviction that unified armed forces should be retained on all CIS territory, even if only Russia and Kazakhstan agreed to this, but added that if efforts to break up the unified armed forces continued, Kazakhstan would be obliged to start forming its own armed forces.[49] On 13 January, on the eve of a visit to Kazakhstan by Shaposhnikov, Nazarbayev stated that he continued to favour retention of a unified military structure, and criticised Ukraine for seeking to split the armed forces.[50] On 10 February he told a correspondent from the newspaper Tyurkie that efforts to break up the former Soviet armed forces could lead to sharp conflicts between CIS members.[51]

Thus Nazarbayev was the only CIS leader who continued to defend the concept of joint CIS armed forces to the bitter end. At the CIS summit in Minsk on 14 February, he proposed a two- or three-year moratorium on creating separate armies and insisted that his proposal on joint armed forces be put to the vote. No other republic displayed much enthusiasm, but eight of them, including Russia, signed an agreement, On Conventional Forces during the Period of Transition, establishing a special command of CIS conventional forces.[52] Nazarbayev tried to portray the agreement as a personal victory, but in reality, as its title indicated, it was only temporary. Nazarbayev had in fact already lost his battle for joint armed forces. Seven weeks later, on 4 April Yeltsin signed a decree establishing a state commission for the formation of a Russian Federation defence ministry, army and navy.[53] Russia would have its own separate armed forces.

On 7 May 1992 Yeltsin issued a decree on formation of a separate Russian armed forces. Russia embarked on dividing the former Soviet armed forces. Nazarbayev could only follow suit. On 8 May he signed a decree, On Formation of the Armed Forces of the Republic of Kazakhstan,[54] according to which all ex-Soviet units and facilities in Kazakhstan came under Kazakhstan's jurisdiction.[55] Thus began the process of formally dividing the armed forces, conducted in accordance with the principles for division of former USSR state property.[56] There was, however, one major complication. The principle could not be applied to nuclear weapons, as it would constitute nuclear proliferation, bringing three more nuclear powers — Kazakhstan, Ukraine and Belorussia — into in the world.

Kazakhstan had 104 heavy ICBMs RC-20 (SS-18), each with ten 550-kiloton nuclear warheads, and 40 Tu 95MC (Bear) strategic bombers, with a total of 240 nuclear cruise missiles, on its territory,[57] as well as an unspecified number of tactical nuclear weapons, a nuclear arsenal greater than that of Britain or France. Kazakhstan's reluctance to relinquish it clearly manifested itself after independence. The emergence of the problem can be traced back to the first days after the unsuccessful August 1991 coup, when some republics declared independence but met with threatening declarations by the RSFSR government on the border issue.

The Kazakh reaction to these declarations was the harshest. In a telegram to Yeltsin, Nazarbayev went so far as to hint at Kazakhstan's nuclear potential, with the phrase "Particular danger lies in the fact that Kazakhstan is a nuclear republic".[58] This could mean nothing but a threat to use nuclear weapons to protect Kazakhstan's territorial integrity. On 16 September 1991, Nazarbayev stated in an interview that Kazakhstan did not intend to relinquish the nuclear weapons stationed on its territory.[59] In his memoirs he referred to the "days following the coup, when voices were heard about territorial changes" as the main reason for his decision to keep the nuclear weapons.[60]

In reality, Nazarbayev was bluffing. Kazakhstan had neither the technical ability to use nuclear weapons nor the power to take physical control of them, because the strategic nuclear forces were manned predominantly by ethnic Russians, who were unlikely to take orders from Alma-Ata. Also, the Kazakhs did not have possession of nuclear launch codes nor the expertise to retarget missiles on Russia. Attacks against Russian units guarding nuclear weapons were unlikely because Kazakhstan did not have an army and the former Soviet army would hardly agreed to follow Kazakh orders. Thus Nazarbayev's tough stance was at most a gamble exploiting the new Russian leadership's inexperience.

But this gamble soon involved the United States, too. U.S. Secretary of State James Baker, who on 16 September was visiting Almaty, linked future Western support for Kazakhstan with a satisfactory solution to the nuclear issue. Nazarbayev, in turn, tried to persuade Baker that nuclear weapons were vital to Kazakhstan's defence and security. In recalling his conversation with Baker, Nazarbayev wrote: "I told J. Baker that in such a situation strategic missiles would stay in Kazakhstan. I simply could not let them go without being given firm security guarantees for my state. . . . When we know that we are secure, when we know that we have firm guarantees, then we will decide on the nuclear issue".[61] Thus, if we believe Nazarbayev, the primary objective of his gamble with nuclear weapons was to obtain security guarantees for his country.

At a joint press conference with Baker, Nazarbayev spoke not of Kazakhstan's sole control of nuclear arms, but of the necessity to have them under unified control, as well as under control by the republics where they are located. "I am opposed to nuclear weapons being owned by any one republic, no matter how large it is", he said. This formula meant that Nazarbayev did not exactly want Kazakhstan to be a nuclear state, but that he objected against Russia's sole ownership of nuclear arms and wanted to have a veto on their possible use. Nevertheless, his pronouncements created quite a stir.[62] On 17 September Soviet Foreign Ministry spokesman Vitaliy Churkin had to make an official statement that Kazakhstan "will not control the nuclear weapons deployed on its territory".[63]

In late September 1991 Kazakhstan state adviser Khitrin was invited to Moscow with an unpublicised mission to prepare an agreement on the status of nuclear weapons on Kazakhstan's territory.[64] The negotiations were obviously unsuccessful, because no formal agreement was concluded at that time. Only a few days later in a speech at a public ceremony, Nazarbayev reiterated his position on nuclear weapons: "We will take all necessary measures to establish reliable control over the strategic missiles located on our territory. This control should be exercised within the context of a unified defence of the country, with mandatory participation by representatives of Kazakhstan".[65] This position remained unchanged until the USSR's final days but did not become politically significant, because de facto control of nuclear weapons remained in the Soviet Defence Ministry's hands.

The situation began changing rapidly after conclusion of the Belovezhskaya accords and Kazakhstan's declaration of independence. Kazakhstan's position on nuclear weapons once again drew Washington's attention. Nonproliferation of nuclear weapons had long been one of the United States' highest foreign policy priorities. The possible emergence of Kazakhstan as a new nuclear power was unacceptable to Washington, because it would create a dangerous precedent for other states to opt for nuclear status. Besides, there were serious doubts that independent Kazakhstan would have sufficient means, expertise and devotion to exercise control over its nuclear arms and technology, including prevention of their leakage to anti-American regimes in the Third World or to terrorist organisations.

Baker once again visited Kazakhstan on 18 December 1991 and had a three-hour meeting with Nazarbayev. After the meeting Baker confirmed that the nuclear problem was discussed widely and in detail. But Kazakhstan's position obviously remained unchanged. At the joint press conference with Baker, Nazarbayev said that Kazakhstan intended to propose an agreement between the four former Soviet republics with nuclear weapons on their territory to insure unified direction, control and non-proliferation of these weapons.[66] Nothing in his position indicated that Kazakhstan was prepared to become a nonnuclear state.

To a large degree Nazarbayev's position found reflection in documents agreed at the Alma-Ata conference of leaders of the former Soviet republics on 21 December 1991. Agreement on Joint Measures with Respect to Nuclear Weapons, signed by the four nuclear republics, specified that nuclear arms were "a part of the Joint Strategic Armed Forces", which ensured "collective security of all members of the Commonwealth of Independent States". The agreement stipulated that by 1 July 1992 Kazakhstan, Ukraine and Belarus would "ensure the removal of tactical nuclear weapons to central factory depots for disassembly under joint control". Tactical nuclear weapons were mobile and relatively easy to relocate to Russian territory even without the consent and cooperation of the authorities of a particular republic. But Nazarbayev effectively avoided any obligations with regard to strategic nuclear systems. The agreement spoke of elimination of nuclear weapons on the territory of Belarus and Ukraine, not Kazakhstan. Kazakhstan did not "pledge to accede to the 1968 Treaty on the Non-Proliferation of Nuclear Weapons as a nonnuclear-weapon state", as stipulated in Article 5 of the Agreement.[67] At that moment it seemed that Kazakhstan was making a bid to become a nuclear power.

This prospect was unacceptable to Russia, because Moscow did not want nuclear-armed neighbours who could challenge its leadership of post-Soviet space. On this question the different factions of Russia's political elite seemed to be unanimous. Liberal ethnic nationalists, then in charge of Russian foreign policy, regarded the Muslim world and particularly Central Asia as a possible strategic threat to Russia. The emergence of Kazakhstan as the first nuclear Muslim state would immeasurably increase the threat and so should be prevented. Conservative ethnic nationalists, seeking unification with the Russian-populated territories of Kazakhstan, anticipated a possible military confrontation with the Kazakhs; therefore the Kazakhs should not be permitted to possess nuclear weapons. Neo-Eurasianists, striving for restoration of the USSR, calculated that Kazakhstan would find it harder to withstand Russian pressure if it was a nonnuclear state.

The task that Russian diplomacy faced was not at all easy. For a number of reasons Russia was unable to apply tough pressure on Kazakhstan. First, Russia's domestic situation was unstable. Yeltsin's administration had been in power for just a short period and was very unsure of itself. Russian pressure on Kazakhstan could lead to a confrontation involving the Russian-speaking population and incite civil war in Kazakhstan, which could spread into Russia, and cause a crisis. This was very undesirable for Yeltsin's government, because its harsh economic measures were making it increasingly unpopular. On the other hand, a rebuff from Kazakhstan would cause serious loss of prestige both domestically and internationally, something the new Russian state, still establishing its position in international affairs, could not afford. Success of its reforms depended on Western cooperation, and the West would not tolerate the use of strong-arm tactics by the former imperial power against what was perceived as former colony.

In these circumstances Moscow chose a two-pronged course of action. The first was to draw the other three nuclear republics into nuclear arms control negotiations, which would force them to discuss the reduction and possible elimination of nuclear weapons in their territories. Toward this end, the Agreement on Strategic Forces was signed on 30 December 1991 at the CIS summit in Minsk. It said that member states "undertake to observe the international treaties of the USSR and to pursue a coordinated policy in the area of international security, disarmament and arms control, to participate in preparation and implementation of programmes of reductions in arms and armed forces". The agreement also established that "the status of strategic forces and procedure for service in them shall be defined in a special agreement".[68]

The second prong was to orchestrate international pressure on Kazakhstan. Here Moscow artfully played on Western fears of nuclear proliferation, already expressed by the United States (Baker had visited Alma-Ata twice and raised the issue with Nazarbayev each time), Germany, France and Britain. In early January 1992 the U.S. State Department announced that Under-Secretary Bartholomew would lead a U.S. team to Russia, Ukraine, Kazakhstan and Belarus to discuss questions of nuclear weapons safety and security, including disabling and dismantling nuclear weapons, and nuclear proliferation, with the aim of establishing strict export controls and ensuring the newly independent republics complied with international agreements.[69] After Bartholomew returned, the U.S. State Department expressed dissatisfaction with Kazakhstan's stance on strategic nuclear weapons.[70]

From Moscow's perspective, Western fears should be nurtured, and so they were. In January 1992 rumours, probably Russian instigated, about the Kazakhs' inability to comply with nuclear nonproliferation rules and exercise effective control over nuclear weapons began to circulate in the Russian and Western media. Kazakhstan's leadership found itself forced to defend its credibility to its Western counterparts. On 17 January, Nazarbayev's press service issued a statement denying allegations that Kazakhstan had begun trading in nuclear technologies, equipment and raw materials, and affirming that Kazakhstan would not help other nonnuclear states to manufacture or purchase nuclear arms.[71] At a press conference following French Foreign Minister Dumas's visit, Nazarbayev said claims that Kazakhstan was exporting nuclear weapons and technology to Arab states were unfounded. But immediately afterwards, the British *Daily Mail* published an article alleging that Iran was trying to buy intercontinental ballistic missiles from Kazakhstan and that Nazarbayev had made at least two visits to Teheran to discuss the deal.[72] This forced Kazakhstan's Foreign Ministry to issue another denial on 28 January.[73]

But reports alleging Kazakhs' involvement in illegal nuclear exports did not cease. In mid-March the German magazine *Stern* claimed that Iran might have obtained two nuclear warheads and medium-range delivery systems from Kazakhstan. *Stern* based its story on information from the German intelligence service, which was quoted as saying that Iran lacked the necessary codes and facilities to launch the weapons.[74] This time both Kazakh and Russian officials issued denials. Nazarbayev's spokesman, Sultan Muratov, described the *Stern* article as just "another canard", adding that "our president has more than once emphasised that our nuclear weapons are under safe control" and that Kazakhstan was living up to its obligations on nonproliferation. Russian Defence Ministry spokesman Ivan Krylnik simply stated that "the information is not true". But interestingly, the concurrent issue of *U.S. News and World Report* magazine quoted an unnamed, high-ranking Russian officer in Moscow who confirmed a U.S. intelligence report that three short-range nuclear weapons had vanished from a former Red Army arsenal in Kazakhstan and said analysts suspected the weapons had been sold to Iran, possibly with cooperation by several Kazakh nuclear specialists recently seen in Teheran.[75] Thus rumours continued to circulate. On 4 May 1992 the chairman of the Kazakh State Security Committee once again denounced foreign media reports that Kazakhstan had sold two nuclear warheads to Iran as a "disinformation plot aimed at poisoning relations between Kazakhstan and Russia", that manifested a clear desire to discredit "the moderate and realistic policies" of Kazakhstan.[76]

Such denunciations obviously did not help much, and Kazakhstan was acquiring a certain notoriety as a country extremely unreliable in nuclear nonproliferation issues. On 5 February in testimony to the Senate Armed Services Committee, U.S. Under-Secretary of State Bartholomew revealed a plan, allegedly devised with Russia, to disable all strategic nuclear missiles outside Russian territory within three years and to eliminate them within seven.[77] This drew an immediate reaction from Nazarbayev. In an interview with the Austrian newspaper *Die Presse* on the next day, he said the West should understand that Yeltsin did not speak for Kazakhstan on nuclear disarmament matters, and Yeltsin's discussions with U.S. President Bush could only be regarded as an initiative.[78] Then Russian diplomacy decided to make a move. On 13 February, *Izvestiya* published an account of a conversation Kozyrev had with journalists aboard his aircraft, in which he allegedly said,

Kazakhstan has no choice but to accede to the Nuclear Nonproliferation Treaty. Maybe someone suggested to Nazarbayev that if this question is left hanging in the air, the republic can score points in the international arena. If so, these are clearly unqualified advisers. The longer the issue remains obscure, the more the country's prestige will suffer. . . . Both credits and foreign aid could be jeopardised. When the Americans began having suspicions about Pakistan's nuclear program, they imposed sanctions against that very close ally.[79]

The statement was quite explicit diplomatically. First, it stated unequivocally to Russia's position in favour of Kazakhstan's nuclear disarmament, indicating to the West that in this important matter Russia would act as an ally. Second, it showed Kazakhstan the potential consequences of noncompliance – the suspension of aid and credits, and imposition of economic sanctions which Kazakhstan would be unable to withstand if Russia participated. Third, by mentioning the United States and its sanctions against Pakistan, it invited Washington to become involved and, moreover, suggested what action it might take.

It is also significant that Kozyrev made his statement on the eve of the CIS summit in Minsk, where Russia raised the question of nuclear weapons once again. Whether or not it was influenced by Kozyrev's statement, Kazakhstan did not object to signing the Agreement on Status of Strategic Forces, which created the position of commander of strategic forces, which would be subordinate to the CIS Council of Heads of State and Commander in Chief of the CIS joint armed forces and would have direct operational control of groupings, formations and units of strategic forces. The command was to organise alert duty, plan and implement operational and combat training, maintain the strategic forces in a combat-ready state, provide for the safety of nuclear weapons on-site and in transit, and operate in accordance with international treaties on nuclear weapons. The agreement retained the previous arrangement that decisions on use of nuclear weapons would be taken by Russia's President in agreement with those of Belarus, Kazakhstan and Ukraine.[80] The summit appointed former USSR Defence Minister Marshal Shaposhnikov as commander in chief of the CIS joint armed forces.

Russia regarded the agreement as an achievement, because it introduced some order into the management of the former USSR's nuclear arsenal and for the time being retained operational control of nuclear arms in Moscow's hands. Nevertheless, the major issue of principle, whether Kazakhstan was a nuclear or nonnuclear state, was not resolved at the summit, and Nazarbayev continued to behave as if it was a nuclear state. On 16 February in an interview to *Ostankino* television broadcasting company he argued that Kazakhstan was a de facto nuclear state "through no fault of our own", because it had been a nuclear test site since 1949, and conditioned the elimination of its strategic nuclear weapons on nuclear disarmament by the United States, China and the rest of the former Soviet Union, meaning of course Russia.[81] These conditions were clearly unrealistic and unacceptable, and could not be regarded as anything but a pretext to avoid relinquishing nuclear weapons. When visiting India in late February, Nazarbayev told reporters during a news conference that Kazakhstan had "a perception of a threat from the U.S., China, Russia, among others" and again linked his country's nuclear disarmament to nuclear disarmament of those states.[82]

In late March new reports from Washington indicated that the U.S. administration was increasingly worried about the positions adopted by Kazakhstan and Ukraine on the nuclear issue and was considering new moves to persuade them to accept nonnuclear status. "We clearly know the agreements we thought we had six or eight weeks ago are not holding up. . . . There is no question it's all deteriorated and we've got to figure out how to get it back on track. . . . We are going to have to tack in a different direction to try to make this happen," a senior U.S. official, who asked not to be identified, told Reuters.[83] In a subsequent move on 31 March, U.S. Defence Secretary Cheney, arriving in Brussels for a meeting of defence ministers of NATO, the CIS and the former Warsaw Pact, said he would urge former Soviet republics to fulfill their promise to transfer all nuclear arms to Russia.[84]

Nazarbayev probably felt that the international community was isolating him and played his last card. He employed a technique often used by small countries when being pressured by great powers. This involved creating and then exploiting differences between two great powers. Kazakh diplomacy had a long tradition of using such diplomatic manoeuvring to exploit rivalry between Russia and China in the eighteenth century. Nazarbayev would capitalise on differences between Moscow and Washington, but first he had to create some. On 28 April he sent a message to President Bush stating that Kazakhstan would like to conclude a strategic alliance with the United States and that Kazakhstan planned to retain the strategic nuclear weapons inherited from the USSR only temporarily.[85] Nazarbayev evidently believed that if the Americans showed the slightest interest in his proposal, it would arouse Russian suspicions, and he could then play one against the other and negotiate the best possible deal.

But Nazarbayev's calculations did not work. On the day his message arrived in Washington, Secretary of State Baker told U.S. reporters that in the event of a threatened nuclear attack against Kazakhstan or Ukraine, the United States would render political support by bringing the issue to the UN Security Council. Even limited political guarantees would depend, he emphasised, on Kazakhstan and Ukraine signing the Nuclear Non-Proliferation Treaty and relinquishing nuclear arms. Also, he firmly ruled out the possibility of extending a formal security guarantee or U.S. military commitment to either country.[86] Baker's statement was obviously intended remove Russian suspicions and make it clear that diplomatic games around a sensitive issue such as nonproliferation were not permissible. Nazarbayev was invited to Washington on 19 May to meet President Bush.[87] The agenda was obviously to persuade Kazakhstan to relinquish its nuclear weapons.

On 2 May 1992 in a telephone conversation with Kozyrev, Baker proposed a way for Kazakhstan, Ukraine and Belarus to undertake legal obligations and become nonnuclear. They would be signatories to an amendment to the Strategic Arms Reduction Treaty (START-1), under which they would agree to remove all nuclear weapons from their territory by 1999, when START was expected to be fully implemented. They should also sign the Nuclear Non-Proliferation Treaty as nonnuclear states as soon as possible. *U.S. News and World Report* quoted senior U.S. officials as saying that Ukraine and Belarus had agreed in principle, but that Kazakhstan was still lagging behind.[88]

Washington's rebuff left Nazarbayev in a diplomatically weak position. In an interview on 6 May, he still claimed that Kazakhstan was a nuclear state, but now suggested that Kazakhstan might agree to nonnuclear status if Russia, China and the United States guaranteed its security.[89] Thus, with his visit to the United States imminent, Nazarbayev laid the groundwork for a retreat from his position, his only realistic option. His advances to the United States had failed and had annoyed Moscow. Now Kazakhstan had two choices. One was running the risk of being left in a security vacuum in potentially unstable Central Asia, and suffering economic sanctions, and possibly blockade, with Russian participation. The other was accepting Russian security guarantees, which would mean that Kazakhstan would remain in the Russian sphere of influence as a junior partner and a nonnuclear state. Nazarbayev chose the latter.

On 15 May in Tashkent Russia, Kazakhstan, other Central Asian states and Armenia signed a collective security treaty, which said specifically that "in the event of an act of aggression being committed against any of the participating states, all the other participating states shall give it the necessary assistance, including military assistance".[90] Thus, the political struggle in the Russian leadership on the prospects for relations with Central Asia ended with a victory for those who advocated a strong military presence there. The shift in favour of such presence was prompted by the break out of civil war in Tajikistan, which Russian military and strategic experts considered capable of destabilising the whole of Central Asia and spreading to Russia's borders. Most of the Russian political establishment then came to see a stabilising Russian military presence in the area as a necessity. The fact that, apart from Russia, only Armenia and the Central Asian states signed the Tashkent Treaty indicated that its primary purpose was to protect the south of the former USSR. The treaty also provided formal security guarantees for Kazakhstan, though only for the relatively short term of five years.

On his way to Washington Nazarbayev stopped in Moscow for a long conversation with Yeltsin, after which he stated at a press conference that Kazakhstan would sign the Nuclear Non-Proliferation Treaty as a nonnuclear state. He added that the Tashkent Treaty provided the security guarantees that Kazakhstan had sought, because Russia had become Kazakhstan's political and military ally. "Now that Kazakhstan has become a member of the Commonwealth collective security committee, and has been provided with a nuclear umbrella. . . . Kazakhstan has changed its position".[91] Nazarbayev's explanation of his change of attitude as motivated by the receipt of security guarantees from Russia under the Tashkent Treaty is unconvincing. Russia had never backtracked on its security obligations to the former USSR republics and had proposed various security arrangements to all CIS states, including Kazakhstan, long before the treaty was signed in Tashkent. Nazarbayev, apparently not satisfied with them, had sought U.S. guarantees instead. Moreover, it seemed that he regarded Russia as the major security threat. In a *Washington Post* interview on the eve of his visit to the United States, he named territorial claims advanced by some Russian politicians as a compelling reason for Kazakhstan to keep its nuclear weapons.[92]

It was not clear why his attitude suddenly changed after the signing of the Tashkent Treaty. Most likely its conclusion facilitated a face-saving diplomatic retreat. This is substantiated by the fact that while in Washington he again pressed very hard for U.S. security guarantees and claimed to have finally extracted from Bush a document promising security guarantees to Kazakhstan.[93] The latter assertion is unsupported by any evidence and may therefore be doubted. According to Russian sources, none of the documents signed in Washington related to security issues[94] Nazarbayev's main achievement there was the signing of an agreement with U.S. oil company Chevron setting up a joint enterprise, Tengizchevroil, to exploit the Tengiz and Korolevskoye oil deposits.[95] Nor did the U.S. administration make any public statements indicating that it had reversed its refusal to give security guarantees to Kazakhstan. Assistant Secretary of State Niles told the press after Nazarbayev's meeting with Bush that full agreement had been reached on all questions involving ratification of the START treaty, and that Nazarbayev had promised to eliminate all nuclear weapons on Kazakhstan's territory during the seven-year period required by the treaty. In his departing remarks, Nazarbayev said Kazakhstan "obligates itself to honour the START treaty as one of the participating parties"[96] but made no mention of receiving any security guarantees from Washington, which he presumably would have done had they really been provided.

In Lisbon on 23 May, Kazakhstan, Ukraine and Belarus signed the special protocol to the START-1 treaty. Article 5 stipulated that they would adhere to the Nuclear Non-Proliferation Treaty as nonnuclear states as soon as possible and would begin immediately to take all necessary actions to this end in accordance with their constitutional practices.[97] Russian diplomacy had scored its first significant victory. As for Kazakhstan, its manoeuvring could hardly be called a success. If its leaders seriously contemplated becoming a nuclear power, their position was unrealistic and untenable. If they wanted to use the nuclear issue as diplomatic leverage to extract some security, political or economic advantages, they failed. Kazakhstan could have had security guarantees from Russia without exploiting the nuclear issue.

Nazarbayev's agreement to accept nonnuclear status for his republic opened the way for signing the Russian-Kazakh treaty, On Friendship, Cooperation and Mutual Assistance. It extended Russian security guarantees to Kazakhstan on a bilateral basis. Article 5 stipulated that in any situation that "threatens peace, or breaches peace in the Eurasian region, or violates essential security interests" of Russia or Kazakhstan, they will consult without delay and if necessary "implement coordinated measures for overcoming such a situation". In case of aggression against either, they pledged "to give each other all necessary assistance, including military".[98] For Kazakhstan this provision was crucial, because the country was not equipped to deal with serious threat to its national security, in the unstable region of Central Asia. The most obvious danger was the civil war in Tajikistan, which could spiral out other Central Asian states, including Kazakhstan. Another possible threat might arise from the involvement of Kazakhstan's Uighurs in the Uighur separatist movement in the adjacent Xinjiang region of China. This involvement might prompt China to launch a limited military action against Kazakhstan. Russia also promised to help Kazakhstan to create its own armed forces (Article 3).

Of course, Moscow received substantial military advantages from the treaty, too. Article 3 stipulated that both sides would "interact in providing for reliable joint defence within the common military-strategic space" and "coordinate the principles and procedure for jointly using means of control of air and outer space", which was tantamount to joint air and space defence. In Article 4, they agreed "to allow joint use of military bases, firing ranges and other defence installations situated on their territories, as well as the use by one side's armed forces of defence installations situated on the other's territory". This provision allowed Russia to station troops in and conduct military operations from Kazakhstan, including southward transit of troops. Article 6 said that they "would not participate in any alliances or blocks directed against one of them". This precluded Kazakhstan's joining a military alliance (e.g., NATO) that could pose a threat to Russia's security. Theoretically, these provisions ensured that Kazakhstan would be effectively kept within the Russian sphere of influence, at least in the military-strategic field.

The provisions on foreign policy coordination were directed toward the same goal. Under Article 2 the contracting parties were to "conduct coordinated foreign policy", "jointly contribute to peaceful settlement of conflicts and situations pertaining to their interests", and consult regularly on international issues. These obligations were less specific than those undertaken by Kazakhstan in the military field, and left Almaty ample room to manoeuvre. For example, Kazakhstan could theoretically avoid participating in the Tajik settlement, by declaring it irrelevant to Kazakhstan's interests. Article 7 bound the parties to coordinate policy in the export and import of military technology and armaments. This provision gave Moscow control over re-export by Kazakhstan of Russian weapons which might end up in the hands of hostile states or organisations. Coupled with the provision in the same article, the parties would "conduct a coordinated military-technological policy". This gave Russia leverage over what weapons Kazakhstan could buy and from whom, an issue of importance for Russian arms exporters.

The treaty also reaffirmed Kazakhstan's obligations in the nuclear field. Article 8 said that the parties "would interact in pursuing precise observance of agreements in the field of reduction of armed forces and armaments, taking account of the Republic of Kazakhstan's obligation to adhere to the Treaty on Non-Proliferation of Nuclear Weapons of 1 July 1968 as a nonnuclear weapon member-state". They also pledged to cooperate for "safe exploitation" of nuclear weapons before their complete withdrawal from Kazakhstan. This meant that until the withdrawal Russian specialists would supervise the nuclear weapons in Kazakhstan, which would deter attempts by Almaty to evade its obligations in the nuclear field. If evasion were discovered, it would be interpreted as violation of the treaty and free Russia of all its obligations under it.

Directly relevant to military and strategic issues, and the source of many difficulties in Russian-Kazakh relations, was the Baykonur cosmodrome (space port). Baykonur, in Kzyl-Orda province of Kazakhstan, was a unique facility, sprawling over an area of 6717 square kilometers, and combining the infra-structure for transportation, storage, assembly and launching of space vehicles and sophisticated communications equipment, especially valuable for launch-ing satellites into high orbits of 20–40 thousand kilometers.[99] It accommodated fifteen launch sites for all seven major types of rockets. All Russian manned space vehicles and telecommunication satellites were launched from there, as were 85% of surveillance satellites, including heavy reconnaissance and early warning satellites. In general, not less than 50% of Russian space launches were conducted from Baykonur. The approximate value of all fixed capital assets there was 7601.8 billion roubles (as valued on 01.01.94).[100]

After the collapse of the USSR, independent Kazakhstan "inherited" Bayko-nur but had neither the technical nor material capabilities to operate it. Russia, on the other hand, was deprived of its major space base, without which it could not properly pursue its space program. Russia had another operational space port, Plesetsk, within its territory, but Baykonur and Plesetsk were designed for different tasks, not duplicating each other's functions, and Plesetsk's geo-graphical position was unsuitable for launches to high orbits. While visiting Plesetsk in April 1992, Yeltsin said that Russia could not afford the 10 billion roubles (100 million dollars) needed for Plesetsk to replace Baykonur.[101] The Kazakh leadership was well aware of this and decided to extract maximum advantage from it.

The documents establishing the CIS made no mention of jurisdiction over Baykonur. At the Minsk summit on 30 December 1991 Yeltsin, Nazarbayev and the leaders of nine other CIS republics signed the Agreement on Joint Ac-tivity in Research and Use of Outer Space. It proscribed that interstate pro-grammes for space research and exploitation would be implemented on the basis of existing space complexes and infrastructure and of those being built. For Russia, this formulation was problematic because there were no interstate programs, and the only country able to conduct a space program was Russia. The agreement also stipulated that "the aforementioned infrastructure for con-ducting independent programs . . . is determined by separate agreements by the interested parties".[102] This meant that if Russia wanted to continue using Baykonur, it would have to negotiate a special agreement with Kazakhstan.

But Moscow was in no hurry to do so because, under the agreement, practi-cal fulfilment of interstate space programmes in the area of military and dual purpose (military and civilian) space facilities was delegated to the CIS joint strategic forces. This effectively left most space activity at Baykonur in the hands of the Russian military, which continued to run it from Moscow as in Soviet days. But this definitely did not suit Kazakhstan.

The first signs of Kazakh discontent with Russian control of Baykonur ap-peared in late January 1991. On 21 January Nazarbayev's press office de-scribed the 20 December launching of a ballistic missile from Baykonur as an experiment in the conversion program. Kazakh officials commented that their newly independent state did not have the technical means to control flights from its own Tyuratam launch site. Nurmagametov, head of Kazakhstan's Defence Committee, said, "Despite the close contacts that now exist between us and the commanders of the strategic forces, only they can give the final answer" about a launch.[103] The statement from Nazarbayev's office reiterated his commitment to the Baykonur facility being used to benefit all members of the Commonwealth.[104] But all this sounded peculiar, since the launch had occurred a month before. This suggests that the statement was intended to prepare the ground for a campaign to take over Baykonur. An initiative to that end was soon implemented. Only two days later, Deputy Prime Minister Evgenii Ezhikov-Babakhanov was quoted as saying that the issue of control over Baykonur would soon be raised with the Commonwealth military.[105]

On 23 February a military construction battalion at Baykonur mutinied. The mutiny lasted for two days and left three soldiers dead. Barracks blocks and food storage warehouses were burned and looted. But it did not look like a spontaneous riot. Members of the battalion seized fifteen trucks, headed in column for Tyuratam launch site and sent emissaries to neighbouring units. They intended to drive to the city of Leninsk, the "capital" of Baykonur, but were blocked by the military and police. At 6 P.M. a rally of about 2000 citizens and soldiers began in Tyuratam. After the arrival of a local television crew and the head of the city administration, the soldiers, mostly ethnic Kazakhs, demanded the removal of a number of Russian officers, creation of "normal" conditions for service and a meeting with Nazarbayev.[106] This gave an air of ethnic conflict to the incident. It is significant that the mutiny occurred less than a week after an official Russian announcement that a joint Russian-German manned mission was to be launched on 17 March.[107] If the soldiers' problems were not resolved in time, the launch could well be jeopardised.

A commission created to investigate the causes of the mutiny promised to improve living conditions and dismissed seven officers for the "unhealthy moral and psychological climate" in the construction battalion that mutinied.[108] What exactly sparked the mutiny was not revealed; however, the dynamics were very reminiscent of methods and techniques used by Kazakhs previously, when they wanted their way and were opposed by Moscow.[109] This similarity suggests that the mutiny may have been orchestrated to warn Russia that the Kazakhs could shut down the space centre if control over it was not transferred to Alma-Ata.

On 23 March, Russian and Kazakh government delegations met in Uralsk in Kazakhstan to discuss a range of bilateral issues, including control over Baykonur.[110] They signed seven protocols, including one on jointly supporting operation of the entire space infrastructure, including Baykonur and Plesetsk, which was to be presented to the other CIS countries for their consideration.[111] This protocol, intended to establish a permanent settlement, hardly suited Kazakhstan; including Plesetsk and the whole space infrastructure caused the Kazakhs' dissatisfaction. Moscow had a definite interest in Baykonur, but Ka-

zakhstan had none in Plesetsk or the other space installations in Russian territory. Thus the issue of control over Baykonur was not resolved.

Soon, new tensions arose regarding the cosmodrome. In an unprecedented
show of force, the Kazakhs blocked the launch of the Cosmos 2185 reconnaissance satellite scheduled for 29 April. This prompted Yeltsin to intervene personally in the dispute. When interviewed while attending the launch of a scientific satellite at Plesetsk, he said, "Kazakhstan is playing up a bit. . . . They
want to show us that we have to have some sort of Russian-Kazakh agreement
on Baykonur" and added that he would raise the issue with Nazarbayev at the
CIS summit in Tashkent on 15 May.[112] Yeltsin's statement was not worded as a
threat, but it reflected Russia's serious concern about the Baykonur situation,
and Alma-Ata could not simply ignore it. Besides, Yeltsin offered specific solutions. He suggested several ways of resolving the dispute, including creation
of a joint venture between Russia and Kazakhstan, or an Russian purchase of a
share of the cosmodrome's real estate.[113]

Yeltsin's conversations with Nazarbayev brought some results. On 25 May
1992 a broad Agreement between the Republic of Kazakhstan and the Russian
Federation on the procedure for use of Baykonur cosmodrome was signed in
Moscow. This separate agreement, specified in Article 25 of the Treaty of
Friendship, Cooperation and Mutual Assistance,[114] was important for Russia
because it meant that both documents were to be taken as inalienable elements
in the Russian-Kazakh settlement. Any Kazakh violation of the agreement on
Baykonur could therefore be regarded as a violation of the Treaty on Friend-
ship, Cooperation and Mutual Assistance.

Though a compromise, the agreement was quite favourable to Russia. The
only concession of principle from Moscow was acknowledgement of Kazakhstan's jurisdiction. Article 2 of the agreement stipulated that "installations
of the cosmodrome 'Baykonur', situated on the territory of the Republic of
Kazakhstan are its property". But Russia managed to insert a formula into the
preamble on the "need to use Baykonur for research and use of outer space in
the interests of economy, science, international cooperation and ensuring security of the Commonwealth".[115] It was not binding, but it reflected the spirit of
the document and left room for further argument that Baykonur should be used
for common purposes, not only those of Kazakhstan.

Another Russian success was the provision that both signatories transferred
the rights to use Baykonur's real estate and movable property to the CIS Strategic Forces, thus effectively keeping its operational management in the Russian military's hands. In addition Russia received the right for unimpeded import, export and transit through Kazakhstan of "technological equipment,
weaponry, military hardware and other material resources necessary for functioning of the Baykonur cosmodrome", free from duties and even customs in-
spection. This provision also covered the arrival and departure of officials, and
technical and military personnel working at Baykonur.[116]

Most importantly, Russia escaped any specific commitment to pay for the
use of Baykonur. Obligations to cover costs of maintenance and use of Bayko-

nur's installations, industrial and social infrastructure were only vaguely expressed, the agreement stipulating only that such expenditures should be submitted by the cosmodrome military command and local authorities "to both
sides" for endorsement and that Kazakhstan's expenditures should not exceed
6% of Russia's.[117] But it was not said what Russian expenses would be and they
could be as little as Russia saw fit. Ironically, failing to gain any substantial
installment from Russia's use of Baykonur, the Kazakhs had to pay for it.

Russia's promise, under Article 7 to pay Kazakhstan not less than 15% of
the profits derived from commercial launches from Baykonur amounted to very
little in practice.[118] First, commercial launches employing Russian boosters
were not yet customary on the international market, and some time would pass
before they were. Second, Russia could make most such launches from Plesetsk
and retain all the profits. As a result, Kazakhstan's potential income from
commercial use of Baykonur was negligible compared to the benefits Russia
derived from its use of the cosmodrome.

The most difficult problem Russian diplomacy had to tackle in relations with
Kazakhstan was that of the Russian minority. Yeltsin's entire political strategy
before the collapse of the USSR had been based on alliance with the national
elites of other Soviet republics against the Union centre. This alliance entailed a
set of mutual obligations, reflected in a number of documents signed by Yeltsin
and other republican leaders. With regard to Kazakhstan, these obligations
were initially confined to the treaty between the Kazakh SSR and RSFSR of 21
November 1990 and the communiqué on the negotiations between the Kazakh
SSR and RSFSR held in Alma-Ata on 30 August 1991 between Nazarbayev
and Russian Vice-President Rutskoy. The treaty contained a guarantee of the
rights and freedoms of Russians in Kazakhstan and Kazakhs in Russia, and the
communiqué confirmed adherence to the treaty, including mutual obligations
under Articles 2 and 6 to observe citizens' rights and territorial integrity.[119]
Thus the major underlying trade-off was Russian recognition of Kazakhstan's
borders in exchange for Kazakhstan's respect for the rights and freedoms of
ethnic Russians in Kazakhstan.

Obligations concerning the rights of ethnic Russians living in other republics
were especially important to Yeltsin. They enabled him to retain his image as a
Russian nationalist in the eyes of the large moderate nationalist wing of the
Russian political elite, which would not otherwise have supported dissolution
of the USSR along the borders carved out by the Bolsheviks. Had the moderate
nationalists turned against Yeltsin, he would have lost his battle with Gorbachev. Even after the collapse of the USSR he needed their support, because
ultimate political power in Russia was vested in the Supreme Soviet, where
moderates in alliance with conservative nationalists and Eurasianists could
have easily toppled him.

Having done so much to gain the support of national elites in other Soviet
republics, Yeltsin found after dissolution of the USSR that the nationalist leaders of the newly independent states had no intention of fulfilling their obligations. There were merely tactical manoeuvres on the road to independence, and

once independence was achieved they proceeded immediately to the next item on their nationalist agenda, *de-russification*. In some instances their policies clearly amounted to ethnic discrimination against their Russian minorities. The anti-Yeltsin opposition artfully capitalised on the events, holding him responsible for the USSR's dissolution, which, they charged, not only failed to bring about a Russian national revival, but also led to the humiliation and suffering of 25 million ethnic Russians who suddenly found themselves beyond the borders of their national homeland.

Initially, Yeltsin's administration tried to improve the situation by purely diplomatic means. In late February 1992 Kozyrev stated in an interview that while Russia respected the sovereignty of the CIS states, it would strictly defend its own interests, including "the protection of the Russian and Russian-speaking population in other CIS states".[120] Kazakhstan had the second largest Russian minority in post-Soviet space and its treatment by the authorities naturally became a primary concern for Russia's leadership. The human rights situation for ethnic Russians in Kazakhstan was not as bad, as in some other post-Soviet states (e.g., Lithuania, Estonia, Moldova, Tajikistan), but nevertheless gave grounds for anxiety. Russia worked at drawing the Kazakh leadership into specific, solid legal obligations toward its Russian minority, by actively exploiting Kazakhstan's need for economic cooperation. At the meeting in Uralsk, the two republics agreed to develop a comprehensive bilateral treaty, which included addressing the protection of rights and freedoms of ethnic Russians in Kazakhstan.

Moscow's attitude to the position of ethnic Russians in other CIS states shifted significantly when the conflict between the Slav majority population along the east bank of the Dnester River and Moldova's government in Chisinau developed into armed clashes. On 1 April Moldovan Interior Ministry special units attacked the city of Bendery, leaving at least ten people dead.[121] This caused public outrage in Moscow, and a number of Russian politicians made bellicose statements that Russia should use military force to protect ethnic Russians in the CIS states. On 6 April Vice-President Rutskoy urged the opening session of the Russian Congress of People's Deputies to take a stand on the question of sovereignty for the breakaway "Dniester Republic" and argued that it must act to defend Russians throughout the former Soviet Union.[122] Subsequent reports revealed that Rutskoy, in charge during Yeltsin's North American visit, had seriously considered sending either the Tula or the Pskov airborne division to Moldova, or the Bolgrad division by land.[123] The first draft of the new Russian military doctrine, which appeared in May 1992, regarded violation of the rights of Russian citizens in former Soviet republics as a casus belli.[124]

Kozyrev's attitude to the situation in Moldova was somewhat more restrained. "We stand for the defence of the Russian population everywhere outside Russia's boundaries, of course, but by methods acceptable within the framework of a present day sense of justice. . . . Of course, one can defend human rights on a CPSU platform, with tanks and special police, or one can do so by lawful methods. I, for example, believe that sometimes one can indeed use forcible methods, but not a gangster plan".[125] Thus Kozyrev was reluctant to use direct military force for protection of ethnic Russians but did not rule out other means. Moreover, the conflict in Moldova caused a certain consensus in the Russian political elite on the question of protecting the Russian diaspora in former Soviet republics to emerge. It became one of the few policy issues on which the entire spectrum of the elite took similar if not identical positions. Russian conservative ethnic nationalists tried to use discrimination against ethnic Russians to justify annexation of territories with compact Russian minorities. Neo-Eurasianists regarded the various national groups which found themselves outside their ethnic states as justification for recreating the empire. Liberal ethnic nationalists initially had a strong dislike for political associations formed by ethnic Russians in other republics, because Russian-speaking groups outside the Russian Federation had strongly favoured maintaining the USSR and were seen as irrelevant after its collapse. But the pro-Western goals proclaimed by the liberals required them to support at least verbally the Western concept of human rights in which discrimination against one group of citizens by another is unacceptable. Major differences among the elite concerned only now to defend the Russian diaspora.

However, events in Moldova proved that Moscow had lost virtually all influence over the post-Soviet republics and its only remaining option, military force, was incompatible with its international image of "democratic Russia". Moreover, the conflict revealed that Russia had no coherent strategy for dealing with the new post-Soviet states and had lost its political advantage in the CIS. Well-known precedents from Russian history were unacceptable for ideological reasons, while ideologically acceptable ones were often unrealistic.

The Moldova conflict forced Yeltsin to search for new ways and means of reasserting Russia's influence. An internal compromise was reached between liberals and conservatives. Moscow probed with a combination of diplomatic means, ranging from novelties such as appealing to international human rights standards and proposing corresponding bilateral and multilateral agreements, to more traditional ones like economic or political pressure, such as the official encouragement of reviving Cossack structures. On 26 April the Congress of People's Deputies passed a law on the rehabilitation of repressed peoples, naming Cossacks among them, which recognised the right of these peoples to restore their territorial integrity, by implementing "legal and organisational measures aimed at re-establishing national-territorial boundaries".[126]

The growth of official Russian interest in the Cossacks was not driven by sentiment or any desire to restore historical justice, but by very pragmatic and immediate interests. To reassert its influence on the post-Soviet space, the Russian government was seeking to establish a reliable political base in other CIS countries. Cossacks were the obvious choice suggested by historical experience and by ideological preference. Yeltsin and his government could not seek a political base in forces such as the Socialist and Communist Parties in the other republics, even though those parties favoured re-establishment of a unitary state over the CIS. Before the 1917 revolution, the tsar had allocated territory to the Cossack forces, and much of it was in Kazakhstan. Though Russian law had no legal status in independent Kazakhstan, it gave a strong moral boost to the Cossack communities there. Besides, the law de facto encouraged the Russian Cossacks' territorial claims against Kazakhstan, because many former Cossack lands covered parts of adjacent provinces in Russia and Kazakhstan.

The role the Russian government allocated to Cossack organisations in its post-Soviet CIS strategy was described in an article by S. Dontsov, deputy head of the main directorate of Cossack forces. He wrote that Russia had met with an "open challenge by nationalist, anti-Russian forces in the republics of Central Asia, Kazakhstan and other states", which, he claimed were seeking to prevent "restoration and strengthening of Russia's influence on territories, which for quite obvious economic and military reasons are a sphere of Russia's vital interests". He argued that, for Russia, Cossacks were "a most important lever for influence" on the situation in a number of post-Soviet states, perhaps the only force capable of countering the policy of squeezing Russians and Russian-speakers out of Kazakhstan.[127] He denied that Cossacks were Russia's fifth column in Kazakhstan and other republics, but his colleague N. Gunkin, ataman of the Semirechye Cossack Union, was less circumspect. He said that the number of people ready for armed struggle in Kazakhstan had substantially increased, and "if tomorrow a certain situation emerges, they will be prepared to resort to most extreme measures. . . . We should work for the goal of making public opinion in Russia start treating calmly the idea that the state can be restored only by military and political means".[128] A. Dolgopolov, chairman of the Subcommittee on Cossacks of the Duma Committee for CIS Affairs and Ties with Compatriots, called the Cossacks "bearers of Russia's primary interest in Kazakhstan, an interest conditioned by the necessity to maintain stability in the environs of the Russian Federation proper, and providing certain guarantees against possible attempts by radical nationalist circles in Kazakhstan to provoke disruption of economic and other ties with Russia".[129]

The Kazakhs well understood the potential dangers emanating from restoration of Russian Cossack organisations. Kazakh historians M. Abdirov and B. Abdirova gave the following account:

From the moment of their arrival in the Kazakh Steppe, Cossacks were actively used by tsarism in its expansionist policy in the East. . . . The Cossacks in Kazakhstan are historically a part of the Russian Cossacks, only located here. Hence the Cossack leadership regards Russian laws as applicable to them, and acts accordingly. And they consider Cossack formations in the republic an organised force of the so-called Russian-speaking population, necessary for advancing Russia's state interests in Kazakhstan.[130]

B. Ayaganov, A. Kuandikov and S. Baymagambetov pointed out that activation of the Cossack movement in Kazakhstan was helped by "Cossack structures of the Russian Federation, which aim to turn the Cossack associations of Kazakhstan into an organised military structure, capable of becoming a destabilising factor at any moment".[131] Almost two-thirds of the participants in the conference Post-Soviet Ethnic Relations: Conflicts and Cooperation, held in Almaty in May 1994, voiced the opinion that establishment of Cossack autonomies in the Russian border regions would stimulate tension in the adjacent areas of neighbouring states.[132]

The Russian Congress of People's Deputies' change of attitude did not escape Nazarbayev's attention, probably because Kazakhstan was mentioned in the debate. Deputy Goryacheva, for example, claimed Guryev and Tselinograd provinces as ancient Russian lands. At the meeting of Central Asian states in Bishkek on 22–23 April, Nazarbayev stated his concern that nationalist declarations at the April session of the Russian Congress of People's Deputies had increased tensions within the CIS.[133] Later, commenting on Goryacheva's speech, he said that any border claims on Kazakhstan would bring "inevitable bloodshed. . . . I want that to be heard. If some people think Nazarbayev is behaving in a 'friendly' way through fear, and may allow part of Kazakhstan's territories to be removed, then they are profoundly mistaken".[134] Nazarbayev also expressed concern over Russia's policy of resurrecting Cossack structures. In an interview he said, "One gets the impression that it suits some people to exploit the Cossacks for their own political purposes. In Kazakhstan such attempts are being made in Uralsk province, where the majority of the population is Cossack".[135]

Nevertheless, the Russian government pursued its Cossack policy. On 15 June 1992 Yeltsin signed a decree, On Measures for Realisation of the Russian Federation Law (On Rehabilitation of Repressed Peoples) with regard to Cossacks. The decree condemned Bolshevik policy towards Cossacks after the 1917 revolution, instructed state authorities to give full support to the movement for Cossack revival, stipulated that in places of compact Cossack settlement "traditional forms of Cossack self-rule can be used". Cossacks "could unite in village, farm and town societies, create regional, assembly and other societies traditional for Cossacks". The Defence and Interior Ministries were instructed to draft proposals on the procedure and specifics for Cossacks serving in the army or protecting the state border and public order.[136] The decree was confirmed on 16 July 1992 by a Supreme Soviet resolution, On Rehabilitation of Cossacks.[137]

It is not known to what extent the tougher Russian policy contributed to Moscow's successfully including a large block of provisions addressing the problems of ethnic Russians in Kazakhstan into the treaty On Friendship, Cooperation and Mutual Assistance. The treaty seemed to reaffirm the basic principles on which Yeltsin and Nazarbayev had formed their alliance while the USSR was still intact. Under Article 10 Moscow formally recognised the inviolability of Kazakhstan's borders, and Almaty undertook to observe the rights of ethnic Russians in Kazakhstan.[138] It was particularly significant for Kazakhstan that Article 10 acknowledged its territorial integrity directly and unequivocally, not within the framework of the USSR or CIS as had previous Russian-Kazakh agreements.

Article 10 also said that the parties would "prohibit and suppress in accordance with their legislation creation and activity on their territories of organisations and groups, as well as activity of individual persons, directed against the independence, territorial integrity of both states, or at escalating tension in inter-ethnic relations". Here Russia virtually conceded that the Kazakh authorities had the right to suppress activities by Russian organisations or individual activists demanding incorporation of Kazakhstan or its Russian-populated northern provinces into Russia, and Russia implicitly undertook to ban similar activities in its own territory.

However, Article 15, despite its similar wording, more addressed Russian concerns. It said each signatory would "undertake effective measures on its territory, including adoption of appropriate legal acts, to prevent and suppress any actions inciting violence against persons or groups, based on national, racial, ethnic and religious intolerance, enmity and hatred, as well as protection of persons and groups which could be subjected to threats and acts of violence, discrimination or enmity on the grounds of their ethnic, linguistic, cultural and religious originality, including protection of their property". Russian was interested in including this provision given experiences in some other post-Soviet states, where Russian minorities had become victims of violent actions by radical nationalistic groups. There were several such organisations in Kazakhstan — Azat, Alash, Azamat and Zheltoksan.

The largest set of provisions in the treaty addressed Moscow's concerns regarding ethnic Russians in Kazakhstan. Article 11 stipulated that the parties "would guarantee equal rights and freedoms to their citizens and persons without citizenship, disregarding ethnic or any other distinctions between them", and "[e]ach Party also guarantees civil, political, social, economic and cultural rights and freedoms in accordance with commonly recognised international norms on human rights, also taking account of the parties' legislation, to citizens of the other Party living on its territory, disregarding ethnic origin, religion or other distinctions". It also gave residents of Russia or Kazakhstan the right to chose citizenship of either.

Article 12 said that the contracting parties could "defend the rights of their citizens living on the territory of the other Party, and give them protection and support in accordance with commonly recognised norms of international law and obligations within the CSCE". But the majority of ethnic Russians in Kazakhstan were not de jure Russian citizens, hence not formally covered by this provision. Their rights were mentioned in Article 14, which had a broader application. It stipulated that the contracting parties would "ensure the development and protection of ethnic, cultural, linguistic and religious uniqueness of national minorities on its territory, and create conditions for encouraging this uniqueness". The following guarantees were provided for national minorities:

1. The right to "freely express, maintain and develop their ethnic, cultural, linguistic and religious uniqueness, support and develop their culture in all its aspects, without being subjected to any attempts at assimilation against their will".

2. The right to "fully and effectively exercise their human rights and basic freedoms
   and use them without discrimination, and under conditions of full equality before the
   law".
3. The right "for participation in state affairs, related to protection and encouragement
   of uniqueness of such minorities, effective and adequate to their needs".

Article 27 stipulated that the parties "would encourage comprehensive development of the languages and cultures of all nationalities and ethnic groups,
living in their territories, teaching of national languages in primary and secondary schools". The Russians wanted this provision, to ensure that the Russian
language maintained a high profile in Kazakhstan. In Article 28 both undertook
"to guarantee the regime of free activity of mass media within the framework
of their legislation". Russia insisted on this in an attempt to secure the right for
Russian organisations in Kazakhstan to express their views without hindrance.

But in general the balance of the treaty was more favourable to Kazakhstan.
The references to national legislation in Articles 11 and 28 substantially undermined all the provisions guaranteeing the rights of the Russian minority in
Kazakhstan, because the Kazakh authorities could enact such laws as they saw
fit and then use them to legitimise ethnic discrimination. The only place where
references to national legislation were beneficial to Russia was Article 10,
which allowed Moscow to refrain from suppressing Cossack organisations on
Russian territory, which were demanding annexation of the Russian-populated
areas of Kazakhstan. Nevertheless, Articles 11 and 12 left Russia some valid
grounds for criticising Kazakh policies on human rights and demanding fulfillment of the treaty. Both articles allowed Moscow to refute Kazakh complaints of interference in internal affairs on human rights issues, and made
protection of Russian citizens a legitimate subject of Russian-Kazakh relations.
It would, of course, be up to the Kazakhs to decide whether to listen to such
criticism or not.

Theoretically, Article 11 benefited Russians in Kazakhstan who preferred to
receive Russian citizenship. In practice this would make them foreigners and
deprive them of the privileges of Kazakhstan citizenship, for example, access to
Public Service posts. Thus, this provision helped only those choosing to emigrate to Russia, a process the Kazakh authorities were happy to encourage.

The guarantees in Article 14 were inadequate, primarily because they limited the participation of ethnic minorities in state affairs to purely cultural matters. Russian diplomacy had failed to consolidate the right of ethnic Russians to
adequate representation in governmental and administrative structures. But
Russia did manage to include in Article 14 an obligation to conclude in the
future a special agreement on cooperation in ensuring national minorities'
rights. Moscow probably hoped to clarify all questions on the status of ethnic
Russians in Kazakhstan during those negotiations. But Kazakhstan was in no
hurry to conclude this agreement.

Overall, Russia made more substantial concessions than Kazakhstan, which
received an unambiguous guarantee of its territorial integrity without making

any firm commitments to its Russian minority. But Moscow accepted Nazarbayev's conditions, obviously impressed by his numerous declarations in favour of interethnic peace and accord, including his strong criticism of mistakes
in nationality policy committed in other multiethnic republics, where, he said,
"[t]he problems of one nation began to be resolved at the expense of others . . . the indigenous nation was put first and all the others occupied second
place".[139] In his Strategy for Kazakhstan's Emergence and Development as a
Sovereign State, published on 16 May 1992, Nazarbayev pledged interethnic
consensus as a fundamental tenet of domestic policy.[140] But leaders of the Russian community in Kazakhstan did not receive the treaty very well. As alleged
by Kachalin, ataman of the Ural Cossack force, at the hearings in the Russian
State Duma in April 1995, Yeltsin fell for Nazarbayev's assurances and signed
the Kazakh version of the treaty, which excluded provisions for dual citizenship and two state languages, Kazakh and Russian.[141]

Dissatisfaction about the provisions of the treaty was expressed on 1 July
1992 by the Cossack Assembly of Siberia (including Cossack unions from
Northern Kazakhstan), which condemned the violation of rights of Russians in
Kazakhstan and called on the Russian and Kazakh parliaments and presidents
to protect the Russian population's rights, pass laws on dual citizenship, and
stop the renaming of Russian settlements and destruction of Russian monuments. The assembly threatened to raise the question of a referendum on
autonomy if no action was taken, and reserved the right to defend its brothers
by all available means.[142]

Despite its shortcomings, the treaty On Friendship, Cooperation and Mutual
Assistance played a very important political role. It created the basis for Russian-Kazakh relations in the post-Soviet period and was Russa's first comprehensive bilateral treaty since the collapse of the Soviet Union. As such it established some essential principles which Russia pledged to adhere to in its relations with Kazakhstan and imposed a number of important obligations on Kazakhstan.

Kazakh official experts generally concur that the treaty manifested completion of the first stage in post-Soviet Russian-Kazakh relations. Thus Mansurov,
Kazakhstan's ambassador to Moscow, characterised the period between December 1991 and May 1992 as one of "emergence of legal inter-state relations
between the two countries". There is no reason to contest his observation that
during this period "in Kazakhstan, as well as in other post-Soviet countries, the
process of defining of inter-state legal relations was under way. Finding themselves in new circumstances, the states were moving by cautiously searching
for initial, urgent and natural contacts, essential for establishing normal interrelations between peoples of what had previously been a single state".[143]

The treaty was received positively in Kazakhstan. Nazarbayev called it an
"equal treaty",[144] and Mansurov described it as "the foundation of qualitatively
new relations at the contemporary stage of history of the two countries. It
opened the first page of official inter-state legal interrelations in the new history of Kazakhstan and Russia, defined principles of bilateral interaction in

political, economic, military-strategic, cultural, spiritual spheres, and gave an impetus to all further processes of negotiations. The treaty establishes that Kazakhstan and Russia build friendly relations as allied states".[143]

These positive evaluations could not, however, obscure the fact that the treaty put on ice rather than solved the major problems in Russian-Kazakh relations. The question of the Russian-speaking population in Kazakhstan was not settled to Russia's satisfaction, nor was that of control of Baykonur. Provisions for coordinating foreign policy could potentially contribute to improving bilateral relations, but much depended on the Kazakh leadership's genuine desire to maintain this form of cooperation. Likewise, the potential of the economic provisions of the treaty depended on Russia's intentions to comply with them. The compromises in the treaty and the vague wording of many of its provisions, left each side free to extract maximum benefits for itself. As a result, subsequent Russian-Kazakh relations were characterised by diplomatic struggles over interpretation of the treaty and fulfillment of its obligations.

NOTES

1.   Crow, S., "Russia's Relations with Members of Commonwealth", *Radio Free Europe / Radio Liberty (RFE/RL) Research Report*, Vol. 1, No. 19, 8 May 1992, p. 9.

2.   *Evropa + Amerika*, No. 1, 1992.

3.   *Nezavisimaya gazeta*, 01.04.92.

4.   *Le Nouveau Quotidien*, 22.01.92.

5.   ITAR-TASS, 10.02.92.

6.   Rahr, A., "'Atlanticists' versus 'Eurasians' in Russian Foreign Policy", *RFE/RL Research Report*, Vol. 1, No. 22, 29 May 1992, p. 20.

7.   Kasenov, U., *Tsentral'naya Aziya i Rossia: ternistiy put' k ravnopravnym vzaimootnosheniyam*, Almaty: KISI, 1994, p. 9.

8.   *Rossiyskie vesti*, No. 2, 1992.

9.   *Krasnaya zvezda*, 21.04.92.

10.   *Rossiyskaya gazeta*, 06.05.92.

11.   Zagorsky, A., ed., *The Commonwealth of Independent States: Developments and Prospect, Report of the Centre for International Studies at the Moscow State Institute of International Relations*, Moscow: MGIMO, 1992, pp. 6, 17–19, 21–22.

12.   Ibid.

13.   Ibid.

14.   *Nezavisimaya gazeta*, 16.01.97.

15.   *Sovetskaya Rossiya*, 14.01.96

16.   *Nezavisimaya gazeta*, 26.03.96.

17.   *Nash sovremennik*, No. 7, 1992, pp. 143–147.

18.   *Den*, No. 42, 1992.

19.   *Pravda*, 30.01.92.

20.   *Rossiyskaya gazeta*, 26.06.92.

21.   ITAR-TASS, 16.07.92.

22.   *RFE/RL Daily Report*, No. 118, 24.06.92.

23.   Checkel, J., "Russian Foreign Policy: Back to the Future?", *RFE/RL Research Report*, Vol. 1, No. 41, 16 October 1992, p. 22.

24. Crow, S., "Russian Peacekeeping: Defense, Diplomacy, or Imperialism?", *RFE/RL Research Report*, Vol. 1, No. 37, 18 September 1992, p. 38.

25. *Izvestiya*, 24.07.96.

26. *Izvestiya*, 22.02.92.

27. *Izvestiya*, 10.03.96.

28. Ibid.

29. "Soglashenie mezhdu Respublikoy Kazakhstan i Rossiyskoy Federatsiey o snyatii ogranicheniy v khozyaystvennoy deyatel'nosti", *Kazakhstansko-rossiyskie otnosheniya, 1991-1995 gody, Sbornik dokumentov i materialov*, Moscow: Posol'stvo Respubliki Kazakhstan v Rossiyskoy Federatsii, 1995, pp. 85–87.

30. *Kazakhstan-Rossiya: sostoyanie i perspektivy ekonomicheskogo sotrudnichestva*, Tsentr Strategicheskikh Issledovaniy Respubliki Kazakhstan, ed., Almaty: Tulga, 1993, pp. 5–6.

31. *Australian Financial Review*, 07.07.92.

32. Puzanov, Yu., Khromov, Yu., "Perspektivy razvitiya integratsionnykh protsessov v ramkakh SNG", *Novaya Evraziya*, No. 4, 1995, p. 63.

33. *Kazakhstan-Rossiya: sostoyanie i perspektivy ekonomicheskogo sotrudnichestva,*. Tsentr Strategicheskikh Issledovaniy Respubliki Kazakhstan, ed., p. 25.

34. Kozhokin, E. M., ed., *Kazakhstan: realii i perspektivy nezavisimogo razvitiya*, Moscow: RISI, 1995, pp. 9, 14.

35. *Kazakhstan-Rossiya: sostoyanie i perspektivy ekonomicheskogo sotrudnichestva*, Tsentr Strategicheskikh Issledovaniy Respubliki Kazakhstan, ed., pp. 6–7.

36. "Kommyunike o vstreche Pravitel'stv Respubliki Kazakhstan i Rossiyskoy Federatsii 23 marta 1992 g. v g. Uralske", *Kazakhstansko-rossiyskie otnosheniya, 1991–1995 gody, Sbornik dokumentov i materialov*, pp. 108–110.

37. Ibid., pp. 108–110.

38. "Soglashenie mezhdu Pravitel'stvom Respubliki Kazakhstan i Pravitel'stvom Rossiyskoy Federatsii o printsipakh sotrudnichestva i usloviyakh vzaimootnosheniy v oblasti transporta", *Kazakhstansko-rossiyskie otnosheniya, 1991–1995 gody, Sbornik dokumentov i materialov*, p. 105.

39. "Nazarbayev on the CIS, Kazakhstan, the Future", *BBC Monitoring Service: Former USSR*, 14.05.92.

40. "Dogovor o druzhbe, sotrudnichestve i vzaimnoy pomoshchi mezhdu Respublikoy Kazakhstan i Rossiyskoy Federatsiey", *Kazakhstansko-rossiyskie otnosheniya 1991–1995 gody, Sbornik dokumentov i materialov*, pp. 87–98.

41. Soglashenie mezhdu Pravitel'stvom Rossiyskoy Federatsii i Pravitel'stvom Respubliki Kazakhstan o pereoformlenii zadolzhennosti po tekhnicheskim kreditam po itogam 1992 goda i yanvarya-iyunya 1993 g. v gosudarstvenniy kredit Pravitel'stvu respubliki Kazakhstan, Moscow [No publisher], 1993.

42. *Kazakhstan-Rossiya: sostoyanie i perspektivy ekonomicheskogo sotrudnichestva*, Tsentr Strategicheskikh Issledovaniy Respubliki Kazakhstan, ed., p. 6.

43. "Soglashenie o sozdanii Sodruzhestva Nezavisimykh Gosudarstv", *Kazakhstansko-rossiyskie otnosheniya 1991–1995 gody, Sbornik dokumentov i materialov*, p. 321.

44. "Agreement on Armed Forces and Border Troops", *BBC Monitoring Service: Former USSR*, 01.01.92.

45. "Nazarbayev: Summit and Documents 'Not Particularly Comforting'", *BBC Monitoring Service: Former USSR*, 16.02.92.

46. "Nazarbayev Insists Oath to Soviet Union", *BBC Monitoring Service: Former USSR*, 13.01.92.

47. "Russian Government Reportedly Ready to Take Control of CIS Forces", *BBC Monitoring Service: Former USSR*, 13.01.92.

48. "Nazarbayev Insists Oath to Soviet Union", *BBC Monitoring Service: Former USSR*, 13.01.92.

49. "Nazarbayev: Republic May Be Forced to Form Own Army", *BBC Monitoring Service: Former USSR*, 14.01.92.

50. *RFE/RL Daily Report* No. 8, 14.01.92.

51. *RFE/RL Daily Report*, No. 28, 11.02.92.

52. "Nazarbayev: Summit and Documents 'Not Particularly Comforting'", *BBC Monitoring Service: Former USSR*, 16.02.92.

53. *RFE/RL Daily Report* No. 77, 22.04.92.

54. On 18 August 1993 Nazarbayev also signed a decree on creation of Kazakhstan's border guard troops to be formed on the basis of the Eastern Border Guard District of the former USSR.

55. Kozhokin, E. M., ed., *Kazakhstan: realii i perspektivy nezavisimogo razvitiya*, p. 123.

56. The agreement on property rights, concluded between the CIS countries at the summit in Bishkek on 9 October 1992, confirmed that contracting parties "mutually recognise the accomplished in accordance with their national legislation transfer into their ownership of the property . . . under the former Union jurisdiction, situated at the territory of the Parties". The agreement covered all property, including military, situated in the territory of the respective republics as on 31 August 1991. Tsibukov, V., *Problemy pravopriemstva v Sodruzhestve Nezavisimykh Gosudarstv*, Moscow: MGIMO, 1994, pp. 44–45.

57. Kozhokin, E. M., ed., *Kazakhstan: realii i perspektivy nezavisimogo razvitiya*, p. 133.

58. "Nazarbayev Warns of the Dangers of Border Claims", *BBC Monitoring Service*, Part 1, The USSR, Third Series, 31.08.91.

59. "Nazarbayev: Kazakhstan Not to Renounce Nuclear Weapons", *BBC Monitoring Service*, Part 1, The USSR, Third Series, 17.09.91.

60. Nazarbayev, N., *Na poroge XXI veka*, Almaty: Oner, 1996, p. 66.

61. Ibid., pp. 64–67.

62. "Further on Nazarbayev's Remarks on Nuclear Weapons Control", *BBC Monitoring Service*, Part 1, The USSR, Third Series, 20.09.91.

63. "Kazakhstan 'Will Not Control Nuclear Arms on Its Territory'", *BBC Monitoring Service*, Part 1, The USSR, Third Series, 18.09.91.

64. "Kazakh State Advisor Visits Moscow", *BBC Monitoring Service*, Part 1, The USSR, Third Series, 28.09.91.

65. *Krasnaya zvezda*, 12.10.91.

66. "Baker and Nazarbayev Hold Press Conference at Conclusion of Talks", *BBC Monitoring Service*, Part 1, The USSR, Third Series, 20.12.91.

67. "Soglashenie o sovmestnykh merakh v otnoshenii yadernogo oruzhiya", *Kazakhstansko-rossiyskie otnosheniya 1991–1995 gody, Sbornik dokumentov i materialov*, pp. 325–326.

68. "Agreement on Strategic Forces", *BBC Monitoring Service: Former USSR*, 01.12.92.

69. Reuters News Service, 09.01.92.

70. Reuters News Service, 27.01.92.

71. "Kazakh Statement Denies Nuclear Weapon Sales", *BBC Monitoring Service: Former USSR*, 20.01.92.

72. *Pravda*, 30.01.92.

73. KazTAG-TASS, 28.01.92.

74. *RFE/RL Daily Report*, No. 53, 17.03.92

75. Associated Press, 16.03.92.

76. ITAR-TASS, 04.05.92.

77. *Washington Post*, 06.02.92.

78. *RFE/RL Daily Report*, No. 26, 07.02.92.

79. *Izvestiya*, 13.02.92.

80. "Agreement on Status of Strategic Forces", *BBC Monitoring Service: Former USSR*, 17.02.92.

81. *RFE/RL Daily Report*, No. 32, 17.02.92.

82. Reuters News Service, 22.02.92.

83. Reuters News Service, 27.03.92.

84. Reuters News Service, 31.03.92.

85. *RFE/RL Daily Report*, No. 82, 29.04.92.

86. *RFE/RL Daily Report*, No. 83, 30.04.92.

87. *RFE/RL Daily Report*, No. 82, 29.04.92.

88. Reuters News Service, 02.05.92.

89. "Nazarbayev on the CIS, Kazakhstan, the Future", *BBC Monitoring Service: Former USSR*, 06.05.92.

90. "Treaty on Collective Security", *BBC Monitoring Service: Former USSR*, 25.05.92.

91. *RFE/RL Daily Report*, No. 95, 19.05.92.

92. *Washington Post*, 06.05.92.

93. Nazarbayev, N., *Na poroge XXI veka*, p. 69.

94. *Izvestiya*, 20.05.92.

95. "Kazakh President Concludes Deal with Chevron Corporation", *BBC Monitoring Service: Former USSR*, 21.05.92.

96. Reuters News Service, 19.05.92.

97. Reuters News Service, 24.05.92.

98. "Dogovor o druzhbe, sotrudnichestve i vzaimnoy pomoshchi mezhdu Respublikoy Kazakhstan i Rossiyskoy Federatsiey", *Kazakhstansko-rossiyskie otnosheniya 1991–1995 gody, Sbornik dokumentov i materialov*, pp. 87–98.

99. See Map A.4 in Appendix.

100. Kozhokin, E. M., ed., *Kazakhstan: realii i perspektivy nezavisimogo razvitiya*, pp. 149, 150–151.

101. Reuters News Service, 29.04.92.

102. "Agreement on Space Research", *BBC Monitoring Service: Former USSR*, 01.01.92.

103. Reuters News Service, 21.01.92.

104. *Izvestiya*, 22.01.92.

105. *RFE/RL Daily Report*, No. 16, 24.01.92.

106. *Trud*, 27.02.92.

107. Reuters News Service, 17.01.92

108. *RFE/RL Daily Report*, No. 43, 03.03.92.

109. Similar events on a larger scale happened in Tselinograd in 1979, in Almaty in 1986, in Novy Uzen in 1989.

110. Reuters News Service, 23.05.92

111. *Izvestiya*, 24.03.92.

112. Reuters News Service, 29.04.92.

113. Ibid.

114. "Dogovor o druzhbe, sotrudnichestve i vzaimnoy pomoshchi mezhdu Respublikoy Kazakhstan i Rossiyskoy Federatsiey", *Kazakhstansko-rossiyskie otnosheniya 1991–1995 gody, Sbornik dokumentov i materialov*, p. 95.

115. Ibid., pp. 99–100.

116. Ibid., pp. 100, 102.

117. Ibid., p. 101.

118. Ibid.

119. *Izvestiya*, 22.11.90; "Kommyunike ob itogakh peregovorov mezhdu delegatsiyami Kazakhskoy Sovetskoy Sotsialisticheskoy Respubliki i Rossiyskoy Sovetskoy Federativnoy Sotsialisticheskoy Respubliki, 30 avgusta 1991 goda", *Kazakhstansko-rossiyskie otnosheniya 1991–1995 gody, Sbornik dokumentov i materialov*, pp. 82–83.

120. *RFE/RL Daily Report*, No. 40, 27.02.92.

121. *RFE/RL Daily Report*, No. 65, 02.04.92.

122. *RFE/RL Daily Report*, No. 68, 07.04.92.

123. *RFE/RL Daily Report*, No. 125, 03.07.92.

124. McMichael, S., "Russia's New Military Doctrine", *RFE/RL Research Report*, Vol. 1, No. 40, 9 October 1992, p. 46.

125. *Rossiyskaya gazeta*, 03.04.92.

126. Zakon Rossiyskoy Sovetskoy Federativnoy Sotsialisticheskoy Respubliki o reabilitatsii repressirovannykh narodov Moscow [No publisher], 1991.

127. Dontsov, S., "Kazachestvo v kontekste vzaimootnosheniy Rossii i stran SNG", *Shturm*, No. 3, 1996, pp. 29–30.

128. "Opasnost' zakliuchaetsya ne v voyne a v samoobmane, kotoriy opravdyvaet nereshitel'nost' rossiyskoy vlasti", *Shturm*, No. 3, 1996, pp. 32, 37.

129. Gosudarstvennaya Duma Federal'nogo Sobraniya Rossiyskoy Federatsii, Stenogramma parlamentskikh slushaniy Komiteta po delam Sodruzhestva Nezavisimykh Gosudarstv i svyazyam s sootechestvennikami "O rossiysko-kazakhstanskikh otnosheniyakh", Moscow [No publisher], 18.04.95, pp. 127–128.

130. Abdirov, M., Abdirova, B., "Kazachestvo v kontekste sovremennikh kazakhstansko-rossiyskikh otnosheniy", *Kazakhstan i mirovoe soobschestvo*, No. 2(3), 1995, pp. 55, 57.

131. Ayaganov, B., Kuvandikov, A., Baymagambetov, S., "Etnopoliticheskaya situatsiya v Kazakhstane: regional'nyy opyt", *Evraziyskoe Soobshchestvo: ekonomika, politika, bezopasnost'*, No. 4–5, 1995, p. 33.

132. Arinov, E., Zhansugurova, Zh., Shedenova, N., *Postsovetskaya Tsentral'naya Aziya: mezhetnicheskie i mezhgosudarstvennie problemy*, Almaty: KISI, 1994, p. 14–15.

133. Reuters News Service, 23.04.92.

134. "Nazarbayev on the CIS, Kazakhstan, the Future", *BBC Monitoring Service: Former USSR*, 14.05.92.

135. Ibid.

136. Ukaz Prezidenta Rossiyskoy Federatsii o merakh po realizatsii Zakona Rossiyskoy Federatsii "O reabilitatsii repressirovannykh narodov" v otnoshenii kazachestva, No. 632, Moscow [No publisher], 15.06.92.

137. Postanovlenie Verkhovnogo Soveta Rossiyskoy Federatsii o reabilitatsii kazachestva, Moscow, Dom Sovetov Rossii, 16 July 1992, No. 3321–1.

138. "Dogovor o druzhbe, sotrudnichestve i vzaimnoy pomoshchi mezhdu Respublikoy Kazakhstan i Rossiyskoy Federatsiey", *Kazakhstansko-rossiyskie otnosheniya 1991–1995 gody, Sbornik dokumentov i materialov*, pp. 87–98.

139. "Nazarbayev on the CIS, Kazakhstan, the Future", *BBC Monitoring Service: Former USSR*, 14.05.92.

140. "Nazarbayev's Strategy for Kazakhstan's Future", *BBC Monitoring Service: Former USSR*, 21.05.92

141. Gosudarstvennaya Duma Federal'nogo Sobraniya Rossiyskoy Federatsii, Stenogramma parlamentskikh slushaniy Komiteta po delam Sodruzhestva Nezavisimykh Gosudarstv i svyazyam s sootechestvennikami "O rossiysko-kazakhstanskikh otnosheniyakh", Moscow [No publisher], 18.04.95, p. 136.

142. *RFE/RL Daily Report,* No. 125, 03.07.92.

143. Mansurov, T., *Razvitie kazakhstansko-rossiyskih otnosheniy*, p. 24.

3

Problem of Ethnic Russians in Kazakhstan

Soon after the conclusion of the treaty On Friendship, Cooperation and Mutual Assistance, it became clear that the issue of ethnic Russians in Kazakhstan had become the greatest problem in Russian-Kazakh relations. Contrary to official declarations defining Kazakhstan as a multi-ethnic state, the Kazakh authorities embarked on developing an ethnically based statehood. On 2 June 1992 Kazakhstan's Supreme Soviet approved first reading of a new draft constitution, drafted by a commission chaired by Nazarbayev.[1] The draft contained some provisions which created anxiety among the Russian-speaking population. Its preamble proclaimed the "inviolability of the Kazakh statehood", and Kazakhstan was defined as a state of the "self-determined Kazakh nation". A meeting of the constitutional commission held on 28 October 1992 under Nazarbayev's chairmanship rejected proposals for a federative structure and state bilingualism.[2] Proposals to proclaim Kazakhstan a state of all its multinational people, to give Russian the status of second state language and to introduce private ownership of land, put forward more than once by Russian deputies in the Supreme Soviet, were always blocked by the Kazakh majority.[3] Despite fierce opposition by the Russian minority in the Supreme Soviet, the new constitution was formally adopted on 28 January 1993.

Analysis of the constitutions of the Central Asian states, prepared by the Russian State Duma in 1995, defined independent Kazakhstan's first constitution as ethnocratic, that is, based on the principle of priority of the titular nationality — Kazakh. It said constitutional provisions were at variance with the proclaimed concept of Kazakhstan as a multinational state, as "[s]uch formulas in fact deny representatives of non-titular nations and nationalities the right to belong to the statehood.[4] Concerns over Kazakhstan's constitution were voiced not only by the Russian community in Kazakhstan, but by Russian officials in Moscow. For example, at Duma hearings on Russian-Kazakh relations in April 1995, Head of the Directorate for Citizenship Questions (in the presidential administration) A. Mikitayev expressed disapproval of the provision defining Kazakhstan as a state of the "self-determined Kazakh nation" and said it would be better if the provision were formulated differently.[5]

The principle of priority of the Kazakh nation was also contained in the Law on Immigration adopted in June 1992. It stipulated that indigenous people could return to their historic homeland without hindrance. The president would establish an immigration quota each year, which would determine "the numbers and types of immigrants, with an indication of the countries from which they come, material and financial resources necessary for receiving and providing for them, and also the regions where they will be resettled, the farms and enterprises where they will be given jobs".[6] By stipulating "indigenous people", Kazakhs, the law explicitly excluded people of other nationalities, for example, Russian Cossacks, many of whom had fled to China after the civil war. Moreover, implementation of the law hardly considered other ethnic groups, for example, Uigurs, Kalmyks and Dungans, who could contend with Kazakhs for indigenous status.

Not surprisingly the law was criticised by the UN High Commissioner for Refugees, but to no avail. Its principles were incorporated in the new constitution, which virtually divided Kazakhstan's citizens into two groups, Kazakhs and non-Kazakhs. On the one hand, Article 4 of the new Constitution established that citizens of Kazakhstan could not hold citizenship of another country "with the exception of cases envisaged by this Constitution and international treaties of the Republic of Kazakhstan". On the other hand, the same article stipulated that "Kazakhs living in other states are entitled to hold citizenship of the Republic of Kazakhstan together with citizenship of other states". The Duma's 1995 report on Central Asian constitutions said that this provision violated the fundamental principle of equality of citizens' rights.[7]

For the Kazakh leadership, ethnically based demographic and migration policies were important elements in attaining the goal of creating a Kazakh national state. In an interview on Kazakh television in connection with the first anniversary of independence, Nazarbayev said, "Kazakhs are coming back to Kazakhstan from various different countries, from Mongolia, Tajikistan, Turkmenistan, Kyrgyzstan, Karakalpakistan. . . . All of them are settling down. There are also people leaving Kazakhstan. . . . If we manage to stand on our feet and keep going on for 15–20 years the demographic situation will be changed".[8] M. Tatimov, a senior expert in the Information and Analytical Centre of the presidential administration, openly called for an effective demographic policy, a major component of which should be "directing flows of new settlers from the desiccating Aral basin, as well as migrants from foreign countries into central and northern regions on the border of Kazakhstan".[9] Kazakhs from Mongolia were indeed sent to north Kazakhstan. Official data indicated that by November 1992 some 30,000 Kazakhs had left Mongolia for Kazakhstan.[10] Another source indicated that in 1991–1992 a total of 41,000 Kazakhs immigrated to Kazakhstan from Mongolia.[11] Thus the primary objective of Kazakhstan's migration and demographic policy was to achieve a decisive shift in the ethnic balance in favour of Kazakhs.[12]

To help bring this about, Nazarbayev proposed in June 1994 to move Kazakhstan's capital from Almaty to Akmola, and the parliament formally adopted the proposal on 6 July 1994. The Kazakh authorities gave numerous justifications for this decision — overpopulation of Almaty, its location in a seismically active zone, proximity to the Chinese border and to politically unstable Tajikistan.[13] But the Russian community in Kazakhstan and many experts in Moscow unambiguously perceived it as an attempt to exercise stricter control over the Russian-populated northern regions and to stimulate an influx of Kazakhs for the purpose of changing the demographic balance there.

Certain elements of the policy of nation building bore clear anti-Russian overtones. One of them was a massive campaign of renaming Russian settlements into Kazakh. In September 1992 the Supreme Soviet Presidium resolved to rename twenty-nine Russian settlements in six provinces,[14] and shortly thereafter renamed Dzhambeytinskiy district in West Kazakhstan province Syrymsky district, in honour of Syrym Datov, widely portrayed in Kazakhstan as a fighter for independence from Russian rule.[15] In the same province, one other city and three villages were renamed.[16] Large cities such as Shevchenko, Ust-Kamenogorsk and Semipalatinsk were renamed Aktau, Oskemen, Semey.[17] In the new Constitution the spelling of the capital, Alma-Ata was changed to Almaty. According to Nazarbayev's secretariat, the change was made to bring the spelling into line with the norms of the Kazakh language.[18] These are only a few examples. In practice the renaming campaign acquired very large dimensions. The Russian Federal Migration Service, in a report to the State Duma, noted with concern that in Kazakhstan "Russian settlements are methodically being renamed".[19]

Renaming Russian settlements was only one element of Nazarbayev's de-russification program. In his perception Moscow exercised control over the periphery through "cultural integration", of which language policy was a tool.[20] Consequently, in building a nation independent of Moscow, the role of Russian culture and language in Kazakhstan's public life must be diminished. Kazakhstan's first post-Soviet constitution (Part 8 of the Fundamentals of the Constitutional System) defined the Kazakh language as the only state language, while Russian was assigned the status of language of inter-ethnic communication. Meanwhile, the situation in Kazakhstan prior to independence was that Russian de facto was the main language in the state apparatus and in the economy. The Kazakh language was used only by Kazakhs, and not in the workplace environment. The number of Kazakhs fluent in Russian was 74.5%. Another 8% could speak and read Russian, but not write it. Thus only 17.5% of Kazakhs could not effectively communicate in Russian. But among Russians only 2.1% were fluent in Kazakh, and another 2.3% could speak and read

Kazakh, but not write it.[21] So 95.6% of Russians could not effectively communicate in the Kazakh language.

In all, language policy was an effective way of sidelining Russians. In particular, introduction of Kazakh language requirements for certain positions in government, public service and some professions could effectively deny the overwhelming majority of Russians access to these jobs.

It is noteworthy that the language provision of the Constitution was adopted while Kazakhs were not even half the population, and Russian was the language of the majority. A sociological survey conducted by the Information and Analytical Centre of the Kazakhstan's parliament in July 1994 showed that 85.5% of all respondents were fluent in Russian. A significant proportion of Kazakhs regarded Russian as the main language. The same survey showed that only 71% of Kazakhs were fluent in the Kazakh language and another 17.5% could speak and read, but not write it.[22] The 1995 Duma report said the inferior status of Russian in Kazakhstan could not be justified because Russians and the generally Russian-speaking population could not be regarded as a national minority: "Its numbers are so large that in this case one should speak about equality of the Kazakh and Russian languages. The Constitutions of Belgium, Canada and Switzerland should serve as examples of how such questions are solved".[23]

The Russian population of Kazakhstan was, naturally, unimpressed by the decision to deny Russian the role of second state language. The problem of the status of Russian became a major irritant in interethnic relations. It must be noted that the majority did in fact support the idea of making Russian the second state language. The July 1994 sociological survey found that 48.7% of respondents positively favoured making Russian the second state language and another 6.6% were more inclined to support than oppose the proposition, while only 23.8% were firmly against it. Among Kazakh respondents alone, 21.7% favoured granting Russian the status of second state language and 47% opposed it.[24]

The major objection to making Russian the second state language was that it would further downgrade the position of the Kazakh language. For example, authors such as M. Arenov and S. Kalmikov admitted that the majority of Kazakhstan's population supported the idea of making Russian a state language, but argued against doing so, claiming that "assigning Russian the status of second state language is not advisable, because it will contribute . . . to further weakening of the position of the Kazakh language, which can cause a negative reaction on the part of Kazakh population". They also maintained that "the Kazakh language can become really dominant only with active state support, expressed in its obligatory use in a number of spheres".[25]

Not all Kazakh experts agree. Professor N. Masanov of Kazakhstan National University argued that official language policy "imposed the language of the minority on the majority", and "[t]ransfer of education into the Kazakh language will turn into universal 'provincialisation' of the population, its alienation from the achievements of world civilisation".[26] Russian authorities expressed dissatisfaction with Kazakhstan's language policy. At the Duma hearings on Russian-Kazakh relations, Head of the Directorate on Questions of Citizenship Mikitayev agreed that many "experience a problem with the Kazakh language", and that "state measures are probably needed, which would allow for active development of the Kazakh language.... But this does not mean that one should discriminate against any other language or other culture". Mikitayev stated that the issue "of the status of the Russian language should be revisited", and Kazakhstan's government should make Russian a state language. He also warned that failure to solve this problem would continue to mar bilateral relations and have a negative effect on economic cooperation between Russia and Kazakhstan. Mikitayev was supported by Russian Deputy Foreign Minister Panov, who said that Russia "supports the movement for granting the Russian language the status of second state language".[27]

Language policy measures were taken in the field of education. The Russian Federal Migration Service in its report to the Duma noted with concern that the number of Russian schools in Kazakhstan was decreasing, and in bilingual schools the number of hours taught in Russian was diminishing.[28]

Table 3.1
Number of Kazakh and Russian Language Secondary Schools in Kazakhstan (1989–1996)

Type of school	1989–1990	1990–1991	1991–1992	1992–1993	1993–1994	1994–1995	1995–1996	Change
Kazakh	2613	2768	2905	3081	3379	3387	3364	+751
Russian	3916	3641	3433	3049	2840	2577	2484	-1438
Mixed	1409	1647	1804	2092	2299	2528	2634	+1225
Other	84	86	89	89	92	98	91	+5
All schools	8022	8142	8231	8311	8610	8590	8573	+551

Source: "Etnokul'turnoe obrazovanie v Kazakhstane: tsifry i fakty", *Mysl'*, No. 9, 1996, p. 67. The publication is based on the data provided by Kazakhstan's Statistical Committee, Ministries of Culture and Education, National Agency of Press and Mass Media.

The decrease in the number of Russian schools was not compensated by the creation of so-called mixed schools, as the drop in the number of Russian schools exceeded the increase in the number of mixed schools by 207 (Table 3.1). This number nearly equalled the difference between the increase in the total number of schools (551) and that of new Kazakh schools (751). Thus 37.6% of the growth in the number of Kazakh schools was provided by closure of Russian schools. The introduction of mixed schools also meant a decrease in the number of classes taught in Russian. Unfortunately, the figures on the proportion of Russian and Kazakh classes in mixed schools is unavailable. But logic suggests that introduction of Kazakh classes in former Russian schools meant abolishing a corresponding number of Russian classes. This conclusion is substantiated by the data in Table 3.2, which shows the reduction in the number of Russian classes.

Table 3.2
Distribution of Pupils in Secondary Schools in Kazakhstan as per Language of Study (1991–1996)

Language	1991–1992		1992–1993		1993–1994		1994–1995		1995–1996	
Kazakh	1063.60	34.1%	1153.9	37.2%	1232.70	39.9%	1302.6	42.7%	1358.5	44.7%
Russian	1975.30	63.3%	1865.2	60.1%	1772.00	57.4%	1655.5	54.3%	1584.9	52.2%
Other	79.01	2.6%	81.5	2.7%	81.13	2.7%	88.7	3.0%	91.2	3.1%

Source: "Etnokul'turnoe obrazovanie v Kazakhstane: tsifry i fakty", *Mysl'*, No. 9, 1996, pp. 67–68.

Table 3.2 also demonstrates that despite vigorous efforts by the government to expand the system of Kazakh language education, the number of pupils attending Russian classes still exceeded those attending Kazakh classes. In 1995–1996 the number of Kazakh schoolchildren attending Russian classes was 327,800.[29]

In higher education the government also embarked on a policy of gradual transfer of more university courses into the Kazakh language. However, in this area the measures were less drastic in the secondary schools, because transferring tertiary education into Kazakh was much more complex, demanding and costly. In 1992–1996 the proportion of university students attending courses taught in Kazakh increased from 22.1% to 30.9%.[30] This, however, did not cause ethnic Russians anxiety, as enough courses were taught in Russian to satisfy demand. But Russians were concerned that ethnic Kazakhs received privileged access to higher education.

Research commissioned by the Kazakhstan government showed that in 1993 more Kazakhs than Russians enrolled as first-year students. In Kazakhstan's National University in Almaty the difference acquired striking proportions. Kazakhs numbered 79.5% of those admitted, Russians only 14.6%. B. Abdigaliev explained this phenomenon with the fact that there are more Kazakhs than Russians under the age of thirty. He claimed that 79.4% of applicants to the National University were ethnic Kazakhs, and only 13.4% ethnic Russians.[31] But it is hardly likely that there are almost six times as many Kazakhs under thirty as there are Russians, especially in Almaty, where Russians comprise 59% of the population, and Kazakhs only 22%.[32] The situation was similar in other Russian-majority regions. For example, in Karaganda in 1994, Kazakhs comprised only 18%–20% of the population, but 85% of the students in tertiary education.[33] In Akmola province, Kazakhs comprised 21.7% of the population, 30% of secondary school students, but

51% of students in tertiary education.[34] Privileged access to higher education would enable Kazakhs to compete successfully against Russians for the more prestigious and better paying jobs, and in the long run would ensure the emergence of a predominantly Kazakh political and business elite. Additionally, the creation of disadvantageous conditions for Russians would compel many of them to seek educational opportunities for themselves and their children outside Kazakhstan and thus indirectly encourage them to emigrate.

The second major element in the de-russification program was the policy on privatisation of state property. Historically, Kazakhstan's major industries had been staffed and managed by ethnic Russians. This was justified, first, by the need for highly qualified managers, engineers and workers and, second, by the fact that Kazakhs preferred agricultural employment, hence, most qualified personnel for industry came from Russia, so that at independence 79% of Kazakhstan's industrial employees were Russians.[35] After the collapse of the USSR, Kazakhstan's Russians remained in control of Kazakhstan's industry. A sociological survey of industrial enterprises in Almaty in 1994 showed that Russians substantially outnumbered Kazakhs at all levels of management. Thus among engineers and officers 67%, were Russians, Kazakhs, 14.3%; among leading specialists, 68.1% and 15.1%, respectively; at the level of directors, 59.5% and 18%, respectively. Even among manual workers, 58.8% were Russians and only 21.3% Kazakhs.[36]

In May 1992, just before conclusion of the Russian-Kazakh treaty On Friendship, Cooperation and Mutual Assistance, Nazarbayev issued a decree that was meant to create the impression that ethnic Russians would receive fair treatment in privatisation. The decree privatisation taking place at the request of the labour force, which would be automatically entitled to 25% of all shares, and senior executives would also be entitled to a certain number of shares.[37]

It soon became clear that the goal pursued by Kazakh elite was to deprive ethnic Russians of economic power in the republic and redistribute national wealth in favour of Kazakhs. As L. Sharonov, entrepreneur and commercial director of the 21st Century Fund in Almaty put it, Russian and Slavic entrepreneurs were driven into a corner: "Joint-stock companies created on the basis of state enterprises, total control by state bureaucrats, who are mainly people of Kazakh nationality or puppets, the dictatorship of the National State Bank in the credit-and-finance sphere—all this signifies that what is actually occurring is a takeover of the republic's economy by a single nationality".[38]

In the opinion of A. Dixon, who made a thorough study of Nazarbayev's economic policy, privatisation in Kazakhstan had a definite ethnic bias favouring Kazakhs.[39] This opinion is shared by Russian experts. According to the Duma report on the Central Asian constitutions, privatisation in Kazakhstan was driven "by attempts by ruling groups and clans of titular nationality to gain leading positions in the distribution of 'public' property . . . and correspondingly take into their hands the main levers of power. . . . In this situation logic leads them along the path of sidelining major competitors, who are thought to be and really are the heads of the largest industrial enterprises and technical-experts, incomers from Russia".[40] As an example of unfair privatisation practices, Russian observers referred to the principle of distribution of privatisation coupons in Kazakhstan. Each urban resident received 100 coupons, those in rural areas 120. Since Russians reside predominantly in urban areas and Kazakhs in rural areas, the distribution of coupons favoured Kazakhs over Russians.[41]

When in April 1993 Kazakhstan launched a national privatisation program for 1993–1995, the authorities could not simply exclude industrial management and labour, predominantly ethnic Russians, from the process. To do so would have caused serious discontent among ethnic Russians and probably provoked massive industrial action, which could have led to industrial collapse, because there were not enough qualified Kazakhs to replace the Russians. Almaty also had to take into account likely international repercussions. Hence, the privatisation program contained important limitations. It was conducted on state initiative and under state control. Privatisation of the largest and usually most lucrative companies — those involved in mining nonferrous, precious and rare metals, or developing oil and gas fields — the government reserved around 70% of shares for itself, thus effectively retaining control, preventing management or labour conducting privatisation to suit their interests, and leaving the decisions to government bureaucrats, mostly Kazakhs.[42]

While retaining control of these enterprises, the government made them available for contract management by foreign companies with a right to further privatisation. Decisions about contracts were made by Kazakh authorities at various levels, and the employees of the enterprises had no say in them. The contracts were concluded without consideration of the efficiency of foreign companies, their business reputation or their ability to operate in the specific conditions of Kazakhstan. According to Nazarbayev, 200,000 workers were employed at enterprises handed over to foreign management or privatised by foreigners in 1997.[43] This is a large proportion of industrial workers for a country like Kazakhstan. Privatisation did not bring noticeable improvements in Kazakhstan's economic performance, even in the industries where most of enterprises were under foreign management.[44] Moreover, some of the foreign companies that took over Kazakhstan's enterprises went bankrupt, stopped their operations and retrenched the workers. Others employed the devious practice of not paying wages. This caused various protest actions by workers, with the most desperate marching on and staging demonstrations in Almaty. The revenue received from privatisation was less than impressive. In April 1997 the Russian weekly *Zavtra* wrote, cited expert opinion that Nazarbayev's government sold to foreigners or handed over to foreign management 98% of the republic's industry for "a ludicrously small sum not exceeding three billion dollars".[45]

All this created serious doubt that handing over Kazakhstan's major industries to foreign companies was motivated by purely economic considerations. It seems that the main reason was political. The tactic was ingenious, because it achieved two major goals simultaneously. First, it deprived ethnic Russian management of the levers of economic power, and transferred them to foreign companies, who were almost totally dependent on the goodwill of the Kazakh leadership, which thus achieved at least indirect control over the enterprises. Second, ethnic Russians were sidelined from privatisation and deprived of property they could legitimately claim. Most of the earnings from the sales were redistributed for ethnic Kazakhs. Moreover, Kazakh bureaucrats who supervised the transfers received their fair share of bribes. Companies from Russia were sidelined from the privatisation, despite having some advantages such as first-hand experience with technological processes at Kazakhstan's enterprises and knowledge of Kazakhstan's business practices. If the enterprises went under Russian control it would increase rather than diminish Russian influence in Kazakhstan, and consequently increase the influence of Russian diasporas in the republic, exactly the outcome that Nazarbayev wanted to avoid.

According to the Russian Minister for Cooperation with CIS States A. Tuleyev, 90% of Kazakhstan's industry was handed over "to many third countries apart from Russia". He also complained that Kazakhstan "is intentionally avoiding solution of questions dealing with establishment of joint enterprises with Russia, financial and industrial groups, is dragging its heels over the adoption of regulations on their forming, while opening unlimited opportunities for the penetration of the country's economy by Western capital". As an example, he pointed to the sale of the controlling share of the republic's chrome industry to a Japanese firm, which he said, was done without prior consultations with the CIS member states. "Now metal producers of Russia and other states have to buy chrome at a higher price, which has badly hit the economics of the entire metal-making industry," he said. The minister added that a similar situation had arisen with Kazakhstan's sale to foreign firms of semifinished titanium, resulting in dozens of production units coming to a standstill in Russia and other CIS states.[46]

A starkly different approach was taken by the Kazakh leadership in relation to land. It decided not to privatise land at all. Behind this decision lay the realisation that land privatisation would benefit mostly Russian farmers engaged in sedentary agriculture and do very little for, or even harm, the interests of Kazakhs engaged in animal grazing. In northern Kazakhstan most agricultural land was worked by Russians, and its privatisation would give Russians control of large areas. This would on the one hand give Russian agricultural producers substantial economic autonomy, and on the other would create difficulties for further resettlement of ethnic Kazakhs in the northern regions. Hence, the first post-Soviet constitution of Kazakhstan established land as "the exclusive property of the state".[47]

On 19 April 1994 Nazarbayev issued a decree on land ownership, which granted citizens the right to lifetime, inheritable possession of plots of land, and instructed local authorities to sell the right to possess, use or lease land to individuals or legal entities. But the land remained state property and could easily be repossessed. [48] Naturally this conferred little security on land users, especially non-Kazakhs, who could expect that in an ethnically based state they would be the first victims of government arbitrariness. Thus private land ownership remained a major issue on which Russian and Kazakh interests clashed.

The most important element of de-russification was the ousting of ethnic Russians from positions of influence in the government, representative bodies and public service. The percentage of Kazakhs in the top echelons of power in Kazakhstan (heads and their deputies of ministries, departments and province administrations) continuously increased, while that of non-Kazakhs decreased. Non-Kazakhs held 50% of such posts in 1985, 49.7% in 1988, 41.5% in 1992, and only 25% in 1994.[49] The Russian Federal Migration Service's 1995 report to the Duma pointed with concern to the continuation of "purposeful ousting of persons of non-Kazakh nationality from leading posts".[50]

Information on the first half of 1994 indicated that there were no non-Kazakhs among the five state advisers. Six of the seven deputy prime ministers were Kazakhs. In the president's offices only one senior official in seven was a non-Kazakh. In certain ministries at the level of minister and deputy minister the ratios were: Ministry of Education 1:6, Finance 3:5, Transportation 2:4, Press and Public Information 1:4, Economics 1:7, Justice 1:4, the National Security Committee 1:6, Committee for State Television and Radio 0:5.[51]

The chairman of the Duma Committee for CIS Affairs and Ties with Compatriots, Konstantin Zatulin, noted in his report on his visit to Kazakhstan in March 1994:

Russians in Kazakhstan in accordance with the tradition introduced in Kunayev's times continue being ousted from the sphere of political and ideological leadership, have almost lost ability and internal tendency to self-organisation, are poorly represented in new entrepreneurial circles. . . . In Kazakhstan we encounter a deliberate, well-thought-out policy of the ruling Kazakh elite, concerned to keep the Russian population as a labouring estate (workers, engineers, specialists) and worried by the prospect of political self-determination of Russians as citizens of Kazakhstan.[52]

Meanwhile, a similar process was occurring at the province level, including northern Kazakhstan. In November 1993 leaders of the Russian community in North Kazakhstan province complained in an interview that the province's entire leadership was being replaced by Kazakhs.[53] In 1994 Kazakhs in senior posts in the Akmola province administration rose from 42.5% to 51.5%.[54] In the same year, in Kokchetau province administration, 5 of 7 departmental heads, 12 of 15 heads of directorates, 8 of 10 committee chairmen, 18 of 19 province procurators, and all the city judges were Kazakhs.[55] At the highest levels (head of administration to chief of staff) in provincial administrations the ratios of non-Kazakhs to Kazakhs were Karaganda 2:6, Pavlodar 3:6, Turgay 3:6, Almaty (province) 2:7, and Almaty (city) 2:9, even though Russians substantially outnumbered Kazakhs in all these provinces.[56] At the 1995 Duma hearings on Russian-Kazakh relations, the Head of the Directorate for Citizenship Questions (in the presidential administration) A. Mikitayev said he considered it unreasonable when in northern provinces of Kazakhstan "leaders of territories are replaced on ethnic grounds and there remain even fewer Russians in leadership positions".[57]

Kazakh officials generally deny the existence of a policy of ousting Russians from key governmental posts. For example, B. Abdigaliev of the Kazakhstan Institute of Strategic Studies wrote, citing State Statistical Committee data, that in state administration Kazakhs comprise 48% of employees, which "is not discriminatory against other ethnic groups".[58] These data, however, did not identify specific occupations and levels of positions held by non-Kazakhs in the public service and government. Some authors try to justify the policy. For example, L. Bakayev, an official in the Kazakhstan Foreign Ministry, claimed that in the years of Soviet power Kazakhs "have acquired large intellectual genetic reserves and possess quite well-trained personnel", and "[t]hat is why increased representation of persons of Kazakh nationality is a quite explainable and logical fact".[59]

The exception is Kazakhstan's elected representative bodies, especially the Supreme Soviet. The Kazakh leadership could not prevent Russians from electing Russians to the Supreme Soviet, and this could theoretically give ethnic Russians and other non-Kazakhs a chance to take control of at least one branch of state power. The first post-Soviet parliamentary elections were scheduled for 7 March 1994, and the most widespread prognosis was that there would be a "Russian parliament", on the grounds that the Russian-speaking population made up the majority of the electorate in Kazakhstan. That conclusion[60] was, of course, based on the assumption that the elections would be free and fair.

The Nazarbayev government did its best to prevent such an outcome. Gross violations of democratic electoral norms became obvious during the early stages of preparations for the elections, most seriously in setting the boundaries of electoral districts. As a result, the numbers of voters per district differed substantially, from 16,000 to 106,000, according to Kazakhstan's Ambassador to Moscow Mansurov.[61] The 176 winning candidates comprised 103 Kazakhs (58%), 49 Russians, 10 Ukrainians and 14 of other nationalities.[62] Thus Kazakhs had a clear parliamentary majority, well above their proportion of the population.

The unfairness and undemocratic nature of the elections was pointed out by international observers, including a CSCE delegation.[63] Konstantin Zatulin, chairman of the Russian Duma Committee on CIS Affairs and Links with Compatriots welcomed the CSCE observers' conclusions and warned that after the elections Kazakhstan "entered a very risky stage of the development of the political situation".[64] In the Russian Federal Migration Service's assessment, the elections "not only consolidated the Kazakh nation's dominant position in the multi-ethnic state, but also deepened the division between the 'indigenous' and 'nonindigenous' population". Their dominance in the parliament "allowed the Kazakh majority practically to block adoption by the Kazakhstan Supreme Soviet of decisions vitally important to the non-indigenous population, capable of stabilising the situation in the Republic".[65]

Overall, the de-russification policy was not an expression of a simple sentimental desire to restore historical justice as seen by the Kazakh leadership, and revive national customs and culture. On the agenda were clear and specific issues of political and economic power. Kazakhstan had a Russian community almost numerically equal to the Kazakhs, generally better educated and qualified, especially for industrial posts, and strategically positioned in Kazakhstan's most important economic sectors. Some official Kazakh political scientists, such as N. Baytenova of the Philosophy Department at the Kazakh National University, overtly described Russians and Kazakhs as "the main competing ethnic groups".[66] In this competition the only advantage Kazakhs had over Russians was control of state power, and they wanted to keep this advantage and use it to the full. Hence, de-russification was aimed at achieving greater consolidation of political and economic power in Kazakh hands, an objective hardly achievable democratically, since the non-Kazakh population notably exceeded that of Kazakhs.

At first sight the de-russification policy was a striking contrast to Nazarbayev's declared aim of maintaining interethnic accord. But in reality there was no contradiction. Analysis of the political program of the pro-Nazarbayev Union of People's Unity of Kazakhstan (UPUK),[67] formed on 6 February 1993, gives a clear indication of his strategy. References to national equality concerned exclusively the cultural rights of ethnic minorities and avoided the issue of their role in political life, state institutions and government. In respect of politics the program had a definite nationalist inclination. It said that UPUK supported "state self-determination of the Kazakh nation and its further endowment with real substance". However, the program, with obvious reference to other Kazakh nationalist parties, criticised radical nationalist tendencies in defending Kazakh national interests. It condemned "radical and rapid change of the balance of interests in favour of its own nation", as "fraught with conflicts. . . . Ethnic and social conflicts can put a brake on the development of all nations". As an alternative the program put forward a concept of "evolutionary development with equality of all nationalities, ethnic groups and reaching concord", but on the basis of recognition that "in a number of issues the Kazakh nation, given the fact that Kazakhstan is the only statehood for Kazakhs, has priority".[68]

Thus the policy advocated by the UPUK program was an evolutionary, gradual transition of Kazakhstan into a Kazakh national state. This policy did not differ in substance from those of other ethnic nationalists in the post-Soviet, post-socialist space. It, however, differed in form by taking into account specific ethnic and geographical conditions of Kazakhstan. Nazarbayev had to act much more subtly and ingeniously than his counterparts in other republics. In fact Nazarbayev had ample opportunity to side with the more radical Kazakh nationalists, who were already well organised in the Zheltoksan, Alash and

Azat parties, but he opted for a more cautious approach, anticipating that radical actions could lead to armed conflict with the Russian population, and to Kazakhstan's being split into two parts along ethnic lines.[69]

Such an outcome was quite possible given ethnic and geographical distribution of population in Kazakhstan where Russians dominated in the northern areas, while Kazakhs prevailed in the central and southern parts of the republic. Table 3.3 shows the regions of Kazakhstan with Russian majority or plurality. (See also Appendix: Map A.3.) It is quite obvious that secessionist potential of these regions is amplified by both their geographical wholeness and adjacency to the Russian border.

Table 3.3
Regions of Kazakhstan with Russian Majority or Plurality (1995)

Province	Russians	Ukrainians	Belorussians	Kazakhs	Others	Population (thousands)
Akmola	46.3%	8.5%	2.7%	21.7%	20.8%	845.8
Kostanay	47.0%	15.8%	-	17.4%	19.8%	1054.9
Kokshetau	36.5%	8.4%	2.6%	28.9%	23.6%	654.9
Karaganda	52.7%	7.9%	2.3%	20.7%	16.4%	1265.6
Pavlodar	44.5%	9.2%	-	31.9%	14.4%	942.2
North Kazakhstan	62.0%	-	-	-	-	601.0
East Kazakhstan	65.9%	-	-	27.2%	6.9%	937.3
West Kazakhstan*	36.3%	-	-	54.1%	9.6%	668.4

Sources: Ayaganov, B., Kuvandikov, A., Baymagambetov, S., "Etnopoliticheskaya situatsiya v Kazakhstane: regional'nyy opyt", *Politika*, No. 1, 1995, pp. 39–42; Karta Kazakhstana, Almaty: PKO "Kartografiya", 1996; Harris, Ch., "Novie russkie menshinstva: statisticheskoe obozrenie [perevod s angliyskogo]", *Evraziyskoye soobshchestvo: ekonomika, politika, bezopasnost'*, No. 2, 1995, p. 40.

* In this province there is a distinct geographical split between the north and the south. Russian population settled compactly in the north prevails in the provincial centre Uralsk and adjacent districts – Zelenovskiy, Priyralniy, Terektinskiy and Burlinskiy, as well the town of Aksay.

Nazarbayev wanted to keep the whole of Kazakhstan for Kazakhs, but understood that the goal of a Kazakh national state within the existing borders could be achieved only by using gradual, evolutionary means, to tip the ethnic balance decisively in the Kazakhs favour. Eruption into a violent ethnic conflict such as in Yugoslavia or Moldova would be disastrous above all for the Kazakhs themselves.

Initially, de-russification seemed to be achieving its goal; Russian emigration from Kazakhstan increased. Accurate figures on emigration, its ethnic, occupational and age composition, geographical distribution among provinces of Kazakhstan and other related details, are difficult to establish. In April 1993 the Kazakh authorities issued a directive classifying the data on emigration.[70] Some figures were released from time to time, but they were not systematic, detailed or verifiable, and were sometimes mutually contradictory. Figures provided by Russia were not accurate either, sometimes bordering on estimates, though for a different reason, namely, not all emigrants from Kazakhstan officially registered as refugees or forced migrants. Many simply moved in with relatives or friends or to prearranged employment, and some Russians or Russian-speakers emigrated not to Russia but to Ukraine, Belarus or countries outside the CIS. Apart from ethnic Germans, however, the overwhelming majority emigrated to Russia.

Nevertheless, combining incomplete data from the various sources can give a rough picture of the emigration process. Thus the excess of emigrants over immigrants in Kazakhstan's case increased from 67,000 in 1991 to 96,000 in 1992, a 43.3% rise.[71] According to Kazakhstan's Ambassador to Moscow Mansurov, 142,000 Russians emigrated from Kazakhstan to Russia in 1992, 145,000 in 1993, and 255,000 in 1994. In the same period 115,000 Russians immigrated to Kazakhstan.[72] Data provided by the Russian Federal Migration Service indicate total emigration from Kazakhstan of 369,000 in 1992, and 333,000 in 1993.[73] According to Kazakhstan's State Statistical Committee, in 1994 the republic lost 410,000 through emigration, 266,637 (65%) of them Russians.[74]

Kazakhstanskaya pravda recently published statistics on migration. In 1992-1996 Kazakhstan lost through emigration 730,000 people. Of there, 344,112 emigrated to Russia in 1994, 187,390 in 1995, and 138,693 in 1996, while immigration in the same three years was 42,426, 46,860 and 31,888 respectively.[75] These figures appear to include all migrants, not only Russians, and relate only to emigration to Russia. They contradict Nazarbayev's May 1997 statement that since independence a total of 2.3 million people had emigrated from Kazakhstan, while 670,000 had immigrated,[76] giving a net negative migration balance of 1.63 million, not the 730,000 cited by *Kazakhstanskaya Pravda*. However, the latter figure may represent only ethnic Russians who emigrated from Kazakhstan to Russia.

Despite the incompleteness of the data, it can be concluded that emigration from Kazakhstan was massive, Russians were a majority among emigrants, and immigration to Kazakhstan in the same period was small by comparison. Emigration peaked in 1994, and then began to subside, clearly because those most anxious and able to leave had already gone. Nevertheless, Kazakhstan's negative migration balance substantially exceeds that of the USSR's last years.

At the 1995 Duma hearings on Russian-Kazakh relations, Zatulin noted with concern that the flow of migrants from Kazakhstan was constantly increasing and was capable of "sweeping away all positive results of any economic growth and any economic reforms in Russian Federation". Kazakh officials did not deny the massive scale of emigration. At the same hearings Kazakhstan's Ambassador Mansurov admitted that migration from Kazakhstan was "acquiring a massive character" and that Kazakhstan's leadership was "concerned about this problem".[77] The RFMS report to the Duma contained the following conclusion: "There are probably no possibilities for satisfactory solution of inter-ethnic problems, if the Republic of Kazakhstan proceeds along the path of further consolidation of sovereignty. Each step in this direction will painfully affect the mass of the Russian-speaking population, pushing it to inevitable exodus".[78]

Nazarbayev's government tried to find various acceptable explanations for the massive scale of emigration, which were not always consistent. On one occasion Nazarbayev in fact admitted that the emigration was caused by errors of nationality policy. In his message to Kazakhstan's parliament on 9 June 1994 he included mistakes in language policy and in determining the status of state language among reasons for the emigration, and declared it "necessary to adopt a new law on languages without delay, and eliminate any discrimination against the Russian language, which Kazakhs and other peoples need for their development just as much as the Russian-speaking population does". He also mentioned "bias in personnel policy" and "imbalance in admissions of applicants to higher and specialised secondary educational institutions" as negative factors stimulating emigration and said the time had come to call attention to manifestations of everyday nationalism, and that "anyone who insults someone else on the basis of nationality should be punished severely".[79]

But nine months later the tune had changed. At the first session of the Assembly of Peoples of Kazakhstan on 24 March 1995, Nazarbayev stated that "it would be naive to seek reasons for emigration in non-existent discrimination on ethnic grounds. . . . The reason for today's emigration is not only economic problems, but also that descendants of forcibly relocated Russians, Ukrainians, Belorussians and other peoples want to return to their historic homelands, to take part in construction of national statehood".[80] The second reason he gave for emigration was unlikely to find much understanding among the Russian community in Kazakhstan, given that many Russians, especially in northern Kazakhstan, regard it as their historic homeland. In numerous opinion polls no Russian ever cited returning to a historic homeland as the reason for emigrating.

Thus most Kazakh experts concentrate on proving that primarily economic reasons stimulated Russian emigration. At the Duma hearings on Russian-Kazakh relations, Mansurov produced results of a sociological survey of 6,000 emigrants, conducted by Kazakhstan's State Statistical Committee (Table 3.4). Obviously, respondents were allowed to name more than one reason, because Mansurov's percentages add up to more than 100%.

Table 3.5 represents the results of a sociological survey conducted by the Information and Analytical Centre of Kazakhstan's parliament in July 1994. This survey was of all ethnic groups, including Kazakhs and this diluted the specific reasons for Russian emigration.

Table 3.4
Reasons for Emigration from Kazakhstan

Reason	% respondents
Dissatisfied with high prices	46.0%
Dissatisfied with low wages	24.6%
Food and consumer goods shortages	19.0%
Lack of prospects in work	16.0%
Problems finding work	12.0%
Poor housing conditions	11.0%

Source: Gosudarstvennaya Duma Federal'nogo Sobraniya Rossiyskoy Federatsii, Stenogramma parlamentskikh slushaniy Komiteta po delam Sodruzhestva Nezavisimykh Gosudarstv i svyazyam s sootechestvennikami "O rossiysko-kazakhstanskikh otnosheniyakh", Moscow [No publisher], 18.04.95, p. 56.

Table 3.5
Reasons for Emigration from Kazakhstan

Reason	% respondents
Inability of authorities to ensure "normal life in future"	14.6%
Higher living standards in country of intended migration	14.0%
Want to reunite with their families	11.0%
Worsening interethnic relations	7.0%
Language problem	5.5%
Discrimination on ethnic grounds	3.0%
Undecided, and other reasons	44.9%

Source: Arenov, M., Kalmykov, S., "Sovremennaya yazikovaya situatsiya v Respublike Kazakhstan" *Politika*, No. 1, 1995, p. 49.

Data provided by pro-Russian organisations presented a different picture. A survey conducted by the Sociological Centre of Ust-Kamenogorsk city administration in late 1994 showed that 39.8% of people emigrated because of ethnic and language discrimination, and 36.3% because of economic problems,[81] thus rating both economic problems and discrimination high, but with discrimination slightly more prominent.

This conclusion is supported by data from independent research. For example, a survey performed in December 1994 by a group of U.S. experts produced the data shown in Table 3.6. The survey took place in eight cities—

Almaty, Atirau, Balikshi, Mamlutk, Petropavlovsk, Talgar, Turkestan, Shimkent—and involved 1061 Kazakh and 1118 Russian respondents. It was financed by the U.S. Science Foundation, Carnegie Corporation and MacArthur Foundation.

Table 3.6
Reasons for Emigration from Kazakhstan

Reason	% of respondents
Unstable economic situation	15.5%
Worsening interethnic relations	13.4%
Adoption of legislation violating human rights	6.0%
Threat of unemployment	5.6%
Rise in prices	4.7%
Discrimination against national minorities	3.1%
Inability to solve the problem of accommodation	2.6%
Difficulties of adaptation to new life	2.6%
Inability to continue education	1.6%
Danger of becoming a victim of physical violence	0.6%
Other	4.7%
Undecided	3.3%
Did not answer	36.3%
Number of respondents	1118

Source: Kozhokin, E. M., ed., *Kazakhstan: realii i perspektivy nezavisimogo razvitiya*, Moscow: RISI, 1995, pp. 275, 291–292.

Figures on the ethnic composition of the migration balance in Kazakhstan tend to support this conclusion. In 1993 total emigration from Kazakhstan exceeded total immigration by 222,000,[82] but ethnic Kazakh immigration exceeded emigration by 23,500.[83] Even in 1994, the year of highest net emigration from Kazakhstan, Kazakh immigrants exceeded Kazakh emigrants by 2,406.[84] In the first nine months of 1996 Kazakh immigrants (12,227) exceeded Kazakh emigrants (7,173) by 5074, though in the same period of 1997 Kazakh emigrants (9,113) slightly exceeded immigrants (8,586).[85] Since independence more Kazakhs immigrated to Kazakhstan, than emigrated from there. If migration flows to and from Kazakhstan were determined exclusively by economic reasons one would not expect Kazakh immigrants to outnumber Kazakh emigrants. If the economic situation had a relatively stronger negative impact on Russians and other non-Kazakhs, there must have been reasons for it.

Although massive, Russian emigration affected primarily only one group of the Russian population in Kazakhstan. This group comprises Russians born in Russia who migrated to Kazakhstan for various, mostly professional, reasons. They have high educational and qualification levels and live in cities, where they are often the majority of the population. This group is most disposed to emigration, because it has the fewest local ties and qualifications that are marketable elsewhere. There is, however, another group, a little larger than the first (66.6% of all Russians in Kazakhstan), consists of Russians whose families have lived in Kazakhstan for two to three generations. These Russians live mostly in rural areas and in the northwest, north and northeast regions. People from this group are far less likely to emigrate than members of the first group; although two-thirds of Kazakhstan's Russian population, they comprise only one-third of Russian emigrants.[86] The July 1994 sociological survey by the Information and Analytical Centre of Kazakhstan's parliament showed that intending migrants are 23% of urban but only 7% of rural populations.[87] Conspicuous within the second group are Cossacks. Migration among them is negligible, mostly young men living to serve in the Russian armed forces.[88]

Another important conclusion that can be drawn from the various surveys is that the majority of Russians intend to stay in Kazakhstan. The July 1994 sociological survey established that throughout Kazakhstan only 25% of Russians contemplated emigration.[89] The survey performed by the team of U.S. researchers in December 1994 established that only 20.8% of Russians see migration as their future, while 36% of Russians indicated definite intent to stay in Kazakhstan and fight to preserve the Russian language and culture. Another 4.5% declared their intention to organise themselves politically for secession of the Russian-populated lands from Kazakhstan.[90]

Self-organisation of those Russians who intended to stay in Kazakhstan started even before the disintegration of the USSR, and Kazakhstan's policy of nation-state building intensified the process, with the Cossacks taking the lead. On 10 August 1992 the Omsk branch of the Cossack Assembly of Siberia sent an appeal to the Russian president and government on behalf of the Cossack groups and the Russian population of northern Kazakhstan, who, they claimed, were being oppressed by the government of Kazakhstan and Kazakh nationalist groups.[91] The Cossacks were followed by other sections of the Russian community. On 24 September 1992, a founding conference of a new Russian organisation, the Republican Public Slavic Movement "Lad" (Concord), was held in Petropavlovsk. Lad's statute defined its objectives as "preservation of the ethnic uniqueness, culture and languages of the Slavs, spiritual revival of the Slavic people of the Republic of Kazakhstan, developing and strengthening of democracy, realisation and defence of political economic, social and cultural rights and freedoms, strengthening of peace and friendship, fraternal relations between peoples of our multinational republic".[92] On 28 May 1993, Lad obtained official registration and a year later, according to its leader A. Dokuchaeva, had 25,000 members.[93] Lad's activities had a clear political direction, though formally it presented itself as a purely cultural organisation, a tactic used to bypass restrictions on the formation of political organisations of ethnic Russians.

In November 1992 another Russian community organisation, Russian Centre, formed in Alma-Ata. It was based on the Russian Cultural Centre there and the Slavic cultural societies in the seventeen provinces. Its declared aims were to help the Slav population through the transition to the market economy and ensure that Slavs stayed in Kazakhstan.[94] It was headed by N. Sidorova. These two new organisations were not directly linked to the Cossack movement and served as important points of consolidation for the non-Cossack Russian and general Slav community in Kazakhstan.

On 7 December 1992 Russian community organisations staged a 15,000-strong rally in Ust-Kamenogorsk (East Kazakhstan province), demanding that Kazakhstan's Supreme Soviet and president restore the political and economic integrity of peoples of the CIS countries. They adopted a resolution demanding recognition of Russian as the second state language and of dual citizenship for residents in the republic, and that the East Kazakhstan provincial authorities be granted "a right of self-government in the spheres of language, culture and exploitation of natural resources". They threatened to call "a general political strike and recall the deputies representing the province" if their demands were not met. Ivan Korbanev, a cochairman of the Slavic Culture Society in East Kazakhstan province, warned that if the parliament refused to consider the demands, the society could raise the issue of forming a Trans-Irtysh republic,[95] an obvious reference to the Transdnistria Republic in Moldova.

When asked about the rally in an interview Nazarbayev dismissed it as of secondary importance. "The population of Kazakhstan must get used to the fact that an independent, sovereign State has come into being. This state has a Constitution. The guarantor of the Constitution is the president, who was elected by general elections, and his institutions of authority. And rallies in towns and villages which put forward ultimatums to the government make no difference", he said. Nazarbayev called for problems to be solved within the constitutional framework, but also warned that public actions by Russians in Kazakhstan could meet with a similar response by Kazakhs. "If one rally presents ultimatums today there will be another rally tomorrow and other peoples will also start asking questions of the government", he said.[96]

De-russification in Kazakhstan did not go unnoticed in Moscow. The first Russian expert to voice concern was probably A. Migranyan, one of Yeltsin's political advisers. He argued that Kazakhstan's declared support for closer integration with Russia was not a long-term strategy, but a tactic to gain time. He noted that while talking of integration, the Kazakh authorities went on resettling Kazakhs in Russian-populated territories of Kazakhstan, gradually squeezing out ethnic Russians.

[In twenty years, Kazakhstan would be an ethnically more homogeneous great power] "able to defend its current territory and borders by itself.... If the CIS falls apart too soon", he continued, "that could provoke a strong separatist movement of Russian-speakers. But that in itself could not play a decisive role; everything will depend on Russia. Will Moscow encourage the departure of ethnic Russians, either directly or indirectly? Or, on the contrary, will it show an interest in keeping Russians in areas that were part of the former Union, where they would be outposts, as it were?"[97]

Migranyan provided no answer to his questions, leaving alternative options open to policy makers.

The important point in Migranyan's argument was that he concentrated not on the immediate negative economic effects of the large Russian immigration from Kazakhstan, but on the strategic perspective. The immigration was disadvantageous for the Russian economy, but only temporarily. Russia was after all large enough to accommodate all Russians leaving Kazakhstan without straining its economy, and Migranyan well understood this. The strategic direction in which Kazakhstan was moving was more important. What would its attitude towards Russia be, say, in 20 years? Would it remain friendly and allied, or make a geopolitical shift and join forces hostile to Russia, creating a serious danger to Russian national security? These questions troubled Russian foreign policy analysts. From the strategic perspective, Moscow obviously saw the presence of a large Russian community in Kazakhstan, with its wide representation in government, public service and major industries, as insurance of Kazakhstan's loyalty.

The attitude to ethnic Russians in Kazakhstan became the main criterion by which the declared and undeclared intentions of the Kazakh leadership were judged. For example, the chairman of a subcommittee on Cossacks of the Duma Committee for CIS Affairs and Ties with Compatriots, A. Dolgopolov, said that the practical settlement of issues related to the activities of Cossack organisations would be "the criterion for the verification of the seriousness of intentions of the sovereign republics' leaders in strengthening ties with Russia".[98] Hence, Russia's primary concern was to encourage Russians not to leave Kazakhstan and to force the Kazakh leaders to restore the participation of ethnic Russian in state institutions.

On 30 November 1992, Yeltsin issued an executive order, On Questions of Protection of Rights and Interests of Russian Citizens beyond the Borders of the Russian Federation, which had direct implications for Kazakhstan. Among other things the document instructed the Foreign Ministry to more active by defending Russian citizens and their interests abroad and authorised the Foreign Ministry and State Committee on Economic Cooperation with CIS "to consider questions of economic relations with republics of the former USSR, depending on their observance of human rights in accordance with universally accepted norms and principles of international law".[99] Thus Moscow established linkage between treatment of ethnic Russians in other republics and Russia's economic relations with those republics. Given Russia's economic dominance in the post-Soviet space this was tantamount to authorising the use of economic pressure against recalcitrant republics. In line with this policy, the RFMS report to the Russian parliament advocated linking every step in the process of integration with Kazakhstan with "adequate shifts in the Kazakhstan leadership's attitude to our compatriots".[100]

One way Moscow chose to exercise political pressure on Kazakhstan was by providing political and diplomatic support for Russian community activists and organisations, especially in cases of persecution by the Kazakh authorities. This capability, conferred by the human rights provisions of the Treaty On Friendship, Cooperation and Mutual Assistance, was not difficult to implement. When Boris Suprunyuk, chief editor of the independent newspaper *Glas*, was arrested in Petropavlovsk 12 April 1994, a massive media campaign was launched in his defence, accompanied by rallies and threats by Russian patriotic organisations directed at the Kazakh authorities.[101]

The Russian authorities acted decisively. The Russian Embassy in Almaty sent diplomatic notes on 12 and 21 April requesting consular access to Suprunyuk, which Kazakhstan's Foreign Ministry ignored. Following the failure of the embassy's demarches, the Duma Committee on CIS Affairs and Ties with Compatriots issued a special statement which said that the Kazakh authorities' actions grossly violated international norms on human rights and the Treaty of Friendship, Cooperation and Mutual Assistance between Russia and Kazakhstan. The Committee expressed "deep concern that such practices with regard to Kazakhstan's Russians may complicate bilateral relations between the Russian Federation and the Republic of Kazakhstan". The statement appealed to the Kazakh authorities to take the necessary steps to settle the situation and "inform state bodies of the Russian Federation about their actions with regard to the Russian Federation citizen Suprunyuk and other Kazakhstan Russians in custody".[102]

At the Duma hearings on Russian-Kazakh relations, Deputy Foreign Minister Panov revealed that the Duma resolution had been arranged at the Russian Foreign Ministry's request.[103] This refutes the well-established misconception that there were some differences of principle between the Russian parliament and Yeltsin's administration over protection of ethnic Russians in the post-Soviet states. Further confirmation can be found in another disclosure by Panov, that "a practice of communicating through confidential letters" had been established between Yeltsin and Nazarbayev, that when difficult questions arose, the presidents wrote to each other, and "[i]ssues such as that of the Cossacks were touched on more than once in letters which Boris Nikolayevich sent to Nazarbayev".[104] So while keeping silent publicly, Yeltsin expressed his concern to Nazarbayev through diplomatic channels. In the Suprunyuk case, Mikitayev acted as Yeltsin's personal envoy and allegedly delivered a personal message from Yeltsin to Nazarbayev.[105] Suprunyuk was released by the end of May.

In similar, later episodes, the Russian government acted along the same lines. When F. Cherepanov, acting ataman of the East Kazakhstan province Cossacks, was kidnapped in Ust-Kamenogorsk in late October 1994,[106] the Russian Foreign Ministry registered dissatisfaction and demanded that Kazakh authorities take all necessary steps to free Cherepanov.[107] The arrest of Gunkin (ataman of the Semirechye Cossacks) on 28 October 1995 provoked a similar reaction. In a letter to Kazakhstan's National Security Committee, the Russian Ministry for Nationalities Affairs and Regional Policy said that the Russian public saw Gunkin's arrest as "an attempt to hold elections to the Kazakh parliament without considering the interests of Kazakhstan's Russian-speaking population".[108] On 17 November the Duma adopted a resolution supporting Gunkin and expressing concern about "the violation of rights and freedoms of both ethnic Russians and Russian citizens in Kazakhstan".[109] When Gunkin was jailed for three months, despite these protests, the Russian Foreign Ministry expressed disappointment.[110] Gunkin served his full three-month sentence and after release was re-elected as Ataman.[111]

Russia also foresaw more active utilisation of Cossack organisations to put psychological pressure on the Kazakh authorities. In early August 1992 a meeting of Cossack atamans from all over Russia was held in Moscow. Rutskoy spoke there in favour of restoring Cossack units in the Russian armed forces and announced that the Russian leadership had decided to draft a special program for a Cossack Force and frontier guard units. Speaking about the position of ethnic Russians in the CIS, he singled out Kazakhstan: "Despite Nazarbayev's rhetoric about internationalism, Kazakhstan's cabinet is adopting decrees barring citizens from certain jobs if they do not speak the Kazakh language. . . . We cannot just sit back and watch the growth of national chauvinism and discrimination against ethnic Russians in the former union republics. In such a situation we must assume a tough position and take measures to prevent such discrimination".[112] After the meeting, Abdildin, chairman of Kazakhstan's Supreme Soviet, stated in a newspaper article that the Cossack atamans' claims to autonomy to protect the interests of the Russian population in Kazakhstan were a provocation, fraught with risk of conflicts.[113]

On 15 March 1993 Yeltsin signed a decree ordering reorganisation of Russian military structures in North Caucasus. The decree included provisions beyond the specific issues of the North Caucasus. Among other things it provided for organisation of Cossack units in the army, internal troops and security forces, and creation of special departments within Defence, Interior and Security ministries to supervise those units. Local authorities in traditional Cossack regions were instructed to form Cossack voluntary nonmilitary structures which were to be used for the purposes of civil and territorial defence as well as ensuring law and order and protecting property.[114] Almaty's reaction to this decree was painful. A lengthy article in the Kazakh language weekly *Orken (Horizon)* said that Yeltsin's decision could hardly be regarded as a purely Russian domestic affair and that it had a direct bearing on the situation in Kazakhstan. Recalling the events prompted by the "celebration on Kazakh sovereign territory of the 400th anniversary of the Cossacks' service to the Russian Tsar", the newspaper said that the Kazakh Justice Ministry had not yet registered a single Cossack organisation, and therefore all their actions were unlawful.[115]

The Cossacks were definitely much more prepared for action than other sections of Kazakhstan's Russian community. A public opinion survey among Russians found that only 17.7% were prepared to take up arms "to defend the interests of their people in inter-ethnic conflicts", whereas 42.9% of Cossacks were so prepared.[116] In some regions, Cossacks have already created shadow structures for organisational deployment in crises. For example, in 1993 Cossacks in northern Kazakhstan divided their territory into twenty Cossack settlements and formed illegal committees to govern them.[117] According to Kazakh sources, unregistered Cossack associations exist in Akmola, East Kazakhstan, Kokshetau, North Kazakhstan and West Kazakhstan provinces.[118]

In March 1994 several villages in Taldy-Kurgan province became an area of sharp confrontation between Kazakhs and local Cossacks, with occasional clashes between Cossacks and Kazakhs taking place and a larger encounter averted only through police interference. In April 1994 the Russian Justice Ministry registered the Siberian Cossack Force. Four of its sixteen subdivisions were located in Kazakhstan.[119] In November 1994 Russian Cossacks started creating an Ural Cossack Force in Orenburg province with headquarters in the town of Tashla. The force was supposed to include Cossacks living in West Kazakhstan.[120]

Not surprisingly, Cossacks in Kazakhstan became the primary target of attacks by the Kazakh authorities, who prevented registration of Cossack organisations, and denied them the right to hold public meeting, rallies and demonstrations. Cossack activists were subjected to regular police harassment, detention and arrest. Some Kazakh authors, such as historians M. Abdirov and B. Abdirova, called on the government to pass laws specifically banning Cossack organisations and the wearing of the Cossack uniform.[121]

At the Duma hearings on Russian-Kazakh relations, Dolgopolov identified three major concessions for Cossacks that Russia should demand from official Almaty: (1) restoration of traditional economic practices, including returning land to possession of Cossack communities, (2) support for Cossack cultural traditions, including wearing the Cossack uniform and restabilising forms of Cossack self-government, and (3) removing restrictions on creation of Cossack organisations.[122]

The Kazakh authorities soon realised that the Cossack movement could not be contained by repression alone and moved to a more flexible approach. The first signs of this appeared in March 1994, when State Counsellor to the President of Kazakhstan Suleymenov proposed convening a republican congress in Almaty of all Cossack formations and communities, to discuss the official status of Kazakhstan's Cossacks.[123]

This tactic was endorsed by some Kazakh experts. M. Abdirov and B. Abdirova wrote, for example,

It is clear that the Cossack problem cannot be solved by prohibitive, punitive measures alone. That is why it is necessary to have a coherent, consistent state policy with regard to them. It may be possible to draft a special program of cultural revival of the Cossacks in the Republic of Kazakhstan, encourage creation of Cossack cultural funds, specific business activities (protection of fish resources, struggle against poaching, etc.), holding Cossack festivals, folklore celebrations, etc.[124]

The authors recommended a logical combination of this policy with harsh measures against recalcitrant Cossack organisations: the carrot-and-stick tactic. The purpose of the recommended policy was to channel the Cossack movement into an innocuous direction by finding a base among Cossacks who would be satisfied with access to various economic and cultural benefits and other incentives.

On 1 June 1994 the Kazakh authorities registered the Society for Assistance to the Semirechye Cossacks, which brought together Cossacks from the Almaty and Taldy-Kurgan provinces of eastern Kazakhstan. While registering it, Justice Ministry officials stressed that it should not be regarded as a military-style formation. However, Kazakh State Counsellor Suleymenov said that it might be possible for Cossack troops to serve on the borders with China, Iran and the Caspian Sea, and that a Cossack platoon might be raised for Kazakhstan's Republican Guards. Suleymenov suggested that the Kazakhstan Cossacks create a multi-ethnic like the Cossack groups in Russia, which have Kalmyks and Osetians in their ranks.[125] The purpose of this manoeuvre was clearly to undermine the ethnic character of the Cossack movement, and dilute its pro-Russian orientation. But the society soon proved to be in nobody's pocket, following the kidnapping of F. Cherepanov, acting ataman of the Cossacks of the East Kazakhstan province. On 19 November it staged a demonstration and rally in the centre of Almaty, after which it was suspended and some Cossack activists were arrested.[126]

The most explosive situation pertaining to ethnic Russians in Kazakhstan emerged in November 1993, when Moscow left the rouble zone and refused Kazakhstan and other Central Asian states fresh deliveries of Russian currency. Russian-Kazakh relations hit their lowest point since the collapse of the Soviet Union. Tension was in the air, with rumours of possible anti-Russian violence in Central Asia. In this electrified atmosphere Yeltsin's government issued a strong warning to Central Asian nationalists. On 16 November 1993 Deputy Prime Minister Shokhin published a statement in the semi-official newspaper *Izvestiya* which said:

In the past few days, in connection with the problems of creating a new rouble zone, threats have been spread around in some former Soviet republics to the effect that Russia should again assume a considerable share of the expense of improving their financial situation, or else things will go especially badly for ethnic Russians who live in those republics. This kind of blackmail can hardly be serious, but such irresponsible statements cannot be ignored. . . . Russia has sufficient means of responding to bullying methods of "people's diplomacy" to make the "architects" of this policy regret it. And there is no need to harp on the old ideological theme of "imperialist practices" — Russia can and will defend its current interests.[127]

Shokhin's statement was echoed by other senior Russian officials, including Foreign Minister Kozyrev.[128] There were angry reactions in Kazakhstan, and Nazarbayev did not hesitate in an interview to show his dissatisfaction by drawing a parallel with Nazi Germany's march into the German-speaking Sudetenland of Czechoslovakia in 1938. "When they talk about protecting people who are not citizens of Russia but of Kazakhstan I recall the times of Hitler, who started with 'protecting' the Sudeten Germans", he said.[129] Yeltsin promptly despatched Kozyrev on a tour of Central Asia. He arrived in Almaty from Uzbekistan on 16 November 1993, but Nazarbayev claimed to be unwell and refused to see him. Instead Kozyrev, conspicuously accompanied by First Deputy Defence Minister General Boris Gromov, held talks with Foreign Minister Suleymenov. Kozyrev was also received by Prime Minister Tereshchenko, to whom he handed a memorandum on the situation of Russians in Kazakhstan listing the issues that caused concern: language policy, problems of Cossacks, personnel policy, situation in education and culture, and the status of Russian military personnel.[130] After the meeting Kozyrev told journalists that Russia's position in favour of dual citizenship remained unchanged. Tereshchenko responded to Kozyrev's calls for additional legal guarantees for Russians by saying that all citizens of Kazakhstan were offered equal rights under the law. "As for additional legal guarantees, that is a far from simple matter which requires detailed examination from all sides", he said.[131]

Meanwhile in Russia Vladimir Zhirinovskiy, leader Liberal Democratic Party of Russia (LDPR), artfully exploited the growth of anti-Kazakh sentiments in his election campaign. In his public statements he supplemented political warnings directed at the Kazakh leadership with offensive remarks about the Kazakhs as a nation. In a television interview on 24 November 1993 he claimed that it was the Russian Cossacks who had introduced civilisation to Kazakhstan. On the subject of discrimination against Russians in the former USSR republics, he said, "We shall not allow any encroachments upon rights, wherever both Russians and people of any other nationality might live. . . . We are opposed to all discrimination in terms of ethnic identity". Zhirinovskiy promised that if he won the election he would grant Russian citizenship to all Russians in former USSR republics and, while resident in Kazakhstan, Uzbekistan or any other region outside Russia, they would be protected by the new Russian government.[132]

Kazakhstan's Foreign Ministry described Zhirinovskiy's pronouncements as "an open provocation aimed at instigating ethnic strife and destabilising the internal situation" in Central Asia, and added that "[i]nstigation of ethnic strife on any level is detrimental both to Kazakhstan and Russia, to the friendly relations which have historically emerged between the peoples of the two countries".[133] Nazarbayev, attending a Global Panel Conference in Maastricht at the time, expressed concern over statements made during the Russian election campaign "which, under the pretext of protecting the Russian-speaking population, sow discord between our countries. . . . Our task is to protect Russians as well as other ethnic groups who live in Kazakhstan because they are our citizens", he said.[134]

Following Zhirinovskiy's address, Nazarbayev's UPUK party circulated a statement expressing indignation and urging the "democratic forces of Russia to rebuff such defenders of the Russian people's interests". A group of Kazakh academics issued a similar statement, and in typical Soviet fashion, the Kazakh authorities arranged a telegram to Yeltsin condemning Zhirinovskiy from leaders of a number of industrial plants in Semipalatinsk, whose jobs naturally depended on Almaty's goodwill.[135] Almaty's harsh reaction was explained by the broad support Zhirinovskiy's ideas found in Russian society. In the elections to the State Duma on 12 December 1993, Zhirinovskiy's LDPR gained 26% of the vote, twice as many as its closest rival.

The last thing the Russian government wanted at that time was an interethnic war in Kazakhstan, which would have put Russia in a very difficult situation. Internal political pressures would have made it impossible not to intervene on the side of the Russian community in Kazakhstan, and intervention would have inevitably caused international outrage and plunged Russia into political and economic isolation. Even if intervention succeeded, any geopolitical advantages for Russia were dubious. Annexation of northern Kazakhstan would have left southern Kazakhstan under the control of anti-Russian forces, gravitating towards Islamic fundamentalism and creating a permanent security threat to Russia's southern borders.

Hence simultaneously with strongly-worded statements targeting the Kazakh and other Central Asian elites Moscow did its best to alleviate the tension. During his visit to Kazakhstan in December 1993, Prime Minister Chernomyrdin, at a joint press conference with his local counterpart, Tereshchenko said he had discussed the problem of the Russian population with Nazarbayev. He stressed that leaders of certain Russian political parties had "made irresponsible remarks, concerning especially the Russian community in Kazakhstan, and not only in Kazakhstan", and continued, "this I do not want, and it cannot be, identified as government policy, or the policy of the President. . . . Russia does not want to foment inter-ethnic tensions, especially by using the Russian-speaking community. . . . I want to use this opportunity to address the Russian-speaking community of Kazakhstan. Don't listen to irresponsible declarations".[136] According to the Russian Federal Migration Service, in 1994 Russia's embassy in Kazakhstan concentrated its efforts "primarily on mitigating the inter-ethnic situation in the country, calming the Russian population and reducing its exodus from Kazakhstan".[137]

Nazarbayev also took steps to reduce tensions. In early January 1994 he announced that he had passed to Yeltsin and Chernomyrdin a draft treaty on basic principles relating to Kazakh and Russian Federation citizenship, in which the contracting parties pledged to adopt without delay legislative acts establishing a simplified procedure for acquisition of citizenship by Kazakhs and Russians, under which applications must be considered within six months of submission. In addition, the signatories would pledge to enact legislation permitting their citizens to serve in each others' armed forces under contract. However, Nazarbayev indicated that he was not at that point prepared to make any concessions on language matters.[138]

The primary purpose of Nazarbayev's announcement was, of course, domestic policy considerations. With parliamentary elections imminent (they were scheduled for 7 March 1994), the ethnic divide in Kazakhstan had become only too obvious. The major differences between the parties and organisations representing the Russian and Kazakh communities remained unchanged – language, citizenship and fair representation in government institutions. With his proposal on citizenship Nazarbayev clearly wanted to play up a little to the concerns of ethnic Russians, not to antagonise them more before the elections, and probably to secure some of their votes for his party's candidates, who would appear moderate compared to the radical Kazakh nationalists. For the Russian community, Kazakhstan's first post-Soviet elections were a chance to shift the balance of power in the republic's leadership somewhat in their favour. But as discussed earlier, they failed due to undemocratic electoral practices.

Zatulin was the head of the Russian parliamentary delegation which visited Almaty on 6–9 March to observe the elections. His report, addressed to Duma Speaker Rybkin, contained the following conclusions and recommendations.

1. Results of the visit allow for an unpleasant conclusion about the state of the Russian community, Russian ethnic and cultural societies and organisations. At present internationalist interests in Kazakhstan are much better expressed by Kazakh public and political figures and academics of democratic orientation (O. Suleimenov, N. Masanov), and not by the leaders of the Russian community, who are little known beyond their own circle. . . . National leaders of the Russian population in Kazakhstan do not exist, though there are undoubtedly grounds for raising them.

2. Unfortunately, Russia has not yet demonstrated a well-conceived policy which would allow it to exercise far-reaching influence on the situation inside Kazakhstan. We think that part of the responsibility for this must be attributed to officials of the Government of the Russian Federation, none of whom has yet once met representatives of the Russian population of Kazakhstan. [The report gave as an example Russian Minister for Culture Sidorov, who ignored Russian community organisations when opening the Days of Russian Culture in Almaty.]

3. Not trying to disavow altogether the results of the elections to Kazakhstan's parliament, in future we should concentrate on stressing its temporary, transitional nature.

4. At inter-state level it is necessary to keep open the questions of dual citizenship and status of the Russian language as second state language. Negotiations that have taken place indicate that among the leaders of Kazakhstan there is not full confidence that they did not overshoot the mark, at least on the Russian language issue. However,

without coordinated pressure from inside and outside Kazakhstan no decision putting the Russian language on an equal footing with Kazakh can be taken, because Russian deputies in the Supreme Soviet of the Republic of Kazakhstan are, as a rule, filtered through representatives of the local population, whose political task is formulated by the republic's leadership. Meanwhile, without demonstrating the will to resist on the issue of language (or dual citizenship), further degradation of Russians in Kazakhstan's political life will continue.

5. Under the emerging trend for ousting Russian and the all-democratic opposition closely connected to it, the possibility of build-up of an explosive political potential in Kazakhstan's northern provinces cannot be excluded. It seems to us that a request to allow Kazakhstan's northern provinces to establish direct economic links with the adjacent regions of Russia is exceptionally important, and can be justified before the Kazakh side itself. Maintaining and strengthening mutual economic integration of these provinces is the best guarantee of closeness of Kazakhstan and its ruling circles, who have an interest in territorial integrity.

6. We should take measures, including demonstrative ones, of support for Russian-speaking ethnic and cultural organisations and Cossacks in Kazakhstan. There is no other way to develop their capabilities, other than doing what we can to render them assistance. We regard the position of the Russian Embassy in Kazakhstan as absolutely correct in this respect. The Kazakhstan leadership's initial negative reaction needs to be outlived and overcome. They are politically and economically incapable of developing a real confrontation with declared Russian interests.

7. Russia's indubitable objective in relation to Kazakhstan is its further integration, closer union with Russia in comparison to the CIS. . . . And if Russia today is not yet fully prepared for integration with Kazakhstan, everything necessary should be done not to exclude such a development in the foreseeable future. [139]

Zatulin's report contained what can be described as a Russian centrist view on future strategy towards Kazakhstan. His conclusions and recommendations found reflection in subsequent Russian policy towards Kazakhstan. Rather than seeking to partition Kazakhstan on ethnic lines and incorporate its northern territories into the Russian state, the policy aimed at gradually and gently drawing the whole of Kazakhstan into a closer relationship with Russia, with the long-term prospect of incorporating it into a new form of union or confederation. For this purpose both external and internal pressure on the Kazakh authorities would be exercised, to achieve ultimately the removal of Nazarbayev's nationalist regime. Kazakhstan's Russian community and democratic, internationalist movements and parties among Kazakhs would be used to exert pressure from within. This strategy envisaged strengthening Russian organisations in Kazakhstan and facilitating their acquisition of a larger share of political power.

Widespread criticism of Kazakhstan's parliamentary elections, domestic and foreign, coupled with the new strain on interethnic relations, that the elections had introduced into the republic's political life, weakened Nazarbayev politically. This may explain his desire to achieve some compromises with Russia. In late March 1994 he went to Moscow with a package of proposals intended to change the negative political attitudes to his regime that were developing in the Russian government and in Russian public opinion. The package included a number of military and strategic matters to appear for the Russian defence establishment and a proposal to create a Eurasian Union of states to replace CIS, intended to appeal broadly to the Russian public in both Russia and Kazakhstan.[140] However, he managed to avoid making any concessions of principle on the rights of ethnic Russians in Kazakhstan, a question of primary importance for his strategy of building a Kazakh national state. The only document on this issue, which Nazarbayev and Yeltsin signed in Moscow on 18 March 1994, was the Memorandum on Basic Principles of Resolving Issues Related to Citizenship and Legal Status of Citizens of the Republic of Kazakhstan, Permanently Residing in the Russian Federation, and Citizens of the Russian Federation, Permanently Residing in the Republic of Kazakhstan.

The memorandum acknowledged the importance of the soonest possible settlement of questions related to "citizenship and legal status of citizens of one state permanently residing on the territory of the other". Both parties agreed to solve these questions through a simplified procedure of granting citizenship to these persons and their relatives; ensuring equality of rights of permanent residents with local citizens, with some agreed exemptions; guaranteeing each other's permanent residents the right to own, use and dispose of their property in accordance with the legislation of the state of residence; to give the right to citizens of one state to serve under contract in the armed forces of the other; guaranteeing visa-free travel to each others' territory by citizens of both states, except for movements to third countries; maximum simplification of customs procedures for citizens travelling between the two countries; creation of conditions for exchange of national currencies and transfers of funds by citizens and legal entities from one country to the other within agreed limits.[141]

Though these provisions addressed practical issues very important for Russia, they were still only a declaration of intent, and not a very precise one. For example, the memorandum did not reflect the major Russian interest, dual citizenship, but neither it exclude it from the agenda for further negotiations. The memorandum instructed the foreign ministries of both states to produce a draft agreement on the subject within a month. Especially important for Nazarbayev was that he managed to include in the memorandum a provision that both sides "confirm determination to prohibit and curb on the territory of their states any actions of organisations and groups, as well as individual persons, provoking inter-ethnic discord and inciting violence against persons and groups of the population on grounds of nationality, religious or political convictions". Nazarbayev agreed to sign the memorandum only with this provision, which he thought gave him Moscow's assent to suppressing opposition organisations in the Russian population.

In May 1994 Almaty was visited by a Russian delegation led by Mikitayev. Its main purpose was to discuss citizenship issues. The talks once again failed to resolve Russian-Kazakhstan contradictions. Almaty still did not accept dual citizenship, while Moscow tried to keep it on the agenda.[142] However, after returning to Moscow Mikitayev was optimistic that an agreement regulating citizenship would be concluded within the next two months. He said Russia was still hoping to persuade Kazakhstan to sign an agreement on dual citizenship, that all problems could be settled through separate bilateral agreements,[143] negotiations between the Russian and Kazakh Foreign Ministers would be continued, and an agreement could be signed by Yeltsin and Nazarbayev as early as in June or July 1994.[144]

Behind Russian insistence on Kazakhstan's acceptance of the principle of "dual citizenship" was a far-reaching political agenda, reflecting primarily strategic considerations, not human rights. Mikitayev was probably quite sincere in telling the Duma hearings on Russian-Kazakhstan relations that "dual citizenship is a bridge of friendship . . . a confirmation that both states intend in future to live in friendship and fraternity".[145] Indeed, Kazakhstan's acceptance of the dual citizenship principle would be an insurance that the republic will stay strategically bound to Moscow, because almost half of its citizens, would simultaneously be Russian citizens. Besides, the issue of protecting Russian citizens in Kazakhstan could serve as a justification for Moscow applying economic and political pressure or taking a military action against Kazakhstan. But considering Russia's and the Soviet Union's past records on human rights, it would be much easier for Moscow to justify any such action not in terms of defending human rights of ethnic Russians, which would lack credibility, but in terms of protecting its citizens. On the other hand, Almaty's awareness of a possibility of a Russian action in defence of its citizens would definitely serve as a deterrent against Kazakhstan's taking certain steps in international relations which could endanger vital Russian interests.

Advantages of dual citizenship for ethnic Russians living in Kazakhstan were mostly psychological. The present generation of ex-Soviets spent most of their lives under a regime which severely restricted the right to leave or enter the country. If Russia at some future date, reimposes tight restrictions, and conditions in Kazakhstan become bad enough to make ethnic Russians want to leave, dual citizenship provides some assurance that Russia will let them in. Some Russians, especially in southern Kazakhstan, might obtain psychological comfort knowing that Russian citizenship could entitle them to protection from Russia in event of interethnic violence in the republic, a real possibility given the civil war in Tajikistan and the continuing instability on the Tajik-Afghan border.

Moscow wanted dual citizenship for the same reasons Almaty did not want it. Kazakhstan's experts produced a whole series of arguments against it. The main one being that it could affect the evolution of the young independent state, bringing divided loyalties into its life.[146] Another argument was that dual citizenship would place ethnic Russians in a privileged position compared to Kazakhs, which would violate the basic constitutional principle of national equality. Also, technical difficulties would arise from differences in national laws when applied to people with dual citizenship.[147] As is often the case in diplomacy, these arguments concealed the basic issue: the Kazakh leadership saw dual citizenship as a major threat to the policy of nation-state building. First, it would discourage Russian emigration. Second, it would augment Moscow's capabilities for interference in Kazakhstan's internal affairs. Third, having 30%–40% of foreign citizens would undermine the very basis of the nation-state.

The Kazakh authorities could not, of course, prevent ethnic Russians in Kazakhstan from applying for Russian citizenship. But to do so would mean losing Kazakh citizenship, and with it the many of social, economic and political rights they had enjoyed as Kazakhstan citizens. This was highly discouraging, so applications for Russian citizenship came only from those who had already decided to emigrate, and were therefore of no further use for Russian strategy towards Kazakhstan. According to the Russian embassy in Almaty, 5,400 acquired Russian citizenship through it in 1993, but in 1994 the figure jumped to 53,000. This was not many, given the size of the Russian community in Kazakhstan. Moreover, most of those who obtained Russian citizenship obviously emigrated to Russia, because the number of Russian citizens officially registered with the embassy as permanent residents remained very low, at 6,516.[148]

Given the diametrically opposed positions of Moscow and Almaty on dual citizenship, the negotiations on the issue went on for much longer than predicted by Mikitayev. They produced some results only in January 1995, when Moscow became embroiled in war with Chechnya. This substantially weakened Russia's negotiating position vis-à-vis Kazakhstan and necessitated a number of major Russian concessions, which opened the way to an agreement.

The agreement on citizenship issues took the form of two documents, both signed on 20 January 1995 during Nazarbayev's visit to Moscow, along with several other agreements. Officially they were called Treaty between the Republic of Kazakhstan and the Russian Federation on the Legal Status of Russian Federation Citizens Residing Permanently on the Territory of the Republic of Kazakhstan, and Citizens of the Republic of Kazakhstan Residing Permanently on the Territory of Russian Federation and Agreement between the Republic of Kazakhstan and the Russian Federation on Simplifying the Procedure for Obtaining Citizenship by Citizens of the Russian Federation Arriving for Permanent Residence in Kazakhstan, and Citizens of the Republic of Kazakhstan Arriving for Permanent Residence in the Russian Federation.

The treaty introduced permanent resident status for citizens of one country on the territory of the other which was generally broader than that existing in international legal practice. Permanent residents were entitled to the same rights as citizens, with some exceptions. Article 3 of the treaty stipulated that "a citizen of one party permanently residing in the territory of the other party maintains legal ties with the party of citizenship, and enjoys the patronage and protection of both parties". According to Article 4 permanent residents were to enjoy "the same rights and freedoms" and bear "the same obligations as citizens of the party of residence, except in instances stipulated by this treaty".

The exclusions are:

a) to vote and be elected to highest state positions or representational bodies of authority of the party of residence;
b) to participate in universal voting (all-state referendum) in the party of residence;
c) to occupy positions in the diplomatic service, security bodies, or internal affairs bodies of the party of residence;
d) to occupy positions in the central bodies of executive authority, as judges, or as procurator in the party of residence;
e) to occupy positions as head or deputy head of regional, district, city, rural and settlement administrations.[149]

In accordance with Article 8 of the treaty, procedures for performance of military service by permanent residents were to be regulated by a separate agreement. Article 6 allowed permanent residents "to occupy positions as heads and deputy heads of structural subdivisions of regional, district, city, rural and settlement administrations, as well as of departments, directorates, committees and other organisations within the system of local bodies of executive authority". Permanent residents were guaranteed the right "to possess, use, and dispose of property" belonging to them. Acquisition of new property by permanent residents was to be regulated by legislation of the party of residence. Permanent residents received the right "to participate in the privatisation of state property of the party of residence on an equal basis with its citizens, in accordance with legislation in effect in the party of residence".

The agreement simplifying procedures for obtaining citizenship said that the parties would afford each other's citizens arriving for permanent residence simplified procedure for acquisition of citizenship through registration. This applied in the following cases: a) when the applicant was a citizen of the Kazakh SSR or RSFSR and simultaneously a USSR citizen in the past, resided in these territories as of 21st December 1991, and has been permanently residing there up to entry into force of this agreement, and/or b) when the applicant has close relatives who are citizens of the parties: husband (wife), parents (adoptive parents), children (including adopted children), sisters, brothers, grandfather or grandmother, permanently residing as citizens in the territory of the party of citizenship to be acquired". The agreement established a time frame of three months for registering acquisition of citizenship.[150]

Article 3 of the agreement guaranteed persons "permanently residing in the territory of one party who was born in the territory of the other party, or at least one of whose parents is or was a citizen of that party permanently residing or formerly residing in the territory of that party" of each side the right who has not yet registered his citizenship affiliation "freely to choose citizenship of either of the parties, at his own discretion, within one year of entry into force of this agreement". This provision covered a substantial number of ethnic Russians in Kazakhstan but by no means all of them.

Article 2 implied, though it did not state directly, that acquisition of citizenship of one side entails relinquishment of citizenship of the other.

However, in Article 5 Russian diplomacy managed to insert a provision, which in principle would allow invalidation of this, at least by Russia. It said that "if the domestic legislation of the parties establishes more advantageous conditions for acquisition of citizenship for a certain category of individuals, the domestic legislation of the parties is applied". Thus, if Russia wanted to waive the requirement for relinquishment of Kazakhstan citizenship, it could do so. However, Russia failed to achieve its goal recognition by Kazakhstan of the principle of dual citizenship. This was a major setback for Moscow and a victory for Nazarbayev.

However, in combination the treaty and the agreement contained a number of provisions which addressed essential interests of the Russian population. Both represented Russian attempts to create more favourable conditions for Russian citizens in Kazakhstan, without introducing the principle of dual citizenship. Moscow obviously hoped that improving the status of Russian citizens in Kazakhstan, as codified in the agreements would encourage ethnic Russians to take up Russian citizenship without emigrating. But this hope did not materialise.

The Russian executive bodies that took part in the negotiations recognised this fact. According to the RFMS, "Documents on citizenship issues signed in Moscow on 20.01.95, do tackle the most pressing issues of ethnic Russians residing in Kazakhstan and their movements between the two states, but at present do not yet solve as such the problem of the Russian-speaking population of Kazakhstan".[151] In particular the RFMS pointed out that provisions on property ownership "extended to some degree" the administrative rights of Russians in Kazakhstan and "introduced more clarity" in their rights with regard to the existing property, but "[a]t the same time this document preserves the existing ban on Russian citizens acquiring property in Kazakhstan, putting them in this on the same level as other "foreigners", and preventing young citizens of the Russian Federation from anchoring themselves in the republic".[152]

The substance of both documents left the Russian community in Kazakhstan unimpressed. In the opinion of Kazakhstan Supreme Soviet Deputy Golovkov, "the treaty confirmed the existing limitations on the rights of Russian citizens residing permanently in Kazakhstan, and the agreement encouraged ethnic Russians to leave".[153] On 2 February 1995 the leaders of Russian community organisations—Lad (A. Dokuchaeva), Russian Commune (Yu. Bunakov), Russian Centre (N. Sidorova), Semirechye Cossack Force (N. Gunkin)—and Russian members of the Kazakhstan parliament—S. Vasilieva, V. Galenko, A. Melnik, and N. Fomich—signed an appeal to the Russian Duma, calling on it not to ratify the agreements and to "continue working on solving issues of dual citizenship between the Russian Federation and the Republic of Kazakhstan". The appeal pointed out that the agreements "only create an illusion of solving the citizenship issue. . . . Ratification of this treaty will not diminish migration from the republic, will augment the process of estrangement of the non-Kazakh population from influencing domestic policy trends, which are going towards strengthening the ethnically oriented state". In conclusion, the authors called on the Duma to unilaterally recognise the right to Russian citizenship for all Russians living in Kazakhstan in the same manner as Kazakhstan's constitution recognised the right for all Kazakhs living abroad.[154]

Some politicians in Moscow also voiced concern. At the April 1995 Duma hearings on Russian-Kazakh relations, A. Dolgopolov, chairman of a Subcommittee on Cossacks of the Duma Committee for CIS Affairs and Ties with Compatriots, stated that it was not clear to him whether the agreements were proof that the Kazakh side had made "a principled choice in favour of establishing close political, economic and military cooperation with Russia", or whether it was an attempt "to remove the existing tension in relations between the two states, secure by formal concessions and declarative agreements an attitude of the Russian people and government which would permit continuance in practice of the strategic line on ousting the Russian-speaking population from Kazakhstan". Konstantin Zatulin, chairman of the Duma Committee for CIS Affairs and Ties with Compatriots, expressed doubts about both documents which seemed directed "to contribute to possible larger migration from Kazakhstan to Russia".

Mikitayev rejected this interpretation. He said the agreements were designed to assist Russians in Kazakhstan to solve many acute problems,[155] and were a positive development because they "approximated" the rights of Russian citizens residing in Kazakhstan to those of citizens of Kazakhstan. Mikitayev called for speedy ratification of both agreements, which the support of Deputy Foreign Minister Panov, who said they gave Russian citizens in Kazakhstan a different status from other foreigners, "the spectrum of rights and duties, including in the social and economic fields, will be much wider".[156] However, both officials made it clear that the issue of dual citizenship was not removed from the agenda. Mikitayev stressed that conclusion of the two agreements did not mean that Russia had resiled from its previous position. "I cannot say that the issue of dual citizenship is taken off the agenda, that this problem has already exhausted itself", he said. Mikitayev said, and Panov agreed, that 600,000–700,000 signatures had been collected in Kazakhstan in support of dual citizenship, and this could not be simply ignored.[157]

The appeals of the treaty's opponents affected the ratification process. Despite the executive branch's strong support, the Duma delayed ratification for more than two years. Not until 26 June 1997 did Russia and Kazakhstan exchange instruments of ratification.[158]

In 1995 Nazarbayev took a number of steps leading to the consolidation of his personal power. On 11 March he dissolved parliament, then called a referendum on extending his term of office until the year 2000.[159] The purpose of his move was clear—to deprive the opposition of its only remaining source of influence on governmental policy, the parliament. This also meant that ethnic Russians would lose their only independent channel of political expression. Not surprisingly, Russian community organisations were swift to react. Lad, Russian Commune and some other organisations issued statements demanding new free and fair parliamentary elections as soon as possible.[160] They received immediate support from the Russian Duma. On 13 March its Committee on CIS Affairs and Ties with Compatriots adopted a statement on political crises in Kazakhstan. It admitted that the previous parliament was illegitimate, but expressed the hope that "the vacuum of legislative power in Kazakhstan will be filled in the nearest future through holding really free and democratic elections". It also expressed the hope that "in the interests of further development of Kazakhstan there may be more active participation in its legislative bodies by members of the Russian community".[161]

The boldness of Nazarbayev's action was due, to a large degree, to Russian preoccupation with Chechnya, where the war was not going well. However, he still needed to attach at least a semblance of legitimacy to his actions. On 24 March he convened what was called the first session of the Assembly of Peoples of Kazakhstan. It was intended to serve as a consultative body under the president and to be formed by proportional representation of every ethnic group. The Russian community organisations supported the idea of holding the Assembly, but voiced reservations about the method of its formation, which they called bureaucratic, as members were selected by heads of province administrations.[162] At the April 1995 Duma hearings, Kazakhstan's Ambassador Mansurov tried to show that delegates to the Assembly were elected, not appointed, but was challenged by Russian activists from Kazakhstan, who disclosed cases of administrative appointments of delegates.[163]

The proceedings of the Assembly were farcical. Lad, the largest Russian community organisation in Kazakhstan, was not even allowed to participate, and Kazakhstan's official media spread false reports that it was taking part. Despite the declared principle of national-proportional representation, the Council of the Assembly comprised 46% Kazakhs and only 16% Russians. Moreover, 44% of places in the Council were taken by government bureaucrats, and 30% by leaders of national and cultural centres, but Russian centres were not represented, and Russian community organisations were represented by only two persons, the head of the Russian Commune and the chairman of the Russian Union.[164]

Speaking at the opening of the Assembly, Nazarbayev touted laid emphasis on Kazakhstan as a multinational state and named the Assembly as "one of the mechanisms of consolidation of our society". He claimed outstanding achievements in the human rights field, and put forward a four-point program for developing national languages, rectifying the national education system, improving national mass media and strengthening legal mechanisms for protection of national culture.[165] But it soon became obvious that the Assembly's main function was to endorse Nazarbayev's call for a referendum, and the hand-picked delegates overwhelmingly approved it.[166]

Lad issued a statement protesting that the Assembly "cannot represent the interests of the people of Kazakhstan, because it has not been elected by the people" and that a referendum on extending Nazarbayev's term of office was "anti-constitutional".[167] On 10 April Russian community organisations proposed collective by that the question of granting Russian the status of second state language be put to a vote at the forthcoming referendum.[168] The Russian Duma supported the appeal by 243 votes for, versus 1 against and 3 abstentions.[169] Nazarbayev rejected the appeal.

The referendum was conducted in a manner reminiscent of Soviet times. According to official Kazakh data, the turnout was 91.3%, and 95.4% of those voting favoured extending Nazarbayev's term of office. Numerous polls taken beforehand had indicated that the turnout would not exceed 70%, and that 17%–26% of those voting would vote against Nazarbayev.[170] If in March 1994 the authorities used unfair tactics to win, in 1995 they saved themselves the trouble. The results were simply decreed from above. Subsequent events with the referendum on the new constitution and elections to the new parliament proved this beyond a doubt.

After the referendum Nazarbayev convened the second session of the Assembly of Peoples of Kazakhstan to legitimise the new constitution prepared by him. At the session Nazarbayev spoke of several issues which were causing concern in the Russian community and promised to introduce some constitutional changes. For example, he admitted that the constitutional provision calling Kazakhstan a state of the "self-determined Kazakh nation" caused "justified concern among our compatriots.... Personally for me Kazakhstan is the result of state self-determination, not only of Kazakhs, but representatives of all nationalities residing in our country". He promised to remove the discriminatory provision allowing dual citizenship only for Kazakhs from the constitution, give official status to the Russian language and introduce limited private land ownership for housing plots, rural houses, dachas and industrial enterprises.[171]

The referendum on the new constitution was held on 30 August, and, like its predecessor, delivered Soviet-style official results, claiming a 90% turnout of the 8.8 million electorate and 89% approval of the new constitution. At a news conference in Almaty on 1 September, opposition organisations said that the vote had been rigged, and the turnout had been only 34%. International observers ignored the referendum.[172] U.S. Representative to OSCE, Sam W. Brown, Jr., said on 31 August that the United States considered it a "second step backward from democracy". Interestingly, U.S. criticisms of the referendum were generally similar to those made by the opposition Russian community organisations.[173]

The new constitution removed a number of the most obvious ethnocentric provisions, but fell far short of Russian expectations. Though references to the ethnic nature of Kazakhstan's statehood were abolished, the preamble to the constitution still said that the people of Kazakhstan were creating their statehood on ancestral Kazakh lands. This served as a reminder to all non-Kazakhs that they were considered guests on Kazakh territory, though this was untrue on many non-Kazakh citizens. Article 10 denied citizenship of any other country to Kazakhstan citizens without exception. This eliminated the privileged status Kazakhs had previously enjoyed with regard to dual citizenship but also explicitly prevented any future agreements on dual citizenship between Russia and Kazakhstan.

Article 6 stipulated that land could be private property "on grounds, conditions and within limits, established by the law".[174] The law would not be a problem for the Kazakh leadership, because Nazarbayev had already decided to establish total control over the legislature, so that he could adopt and amend laws as he wished. Article 7 reiterated the role of Kazakh as the only state language. Russian was upgraded to an official language[175] but was denied equal status with Kazakh, which was one of the Russian community organisations' primary demands.

The main issue of concern, that provisions in the new constitution concentrated almost unlimited power in the president's hands, attracted the bulk of the Russian community organisations' criticisms.[176] Russians in Kazakhstan understood only too well from their experience with previous Soviet constitutions that whatever improvements the new constitution might contain, in the absence of basic democratic guarantees those improvement would remain on paper and serve only to camouflage continuation of ethnocentric policies. Excessive concentration of power in the president's hands without effective checks and balances to his authority, meant that the Russian community lost the little leverage on government policy which it previously possessed.

Throughout 1995 Nazarbayev justified establishment of authoritarian rule as a necessity to achieve interethnic consolidation. This, however, soon proved only empty promises. A major consequence of the political transformation in 1995 was even greater sidelining of ethnic Russians from politics and government. By late 1995 Kazakhs held 81.4% of posts at the level of ministers, heads of state committees, committees and departments, and Russians held only 14%, compared to 64.2% and 21%, respectively, in 1994.[177] During the elections to the new two-chamber parliament,[178] held on 5 and 9 December 1995, candidates for the Senate were nominated directly from Almaty. As a result 28 were unopposed, and 26 of the 38 elected (68%) were Kazakhs.[179] In the elections to the Majilis, the government did its best to eliminate opposition candidates, sometimes employing overtly oppressive measures.[180] As a result 53 (79%) of the 67 Majilis seats went to progovernment candidates.[181] Data on the ethnic composition of the Majilis are not available, but officially selected deputies, whatever their ethnicity, obediently followed Nazarbayev's political line.

In an interview with Moscow's NTV television on 22 October 1997, Nazarbayev disclosed that Kazakhs comprised 70% of government members and provincial governors,[182] substantially more than the percentage of Kazakhs in the population. Besides, this remark referred only to a very small circle of top officials and did not include other senior positions in the state apparatus such as deputy ministers, deputy province governors, mayors of large cities, or post within the presidential administration. In the latter, for example, Kazakhs held 75% of the leading positions by January 1997.[183] Nazarbayev produced no figures for the ethnic composition of personnel in the most important government departments such as the Foreign, Defence and Interior Ministries and the National Security Committee, nor did he evince any desire to conduct new free and fair parliamentary elections which would adequately reflect the ethnic balance in Kazakhstan.

On 22 December 1995 Nazarbayev issued the decree On Land, which had the force of law. It established that all land in Kazakhstan remained state property, except for plots adjacent to or allocated for construction of residential buildings, installations and their compounds, for gardening or vegetable growing or production, or any other facilities specific to the land. The edict specifically excluded private ownership of agricultural land or peasants' private plots. Peasants would receive the right to permanent land use, but the land remained state property. This meant rejection of the farmers' demands for private ownership of agricultural land, the moods particularly widespread among Russians, and especially among the Cossacks, who were trying to resurrect the *stanitsa* with its specific form of private property in land.

Formally, the "buy-out" procedure established by the edict for alienation of privately owned land for state needs appeared to correspond to international norms, with the final decision on disagreements between the government and a landowner left to the courts. But in Kazakhstan, where courts are government instruments without the relative independence they have in democratic countries, this provision would in no way hamper the government's arbitrariness, and no landowner could be sure that he would be fairly compensated (if at all) for his property.

Moreover, the edict contained clear discriminatory provisions against ethnic Russians by stipulating in Article 33 that land plots "which are granted (to be granted) for keeping personal land plots for gardening and vegetable growing and dacha construction may not be in private ownership by foreign citizens". This meant that any ethnic Russian who chose Russian citizenship would lose the right to own any land he held. Moreover, Article 40 stipulated that "right to permanent use of land may not be granted to foreign land users", so Russian citizens in Kazakhstan would have only the right of temporary land use, for which, under Article 8, they would be obliged to pay "to the extent to which that right was not previously purchased". Since in Soviet times land plots were allocated free of charge, this would require paying the full market value. In all, the land decree created strong material disincentives for ethnic Russians to take up Russian citizenship.

The Kazakh authorities continued persecution of Russian community activists, adding new fuel to the existing tensions in bilateral relations with Russia. On 20 August 1996 Nina Sidorova, head of the Russian Centre in Almaty, was arrested on charges of insulting judges and guards during Gunkin's trial. Again, a Russian reaction followed. On 16 September protestors demonstrated outside the Kazakh Embassy in Moscow.[184] On 18 September 1996 the Duma Committee for CIS Affairs and Ties with Compatriots issued a statement expressing concern about "the continuing persecution of the Russian population in Kazakhstan", and calling on the Kazakh authorities to "cease persecution and harassment of the Russian population, Cossacks in particular".[185] Sidorova was convicted of contempt of court and injuring an official of the Procurator's Office, and sentenced to two years' imprisonment, but the sentence was immediately suspended under an amnesty to mark the anniversary of Kazakhstan's constitution.[186] In May 1997 Petr Kolomets, deputy ataman of the Semirechye Cossack Force, was arrested in Almaty. Russian Cossacks held protest rallies demanding Kolomets's release in Moscow, Kurgan and some other Russian cities, including a small demonstration in June 1997 outside Kazakhstan's embassy in Moscow.[187]

The policy of administratively restricting use of the Russian language also remained unchanged. On 4 November 1996 Nazarbayev endorsed the Concept of Language Policy of the Republic of Kazakhstan, which advocated altering the hierarchy of languages and giving priority to development of the Kazakh language. It did not envisage a wide sphere of long-term use of Russian, and contained provisions that could be interpreted as establishing administrative barriers to employment in certain professions outside public service by requiring knowledge of the Kazakh language.[188] Nazarbayev's endorsement of the concept prompted criticism by the Russian government. On 20 November 1996 Russian Minister for Cooperation with CIS States Tuleyev warned that its implementation could lead to a massive exodus of Russian-speakers, and sent a message to this effect to Nazarbayev and to the speakers of both houses of the Kazakh parliament. He said that the concept "limits the already curtailed rights of the Russian-speaking part of the population", and called for revision of some of the concept's provisions on the grounds that they contradicted the principles of the Treaty on Friendship, Cooperation and Mutual Assistance. "It has become increasingly necessary to speed up creation in Kazakhstan of Russian consular services and a committee on human rights," he said.[189]

Despite this, on 18 June 1997 Kazakhstan's parliament passed the law On Languages in the Republic of Kazakhstan, which was based on the concept and confirmed the Kazakh language as the only state language in Kazakhstan. Russian was to be officially used equally with Kazakh in state and local administrations. But the notion of equality was undermined by Article 23 of the law, which established a special state program "providing for priority of the state language and stage-by-stage transfer of administrative work into the Kazakh language", and by Article 9, under which Kazakh was to be the main language in drafting and adopting state legislation and other acts of state bodies. Kazakhstan's diplomatic missions were to function in Kazakh and in other languages when necessary, official diplomatic receptions were to be conducted in Kazakh, and bilateral treaties were to be written in the state languages of the contracting parties.

Notably, the law went beyond the sphere of official relations into that of private communication. It said that Kazakh was to be used in nongovernmental organisations, though other languages could also be used "in case of necessity"

(Article 8), that internal documentation in state and private organisations must be in both Kazakh and Russian (Article 10), as must all contracts between individuals or companies (Article 15). Thus private deals between two or more Russians, or between companies in Russian-populated areas would have to be in both languages, requiring a complicated bureaucratic process of certified translation into Kazakh, and companies in Russian-populated areas would have to employ Kazakh interpreters and translators, which would impose extra difficulties on their work.

Moreover, coupled with the provision on nonimpediment to functioning of languages in Kazakhstan (Article 7), it created potential for government interference with the activity of private companies controlled by ethnic Russians. Theoretically, any individual Kazakh employed by a company could demand that documentation and communication therein must be conducted in Kazakh. Of course, the likelihood of such a demand would be low, except when authorities would incite Kazakh employees to behave in such a way for the purposes of disrupting work of particular companies, for example, those involved in financing Russian community organisations.

Also, the law laid down that Kazakh-language television and radio broadcasts should not be less than half of all broadcast time. Formally, this provision corresponded with established international practice that individual television and radio stations could be assigned quotas for broadcasts in specific languages. But Kazakhstan's law applied this practice excessively, way covering all television and radio stations, both government and private, for the purpose of creating difficulties for Russian electronic mass media.

Another unprecedented requirement was that cultural events should be conducted in Kazakh and when necessary in other languages, but did not state how necessity would be determined, thereby leaving the final decision to bureaucratic arbitrariness. Due to strong opposition from the non-Kazakh population, the law did not go as far as establishing a list of professions where knowledge of Kazakh would be obligatory, but it foreshadowed future adoption of such legislation.[190] Not surprisingly, the law was harshly criticised by the Russian community. At a press conference on 21 August 1997, members of the Society of Ethnic Russians in Kazakhstan urged the Russian Duma to take concrete measures to protect the rights of Russian-speakers in Kazakhstan, who, they said, were more than half the population.[191]

The intensification of the ethnocentric policy can be explained by the fact that the Kazakh leadership's hope for early resolution of the interethnic situation in the Kazakhs' favour did not materialise. The main failure was in the economic sphere, where expectations of an early economic revival proved unfounded.[192] In addressing the nation in October 1997, Nazarbayev admitted that over the past eight years Kazakhstan's economic output had shrunk more than twice and the "standard of living of the majority of citizens deteriorated".[193]

Despite various administrative limitations imposed by the Kazakh authorities, Russian remains Kazakhstan's de facto first language. This was conceded by S. Orazalinov, director of the Department for Coordinating Language Policy in Kazakhstan's Ministry of Education and Culture at a representative conference in Almaty in July 1997. He admitted that the Kazakh language had not yet acquired "worthy positions in education, science and public administration", and "Kazakh remains a language which is more or less actively used only among the indigenous population, and at that more often in the non-work environment". He said that many Kazakh language study courses established several years before, had disappeared without trace, and complained that while three to five years before, enrolments to Kazakh-language secondary schools were very high, "and not only among the indigenous nationality", now a reverse trend was underway. He went on to say that newspapers, journals and books in Kazakh, "which already have low circulation", failed to sell, since there was no demand for them. Not all television and radio channels, especially commercial ones, used Kazakh in their broadcasts, and in many ministries and departments the requirement to conduct business in both Kazakh and Russian was being ignored, and only Russian used.[194]

The Kazakh leadership failed to achieve a decisive shift in the demographic balance in favour of Kazakhs. Nazarbayev's policies indeed led to a dramatic fall in the Russian population from 40.8% in 1990 to 36.4% in 1994 and 29% in 1997.[195] In 1997 emigration continued, and even increased compared to 1996. In the first nine months of 1997, 230,786 people emigrated from Kazakhstan, 57.5% of them ethnic Russians.[196] However, in combination with other Slavs and non-Kazakhs who perceive themselves as Russian-speakers, they still comprise more than 40% of the population.

At the same time, the post independence years registered a rapid decrease in the growth rate of the ethnic Kazakh population. One contributing factor may have been the difficult economic situation. M. Tatimov, a senior expert in the Information and Analytical Centre of the presidential administration, noted with concern that the Kazakh birth rate was falling "even faster than in the years of destruction, famine and war (the 1920s, 30s, 40s)".[197] In his address to the nation in October 1997, Nazarbayev pointed to a real danger of demographic depopulation in Kazakhstan, noting that for the first time in the past fifty years "our population has begun to shrink". He called for "immediate termination of this trend", and identified demographic and migration policy as "a leading priority of national security".[198]

Besides, Russian emigration from Kazakhstan had a specific character, which accentuated the interethnic divide. It affected primarily the southern, Kazakh-populated provinces. According to A. Galiev, head of the Chair at the Interior Ministry Higher School in Almaty, the extent of emigration from northern and southern provinces varied substantially. The largest emigration took place from seven provinces—Mangistau, Kzyl-Orda, Atirau, Zhambul, South-Kazakhstan and Taldy-Kurgan. The lowest migration was from North-Kazakhstan, West-Kazakhstan, Kostanay, Kokshetau, East-Kazakhstan, Akmola, Aktyubinsk and Pavlodar provinces.[199] The second group comprised mostly provinces with a Russian-majority population, and the trend indicated that Russians there were not particularly keen to emigrate. The prospect of recolonisation of the northern provinces by Kazakhs, given their poor demographic situation, does not look very promising, at least in the short term.

In the RFMS assessment exacerbation of the problem of the northern territories can be expected. "The predominantly Russian-speaking population there can choose secession from Kazakhstan instead of a massive exodus, and this could cause serious complications in Russian-Kazakhstan inter-state relations".[200] Another disturbing fact is the finding in a sociological survey which established that secessionist attitudes are much stronger among younger-generation ethnic Russians. According to N. Baytenova, a political scientist from the Kazakh National University, separatist attitudes among Russians are more characteristic of those under thirty-five years of age, while those over fifty are indifferent or against secession.[201] This suggests that as time goes by, Russian secessionist potential in Kazakhstan is likely to increase.

The policy directed at neutralising the Cossack movement also failed, and attempts to split the Cossack organisations had very limited results. The failed attempt in Uralsk provides a telling example. According to *Zavtra*, Nazarbayev's secret services managed to neutralise the former leadership of the Ural Cossacks, and put their agents into leading positions in major Cossack organisations, which then proclaimed that the Cossack movement's main objective must be the solution of economic problems. The newspaper identified leaders of the Ural Cossacks, such as Bukin and Solodilov, as agents who secured the support of the majority of Cossacks through promises of funds, allegedly opened for them in Almaty.[202] Those Cossacks who opposed Bukin and Solodilov were grouped around A. Kachalin, the pro-Moscow ataman of the Ural Cossack Force.

The Union of Cossacks of Semirechye (to be differentiated from the Semirechye Cossack Force), supported by official Almaty and headed by Ovsyannikov, provides another example of infiltration. Ovsyannikov promoted the idea that Cossacks should be loyal to Nazarbayev, since they always served sovereign Kazakhstan. His union, which initially had a following of only fifty, began to compete with Gunkin's organisation for influence over the Semirechye Cossacks. In July 1997 Ovsyannikov's deputy, Shikhotov, published an article in *Kazakhstanskaya Pravda* bitterly attacking Gunkin, saying that he "should not be associated with the Semirechye Cossacks, because nobody mandated him to solve our problems, or, moreover, call himself Ataman".[203] Gunkin in turn claimed that he possessed evidence proving that Ovsyannikov had always been an officer of Kazakhstan's Interior Ministry and had deliberately tried to hinder development of the Cossack movement.[204] Despite this interference, most Cossack organisations in Kazakhstan maintained their independence and remained opposed to the regime.

The First Division of the Siberian Cossack Force decided to hold its Assembly in Kokchetau on 2 May 1997. This was clearly a provocative move, deliberately scheduled for the May holidays and celebrations. The main issue on the agenda was "determination of the status of the lands of the Siberian Cossack Force located at present on the territory of Kazakhstan". Cossacks from other areas of Kazakhstan and from Russia were expected to attend. The organisers planned to use the Assembly to proclaim creation of a South Siberian Republic, which would include Kokchetau, Pavlodar and North-Kazakhstan provinces. The Kazakh authorities knew of the planned action and prepared for it well in advance. The Assembly was, naturally, banned, some Cossack activists were summoned to the local police and Committee of National Security (CNS), extra police and troops were deployed in Kokchetau, and reinforced units patrolled the streets during the May holidays. Russian representatives arriving for the Assembly were intercepted at the railway station and forcibly turned back. Ten of them were arrested by the local police. When groups of Cossacks gathered in the centre of the city on 2 May, they were surrounded by Interior Ministry troops and driven out of the city. They managed to hold their meeting on the outskirts, but obviously failed to produce any strong political effect.[205] Nevertheless, the action served to show that the Cossack movement was still alive, and prepared to defy the authorities.

The Russian leadership was disappointed by its inability to induce Nazarbayev to change his political course. On 23 November 1996, during a meeting with Nazarbayev, Yeltsin proposed drawing up a new, broader agreement on the status of ethnic Russians in Kazakhstan. According to presidential spokesman Yastrzhembskiy, "Yeltsin suggested to Nazarbayev that a joint document be drafted on the status of the Russian-speaking population in Kazakhstan, defining personal guarantees and the status of the Russian language there.... Such a document will put an end to speculation and discrimination in this field".[206] Yeltsin's proposal acknowledged that there were weaknesses in the previous agreements with Kazakhstan and Yeltsin wanted to improve the situation. But Nazarbayev showed no inclination to negotiate a new treaty.

In January 1997, as a clear signal of dissatisfaction with Kazakhstan's attitude, Moscow deployed Cossack units along the Russia-Kazakhstan border. Their functions included checking documents and inspecting the baggage of persons entering Russia from Kazakhstan. To manage these units, Russia's Federal Border Guards Service (RFBGS) established a new Border Watch Directorate.[207] This was a basic policy reversal, because previously Russia had made rather firm commitments to the principle of open borders with Kazakhstan. RFBGS naturally tried to downplay the event, describing it as an experiment to combat drug trafficking and smuggling, and involving unarmed volunteers.[208] The "experiment" embraced at least four large Russian provinces—Saratov, Orenburg, Chelyabinsk and Omsk—and would extend the whole 7,500-km length of the joint border after the trial period ended in June.[209] Moreover, by late March 1997 it was already known that the volunteers were in fact light-armed units.[210]

Russia's move provoked an angry reaction in Almaty. On 25 March 1997, Beksultan Sarsekov, secretary of Kazakhstan's Security Council, criticised the decision, pointing out that it was at odds with an open borders agreement with Russia. "In some Russian regions along the Kazakh border, the Russian Federation has set up Cossack posts. These Cossacks received uniforms and weapons. These Cossacks are a prototype border guard force," he told a news conference in Almaty.[211] On 16 April formal statement by the Kazakhstan Foreign Ministry press service, expressed regret at the Russian move. The statement said that "serious concern has been provoked by an experiment by Russia's Federal Border Guards Service to place non-regular units manned by Cossacks to guard the border". The statement claimed that this was a "serious breach" of existing bilateral accords on the regime of the common border, and drew particular attention to the Cossack involvement, stating "The history of Cossacks on Kazakhstan's territory is well known to all. Thus one should be very cautious in approaching such a delicate issue as involving Cossacks in guarding the border".[212]

On 16 May, Nazarbayev addressed a group of Russian journalists in Almaty and blamed Russia for what he described as the loss of trust in the CIS among its members.[213] He devoted a substantial part of his statement to Cossacks, saying that he was alarmed that Cossack units had been deployed to guard the Russian-Kazakh border and announcing that he had sent a special memorandum on this issue to Yeltsin, but still had received no reply. In a veiled warning, Nazarbayev said that in Kazakhstan "under the sultans and khans there were Sardars, military formations similar to Cossacks under the Tsars", and that pressure was mounting on him to recreate such formations and deploy them in all provinces of Kazakhstan.[214]

Tuleyev, Russian minister for Cooperation with CIS Member States, and himself a Kazakh, reacted sharply to Nazarbayev's comments calling them anti-Russian. On 20 May 1997 he issued a statement in which he stressed that Russia "will continue to condemn Kazakhstan's policy towards Russian and Russian-speaking citizens", criticised Kazakhstan's decision to reduce the quantity of Russian television and radio broadcasts, and opposed the adoption of "a discriminatory language law, which infringes the interests of the Russian-speaking population".[215] In an interview on 27 May, Tuleyev said that since 1992 more than a million Russians had run away from Kazakhstan, and mentioned oppression of the Russian minority as a reason for the exodus. Now it was Almaty's turn to feel offended. A diplomatic protest was sent to the Russian Foreign Ministry. Tuleyev revealed in an interview that Nazarbayev personally asked Yeltsin to dismiss him.[216] Nazarbayev did not stop at that. In an interview shown on Kazakh television on 27 June 1997, he warned that Kazakhs "should be ready to preserve the country's independence and integrity", because many "ill-wishers" had emerged in Russia, and "have drawn up different programs, if not to go back to the Soviet Union, then to bring Kazakhstan back under Russia's wing", programs which included as a last resort "stirring up ethnic Russians living in Kazakhstan with the idea of separatism, and setting them against ethnic Kazakhs".[217]

Simultaneously, Almaty continued pressing Moscow to revoke the decision on Cossack-manned border posts. On 4 June 1997 at a meeting of the Council of CIS Border Troops commanders in Moscow, the Kazakh representative called the Cossack involvement an "experiment [which] caused certain tension . . . in Kazakhstan" and urged Moscow to terminate it.[218] But Moscow was in no hurry to accommodate the Kazakh demands, obviously finding the border patrols an effective instrument of diplomatic leverage over Kazakhstan on human rights issues.

On 26 June 1997, while returning from New York, Kazakhstan's Foreign Minister Tokayev had a brief meeting with his Russian counterpart, Primakov, during a stopover in Moscow, and again raised the Cossack issue. Primakov replied that "the experiment" was temporary, and that the Russian Foreign Ministry was recommending that it be abandoned in view of Kazakhstan's concern, but he gave no clear indication of when this might happen. Primakov specifically linked the issue of Cossack border guards with practical fulfilment of Nazarbayev's proposal to create a public council of the two states for solving humanitarian problems "in the spirit of the treaty on Friendship, Cooperation and Mutual Assistance".[219] But the initiative, like many others before it, proved purely declaratory, and did not materialise.

Nazarbayev discussed the issue of border controls with Yeltsin on 6 September 1997, while attending Moscow's 850th anniversary celebrations. Yeltsin promised that Chernomyrdin and other high-ranking Russian officials would visit Kazakhstan and sign a number of bilateral agreements on that and other issues.[220] On 29 September A. Nikolayev, Russian Federal Border Service Director, arrived in Almaty and met Nazarbayev, obviously to discuss the Russian Cossack border guards issue. After the meeting Nazarbayev told journalists that the two countries' border guard services would prepare and sign an agreement on the regime and status of the Russian-Kazakh border, which would provide for elementary security along it. Nikolayev added that Kazakhstan had agreed on joint measures with Russia to reinforce its outer (non-CIS) borders.[221] But Nikolayev's visit did not solve the Cossack problems, which is unlikely to be solved until a broader agreement providing for Russia's increased role in Kazakhstan's border protection is negotiated, a process likely to be prolonged. In fact, Russia may well prolong the process by putting forward more and more conditions, and linking success of the negotiations to Kazakh concessions on the status of ethnic Russians in Kazakhstan.

This is substantiated by the results of Chernomyrdin's visit to Kazakhstan on 4 October 1997. He and Nazarbayev agreed to form an intergovernmental commission on cooperation between the two countries. Its main task is to prepare Yeltsin's official visit to Kazakhstan, and negotiate a new basic treaty to replace the Treaty on Friendship, Cooperation and Mutual Assistance, because, as it was said, "time requires clarification of many notions which emerged five years ago, when the previous document was adopted".[222] The understanding was probably a development of Yeltsin's 1996 proposal for a new agreement with Kazakhstan on the status of ethnic Russians. In any event,

Russia has managed to draw Kazakhstan into re-negotiating the previous basic agreement, which it saw as inadequately serving Russian interests, especially on the question of ethnic Russians in Kazakhstan. Agreement to negotiate was itself a major Kazakh concession, but the results of previous negotiations between Russia and Kazakhstan suggest that they are hardly likely proceed without major difficulties, or to have an outcome both early and successful. Moreover, the negotiation process itself is likely to have further adverse effects on bilateral relations, result in additional diplomatic complications and not remove the major differences over the status of ethnic Russians. To overcome these differences, either Russia's or Kazakhstan's policies on the matters of principle must change, but there are no indications that this can be expected, at least not in the foreseeable future.

NOTES

1. *Radio Free Europe / Radio Liberty (RFE/RL)* Daily Report, No. 105, 03.06.92.
2. "Nazarbayev Finalises Last Revisions to New Draft Constitution", *BBC Monitoring Service: Former USSR*, 31.10.92.
3. Yazkova, A., Lafitskiy, V., "Analiz konstituciy sredneaziatskogo regiona i praktika mezhnacionalnikh otnosheniy v Respublike Kazakhstan (analiticheskaya razrabotka)", Moscow [No publisher], 1995, p. 1(b).
4. Ibid., p. 3.
5. Gosudarstvennaya Duma Federal'nogo Sobraniya Rossiyskoy Federatsii, Stenogramma parlamentskikh slushaniy Komiteta po delam Sodruzhestva Nezavisimykh Gosudarstv i svyazyam s sootechestvennikami "O rossiysko-kazakhstanskikh otnosheniyakh", Moscow [No publisher], 18.04.95, p. 33.
6. "Immigration Law Published", *BBC Monitoring Service: Former USSR*, 28.08.92.
7. Yazkova, A., Lafitskiy, V., "Analiz konstitutsiy sredneaziatskogo regiona i praktika mezhnatsional'nykh otnosheniy v Respublike Kazakhstan", pp. 9–10.
8. "Nazarbayev on Kazakh TV: Talks about Economy, Religion, Nationality Mix", *BBC Monitoring Service: Former USSR*, 18.12.92.
9. Tatimov, M., Vliyanie demograficheskikh protsessov na vnutripoliticheskuyu stabil'nost' Respubliki Kazakhstan", *Politika*, No. 5, 1995, p. 22.
10. *Izvestiya*, 11.11.92.
11. Bakaev, L., "Mezhetnicheskie otnosheniya v Kazakhstane: istoricheskiy opyt, problemy i protivorechiya," *Evraziyskoye soobshchestvo: ekonomika, politika, bezopasnost'*, No. 2, 1995, p. 7.
12. One official at the Kazakhstan's Ministry of Foreign Affairs told the author of that Kazakh objective was to increase the Kazakh numbers to as many as 30 million.
13. *Izvestiya*, 11.06.94; *Segodnya*, 07.06.97.
14. In East Kazakhstan province Dirizhabl became Kyzylsu; Kirovo, Zhanalyk; Andreyevka, Zhanatileu; Komsomol, Zhetyaral; Priozernyy, Tugyl; Pokrovka, Manyrak; Sergeyevka, Kaynar; Budenovka, Toskayyn; Vysokogorka, Karabulak; Maralikha, Maraldy; Pugachevo, Ushbulak; Platovo, Sarytau; Zelenoye, Algabas; Kalinino, Yegindybulak; Tochka, Bayash; Utepova Skalistoye, Izgutty Aytykova. In Kustanay province Aktobe became Maylin. In Mangistau province Kuybyshevo became Zhyngyldy. In Semipalatinsk province Yernazar became Zhantikey; Igorevka, Sulusary;

Saratovka, Koytas; Filippovka, Shymyldyk; Ilyinka, Birlikshil. In Taldy-Kurgan province Andreyevka became Kabanbay; Saratovka, Kyzylkayyn; Glinovka, Ushbulak; Tridtsat Let Kazakhskoy SSR, Nadirizbek. In Akmola province Budennoye became Khadzhimukana. In South Kazakhstan province Galkino became Zertas. "Places Renamed in Kazakhstan", *BBC Monitoring Service: Former USSR*, 19.09.92.

15. "Rayon in West Kazakhstan Renamed after Kazakh National Hero", *BBC Monitoring Service: Former USSR*, 02.10.92.

16. *Megapolis-Express*, 05.05.93.

17. Kuzmin, N., "Nochnyye besedy", *Molodaya Gvardiya*, No. 2, 1997, p. 339.

18. "Supreme Kengez Votes to Change Spelling of Alma-Ata", *BBC Monitoring Service: Former USSR*, 12.02.93.

19. Federal'naya Migratsionnaya Sluzhba Rossii, O rabote migratsionnoy sluzhby posol'stva Rossiyskoy Federatsii v Respublike Kazakhstan v 1994 godu, Doc. No. 722, Moscow [No publisher], 13.04.95, p. 14.

20. Nazarbayev, N., *Na poroge XXI veka*, Almaty: Oner, 1996, p. 39.

21. Arenov, M., Kalmykov, S., "Sovremennaya yazikovaya situatsiya v Respublike Kazakhstan", *Politika*, No. 1, 1995, pp. 43–48.

22. Ibid., pp. 43–44.

23. Yazkova, A., Lafitskiy, V., "Analiz konstituciy sredneaziatskogo regiona i praktika mezhnacionalnikh otnosheniy v Respublike Kazakhstan", pp. 6, 7, 9.

24. Arenov, M., Kalmykov, S., "Sovremennaya yazikovaya situatsiya v Respublike Kazakhstan", p. 48.

25. Ibid., pp. 51–52.

26. Masanov, N., "Kazakhstan: etnicheskiy aparteid i novaya gosudarstvennost", *Rossiya i musulmanskiy mir*, No. 3(33), Moscow: INION, 1995, p. 43.

27. Gosudarstvennaya Duma Federal'nogo Sobraniya Rossiyskoy Federatsii, Stenogramma parlamentskikh slushaniy Komiteta po delam Sodruzhestva Nezavisimykh Gosudarstv i svyazyam s sootechestvennikami "O rossiysko-kazakhstanskikh otnosheniyakh", Moscow [No publisher], 18.04.95, pp. 10, 28.

28. Federal'naya Migratsionnaya Sluzhba Rossii, O rabote migratsionnoy sluzhby posol'stva Rossiyskoy Federatsii v Respublike Kazakhstan v 1994 godu, Doc. No. 722, Moscow [No publisher], 13.04.95, p. 14.

29. "Etnokul'turnoe obrazovanie v Kazakhstane: tsifry i fakty",: *Mysl'*, No. 9, 1996, p. 68.

30. The total number of university students in Kazakhstan was 280,700 in 1992–1993 and 260,000 in 1995–1996. "Etnokul'turnoe obrazovanie v Kazakhstane", pp. 71–72.

31. Abdigaliev, B., "Russkie v Kazakhstane: problemy, mify i realnost", *Kazakhstan i mirovoe soobshchestvo*, No. 1(2), 1995, pp. 74–75.

32. Harris, Ch., "Novie russkie menshinstva: statisticheskoe obozrenie [perevod s angliyskogo]", *Evraziyskoye soobshchestvo: ekonomika, politika, bezopasnost'*, No. 2, 1995, p. 44.

33. *Megapolis-Express*, 02.02.94.

34. Gosudarstvennay Duma Federalnogo Sobraniya Rossiyskoy Federatsii, Komitet po delam Sodruzhestva Nezavisimikh Gosudarstv i svyazyam s sootechestvennikami, Spravka o polozhenii v Kazakhstane, Moscow [No publisher], 1995.

35. Harris, Ch., "Novie russkie menshinstva", p. 53.

36. Abdigaliev, B., "Russkie v Kazakhstane", p. 76.

37. "Privitization Decree Leaves State with Controlling Role", *BBC Monitoring Service: Former USSR*, 14.05.92.

38. *Rossiyskaya gazeta*, 05.06.93.

39. *See*: Dixon, A., *Kazakhstan: Political Reform and Economic Development*, London: Royal Institute of International Affairs, 1994.

40. Yazkova, A., Lafitskiy, V., "Analiz konstituciy sredneaziatskogo regiona i praktika mezhnacionalnikh otnosheniy v Respublike Kazakhstan", p. 12.

41. Kozhokin, E. M., ed., *Kazakhstan: realii i perspektivy nezavisimogo razvitiya*, Moscow: RISI, 1995, p. 32.

42. Ibid., pp. 30–32.

43. *Kazakhstanskaya pravda*, 28.05.97.

44. For example, in ferrous and nonferrous metallurgy production continuously fell in 1993–1994. In 1995 it managed to regain some ground, which, however, fell far short of the recovery of the level of production in the last years of the USSR. *See*: *Kazakhstan: Transition of the State, A World Bank Country Study*, Washington: World Bank, 1997, p. 226.

45. Boroday, A., "Ray Nazarbayeva", *Zavtra*, No. 13(174), 1997.

46. "Russian Minister Responds to President Nazarbayev's Remarks", *BBC Monitoring Service: Former USSR*, 22.05.97.

47. Kozhokin, E. M., ed., *Kazakhstan: realii i perspektivy nezavisimogo razvitiya*, p. 31.

48. *Izvestiya*, 13.04.94.

49. Gosudarstvennay Duma Federalnogo Sobraniya Rossiyskoy Federatsii, Komitet po delam Sodruzhestva Nezavisimikh Gosudarstv i svyazyam s sootechestvennikami, Spravka o polozhenii v Kazakhstane, Moscow [No publisher], 1995.

50. Federal'naya Migratsionnaya Sluzhba Rossii, O rabote migratsionnoy sluzhby posol'stva Rossiyskoy Federatsii v Respublike Kazakhstan v 1994 godu, Doc. No. 722, Moscow [No publisher], 13.04.95, p. 14.

51. *Nezavisimaya gazeta*, 02.04.94.

52. Zatulin, K., "Otchet ob itogakh poezdki gruppy deputatov Federal'nogo Sobraniya, nablyudavshikh za vyborami v Verkhovniy Sovet Respubliki Kazakhstan", Doc. No. 316/333, Moscow [No publisher], 01.04.94, p. 4.

53. *Nezavisimaya gazeta*, 27.11.93.

54. Gosudarstvennay Duma Federalnogo Sobraniya Rossiyskoy Federatsii, Komitet po delam Sodruzhestva Nezavisimikh Gosudarstv i svyazyam s sootechestvennikami, Spravka o polozhenii v Kazakhstane, Moscow [No publisher], 1995.

55. *Megapolis-Express*, 02.02.94.

56. *Nezavisimaya gazeta*, 02.04.94.

57. Gosudarstvennaya Duma Federal'nogo Sobraniya Rossiyskoy Federatsii, Stenogramma parlamentskikh slushaniy Komiteta po delam Sodruzhestva Nezavisimykh Gosudarstv i svyazyam s sootechestvennikami "O rossiysko-kazakhstanskikh otnosheniyakh", Moscow [No publisher], 18.04.95, p. 38.

58. Abdigaliev, B., "Russkie v Kazakhstane", p. 76.

59. Bakaev, L., "Mezhetnicheskie otnosheniya v Kazakhstane", p. 17.

60. *Nezavisimaya gazeta*, 02.04.94.

61. Gosudarstvennaya Duma Federal'nogo Sobraniya Rossiyskoy Federatsii, Stenogramma parlamentskikh slushaniy Komiteta po delam Sodruzhestva

Nezavisimykh Gosudarstv i svyazyam s sootechestvennikami "O rossiysko-kazakhstanskikh otnosheniyakh", Moscow [No publisher], 18.04.95, p. 64.

62. *Nezavisimaya gazeta*, 15.03.94.

63. *Segodnya*, 11.03.94.

64. Zatulin, K., "Otchet ob itogakh poezdki gruppy deputatov Federal'nogo Sobraniya, nablyudavshikh za vyborami v Verkhovniy Sovet Respubliki Kazakhstan", Doc. No. 316/333, Moscow [No publisher], 01.04.94, pp. 1–3.

65. Federal'naya Migratsionnaya Sluzhba Rossii, O rabote migratsionnoy sluzhby posol'stva Rossiyskoy Federatsii v Respublike Kazakhstan v 1994 godu, Doc. No. 722, Moscow [No publisher], 13.04.95, p. 2.

66. Baytenova, N., "Mezhetnicheskaya integratsiya v Kazakhstane: sostoyanie i perspektivy", *Politika*, No. 3, 1995, p. 30.

67. Most of the provisions of the program were later incorporated into Nazarbayev's brochure "Ideological Consolidation of the Society as a Condition of Progress of Kazakhstan". *See:* Nazarbayev, N., *Ideynaya konsolidatsiya obshchestva - kak uslovie progressa Kazakhstana*, Almaty: Kazakhstan - XXI vek, 1993.

68. Zaslavskaya, M., "Programma Soyuza Narodnoe edinstvo Kazakhstana (pervonachal'nyy proekt)", *Politicheskie partii i obschestvenyye ob'edineniya Kazakhstana na sovremennom etape razvitiya*, Almaty: KISI, 1994, pp. 208–211.

69. For ethnic-geographical division of Kazakhstan see the Map A.3 in Appendix.

70. "'Russia' TV Says Russians Still Emigrating from Kazakhstan", *BBC Monitoring Service: Former USSR*, 03.01.94; *Megapolis-Express*, 02.02.94.

71. Khroustalev, M., *Tsentral'naya Aziya vo vneshney politike Rossii*, Moscow: MGIMO, 1994, p. 34.

72. Gosudarstvennaya Duma Federal'nogo Sobraniya Rossiyskoy Federatsii, Stenogramma parlamentskikh slushaniy Komiteta po delam Sodruzhestva Nezavisimykh Gosudarstv i svyazyam s sootechestvennikami "O rossiysko-kazakhstanskikh otnosheniyakh", Moscow [No publisher], 18.04.95, p. 54.

73. Federal'naya Migratsionnaya Sluzhba Rossii, O rabote migratsionnoy sluzhby posol'stva Rossiyskoy Federatsii v Respublike Kazakhstan v 1994 godu, Doc. No. 722, Moscow [No publisher], 13.04.95, pp. 3–4.

74. Gosudarstvennay Duma Federalnogo Sobraniya Rossiyskoy Federatsii, Komitet po delam Sodruzhestva Nezavisimikh Gosudarstv i svyazyam s sootechestvennikami, Spravka o polozhenii v Kazakhstane, Moscow [No publisher], 1995.

75. *Kazakhstanskaya pravda*, 07.11.97.

76. *Kazakhstanskaya pravda*, 28.05.97.

77. Gosudarstvennaya Duma Federal'nogo Sobraniya Rossiyskoy Federatsii, Stenogramma parlamentskikh slushaniy Komiteta po delam Sodruzhestva Nezavisimykh Gosudarstv i svyazyam s sootechestvennikami "O rossiysko-kazakhstanskikh otnosheniyakh", Moscow [No publisher], 18.04.95, pp. 4, 54.

78. Federal'naya Migratsionnaya Sluzhba Rossii, O rabote migratsionnoy sluzhby posol'stva Rossiyskoy Federatsii v Respublike Kazakhstan v 1994 godu, Doc. No. 722, Moscow [No publisher], 13.04.95, pp. 10–11.

79. *Izvestiya*, 15.06.94.

80. Nazarbayev, N., "Za mir i soglasie v nashem obshchem dome, Doklad na pervoy sessii Assamblei narodov Kazakhstana, Almaty, 24 March 1995", *Kazakhstan i mirovoe soobshchestvo*, No. 1(2), 1995, pp. 8, 16.

81. Gosudarstvennay Duma Federalnogo Sobraniya Rossiyskoy Federatsii, Komitet po delam Sodruzhestva Nezavisimikh Gosudarstv i svyazyam s

sootechestvennikami, Spravka o polozhenii v Kazakhstane, Moscow [No publisher], 1995.

82.   Federal'naya Migratsionnaya Sluzhba Rossii, O rabote migratsionnoy sluzhby posol'stva Rossiyskoy Federatsii v Respublike Kazakhstan v 1994 godu, Doc. No. 722, Moscow [No publisher], 13.04.95, pp. 3–4.

83.   Galiev, A., "Etnodemograficheskie i etnomigratsionnyye protsessy v Kazakhstane", Evraziyskoye soobshchestvo: ekonomika, politika, bezopasnost', No. 2, 1995, p. 61.

84.   Gosudarstvennay Duma Federalnogo Sobraniya Rossiyskoy Federatsii, Komitet po delam Sodruzhestva Nezavisimikh Gosudarstv i svyazyam s sootechestvennikami, Spravka o polozhenii v Kazakhstane, Moscow [No publisher], 1995.

85.   Information was provided by Merhat Sharipzhan from RFE/RL Kazakh Broadcasting Service with reference to Radio Free Europe/Radio Liberty's Bureau in Aqmola and Kazakh State Agency on Statistics.

86.   Federal'naya Migratsionnaya Sluzhba Rossii, O rabote migratsionnoy sluzhby posol'stva Rossiyskoy Federatsii v Respublike Kazakhstan v 1994 godu, Doc. No. 722, Moscow [No publisher], 13.04.95, pp. 15–16; Ribakovskiy, L., "Migratsionniy obmen naseleniem mezhdu Centralnoy Aziey i Rossiey", Rossiya i musulmanskiy mir, Bulleten referativno-analiticheskoy informaacii, No. 12(42), Moscow: INION, 1995, p. 37.

87.   Arenov, M., Kalmykov, S., "Sovremennaya yazikovaya situatsiya v Respublike Kazakhstan", p. 49.

88.   Federal'naya Migratsionnaya Sluzhba Rossii, O rabote migratsionnoy sluzhby posol'stva Rossiyskoy Federatsii v Respublike Kazakhstan v 1994 godu, Doc. No. 722, Moscow [No publisher], 13.04.95, pp. 15–16.

89.   Arenov, M., Kalmykov, S., "Sovremennaya yazikovaya situatsiya v Respublike Kazakhstan", p. 49.

90.   Other respondents named different modes of behaviour or had difficulties in answereing the question. Kozhokin, E. M., ed., Kazakhstan: realii i perspektivy nezavisimogo razvitiya, p. 277].

91.   RFE/RL Daily Report, No. 153, 12.08.92

92.   Zaslavskaya, M., "Ustav Respublikanskogo Obschestvennogo Slavyanskogo Dvizheniya 'Lad'", Politicheskie partii i obschestvennie obiedineniya Kazakhstana na sovremennom etape razvitiya, pp. 217–219.

93.   Zaslavskaya, M., Politicheskie partii i obschestvennie obiedineniya Kazakhstana na sovremennom etape razvitiya, p. 32.

94.   "Russian Organisation Launched in Alma-Ata", BBC Monitoring Service: Former USSR, 27.11.92.

95.   "Slavs in East Kazakhstan Threaten Secession", BBC Monitoring Service: Former USSR, 09.12.92.

96.   "Nazarbayev Answers Viewers' Questions on TV Phone-in", BBC Monitoring Service: Former USSR, 11.12.92.

97.   Megapolis-Express, 28.10.92.

98.   Gosudarstvennaya Duma Federal'nogo Sobraniya Rossiyskoy Federatsii, Stenogramma parlamentskikh slushaniy Komiteta po delam Sodruzhestva Nezavisimykh Gosudarstv i svyazyam s sootechestvennikami "O rossiysko-kazakhstanskikh otnosheniyakh", Moscow [No publisher], 18.04.95, p. 126.

99.   "Rasporyazhenie Prezidenta Rossiyskoy Federatsii o voprosakh zaschity prav i interesov rossiyskikh grazhdan za predelami Rossiyskoy Federatsii", Diplomaticheskiy vestnik, Nos. 1–2, 1993, p. 8.

100. Federal'naya Migratsionnaya Sluzhba Rossii, O rabote migratsionnoy sluzhby posol'stva Rossiyskoy Federatsii v Respublike Kazakhstan v 1994 godu, Doc. No. 722, Moscow [No publisher], 13.04.95, p. 18.

101. "Leader of Russian Community Arrested in Northern Kazakhstan", *BBC Monitoring Service: Former USSR*, 19.04.94.

102. Zayavlenie Komiteta Gosudarstvennoy Dumy po delam SNG i svyazyam s sootechestvennikami v svyazi s arestom grazhdanina Rossiyskoy Federatsii B. F. Suprunyuka 12 aprelya 1994 g. v g. Petropavlovske, Moscow [No publisher], 1994.

103. Gosudarstvennaya Duma Federal'nogo Sobraniya Rossiyskoy Federatsii, Stenogramma parlamentskikh slushaniy Komiteta po delam Sodruzhestva Nezavisimykh Gosudarstv i svyazyam s sootechestvennikami "O rossiysko-kazakhstanskikh otnosheniyakh", Moscow [No publisher], 18.04.95, p. 12.

104. Ibid., p. 11.

105. "Problems Remain in Russo-Kazakh Citizenship Accord", *BBC Monitoring Service: Former USSR*, 31.05.97.

106. Reuters News Service, 01.11.94.

107. Reuters News Service, 03.11.94.

108. "Russia Concerned over Arrest of Cossack Chieftain in Kazakhstan", *BBC Monitoring Service: Former USSR*, 16.11.95.

109. "Duma Voices Concern over Human Rights in Kazakhstan", *BBC Monitoring Service: Former USSR*, 20.11.95.

110. "Cossack Chief Sentenced to Three Months in Prison", *BBC Monitoring Service: Former USSR*, 23.11.95; "Russia Expresses Regret at Court Sentence on Cossack Chief", *BBC Monitoring Service: Former USSR*, 23.11.95.

111. "Opasnost' zakliuchaetsya ne v voyne a v samoobmane, kotoriy opravdyvaet nereshitel'nost' rossiyskoy vlasti", *Shturm*, No. 3, 1996, p. 31.

112. "Cossack Council of Atamans ends session in Moscow", *BBC Monitoring Service: Former USSR*, 17.08.92.

113. "Cossack Atamans' Claims to Autonomy in Kazakhstan are a 'Provocation'", *BBC Monitoring Service: Former USSR*, 15.08.92.

114. Ukaz Prezidenta Rossiyskoy Federatsii o reformirovanii voennikh struktur pogranichnikh i vnutrennikh voysk na territorii Severo-Kavkazskogo regiona Rossiyskoy Federatsii i gosudarsvennoy podderzhke kazachestva, No. 341, Moscow [No publisher], 15.03.93.

115. "Yeltsin Decree on Cossacks Sparks off More Debate on Attitudes to Russia", *BBC Monitoring Service: Former USSR*, 17.04.93.

116. Abdirov, M., Abdirova B., "Kazachestvo v kontekste sovremennikh kazakhstansko-rossiyskikh otnosheniy", *Kazakhstan i mirovoe soobschestvo*, No. 2(3), 1995, p. 59.

117. Kozhokin, E. M., ed., *Kazakhstan: realii i perspektivy nezavisimogo razvitiya*, p. 209.

118. Ayaganov, B., Kuandikov, A., Baymagambetov, S., "Etnopoliticheskaya situatsiya v Kazakhstane: regionalniy opit," *Evraziyskoe Soobschestvo*, No. 4–5, 1995, p. 7.

119. *RFE/RL Report*, No. 67, 08.04.94; Kozhokin, E. M., ed., *Kazakhstan: realii i perspektivy nezavisimogo razvitiya*, p. 210.

120. Ayaganov, B., Kuandikov, A., Baymagambetov, S., "Etnopoliticheskaya situatsiya v Kazakhstane", p. 7; Abdirov, M., Abdirova, B., "Kazachestvo v kontekste sovremennikh kazakhstansko-rossiyskikh otnosheniy", p. 59.

121. Abdirov, M., Abdirova, B., "Kazachestvo v kontekste sovremennikh kazakhstansko-rossiyskikh otnosheniy", p. 62.

122. Gosudarstvennaya Duma Federal'nogo Sobraniya Rossiyskoy Federatsii, Stenogramma parlamentskikh slushaniy Komiteta po delam Sodruzhestva Nezavisimykh Gosudarstv i svyazyam s sootechestvennikami "O rossiysko-kazakhstanskikh otnosheniyakh", Moscow [No publisher], 18.04.95, pp. 127–128.

123. "Kazakhstan's Cossacks to Meet to Discuss Status", *BBC Monitoring Service: Former USSR*, 29.03.94.

124. Abdirov, M., Abdirova, B., "Kazachestvo v kontekste sovremennikh kazakhstansko-rossiyskikh otnosheniy", p. 62.

125. "Cossack Group Given Official Status by Kazakh Authorities", *BBC Monitoring Service: Former USSR*, 12.07.94.

126. "Kazakh Justice Minister Suspends Cossack Society, Rutskoy Alleges Discrimination", *BBC Monitoring Service: Former USSR*, 08.12.94.

127. *Izvestiya*, 16.11.93.

128. Ibid.

129. Reuters News Service, 26.11.93.

130. *Megapolis-Express*, 02.02.94.

131. "Russian Foreign Minister Visits, Discusses Cooperation And Tajikistan", *BBC Monitoring Service: Former USSR*, 19.11.93.

132. "'Over to The Voter' Presents Zhirinovskiy and Party of Russian Unity and Accord", *BBC Monitoring Service: Former USSR*, 26.11.93.

133. "Foreign Ministry Criticizes Zhirinovskiy for Remarks on Former Soviet States", *BBC Monitoring Service: Former USSR*, 30.11.93.

134. "President Nazarbayev Visits Maastricht Conference", *BBC Monitoring Service: Former USSR*, 04.12.93.

135. "Foreign Ministry Criticizes Zhirinovskiy for Remarks on Former Soviet States", *BBC Monitoring Service: Former USSR*, 30.11.93.

136. "Russian Premier Calls on Ethnic Russians Not to Heed Provocation", *BBC Monitoring Service: Former USSR*, 30.12.93.

137. Federal'naya Migratsionnaya Sluzhba Rossii, O rabote migratsionnoy sluzhby posol'stva Rossiyskoy Federatsii v Respublike Kazakhstan v 1994 godu, Doc. No. 722, Moscow [No publisher], 13.04.95, p. 6.

138. *Nezavisimaya gazeta*, 06.01.94.

139. Zatulin, K., "Otchet ob itogakh poezdki gruppy deputatov Federal'nogo Sobraniya, nablyudavshikh za vyborami v Verkhovniy Sovet Respubliki Kazakhstan", Doc. No. 316/333, Moscow [No publisher], 01.04.94, pp. 1–3.

140. Analysis of the Nazarbayev's concept of Eurasian Union is given in Chapter 4, his concessions on military and strategic issues are described in Chapter 5.

141. "Memorandum ob osnovnikh principakh resheniya voprosov, sviyazannikh s grazhdanstvom i pravovim statusom grazhdan Respubliki Kazakhstan, postoyanno prozhivaiuschikh na territorii Rossiyskoy Federatsii, I grazhdan Rossiyskoy Federatsii, postoyanno prozhivaiuschikh na territorii Respubliki Kazakhstan", *Kazakhstansko-Rossiyskie otnosheniya, 1991–1995 godi, Sbornic dokumentov i materialov*, Moscow: Posol'stvo Respubliki Kazakhstan v Rossiyskoy Federatsii, 1995, pp. 160–161.

142. "Problems Remain in Russo-Kazakh Citizenship Accord", *BBC Monitoring Service: Former USSR*, 31.05.97.

143. Ibid.

144. "Russia to Persuade Kazakhstan to Sign Dual Citizenship Agreement", *BBC Monitoring Service: Former USSR*, 02.06.94.

145. Gosudarstvennaya Duma Federal'nogo Sobraniya Rossiyskoy Federatsii, Stenogramma parlamentskikh slushaniy Komiteta po delam Sodruzhestva Nezavisimykh Gosudarstv i svyazyam s sootechestvennikami "O rossiysko-kazakhstanskikh otnosheniyakh", Moscow [No publisher], 18.04.95, p. 41.

146. *RFE/RL Report*, No.224, 29.11.94.

147. Kotov, A. "Edinoe grazhdanstvo – konstitucionnaya osnova ravnopraviya v Respublike Kazakhstan", *Politika*, No. 3, 1995, pp. 21–23.

148. Federal'naya Migratsionnaya Sluzhba Rossii, O rabote migratsionnoy sluzhby posol'stva Rossiyskoy Federatsii v Respublike Kazakhstan v 1994 godu, Doc. No. 722, Moscow [No publisher], 13.04.95, p. 7.

149. "Dogovor mezhdu Respublikoy Kazakhstan I Rossiyskoy Federaciey o pravovom statuse grazhdan Rossiyskoy Federatsii, postoyanno prozhivaiuschikh na territorii Respubliki Kazakhstan, i grazhdan Respubliki Kazakhstan, postoyanno prozhivaiuschikh na territorii Rossiyskoy Federatsii", *Kazakhstansko-Rossiyskie otnosheniya, 1991–1995 godi*, pp. 216–221.

150. "Soglashenie mezhdu Respublikoy Kazakhstan I Rossiyskoy Federaciey ob uproschennom poryadke priobreteniya grazhdanstva grazhdanami Rossiyskoy Federatsii, pribivaiuschimi dlya postoyannogo prozhivaniya v Respubliku Kazakhstan, i grazhdanami Respubliki Kazakhstan, pribivaiuschimi dlya postoyannogo prozhivaniya v Rossiyskuiu Federaciu", *Kazakhstansko-Rossiyskie otnosheniya, 1991–1995 godi*, pp. 221–224.

151. Federal'naya Migratsionnaya Sluzhba Rossii, O rabote migratsionnoy sluzhby posol'stva Rossiyskoy Federatsii v Respublike Kazakhstan v 1994 godu, Doc. No. 722, Moscow [No publisher], 13.04.95, p. 11.

152. Federal'naya Migratsionnaya Sluzhba Rossii, O rabote migratsionnoy sluzhby posol'stva Rossiyskoy Federatsii v Respublike Kazakhstan v 1994 godu, Doc. No. 722, Moscow [No publisher], 13.04.95, p. 17.

153. Gosudarstvennaya Duma Federal'nogo Sobraniya Rossiyskoy Federatsii, Stenogramma parlamentskikh slushaniy Komiteta po delam Sodruzhestva Nezavisimykh Gosudarstv i svyazyam s sootechestvennikami "O rossiysko-kazakhstanskikh otnosheniyakh", Moscow [No publisher], 18.04.95, p. 46.

154. "Obraschenie k predsedateliu frakcii Agrarnoy Partii Rossii M.I. Lapshinu". Gosudarstvennay Duma Federalnogo Sobraniya Rossiyskoy Federatsii, 04.02.95, Moscow [No publisher], 1995.

155. Gosudarstvennaya Duma Federal'nogo Sobraniya Rossiyskoy Federatsii, Stenogramma parlamentskikh slushaniy Komiteta po delam Sodruzhestva Nezavisimykh Gosudarstv i svyazyam s sootechestvennikami "O rossiysko-kazakhstanskikh otnosheniyakh", Moscow [No publisher], 18.04.95, pp. 39–40, 125.

156. Ibid., pp. 9, 24.

157. Ibid., pp. 18–19, 24–25, 41.

158. *Kazakhstanskaya pravda*, 28.06.97.

159. Nazarbayev's decision showed his particular dislike for contested elections. In the first presidentiaal elections in Kazakhstan on 1 December 1992 he was the only candidate.

160. *See*: Politicheskoye zayavlenie respublikanskogo obschestvennogo slavyanskogo dvizheniya "Lad" o rospuske Verkhovnogo Soveta Respubliki Kazakhstan, Almaty [No publisher], 19.03.95. Russkaya Obschina protestuet, Resoluitsiya obschego sobraniya, Almaty [No publisher], 20.03.95.

161. Gosudarstvennay Duma Federalnogo Sobraniya Rossiyskoy Federatsii, Komitet po delam Sodruzhestva Nezavisimikh Gosudarstv i svyasyam s

sootechestvennikami, Zayavlenie o politicheskom krizise v Kazakhstane, Doc. No. 316/492, Moscow [No publisher], 13.03.95.

162. Zayavlenie russkikh, slavyanskikh i kazachikh organizatsiy po povodu Assamblei narodov Kazakhstana, Almaty [No publisher], 1995.

163. Gosudarstvennaya Duma Federal'nogo Sobraniya Rossiyskoy Federatsii, Stenogramma parlamentskikh slushaniy Komiteta po delam Sodruzhestva Nezavisimykh Gosudarstv i svyazyam s sootechestvennikami "O rossiysko-kazakhstanskikh otnosheniyakh", Moscow [No publisher], 18.04.95, pp. 61–65.

164. Politicheskoye zayavlenie respublikanskogo obschestvennogo slavyanskogo dvizheniya "Lad" o rospuske Verkhovnogo Soveta Respubliki Kazakhstan, Almaty [No publisher], 19.03.95.

165. Nazarbayev, N., "Za mir i soglasie v nashem obschem dome, Doklad na pervoy sessii Assamblei narodov Kazakhstana, sostoyavsheysya v Almaty 24 marta 1995 goda", *Kazakhstan i mirovoe soobschestvo*, No. 1(2), 1995, pp. 9, 13–16.

166. Politicheskoye zayavlenie respublikanskogo obschestvennogo slavyanskogo dvizheniya "Lad" o rospuske Verkhovnogo Soveta Respubliki Kazakhstan, Almaty [No publisher], 19.03.95.

167. Ibid.

168. Otkritoe pismo Presidentu Respubliki Kazakhstan N. A. Nazarbaevu, Almaty [No publisher], 10.04.95.

169. "Russian MPs Urge Kazakh Leader to Move on Russian Language", *BBC Monitoring Service: Former USSR*, 28.04.95.

170. *Segodnya*, 04.05.95.

171. Nazarbayev, N., "Osmislenie proydennogo i dalneyshee demokraticheskoe reformirovanie obschestva, Doklad na vtoroy sessii Assamblei Narodov Kazakhstana", *Politika*, No. 2, 1995, pp. 11–13.

172. *OMRI Daily Report*, No. 170, Part I, 31.08.95; "Opposition Says Referendum Turnout 34%", Result Invalid, *BBC Monitoring Service: Former USSR*, 04.09.95.

173. The U.S. statement said: "On August 1, the Kazakstani government published the final version of its new draft constitution. In the view of democracy and human rights activists in Kazakhstan, the new constitution does not adequately protect civil and human rights. . . . The U.S. and other countries urged Kazakstan to approach the OSCE's Office for Democratic Institutions and Human Rights to solicit technical assistance to bring the draft constitution more closely into line with democratic norms. The U.S. regrets that the government of Kazakstan pressed forward with the 30 August referendum. In view of the predictable and frankly unbelievable Soviet-style results of the 29 April referendum which extended President Nazarbayev's term in office, there is little reason to doubt that official results of the 30 August vote will show the draft constitution winning by a vast overwhelming and equally unbelievable margin. The term extension referendum was a step backward from democracy in Kazakstan. The U.S. regrets that the constitutional referendum is a second step backward from democracy. The U.S. expresses these concerns as a friend of Kazakstan. Democracy is essential to Kazakstan's long-term stability, unity, and prosperity. Kazakstan is a young, multi-ethnic state facing a range of challenges and only participatory government can give Kazakstani citizens the sense of common destiny essential to maintaining political cohesion during a painful political and economic transition. The U.S. government did not send observers to monitor the constitutional referendum on 30 August" (U.S. Disappointed in Constitutional Referendum in Kazakhstan, File ID: 95083103.WWE, USIA Database, 31.08.95).

174. *Konstituciya Respubliki Kazakhstan*, Almaty: Kazakhstan, 1995, pp. 3, 6–7.

175. Ibid.

176. "Kazakh Protest Rally over New Draft Constitution", *BBC Monitoring Service: Former USSR*, 29.07.97.

177. *Moskovskiy Komsomolets*, 24.08.95.

178. Deputies to the upper house, the Senate, were to be elected by province electoral colleges made up of all members of representative bodies of each province. Two senators were to be elected from each province, cities under republic's jurisdiction and the capital. Seven senators were to be appointed by the president. This should have brought the total number of senators to 47. To the lower chamber, the Majilis, 67 deputies were to be elected on the basis of direct voting in electoral districts.

179. *Nezavisimaya gazeta*, 08.12.95.

180. The most outrageous episode took place with Ataman Gunkin, who was abducted by police officers at the headquarters of an election precinct where he came to register (Nezavisimaya gazeta, 03.11.95).

181. Calculation is made on the basis of statistics, provided in Mashanov, M. S., *Sravnitelniy analiz partiynogo aspekta parlamentskikh viborov 1994 i 1995 godov*, Almaty: IRK, 1996, pp. 14–15.

182. "President Nazarbayev Denies Breach of Ethnic Russians' Rights", *BBC Monitoring Service: Former USSR*, 28.10.97

183. "Struktura administratsii Presidenta Respubliki Kazakhstan i perechen dolzhnostnikh lits, obespechivaiuschikh ego deyatelnost", *Kazakhstanskaya pravda*, 10.01.97.

184. "Protest in Moscow about Treatment of Kazakhstan's Russian Population", *BBC Monitoring Service: Former USSR*, 18.09.96.

185. "Russian MPs Concerned about Treatment of Russians in Kazakhstan", *BBC Monitoring Service: Former USSR*, 23.09.96.

186. "Ethnic Russian Activist Found Guilty, but Sentence Lifted", *BBC Monitoring Service: Former USSR*, 23.12.96.

187. *Zavtra*, 27.05.97, 30.06.97, 22.07.97.

188. *Kazakhstanskaya pravda*, 06.11.96.

189. "Russia Warns against Change in Kazakhstan's Language Policy", *BBC Monitoring Service: Former USSR*, 23.11.96.

190. "Zakon Respubliki Kazakhstan o Yazikakh v Respublike Kazakhstan", *Kazakhstanskaya pravda*, 15.07.97, p. 2.

191. *RFE/RL Newsline*, Vol. 1, No. 101, Part I, 22.08.97.

192. Tables A.6 and A.7 (Appendix) contain some economic indicators of Kazakhstan's agricultural and industrial development from 1985–1995.

193. Nazarbayev, N., "Kazakhstan – 2030: protsvetanie, bezopasnost i uluchshenie blagosostoyaniya kazakhstantsev, Poslanie Presidenta strani narodu Kazakhstana", *Kazakhstanskaya pravda*, 11.10.97, p. 8.

194. *Kazakhstanskaya pravda*, 11.07.97.

195. *Russia*, No. 19, 1994, p. 4; *Kazakhstanskaya pravda*, 28.05.97.

196. Information was provided by Merhat Sharipzhan from RFE/RL Kazakh Broadcasting Service with reference to Radio Free Europe/Radio Liberty's Bureau in Aqmola and Kazakh State Agency on Statistics.

197. Tatimov, M., "Vliyanie demograficheskikh processov na vnutripoliticheskuiu stabilnost Respubliki Kazakhstan", *Politika*, No. 5, 1995, p. 22.

198. Nazarbayev, N., "Kazakhstan – 2030", pp. 8, 14–15.

199. Galiev, A., "Etnodemograficheskie i etnomigratsionnie processi v Kazakhstane", p. 61.

200. Federal'naya Migratsionnaya Sluzhba Rossii, O rabote migratsionnoy sluzhby posol'stva Rossiyskoy Federatsii v Respublike Kazakhstan v 1994 godu, Doc. No. 722, Moscow [No publisher], 13.04.95, pp. 10–11.

201. Baytenova, N., "Mezhetnicheskaya integraciya v Kazakhstane", p. 29.

202. Boroday, A., "Ray Nazarbaeyva", *Zavtra*, No.11, 1997.

203. *Kazakhstanskaya pravda*, 05.07.97.

204. "Opasnost' zakliuchaetsya ne v voyne a v samoobmane, kotoriy opravdyvaet nereshitel'nost' rossiyskoy vlasti", *Shturm*, pp. 33–34.

205. *Zavtra*, 22.04.97, 05.05.97.

206. "Yeltsin Proposes Accord on Ethnic Russians in Kazakhstan", *BBC Monitoring Service: Former USSR*, 27.11.96.

207. Reuters News Service, 16.04.97.

208. Reuters News Service, 16.04.97.

209. "Russia Denies Breaking Accords with Kazakhstan over Border Guards", *BBC Monitoring Service: Former USSR*, 28.03.97.

210. "Cossacks Reject Protests at Their Role on Kazakh-Russian Border", *BBC Monitoring Service: Former USSR*, 28.03.97.

211. Reuters News Service, 25.09.97.

212. *Kazakhstanskaya pravda*, 17.04.97.

213. "Russian Minister Responds to President Nazarbayev's Remarks", *BBC Monitoring Service: Former USSR*, 22.05.97.

214. *Kazakhstanskaya pravda*, 28.05.97.

215. "Russian Minister Responds to President Nazarbayev's Remarks", *BBC Monitoring Service: Former USSR*, 22.05.97.

216. Tuleyev, A., "SNG: blef ili integraciya? Beseda s Aleksandrom Prokhanovim i Valentinom Chikinim", *Zavtra*, No. 21, 1997.

217. "Kazakh President Warns of Possible Threat from Russia", *BBC Monitoring Service: Former USSR*, 30.06.97.

218. *Kommersant-Daily*, 06.06.97.

219. *Kazakhstanskaya pravda*, 28.06.97.

220. *Kazakhstanskaya pravda*, 09.09.97.

221. *Kazakhstanskaya pravda*, 02.10.97.

222. *Kazakhstanskaya pravda*, 07.10.97.

4

Russian and Kazakh Approaches to CIS Integration

Relations between Russia and Kazakhstan in the post-Soviet era very much depended on their interaction within the multilateral CIS framework. The importance of this element in Russian-Kazakh relations can hardly be exaggerated. The future of the CIS will play a crucial role in determining which way the whole political situation on the Eurasian continent will go, whether it will develop along an integrative path towards formation of a new supranational entity or move towards greater separation and consolidation of national states. The positions of Moscow and Almaty as major players in the CIS are therefore paramount not only for their bilateral relations (as an indicator of the level of cooperation between them), but for the future geopolitical architecture of the Eurasian mainland.

Kazakhstan's attitude to the CIS was predetermined by its very large dependence on economic relations with other CIS states. According to expert assessments, in a fully isolated situation Kazakhstan could manufacture only 27% of the products it manufactured in 1991, whereas the figure for Russia would be 64.5%. Kazakhstan's economy could produce only 42% of the consumer goods sold there.[1] Before independence Kazakhstan ran regular trade deficits with the rest of the USSR, which in 1990 reached 7 billion roubles.[2] Besides, in Soviet times Kazakhstan's economy relied heavily on subsidies from the USSR central government, which, according to the *Economist*, in 1991 covered 23% of its budget.[3] Thus Kazakhstan's immediate transition to economic self-reliance was not possible even in theory. Consequently, by the need to maintain the system of CIS economic interrelationships as much as possible and utilise its benefits to restructure and modernise Kazakhstan's economy shaped Nazarbayev's diplomatic tactics.

Even before the collapse of the USSR, Nazarbayev persistently insisted on preserving economic union, while actively pursuing the dismantling of the

Union's central political structures, which limited Kazakhstan's sovereignty. From the very first days after dissolution of the USSR, Nazarbayev stood firmly for economic integration within the CIS. At the CIS heads of state meeting in Moscow on 16 January 1992 he suggested renouncing import restrictions and restrictive licensing of products intended for industrial and technical purposes, and repealing taxes on imports and exports in transit through CIS states.[4] Some other CIS members greeted these proposal unenthusiastically, especially Ukraine, and even Yeltsin's support failed to secure their acceptance.[5]

When the CIS summit in Minsk on 14 February 1992 ended without any major breakthroughs in the economic areas, Nazarbayev did not conceal his frustration. In an interview immediately after the summit he criticised "paralysis of economic links, closure of trade borders by way of licences and quotas, economic disintegration", and put forward a program of economic integration:

1. Setting up "a good and powerful coordinating centre ... perhaps an assembly like the European Parliament".
2. Creation of a banking union for those within the rouble currency zone.
3. Coordination of pricing policy for the basic sectors of economy, especially for power and fuel; examine coordination of monetary and credit procedures, investment procedures, and so forth.
4. Lifting all customs barriers.
5. Harmonising legislation to create a normal environment for businessmen.[6]

Explaining his position on CIS integration during his visit to Austria several days later, Nazarbayev said that each CIS member should be politically independent and free, but the CIS should remain a single economic area similar to the European Community.[7]

The program proposed by Nazarbayev was very pragmatic and directed not so much at strategic objectives of CIS integration, but at meeting Kazakhstan's immediate economic needs. The idea of creating a powerful coordinating centre like the European parliament was devoid of logic, because the European parliament never was and still is not such a coordination centre. Thus, Nazarbayev proposed a largely symbolic supranational body that would be unable to limit Kazakhstan's sovereignty in any way or impose any guidelines, which Kazakhstan itself was not prepared to follow. On the other hand, the proposals to create a banking union and coordinate monetary and credit procedures reflected Nazarbayev's desire to have a say in decisions on rouble emission. After the collapse of the USSR, the emission of roubles remained in Moscow's hands, and it could supply other republics with cash at its own discretion. In the first quarter of 1992 the Russian Central Bank raised the percentage emission allocated to Russia from 66% in 1990–1991 to 80%. It also refused to accept bills of exchange or cheques from other rouble zone states.[8] Nazarbayev obviously hoped that the introduction of a coordinating structure such as a banking union would impose some restrictions on Moscow and perhaps subordinate it to the combined will of the other CIS states.

Russia in its turn was extremely dissatisfied with the policies of central banks of other CIS states, including Kazakhstan. Finding themselves free of Moscow's control, they embarked on unrestrained non-cash emission of roubles. Russia was the only republic which printed roubles, but all central banks in the rouble zone could issue rouble credits. Local central banks lent to local commercial banks, commercial banks lent to local companies, and the latter used the money to buy imports, mostly from Russia itself. As a result, this mass of credit roubles ended up in Russian exporters' bank accounts. Russia was immediately awash with devalued money, which was spurring inflation, while massive amounts of goods and resources were flowing out to other CIS. Russia countered by introducing restrictions on exports of fuel and energy resources, and on some essential raw materials and manufactures. This limited Kazakhstan's ability to buy the resources and goods it needed freely from Russia. Hence, Nazarbayev's proposal to lift all customs barriers.

Moscow's decision to free fuel prices was very painful for Kazakhstan. These were much below world market prices, and the Soviet economy in general and Kazakhstan's in particular had become dependent on cheap energy and fuel. Freeing prices overnight Would have a destabilising effect on Kazakhstan's economy, hence Nazarbayev's proposal to coordinate pricing policy for the basic sectors of the economy, especially power and fuel. Almaty pleaded with Moscow to postpone freeing oil prices until mid-summer, when most of the agricultural work would be over, but Moscow agreed only to a one-month delay, until mid-May.[9] Kazakhstan then mobilised Belarus, Kyrgyzstan, Moldova, Uzbekistan and Ukraine to issue a joint appeal to Russia to delay the freeing of oil prices until October, when sowing and harvesting would be over.[10]

At the meeting of Central Asian states in Bishkek on 22–23 April 1992, Russia was criticised for failing to consult its CIS partners on monetary policy such as price formation and meeting their increased needs for roubles.[11] Following the meeting Nazarbayev announced that his "confidence in the stability of the Commonwealth had decreased of late", and said he was dissatisfied over progress in establishing joint cooperation bodies, putting the blame on Russia and Ukraine.[12] At that time, reports on Kazakhstan's intention to introduce its own currency began to circulate in the media. In an article that appeared in several Kazakhstan newspapers on 17 May, Nazarbayev was quoted as saying that Kazakhstan might have to introduce its own currency "without waiting for economic stabilisation". He reportedly argued that in the medium term preserving the rouble could jeopardise Kazakhstan's economic development and that the behaviour of "the countries in the rouble zone is hardly predictable and does not respect their partners' needs".[13]

These rumours were not without foundation. In early 1992 Nazarbayev signed a top secret decree on preparing for the introduction of Kazakhstan's own currency. Nazarbayev himself approved the design, and the master was kept in a safe in a British bank. An agreement was reached with a British company to print the money promptly when ordered.[14] But Kazakhstan had as yet no intention of introducing its own currency. Staying in the rouble zone gave some substantial advantages, especially the ability to buy goods and services from Russia in excess of goods and services sold to Russia by Kazakhstan. The rouble zone in fact constituted a new form of Russian subsidy to other republics of the former USSR. While the system existed, Nazarbayev wanted to take full advantage of it. But many in the Russian government started to voice objections and insist that the rouble zone be abolished. Only then did Nazarbayev order 20% of the Kazakh currency to be printed, "just in case".

In Russia influential Eurasianist-orient forces, insisted that the rouble zone should be preserved, to facilitate the integration process within the CIS. Since the parliament controlled the Russian Central Bank, it could exercise strong leverage over Russian monetary policy. There were two solutions to the monetary problem: either Russian control of currency over all participants in the rouble zone, or introduction of national currencies by individual CIS countries. The Russian Central Bank obviously tried to explore the option of maintaining the rouble zone without disadvantage to the Russian economy. In an attempt to realise this alternative it was agreed at the meeting of CIS central banks in Bishkek on 7–8 May to create an Interbank Coordinating Council of the rouble zone states' central banks. The council was charged to coordinate monetary policies, agree limits on budget deficits, and set the level of currency emission each quarter.[15] At the Tashkent summit on 15 May, member-states agreed to make mutual repayments of a proportion of their debts where possible, and introduced tougher penalties for nonpayment. But the summit failed to agree on guidelines for the functioning of states in the rouble zone or on the introduction of national currencies.[16] On 21 May at a conference in Tashkent, the CIS national banks consented to coordinate their efforts, exchange information, limit issuing credits to republican governments and commercial banks, and make a gradual transition to a unified currency rate. Guidelines for monetary policy in the rouble zone were worked out, to be coordinated with member governments and endorsed at the next meeting of the Interbank Coordinating Council.[17]

None of the decisions adopted in May produced substantial results. By 1 June 1992 the other CIS republics' debt to Russia reached 214.7 billion roubles and was growing rapidly.[18] On 11 June 1992, First Deputy Prime Minister Gaidar told a government meeting that former Soviet republics that chose to retain the rouble would have to respect "very tough terms . . . in particular, Russian control over their central banks". Moreover, Gaidar signaled that Moscow was ready to help states that wanted to introduce their own currencies. But the meeting failed to agree on crucial procedures to establish separate currencies.[19] On 21 June, a presidential decree on protection of Russia's monetary system established account settling on reciprocal goods deliveries between Russia and other countries in the rouble zone in accordance with the principle of balanced accounts, ruling out any possibility of automatic crediting of deliveries. The Russian Central Bank was instructed to hold talks with states intending to stay in the rouble zone to provide for coordinating economic policy.[20] The new system provided that other CIS republics could make purchases in Russia only through special accounts at the Russian Central Bank. The system was designed to shield Russia from uncontrolled granting of credit by creating a regime under which CIS countries could buy in Russia only with roubles earned from their own sales, or credits legally granted by the Russian Central Bank. The decision de facto split the rouble zone into subzones with roubles of different values. Thus the rouble in Kazakhstan was no longer equivalent in value to the rouble in Russia. The arrangement drew a sharp reaction from the Central Banks of Kazakhstan, Ukraine and Belarus, which demanded an extraordinary meeting of the Interbank Coordinating Council.[21] But Moscow refused to comply with other CIS members' demands. The first serious crack appeared in the rouble zone.

In August 1992 Nazarbayev proposed a new package of initiatives on economic integration within the CIS, including:

1. Establishment of a CIS Economic Council
2. Creation of a banking union of rouble zone states
3. Establishment of the rouble as a supranational currency, allowing other republics a say in emission and credit issues
4. Establishment of a CIS Economic Court
5. Strengthening the defence alliance and making it functional
6. Organising the work of the Inter-Parliamentary Assembly.[22]

The initiatives were very reminiscent of those he had advanced in February 1992 and reflected a similar set of economic and political priorities. They were limited and pragmatically oriented toward helping Kazakhstan solve its most acute problem, economic survival in the post-Soviet era, while avoiding any real limitations on its sovereignty. Conversely, they imposed real limitations on Russia's freedom to manoeuvre in economic policy, making it dependent on attitudes in Almaty, Tashkent or Kiev. As the largest country in the CIS, with economic potential far exceeding that of all the other members combined, Russia had no desire to become subordinate to decisions imposed by its smaller partners. No agreement other than acceptance of its own terms would be acceptable to Moscow, and Nazarbayev's proposals were no exception.

Not surprisingly at the CIS summit in Bishkek on 9 October, Russia's position on Nazarbayev's initiatives was very reserved. Yeltsin rejected the idea that other republics should control rouble issuing and credits. When the question of an interstate bank was discussed, he rejected the proposal that each member have one vote.[23] It was decided to refer the interstate bank question to a working group. Russia's Economic Minister Nechaev noted after the summit that creation of a single currency-issuing bank would necessitate a single budget policy, which would infringe the rights of parliaments, and they would never agree to it.[24] Russian officials said they saw the bank's role as a clearing house for interstate payments rather than as a new rouble-zone central bank.[25]

The CIS Economic Council's proposal was watered down and replaced by a coordinating committee with unspecified powers and the decision on it was postponed.

However, the summit reached an important agreement, On the Single Monetary System and Coordinated Credit and Currency Policies of States Which Retain the Rouble as Legal Tender. Nine CIS republics signed the agreement, including Russia and Kazakhstan, but not Ukraine, and declared the rouble the only legal tender in the signatories' territories. Limitations to rouble circulation were declared illegal, and the parties authorised the Central Bank of Russia to control cash and credit issuance pending establishment of an Interstate Bank. Credit quotas were to be fixed by the Interbank Coordinating Council. Russia would provide the signatories' central banks with adequate amounts of cash.[26] Moscow gave its CIS partners two-and-a-half months to determine their monetary and credit policy and reserved the right to raise the question of making the rouble Russia's currency only, unless this demand was met.[27] For Nazarbayev this outcome was unpromising. The major objectives of his integration policy had not been achieved.

When on 14 December 1992 Viktor Chernomyrdin was elected Russian prime minister, Nazarbayev's hopes of preserving the rouble zone were revived. In contrast to the young and liberal-minded Gaidar, Chernomyrdin was an experienced old-school Soviet bureaucrat and a personal acquaintance of Nazarbayev. On the day after Chernomyrdin's election, Nazarbayev spoke in an interview on *Ostankino* television channel in favour of a smaller and tighter Commonwealth, comprising only the states which supported the rouble zone and joined the defence alliance.[28] During Chernomyrdin's visit to Alma-Ata on 19 December, Nazarbayev exploited their personal relationship. He asked Chernomyrdin if Kazakhstan could count on staying in the rouble zone, and Chernomyrdin promised that Kazakhstan could "definitely stay in the rouble space".[29] Nazarbayev agreed to send an official delegation to Moscow to draft an accord on payments and deliveries of oil, nonferrous metals and timber.[30] Knowing Chernomyrdin's background in the Russian oil and gas industry, Nazarbayev wanted to use his interest in Kazakhstan's energy resources to facilitate agreements in other fields. Both agreed to proceed with plans to create CIS banking and economic unions, whatever the results of the next Commonwealth summit.[31] During the negotiations in Moscow on 24 December, Russia and Kazakhstan signed several documents, including agreements on cooperation in the power and energy industry, and on procedures for debt settlement for 1992 and implementation of intergovernment credit; a protocol on the meeting between the leaderships of Russia's and Kazakhstan's national banks; a protocol on implementing accords in monetary and credit relations; and an agreement on mutual deliveries of production and technical goods and cooperation between the two countries' metallurgical industries in 1993.[32] Soon afterwards, Chernomyrdin made another gesture of accommodation to Nazarbayev. On 9 January 1993 he arranged a representative meeting in Omsk between Russian and Kazakh governmental delegations with participation of the heads of adjacent provinces of both countries. The Kazakhstan delegation was led by Prime Minister Tereshchenko. The sides agreed to coordinate their actions in pricing, monetary, credit, fiscal and customs policy, and support for entrepreneurial activity. The joint communiqué emphasised that "closeness of the two countries and long-term cooperation of their economies are a solid basis for strengthening integration processes and helping to overcome difficulties of the transitional period".[33] After the meeting Tereshchenko stressed the significance of economic cooperation and expressed the hope that customs barriers between the two countries would be lifted and the problem of mutual payments between enterprises solved.[34]

It is significant that the Omsk meeting preceded the CIS summit in Minsk, where Nazarbayev hoped to have his integration program finally approved. In preparation for the summit, Nazarbayev worked to secure maximum political support. On 4 January 1993 he attended a summit of Central Asian leaders in Tashkent. Its declared purpose was inter-regional economic cooperation in Central Asia, but actually the emphasis was on economic cooperation within the entire CIS. Expressing his colleagues' shared opinion at a press conference, Nazarbayev stressed that their support of the rouble zone would be conditional on the rouble being a supranational currency; on creation of a banking union consisting of executives of all the republics' central banks, each having one vote; and on the establishment of a common investment policy. Leaders also discussed alternatives to CIS integration, including setting up a separate Central Asian economic bloc. Nazarbayev said that under certain conditions, creation of a regional market was entirely possible and hinted at the possibility of forming a military alliance between the Central Asian states. The Central Asian leaders believed such a bloc would reorient their interests toward the Asian world, initially Iran and Turkey, building routes through their territories for export of raw materials.[35]

The decisions made at the summit had little practical meaning. Participants simply instructed their governments "to study questions involving pricing policy, development of transportation and communication lines, and provision of energy resources".[36] This lack of results and plethora of general declarations was a clear sign that the Tashkent conference was designed less for fostering Central Asian inter-regional cooperation than for an outside audience. The notion of creating a Central Asian bloc with close links to Iran and Turkey was obviously meant to pressure Russia into making concessions regarding financial policy.

It is difficult to say to what extent Nazarbayev's diplomatic manoeuvres influenced Russia's position, but the Minsk summit of 22 January 1993 brought about some results in economic matters. The participants adopted an agreement on setting up the CIS Interstate Bank and endorsed its charter.[37] The latter provided for establishment of the Coordination and Consultative Committee (CCC) as the CIS permanent executive body and of the Economic Court,[38] both proposed in Nazarbayev's program. But the outcome of the summit fell far short of Nazarbayev's hopes. Russia still rejected CIS control of rouble emission, and the Interstate Bank was set up in a form suggested by Moscow that limited its role to facilitating trade and clearing between member states, and coordinating the monetary-credit policies of the participating countries. The bank's governing body was its council, comprising one representative from each member with a correspondent account. Settlements would be in roubles issued by the Russian Central Bank, and clearing settlements in freely convertible or other currency. Members would contributed the bank's initial statutory capital of 5 billion roubles.[39] The Interstate Bank Charter, signed by all ten CIS members, specified that Russia would contribute more capital than other CIS states and would have 50% of its shares, but decisions required a two-thirds majority.[40]

The voting arrangements confirmed Russia's central role in implementing monetary policy in the CIS. Other CIS states received a guarantee that Russia would be unable to impose decisions against their combined will, but correspondingly they could not impose their combined will on Russia. The voting procedure simply institutionalised the status quo: Russia could continue to frame its monetary policies more or less as it wished. More importantly, the Interstate Bank had no power to re-establish a single rouble space. The republics made so many amendments to the draft charter that they emasculated the very idea of coordinating credit and monetary policy. In creating the bank, none of the CIS countries seriously intended to have their national banks coordinate credit and currency-emission policy with it. Thus the provision for coordination remained on paper. Vice-Chairman of the Russian Central Bank Solovov commented that the Interstate Bank would not even be able to solve the painfully urgent problem of settling accounts between enterprises in different republics. The only area in which it could play a role was in organising account-settling operations under intergovernmental agreements.[41] The emerging monetary environment had no parallel in the world. A number of republics used their own variously weighted roubles in noncash transactions, but used a common rouble in cash circulation. Meanwhile, Russia continued supply cash to other CIS states. Thus, the difference between the cash and noncash roubles continued to grow. This flew in the face of all economic logic and was fraught with serious complications for relations between members of the zone. The CIS leaders' lack of political will to limit the sovereignty of their states doomed the rouble zone.

After the unimpressive results of the Minsk summit, Nazarbayev looked for a way to preserve the rouble zone by uniting a narrower circle of participants, namely Russia, Kazakhstan, Belarus and Uzbekistan. On 26 February he arrived in Moscow and discussed this with Yeltsin and Chernomyrdin. After meeting with Chernomyrdin, Nazarbayev said that the two countries' leaderships "steadfastly support integration processes in the Commonwealth. . . . The countries which want to enter the rouble zone must reach agreement and honour the single rules of the rouble zone", he continued, adding that he thought these rules should include a concerted credit, emission and tax policy. "They will have to sacrifice some of their sovereignty in this case for the sake of improving the living standards of their peoples and strengthening the rouble".[42] This was perhaps the first time that Nazarbayev referred to self-limitation of sovereignty; previously, he had spoken only of strengthening Kazakhstan's sovereignty.

On 27 February Nazarbayev met Yeltsin, and they agreed on a joint communique voicing support for early ratification of the CIS Charter adopted at the Minsk summit, calling for implementation of decisions on the Interstate Bank and CCC. They reiterated their support for the rouble zone and agreed to take additional joint action in the field of monetary emission, budget policy and taxation, and resolved to pursue a coordinated customs policy. Kazakhstan's Deputy Prime Minister Daulet Sembayev told a press conference that custom duties would be introduced for the first time ever in bilateral trade; that was why it was vital for Russian and Kazakh businesses to be abreast of times and "update their performance", and for the two governments to act to avert any possible misunderstandings.[43]

Sembayev's statement disavowed the many declarations in support of CIS integration made by the leaders of both countries. While talking of integration, they in practice further disengaged the national economies of Russia and Kazakhstan by introducing customs duties. Nevertheless, the atmosphere of the meeting and some of the decisions made there gave some impetus to the process of CIS integration. Deputy Prime Minister Shokhin later revealed that some time in March or thereabouts Russia, Belarus and Kazakhstan began confidential discussions on a possible deeper economic agreement within the CIS framework. Though Belorussian Prime Minister Kebich initiated the talks, the Kazakh leadership took an active part in them. According to Shokhin, "[T]he idea was that instead of trying to agree with all the states on the provisions of various documents, and implementing them immediately, we tried to show how cooperation should be built in reality", and "the states which were sincerely interested in deepening integration and economic cooperation could best do this".[44] Thus the idea of a CIS economic union was born.

Yeltsin and Nazarbayev agreed at this meeting to coordinate moves to strengthen the CIS, and this became clear in their subsequent actions. On 17 March Yeltsin advanced a set of proposals for closer CIS integration. In a declaration read by Foreign Minister Kozyrev, Yeltsin described the association of former Soviet republics as amorphous and "unable to fulfill the hopes invested in it". He said the move primarily intended to address the burgeoning conflicts on Russia's borders and to establish some financial discipline over those states which remained in the rouble zone. Kozyrev said the initiative was designed to increase economic cooperation, particularly through modern market techniques — setting up multinational companies and encouraging investment in each other's projects.[45]

The next day Nazarbayev sent a telegram to Yeltsin stating his support for "strengthening the commonwealth, deepening economic reforms and democratic changes". He sent similar telegrams to the heads of states which had signed the CIS Charter. Nazarbayev proposed to hold in late March or early

April a summit of the CIS states who had signed the Charter to discuss issues such as: ensuring a viable economic space, a single supranational currency, free trade and a customs union; forming an interstate economic committee to which the states supporting this decision would delegate the necessary powers; and drawing up principles for relations with those states which did not sign to the CIS Charter.[46]

The summit met a little later than proposed, on 16 April 1993, in Minsk, and was the result of a combined Russian-Kazakh initiative. The agenda was devoted exclusively to CIS integration. Russia and Kazakhstan acted in unison, presenting similar proposals, obviously agreed to beforehand. The leading role, of course, was assigned to Yeltsin. He delivered an explicit speech, advocating a number of initiatives in various fields of CIS integration. He spoke in favour of coordinating foreign policy and setting up a CIS defence union, but devoted most of his speech to economic matters. He formally presented the concept of a CIS economic union, based on customs and currency unions. He warned that while Russia would continue talks on monetary union, a decision had to be made on "either demarcating and creating our own monetary systems, or integrating. . . . There is no third option: preserving the present situation would be dangerous for the economies of the commonwealth countries".[47] Nazarbayev also called for stronger economic links, a financial and currency union, coordinated credit and budget policies. He again raised the issue of setting up an economic coordination committee, but consideration was again postponed until the next summit.[48]

In practice the summit did not produce any results. But it provided an important platform for Yeltsin, who, because of the internal political struggle in Russia, was locked in deadly confrontation with the parliament. Facing a referendum on his rule and political course, Yeltsin needed something to counter accusations of having been responsible for dissolving the USSR and failing to do enough for CIS integration. Suggestions worked out in secret negotiations with Nazarbayev and Kebich proved useful for polishing Yeltsin's political image. It was no accident that the concept of Russian foreign policy approved by Yeltsin and made public in late April emphasised the importance of achieving the greatest possible degree of integration in all spheres among the former Soviet republics on the bases of voluntary participation and reciprocity. Moreover, the concept treated attempts by outside forces to undermine the integrative processes in the CIS as a threat to Russia's national security.[49]

On 25 April Yeltsin won the referendum, which diminished his enthusiasm for CIS integration. The CIS summit in Moscow on 14 May 1993 was held in a slightly different atmosphere from the previous one. Yeltsin declared that "the rouble zone has in fact collapsed" and suggested that other republics' debts to Russia be settled by transferring debts resulting from technical credits to an interstate debt to be repaid according to internationally recognised norms. This was another step away from preserving the common CIS economic complex. Yeltsin claimed that Russia was "ready for setting up a currency union as an inalienabie part of the economic alliance". However, he considered such an alliance impossible "without a uniform economic space, without an agreed strategy for economic reforms, without coordination of our actions in the sphere of economic policy". The first step towards creating an economic union should be formation of a customs union, which would make it "possible to remove all barriers to movement of goods, capital and services". He advocated accelerating the setting up of the Interstate Bank to make it operational before 1 October 1993.[50] The summit adopted the declaration, On Economic Cooperation, which called for establishment of an economic union within the CIS. But first a treaty had to be drafted and then signed at the next CIS summit.

Nevertheless, Nazarbayev's assessment of the summit was explicitly positive, probably because it decided to go ahead with practical establishment of the CCC. The summit decided that the CCC would operate at the level of Deputy Prime Ministers for the Economy and would be entrusted with coordinating and preparing documents and decisions in the economic, foreign policy and military fields. Nazarbayev hailed the concept of economic union, but warned that it should avoid functioning like the former Soviet-dominated Council of Mutual Economic Assistance and act more like the European Community of equal, sovereign states. Nazarbayev also managed to include in the draft documents on the economic union a special protocol, signed by the heads of government, recommending deeper integration between the states remaining in the rouble zone.[51]

Nazarbayev's positive perception of the summit suggests that he probably had not grasped that a major change in the political situation had taken place between April and May, even though Yeltsin's speech contained obvious indications of a political turnaround. First, there he declared the collapse of the rouble zone and the necessity to replace existing credit relations in the CIS with recognised international practices. Second, he proposed a currency union, which might mean either a new definition of the rouble zone or an arrangement that was new in principle. Third, Yeltsin conditioned implementation of economic union on so many "ifs" to make it virtually unfeasible under the circumstances then prevailing in the CIS. Of course, Yeltsin could not change course 180 degrees, because his opponents in parliament were still strong. So he continued to pay verbal tribute to CIS integration, while hatching an absolutely different policy.

In June 1993 Russia informed Kazakhstan and other members of the rouble zone that it would no longer extend credit by means of Central Bank technical credits. Instead, Moscow advised that from now on it would provide Kazakhstan and other CIS countries with state credits, effectively equivalent to loans given by foreign creditors. Among 800 billion roubles of such credits approved by the Duma for the forthcoming financial year, 150 billion were reserved for Kazakhstan.[52] At the same time Moscow demanded that the balances in correspondent accounts of other CIS countries in the Russian Central Bank be converted into state debt to Russia.

Russia's move was caused by its obvious inability and unwillingness to continue subsidising other CIS republics at previous levels. Official Russian estimates showed that in 1992 the Russian Central Bank transferred 1.5 trillion roubles, equivalent to 8% of the Russian GDP, to other CIS members. In the first seven months of 1993 this sum increased to 2.3 trillion, mostly because of inflation, but in real terms roughly equal to the amount for the same period in 1992. Granting credit to CIS republics accounted for 25% of Russia's inflation. Kazakhstan was the second largest per capita recipient (after Turkmenistan) of Russian currency. In 1993 cash deliveries to Kazakhstan equalled 38,000 roubles per head, 30.1% higher than per capita emission in Russia. In 1992 Russian subsidies equalled 25.1% of Kazakhstan's GDP, and 48.8% in January–July 1993.[53]

On 16 June 1993 difficult negotiations held in Moscow between Tereshchenko and Russian Deputy Prime Ministers Fedorov and Shokhin resulted in the signing of the agreement on monetary-credit relations in 1993 and on the size of Kazakhstan's debt to Russia in 1992. Kazakhstan acknowledged debts of 247 billion roubles for 1992, and this sum was defined as Kazakhstan's state debt to Russia. The signatories also noted that Russian state enterprises owed 78.5 billion roubles more to their Kazakhstan counterparts than Kazakhstan enterprises owed to their Russian equivalents, and that this difference might be used to offset part of Kazakhstan's state debt.

Kazakhstan decided that its cash emission in the forthcoming quarter would not exceed 15% of the Russian emission for the same period. But the negotiators failed to settle the issue of Kazakhstan's debt to Russia for January–April 1993 and postponed the matter until signing of a bilateral agreement, due before 1 October 1993, on coordinated financial, monetary-credit and currency policy, based on use of the Russian rouble as the legal tender in Kazakhstan. If the agreement was not signed by that date, the sides agreed to conclude another agreement on terms and periods of Kazakhstan's repayment of the Russian state credit.[54] That provision demonstrated Russia's blatant use of the debt-credit issue as leverage to force Kazakhstan and, implicitly, other CIS states to accept common rules of monetary policy established in Moscow.

According to Tereshchenko the key disagreement in the negotiations was that Almaty was willing, but Moscow was not, to take responsibility for debts incurred by state-owned enterprises. It was not therefore accidental that the provision on enterprise debts was subjectively formulated. The Russians allegedly told their Kazakhstan counterparts to settle all questions of enterprise debt via the economic courts. Russia also put forward special terms for provision of credits in 1993, effectively equating them with loans by foreign creditors.[55] As a result Kazakhstan refused to sign an agreement on state-to-state credits and remained the only rouble zone country without such an agreement. Kazakhstan probably refused to sign the agreement because of the very modest sum of 150 billion roubles reserved for it. Back in Almaty Tereshchenko stated, "On the whole we were given a clear indication that they do not want to see Kazakhstan in the rouble zone. We are being told to introduce our own currency." In turn, Nazarbayev began to accuse Russia of denying state credits to Kazakhstan while giving them to everyone else.[56]

After Tereshchenko's return Nazarbayev promptly arranged a conference, which took place in Almaty on 21 June, on the economic situation in Kazakhstan and the state of credit and monetary relations within the CIS. Members of the government, heads of province administrations, chairmen of parliamentary committees, and executives of banks and major industrial enterprises attended the conference. Summing up its results, Nazarbayev said that he had no radical change of policy in mind; "whether we want it or not the integration processes will continue". At the same time he emphasised the need for urgent steps to reduce Kazakhstan's dependence on imports, improve domestic product quality to equal that of imported goods, introduce tough control over the use of strategic raw materials, and develop a specific action plan to meet the current difficult conditions. Nazarbayev recommended that Kazakhstan's enterprises satisfy the republic's needs first, before entering into cooperation with foreign partners, meanting Russian firms.[57] According to Shokhin, the Kazakh government sent telegrams to major enterprises ordering them to cease sending goods to Russia and other CIS states.[58]

In addition, Nazarbayev prepared a diplomatic offensive to be launched at the second meeting of heads of state and government of the Organisation for Economic Cooperation (OEC) in Istanbul on 7 July. The OEC summit presented a unique opportunity to put political pressure on Russia, because it brought together all the post-Soviet Central Asian states with three non-CIS Muslim countries, Turkey, Iran and Pakistan. Nazarbayev's speech at the summit was shrewdly constructed. He did not miss a chance to mention Russia and CIS as potential OEC partners, but constantly emphasised the trade and economic advantages of Kazakhstan's cooperation with OEC and spoke very strongly in favour of new transport and pipeline routes to link Kazakhstan with the Persian Gulf through Iran and with the Mediterranean Sea through Turkey. Nazarbayev obviously tried not to overdo it, but clearly warned Moscow of the possible repercussions of disengagement from Kazakhstan. The text of the summit's final communiqué referred to "giving priority to creation of an effective infrastructure network that not only links the OEC member-states, but also gives them access to other parts of the world".[59]

This time the Russians did not hesitate to call Nazarbayev's bluff. The counteroffensive came on 10 July, when the Prime Ministers of Russia, Ukraine and Belarus signed a joint statement on urgent measures for closer economic relations. The statement said that they still remained committed to the treaty on CIS economic union, but "believe that measures for closer trilateral integration of their economies will help accelerate the implementation of this treaty's goals and principles". Deputy prime ministers were instructed to prepare by 1 September 1993 a draft treaty on deepening economic integration among the three republics.[60] The event later proved to be purely declaratory, but neither consulting Kazakhstan nor inviting Kazakhstan to the meeting delivered a serious rebuff, especially since Nazarbayev had been a very active proponent of the concept of the economic union.

The Slav republics' trilateral accord caused bewilderment in Kazakh government circles, especially after Russian Deputy Prime Minister Shokhin explained Russia's move at a press conference on 13 July. Shokhin said that the decision made at the trilateral summit resulted from news from Turkey that a customs union, common market in goods, capital, services and manpower, and a single bank were being established within the OEC framework, and "[s]ince Kazakhstan has decided to enter a Customs Union with Turkey, it can no longer join our union".[61] Shokhin's statement drew a harsh response from Almaty. State Counsellor Zhukeyev said that "Shokhin's attempt to attribute what happened to 'the desire of the Central Asian states to create an economic union with Turkey and Pakistan' is tactless, to put it mildly. And his proposal that Kazakhstan and the other CIS partners chose between entering one of these two economic unions simply does not stand up to any common-sense criticism—if only because in Istanbul there was no discussion at all about creation of an economic union". In addition, Zhukeyev ascribed to Shokhin something he never said, that Russia intended to block the setting up of a free transportation system in Asia and "restrict the Central Asian states' possibilities for future free development".[62]

The Russian move caused genuine concern in Almaty not least because it was very reminiscent of the Belovezhskaya Puscha agreement, when the three Slavic republics had easily dissolved the Soviet Union without inviting or even consulting Kazakhstan, and could be taken to imply that it was now time to dissolve the CIS. In all Kazakhstan's diplomatic position was substantially weakened. Thus Nazarbayev's bluff in Istanbul backfired, and gave Moscow a convenient justification for putting an end to the rouble zone. On 22 July he made a gesture of rapprochement to Moscow, in a press release entitled "Kazakhstan is for Economic Partnership". The statement said it was important "to overcome the individual differences in approaches to interstate economic cooperation that were reflected in conclusion of a treaty on economic alliance by the governments of Belarus, Russia and Ukraine", denied that there were any undercurrents with regard to Kazakhstan's membership in CIS and trade and economic cooperation with the countries of the Asian continent, and insisted that the recent OEC meeting was to serve the interests not only of Central Asia, but of the entire CIS.[63]

But it was too little too late. Those members of the Russian government who were suspicious of Kazakhstan's and other Central Asian states' intentions with regard to the rouble zone got the upper hand in the internal struggle and succeeded in portraying Kazakhstan and other republics that attended the OEC conference as disloyal to the CIS. Obviously, not all their suspicions were groundless. Besides Nazarbayev's declarations, which were probably a diplomatic gambit, there were other worrying facts. As later revealed by Shokhin, Moscow knew that, during the OEC conference in Istanbul in July, Nazarbayev, Karimov and Niyazov had agreed to simultaneous introduction of national currencies.[64] Moscow probably also knew that Kazakhstan had already ordered printing of its national currency in Britain, despite its being among

Nazarbayev's most closely guarded secrets. In combination, these facts could easily lead Russia's leadership to conclude that Kazakhstan participated in the rouble zone to obtain maximum advantage from Russian credits, until, at aan opportune moment, Kazakhstan introduced its national currency, leaving Russia to bear the economic consequences.

On 26 July Russia introduced new types of rouble banknotes into circulation, which was tantamount to introducing its own separate currency. All CIS states had stocks of the old notes, but could obtain new ones only on the basis of state-to-state credits or through sales to Russia. Now Kazakhstan and the other rouble zone states faced a very restricted choice: either opt for their own currency or agree to Russia's conditions. Nazarbayev decided to keep both options open. On the same day he ordered Kazakhstan's National Bank to accelerate the printing of the whole amount of national currency. Simultaneously, he telephoned Chernomyrdin and asked when Kazakhstan would get the new roubles. Chernomyrdin said very soon, and Russian Central Bank Chairman Gerashchenko confirmed that he was only waiting for orders to release the money.[65] Speaking in Akmola on 19 August, Nazarbayev announced that Kazakhstan was technically prepared to leave the rouble zone, but that he believed it would be more profitable to stay in it.[66]

Very probably Moscow wanted to use Kazakhstan's rwquest for new banknotes as a negotiating tool to force Kazakhstan into concessions on outstanding issues of economic cooperation. In Moscow on 29 July, Russia and Kazakhstan signed tow agreements on settling debt and credit matters. The first dealt with restracturing of Kazakhstan's debts, incurred through Russian technical credits, into state debt to Russia. Under the agreement Kazakhstan acknowledged 300 billion roubles in debt for the period January–May 1993 and agreed to its conversion into state debt to Russia. Thus Kazakhstan's debt to Russia for 1992–1993 was established at 547.6 billion roubles, confirmed as equivalent to U.S.$1.25 billion. The state credit was to be paid off from 1996–2000 in quarterly instalments.[67] The second agreement, On State Credit in 1993, allotted Kazakhstan the above-mentioned 150 billion rouble credit, to be paid off during 1995–1997.[68] Both agreements provided a very mild repayment regime. The interest rate was defined as Libor + 1% per year and Libor + 2% for overdue payments. The agreement provided that forms of repayment be determined annually when concluding trade and economic agreements for each year.

The credit for 1993 was substantially less than Kazakhstan had previously obtained through the Russian Central Bank, especially after taking into account high inflation and the steady fall in the rouble's value. For Moscow, both agreements ensured transformation of Russian-Kazakh financial relations into normal interstate relations, a necessary precondition not for unification but for divorce of monetary systems. The agreements also equipped Moscow with a powerful instrument of influence over Kazakhstan, as if preparing the ground for a future dependent relationship.

On 7 August Yeltsin met Nazarbayev and Uzbek President Karimov in Moscow, and they adopted a joint statement favouring setting up "a common monetary system with the Russian Federation by using the rouble". The presidents instructed their governments and central banks to hold " special negotiations within a period of two weeks to consider general and technical questions of setting up a collective monetary system" and "to sign an agreement on practical measures to set up a new kind of rouble zone". Other CIS members were invited to participate in the agreement.[69] On 11–12 August, Gerashchenko and Mashits, chairman of Russia's State Committee for CIS Economic Cooperation, made a hasty visit to Almaty, where they held meetings with the Kazakh government and National Bank on creating a Kazakh-Russian monetary system. In particular, they discussed the general concept of a new type of rouble zone and settled the problem of urgent cash deliveries to Kazakhstan.[70]

At that time, some Kazakh experts began expressing concern that Russia's conditions for creating a common monetary system and providing Kazakhstan with 1993 banknotes were difficult to meet. Nazarbayev also expressed doubts. At the republican conference of local leaders in Akmola on 19 August, he made it clear that Russia would infringe on Kazakhstan's sovereignty if it set terms which obliged Kazakhstan to receive new rouble banknotes as credit, and to coordinate its budget, taxation and investment policies with Russia's Central Bank, and said that only Kazakhstan's parliament could decide how much of its sovereignty Kazakhstan might delegate to Russia.[71] The next day the head of Kazakhstan's National Bank, Baynazarov, echoed these concerns, complaining that Russia's conditions, if accepted, would virtually turn Kazakhstan's National Bank into a branch of the Central Bank of Russia. He also said that parliamentary approval must be obtained join a Russian rouble zone.[72] However, on 20 August Nazarbayev met Yeltsin in Moscow and signed the second declaration that Kazakhstan would stay in the rouble zone. According to Nazarbayev, by that time Kazakhstan had changed its customs and financial laws and the law on the National Bank to comply with Russian demands.[73]

On 7 September representatives of the governments and central banks of Russia, Kazakhstan, Tajikistan, Uzbekistan, Belarus and Armenia meting Moscow and signed a document, On Practical Measures to Establish a New-style Rouble Zone, to be approved by their parliaments. The agreement referred to the signatories' desire for "a common monetary system using the Russian Federation rouble as the legal means of payment". It proposed strict coordination of monetary, credit, interest and customs policing and involved relevant changes in the member countries' legislation. Once implemented, access to the Russian rouble as the only legal tender would be open. Bilateral agreements were to define the conditions of the new rouble zone and mechanisms for harmonising and unifying legislation on monetary and credit relations. They were to be followed by a comprehensive multilateral treaty on economic union, scheduled for signing on 24 September at the CIS summit in Moscow.[74] Nazarbayev expressed satisfaction with the deal. Before leaving Moscow on 7 September he told journalists, that his visit had not been in vain and had convinced him that there was no alternative to integration. He underlined that the states needed at least a month and a half to abandon old roubles and introduce temporary coupons or other monetary units.[75]

On 23 September in Moscow the prime ministers of Russia and Kazakhstan signed a bilateral agreement on unification of their monetary systems. Kazakhstan was the last of the five participants in the rouble zone to do so. Answering journalists' questions after the ceremony Tereshchenko noted that the agreement was very important for stabilising the economic situation in his republic.[76] Strangely, the next day saw the signing in Moscow of another document which to some extent contradicted it. On 24 September a treaty, On Creation of Economic Union, was signed by all CIS members except for Ukraine and Turkmenistan, which joined it as associate members.[77] The treaty defined aims and principles of the economic union, codified trade relations, entrepreneurial and investments activities, dealt with monetary, financial and currency issues, social policies and legal regulation of economic relations. Under the treaty economic union provided for "free movement of goods, services, capital and labour; coordinated monetary-credit, budget, taxation, prices, foreign economic, customs and currency policies; harmonisation of national economic legislation of the contracting parties; common statistical base". The treaty provided for creation of economic union in four stages: free trade association; customs union; common market of goods, services and labour; and finally monetary union.[78] Thus the treaty regarded monetary union not as the initial but as the most advanced stage of economic integration, scarcely achievable in the immediate future.

True, Article 15 established that at the stage of free trade association the parties would use in their monetary-credit and financial relations either a multi-currency system, embracing national currencies circulating in individual states or a system based on the Russian Federation rouble. Thus in principle the treaty did not exclude the possibility of CIS members using the Russian rouble at the first, lowest stage of economic integration. Ironically, this stage in Russian-Kazakh integration had not yet been achieved, and it was far from clear when it would be. Being a framework document only, the treaty itself did not introduce a free trade zone; therefor for each stage of integration special agreements had to be reached and practical measures implemented. In expert assessment, to implement the treaty's provisions, all sides would have to sign more than thirty special agreements. Most of these agreements remained unsigned or unratified for at least two years.[79] Thus the treaty provisions obviously contradicted the ongoing negotiations on monetary union between Russia and Kazakhstan.

This contradiction supports the argument that Yeltsin and his entourage did not take the economic union treaty and rouble zone agreements seriously, regarding them not as instruments for real integration but as propaganda ploys in the domestic political struggle. The Kazakhs did not know, any more than the majority of government officials in Russia and the other CIS members, that these agreements had become an element in a subtle combination prepared by Yeltsin for his showdown with the Duma. Their solemn signing in Moscow coincided with Yeltsin's controversial decree of 21 September on dissolving parliament. Yeltsin employed a similar strategy in April, preceding the Russian referendum, but now the stakes were much higher. Yeltsin's move went beyond constitutional bounds, because he had no legal power to dissolve parliament. To boost his popularity and refute opposition claims that he was betraying Russian interests, Yeltsin needed to demonstrate real achievements in CIS integration.

But the parliament fought back, and on 3–4 October armed clashes took place between its supporters and Interior Ministry troops. Then tanks shelled the parliament building. Yeltsin, who enjoyed the loyalty of the army command, prevailed. The parliament was dissolved, and gone with it were the majority of Eurasianists in Russia's leadership. Ethnic nationalists enjoyed an unequivocal victory. A week later a new tone in Russian policy appeared. On 11 October Finance Minister Fyodorov expressed his fear that his country's currency could be weakened by a too hasty expansion of the rouble zone:

The biggest problem is the policy on the rouble zone, which has not been fully thought out. . . . We have agreements with neighbouring countries which are not bad, but there is a tendency to press for integration too quickly. The biggest danger would be to deliver cash to the CIS countries before they have coordinated their economic policies. We will risk importing inflation, our rouble will sharply lose its value, and our ability to influence the situation through our own Central Bank will be severely limited.[80]

The statement came just a day before Kazakhstan's parliament was due to ratify the rouble zone agreement, but did not influence the vote. After ratification, Nazarbayev issued a decree on the monetary system that established a legal basis for recognition of the Russian rouble as the sole legal tender in Kazakhstan.[81] This, however, could not save Russian-Kazakh negotiations on monetary union, which began to founder. Moscow advanced tough new conditions for providing new banknotes to Kazakhstan. Russia insisted that the cash be given as a state credit for six months, charging normal interest established by the Russian Central Bank, and with Kazakhstan making a deposit equal to 50% of the credit. If in six months Russia was satisfied that Kazakhstan's economy could function jointly with Russia's, the deposit would be returned, the interest discarded, and the credit would not have to be repaid. Russia's second condition prohibited Kazakhstan from introducing a national currency within five years.[82] Kazakhstan perceived the new conditions as exceptionally harsh and as deliberately aimed at ensuring failure of the negotiations. Deputy Prime Minister Sembayev stated in an interview that "principally new conditions unexpectedly presented by Russia" were "purposefully designed to be unacceptable". He felt Kazakhstan was simply being "pushed out of the rouble zone".[83]

On 26 October Shokhin arrived in Almaty and met Nazarbayev. Negotiations faltered. Shokhin sincerely asked Nazarbayev what would be the advantage for Kazakhstan "of jumping into the last carriage of the departing Russian train". According to Nazarbayev he was outraged, and asked Shokhin if he had authority from Chernomyrdin to negotiate. Shokhin replied that did and told Nazarbayev that Kazakhstan could not be in the rouble zone.[84] Shokhin's account differs. When he asked Nazarbayev if he could give a 100% guarantee that Kazakhstan would not introduce its own currency within a year, Nazarbayev allegedly replied that he could not.[85] The rouble zone between Russia and Kazakhstan was no longer feasible.

On 28 October Kazakhstan's parliament gave Nazarbayev power to introduce a national currency. In a secret operation he hired four cargo aircraft, to bring 60% of the new currency from London.[86]

On 3 November Tereshchenko arrived in Moscow for talks on disengagement from the rouble zone. He signed a protocol recognising that "the present state of the monetary system of the Republic of Kazakhstan does not allow for its immediate practical merging with the monetary system of the Russian Federation". The sides "agreed that the optimum way out of the existing situation was introduction by Kazakhstan of its own banknotes and implementation in the nearest future of measures for strengthening the monetary system". A Russian-Kazakh commission (Shokhin and Sembayev) would within ten days draft agreements on a payment union between the two countries and "on the mechanism for realisation in bilateral relations of the regime of free trade and customs regulation". Russia promised to give Kazakhstan technical assistance in drafting documentation for introducing the national currency and to release within a week 10 billion roubles of the state credit for 1993. In addition, Russia expressed readiness to help Kazakhstan stabilise its monetary system by assisting in covering the debts of Russian enterprises to their Kazakhstan counterparts, postponing interest payments on the state credits until 1995 and returning foreign currency to Kazakhstan from its accounts in the former USSR Bank for Foreign Economic Relations.[87]

In a television address on 12 November Nazarbayev announced introduction of its national currency, the Tenge, as of 8 A.M. on 15 November. The rouble zone collapsed, highlighting another stage in the process of separation of the CIS states. This event received contradictory interpretations in Kazakhstan and Russia. Recalling those dramatic days, Nazarbayev said in a recent interview: "The Russian government's economic egoism manifested itself in the first place in abolishing the common currency, common economic complex. This did irreparable damage first of all to the integrative processes. . . . I did everything possible and impossible to keep Kazakhstan in the common monetary and technological space with Russia and other CIS states. But alas, the vector of Russian development was pointed in a different direction".[88] Strangely, Nazarbayev gave a slightly different interpretation in his memoirs. He said that Shokhin had been "probably right at that moment. . . . Building your statehood, it is impossible to do without your own currency. Sooner or later it should have been introduced".[89] A similar view is voiced by Mansurov, Kazakhstan's ambassador to Moscow: "[w]hen Kazakhstan and Russia—two independent states . . . are not united into a common form of statehood, be it federation or confederation, the single rouble could exist only for a certain transitional period with the objective of mitigating the destructive consequences of the collapse of the overcentralised state which the Soviet Union was".[90] Thus Mansurov recognised the objective, inevitable, breakup of the rouble zone in the absence of a common union statehood.

In Russia politicians of Eurasianist orientation condemned the abolition of the rouble zone, while liberal ethnic nationalists welcomed it and castigated the mostly egoistic motives behind Kazakhstan's and other Central Asian states' approach to the rouble zone. Khroustalev, director of the MGIMO Centre for International Studies wrote that these countries were interested primarily in "keeping up and strengthening the preferential economic structure, because it was through it that the major portion of Russian aid goes". He welcomed Russia's disengagement from the rouble zone, because he claimed it would permit Moscow to "not only regulate the size of its donations, but no less important, tie it to certain rather tough economic and political conditions".[91] On the other hand, Dzasokhov, an influential member of the Duma International Affairs Committee, speaking at a Russian Foreign Policy Council conference on issues of CIS integration in November 1994, expressed a different view: "Let us recall the proposals put forward by Alma-Ata and Tashkent when the issue of a common currency system was at the stage of fairly substantive discussion. I think we acted overhastily at the time by rejecting them, by distancing ourselves from those calls. Thereby we encouraged some Central Asian republics to carry forward their sovereignty in forms that were far from justified in every case".[92]

Both points of view seem correct. They simply have two different criteria for assessment. To Eurasianists, seeking reintegration of the union state at almost any cost, the obstacles in the way of the rouble zone mentioned by their opponents looked secondary and artificial. For ethnic nationalists other issues dominated. Each side thought not so much of integration, but of a desire to extract maximum benefit for itself at its partner's expense. Russia's interest in "integration" was determined by primarily political considerations—maintaining indirect control of the periphery through economic means, but as cheaply as possible. Kazakhstan's primary interest lay in economics—getting cheap Russian credits and living on them without putting much effort into economic revival, while maintaining full independence from Moscow. Also, both Yeltsin and Nazarbayev experienced serious domestic political pressure for integration, and could not simply reject the idea without damaging their political standing. Consequently, they created an impression of actively pursuing integration, with each playing into the other's hand. But when the process reached the point where real decisions had to be made, both sides showed a lack of desire to follow through.

The breakup of the rouble zone placed the CIS in the most serious crisis in its brief history. It seemed on the verge of total disintegration, and Russian-Kazakh relations hit their lowest point since the collapse of the Soviet Union. To avert irreparable damage, the CIS had to take urgent measures to restore trust between its members. From this angle the upcoming summit in

Ashgabad scheduled for 23–24 December would be decisive in either deepening the rift between the former Soviet republics or reversing the trend by favouring integration. Nazarbayev obviously understood this and showed some strategic savvy by avoiding another round of score-settling with Moscow.

On 20 December ITAR-TASS news agency, quoting sources close to Nazarbayev, report that Kazakh economic experts felt there was no need to "overdramatise" the failure to create a common rouble zone: "This is a temporary measure, but despite all its minuses, it should eventually lead to the introduction of a single common currency in the CIS".[93] At the Ashgabad summit the CIS countries reached agreement on temporary application of the economic union treaty as Nazarbayev had insisted.[94] They agreed to support cooperation between industrial enterprises of the CIS states and to cooperate in investment activity, and they approved the status of the Council of Heads of CIS customs services.[95] The summit helped to reduce tensions and laid the foundation for the re-emergence of impulses for integration within the CIS.

On 22 March 1994 Nazarbayev announced his most conspicuous integration initiative — the project for a Eurasian Union (EAU). At the Royal Institute of International Affairs in London he said that the need had matured for reform of the CIS itself, "to provide for the creation in this region of a belt of stability and security". He suggested reviving the CIS as a Eurasian Union of sovereign states, drawing on both the European Union and British Commonwealth as models.[96] It remains unclear why Nazarbayev chose London for advancing his initiative. Perhaps he wanted to test both Western and Russian reactions on the eve of a crucial meeting with Yeltsin scheduled for 28 March. If this was Nazarbayev's intention, it failed, because no substantial reaction followed either from Moscow or from Western capitals, and he had no alternative but to use opportunities presented during his visit to Moscow to advance his initiative. He actively promoted it at meetings with academicians and students of Moscow State University, businessmen and intelligentsia at the Moscow mayor's office and chief editors of Russian's leading newspapers.

He explained his reasons for initiating the EAU concept with his dissatisfaction with the CIS. The CIS had become an organisation for "civilised divorce" and attempts "to channel the process along the route of integration" had failed. His dissatisfaction was based on two premises. (1) "political dynamics" started to damage "not only the obsolete and economically invalid forms" of relations between the former Soviet republics, but also "quite rational and mutually beneficial links"; and (2) prompt integration with other economic groupings and "hopes for foreign aid" did not materialise. "The EAU project was prepared taking account of the fact that in the near future CIS countries would not join developed economic blocs as equal partners".[97]

He disclosed that he had reached the conclusion that CIS integrative processes must be activated "only after extensive study of the experience of other international associations, analysis of the situation in the CIS states and consultations with experts". He argued that the lack of success in CIS integration resulted from the misconception that integration contradicted and even threatened national sovereignty. But he believed notions of sovereignty and integration were interconnected, "not excluding, but augmenting each other",[98] and advocated "combining the process of national-state construction with preservation and development on this basis of inter-state integrative processes".[99]

The EAU project, published on 6–8 June 1994 in Kazakhstan and Russia, started from the assumption that the existing CIS structure "did not allow for full realisation of the integrative potential" of the former Soviet republics. Also, previous CIS performance "showed the need to move to a new level of integration, which would guarantee fulfilment of jointly undertaken obligations by all member-states". Without excluding further improvement of CIS mechanisms, the plan suggested that the CIS "should not be regarded as the only form of unification". A Eurasian Union would be compatible with the CIS and would take into account "multi-variant integration, different tempos, non-homogeneity and divergence in the development of the CIS states".[100]

At the heart of the project was support for political integration: "Resolution of questions of economic integration dictates the need for setting up political institutions, possessing ample authority. They must include functions for regulating relations between states in the economic, political, legal, ecological, cultural and educational spheres".[101] The new entity, regarded as an "economic, currency and political union", represented a significant shift in Nazarbayev's position. Previously, he had defined integration exclusively in economic terms.

Eurasian Union would be comprised of equal independent states, aimed at realisation of their national interests and "strengthening stability and security, social and economic modernisation in the post-Soviet space". The international association would come into being through referendums in countries wishing to join and subsequent signing of a treaty. Decisions in the EAU would require a four-fifths majority, another breakaway from CIS principles, where decisions required unanimity. The project also established preconditions for joining the EAU, including mandatory observance of international obligations, acceptance of the existing state and political institutions of the EAU member-states, recognition of territorial integrity and inviolability of borders, repudiation of economic, political and other forms of pressure in interstate relations; termination of military activities against each other. The project allowed EAU member-states to participate in other integrative associations, including CIS. Each member could leave the EAU after giving six months' notice.

The project provided for setting up supranational institutions. It named the Council of Heads of State and of Government as EAU's highest political authority. Chairmanship of EAU would rotate at six-month intervals. In addition, the union would have a Council of Foreign Ministers for foreign policy coordination. A EAU legislature, described as a consultative and counselling body, would be established by equal representation from each member state, or by way of direct elections. To be legally binding the parliament's decisions would have to be ratified by the member-states' parliaments. Another proposed supranational structure was an Interstate Executive Committee, a permanently functioning executive and controlling body. The proposal did not define its powers, specifying only that it should be composed of representatives of all member-states, and that its chairmanship should rotate.

An interesting provision, reflecting Kazakh official policy, concerned citizenship. The project did not promote common union citizenship, but suggested that persons changing their country of residence within EAU should be automatically granted citizenship of the receiving state. It proposed that a capital of the new union be a city at the juncture of Europe and Asia and named two possible candidates (both in Russia), Kazan, capital of Tatarstan, and Samara. In the economic area, the project envisaged a number of supranational coordinating structures: an Economic Commission under the Council of Heads of State and of Government, a Raw Materials Commission of EAU Exporter-States, a Fund for Affairs of Economic and Technical Cooperation, a Commission on Interstate Financial and Industrial Groups and Joint Ventures, International Investment Bank, Interstate Arbitrage, and a commission on introduction of a new currency, the transferable rouble. The project also called for creation of a common defence space to coordinate defence activities, and made a number of proposals for cooperation in other spheres, such as science, culture, education and ecology.[102]

The concept of the Eurasian Union represented a reversal in Nazarbayev's way of thinking. In 1991 he had ardently advocated Kazakhstan's economic independence and application of imported economic development models, but by 1994 his outlook had become more realistic. He went so far as advocating not only economic but political integration of the post-Soviet space. He admitted that disintegration of the single economic space had damaging results and that building economic strategy on expectations of foreign economic assistance or of penetration of nontraditional markets already firmly controlled by other nations had been naive.

Nazarbayev's initiative received a positive reaction from a number of influential Russian politicians. On 30 March 1994 Shumeyko, chairman of the Russian Federation Council and head of the Council of the CIS Interparliamentary Assembly, told journalists that recreating a new union, unlike the former USSR, was quite possible. He said it did not matter what it was called, but noted that the new association could be based on existing CIS institutions, such as the Council of Heads of State, Council of Heads of Government and Interparliamentary Assembly. He also expressed the opinion that supranational institutions would have to be established gradually, adding there could be discussion about united armed forces, a single monetary system, and abolition of borders.[103]

On 4 April, at a news conference at the State Duma, Shakhray, Russia's minister for Nationalities Affairs and Regional Policy, presented for discussion a draft confederation agreement which envisaged establishing a union of Eurasian states on the basis of the CIS. The draft envisaged establishment of a "confederative economic community" to ensure "revival and development of a common market of member countries as a single economic space without customs barriers . . . creation of a common currency and banking system, based on

preservation of the national currencies of these countries and the agreed principles of credit and monetary regulation". It also provided for setting up a community governmental committee, a defence union formed by the members'
national armies, a general political council, a security council and a court of the
confederation. Shakhray proposed to form an international working group to
compose a confederation treaty, made up of representatives of countries which
were ready to join the Eurasian Union.[104] Kazakh Prime Minister Kazhegeldin
appraised Shakhray's proposal as "similar to the EAU project in a whole number of provisions".[105]

The Kremlin's reaction was much less enthusiastic. On 31 March Kostikov,
Yeltsin's press secretary, described Nazarbayev's initiative as "unexpected".
He said Yeltsin had heard about the EAU proposal with reserved interest, and
that Nazarbayev's idea was geopolitically logical but so were the CIS principles, "so there is hardly any need to replace one strong idea with another,
though their mutual improvement would make sense". Kostikov said that Yeltsin reserved judgment until he had further studied the pros and con of Nazarbayev's initiative.[106] Nazarbayev's project could at least serve as a basis for
further negotiations, but this did not happen either. The official joint communiqué on Nazarbayev's visit to Moscow did not even mention the Eurasian
Union. It said he and Yeltsin discussed prospects for CIS development, that
they welcomed CIS expansion through accession of new members, and saw
this as evidence of growing understanding of the importance of multilateral
cooperation within the CIS. They confirmed readiness to cooperate in further
strengthening the CIS and increasing its efficiency, specifically by accelerating
the formation of an economic alliance, and strengthening the role of coordinating institutions.[107]

Thus Yeltsin was prepared to proceed with economic integration only at that
stage. This found reflection in the treaty On Further Deepening of Economic
Cooperation and Integration between the Republic of Kazakhstan and the Russian Federation, signed during Nazarbayev's visit. The treaty contained a number of general provisions which needed to be made more specific. Article 1 said
that both countries would cooperate closely "in fulfilling economic integration,
creating a joint economic space and forming a common market". They agreed
to "steadily lower customs tariffs in mutual trade, taxes, duties and other tariff
and non-tariff restrictions, make a transition to a joint trade regime in relations
with third countries, unify economic legislation on the most acute issues of
trade and economic relations, implement unification of customs tariffs, rules
and procedures and customs documentation" (Article 3). The treaty contained
an obligation to implement by the end of 1994 "conditions for transition from a
free trade zone to creation of a fully fledged Customs Union, taking into account steps taken in this field on a multilateral basis within the Economic Union".[108]

Not only Russia but other CIS states, including Kazakhstan's closest allies
from Central Asia received the EAU proposal coolly. At the CIS summit in
Minsk on 15 April, which Nazarbayev did not attend allegedly for health rea-

sons, Nazarbayev's Central Asian counterparts were the first to criticise the concept of a Eurasian Union. Rahmonov, chairman of the Supreme Soviet of Tajikistan, said the EAU idea was good, but the CIS had not yet exhausted its possibilities and reserves. Karimov, president of Uzbekistan, voiced the strongest criticism. He stated that the concept of Eurasian Union "had no serious foundation" and that "it would be incorrect to jettison the idea of strengthening the Commonwealth primarily via economic structures, via economic union, when we have only reached half-way, although we all put our signatures to this, and to put forward the new idea of a Eurasian Union. In general it smacks of populism".[109] Thus both leaders aligned themselves with Yeltsin's position, not Nazarbayev's. Nobody spoke in support of Nazarbayev's plan.

Given the generally unfavourable reaction to the EAU project, it is perhaps surprising that Nazarbayev did not discard the initiative, but continued to advance it. On 3 June 1994 he officially forwarded the Project for Formation of a Eurasian Union of States to the CIS heads of state.[110] On 1 July Kazakhstan circulated a draft paper describing the EAU proposal as an official UN General Assembly document. The EAU initiative figured high on the agenda of the Uzbek-Kazakh-Kyrgyz summit in Almaty on 8 July. Nazarbayev's hoped to reverse his Central Asian colleagues' negative attitude to the EAU and planned to use the occasion to promote it further. He at least partially achieved this aim. Karimov refrained from repeating his numerous previous criticisms of the EAU idea, and Akayev said at the press conference after the meeting that he supported the EAU initiative "first and foremost because I consider it as the final goal of our commonwealth. . . . I believe that all the topical and disputable problems within the CIS could be settled as a part of this program: the program of changing from passive union to the Eurasian union. I believe that the documents that we signed today could serve as . . . a crystallisation point for this kind of Eurasian union".[111]

Besides making statements supporting deeper integration of the post-Soviet space, the three presidents signed a number of documents directed to achieve it. They included agreements on setting up a common bank and joint ministerial councils intended to help implement creation of a common economic zone. The major accord reached at the meeting was a decision to set up an Interstate Council of the three countries, and structures for this council, later termed the "Central Asian Union" by some Russian analysts. They also agreed to create an intergovernmental commission to deepen economic integration. An executive committee and councils of the ministries of foreign affairs and defence were to become operational under the aegis of this commission. But this time the Central Asians carefully avoided provoking accusations of economic separatism, specifically emphasising that this economic integration existed exclusively within the CIS framework and in no way contravened its charter.[112] In fact the major objective of these accords was to stimulate further integration between CIS states and through this give an indirect boost to the EAU concept.

Continuing his diplomatic offensive, Nazarbayev tried to secure support from Belarus, the Slavic republic most disposed to CIS integration. On 11

August, while visiting the Ukrainian capital Kiev, Nazarbayev made an unexpected phone call to President Lukashenko of Belarus and discussed further integration between the post-Soviet republics. Nazarbayev spoke about his idea of a Eurasian Union and said that he saw Lukashenko as "an ally and partner in joint efforts aiming to achieve close integration among the CIS memberstates".[113] But Lukashenko, probably afraid of being drawn into some sort of anti-Russian scheme, was cautious, giving the opinion that when moving towards integration it was important to avoid "piling up of ideas" and to try to use all CIS possibilities.[114] Thus Nazarbayev failed to obtain Belorussian support.

On 19–21 September an international conference, The Eurasian Space: Integrative Potential and its Realisation, arranged by the Kazakh authorities, was held in Almaty. Nazarbayev addressed the conference, attended by 140 officials, politicians, diplomats, scholars, writers and publicists from several CIS countries. His Eurasian Union proposal was the centerpiece of the conference,, and many of the Russian politicians and public figures present voiced their approval of it. The final document adopted by the conference suggested "taking steps to strengthen the CIS's integrative potential, using the idea of Eurasian Union of states and other integration projects".[115] The conference was conveniently timed before the forthcoming CIS summit, to give a boost to the EAU concept, which had been put on its agenda.

However, the CIS summit, held on 21 October in Moscow, clearly remained unconvinced. As Yeltsin said, "We all studied it very carefully. However we all came to the conclusion that this is perhaps a good idea, but premature. Today the peoples are not ready to enter a new union".[116] The summit adopted a resolution on the EAU proposal which said that the Council of Heads of State had taken note of President Nazarbayev's information on creating a Eurasian Union of States and had decided "to use the major ideas, enunciated in the Republic of Kazakhstan's proposal, for deepening integrative processes in the Commonwealth of Independent States".[117] Nazarbayev expressed his displeasure at this decision at a press conference after the summit. Speaking about the other CIS leaders he said, "I started to ask my colleagues some questions: 'What's going to happen to everything we're deciding on? We've passed 451, 452, 453 resolutions since the creation of the CIS, but how will they be implemented?'. . . . When I talk to them separately, especially if it's over a friendly lunch . . . they all agree that we can't live without each other. They even say we're doomed to togetherness. So why do they say something different to the press?"[118]

The summit decision clearly represented dominance of Yeltsin's approach of continuing to develop integration within the CIS framework. If Yeltsin had supported Nazarbayev's initiative the outcome could have been quite different. Of course, Ukraine, Azerbaijan, Georgia and Turkmenistan still would have actively opposed the EAU concept. But it might have acquired support from Kyrgyzstan and Belarus, and that would have been enough to create the nucleus of a future union between the four CIS nations which were inclined to go deeper in their integration than the others. But Yeltsin evidently opposed the whole EAU concept.

Yeltsin's restrained attitude can be explained to a large degree by personal reasons. The personal element was always evident in Yeltsin's behavioural patterns, and Nazarbayev committed a major tactical error by not taking account Yeltsin's extreme ambitiousness. Yeltsin could not accept someone other than himself as the author of an initiative as important and potentially historic as the Eurasian Union. As a creator of the CIS, he had no intention of passing over the historical leadership to anyone else, even if it was in Russia's interest to do so. Thus Yeltsin did not support Nazarbayev's proposal, even though some influential members of his own team received it warmly. Of course, some considerations of principle also determined the Russian position.

Foreign Minister Kozyrev voiced Russia's concerns over the EAU proposal at the summer meeting of the Russian Foreign Policy Council devoted to CIS integration. On one hand, Kozyrev made it clear that Russia wanted "a more closely-knit Commonwealth, one advancing to integration. . . . If some republics, or several republics, are willing to join a confederation or some other union with us on a bilateral or multilateral basis, they are welcome. I can say right away that our response would be positive. If anyone is ready to accept a Eurasian Union, our answer will be yes in this case as well". On the other hand, Kozyrev expressed scepticism of the seriousness of the Nazarbayev's proposal. "If we try to imagine what the proposed Eurasian Union would be like this would be somewhat strange, because we still cannot implement specific accords reached with, say, Kazakhstan, which were reaffirmed during Nursultan Nazarbayev's official visit to Moscow", he said.[119] Thus Russia suspected that the EAU concept was nothing more but another gesture of self-promotion by Nazarbayev, lacking any serious desire to achieve concrete results. Existing difficulties in bilateral relations, particularly involving ethnic Russians in Kazakhstan, but also implementation of the bilateral agreements already concluded, gave rise to these suspicions.

One anti-EAU argument put forward by Russian experts explained Nazarbayev's various integration initiatives by the desire to remove the problem of human rights of ethnic Russians in Kazakhstan from the agenda. Mark Khroustalev, director of the Moscow State Institute of International Relations (MGIMO) Centre for International Studies, held this view.[120] Some Russian foreign policy analysts saw the EAU proposal as a plan to change the rules of the game in the CIS. Andrey Zagorsky, deputy vice-chancellor of MGIMO, argued that the principal innovation in Nazarbayev's project consisted almost exclusively in changing the decision-making rules, from unanimity to a four-fifths majority, a voting procedure which he felt would prevent Russia from blocking decisions detrimental to her interests.[121] Zagorsky said that "[t]he strategy of the CIS 'junior partners' is well seen in the instance of Kazakhstan's proposal for Eurasian Union — this is a strategy of subordinating Russia to the collective will of the union members, which would be ensured first of all by the rules for adopting binding decisions by a four-fifths majority of votes, while the strategic aim of the majority of the CIS states consists in consolidating their own statehood, overcoming their fated dependence on Russia".[122] LDPR leader Zhirinovskiy wrote in a recent book

As for projects for an Eurasian Union, they have an anti-Russian character, because they are designed to diminish Russia's role to that of a third-rate country within a framework of the multiple components of a Eurasian association. To put it bluntly... this project contains vain plans by nationalists of Turkic origin to recreate the Golden Horde in a new form. . . . Russians and other Slavic peoples comprised the overwhelming majority of Russia's (USSR's) population, and their incorporation into some "Eurasian people" carries an anti-Russian, anti-Slav meaning.[123]

All these opinions in fact represented a basic point of view. Russia, a great power, had no intention of having its policy subordinated to some supranational structure controlled by former Russian dependencies, thereby diminishing Russia's own role in CIS and internationally. This posture may have been assumed in response to some extravagant geopolitical constructions advanced by some Kazakh foreign policy officials. For example, an article by Dulatbek Kiderbekuli, a Kazakh diplomat, on formulation of Kazakhstan's foreign policy asserted that the economic union of Kazakhstan, Kyrgyzstan and Uzbekistan was no less than "the axis of the Organisation of Economic Development". Kiderbekuli regarded Kazakhstan as playing the linking role between it and the Customs Union of Russia, Belarus and Kazakhstan. This led him to the stunning conclusion that "Kazakhstan is the core of the Eurasian Union, with a prospect for its extension in Eurasia to the whole system of the Organisation for Economic Development".[124] Such extravaganzas were not officially proclaimed but obviously discussed within Kazakhstan's foreign policy establishment, and this provided ammunition for those in Moscow who saw anti-Russian designs behind the EAU project.

Nazarbayev later claimed that his proposal had not been well received because it had not been properly understood. He wrote in his memoirs: "At that moment the project for an Eurasian Union was not fittingly received, though not categorically rejected. This attitude has prevailed for the two years since this project's publication. In general the position of many politicians reminded me then of the old bureaucratic principle, everything seems all right, but may it not lead to something wrong?".[125] Nazarbayev explained the restrained response to his plan by the other leaders' reluctance to embark on CIS integration, an assertion obviously designed to divert attention from the project's merits and defects. Meanwhile, Kazakh officials and progovernment experts tried their best to substantiate this assertion. Askar Akhmedzhanov, head of a Department at the Kazakhstan Institute of Strategic Studies and Alma Sultangalieva, a senior fellow at the Centre for Oriental Studies of the Kazakhstan Academy of Sciences, claimed in an article that the dubious reaction to Nazarbayev's proposal was caused by its being perceived as an "encroachment on sovereignty. . . . The ruling elites of the majority of post-Soviet states were alarmed by the possibility of reintegration of the post-Soviet space, which could lead to their losing power". The authors obviously did not include Nazarbayev and his regime among these ruling elites; on the contrary, they tried to prove his staunch adherence to reintegration, claiming "[t]he EAU project conscientiously proposed rather firm forms of integration — supranational bodies not only in the economic, but also in the political sphere. It is possible that it also took account of public opinion, which could put pressure on political elites through the mass media".[126]

The most ardent promoter of the EAU concept was Mansurov, Kazakhstan's ambassador to Moscow. In one article he called it "the most promising among integrationist ideas proposed up to now, which meets the hopes of the majority of the population in the CIS states. . . . It is the project for forming a Eurasian Union of states which has recently acquired a reputation as the most comprehensive and popular integrationist initiative not only among politicians and scholars, but also among the broad public of a number of CIS states".[127] The falsity of this statement is obvious, given the generally negative reaction of most CIS leaders and of political scientists and other experts in Russia to Nazarbayev's initiative. It is not surprising that at Mansurov's defence of his doctoral thesis one of the examiners, Nikolay Bugay, head of a Department of the Russian Ministry for Nationalities Affairs and Regional Policy, convincingly dismissed Mansurov's praise of the EAU concept, describing it as "disputable" and "not scientifically researched in depth". He added,

It is hardly desirable to overstate the role and significance of the Eurasian Union idea advanced by Nazarbayev. In my opinion all these postulates downgrade the role of the Russian people (Nazarbayev proclaims one thing, but does another, hammering in the notion that Kazakhs were a "repressed" people). . . . In my assessment, the state policy conducted by the government of Kazakhstan and President Nazarbayev himself in the sphere of inter-ethnic relations, and so much discussed in the dissertation, contributes to creation of a "new belt" of tensions on Russia's southern borders.[128]

Only a few Russian experts welcomed the EAU project, most notably Professor Bagramov, whose journal *Eurasia* was financially supported by Kazakhstan's government. He hailed Nazarbayev's initiative as "an adequate answer to the actual situation in which the peoples of the former USSR found themselves". Bagramov argued that the Eurasian Union could be of substantial benefit to Russia and argued that (1) creation of the Eurasian Union would mean the end or substantial weakening of centrifugal tendencies in the post-Soviet space; (2) Russia in alliance with the other CIS states would have a chance to revive itself as a mighty world power; (3) Russia would be able to overcome internal separatist trends more easily and settle interethnic conflicts in other parts of the CIS; and (4) Russia would be able to provide for better protection of human rights of ethnic Russians discriminated against in the new independent states. Bagramov to refuted claims that ideas of Eurasianism belit-tled the role of the Russian people. He argued that those making such claims "ignore the Eurasian nature and Eurasian mission of the Russian people, whose national idea cannot be implemented in the narrow ethnic space and includes the array of peoples historically formed around the Russian nation".[129]

Thus Bagramov's position reflected a common tendency among contemporary scholars in Russia to equate Nazarbayev's EAU concept with an ideology of neo-Eurasianism. This tendency is characteristic authors such as Senior Fellow at the Institute of History of the Russian Academy of Science Narochnitskaya, Corresponding Member of the Russian Academy of Sciences Myasnikov, or political scientist Iordanskiy. For example, Iordanskiy wrote that Nazarbayev's proposals "fill the Eurasianist idea with specific political and economic substance".[130] Bagramov, on the other hand, made the qualification that "modern Eurasianism and the Eurasianism of the 1920s are different phenomena" and that "this concept applied to present day conditions still waits to be worked out".[131] But by dwelling on the EAU concept in the context of Eurasianism, Bagramov placed Nazarbayev's idea in the general stream of neo-Eurasianist thinking, which not only created a misleading impression, but led to inappropriate conclusions.

In reality, Nazarbayev's proposals had nothing in common with the ideology of Eurasianism, and his use of a similar term was an attempt to capitalise on an ideological concept becoming increasingly popular in Russia. Eurasianists called for recognising the cultural and historical specificity of Russia, which they considered represented neither Europe, with its Romano-Germanic civilisation, nor Asia. Russia's uniqueness allegedly permitted singling it out as a separate geopolitical entity, Eurasia, which in geographical terms embraced not the whole Eurasian continent, but only its central part, within the boundaries of the former Russian empire.[132] One of the founders of the Eurasianist philosophy, Trubetskoy, wrote: "The destinies of the Eurasian peoples have interlinked with each other, have firmly bound together into a single gigantic knot, which can no longer be disentangled. Hence disengagement of one people from this entity could be achieved only through unnatural compulsion and would lead to suffering". To counter the threat of ethnic nationalism Trubetskoy suggested a concept of common Eurasian nationalism. He argued that "individual parts of the former Russian empire need a single substratum of statehood to be able to continue to exist as parts of one state", and neither the Russian nor any other individual people in Eurasia could play the role of substratum. "Only all the conglomerate of peoples living in this state, perceived as a special multi-ethnic nation, and in this capacity possessing its own nationalism" could be the national substratum of the future Eurasian state, and "common Eurasian nationalism must be a sort of expansion of the nationalism of each of the Eurasian nationalities, a sort of integration of all these individual nationalisms into one whole. . . . We call it the Eurasian nation, its territory Eurasia, its nationalism Eurasianism. . . . Only the awakening of the multi-ethnic Eurasian nation can give Russia-Eurasia the ethnic substratum of statehood, without which it will sooner or later start to fall apart, causing grief and suffering of all its parts", he concluded.[133]

Nazarbayev's proposal avoided addressing the main issue of Eurasianist philosophy — common Eurasian nationalism — which was the core of the whole Eurasianist concept. Some Russian scholars noticed the omission. Professor Titarenko, director of the Institute of the Far East of the Russian Academy of Sciences characterised Nazarbayev's plan as follows:

In our opinion, President Nazarbayev of Kazakhstan's initiative for creating a Eurasian Union (EAU) takes account only of Eurasinaism's geopolitical, economic and geographical constants, i.e. envisages creation of a union mostly for solving economic problems, getting access to energy resources, raw materials, etc. However, from the viewpoint of inter-ethnic, inter-civilisation relations, this proposal has very little in common with the spiritual principles of Eurasianism, and this is very clearly manifested in the light of the actual policy of administratively establishing domination by the titular Kazakh nationality, ignoring the multi-ethnic culture and multi-ethnic composition of the population of Kazakhstan.[134]

Eurasianists indeed promoted the idea of a common Eurasian nation, while Nazarbayev's plan did not envisage a common state nor even common union citizenship. Nor could Nazarbayev's policies in regard to nationality relations in Kazakhstan be interpreted as directed at creating a multiethnic nation. The Kazakh leaders themselves did not deny that primarily economic considerations lay behind the EAU initiative. Thus Prime Minister Kazhegildin, at a conference on foreign policy issues held in Almaty on 15 February 1995, stressed that "bringing forward the EAU project was dictated first of all by economic motives".[135]

It seems that a combination of factors rather than a single factor prompted the EAU initiative. Of course, domestic policy considerations were paramount, with a desire to play up to the aspirations of Kazakhstan's Slavic population and thereby make them more tolerant towards the policy of Kazakh nationstate building. The other intention was to divert attention of Russian government and public from the situation with ethnic Russians in Kazakhstan.

Yet there is little doubt that Nazarbayev sincerely wanted economic integration, along lines he had already proposed more than once, on his own terms, with no concessions of principle on the issues of Kazakh sovereignty or the role of Russians in the republic, a position unacceptable to Russia. The EAU concept's major shortcoming was Nazarbayev's basic formula of integration and sovereignty. This in fact meant only token integration, because real integration requires acceptance of limitations on national sovereignties for the common good. In his project Nazarbayev did mention the necessity to delegate sovereignty, but analysis of his proposal shows that he did not mean it. His suggested decision-making process differed little from that already existing in the CIS, except that it substituted a four-fifths majority for unanimity. It is doubtful that such a procedure could make acute problems within the union easier to resolve, especially over enforcement of decisions, given the CIS experience of an exceptionally broad spectrum of different opinions on almost any issue. Russia especially found of it unacceptable, since it would endanger Russia's central role in the CIS, subordinating it to the collective will of the other members. Russia would want to be the leader, not just another member, of the proposed EAU.

Despite its rejection by Russia, the EAU project stimulated further discussion on re-integration of the post-Soviet space and built up internal and external pressures on Yeltsin's administration in favour of increased integration. Besides, Nazarbayev's proposal created an effect perceived in the Kremlin as a threat to Russia's ideological leadership in the CIS. This forced the Russian government to seek ways of countering the EAU project. Consequently, Russia prepared a special memorandum proposing tighter CIS integration in areas such as politics, defence and border protection, and Yeltsin presented it to the next CIS summit, held in Moscow on 21 October.[136] The memorandum, entitled Major Directions of Integrative Development of the Commonwealth of Independent States, was unanimously approved at the summit, together with the related Prospective Plan for Integrative Development of the Commonwealth of Independent States. The summit voted to acknowledge Nazarbayev's proposal on EAU "and use major ideas, conveyed in the Republic of Kazakhstan's proposal for strengthening integration processes in the Commonwealth of Independent States".[137]

The CIS leaders, except Niyazov of Turkmenistan, also concluded an agreement to establish an Interstate Economic Committee of the Economic Union (IECEU), a measure long advocated by Nazarbayev. It would be based in Moscow; its voting system gave Russia 50% of the votes and required an 80% vote for decisions. This effectively gave Russia the right to veto.[138] The full text of the agreement was, however, never released to the press. A brief communique from the CIS Secretariat indicated that the IECEU had powers "to adopt binding decisions on a specific range of issues", including management of facilities which were transnational in nature, such as "energy systems, transportation, gas and oil pipelines, and jointly owned installations".[139]

Another achievement of the summit was an agreement on a Payments Union, signed by all CIS members, and aimed at securing continual payments between CIS states in their national currencies. The agreement was based on acceptance of the members' national currencies as means of payment for trade and nontrade operations, and banned administrative limitations on the choice of currencies to be used by enterprises when concluding contracts. The exchange rates between national currencies were to be established by supply and demand on the currency markets of the member-states. They undertook to apply coordinated measures to maintain the stability of their national currencies. The agreement assigned an important role to the Interstate Bank as a "specialised body of the Payments Union", whose major task was to arrange multilateral clearing payments between the central banks of the CIS members. They also agreed to establish an International Currency Committee to facilitate multilateral cooperation in currency payments and credit relations.[140]

In an interview after the summit, Nazarbayev claimed that his idea of a Eurasian Union "pushed all the politicians and presidents to take fair decisions to set up the CIS Interstate Economic Committee, work out a customs and payments union, and for more vigorous activity by the CIS Interparliamentary Assembly".[141] He exaggerated the degree of his success. As usual, decisions made by the CIS were largely symbolic. The agreement on the Payments Union provided only for very gradual introduction of the new payments regime through conclusion of special bilateral and multilateral agreements, a process which would take years.[142] The IECEU had little chance of becoming an effective structure, because each national government and president would decide how much power to delegate to it. Also, the IECEU could not start work for at least several months due to disagreements over its chairmanship; some republics objected to the recommendation of a representative of Russian Deputy Prime Minister Bolshakov for the post.[143]

Only with the completion of negotiations on the Customs Union did a real opportunity for mutually beneficial and solid economic integration between Russia, Kazakhstan and other CIS members finally arrive. According to the treaty On Creation of an Economic Union, signed in 1993, the Customs Union was to be the first step in movement to a full-fledged economic union. On 20 January 1995 Russia, Kazakhstan and Belarus took this first step by signing an agreement, On Customs Union. Actually, Russia and Belarus signed a bilateral agreement on Customs Union on 6 January 1995, and Kazakhstan joined it on 20 January, pledging to abide by its provisions. The three countries agreed that two Russian-Kazakh bilateral accords, On Single Procedure of Regulation of the Foreign Economic Activity and Protocol on Introduction of Free Trade Regime without Exemptions and Limitations, would serve as unalienable parts of the agreement, and resolved to create a special executive body for the Customs Union. Article 7 contained an important provision, with consequences for the Customs Union's future. It said that the agreement would not affect the three countries' obligations under other international treaties which "do not contradict the present agreement". The duration of the agreement was not specified, and it provided for the possibility of unilateral withdrawal, on one-year's prior notice.[144]

The memorandum signed by Russia, Kazakhstan and Belarus on 28 January stipulated that the Customs Union would be created in two stages. In the first stage, participants would abolish customs duties and quantitative restrictions on trade between themselves and establish common customs schedules with regard to third countries. In the second stage the territories of the members would become a single customs space, and customs control would be imposed only along their external borders. Prime Ministers Chernomyrdin, Chigir and Kazhegeldin also signed a memorandum to standardise foreign trade, customs, monetary and price laws, a special executive body of the Customs Union would be formed to control the process. The signatories also undertook to meet the conditions necessary for creation of the common customs space, including unification of foreign trade, customs, currency, taxation and other economic legislation; working out common rules for organising currency markets, access to them by authorised banks and achievement of mutual convertibility of national currencies; conduct of coordinated foreign economic policy; and ensuring effective joint protection of external borders. Russia, Kazakhstan and Belarus declared that other CIS members could join once they met the above conditions.[145] Kazakh Prime Minister Kazhegeldin gave a high assessment to the agreement: "The Customs Union is a most important component part of the Treaty on Creation of the Economic Union signed earlier, an important step along the way of creating a common market of goods, services, capital and labour. This agreement must influence the further process of development toward real integration".[146]

On 16 May 1995 in Moscow, Chernomyrdin and Kazhegeldin signed an agreement on joint administration of their customs services. It provided for each country to send a customs mission to the other's customs services. The missions would coordinate decisions of the customs services, organise information exchange and interaction between the services, including joint customs control, and draft proposals on unification of the customs legislation.[147]

It took six months to standardise the regulations so that the Customs Union could begin functioning; it formally became effective on 20 July 1995, thereby completing the first stage of implemention. On 19 July, at a news conference held to mark this event, Kazakh First Deputy Prime Minister Isingarin said the signing of the agreement had had a definite positive effect on Kazakhstan, because since January its exports of goods to Russia had increased by almost 50%.[148] On 18 August 1995 Nazarbayev met with visiting Russian Deputy Prime Minister Bolshakov, and they discussed further steps in implementing the agreement. Bolshakov also passed to Nazarbayev a personal message from Yeltsin, welcoming completion of the first stage of the Customs Union. "In this way", said Yeltsin, "comprehensive integration in the framework of an Economic Union Treaty becomes reality".[149] The next day Bolshakov and Kazhegeldin signed a document initiating implementation of the second stage of the Customs Union.[150]

On 20 September 1995 Nazarbayev issued a decree "On cancelling customs control on the border of the Republic of Kazakhstan with the Russian Federation". This lifted customs controls on Russian goods; in future only shipments in transit from third countries would be checked. The decree also provided for joint Russian-Kazakh customs controls on the external borders of the Customs Union.[151] Russia, however, did not follow with any reciprocal action. Moscow still doubted whether Kazakhstan would be able or willing to abide by its obligations undertaken within the Customs Union. There were some grounds for concern. One of them may have been Nazarbayev's position at the Shymkent summit of Kazakhstan, Kyrgyzstan and Uzbekistan held on 14 April. The summit agreed to a communiqué, which said: "The presidents of Kazakhstan, Kyrgyzstan and Uzbekistan considered the key aspects in the process of implementing the Treaty on Creating a Single Economic Space. Specific recommendations were made for further strengthening cooperation within the treaty framework. The program for economic integration between the Republic of

Kazakhstan, the Kyrgyz Republic and the Republic of Uzbekistan up to 2000 was considered in detail and approved".[152]

The text of the communiqué made a controversial impression in view of the obligations previously accepted by Kazakhstan under the Customs Union agreement. Sometime later Kazakh First Deputy Prime Minister Isingarin denied any contradiction between the two documents.[153] But this economised on truth. Kazakhstan, on the one hand, agreed on joint customs and foreign trade policies with Russia, and on the other undertook less than three months later to integrate economically and consequently to open its market to countries outside the Customs Union. The Shymkent communique did contain a reference to Kyrgyzstan's and Uzbekistan's desire to join the Customs Union. But for the time being they were outside it, so Kazakhstan had accepted international obligations which contravened Article 7 of the Customs Union agreement.[154] This suggested a somewhat nonchalant attitude to the Customs Union.

On 26 September an unidentified but high-ranking customs official in Moscow was quoted as saying that Russia "does not think it possible to cancel customs control on its border with Kazakhstan as long as the latter does not bring its system of regulating foreign economic relations in line with that of Russia and Belarus".[155] On 23 November 1995, the tripartite intergovernmental commission met in Moscow and approved a list of rules for new members joining the Customs Union. The conditions included signing agreements on a single procedure for regulating foreign economic activities, integrated management of customs agencies and cargo transportation, joint efforts to safeguard frontiers of the Customs Union, and a protocol on introduction of a free trade regime. They also signed joint protocol on completion of the first phase of accords on the Customs.[156]

On 2 January 1996 Russian First Deputy Prime Minister Soskovets told journalists that the first stage of economic union should be completed during the year, and the next day Yeltsin issued a decree lifting customs controls on the Russia-Kazakhstan border, instructing that henceforth only transit cargoes from third countries be checked at that border, and adding that this marked completion of the first stage of the Customs Union. Yeltsin instructed his government to work with the Kazakh authorities on a plan for joint enforcement of customs controls on both countries' external borders.[157] The reason for this move was not so much Moscow's satisfaction with Kazakhstan's observance of the Customs Union rules, but the new political situation that emerged in Russia after the Communist Party's strong performance in the elections to the State Duma in December 1995. The Communists' strong performance in these elections created a high probability that their candidate would win the forthcoming presidential election.[158] Yeltsin's team was close to panic.

One of the Communists' most effective pre-electoral tactics was active exploitation of the issue of integration of the post-Soviet space. They accused Yeltsin of breaking up the Soviet Union and failing to achieve real unification within the CIS. But this was not only a tactical ploy. The Communist Party program, adopted at the party congress on 22 January 1995, proclaimed as one of its immediate goals "denunciation of the Belovezhskaya agreements and stage by stage restoration of a single union state on a voluntary basis".[159] On 15 March 1996 the Duma passed a Communist-sponsored resolution revoking the RSFSR Supreme Soviet's decision of 12 December 1991 to abrogate the 1922 treaty forming the USSR. The Duma then passed a second resolution affirming the legal force of the 17 March 1991 referendum on preservation of the USSR, in which 71% of those voting in Russia supported retaining the union. Taken together the Duma resolutions asserted that the USSR legally continued to exist, and rejected the December 1991 accords that formed the CIS.[160] This fulfilled the first part of the above provision of the Communist Party program. The second part — restoration of a single union state — was to be fulfilled if the Communist candidate won the presidential elections.

Nazarbayev was seriously disturbed by the Duma decision. During a telephone conversation on 16 March, Yeltsin assured Nazarbayev that the Duma's resolutions had no legal force. The next day, obviously in agreement with Yeltsin, Nazarbayev issued a statement that Kazakhstan would never relinquish its sovereignty and independence. He also warned that "any actions of political movements, parties and individual persons going against the constitution and pursuing the task of destabilising the situation in our country will be regarded as illegal and resolutely terminated". However, Nazarbayev could not simply ignore the political pressure created by the Duma's resolutions in favour of restoring the USSR. He, Yeltsin and other leaders had to demonstrate progress towards CIS integration, and beyond a barely functional Customs Union. During their telephone conversation Yeltsin and Nazarbayev presumably discussed how to counter the Duma's challenge and came up with the idea of a union of four. Nazarbayev advised that by the end of March he and Yeltsin would sign "a comprehensive document, which would bring integration to a new level".[161]

That document — a treaty On Deepening Integration in Economic and Humanitarian Spheres between Russia, Kazakhstan, Belarus and Kyrgyzstan — was signed in Moscow on 29 March 1996.[162] It covered a number of issues in areas such as economic, social and cultural cooperation, financial and legal framework and management of integration. The parties pledged to coordinate directions and timing of economic reforms, and establish conditions for a common market; to coordinate financial and monetary policy with a view to achieving convertibility of their national currencies and, at later stages, common regulatory standards and practice of banking activity, with introduction of a common currency as the ultimate objective, if the necessary level of integration were achieved. To achieve these goals the parties instructed their Central Banks to create a banking union. Other undertakings included "preservation and strengthening of the common cultural space", "coordination of actions in planning and realisation of foreign policy" and establishing and strengthening a common system of border protection".[163]

They also agreed to create three bodies to manage integration processes. The highest, the Interstate Council, would consist of the heads of state and of government, the foreign ministers, and the chairman of the Integration Committee with a right to put forward initiatives, but not to vote. The Integration Committee was established as a permanent executive body, comprising deputy heads of government and ministers responsible for cooperation with other CIS members.[164] The Inter-Parliamentary Committee would be composed of equal numbers of members of parliament of each country. Its major objective was to draft model legislation to serve as a basis for national legislation. The text of the treaty was declaratory; it contained generalities, expressing intentions of the parties, not binding obligations. The bodies of integration and the decision-making process resembled those within the CIS, and it was difficult to say what new they could contribute to the integration process. The Interstate Council could take binding decisions only by unanimous vote of all the presidents at the Interstate Council. Nevertheless, official Kremlin propaganda hailed the treaty as establishing a much tighter-knit community of four, and Nazarbayev described it as 98% comprised of his proposals.[165] But both Russian and foreign experts dismissed it as an artificial arrangement designed to boost Yeltsin's image with some of the Russian electorate. Presidential candidates Yavlinsky, Fyodorov and Lebed denounced the treaty as a hasty election ploy. "The political games over the integration of CIS countries are becoming increasingly dangerous," they said in an unusual joint statement.[166] Later events showed that neither the treaty nor the bodies created by it produced anything useful to foster CIS integration.

Nazarbayev's willingness to play up to Yeltsin by joining the community of four pointed to two things: (1) that Nazarbayev had a vested interest in keeping Yeltsin in the Kremlin, thereby perpetuating his own future as Kazakhstan's leader; and (2) Nazarbayev, representing the Kazakh national elite, had become seriously alarmed at the prospect of real integration. After the signing ceremony he made an important statement, which indicated reversal of his position on the CIS integration. He said the time might be right to steady the pace of integration: "Now I say don't rush with integration. Don't whip the horses". He also rejected the Duma's denunciation of the Belovezhskaya agreements and hit out at Cossack activists for trying to destabilise ethnically diverse Kazakhstan. "What the Duma decides about foreign countries does not concern us in any way. . . . There can be no talk about recreating the Soviet Union. Kazakhstan will never support it — it makes no sense".[167]

At the third session of the Assembly of Peoples of Kazakhstan, held in Almaty on 29 April 1996, Nazarbayev was even more precise. On the issue of integration he said:

Kazakhstan is prepared to accept a level of integration which does not infringe its independence. Our republic will never agree, first of all on the basis of its constitution, to formation of any former unified state. We can only envisage close, friendly integrative ties of states in all spheres of people's life. But these are relations of independent states, and not some unknown and utopian federation. All irresponsible calls . . . in favour of restoration of the USSR or joining Kazakhstan to another state are a call for liquidation

of Kazakh statehood, which cause righteous indignation and leads to serious confrontation.[168]

Nazarbayev's position clearly demonstrated no difference from the principles
of relations already established in the CIS, and no desire for a more advanced
integration model. Moreover, he once again demonstrated his allegiance to Kazakh statehood, contrary to many official pronouncements that Kazakhstan was
a multinational state. In his speech to the CIS summit in Moscow on 28 March
1997, Nazarbayev reiterated his position against more advanced forms of integration, stating that for the new independent states "national-state interest is
higher than everything else, including chimerical associations and confedera-
tions".[169]

Nazarbayev's anti-integration stance fully revealed itself in his reaction to
the conclusion on 2 April 1997 of the Union Treaty between Russia and Belarus. Nazarbayev's spokesman Kusherbayev said Kazakhstan was happy to see
a union between Russia and Belarus, but warned that it was concerned by some
aspects of the treaty and by the speed of its adoption. To justify his stance Kusherbayev put forward a rather tenuous argument that "instead of working for
the cause of unification, the union treaty may cause disagreements within Russia", and "a number of Russia's regions, Chechnya, for example, may demand
a similar treaty for themselves".[170] In reality the Kazakh authorities were concerned primarily with the effect that conclusion of the treaty could have on the
internal situation in Kazakhstan. They obviously expected it to increase internal
pressures, especially among the non-Kazakh population, in favour of following
the Belarus example.

Nazarbayev's interest in integration with Russia and other CIS states was
motivated by the desire to extract immediate political and economic benefits
for himself or Kazakhstan, while avoiding or ignoring obligations of substance.
When the Kazakh leadership saw integration becoming an issue of real policy,
their enthusiasm for it vanished. What contributed to this about-face was the
Russian leadership's early 1996 change of mood towards favouring real integration, prompted by the very strong Communist showing in the Duma elections. At earlier stages Nazarbayev could readily advance integrative initiatives
without worrying that they might be accepted. He could always be sure that
someone would block them, and this gave him opportunities to portray himself
as a staunch proponent of integration without running risk of becoming involved in any agreements that would undermine Kazakhstan's sovereignty.
When, however, Yeltsin pursued real integration and achieved a positive result
with Belarus, Nazarbayev understood that he could no longer proclaim initiatives and then blame Moscow for their failure.

Kazakhstan's more reserved approach to integration was immediately trans-
lated into practical policies. In March 1996 the government issued a number of
decrees relaxing trade controls and introducing new tariff rates. They took effect in two stages, from 14 April and 1 June. Export tariffs on many key commodities were halved, while duties on imported consumer goods such as

clothing, furniture and vehicles were slashed. Joint tariffs within the Customs Union were higher than Kazakhstan wanted, and regulation was too tight, so Almaty decided to take advantage of Yeltsin's preoccupation with the elections and reneged upon the previously accepted obligations within the Customs Union. Kazakhstan's Deputy Economics Minister Begakhmetov revealed that Kazakhstan had asked Russia in the previous year to agree to lower import tariffs for these items, but opted to go it alone when Russia declined. "We gained a lot from the Customs Union. . . . But Kazakhstan is a sovereign state and has its own interests to defend. We don't produce cars. We were basically defending Russian industry".[171] The Kazakh authorities artfully exploited Yeltsin's dependence on them in the election campaign. He could not afford even moderate criticism of Kazakhstan's decisions, because the image of the Customs Union was one of CIS integration's few success stories.

When the election fever subsided and the political situation in Russia stabilised, following Yeltsin's successful heart operation, Moscow revisited the issue of Kazakhstan's compliance with the Customs Union obligations. On 14 January Yeltsin's press service issued a release saying he had informed the Duma that he had not signed a law on Customs Union between Russia and Kazakhstan. The law, ratifying the Customs Union and common foreign trade regulations of Russia and Kazakhstan, had been passed by the Duma on 15 December 1996, and by the Federation Council, the upper house of parliament, on 25 December. The release said that in Yeltsin's opinion the law contained several inconsistencies.[172] Yeltsin's action amounted to temporarily freezing the Customs Union with Kazakhstan and coincided with the Russian Federal Border Guard Service's decision to deploy Russian Cossack units along the Russian-Kazakh frontier, effectively reintroducing border controls. This caused a painful reaction in Kazakhstan, and not only because Cossacks were involved.

On 18 March Kasymov, chairman of Kazakhstan's State Customs Committee, told a news conference that Kazakhstan "cannot allow our borders to be as open as they have been until now", and "[t]he economic security of our state is suffering, huge amounts of contraband goods are being brought in". He said the other members of the Customs Union — Russia, Belarus and Kyrgyzstan — had not complied with the union's constrictions, which in turn entitled Kazakhstan to turn its back on it. "Our neighbours in all geographical directions are strengthening their own borders, their customs posts are now armed with armoured vehicles", he said, and added that Kazakhstan would begin tightening its customs regime at its nineteen airports, then establish customs posts along its lengthy borders.[173] This was obviously a retaliation against the Russian action. At a press conference in Moscow on 25 March, at the end of the CIS summit, Nazarbayev described the Customs Union as a temporary arrangement, and stated that it would no longer be needed once its members joined the World Trade Organisation.[174]

Exchanges of blows did not stop at that. In a statement on 20 May 1997 Tuleyev, Russia's minister for Cooperation with the CIS States, criticised Kazakhstan's unilateral introduction of customs inspections at airports, railway stations and roads as "defiance of agreements reached among the four members of the Customs Union". He characterised Nazarbayev as "an energetic initiator of and participant in many blocs, projects and actions clearly of anti-Russian orientation", whose political and economic decisions are "aimed at CIS' further disintegration".[175] Thus the Customs Union, launched with widespread enthusiasm, proved a failure. In the first half of 1997 trade between its members fell by 33%.[176]

In September 1997 Kazakhstan and Russia attempted to revive the Customs Union. During Nazarbayev's visit to Moscow's 850th anniversary celebrations, both he and Yeltsin advocated more efficient integration between the members of the Customs Union and strengthening interaction within CIS. They discussed preparations for a session of the Interstate Council of the "four" and for the next CIS summit.[177] Nazarbayev spoke in favour of removing border controls, creating common economic space, coordinating foreign trade and questions of joint security and said, "Integration of the "four" should move in the direction of a Eurasian Union being created on the same lines as European Union".[178] Following the meeting Russian presidential spokesman Yastrzhembsky told journalists that Moscow was dissatisfied with the working of the Customs Union and expected to hold a session of the Interstate Council of the "four" prior to the CIS summit in Chisinau, to give a boost to CIS integration.[179]

The session took place in Moscow on 22 October. Nazarbayev's speech at the session is of interest, because it contained a set of Kazakhstan's complaints against Russia over the Customs Union and a program for its future development. Nazarbayev made the following charges: introduction of "rates of customs tariffs", which "violated the procedure for changing customs duties"; application of excise duties to Kazakhstan's goods; tightening the regime for transit of alcohol, including temporary depositing of customs duties as security; tightening of customs controls at the Russian-Kazakh border; and introduction of customs controls on citizens of Kazakhstan, which "creates unwarranted social tensions and additional inconveniences". Nazarbayev also complained about high Russian railway tariffs, which increased the costs of Kazakhstan's exports, making them less competitive. He proposed an explicit set of measures to facilitate trade between the member-states, including introduction of norms common in international practice for levying indirect taxes on import and export of goods, and abolishing such taxes altogether on transit of goods between members of the Customs Union; bringing closer trade regimes with third countries; establishing common approaches to tariff and nontariff regulations, and common rules for foreign currency controls and regulations; to establish free transit of goods through the territory of the Customs Union; strict control over observance of treaties, agreements and decisions; and decisions of the Interstate Council to be adopted by qualified majority, not unanimity.[180]

Although Nazarbayev's initiatives pragmatically suited Kazakhstan's immediate economic interests, the Interstate Council supported most of them. The council accepted a plan of action for bringing closer regulations on trade regimes with third countries, unifying approaches to tariff and nontariff regulation, and introducing common currency controls and freedom of transit, provided that the unified rules for commodity shipment under customs surveillance were observed. Decisions on a free trade zone for Customs Union member-states and on coordinated principles for calculating and collecting indirect taxes were also signed. The latter implied switching to a new tax system as of 1 January 1998, which envisaged mutually compatible systems of calculating and collecting taxes. Value added tax (VAT) was to be collected in the country of destination within the union, and manufacturers were to be exempt from VAT on goods exported to other union members. The prime ministers issued a ruling on a draft treaty on common measures of nontariff regulation to enable member-states to start compiling unified lists of goods in relation to which measures of nontariff settlement would be applied.

The Interstate Council approved priority guidelines for implementing the "treaty of the four", which included forming a common market of goods, services, labour and capital, further development of the union and progress in the drafting of laws encouraging integration. The council reacted positively to Tajik President Rahmonov's appeal for Tajikistan's admission to the Customs Union, and instructed the Integration Committee to examine the matter carefully and submit its findings to the council's next session. One procedural decision established a Council of Heads of Government attached to the Interstate Council. The council elected Nazarbayev chairman of the Interstate Council, but postponed selection of a chairman of the Integration Committee until their next session.[181]

Though the session managed to stabilise the situation in the Customs Union and curbed the negative trends that had developed in the field of integration in summer 1997, it added very little of practical value to the Customs Union. It seemed that the "four" just returned to the very basics from which any Customs Union should have started, and from what could have been achieved in 1995, had the members had sufficient desire and political will. But both remained in short supply, because disagreements resurfaced immediately after the session of the Interstate Council. On 24 October A. Kruglov, head of the Russian Customs Committee, told a news conference that the Russian customs service did not favour introduction of the international practice of collecting VAT in the Customs Union. "In this case, customs control will have to be imposed on the borders between the countries of the union," he said. Therefore, other methods for unifying taxation principles must be found. Unifying excises, or indirect taxes, in the four countries would not lead to altering their rate in Russia. "Unification of excises in the union will most likely be based on the current rates in Russia," he said.[182] The Interstate Council session scheduled for 18 December 1997 was postponed, allegedly due to changes in Yeltsin's work schedule,[183] but the real reason may have been lack of progress in implementing decisions on the Customs Union.

It seems that Russian and Kazakh diplomatic moves in the autumn of 1997 were directed less at achieving a breakthrough in the integration process than at repairing the damage done to bilateral relations in previous months and stopping centrifugal tendencies pushing the two countries further and further apart. Events developed in the cyclical pattern, which had become traditional in Russian-Kazakh relations: expectations and projects for deeper integration, failure to implement concluded accords, deterioration of relations and revival of hopes for further integration. A prospect of further disintegration suited neither Yeltsin nor Nazarbayev, for domestic political reasons. Yet, there were no visible signs that Nazarbayev was prepared to jettison his policies of nation-state building and turn towards real integration with Russia. So the Interstate Council's decisions were no more than applications of previous practices of observing civilities and preserving a semblance of integration. In reality, the Customs Union remains barely functional. If not completely dead, it drags on as a secondary commitment, whose provisions nobody intends to fulfill. It is difficult to imagine when and under what circumstances relations within the Customs Union could be restored and turned towards real integration. Until this happens, potential broad CIS integration is not likely to be realised.

NOTES

1. Kozhokin, E. M., ed., *Kazakhstan: realii i perspektivy nezavisimogo razvitiya*, Moscow: RISI, 1995, pp. 14, 138.
2. *Kazakhstan-Rossiya: sostoyanie i perspektivy ekonomicheskogo sotrudnichestva*, Tsentr Strategicheskikh Issledovaniy Respubliki Kazakhstan, ed., Almaty: Tulga, 1993, p. 4.
3. *Economist*, Vol. 325, No. 7791, 1993, p. 81.
4. *Izvestiya*, 18.01.92.
5. *Izvestiya*, 18.01.92.
6. "Nazarbayev: Summit and Documents 'Not Particularly Comforting'", *BBC Monitoring Service: Former USSR*, 18.02.92.
7. "Nazarbayev Refuses to Enact Unilateral Nuclear Disarmament", *BBC Monitoring Service: Former USSR*, 26.02.92.
8. *Radio Free Europe/Radio Liberty (RFE/RL) Daily Report*, No. 96, 20.05.92.
9. "Gaydar Tells Viewers of Postponement of Oil Price Liberalization", *BBC Monitoring Service: Former USSR*, 30.03.92.
10. Reuters News Service, 02.04.92.
11. *Izvestiya*, 25.04.92.
12. Reuters News Service, 23.04.92.
13. *RFE/RL Daily Report*, No. 96, 20.05.92.
14. Nazarbayev, N., *Na poroge XXI veka*, Almaty: Oner, 1996, pp. 143–144.
15. *RFE/RL Daily Report*, No.96, 20.05.92.
16. "Yeltsin Adviser on Finance Agreements Reached at Tashkent Meeting", *BBC Monitoring Service: Former USSR*, 18.05.92.
17. "Bankers in Rouble Zone Agree on Need to Coordinate Emission and Credit", *BBC Monitoring Service: Former USSR*, 29.05.92.
18. *Izvestiya*, 09.07.92.

19. Reuters News Service, 11.06.92.

20. "Yeltsin Decree to Maintain Russian Control of Rouble in Rouble Zone", *BBC Monitoring Service: Former USSR*, 23.06.92.

21. *Izvestiya*, 09.07.92.

22. Valovoy, D., *Kremlevskiy tupik i Nazarbayev*, Moscow: Molodaya gvardiya, 1993, pp. 168–169.

23. *Megapolis-Express*, 14.10.92.

24. *Nezavisimaya gazeta*, 10.10.92.

25. Reuters News Service, 22.01.93.

26. *Ekonomika i Zhizn*, 22.10.92.

27. *Nezavisimaya gazeta*, 10.10.92.

28. "Nazarbayev: CIS Leaders Should "Carry Out Divorce" at Minsk in Civilized Manner", *BBC Monitoring Service: Former USSR*, 21.12.92.

29. Nazarbayev, N., *Na poroge XXI veka*, pp. 144–145.

30. *RFE/RL Daily Report*, No. 244, 21.12.92

31. Reuters News Service, 19.12.92.

32. *Kazakhstansko-Rossiyskie otnosheniya, 1991–1995 gody, Sbornik dokumentov i materialov*, Moscow: Posol'stvo Respubliki Kazakhstan v Rossiyskoy Federatsii, 1995, pp. 47–48.

33. "Communique of Results of Russo-Kazakh meeting in Omsk", *BBC Monitoring Service: Former USSR*, 12.01.93.

34. "Kazakh and Russian Premiers on Omsk Meeting", *BBC Monitoring Service: Former USSR*, 12.01.93.

35. *Trud*, 06.01.93.

36. *Nezavisimaya gazeta*, 05.01.93.

37. The Charter was initially signed by Russia, Kazakhstan, Armeniya, Belorus, Tadjikistan, Kyrgyzstan, Uzbekistan.

38. "Ustav Sodruzhestva Nezavisimykh Gosudarstv", *Kazakhstansko-rossiyskie otnosheniya, 199--1995 gody, Sbornik dokumentov i materialov*, Moscow: Posol'stvo Respubliki Kazakhstan v Rossiyskoy Federatsii, 1995, pp. 271, 273.

39. "Banking—CIS Interstate Bank", *BBC Monitoring Service: Former USSR*, 29.01.93.

40. Reuters News Service, 22.01.93.

41. *Izvestiya*, 25.01.93.

42. "Russia and Kazakhstan Agree on Closer Economic and Military Cooperation", *BBC Monitoring Service: Former USSR*, 03.03.93.

43. Ibid.

44. "Shokhin on Economic Union's History, Details and Prospects", *BBC Monitoring Service: Former USSR*, 16.07.93.

45. *Financial Times*, 18.03.93.

46. "Nazarbayev Telegram to Yeltsin with Proposals for Strengthening CIS", *BBC Monitoring Service: Former USSR*, 26.03.93

47. "CIS Summit in Minsk—Yeltsin Proposes Greater Economic, Industrial and Military Integration", *BBC Monitoring Service: Former USSR*, 19.04.93.

48. Reuters News Service, 17.04.93.

49. *Nezavisimaya gazeta*, 29.04.93.

50. "Yeltsin Speaks in Favour of Economic Integration", *BBC Monitoring Service: Former USSR*, 17.05.93.

51. "Yeltsin, Kravchuk and Nazarbayev Answer Journalists' Questions—Post Summit Press Conference", *BBC Monitoring Service: Former USSR*, 17.05.93.

52. *Megapolis-Express*, 28.07.93.

53. *Izvestiya*, 16.09.93.

54. Soglashenie o denezhno-kreditnykh otnosheniyakh v 1993 godu i o razmere zadolzhennosti Respubliki Kazakhstan po tekhnicheskomu kreditu po rezultatam torgovo-ekonomicheskikh otnosheniy s Rossiyskoy Federatsiey za 1992, Moscow [No publisher], 1993.

55. *Izvestiya*, 23.06.93.

56. *Izvestiya*, 23.06.93; *Megapolis-Express*, 28.07.93.

57. "President and Premier Address Meeting on Economy and Relations with Russia", *BBC Monitoring Service: Former USSR*, 07.07.93.

58. *Megapolis-Express*, 28.07.93.

59. *Nezavisimaya gazeta*, 14.07.93.

60. *Izvestiya*, 13.07.93.

61. *Megapolis-Express*, 28.07.93.

62. *Izvestiya*, 15.07.93.

63. *Nezavisimaya gazeta*, 22.07.93. Formal Central Bank announcement was made on 24 July 1992.

64. *Moskovskie novosti*, 21.11.93.

65. Nazarbayev, N., *Na poroge XXI veka*, p. 145.

66. "Kazakh President Visits Akmola Oblast; Talks of Rouble Zone and Grain Harvest", *BBC Monitoring Service: Former USSR*, 28.08.93.

67. Soglashenie mezhdu Pravitel'stvom Rossiyskoy Federatsii i Pravitel'stvom Respubliki Kazakhstan o pereoformlenii zadolzhennosti po technicheskim kreditam po itogam 1992 goda i yanvarya-iyunya 1993 g. v gosudarstvenniy kredit Pravitel'stvu respubliki Kazakhstan, Moscow [No publisher], 1993.

68. Soglashenie mezhdu Pravitel'stvom Rossiyskoy Federatsii i Pravitel'stvom Respubliki Kazakhstan o gosudarstvennom kredite na 1993 god, Moscow [No publisher], 1993.

69. "Statement on New Monetary System Involving Russia, Kazakhstan, Uzbekistan", *BBC Monitoring Service: Former USSR*, 10.08.93.

70. "Russia's Central Bank Chairman Holds Talks in Alma-Ata", *BBC Monitoring Service: Former USSR*, 14.08.93.

71. "Kazakh President Visits Akmola Oblast; Talks of Rouble Zone and Grain Harvest", *BBC Monitoring Service: Former USSR*, 28.08.93.

72. "Bank Head Says Too Early for Republic to Introduce National Currency", *BBC Monitoring Service: Former USSR*, 02.09.93.

73. Nazarbayev, N., *Na poroge XXI veka*, p. 146.

74. "Text of Six CIS States' Agreement on a 'New-Style Rouble-Zone'", *BBC Monitoring Service: Former USSR*, 08.09.93.

75. "Nazarbayev Convinced That There Is No Alternative to Integration", *BBC Monitoring Service: Former USSR*, 11.09.93.

76. "Russia and Kazakhstan Sign Agreement on Rouble Zone and Use of Nuclear Power", *BBC Monitoring Service: Former USSR*, 27.09.93.

77. *Izvestiya*, 25.11.93.

78. "Dogovor o sozdanii Ekonomicheskogo soyuza", *Kazakhstansko-Rossiyskie otnosheniya, 1991–1995 gody*, pp. 335–338.

79. Puzanov, Yu., Khromov, Yu., "Perspektivy razvitiya integratsionnykh protsessov v ramkakh SNG", *Novaya Evraziya*, No. 4, 1995, p. 69.

80. Reuters News Service, 11.10.93.

81. *Izvestiya*, 16.11.93.

82. *Moskovskie novosti*, 21.11.93.

83. *Izvestiya*, 03.11.93.

84. Nazarbayev, N., *Na poroge XXI veka*, pp. 146–147.

85. *Moskovskie novosti*, 21.11.93.

86. Nazarbayev, N., *Na poroge XXI veka*, p. 147.

87. Protokol rabochey vstrechi pravitel'stvennikh delegatsiy Rossiyskoy Federatsii i Respubliki Kazakhstan s uchastiem Tsentral'nogo banka Rossiyskoy Federatsii i Natsional'nogo banka Respubliki Kazakhstan, Moscow [No publisher], 03.11.93

88. *Nezavisimaya gazeta*, 16.01.97.

89. Nazarbayev, N., *Na poroge XXI veka*, p. 147.

90. Mansurov, T., *Razvitie kazakhstansko-rossiyskih otnosheniy v protsesse suverenizatsii Kazakhstana (1991–1995 gody), Avtoreferat dissertatsii na soiskanie uchenoy stepeni doktora politicheskikh nauk*, Moscow: Institut Rossiyskoy Istorii, 1996, pp. 27–28.

91. Khroustalev, M., *Tsentral'naya Aziya vo vneshney politike Rossii*, Moscow: MGIMO, 1994, pp. 25–26.

92. "Russian Interests in the CIS", *International Affairs*, No. 11, 1994, p. 18.

93. "Kazakhstan to Push for Closer Economic Union at CIS Summit", *BBC Monitoring Service: Former USSR*, 23.12.93.

94. *Nezavisimaya gazeta*, 25.12.93.

95. *Kazakhstansko-Rossiyskie otnosheniya, 1991-1995 gody, Sbornik dokumentov i materialov*, Moscow: Posol'stvo Respubliki Kazakhstan v Rossiyskoy Federatsii, 1995, pp. 305–306.

96. *Times*, 23.03.94.

97. Nazarbayev, N., *Na poroge XXI veka*, pp. 102–103, 108.

98. Ibid.

99. "Proekt o formirovanii Evraziyskogo Soyuza Gosudarstv", *Kazakhstansko-Rossiyskie otnosheniya, 1991–1995 gody*, p. 367.

100. Ibid., pp. 367–369.

101. Ibid.

102. "Proekt o formirovanii Evraziyskogo Soyuza Gosudarstv", *Kazakhstansko-Rossiyskie otnosheniya, 1991–1995 gody*, pp. 370–376.

103. "Federation Council Speaker Supports Nazarbayev's Idea of a Eurasian Union", *BBC Monitoring Service: Former USSR*, 01.04.94.

104. "Shakhray Puts Forward Draft Eurasian Confederation Agreement", *BBC Monitoring Service: Former USSR*, 06.04.94.

105. Kazhegildin, A., "'Evrasiyskiy Soyuz': teoreticheskie discussii i prakticheskie shagi", *Vneshniaya politika Kazakhstana, Sbornik statey*, Moscow: Ministerstvo Inostrannikh Del Respubliki Kazakhstan, 1995, p. 19.

106. "Yeltsin's Reaction to Plans for Eurasian Union Described by Press Secretary", *BBC Monitoring Service: Former USSR*, 04.04.94.

107. "Russian and Kazakhstan Issue Joint Statement on Nazarbayev's Visit", *BBC Monitoring Service: Former USSR*, 05.04.94.

108. "Dogovor o dalneyshem uglublenii economicheskogo soTrudnichestva i integratsii Respublici Kazakhstan i Rossiyskoy Federatsii", *Kazakhstansko-rossiyskie otnosheniya, 1991–1995*, pp. 150–151.

109. "CIS Leaders Give Press Conference on Results of Summit", *BBC Monitoring Service: Former USSR*, 18.04.94.

110. "Razvitie idei Evraziyskogo Soyuza Gosudarstv", *Kazakhstansko-rossiyskie otnosheniya, 1991–1995*, p. 378.

111. "Uzbek-Kazakh-Kyrgyz Summit Held in Alma-Ata", *BBC Monitoring Service: Former USSR*, 12.07.94.

112. Ibid.

113. "Belarussian and Kazakh Presidents Discuss Integration", *BBC Monitoring Service: Former USSR*, 15.08.94.

114. Plishevskiy, B., "Evraziyskie manevri Nursultana Nazarbayeva nravyatsya ne vsem", *Vek*, No. 34, 1994, p. 7.

115. Nazarbayev, N., *Na poroge XXI veka* p. 104.

116. Reuters News Service, 21.10.94.

117. "Reshenie po predlozheniiu Respubliki Kazakhstan o formirovanii Evraziyskogo Soyuza Gosudarstv", *Kazakhstansko-rossiyskie otnosheniya, 1991–1995*, p. 356.

118. Reuters News Service, 22.10.94.

119. "Russian Interests in the CIS", *International Affairs*, No. 11, 1994, pp. 12–13.

120. Khroustalev, M., *Tsentral'naya Aziya vo vneshney politike Rossii*, Moscow: MGIMO, 1994, p. 27.

121. *Rossiyskaya gazeta*, 25.03.95.

122. Zagorsky, A., "Rossiya - SNG i Zapad", *Mezhdunarodnaya zhizn'*, No. 10, 1994, p. 83.

123. Zhirinovskiy, V., *Ideologiya dlya Rossii*, Moscow: LDPR, 1997, pp. 62–63.

124. Kiderbekuli, D., "Formirovanie strategii vneshney politiki Kazakhstana", *Evraziyskoe Soobschestvo: ekonomika, politika, bezopasnost'*, No. 4–5, 1995, p. 159.

125. Nazarbayev, N., *Na poroge XXI veka* p. 107.

126. Akhmedzhanov, A., Sultangalieva, A., "Ideya Evraziyskogo Soyuza dlya SNG i Kazakhstana (Popytka reintegratsii postsovetskogo prostranstva na printsipakh partnerstva)", *Kazakhstan i mirovoe soobshchestvo*, No. 1(2), 1995, p. 31.

127. Mansurov, T., "Integratsiya i suverinitet - strategicheskie prioritety kazakhstansko-rossiyskikh otnosheniy", *Kazakhstan i mirovoe soobshchestvo*, No. 2(3), 1995, p. 14.

128. Bugay, N., Otzyv na rukopis doktorskoy dissertatsii Mansurova Taira Aymukhametovicha "Razvitie kazakhstansko-rossiyskikh otnosheniy v protsesse suverenizatsii Kazakhstan (1991–1995 gg.)", Moscow [No publisher], 1996, pp. 6–7.

129. Bagramov, E., "Rossiya i proekt Evraziyskogo Soyuza", *Evraziya: narody, kultury, religii*, No. 1(3), 1995, pp. 21–22.

130. Iordanskiy, V., "Evraziyskaya perspektiva: realnost ili mirazh?", *Rossiya na novom rubezhe*, 1995, p. 14; Myasnikov, V., "Evraziyskaya ideya i ee perspektivy", *Biznes i politika*, No. 5, 1995, p. 8.

131. Bagramov, E., "Rossiya i proekt Evraziyskogo Soyuza", *Evraziya: narody, kultury, religii*, No. 1(3), 1995, pp. 21–22.

132. Semenkin, N., "Kontseptsiya 'pravyaschego otbora' kak politicheskaya ideya evrasiystva", *Etnopoliticheskiy vestnik*, No. 1, 1994, pp. 180–182.

133. Trubetskoy, N., "Obscheevraziyskiy natsionalism", *Etnopoliticheskiy vestnik*, No. 4, 1995, pp. 218–221.

134. Titarenko, M., "Aziatskiy aspekt evraziystva", *Etnopoliticheskiy vestnik*, No. 5, 1995, pp. 114–115.

135. Kazhegeldin, A., "'Evrasiyskiy Soyuz': teoreticheskie diskussii i prakticheskie shagi", p. 25.

136. Reuters News Service, 21.10.94.

137. "Reshenie po predlozheniyu Respubliki Kazakhstan o formirovanii Evraziyskogo Soyuza Gosudarstv", *Kazakhstansko-rossiyskie otnosheniya, 1991–1995 gody*, p. 356.

138. Reuters News Service, 21.10.94.

139. *Segodnya*, 22.10.94.

140. "Soglashenie o sozdanii Platezhnogo soyuza gosudarstv-uchastnikov Sodruzhestva Nezavisimykh Gosudarstv", *Kazakhstansko-rossiyskie otnosheniya, 1991–1995 gody*, pp. 357–362.

141. "Nazarbayev on Greater Integration Among CIS States", *BBC Monitoring Service: Former USSR*, 05.01.95.

142. "Soglashenie o sozdanii Platezhnogo soyuza gosudarstv-uchastnikov Sodruzhestva Nezavisimykh Gosudarstv", *Kazakhstansko-rossiyskie otnosheniya, 1991–1995 gody*, pp. 357–362.

143. Reuters News Service, 10.02.95.

144. "Soglashenie o Tamozhennom soyuze", *Kazakhstansko-rossiyskie otnosheniya, 1991–1995 gody*, pp. 230–231.

145. "Memorandum Pravitel'stv Respubliki Belarus, Respubliki Kazakhstan i Rossiyskoy Federatsii ob uchastii v troystvennom Tamozhennom soyuze drugikh zainteresovannykh gosudarstv Economicheskogo soyuza", *Kazakhstansko-rossiyskie otnosheniya, 1991–1995 gody*, p. 241.

146. Kazhegeldin, A., "'Evrasiyskiy Soyuz': teoreticheskie diskussii i prakticheskie shagi", p. 23.

147. "Soglashenie mezhdu Respublikoy Kazakhstan i Rossiyskoy Federatsiey o edinstve upravleniya tamozhennymi sluzhbami", *Kazakhstansko-rossiyskie otnosheniya, 1991–1995 gody*, pp. 247–248.

148. "Kazakh-Russian-Belarus Customs Union Comes into Effect on 20th July", *BBC Monitoring Service: Former USSR*, 21.07.95.

149. "Kazakh President Discusses Customs Union with Russian Envoy", *BBC Monitoring Service: Former USSR*, 21.08.95.

150. "Kazakhstan and Russia Sign Customs Union Agreement", *BBC Monitoring Service: Former USSR*, 21.08.95.

151. "Kazakhstan Lifts Customs Control on Russian Borders", *BBC Monitoring Service: Former USSR*, 22.09.95.

152. "Central Asian Summit—Text of Communique", *BBC Monitoring Service: Former USSR*, 17.04.95.

153. "Kazakh-Russian-Belarus Customs Union Comes into Effect on 20th July", *BBC Monitoring Service: Former USSR*, 21.07.95.

154. "Central Asian Summit—Text of Communique", *BBC Monitoring Service: Former USSR*, 17.04.95.

155. "Russia Not Yet Ready to Cancel Customs Control on Kazakh Border", *BBC Monitoring Service: Former USSR*, 28.09.95.

156. "Kazakhstan, Russia and Belarus Agree on Customs Union Terms", *BBC Monitoring Service: Former USSR*, 25.11.95; *Commersant*, 25.11.95.

157. "First Deputy Premier Soskovets Stresses Need to Develop Cooperation with CIS", *BBC Monitoring Service: Former USSR*, 04.01.96; "Yeltsin Orders End to Customs Controls on Russian-Kazakh Border", *BBC Monitoring Service: Former USSR*, 04.01.96.

158. Presidential elections were to take place on 16 June 1996.

159. "Programma Kommunisticheskoy Partii Rossiyskoy Federatsii", *Pravda*, 31 January 1995, p. 2.

160. *OMRI Daily Digest*, No. 55, Part I, 18.03.96.

161. "Zayavlenie Prezidenta Respubliki Kazakhstan N.A.Nazarbayeva po povodu resheniya Gosudarstvennoy Dumy Rossiyskoy Federatsii ot 15 marta 1996 goda (17 marta 1996 goda, g.Almaty)", *Diplomaticheskiy kurier*, No. 2, 1996, pp. 31–32.

162. The accession of Kyrgysztan to the treaty became possible after in March 1996 it joined the Customs Union.

163. "Dogovor mezhdu Respublikoy Kazakhstan, Respublikoy Belarus, Kyrgyzskoy Respublikoy i Rossiyskoy Federatsiey ob uglublenii integratsii v ekonomicheskoy i gumanitarnoy oblastyakh", *Diplomaticheskiy kurier*, No. 2, 1996, pp. 46–49.

164. On 18 October 1996 the Integration Committee was also designated as the executive body of the Customs Union (*Kazakhstanskaya pravda*, 08.01.97).

165. Reuters News Service, 01.04.96.

166. *The Times*, 30.03.96.

167. Reuters News Service, 01.04.96.

168. Nazarbayev, N., "Obschestvennoe soglasie - osnova demokraticheskogo razvitiya Kazakhstana, Doklad na tret'ey sessii Assamblei narodov Kazakhstana", *Kazakhstan i mirovoe soobshchestvo*, No. 1, 1996, p. 7.

169. *Kazakhstanskaya pravda*, 24.04.97.

170. Reuters News Service, 02.04.97.

171. Reuters News Service, 25.03.96; *Financial Times*, 17.04.96.

172. "Yeltsin Vetoes Several Laws, Including One on Customs Union with Kazakhstan", *BBC Monitoring Service: Former USSR*, 16.01.97.

173. Reuters News Service, 18.03.97.

174. *Kazakhstanskaya pravda*, 01.04.97.

175. "Russian Minister Responds to President Nazarbayev's Remarks", *BBC Monitoring Service: Former USSR*, 22.05.97.

176. *Kazakhstanskaya pravda*, 30.10.97.

177. "Yeltsin, Nazarbayev for Making Integration More Efficient", *ITAR-TASS World Service*, 06.09.97.

178. *Kazakhstanskaya pravda*, 09.09.97.

179. "Kremlin Unpleased with CIS Customs Union's Work", *ITAR-TASS World Service*, 10.09.97.

180. *Kazakhstanskaya pravda*, 30.10.97.

181. "Russian, Belorussian, Kazakh, Kyrgyz Leaders Agree on Further Integration Steps", *BBC Monitoring Service: Former USSR*, 24.10.97; "Quadrilateral Customs Union Likely to Accept Tajikistan", *ITAR-TASS World Service*, 23.10.97.

182. "Customs Chief Sceptical of New VAT Rules for Customs Union Members", *BBC Monitoring Service: Former USSR*, 27.10.97.

183. "Four CIS Presidents to Meet in January Ahead of CIS Summit", *ITAR-TASS World Service*, 17.12.97.

5

Relations Between Russia and Kazakhstan in the Military and Strategic Spheres

The conclusion of the Treaty on Friendship, Cooperation and Mutual Assistance did not immediately lead to a military alliance between Russia and Kazakhstan. In 1992–1993 major difficulties, contradictions and tensions characterised Russian-Kazakh relations in the military sphere. Russian Deputy Foreign Minister Panov described negotiations with Kazakhstan on military questions as very hard.[1] Both countries were preoccupied with wrangling over the future of former Soviet military assets located in Kazakhstan. The Kazakh authorities complained that Russia's Defence Ministry and other departments constantly violated the property division principles agreed upon at the CIS October 1992 summit in Bishkek and systematically removed military equipment to Russia.[2] Russian surface-to-air missile tests near the border with Atirau province, some of which resulted in Russian missiles falling in Kazakhstan, provided another cause for Kazakh dissatisfaction. The Kazakh side regarded such incidents as violations of its sovereignty, and more than once protested to Russia, which made formal apologies but did not change the direction of missile launches.[3] By December 1992 Kazakhstan had closed four major military test ranges, depriving the Russian military of the ability to use them.[4] Russia in turn refused to satisfy Kazakhstan's 1993 request for arms supplies totalling 14.6 billion roubles (at 1 July 1993 prices) due to Kazakhstan's chronic inability to pay its bills.[5]

On 19 August talks on a wide range of military issues were held in Alma-Ata with a Russian military delegation, headed by Chief of General Staff General V. Dubinin. Altogether twelve draft agreements were discussed covering issues such as the legal status of Russian Strategic Nuclear Forces (SNF) units stationed in Kazakhstan, the procedure for their withdrawal and joint use of Kazakhstan's test ranges for the benefit of both countries' armed forces. But only two agreements were signed.[6] The first dealt with the training of Kazakh officers in Russian military educational establishments, and granted free training for officer cadets from Kazakhstan, a privilege accorded to no other CIS member. The second agreement, signed on 19 August 1992, dealt with transfers of officers and warrant officers between the two countries' armies, and stipulated that such transfers were to be free from interference by either country's military authorities.[7] This agreement was mostly of interest to Russian, because many officers in Kazakhstan's army were ethnic Russians, and preferred to continue their careers in Russia's army. This of course did not suit Kazakhstan, but Almaty realised that lack of an agreement on personnel transfers could not stop the exodus of Russian officers, and would only harm relations with Moscow by attaching an air of anarchy and illegality to it. The other ten draft agreements were referred to the political leadership for consideration, and shelved for a long time.

In 1993 Russia and Kazakhstan concluded three more military agreements, two of which were signed by their prime ministers on 22 January 1993 at the CIS summit in Minsk. The first regulated the procedure for using the remaining test ranges in Kazakhstan, the second established principles for mutual material and technical maintenance of both countries' armed forces. The third agreement, signed by the prime ministers on 25 February 1993 in Almaty, covered cooperation and interaction on border issues. These agreements were of secondary importance, and did not establish a framework for comprehensive military cooperation. During Nazarbayev's visit to Moscow on 26–27 February, Russia and Kazakhstan reached an understanding to draft a bilateral agreement on military cooperation within a month.[8] But the subsequent negotiations dragged on for over a year.

The major disagreement during this period remained the issue of control over nuclear weapons. In the second half of 1992, after Kazakhstan, Ukraine and Belarus signed the Lisbon Protocol, Russia proceeded to the next stage of the plan, their nuclear disarmament. A key foreign policy directive, Basic Provisions of the Russian Federation's Foreign Policy Concept, signed by Yeltsin in April 1993, reflected his strategic objective. It identified "ensuring Russia's status as the only nuclear power in the CIS" as a foreign policy priority.[9] At the CIS summit in Moscow in July 1992, Russia pushed through a decision to "immediately initiate talks" aimed at ridding Belarus, Kazakhstan and Ukraine of nuclear weapons.[10]

But Moscow's task was not easy. Though Kazakhstan, Ukraine and Belarus pledged adherence to the Nuclear Non-Proliferation Treaty as non-nuclear states, the state property division principles inside the CIS entitled them to full ownership of nuclear weapons on their territory. This gave them strong diplomatic leverage to counter Russia's bid for sole control of nuclear weapons. The disagreements revealed themselves at the CIS summit in Bishkek on 9 October 1992, when Russia made its first official proposal to take full control of CIS nuclear weapons. CIS Commander-in-Chief Air Marshal

Shaposhnikov said in an interview preceding the summit that "you cannot leave such terrible weapons without control by a specific national state", and that Yeltsin fully agreed with his initiative.[11] In Bishkek, Shaposhnikov suggested that Russia be given sole control over launch codes and dismantling of nuclear weapons. Belarus supported this proposal, but it met strong resistance from Ukraine.[12]

Before the summit Russia and Kazakhstan had finalised all provisions of a draft agreement on the status of SNF units stationed in Kazakhstan except one: who would have jurisdiction over them until their withdrawal? Russian Defence Minister Grachev said that if Yeltsin and Nazarbayev agreed, the issue could be resolved on the Belorussian pattern, and the strategic forces transferred to Russian jurisdiction.[13] But Nazarbayev refused. On the eve of the summit he indicated he was against changing the status of the nuclear forces.[14]

After the summit Russia continued to pursue obtaining sole ownership of nuclear weapons. For that purpose the CIS Joint Armed Forces High Command scheduled a meeting of the defence ministers of Russia, Ukraine, Belorussia and Kazakhstan (the Nuclear Policy Committee) for 21 January, immediately before the CIS summit in Minsk.[15] Before the meeting Shaposhnikov reiterated Russia's position that "according to the spirit and letter of the Lisbon Protocol, all nuclear weapons in what was the USSR are Russian".[16] At the meeting Russia counted very much on winning Kazakhstan's support and diplomatically isolating Ukraine. Grachev even praised Kazakhstan's position, saying it was close to that of Belarus.[17] This was clearly wishful thinking. At the meeting Kazakhstan sided with Ukraine, not Russia. After the meeting, Kazakhstan's Defence Minister Nurmagambetov told reporters, "We do not say the nuclear weapons are under Russian control. They are under unified command. . . . This is implemented through the Supreme Command of CIS Strategic Forces." According to L. Ivashov, secretary to the CIS Council of Defence Ministers, there had been tough talk between the four members of the nuclear club. The meeting failed to resolve the issue of ownership and control of the SNF.[18]

Squabbling continued at the CIS Defence Ministers' meeting in Moscow on 13 May 1993, with Russia on one side, and Kazakhstan and Ukraine on the other. Russia rejected draft agreements on the structure, functions and responsibilities of the CIS Joint Armed Forces Command. Grachev said that the provisions in them which left the right to control nuclear weapons to the CIS Joint Armed Forces Command did not suit Russia. "The Command, like the CIS, is not a state, and cannot have the right to control and use nuclear weapons", he said, pointing out that the signing of the Lisbon protocol and concomitant statements by the leaders of Kazakhstan and Ukraine amounted to acknowledgment that Russia alone had ownership rights over the former Soviet nuclear arsenal. Both Kazakhstan and Ukraine denied this and maintained that the original agreements establishing CIS control over nuclear weapons held sway.[19] The situation appeared deadlocked.

The Kazakh position expressed sincere anxiety about Russia's future policies toward Kazakhstan, anxiety that conclusion of the Russian-Kazakh Treaty on Friendship, Cooperation and Mutual Assistance had failed to dispel. Publications by official Kazakh experts gave a clear insight into the line of thinking adopted by Nazarbayev's leadership. One such publication, *Kazakhstan and the Nuclear Non-Proliferation Treaty*, was prepared by a team from the Kazakhstan Institute of Strategic Studies, a subdivision of the presidential administration. The authors argued that "[i]f the democratic process in Russia is terminated, and neo-Bolshevik forces come to power, they will try to turn back the wheel of history and reanimate the previous totalitarian system and the Empire within the boundaries of 1917. . . . It is absolutely clear that they will rely primarily on military strength, including nuclear weapons. . . . Will it not be an error of strategic dimensions to confirm Russia's monopoly control over nuclear weapons, deployed on the territory of Ukraine, Belarus and Kazakhstan and to recognise Russian status of these weapons and not the collective one envisaged in the Alma-Ata and Minsk agreements"?[20]

Thus security issues drove Nazarbayev's agenda, when he fought so hard to retain control of part of the former USSR's nuclear arsenal. But he lost the battle. On 11 June 1993 in a diplomatically ingenious move Yeltsin appointed CIS Commander-in-Chief Air Marshal Shaposhnikov to the post of secretary of the Russian Security Council. In an interview on the next day, Yeltsin said that Shaposhnikov had become available because the responsibilities of the CIS Command were shrinking as the former Soviet states built their own armies, and added that the SNF were being subordinated to the Russian Defence Ministry.[21] This move nearly breached Russia's international obligations. The ingenuity was that Shaposhnikov relinquished the Command of his own free will and nobody could prevent his doing so. No successor could be appointed because the post could be filled only by unanimous vote of the CIS Council of Heads of State, and Russia would not approve any candidate. Shaposhnikov's resignation therefore ensured de facto elimination of the post, and without a Commander-in-Chief the High Command of CIS Joint Armed Forces could not function. This effectively transferred operational control of the SNF to the Russian Defence Ministry. The ingenuity of the Russian manoeuvre was well understood in Almaty. L. Bakaev, Head of the International Security Department of Kazakhstan's Foreign Ministry, wrote "to coerce Kazakhstan into withdrawing nuclear weapons from its territory and recognising Russia's right to possess all the nuclear weapons, Russia embarked on the policy of abolishing the post of CIS Commander-in-Chief".[22] But Kazakhstan and the rest of the CIS, faced with a fait accompli, had nothing to counter to it.

The CIS Defence Ministers' meeting in Moscow on 15 June therefore had no alternative but to accept Russia's proposal to abolish the CIS High Command[23] and to replace it with a Staff for Coordination of Military Cooperation of CIS Member States, a looser body with only consultative functions, no authority over CIS nuclear weapons. Russia's move also deprived Kazakhstan of any decision-making role regarding the use of nuclear weapons.

Now Moscow had to solve only the final problem, physical removal of the nuclear weapons from Kazakhstan. And Almaty had only one option left – to exact the highest possible price for their removal.

In a speech at the UN on 5 October, Suleimenov, Kazakhstan's foreign minister, indicated the estimated price for Kazakhstan's nuclear disarmament – $2 billion in aid to dismantle the nuclear systems and clean up the Semipalatinsk nuclear test site.[24] But Russia, with its own economic problems, had no intention of paying the bill. Russian diplomacy applied the tactic, which by then had become typical, sustaining international fears of possible nuclear proliferation from Kazakhstan, while referring the financial aspects of the problem to the West.

In December 1993 U.S. Vice President Gore visited Almaty, bringing an offer of $88 million in financial assistance for Kazakhstan's expenses in dismantling nuclear missiles. Kazakhstan also won recognition of its right to part of the proceeds from the sale of highly enriched uranium extracted from the warheads. On 13 December 1993, three hours after the U.S. delegation landed at Almaty airport, Kazakhstan's parliament ratified the Nuclear Non-Proliferation Treaty and accepted a loan of $214 million obtained from the International Bank for Reconstruction and Development with American help.[25] In return Kazakhstan signed a framework agreement on dismantling intercontinental ballistic missile launching silos.

Final details of the U.S. denuclearisation aid package were formalised on 15 February 1994, during Nazarbayev' s visit to the United States. Nazarbayev formally handed documents on Kazakhstan's accession to the Nuclear Non-Proliferation Treaty to President Clinton, who more than tripled U.S. aid to Kazakhstan, from $91 million in 1993 to $311 million in 1994.[26] To further encourage Kazakhstan's nuclear disarmament, US Secretary of Defence Perry visited Almaty on 19–20 March and signed another agreement providing $15 million in aid for defence industry conversion. Perry also received assurances from Nazarbayev that all SS-18 ICBMs in Kazakhstan would be shipped to Russia for dismantling.[27]

The total sum received by Kazakhstan did not approach the $2 billion initially requested, but did at least sweeten the disarmament pill. In any case, it helped Moscow to reach formal agreements with Almaty on the nuclear issue. A preliminary understanding had been reached in December 1993, when Chernomyrdin arrived after Gore had left. His talks with Tereshchenko resulted in the signing of a memorandum which provided for negotiations to begin "in the immediate future on the timetable for detachment and withdrawal of all nuclear warheads from Kazakhstan to the territory of Russia, as well as to determine the procedure for elimination of the strategic offensive weapons, deployed in the Republic of Kazakhstan". Unlike the United States, Russia managed to avoid any specific obligation to pay for Kazakhstan's nuclear disarmament. The memorandum contained only the vague provision that Russia was prepared "to consider and solve questions of compensating the Republic of Kazakhstan with equivalents of the cost of fissionable materials and other components of nuclear weapons through separate agreements, taking account of Russia's expenses on their storage, transportation, dismantling and reprocessing".[28] Meanwhile, Russia could prepare a large bill of its own expenses to offset Kazakh claims. For example, in a February 1995 interview General Sergeev, commander of the Russian Strategic Rocket Forces, stated that Almaty was in no hurry to resolve the issue of how much to pay Russia for the housing facilities and other infrastructure that it would leave in Kazakhstan.[29]

On 28 March 1994, during Nazarbayev's visit to Moscow, Russia and Kazakhstan settled the legal issues related to the SNF in Kazakhstan. The first document signed, the Treaty on Military Cooperation between the Republic of Kazakhstan and the Russian Federation, covered a wide range of military and strategic issues, and contained several provisions on SNF units' status in Kazakhstan. Article 3 of the treaty stipulated that Kazakhstan "taking into account the existing system of functioning of Strategic Nuclear Forces situated on its territory, recognises that the above military formations of the Strategic Nuclear Forces should have the status of Strategic Nuclear Forces of the Russian Federation". In turn, Russia, under Article 3, recognised Kazakhstan's right "to receive the equivalent (in cash or other form) of the cost of the materials of nuclear forces, agreed by the Parties". The protocol on talks between Chernomyrdin and Tereshchenko contained special provisions instructing the respective ministries to prepare within three months an agreement on compensation to Kazakhstan for the uranium, and proposals on compensation for strategic bombers and air launched cruise missiles transferred to Russia.[30] Neither directive was fulfilled in time.

The second agreement, On the Strategic Nuclear Forces Temporarily Stationed on the Territory of Republic of Kazakhstan, covered the period up to the liquidation of all SNF presence in Kazakhstan. It addressed a number of technical issues related to the SNF's status and functioning during the transition period. The procedure for employing strategic nuclear weapons provided for consultations between the Russian and Kazakh presidents. General SNF activities in Kazakhstan were to be subject to consultation with Kazakhstan's Defence Ministry. Kazakhstan undertook not to impede the SNF's performance of its functions and promised to provide the SNF with communal services, electricity, gas, accommodation and medical care pending withdrawal.[31]

Meanwhile, withdrawal was already under way. On 22 February 1994 Colonel-General Deinekin, Commander-in-Chief of Russia's Air Force, advised the press that the last four Russian Tu-95MS (NATO designation: Bear H) bombers had been moved to Russia.[32] Then the Kazakhs resumed delaying tactics, by hampering the transfer to Russia of the remaining 1040 ICBM warheads. As witnessed by Colonel-General Merkulov, Russian Defence Ministry representative at the hearings on Russian-Kazakh relations in the Russian State Duma in April 1995, the withdrawal of nuclear weapons from Kazakhstan had been proceeding with great difficulties; the Kazakhs "systematically linked this issue with compensation for the aircraft and highly enriched uranium being withdrawn".[33]

Not until early 1995 did the controversy over compensation resolve. At that time, as stated by SNF Commander-in-Chief General Sergeev, only 266 strategic nuclear warheads remained in Kazakhstan.[34] On 20 January 1995 Moscow and Almaty concluded the agreement, On Cooperation and Settling Mutual Accounts during Reprocessing of Nuclear Weapons, which stipulated that highly enriched uranium would be transferred to Russia for recycling into low-grade uranium to be sold later to the United States. Kazakhstan was entitled to a fixed share of the profit from each sale. Russia's expenses incurred in dismantling nuclear warheads, transporting and recycling the uranium, and sales-related costs would be deducted from the Kazakh share. Details of calculating these expenses and determining dates and terms of payments were to be specified in a special Russian-Kazakh contract. Plutonium extracted from the warheads was to be stored in Russia, pending a joint decision on its future use. The agreement would be considered fulfilled once all the uranium was sold and Kazakhstan received its share of the profits.[35] Implementation of the agreement ran into difficulties immediately after signing, because the Russian Finance Ministry declined to make advance payments for work connected with recycling the uranium.[36] How much compensation Kazakhstan has received for the uranium is still unknown.

A more precise agreement was reached with regard to compensation for strategic bombers and cruise missiles. In January 1995 Russian Deputy Prime Minister Soskovets authorised an interdepartmental commission, comprising representatives of the Ministries of Defence, Foreign Affairs and CIS Affairs, to draft an agreement with Kazakhstan to assist it in creating two air force regiments as a form of compensation.[37] The agreement was concluded at the meeting of CIS heads of government in Moscow on 3 November 1995.[38] It provided for the transfer of seventy three combat aircraft (21 MIG-29s, 14 SU-25s and 38 SU-27s) to Kazakhstan, as compensation for strategic bombers withdrawn to Russia. However, by October 1997 only forty-one planes had been transferred.[39]

It took Russia more than a year to complete the withdrawal and elimination of nuclear weapons from Kazakhstan. Given the complexity of the task, the Russians acted expeditiously. Finally, on 25 April 1995 Colonel General Yesin, Russian Strategic Rocket Forces Chief of Staff, made an official statement that all Soviet-era nuclear warheads had been transferred.[40] President Nazarbayev confirmed this in his 26 May address to the nation, in which he stated that "all deadly warheads have been removed from the republic's territory".[41] Kazakhstan had become de facto a non-nuclear weapon state. The diplomatic struggle between Russia and Kazakhstan had not ended to Kazakhstan's advantage, though Nazarbayev tried to prove otherwise in his memoirs.

Nazarbayev claimed that the primary objective of his diplomatic manoeuvring on the nuclear issue was to force the nuclear powers, including the United States, to provide Kazakhstan with security guarantees, and

Kazakhstan renounced the nuclear weapons on its territory only after it received them. He wrote, "My position was clear — first security guarantees from great powers, and then we will relinquish all nuclear weapons. . . . I understood that there could be no alternative to non-nuclear status for our state. But I faced a task — to ensure Kazakhstan's security in very difficult conditions of system instability embracing the whole world". He claimed that the guarantees were provided in the Memorandum on Security Guarantees signed by the United States, Great Britain and Russia at the CSCE summit in Budapest in December 1994.[42]

It seems, however, that Nazarbayev overstates the case in claiming he obtained real security guarantees from the great powers including the United States. The Budapest memorandum does indeed contain a provision that the United States, Great Britain and Russia "confirm their obligations to seek immediate UN Security Council action in providing assistance to the Republic of Kazakhstan. . . if the Republic of Kazakhstan becomes a victim of aggression or subject to a threat of aggression with use of nuclear weapons".[43] This provision, however, can not be regarded as a real security guarantee. First, the memorandum deals exclusively with the possibility of a nuclear attack against Kazakhstan. But neither Russia nor China,[44] the countries Kazakhs were most concerned about, would need nuclear weapons in any conflict with Kazakhstan, because their military potential is immeasurably stronger than Kazakhstan's. Besides both are permanent members of the UN Security Council and can veto any decision directed against their actions. Second, the only obligation contained in the memorandum is to ask the UN Security Council to do something. With this accomplished, the signatories of the memorandum can claim that they have fulfilled their obligations, without taking any practical actions. On the other hand, if they decide to take the matter further, they can. In all, the memorandum gave the signatories the right to act as they wished, if and when such a situation arises.

It is important to look at the difference between the Kazakh and U.S. interpretations of the document. When visiting Kazakhstan in March 1994 U.S. Secretary of Defence Perry made a statement about the memorandum at a news conference. He said that an agreement involving the United States, Britain and Russia was being prepared which would give Kazakhstan a security assurance from the nuclear states, which would assure consultations and help stabilise any dangerous situations. Perry also clarified that an important distinction exists between security *guarantee* and security *assurance*: "It is an assurance — it is not a guarantee. It is not a statement that we would go to war on any issue that arose with Kazakhstan."[45] In practice Perry's statement did no more than confirm the stance taken by Bush administration in May 1992. This was the most the United States was prepared to offer to Kazakhstan.

Some nonofficial Kazakhs have also pointed this out. E. Abenov, a scholar at the Institute for Development of Kazakhstan, wrote: "It is inappropriate to rely unreservedly on the security guarantees received by Kazakhstan from the US, Britain, France, China and Russia. For the time being Moscow still has the right of veto in the Security Council, just in case".[46] Thus for the time being Kazakhstan enjoys a formal security guarantee from only one nuclear power — Russia. This is confirmed not in the Budapest memorandum but in the Russian-Kazakh Treaty of Friendship, Cooperation and Mutual Assistance.

The diplomatic struggle between Russia and Kazakhstan over the nuclear issue was closely linked to the problem of Baykonur cosmodrome. The new Russian policy of taking sole control of the CIS nuclear arsenal and abolishing the CIS Joint Armed Forces Command inevitably had negative repercussions on the Baykonur issue. The Russian-Kazakh agreement on Baykonur of 25 May 1992 stipulated that possession and operational management of the cosmodrome's facilities and equipment would be transferred to the CIS Strategic Forces.[47] While the CIS Joint Armed Forces Command existed, everything complied with the agreement. On 2 October 1992 Russia and Kazakhstan signed a document defining the facilities to be handed over to the CIS Strategic Forces, and the conditions for their use and maintenance.[48] In February 1993 Russia and Kazakhstan agreed to cofinance that year's running costs of the cosmodrome, assessed at 32 billion roubles ($32 million).[49]

In reality, however, the situation was much more complex. According to information provided by Koptev, director-general of the Russian Space Agency (RSA), at the Duma hearings on Russian-Kazakh relations in April 1995, the period 1992–1993 had a most negative effect on Baykonur. Koptev said that on paper the cosmodrome was given for use to the Russian military, but "in reality everything worked vice-versa. . . . The mechanism of maintenance through the Defence Ministry was destroyed. The local civil administration appeared. It had no resources. It must be said that it is a miracle we survived the winter of 1993. . . . We were losing houses, water, people were living without water, heating or sewerage".[50]

Obviously, Moscow withheld payments for maintenance. it had undertaken to finance in accordance with the agreement of 25 May 1992 because Kazakhstan established its own administration at Baykonur. For the first quarter of 1993 it paid only half of the 9 billion roubles it promised toward covering 96% of the cosmodrome's running costs.[51] Meanwhile, the cosmodrome's infrastructure was gradually disintegrating. In an attempt to resolve the problems, Yeltsin, in early April 1993, invited Nazarbayev to a meeting in May to discuss the cosmodrome's future. Yeltsin noted that maintaining it was in the interests of the whole world, not just of Russia and Kazakhstan, but that its future would be threatened if the two states could not agree on ways to implement signed treaties that covered key issues such as the legal status of the Russian military units (without which the cosmodrome could not function), the principles of shared financing, manning, and maintenance of safety, law and order.[52] Moscow wanted the military space forces (MSF) deployed at Baykonur to have Russian status, and the launch facility's defence installations accorded the status of a military space base under Russian jurisdiction.[53]

Kazakhstan could not accept Yeltsin's proposals, given its position on the need to maintain the CIS Joint Armed Forces Command. Not surprisingly in May the Kazakh side counterproposed that the MSF formations at Baykonur have joint status, that an interstate joint command and cosmodrome administration be set up to run Baykonur, and a coordinating council set up to manage it, headed by one of Kazakhstan's deputy prime ministers.[54]

In mid-May 1993 the Kazakhstan government placed Baykonur under guard by special formations of its Interior Forces, allegedly to prevent the theft of equipment and other valuable items.[55] But this did not prevent riots taking place on the night of 3–4 June, when 450 military construction personnel went on the rampage, setting offices and barracks on fire, and looting shops and warehouses.[56] As in the riots in February 1992, nobody, including the servicemen themselves, could explain what caused the disturbances. But as in the previous case, the riots occurred just three weeks before a scheduled joint Russian-French mission to the *Mir* space station.

On 9 June 1993, while visiting Serebryansk in East Kazakhstan province, Nazarbayev met officers of the local air defence regiment and told them that his upcoming meeting with Yeltsin would take place at the cosmodrome, where they intended to sign a treaty on military cooperation.[57] But Yeltsin did not go to Baykonur. Unfortunately, the meeting coincided with Yeltsin's unilateral decision to appoint Air Marshal Shaposhnikov Secretary of the Russian Security Council, which, as mentioned above, brought about the abolition of the CIS Joint Armed Forces Command. Almaty was also frustrated at the transfer of the MSF, including those at Baykonur, to the jurisdiction of the Russian Defence Ministry, without coordinating it with the other CIS members. Yeltsin presumably thought the atmosphere unpropitious for him to meet with Nazarbayev, so he sent Defence Minister Grachev and Deputy Prime Minister Soskovets, who were also to attend the launching of the joint Russian-French mission on 1 July.

During their visit Grachev and Soskovets had discussions with Tereshchenko and Defence Minister Nurmagambetov. The negotiations, mainly about Baykonur, failed to resolve the disagreements. Grachev said at a press conference on arrival that Kazakhstan's proposals to put the cosmodrome's military units under joint control, and to set up an interstate constitutional council headed by a deputy premier of Kazakhstan to manage them were unacceptable. He noted that Russia financed the cosmodrome entirely, that the cosmodrome could not exist without Russia's technical and financial resources, and that any change in its status might disrupt space programs. Grachev stated that he would insist on Russian status of the cosmodrome's military units being recognised. But the Kazakh side did not acknowledge Russian jurisdiction over the MSF units at the cosmodrome. "The cosmodrome is on Kazakhstan's territory and we consider it our property," Nurmagambetov said, "We insist on making it a joint facility. Both police and the court on its territory should be Kazakh".[58]

The Kazakhs' position could be explained only by a desire to exclude from the republic any permanent Russian military presence, which they apparently regarded as a breach of their new sovereignty. The abolition of the CIS Command gave Kazakhstan a viable legal excuse to renege on its previous undertakings with regard to Baykonur. The May 1992 agreement stipulated that Baykonur's facilities were for use by the CIS Strategic Rocket Forces, not Russian military units. The de facto difference was minimal, but formally Kazakhstan was entitled to demand withdrawal of Russian troops, especially since Kazakhstan's postindependence constitution banned foreign military bases. This probably contradicted the spirit, but not the letter, of Article 4 of the Treaty on Friendship, Cooperation and Mutual Assistance, which provided that Russia could use military installations on the territory of Kazakhstan, as the Kazakhs could argue that the article did not specify whether such use was to be permanent or temporary.

However, they did not want to lose the substantial economic benefits that exploitation of Baykonur could bring to Kazakhstan. Politically, they understood that complete exclusion of Russia could irreparably damage bilateral relations, which Almaty wanted to avoid. Moreover, exclusion would violate the Treaty on Friendship, Cooperation and Mutual Assistance, automatically allowing Russia to renege on its obligations to Kazakhstan. The Kazakhs therefore developed a concept for Baykonur which they thought would allow them to achieve both aims, ousting the Russian military and securing the cosmodrome's future. The best possible option, as they saw it, was to create an international space company with participation primarily by Russia, Kazakhstan and Ukraine, and possibly other countries. This, they felt, could attract considerable foreign resources as well as help demilitarise the complex.[59]

The concept of internationalisation of Baykonur was clearly designed to counterbalance Russia's influence by that of others, such as Ukraine. But more importantly, the arrangement focused primarily on commercial space programs, marginalising its military role and prospectively leading to full demilitarisation. Russia, with its military space program heavily dependent on Baykonur, inevitably could not agree to this arrangement. Another consideration behind the Kazakh move may have been euphoria undamped by technical expertise. They perhaps thought that opening Baykonur to foreign economic interests would cause a stream of investment to pour into Kazakhstan. But in reality, technological differences between Russian and Western rockets made it impossible to employ Baykonur for launching both.

The Russian military found Kazakhstan's desire to internationalise Baykonur unacceptable, which led to a new round of diplomatic wrangling. On 20 July 1993 Kazakhstan's Deputy Prime Minister Abilsiitov arrived in India to attend the first session of the Indo-Kazakh Joint Commission. He told Indian industrialists that Kazakhstan was ready to offer India use of the cosmodrome for launching satellites, rockets and manned space vehicles. At a meeting organised by the Confederation of Indian Industry, he said that Kazakhstan wished to convert Baykonur for civilian use and wanted Indian firms interested in space technology to invest in the company for use of it.[60] Simultaneously, Aubakirov, director-general of Kazakhstan's National Space Agency, announced that Kazakhstan intended to train experts for Baykonur independently of Russia.[61]

Kazakhstan's diplomatic manoeuvre took Moscow by surprise. Russia's leadership was evidently confused about what to do next, what countermeasures Russia could possibly undertake. This resulted in rather contradictory behaviour during Nazarbayev's visit to Moscow in early August 1993. He came for a CIS conference of Central Asian states and Russia on the situation in Tajikistan, but had a separate meeting with Yeltsin to discuss the problem of Baykonur. On 6 August Yeltsin's press service circulated the text of a joint statement, which stressed the need to preserve Baykonur as a single entity in the interests of Russia, Kazakhstan and the whole CIS.[62]

But Nazarbayev revealed to a Russian television interviewer that, while meeting with Yeltsin, he had proposed creation of an international company to run Baykonur with participation by Russia, Ukraine, Kazakhstan and foreign investors, and that they had ordered their defence and foreign ministries to draw up a military cooperation treaty within a month, including provision for joint use of the cosmodrome.[63] Clearly, Nazarbayev's statement went beyond Yeltsin's press release. Nothing in the agreed formula suggested joint management or foreign participation in running Baykonur. Yeltsin's personally agreeable attitude to Nazarbayev's proposal probably made Nazarbayev overoptimistic. But he was immediately rebuffed. A Russian Foreign Ministry statement merely reaffirmed that Russia and Kazakhstan had agreed that the cosmodrome should be preserved as a single unit acting in the interests of the whole CIS, and made no mention of an international company or foreign participation.[64]

Meanwhile Almaty persevered with its campaign of diplomatic pressure on Moscow, utilising every opportunity that arose. On 18 August Vice President Asanbayev told a delegation from the U.S. Aerojet aerospace company that the Kazakh government wanted to convert Baykonur into an international space company. According to Russian press reports, Aerojet's president, W. Rorer, and its chief engineer, J. Thomson, expressed interest in cooperating with such a company.[65] Also in late August a preliminary Kazakh-Ukrainian agreement signed in Almaty envisaged transformation of the space centre into an international space company.[66]

On 21 September Kazakh television gave extensive coverage to the visit by E. Reuter, chairman of the board of Daimler-Benz, claiming that he had displayed enormous interest in using Baykonur. The heads of Leninsk town administration and of the cosmodrome showed him the missile-assembly shops and experimental departments, and he was reported as saying his company was interested in manufacturing aircraft and undertaking space investigation programs as well as in setting up joint ventures, using the existing facilities. Daimler-Benz experts would visit Baykonur to study the situation.[67] On 3

December Nazarbayev himself received a group of U.S. congressmen, led by George Brown, chairman of the Congressional Committee on Science, Space and Technology. Nazarbayev told them that Kazakhstan aimed at open and mutually beneficial use of Baykonur's potential and was ready to participate in international space projects with the United States, Russia and other countries.[68] The congressmen then went on to Baykonur, where they studied possibilities for international cooperation on the Project Alpha space station. According to Deputy Prime Minister Abilsiitov, their visit might have a decisive effect on Baykonur's fate.[69]

The Russian leadership was divided on how to react to the Kazakhs' diplomatic offensive. Symptoms of political contention around the issue were revealed in contradictory statements by Russian officials. On 5 September *Nezavisimaya gazeta*, citing a government source, reported that Russia had decided to sever all links with Baykonur space centre and cease to use it. But a Glavkosmos spokesman denied this, saing Russia had too great an interest in the cosmodrome to make such a decision.[70] However, the controversy did not end there. On 9 September Assistant Director of the Transmash Design Office Bondarenko told the press that Russia had decided to stop using Baykonur. Glavkosmos again denied this.[71]

One of the two opposing camps was represented by the Russian Space Agency (RSA), which advocated putting Baykonur under civilian administration, generally in line with Kazakhstan's position. The other camp was represented by the Defence Ministry which wanted Baykonur split into two parts, civilian and military, keeping for itself only launches for military purposes.[72] Koptev, director-general of RSA, stressed more than once that Baykonur was irreplaceable for Russia. At the April 1995 Duma hearings on Russian-Kazakh relations he eloquently defended this position: "I can say once again that today exclusion of Baykonur from Russian space activities will cause irreparable damage, for which nothing can compensate. That is Russia will terminate, in principle, the possibility of major directions of space activity".[73]

The Russian military had only one issue of principle at stake: they wanted to retain full control of their programs and exclude any possible outside interference with them. Hence, the Defence Ministry insisted that all or part of the cosmodrome should remain under its control as a Russian military base. If their conditions were not met, they were prepared to leave Baykonur. MSF Commander Colonel-General Ivanov, during his visit to the second Russian cosmodrome at Plesetsk in September 1994, said bluntly that the Russian Defence Ministry did not want launching its space hardware to be dependent on the policies of any foreign state, including Kazakhstan.[74]

Initially, the civilians appeared to be winning. Press reports on 9 September, quoting a RSA spokesman, indicated that a document determining Russia's position on Baykonur would be submitted to the government before 15 September, and that it acquiesced to transformation of Baykonur into an international space company. The three interested states—Russia, Kazakhstan and Ukraine—were to be sponsors of the company, and their presidents would sign an appropriate tripartite agreement during their meeting in Moscow on 24 September.[75] But dramatic events of a higher order suddenly intervened and changed the entire picture.

On 21 September Yeltsin issued a decree dissolving the Russian parliament. This led to armed clashes with the parliament's defenders in the streets of Moscow on 3–4 October. It was only personal loyalty to Yeltsin of Russia's military command that saved the presidential side from defeat. But before moving to rescue Yeltsin, the military exploited the situation to wrest some substantial concessions from him, most importantly a new version of the military doctrine. It is likely that support of the Defence Ministry's position on Baykonur was part of the package. In any case, the October events increased the Defence Ministry's influence in the Russian leadership, evidenced by the fact that advocates of a tougher line on Baykonur prevailed. As a result Moscow initiated diplomatic countermoves to put pressure on Kazakhstan.

In November the Council of Ministers decided to order a feasibility study for a new space centre.[76] Also in November a delegation of Russian space officials suddenly visited Papua New Guinea (PNG), which being close to the equator was ideally situated for launching heavy space vehicles to high orbits. The visit resulted in the signing of a protocol with an Australian company, Space Transportation Systems (STS), for a planned billion-dollar spaceport in PNG. STS Chairman Mike Ahern told journalists that the delegation had endorsed two sites as technically suitable for a Proton launch facility. The protocol confirmed the start of phase one of the site selection process. STS planned to begin construction in 1996, though, interestingly, Russian space officials had said earlier in Moscow that site selection was to be completed by March 1994.[77] This indicated that Russia wanted to convey the impression that construction of the new cosmodrome in PNG would begin very soon, while in reality it was only in the planning stage. It is most likely that Russia's approach to PNG was not a real business proposition, but a means to put diplomatic pressure on Kazakhstan, as Moscow abandoned the PNG project only four months after reaching the Russian-Kazakh settlement on Baykonur. On 4 August 1994 Russian officials told journalists that the project had run into problems because the companies had failed to attract the estimated $900 million needed to fund construction of the new cosmodrome. After that the project was virtually forgotten, and the idea of turning PNG into a new space power quietly died.[78]

The Russian diplomatic countermove apparently produced the desired result. Almaty could not be sure that Russia had no alternative to Baykonur. The signing of a protocol with STS looked real. The Kazakh leadership knew of the potential loss to the national economy if Russia withdrew from Baykonur and that it could not manage or finance the cosmodrome on its own. Without Russian participation Baykonur would also be useless for foreign investors. First, Baykonur was designed to suit Russian space vehicles and not those of third countries, and all space powers had custom-built launch sites for their technology. It is hard imaging any of them spending the vast amounts of money that would be needed to adapt existing facilities or build new ones at Baykonur. Second, most of the tracking facilities needed to monitor and control space vehicles were situated in Russia, and without them successful launches would be virtually impossible.

Symptoms of a softening Kazakh position appeared on 25 December during Chernomyrdin's visit to Almaty. He and Tereshchenko signed a memorandum that dealt with a number of bilateral issues, including the cosmodrome. For the first time the possibility of its lease by Russia was mentioned in a bilateral document. The memorandum also stated that exploitation of the Baykonur cosmodrome would be conducted by the Russian government, which implied that it would remain under Moscow's sole control. However, the memorandum did not specify either the duration of the lease or the amount Russia would pay in rent. These were quite complex questions. The status of Russian military units in Baykonur, a question of primary importance for Russia, was defined only vaguely. The sides agreed that "Russian military formations, conducting exploitation of the Baykonur cosmodrome . . . are deployed on the territory of the Republic of Kazakhstan on a temporary basis, and their status will be defined in separate agreements".[79] In principle this formula did not conflict with Moscow's intention to turn Baykonur into a Russian military base, but neither did it impose any particular obligations on the Kazakh side.

Thus the optimism voiced by Russian officials who participated in the Almaty talks was premature.[80] No real breakthrough was achieved. A long and intensive period of further tough bargaining on the specific terms of the lease lay ahead. This soon revealed itself. The memorandum provided for establishing a special working commission to prepare an agreement on Baykonur by March 1994, for the summit meeting between Yeltsin and Nazarbayev. When the Russian and Kazakh delegations began to negotiate in January 1994, disagreements immediately came to the fore. One concerned the rent that Russia would pay for use of Baykonur. T. Zhukeyev, a state councillor of Kazakhstan, hinted at a figure of $7 billion for two years, much more than Moscow wanted to pay.[81] Its initial offer was $80 million a year.[82]

It soon became obvious out that in signing the memorandum Kazakhstan intended to hand over only part of Baykonur to the Russian military. The Kazakhs continued to insist that the cosmodrome should be used primarily for economic and scientific purposes. Zhukeyev clearly stated at a special meeting with journalists that the Kazakh side rejected the Russian government's proposals for military units to be stationed in Kazakhstan with military base rights, and that the Russian government's conception of Baykonur as a military installation was wrong. The Kazakhs refused to abandon the idea of turning Baykonur into an international joint-stock company, even though the Russians more than once made it clear that that arrangement was absolutely unacceptable. In late January 1994 Nazarbayev made an official visit to Ukraine, where he concluded a number of economic agreements, including one on joint use of Baykonur.[83]

On 8–10 February 1994, Russian Foreign Minister Kozyrev made an urgent trip to Kazakhstan in the vain hope of settling the most complex bilateral problems, including Baykonur. The talks proved fruitless. Proposals for Baykonur's future outlined by Nazarbayev included the withdrawing Russian troops and selling military equipment cheaply to Kazakhstan in return for Russia's right to lease some facilities there.[84] On 24 February, Kalybaev, deputy director-general of Kazakhstan's Space Agency, said that Kazakhstan would not agree to lease Baykonur space to Russia until the status of Russian troops servicing the facility was resolved, because Nazarbayev refused to have foreign military bases in Kazakhstan.[85]

The Kazakhs were apparently raising the stakes. On 14 February a meeting of the president's administration and cabinet of ministers was held to assess the ecological damage caused by use of Baykonur. At a press conference the same day, the ecology department of the administration reported that the cosmodrome had influenced the ecological situation in the Aral Sea basin in a harmful, even catastrophic way. It reported that rocket fuel had polluted the subsoil water, and that the cosmodrome used subsoil water for technical purposes without any control whatsoever. The radiological situation in the region was said to be critical. Simultaneously, it was pointed out that the proposed Kazakh-Russian agreement on Baykonur did not mention ecology, while Russia as successor to the USSR had to provide at least partial compensation for the losses inflicted on the region. The head of the ecology department, A. Shamenov said that all accords with regard to the cosmodrome should include ecological issues.[86]

By now the Russians were accustomed to Almaty's tough negotiating techniques and to responded in kind. First, Moscow linked the problem of Baykonur with the bilateral treaty on military cooperation and other important bilateral documents then under negotiation. Yeltsin refused to meet Nazarbayev and sign any agreement of substance until they settled the question of Baykonur. The scheduled meeting between them was postponed more than once.[87] Second, the Russian side began to create the impression that it was seriously considering switching preferences to a cosmodrome in Russia proper. In early February an unidentified Missile Space Forces official told journalists that the Russian authorities were considering building a new cosmodrome on Russian territory, and named a former ballistic missiles base in the Far East, 300 km from the Russia-China border, as the likely site.[88] This was confirmed on 9 March by MSF Commander Colonel-General Ivanov, who stated officially that Russia would build a major new cosmodrome near the settlement of Svobodnyy in the Far East by the year 2000 to ensure the independence of its space program. He added that the new base would be able to launch manned rockets and heavy Proton boosters, because of its favourable geographical location (just several degrees north of the equator in comparison to Baykonur). Ivanov added, in an obvious bluff,[89] that it would not be expensive to set up the site, because the former ballistic missiles base already had launching equipment.[90] The statement was carefully timed to coincide with the arrival in

Almaty of a RSA team led by Director-General Koptev for a new round of talks on Baykonur.

Russian pressure continued to build throughout the following stages of the negotiations. On 14 March General Ivanov flew to the Amur province with a group of officers and industrialists for talks with the local administration on building Russia's new cosmodrome by the year 2000. After arriving at Svobodnyy, Ivanov claimed that the new cosmodrome would start launching Rokot lightweight booster rockets as early as 1996, and the new generation of Angara heavyweight booster rockets, used for placing satellites in geostationary orbit, in the year 2000. He also said that a decision to construct the new cosmodrome was expected to be signed by the Russian government at the end of March. In a new development, the RSA suddenly dropped its opposition to the new cosmodrome.[91]

Tough bargaining continued until the eleventh hour. Finally, signs appeared that the Kazakhs were beginning to yield ground. On 17 March Tereshchenko arrived in Moscow and met Chernomyrdin to discuss Baykonur.[92] On 18 March a senior Russian representative at the Russian-Kazakh talks on Baykonur advised that complete success had been achieved. The delegations had found solutions to a whole series of points on which they had earlier disagreed. In particular, Kazakhstan's representatives responded favourably to Russia's arguments that the term of lease should be at least thirty years. A positive solution also emerged regarding the status of Russian military personnel and civilians at Baykonur.[93] This breakthrough paved the way for the Russian-Kazakh presidential summit and signing on 28 March of the Agreement between the Republic of Kazakhstan and the Russian Federation on the Major Principles and Conditions for using Baykonur Cosmodrome.

Russia's initial position dominated the agreement. Russia leased Baykonur for twenty years, with an automatic extension for another ten years if neither side objected. It was probably not as long as Moscow would have preferred, but was at least a long-term arrangement, a major Russian requirement. The conditions of the lease were as follows: Operational management of the complex passed to the Russian MSF (Article 4). The cosmodrome's commander would be appointed by the Russian president, but approved by the president of Kazakhstan (Article 3). Article 4 stipulated that "military formations of the Russian Federation, providing for implementation of space programs using the facilities of the Baykonur cosmodrome . . . have the status of Russian military formations, deployed on the territory of the Republic of Kazakhstan on a temporary basis", and continued, "Russian military formations conduct their activities in accordance with the legislation of the Russian Federation, procedures and rules in force in the Armed Forces of the Russian Federation taking account of the legislation of the Republic of Kazakhstan. On the territory of the Baykonur complex, the legislation of the Russian Federation is in force, and its appropriate services operate in relation to the servicemen, civilian personnel of Russian Federation and members of their families. In other cases the legislation of the Republic of Kazakhstan is in force, and its appropriate authorities operate".[94] Thus the agreement de facto gave Baykonur the status of a Russian military base without mentioning the word "base".

The annual rent was established at $115 million, much closer to Russia's initial $80 million offer than to the initial Kazakh bid for $3.5 billion. Part of it could be paid on a compensatory basis, that is, by simply deducting it from Kazakhstan's debt to Russia. (Article 4). Nothing was said about previous ecological damage or Russian compensation for it. The only success the Kazakh side achieved was Russia's agreeing to cover the costs of Baykonur's exploitation in 1992–1993. Other Russian concessions included the provision that the Baykonur commander's appointment would require the consent of the president of Kazakhstan, who would also have a permanent representative at the cosmodrome (Article 3). Russia also agreed to assist Kazakhstan in "implementing its space projects, first of all in the field of satellite communications and survey of the earth's natural resources, in creating joint structures and in training specialists in space technology" (Article 4). Moscow did not object to Kazakhstan's currency being the only legal tender at Baykonur (Article 5). These were all minor concessions. It is clear that the Kazakh side had to make the bigger to compromise, if it can be called compromise. The Kazakh side's lack of diplomatic experience, probably led it to assume an unrealistic and unsustainable position at the outset, which accounted for their ultimate capitulation.

The agreement on Baykonur substantially reduced the tensions between Moscow and Almaty but failed to remove them altogether, because it left a number of technical issues unsettled. These were to be regulated by other agreements, the principal one being the Lease Treaty, to be concluded within three months after the Baykonur agreement came into force. Nevertheless, the initial impression was that the agreement on Baykonur would be implemented without difficulties. The Duma ratified it in June 1994, at the second attempt, and Kazakhstan's parliament did so in July.

The Treaty of Lease of the Baykonur complex was formally signed by Chernomyrdin and Kazhegeldin in Moscow on 10 December 1994. It was largely based on provisions of the agreement of 28 March 1994 and contained a number of clarifications of that agreement's provisions, as well as some new elements. The latter included mentioning the town of Leninsk, the main residential area for the cosmodrome's personnel. In 1994 it had a population of 150,000, of which 60,000 were Russians, including 7,000 commissioned and noncommissioned officers, 17,000 members of their families, and 36,000 civilians.[95]

The treaty envisaged financing of Leninsk by Russia, with Kazakhstan's participation limited to ensuring social rights of the Republic of Kazakhstan. The head of the administration was to be appointed jointly by the presidents of Russia and Kazakhstan and would "form the administration of Leninsk". (Article 6, §-6.9, §-6.10). For the purpose of ensuring interaction of organisations, enterprises and military units of Russia and Kazakhstan at Baykonur, the treaty established a Coordinating Council of the Baykonur complex, consisting of the commander, the head of the Leninsk administration, Kazakhstan's representative at Baykonur, and one representative each from the RSA, MSF and Kazakhstan's National Space Agency, (Article 6, §-6.14).

Another point of importance was that the production and profit received by Russia from exploitation of the cosmodrome would be Russian property (Article 6, §-6.5). This meant that all commercial launches and other commercial projects conducted without financial participation by Kazakhstan were unequivocally regarded as belonging to Russia, removing one of the major ambiguities created by Kazakhstan's earlier proposal to turn Baykonur into a joint-stock company. Kazakhstan promised not to hamper directly or indirectly Russian use of Baykonur's facilities, to ensure the supply of electricity, fuel, construction materials, medical equipment and other material means, and to provide transportation and other services. The Kazakh side also undertook to allow duty-free entry of equipment, fuel and other materials necessary for Baykonur's functioning (Article 8, §-8.2).

Article 5 described in detail the procedure for making rental payments to Kazakhstan. Russia also undertook to "make rental payments in the amounts and time provided for in the Treaty" (Article 8, §-8.4). The treaty contained an attachment listing the objects and facilities to be leased by Russia. Russia secured the right to make improvements to Baykonur's facilities, with the understanding that their cost could be reclaimed after expiration of the lease (Article 8, §-8.3).[96] This was obviously to ensure that Russia could invest in Baykonur's infrastructure without concern that the cost might never be recovered. However, later events showed that this provision did little to remove Russian apprehensions about investment in Baykonur.

On 4 August 1994, before the Lease Treaty was formally signed, the question of Baykonur was discussed by the presidium of the Russian government, which approved the main principles and conditions for using the cosmodrome.[97] On 29 August 1994 Chernomyrdin signed government order No. 996, which became the legal document governing Russian activities on Baykonur. It included the following major elements:

1. The Defence Ministry would transfer facilities at Baykonur employed in the Russian federal civil space program to use and possession of the RSA.
2. The Defence Ministry in conjunction with RSA, and by agreement with the Kazakh side, would set up a coordinating body headed by the chief of the space centre.
3. The Defence Ministry would continue under the established system and on a contract basis to supply facilities at the Baykonur space centre with electricity, water, heat, rocket fuel, fuels and lubricants and other materials; organise rail transport of workers and freight within the space centre precincts; provide aviation services at the Krayniy airfield (landing clearance, servicing, refuelling, security and dispatch of air transport enterprises' assets); and meteorological, medical and other services.
4. The Defence Ministry was authorised to recruit civilian specialists paid under the procedure laid down by Russian legislation to operate power, heat and water supply systems, and sewage and communications systems at general space centre installations.

5. The Finance Ministry was authorised to allocate $115 million in 1994 to pay for the lease. Within the 1994 federal budget allocations for maintenance of the Baykonur complex consisted of 191.2 billion roubles for the MSF; 179.2 billion for the RSA; 17.6 billion for the purchase of series-produced space equipment; 15.8 billion for capital construction; and 91 billion for upkeep of the town of Leninsk.

6. The Foreign Ministry, Defence Ministry, Ministry of Internal Affairs, Counterintelligence Service, Ministry of Justice, Ministry of Social Protection of the Population and the RSA were to elaborate in conjunction with the Kazakh side the possibility of creating in the town of Leninsk a closed administrative-territorial unit in line with the Russian Federation law on closed administrative-territorial units and to draw up proposals on candidature for the head of the Leninsk town administration.

7. The Ministry of Education was requested to ensure organisation of the education of schoolchildren at educational establishments in Leninsk under Russian Federation plans and programs; and to coordinate with the Kazakhstan Ministry of Education questions of education of Kazakhs under national programs.[98]

The order showed that Russia wanted more than a simple lease of Baykonur. Moscow obviously aimed to take full control of Leninsk by making it a closed town under Russian supervision, and managed to do so without much effort. On 16 June 1995 Russian Deputy Prime Minister Bolshakov and his Kazakh counterpart Isingarin initialled an agreement effectively putting Leninsk under Russian jurisdiction for twenty years as of 1 August 1995. Despite some mild Kazakh press criticism of this decision as violating Kazakhstan's sovereignty,[99] Almaty was probably only too happy to shift the burden of supporting Leninsk onto Moscow. Under the agreement Russia undertook to maintain and develop the city's infrastructure and to assist in supporting two nearby population centres. Notably, the agreement envisaged that Leninsk would be financed entirely from the Russian federal budget.[100]

This, however, did not help the town very much. Leninsk, which on 2 December 1995 was renamed Baykonur,[101] remains in a catastrophic situation. Military-construction units cannot manage the town's infrastructure, because works already completed have not been paid for. They lack funds not only for widening the spectrum of works but for buying soldiers' uniforms. According to the mayor, there were approximately 2,000 empty and looted flats in town; the water supply is almost completely destroyed, the electric power plant hardly functions, the roads are in awful condition and there are regular bread shortages. Officers and other specialists have not been paid for three months. Uncontrolled emigration occurred — about half of the space specialists have left.[102] All this has created problems for successful functioning of the cosmodrome, as well as a number of serious accidents. In February 1995, a major fire destroyed an expensive satellite which was intended for launching.[103] On 27 September 1995, another accident threatened the launch of the Progress M-29 cargo craft. The transporter, an open freight wagon transporting the rockets to the launch site, derailed, damaging the wagon and twenty metres of the single-track railway.[104] On 6 September 1996, a power cut raised fears that the forthcoming launch of the $36 million Immarsat satellite might not take place.[105]

On 24 April 1995 the crisis at Baykonur was discussed at a conference in Moscow chaired by Deputy Prime Minister Soskovets. The participants described the conditions at Baykonur launch site and in Leninsk as critical. It was pointed out that repair and maintenance of the site's facilities had halted due to lack of funds, and that nonindustrial workers in Leninsk had not been paid since January and were abandoning the town in large numbers. It was particularly noted that Moscow had failed to remit the funds allocated for maintenance of the town.[106] Despite the criticisms, the situation failed to improve. By April 1996 it had become so desperate that the coordinating council of the Baykonur complex (which includes the town's mayor, the head of the space centre and the Kazakh president's representative) made a joint appeal to the two first deputy prime ministers, Soskovets of Russia and Isingarin of Kazakhstan, who handled Baykonur's affairs. The appeal said that social tension was spreading from Baykonur to the whole of Kzyl-Orda region, and if the governments did not provide funds to meet the space centre's debts, a social explosion would be added to the constant disruptions of rocket launches.[107] But the appeal was not followed by any visible improvements.

Basically, Russia has no incentive to maintain the quality of Baykonur, because it regards the cosmodrome as Kazakhstan's property which it will have to return. Thus from the very beginning, Russian policy was to squeeze as much as possible from Baykonur, while refraining from making any long-term investment in it. Russian-Kazakh relationships with regard to Baykonur are characterised by continuous wrangling over the financial terms of the lease. In 1994 the Russian draft budget envisaged allocation of $115 million in rent to Kazakhstan, but it was never paid. In 1995 these allocations were not even included in the Russian budget. Moscow insisted that Kazakhstan should pay its debts to Russia, which Russia assessed at $1.25 billion.[108] Kazakhstan, in turn, revived counterclaims, including compensation for ecological damage caused by previous use of Baykonur. Kazakh experts assessed this damage at around $2 billion, while the Russian Defence Ministry argued that it could hardly exceed $40 million.[109]

To avoid endless negotiations, Russia and Kazakhstan decided to agree on a zero-option solution, that is, to cancel all debts to each other. This formula provided the basis for the Protocol on Settlement of Mutual Financial Claims Between the Republic of Kazakhstan and the Russian Federation, signed by the prime ministers on 20 January 1995. It stated that the sides "revoke their claims on each other: the Kazakh side on compensation for the damage, connected with exploitation of the Baykonur complex in 1991–1993; the Russian side on debts of, and credit to, the Republic of Kazakhstan in 1991–1994".[110] But this accord soon eroded due to its broad interpretation by the Kazakhs, who tried to include Kazakhstan's $275 million of debts to two Russian companies, Roskontrakt and Rosenergo, in the settlement. Russia rejected these demands on the grounds that debts between companies, state owned or not, were not covered by the protocol.[111] By the end of 1997 the problem of mutual debts remained unresolved. Moscow has not allocated a single dollar for rent payments. The problem of settling mutual debts was discussed by Chernomyrdin and Nazarbayev at their meeting on 4 October 1997, but they again failed to reach agreement.[112]

Many Russian experts see the lease of Baykonur as disadvantageous to Russia. Some of them point to its unreliability as a prospective Russian launch site, given the expected onset of political instability in Kazakhstan due to economic depression and deterioration of administrative control.[113] Others argue that Russia spends much more on the cosmodrome than it receives from it. Given the poor condition of the real estate at Baykonur, including the social infrastructure, Russia's obligation to maintain and develop the material and technological base of a complex which remains Kazakhstan's property entails substantial financial loss. According to some assessments, in 1994 Russia spent $185 million on the cosmodrome's upkeep, on top of the annual rent. Other estimates indicate that over the twenty years of the lease, Russia's expenditure on Baykonur will be more than double the value of its fixed capital, or more than enough for Russia to build two similar cosmodromes on its own territory.[114] These estimates were however rejected by RSA Director-General Koptev, who said that the rental payments for twenty years would be roughly equal to the value of Baykonur's fixed capital and that such payments would be economically justifiable in comparison to a cost of building a new cosmodrome.[115]

Given this difference of opinion, on 4 August 1994 the presidium of the Russian government linked discussion of the problem of Baykonur to the proposition of building a new Russian cosmodrome near Svobodnyy in the Far East. Although originally a diplomatic tool for bargaining with Kazakhstan, this idea clearly had acquired its own momentum. After the closed part of the sitting ended, Koptev told journalists that the possibility of building a new Russian cosmodrome was under consideration. He noted without much optimism that a total of 4–4.5 trillion roubles at present prices would be needed to implement such a project, that it would take ten to twelve years, and that the issue would be decided by 1 November.[116] A divergence of views had emerged in Russia's leadership on how to treat Baykonur over the long term.

Interestingly, the Russian military continued to push for the new cosmodrome. This soon became apparent through statements made by the Missile Space Forces leadership. In December 1994 Major-General Venediktov said in Blagoveshchensk that Svobodnyy must fully replace Baykonur as Russia's main space port. He said that Baykonur could be fully operational for another few years, a decade at most, after which all its technical structures would no longer satisfy safety requirements. Venediktov made no bones about the fact that the new space centre would be used primarily for military purposes.[117] On 26 January a similar statement was made by MSF Commander Colonel-General Ivanov in a speech to the Duma. He stressed that Russia wanted to phase out Defence Ministry satellite launchings from Baykonur by the year 2003.[118]

Distrust of the Kazakh leadership and doubts as to Kazakhstan's reliability as an ally lay behind the Russian military's position. These fears grew out of certain Kazakh actions. In January 1994, when Russian-Kazakh negotiations over Baykonur were in full swing, Kazakhstan unexpectedly signed an agreement with the United States on joint monitoring of outer space and space debris which could pose a threat to orbiting satellites. During Nazarbayev's visit to Washington in February 1994, Kazakhstan and the United States allegedly concluded an unspecified space agreement which dealt with joint use of Baykonur.[119] Despite direct questions from journalists, Nazarbayev refused to disclose details of the agreement and confined his remarks to saying that it related only to know-how and to nonproliferation of U.S.-provided space technology.[120] Some Russian experts saw these actions as "an element of blackmail with regard to Russia".[121] Undoubtedly they increased Russian suspicions of the Kazakh leadership's policies.

This may explain why the Russian MSF began moving military space programs from Baykonur to Plesetsk. On 21 September 1994 a group of military experts and engineers led by MSF Commander Colonel-General Ivanov arrived at Plesetsk to discuss the transfer of a number of facilities belonging to the missile troops. New launch sites for Zenit and for new Rus booster rockets began to be built at Plesetsk.[122] On 19 March 1996 the Plesetsk cosmodrome's head, Major-General Ovchinnikov, told reporters the space centre was being refurbished to make room for military and research space programs being transferred from Baykonur. He added that two launching sites for Zenit boosters would soon be completed. One of them, he claimed, was 70% ready, and expected to become fully operational in 1997. He also advised that four launching sites for Soyuz boosters were being reconstructed to accommodate a new booster, Rus, and that after the year 2000, a universal launching site would be built for the Angara, an upgraded second-generation version of the Proton booster.[123]

Among other things, the Russian military's insistence on the new cosmodrome indicated of the Defence Ministry's lack of intent to treat Baykonur as a form of Russian military presence in Kazakhstan. Reliability of the military space program was obviously a much higher priority for the Russian military. But it was difficult for the Defence Ministry to get its own way, for two reasons. The first was that at that time all military programs were very unpopular with the public and could not generate massive political support. The other reason was opposition from officials involved in the civil space program, above all RSA. The temporary alliance that had emerged between the Defence Ministry and RSA during the negotiations with Kazakhstan broke down after conclusion of the agreement on Baykonur. RSA was quite satisfied with Baykonur and feared that construction of a new cosmodrome would divert funds from the civil space program, already under severe financial stress. This predetermined active political manoeuvring around the issue of Svobodnyy, and the question consequently remained unresolved for some time to come.

Contradictory reports about the future of the Svobodnyy project began to arrive in late October 1994. On 24 October the Defence Committee of the Duma dismissed the Space Forces' arguments in favour of Svobodnyy as unconvincing, and decided that Baykonur's four launch pads for Proton heavy rockets and its other facilities were enough for all Russia's space programs, including military ones. Nevertheless, a MSF spokesman expressed optimism about the Svobodnyy plan. He said President Yeltsin had already received the draft of a decree ordering construction of the Far Eastern complex to begin in 1995 and was due to sign it early in the next month.[124] In December Major-General Venediktov stated that the federal government would take the decision to begin construction at Svobodnyy in the very near future and that construction work had already begun.[125] This statement was echoed on 26 January 1995 by MSF Commander Colonel-General Ivanov, who told the Duma that work to build a new launch-pad at Svobodnyy was on schedule and the first launches would take place by early 1996.[126] But on 12 May 1995 MSF spokesman Gorbunov said plans to convert the Svobodnyy base had been halted for lack of funds.[127]

At that point, a compromise between the MSF and RSA emerged. A document, Program of Development of the Surface Cosmic Infrastructure of the Russian Federation (for the period until 2014), submitted to the Duma in connection with ratification of the Baykonur Lease Treaty, was signed by RSA Director-General Koptev and MSF representative Borisiuk. It contained the following conclusions:

Implementation of Russian space programs within several forthcoming decades is practically impossible without the use of Baykonur cosmodrome. . . . Together with using Baykonur cosmodrome and allocating funds for its maintenance and modernisation, Russia should ensure further development of the infrastructure for preparing and launching space vehicles from Russian cosmodromes. For this purpose the Plesetsk range must be developed further, and analyses made of the possibility and practicability of preparing and launching medium- and heavy-class rockets from Svobodnyy cosmodrome.[128]

The program stipulated that Svobodnyy be assessed as a prospective launching site for heavy launch vehicles "sending military space apparatus into orbit" starting in 2011. The draft plan proposed that in 2014 Svobodnyy should have five launching pads for three classes of boosters. Functions of space apparatus launched from the cosmodrome would cover areas such as strategic reconnaissance, navigational support, communications and television broadcasting from geostationary orbits, as well as the Rokot program. The plan also indicated that in 2014 Baykonur would continue fulfilling all aspects of the Russian space program, including those designed for Svobodnyy and Plesetsk, and would retain two not duplicated by the other two cosmodromes—piloted space flights and international commercial space launches.[129] This could be interpreted to mean that Russia does not completely discard the possibility of using Baykonur for military purposes in the future. Yet, the duplication of all Baykonur's military functions by two Russian cosmodromes gives reason to believe that the proportion of military launches from Kazakhstan would substantially decrease or cease altogether, and Baykonur would be employed for military purposes only in extraordinary circumstances.

Thus the Russian military managed to defend their position and keep Svobodnyy in the governmental plans. On 1 March 1996 Yeltsin signed a decree endorsing the establishment of the second Russian cosmodrome at Svobodnyy. The MSF press service commented that a new cosmodrome, capable of full-weight space launches, would help to completely eliminate Russia's dependence on other countries for launching spacecraft to various orbits.[130] On 4 March 1997, Russia carried out its first launch from Svobodnyy of a Zeya military satellite on a Start-1 booster rocket.[131] There have been several other launches of low, earth orbit satellites from there, indicating that the new cosmodrome's development program is on schedule.

At present Russian policy on Baykonur can be described as gradual disengagement. Russia's military is diminishing its reliance on the Kazakh cosmodrome, pending full withdrawal of military programs, facilities and personnel. In the short term Russia is likely to continue relying on Baykonur for its civil space program, including commercial launches, and it remains Russia's only launching site for manned space flights. Baykonur's role will be crucial for the successful launching of many components for the International Space Station, but once that station's program is complete, further Russian withdrawal can be expected. Given the previous and current difficulties with Kazakhstan over Baykonur, Russia is unwilling to commit significant funds for future maintenance and upgrading. Hence much will depend on Kazakhstan's ability to maintain the cosmodrome's operational potential, but there are serious doubts whether it can. Moreover, unfavourable conditions for renting Baykonur forced Russia to search actively for alternative commercial launching sites in other countries. RSA and Russian commercial launch operators have already approached other countries (e.g., Australia, Brazil and India) with a view to setting up a commercial cosmodrome on their territory. Launch sites in these countries are geographically advantageous because they are nearer the equator, they require much lower rent than that paid for Baykonur, and they have a more stable and predictable political environment. Russia also intends to solve the problem of manned space flights by developing a new heavy-lift launch vehicle, "Rus" (also known as Soyuz 2), designed for launch from Plesetsk.

After the collapse of the Soviet Union, Russia had three options for securing its military and strategic interests in the post-Soviet space: maintaining and developing bilateral military relations with the countries of the region, acting within the legal framework provided by CIS, or a combination of both. But in the independence euphoria that engulfed the post-Soviet space, bilateral military cooperation between Russia and other CIS members presented major difficulties. Any Russian proposal for stationing troops, weapons and military facilities in other former Soviet republics could be interpreted as a continuation of Russia's "imperial" policy, with likely negative effects not only in the republics but internationally. This was why Russia initially decided to put the major emphasis on multilateral military cooperation within the CIS, though only to the extent that it served Russia's own interests. The Basic Provisions of the Russian Federation's Foreign Policy Concept, signed by Yeltsin in April 1993, specifically mentioned Russia's responsibility for strengthening stability and security on the territory of the former USSR. It contained provisions for developing military and political cooperation with other CIS members with a view to creating an effective collective security system, for protecting CIS external borders, and for preserving the military infrastructure and installations that constituted an integrated system for ensuring CIS members' military security. The directive attached special importance to developing and improving peacekeeping mechanisms within the CIS with Russian participation.[132]

The signing of the Tashkent Collective Security Treaty indicated that Central Asia had become a priority for Russian defence strategy. Russian military and strategic interests in Central Asia can be summarised as follows:

Forward defence. Russia is interested in denying anti-Russian political forces (such as the Taliban in Afghanistan) ability to penetrate the region and advance to Russia's borders. In the longer term, Russian presence in Central Asia could serve to contain expansionist ambitions of China, should such appear in the future.

Maintenance of stability. Russia genuinely perceives Central Asia as a zone of potential political instability, which could spiral out into Russian territory. From this angle, a Russian military presence in the region plays a triple role. First, it blocks attempts by external destabilising influences, such as Tajik opposition forces based in Afghanistan, from consolidating a hold in the region. Second, it deters opposition forces inside the Central Asian countries from resorting to force in pursuit of power. Third, should such deterrence fail, Russian forces can be used to defend the Russian-speaking population against massacres by nationalists.

Strategic denial. Russia is determined to ensure that the Central Asian states are not drawn into military and political alliances with countries it perceives as hostile, such as Turkey, Pakistan or Saudi Arabia. This is important in the broader context of Russia's Eurasian strategy.

Projection of power. Central Asia is a potential springboard for military intervention in the Persian Gulf and Middle East, regions of utmost importance to the West. Such power projection could become important if Russia's future relations with the West deteriorate into a new round of confrontation. Having lost its positions in Europe, Russia would probably try to compensate by applying pressure on Western interests in other areas, rather as nineteenth-century Tsarist Russia, when frustrated in its designs on the Ottoman Empire's

Balkan provinces, turned south-eastward to put strategic pressure on the British in India.

Economic considerations. Russia's Defence Ministry is interested in continued access to military installations in other republics, which were built in Soviet times for strategic defence and are impossible in current economic conditions to replace by building new facilities in Russia.

Kazakhstan plays a central role in securing Russia's military and strategic interests in Central Asia. First, it is the largest and most influential of the former Soviet Central Asian republics. Second, apart from limited access via the Caspian Sea and Turkmenistan, all surface routes from Russia to Central Asia pass through Kazakhstan. Third, Kazakhstan has the largest Russian-speaking community in post-Soviet Central Asia. Finally, Kazakhstan inherited from the Soviet era the largest and most important military infrastructure in all Central Asia. Moscow therefore sought to secure Kazakhstan's support in establishing a collective security structure for Central Asia, and Kazakhstan responded positively.

Kazakhstan joined Russia as cosponsor of the Tashkent Treaty, and was one of the first to ratify it (23.12.92), six months before the Russian parliament.[133] Nazarbayev was also the most ardent supporter of a CIS defence alliance, an idea he first proposed at the CIS summit in Bishkek in October 1992.[134] "Kazakhstan's leadership is firmly convinced, even today, that the security of every sovereign state will be more reliably ensured through collective defence by the countries of the Commonwealth", S. Nurmagambetov, Kazakhstan's Defence Minister, wrote in a program-style article in November 1992.[135] In a telegram sent to Yeltsin and heads of other CIS members on 18 March 1993, Nazarbayev specifically proposed "establishing clearly functional bodies in a defence alliance, in accordance with the Collective Security Treaty".[136] Nazarbayev's project for a Eurasian Union, put forward in March 1994, contained a special section on defence which envisaged conclusion of a treaty on joint measures to strengthen the EAU member-states' national armed forces and protection of EAU's external borders; creation of a common defence space for the purpose of coordinating defence activities; and formation of collective EAU peacekeeping forces, assigned official peacekeeping status by the UN Security Council.[137]

Kazakhstan supported the concept of CIS collective security for several reasons. The main one being that it lacked the potential to provide for its own defence. After the collapse of the Soviet Union it met a number of problems in creating its own army. On top of the economic difficulties, Kazakhs, like the other Central Asian peoples, lacked a modern tradition of military service, few pursued military careers and hardly any reached senior rank.[138] Therefore, no pool of trained indigenous officers existed to fill the gaps created by the massive postindependence exodus of Slav officers who chose to continue their service in the armed forces of Russia, Ukraine or Belarus. Kazakh military officials admitted that this exodus "caused an irremediable shortage of command, engineer and technical cadres".[139] Some independent Kazakh experts even went so far as to question the rationality of the decision to form a national army. For example, political scientist Asker Kusmanuli wrote that Kazakhstan had the option of asking the Russian army to assume the defence of Kazakhstan, but its political leadership could not accept the loss of sovereignty; the decision to create a national army was "politically right, but economically absolutely unfounded".[140]

The Kazakh leaders saw potential, clear danger of instability in neighbouring Tajikistan, easily spreading into their own territory and needed military support to counter it. On 4 November 1992 the leaders of Kazakhstan, Kyrgyzstan, Uzbekistan and Tajikistan met in Almaty to discuss how to end the fighting in Tajikistan and issued a five-point statement, calling for the Russian 201st Motorised Rifle Division stationed in Tajikistan to maintain a peacekeeping role until a joint CIS peacekeeping force could be formed.[141] Russian Foreign Minister Kozyrev attended the meeting as an observer, though it is safe to assume his role was not limited to listening to the others. As Nazarbayev later explained: "Bloody conflict, which engendered real danger of penetration into that country [Tajikistan] of extremism from neighbouring Afghanistan, mobilised us into forming collective peacekeeping forces to protect the Tajik-Afghan border".[142]

On 30 November 1992 at a meeting in the Uzbek town of Termez, the defence ministers of Russia, Kazakhstan, Uzbekistan, Kyrgyzstan and then CIS Armed Forces Commander-in-Chief Shaposhnikov took a decision on a combined CIS peacekeeping force for Tajikistan, including the Russian 201st division, a motorised regiment from Uzbekistan and a battalion each from Kazakhstan and Kyrgyzstan.[143] For Russia it was essential that the operation in Tajikistan be collective, to legitimise it internationally, and to spread its costs. Kazakhstan's willingness to provide a battalion demonstrated its leaders' apprehensions of the danger emanating from Tajikistan. Nevertheless, Nazarbayev faced strong domestic opposition, primarily in Kazakhstan's parliament. At that time, presidents in the CIS states had not yet acquired enough power to proceed with implementation of such sensitive agreements without parliamentary approval. And parliaments resisted sanctioning deployment of troops beyond national borders, especially to areas of interethnic conflict. This delayed the establishment of a CIS peacekeeping force in Tajikistan.

On 22 December 1992 Nazarbayev presented the agreement On Contingents of Military Observers and CIS Collective Peacekeeping Forces, which had been signed at the March 1992 CIS summit in Kiev for ratification by Kazakhstan's Supreme Soviet. Ratification would have opened the way for formation of Kazakhstan's peacekeeping unit for Tajikistan.[144] But two days later the parliament voted to table the issue on grounds of insufficient information regarding the state of affairs in Tajikistan.[145] It then adjourned for the holidays, and Nazarbayev's first attempt to send Kazakh peacekeeping troops to Tajikistan ended in failure.

In January 1993 Marshal Shaposhnikov had to admit that the Tashkent Treaty was "to all intents and purposes inoperative".[146] On the eve of the CIS summit in Minsk he again complained that not all states had ratified the treaty, and that only Russian troops were acting as peacekeepers. He said that it was very important to ensure joint participation in peacekeeping actions. When Yeltsin arrived in Minsk he stated firmly that he would raise the question of Tajikistan and specifically emphasised that besides Russia "other states must take part in the peace-keeping process".[147]

The CIS Charter adopted by the summit contained a number of provisions on military issues. Article 12 provided for consultations and measures directed at the "removal of the emerged threat" by peacekeeping operations and if necessary use of armed forces. Article 13 stipulated that member-states must take adequate steps to ensure stability of their external borders, and coordinate activities of their border guard forces and other services responsible for border controls.[148] The Charter was signed by seven states, including Russia and Kazakhstan, as well as other Central Asian states with the exception of Turkmenistan. The important element in the Charter was that it was of indefinite duration and was to automatically substitute for the Tashkent Treaty after the latter expired.

The signing of the Charter did not however establish the defence union. Article 15 specifically pointed out that concrete issues of military-political cooperation between member-states would be regulated by special agreements. The absence of such detailed agreements regulating cooperative defence measures doomed the Charter's provisions to remain another empty declaration. Nevertheless, it accomplished the first step towards realisation of Nazarbayev's idea. To move the process ahead, he needed to prove Kazakhstan's commitment to joint peacekeeping operations within the CIS. Correspondingly, before the forthcoming CIS summit in Minsk Nazarbayev applied strong pressure on Kazakh deputies, and on 14 April they voted in closed session in favour of sending a battalion to the Tajik-Afghan border, provided it consisted entirely of volunteers.[149] A Kazakh Border Guard battalion was deployed to the border of the Gorno-Badakhshan Autonomous Region of Tajikistan.[150]

On 7 August 1993 the leaders of Russia, Kazakhstan, Kyrgyzstan and Tajikistan met in Moscow to discuss the deteriorating situation on the Tajik-Afghan border. Yeltsin told the Central Asians that unless they increased their contributions of men, material and money to the peacekeeping force, he would withdraw the Russian troops. The Central Asian leaders accepted his terms in full.[151] On 24 August the Foreign and Defence Minsters of Russia, Kazakhstan, Kyrgyzstan, Uzbekistan and Tajikistan met in Moscow, and agreed to establish collective peacekeeping defence forces in Tajikistan, under command of a Russian officer, Colonel-General Boris Pyankov, and with headquarters in Dushanbe. The defence ministers also decided to set up the main supply base in Tajikistan and a standby base in Khorog, capital of Gorno-Badakhshan. Each signatory would finance its own contingent.[152] Russia would contribute 50% of funds to maintain the force, Kazakhstan and Uzbekistan 15% each, Tajikistan and Kyrgyzstan 10% each.[153] On 24 September 1993 the CIS heads of state summit in Moscow formally endorsed these decisions.[154]

During the period 1993–1995 Kazakh combat losses comprised thirty six dead and at least thirty eight wounded.[155] The Kazakh leadership threatened several times to withdraw the battalion, but did not do so, and remained committed to joint CIS protection of the Tajik-Afghan border. Kazakhstan signed almost all the CIS collective security agreements, including important ones such as The Statute of the Council of Collective Security (06.07.92), and Agreements on the Statute of the Council of CIS Defence Ministers (22.01.93), Collective Peacekeeping Defence Forces and Joint Measures for Their Material and Technical Support (24.09.1993), The Statute of the Council of Commanders of Border Troops (24.09.1993), Decision on the Staff for Coordination of Military Cooperation of the CIS Member States (24.12.93), Memorandum on Cooperation in Protecting External State Borders (24.12.93), Agreement on Creation of Joint System of Air-Defence (10.02.95), and Concept of Collective Security of the Member-States of the Collective Security Treaty (10.02.95).

The Russian Defence Ministry approved of Kazakhstan's position on collective security, assessing Kazakhstan as "an active participant in the Collective Security Treaty", which "supports the idea of creation of a collective security system on the basis of it". It further stated that Kazakhstan's and Russia's positions on a collective security system generally coincided, including: unification of main legislative provisions in the fields of defence and security; devising common approaches to issues of putting troops on higher stages of alert, forms and methods of training, operational and combat use, and coordinated mobilisation preparedness of the member-states' economies; reaching agreements on joint use of elements of infrastructure, airspace and waterways; permanent consultations on problems of military construction and armed forces' training; coordinating questions of operational preparation of members' territory for purposes of collective defence; joint operational and combat-training exercises of armed forces and other troops; coordinating military personnel training programs; coordinating plans for developing, producing, supplying and maintaining arms and equipment; working out common approaches to parameters of stockpiling and storing material resources; creating common (joint) air defence and other systems.[156] The ministry's opinion is shared by experts at the Russia Institute of Strategic Studies.[157]

But in reality the Russian and Kazakh approaches to the collective security system in Central Asia are far from concurrent. From the very beginning there were obvious problems and contradictions. Kazakhstan tried to evade some of its obligations to contribute to the peacekeeping force in Tajikistan. At the CIS defence ministers' meeting in Ashgabat in December 1993, the force commander, Colonel-General Pyankov, openly criticised Kazakhstan for failing both to send the required number of troops and to allocate funds stipulated by the agreement.[158] This behaviour clearly indicated that Almaty regarded the collective peacekeeping force largely as a convenient way to shift responsibility for fighting and finance onto Russia.

Also, although formally allied to Russia, the Kazakh leadership was still suspicious of Moscow's intentions in Central Asia. Some of Nazarbayev's staff, including U. Kasenov, director of Kazakhstan's Institute of Strategic Studies (a subdivision of the presidential administration) openly voiced their suspicions that Russia "seeks to keep its military presence not so much to prevent external threats, as to maintain and strengthen its control over development of the internal situation in the Central Asian states and limit their sovereignty, especially in foreign policy and foreign trade".[159] In his address to Britain's Royal Institute of International Affairs on 22 March 1994, Nazarbayev made it clear that he opposed deployment of entirely Russian peacekeeping forces in CIS trouble spots, warned of hard-line tendencies in Moscow and said the time had come for the Russians to reconcile themselves to the existence of truly independent neighbours.[160]

Reluctant to accept a Russian military presence in Kazakhstan, but unable to provide for Kazakhstan's security with its own resources, Nazarbayev tried to solve the problem by invoking various concepts of alternative collective security mechanisms for Central Asia. At the 47th session of the UN General Assembly on 5 October 1992, he suggested establishment of a new collective security organisation in Asia — a Conference on Interaction and Confidence Measures in Asia (CICMA) — clearly based on OSCE. The essence of this initiative was "creation of an effective mechanism of preventive diplomacy in Asia". CICMA would be a system of relations between the states of the region established to guarantee their political and economic independence, territorial integrity and security.[161]

Ideas expressed by Kazakh experts such as Abenov, of the Kazakhstan Development Institute, obviously motivated Nazarbayev to embark on this plan. Abenov proposed creation of an alternative collective security system in Central Asia without Russia:

International legal acts to create an intra-CIS collective security system, such as the Collective Security Treaty and the Concept and Declaration on Collective Security have remained on paper only. In this situation Kazakhstan has no alternative but to establish its own subregional or regional collective security system on the basis of existing interstate alliances. . . . Russia, which in pursuing its foreign policy interests is putting its bets . . . on ethnic Russians and multiple Cossack enclaves in the former Soviet republics, and openly claiming 'responsibility' for their protection, is not a very serious partner in maintaining collective security within the framework of the new independent states.[162]

However, progress in implementing Nazarbayev's initiative was unimpressive. The first CICMA preparatory meeting took place in March 1993, attended by representatives of ten states and two international organisations. At its third meeting, in October 1993, twenty six states and four international organisations were represented. They decided to create a working group, with a view to preparing a CICMA conference of foreign ministers. The group, initially of fourteen and later fifteen permanent members and two or three observers, met three times in 1995, but failed to reach a decision on the foreign ministers' conference. Instead, a conference of deputy foreign ministers was held in Almaty on 7–8 February 1996, attended by representatives from twenty three states (fifteen members and eight observers)[163] and observers from the UN and OSCE. The conference decided to complete the drafting of founding documents, and to convene a foreign ministers' conference not later than the second half of 1997.[164]

But the conference did not materialise. Instead, deputy foreign ministers from sixteen countries once again met in Almaty on 3 December 1997. In their final statement they confirmed their commitment to the goals and principles of the UN Charter and expressed preparedness to implement a mechanism of confidence measures and promote cooperation in Asia in order to increase production, develop technologies, encourage international trade and set up joint economic and financial institutions. They decided to hold a conference at the level of foreign ministers in Almaty in 1998.[165] In all the political dynamics surrounding the CICMA initiative show clearly decreased international interest.

Another element in Kazakhstan's national security strategy can be described as diversification of alliances. Philosophically, this concept was clearly represented in Nazarbayev's address to the nation in October 1997 as a priority "initiation stability, through the state's foreign policy bodies, of the already emerging strategic parity around Kazakhstan, which would meet our country's long-term strategic interests".[166] Nazarbayev found the balance of power desirable, because it permitted manoeuvring between the different poles of world power and avoidance of slipping into unilateral dependence on any particular country, especially Russia.

The works of some Kazakh military analysts expressed these ideas in more precise terms. L. Bakaev, for instance, did not hide his concern about some elements of Russian military doctrine, considering that "increased military danger for Kazakhstan" could arise from its proviso that Russia regards "suppression of the rights, freedoms and legitimate interests of Russian Federation citizens in foreign countries" as a major source of military threat.[167] Asker Kusmanuli shared these concerns, but saw the above proviso as "not a military danger to Kazakhstan, more an attempt to psychologically influence the situation in the republic".[168] Despite this difference, both analysts evidently saw military alliance with Russia as insufficient to ensure Kazakhstan's national security, and called for increased military cooperation with NATO, with eventual membership.[169]

Nazarbayev officially outlined the strategy of expanding Kazakhstan's links with NATO as early as May 1992, in his program work Strategy for Kazakhstan's Emergence and Development as a Sovereign State.[170] Although formally in alliance with Russia, and despite its vigorous opposition,

Nazarbayev opened contacts with NATO, and even welcomed its expansion to the east. In a speech at Columbia University in New York on 16 February 1994 he said, "We regard the initiative of the 'sixteen' to expand NATO as a timely and entirely prospective action, which would serve to strengthen the security system in Europe and adjacent areas. Of special importance for us are the opportunities which are being opened within NATO's Partnership for Peace program for strengthening regional security and the defence potential of states participating in it".[171] Meanwhile, Russia's concerns were aroused by precisely that program's possible negative effects on the CIS collective security system. The Duma Committee on CIS Affairs concluded that the program "will block the prospects for military and political consolidation of the CIS space around Russia" and "invalidate the Treaty on Collective Security, concluded between the CIS member-states". The committee recommended support for Yeltsin's postponement of Russia's adherence to the program, and use of "all possible means ... to achieve coordination and a joint position within the CIS in relation to the NATO initiative".[172] These means obviously had no effect on Kazakhstan.

On 24 January 1995, after a meeting in Brussels with NATO Secretary-General, Willy Claes, Nazarbayev disclosed that they had discussed drawing up an individual partnership programme for Kazakhstan and NATO, as well as issues pertaining to security on the Eurasian continent. During the meeting Nazarbayev allegedly stated that increasing military cooperation between Kazakhstan and Russia did not conflict with the Partnership for Peace program.[173] At a conference on foreign policy issues held in Almaty on 15 February 1995, Kazakhstan's Foreign Minister Tokaev stated that Kazakhstan had "no intention of declining to cooperate with NATO within the Partnership for Peace program. . . . NATO's leadership agrees that rapprochement between Kazakhstan and Russia does not contradict this program, because the Russian and Kazakhstan armies remain separate armed forces".[174]

The same strategy underlay Nazarbayev's proposal to create a Central Asian peacekeeping battalion without Russian participation, advanced at his meeting with the presidents of Kyrgyzstan and Uzbekistan in the Kazakh town of Dzhambul on 15 December 1995. The presidents agreed that the battalion should be created as a UN reserve force,using UN financial, material and technical assistance to form it. They sent an appeal to UN Secretary-General Boutros Boutros-Ghali, saying that Kazakhstan, Kyrgyzstan and Uzbekistan were ready to join the UN's system of agreements on military reserves and to start consultations with UN experts. They wanted to deploy the new force in southern Kazakhstan, near the border with Uzbekistan, but said it would not just have a regional remit. "This battalion will not be formed for maintaining stability in Tajikistan, where CIS-mandated troops are already acting," said Kazakh presidential spokesman Daulet Kuanyshev. "It will not be created just as a regional unit, and could even be used in Bosnia or other hot spots."[175]

From the diplomatic angle, a Central Asian battalion under UN auspices was an ingenious idea. It did not have the direct anti-Russian implications of, say, an approach to NATO. In addition, it sought to acquire non-Russian material support, combat training and equipment, probably free of charge, and to diminish the Central Asia's military dependence on Moscow. At the same time it opened the way for other powers, primarily the United States, to increase their presence in the region under UN auspices. Not surprisingly, the United States immediately spotted the initiative and offered help. On 3 April a U.S. military delegation led by Robert Hunter, U.S. Ambassador to NATO, arrived in Kazakhstan for talks on international and regional security issues and on cooperation on defence issues. Hunter was reported to have told First Deputy Foreign Minister Nurlan Danenov that the United States was willing to assist financially in creation of a Central Asian peacekeeping battalion under UN auspices. He also approved of Kazakhstan's plans to join NATO's Partnership for Peace program.[176]

On 5 May 1996, at a meeting in the Kyrgyz capital Bishkek, the presidents of Kazakhstan, Kyrgyzstan and Uzbekistan agreed to create a 500-strong Central Asian battalion, to be trained under the Partnership for Peace program. Kazakhstan and Uzbekistan would each provide 40% of its funding, and Kyrgyzstan 20%.[177] At a press conference after the meeting, Nazarbayev said that the battalion would be able to acquire vital military know-how, and help quell any disturbances in the three participating states, as well as operate as UN peacekeepers abroad. "We don't have any territorial claims against other states, but we don't want other states to have territorial claims against us," he said.[178] His statement indicated first, that Kazakhstan was dissatisfied with existing collective security arrangements and second, that the battalion might be used to quell internal ethnic unrest. It was not hard to guess against whom it would be used in that event. This also explained why Nazarbayev preferred it to be trained by NATO: absence of Russian connections would be crucial if the force were ever used against Russian separatists. In August 1996 the battalion, including troops from all three countries, took part in the cooperative Osprey-96 military exercise under the Partnership for Peace at Camp Lejeune, North Carolina. The decision to send it to the United States was taken despite Russia's refusal to participate in the exercise.[179]

From 1994 the emphasis in Russian-Kazakh military relations began to shift to a bilateral basis. In mid-1993 the CIS Joint Armed Forces High Command was abolished, and the Tashkent Treaty provided no effective alternative mechanisms for military cooperation. During 1994 the Russian Defence Ministry actively worked with Kazakhstan to find solutions to the following problems: organisation of communications and warning; procedure for interaction between Kazakh and Russian air defences; joint planning and use of military formations; interstate military transportation; status of Russian military formations in Kazakhstan; training of Kazakhstan officers in Russian military-educational establishments; social guarantees to personnel serving in Kazakhstan; and status of several military installations in Kazakhstan, including four test ranges and the Balkhash Missile Attack Warning Centre.[180] Some of these questions were mentioned in two key documents, the Treaty between the Republic of Kazakhstan and the Russian Federation on Military Cooperation and the Agreement between the Government of the Republic of Kazakhstan and the Government of the Russian Federation on Military and Technological Cooperation concluded in Moscow on 28 March 1994. The first was signed by Yeltsin and Nazarbayev, the second by prime ministers Chernomyrdin and Tereshchenko.

Besides a large block of provisions on nuclear weapons (which duplicated formulas contained in the agreement on strategic nuclear forces) the treaty mentioned a number of issues which Russia had actively sought to resolve. Article 4 permitted the signatories to lease military installations and facilities to each other, thus opening the way to agreements on the test ranges. Article 8 envisaged concluding special agreements on joint planning and use of troops and joint training of control bodies and troops. Article 10 bound them to coordinate their activities in the military intelligence field, and not to conduct military operations or espionage against each other. Article 12 stipulated that a special agreement be concluded on social guarantees and pensions for servicemen from one country serving on the other's territory. Article 19 dealt with communications, warning and interstate transportation, and said that "the sides will keep all existing systems of liaison, anti-aircraft and anti-missile defences, warning and communications, and will take agreed measures for their development". The signatories undertook to cooperate in military interstate transportation, and to conclude a special agreement on this issue, to retain joint airspace for military and civil flights, and a unified system for controlling them.[181]

Kazakhstan also obtained some advantages. Article 11 provided for agreement on joint use of naval forces in the Caspian Sea. Kazakhstan had neither a navy nor trained sailors, so Russian assistance in this area was essential. Article 17 stipulated that arms and military equipment be supplied at domestic, not world, prices, thus giving Kazakhstan access to Russian weaponry and spare parts at the lower domestic prices used in Russia. Article 18 included a provision that the signatories retain the same regime for educating and training officers and warrant officers established in earlier agreements. This was added at Kazakh insistence, obviously to retain the freedom from fees provided by the accord concluded on 25 July 1992.

Article 1 of the Agreement on Military and Technological Cooperation stipulated that the signatories ensure coordination and interaction in implementing bilateral military and technological cooperation, by: maintaining and developing ties between designers and manufacturers of military equipment; supplying each other with military products and material means needed for defence and security; coordinating mobilisation plans; and providing services in the military field, including supplying each other with technical documentation on manufacturing, maintenance and exploitation of military equipment. Article 2 obliged them to define the types and quantities of military supplies for each other, and the conditions and forms of payment for them, in special annual agreements to be signed by 15 November of each year.

Under Article 4 they agreed to cooperate in the arms trade with third countries, to assist each other in securing and defending mutual interests, and to conclude a special agreement defining the terms and procedure for re-export of arms. Each also undertook not to sell or give military equipment supplied by the other, nor information about it, to third countries without previous written consent of the supplier.[182] These conditions for re-export of military equipment were aimed at preventing damage to Russian arms exports in world markets, and leakage of sensitive technological information on weapons design and characteristics.

The Agreement on Military and Technological Cooperation was mostly tailored to satisfy Kazakhstan's needs. Kazakhstan needed Russian military supplies, not vice-versa. Although (and because) it inherited a large part of the former Soviet arsenal, Kazakhstan remains highly dependent on Russia for military hardware and spare parts. Kazakhstan's military- industrial complex is poorly developed. It has neither enterprises manufacturing complete military equipment, nor the material base for repairing them.[183] One major problem is that most weapons systems produced in Kazakhstan in Soviet times were intended for the Navy.[184] Russia, however, is happy to continue receiving naval weapons from Kazakhstan, because this saves it the trouble and expense of converting enterprises to produce them itself. At present defence enterprises in Kazakhstan continue to supply 200 types of naval weapons, equipment and components to 45 Russian plants, including torpedoes, mine-torpedo and mine-rocket complexes, air- and ship-laid sea-bed mines, contact and noncontact trawls, shore defence missile complexes, onboard equipment for cruise missiles, and steering-control systems for submarines.[185] Russia is also interested in supplies of strategic raw materials from Kazakhstan; were there no agreement, it could still purchase them, but would have to pay higher free market prices.

The general impression is that the Treaty on Military Cooperation and the Agreement on Military and Technological Cooperation were comprehensive but not well prepared, and resembled mere declarations of intent. They defined spheres of interest of both Russia and Kazakhstan in military cooperation, and indicated potential agreements of substance, but they contained very few specific obligations. Their shortcomings soon revealed themselves, and many important provisions simply remained on paper. For example, in 1994 Russia again refused to fulfil Kazakh requests for weapon and equipment supplies, because of Kazakhstan's inability to pay.[186] Kazakhstan accused Russia of failing to adhere to the letter of the treaty, alleging that Moscow had demanded payment at world, not domestic, prices.[187]

Kazakhstan also complained that immediately after signing the Treaty on Military Cooperation, the Russian Defence Ministry issued an order providing Russian pensions only to servicemen who would have retired from other CIS member-states' armed forces and returned to Russia by the end of 1994. This order caused an upheaval among the Slavic officer corps in Kazakhstan, and virtually stripped it of personnel. Kazakh attempts to stabilise the situation by signing a special agreement on military service with Russia did not succeed until January 1995; by then, many officers had already left Kazakhstan. Disagreements also spread into the sphere of military education. Kazakhstan expected that under Article 18 free education of Kazakhs in Russian military-educational institutions, provided under the 1992 agreement, would continue. But the Russian Defence Ministry suddenly began demanding payment of fees. Nor was the Kazakh side fully satisfied at the attitude towards Kazakh cadets in the Russian establishments, alleging that they were treated as foreigners and grouped with other non-Russian cadets, and that some of them had been unjustifiably dismissed.[188]

According to Kazakh military experts, in 1994 achievements in military cooperation between Russia and Kazakhstan found reflection "primarily in a number of mutually signed agreements, leaving general military problems practically unsolved".[189] This conclusion seems to be justified. It is also important to recognise that Russia's uncooperativeness may have been deliberate policy. Moscow put restraints on bilateral military cooperation while waiting for progress on a number of issues of primary importance for Russia, such as test ranges, status of military formations and interstate transportation. Moreover, Russia obviously conditioned its military cooperation with Kazakhstan on progress in negotiations on Baykonur and fulfillment of Kazakhstan's obligations to remove nuclear warheads to Russia. It was only after considerable progress was made on these matters that Russian-Kazakh military relations experienced a real turn for the better.

Russian-Kazakh bilateral military relations showed signs of improvement in late 1994. On 8 September 1994 Russia and Kazakhstan signed an agreement of principle importance to Moscow, dealing with transportation through Kazakhstan of border guard troops, materials and equipment in the interests of protecting CIS external borders. In accordance with this agreement, Kazakhstan pledged unimpeded and free transit to Russian border guards protecting the external borders of Tajikistan, Kyrgyzstan and Turkmenistan, and undertook to ensure fulfillment of schedules and security of transportation through its territory. The agreement covered all forms of transit — air, rail road, sea and rivers.[190]

This agreement was followed by another substantial document, the Treaty between the Russian Federation and the Republic of Kazakhstan on Cooperation in Protecting External Borders, signed on 21 October 1994. The sides agreed that with open borders between them, protection of the external borders was their common duty (Article 3). In the event of destabilisation or threat of destabilisation anywhere along the external border, they pledged immediate consultation and joint measures to restore stability (Article 4). They would coordinate their activities and take joint measures against terrorist acts, illegal traffic in drugs, weapons and other contraband, illegal entry to and exit from Russia and Kazakhstan (Article 4), and to cooperate in conducting intelligence operations in the interests of protecting the external borders (Article 7). Russia promised to assist Kazakhstan in training officers and

warrant officers for border guard service, and to supply Kazakh border troops
with military and technical equipment (Articles 8 and 9).

A Consultative Control Council would be formed, consisting of the
commanders-in-chief of Russia's and Kazakhstan's Border Guard Forces, their
deputies and other persons appointed by them. Its main functions would
include: ensuring fulfillment of the treaty; consultations on measures for
improving efficiency of border protection; determining current and prospective
needs for officers; exchanging information on questions of common interest;
organising cooperation between Border Guard troops in situations of
destabilisation or threat of destabilisation at the external borders; developing
and implementing proposals to unify legislation on border guards' functioning;
taking decisions on training at border guard military-educational
establishments; and consultations on questions of military equipment
deliveries.[191]

On 14 December 1994, during Chernomyrdin's visit to Almaty, he and his
Kazakh counterpart Kazhegeldin signed an agreement regulating the procedure
for Russia's use of the Balkhash Missile Attack Warning Centre. On 30
December their Defence Ministers concluded two accords, On Air Defence
Facilities of the Russian Federation and Kazakhstan, and their Joint Operation
and On Issues of Joint Planning of the Armed Forces in the Interest of Mutual
Security of the Russian Federation and Kazakhstan. But all this was only a
prelude to the Yeltsin-Nazarbayev meeting in Moscow on 20 January 1995,
which was meant to be a real breakthrough in bilateral military cooperation.

The Declaration on Expansion and Deepening of Russian-Kazakh
Cooperation, adopted by the two presidents expressly defined obligations
undertaken in accordance with the Treaty on Military Cooperation as "a long-
term basis for cooperation between Russia and Kazakhstan within the common
military and strategic space", and went as far as proclaiming "the formation,
beginning in 1995, of joint armed forces on the principles of joint planning of
preparation and use of forces, and providing them with armaments and military
equipment".[192] Another important point concerned CIS external borders, and
stressed that "protection of the external borders of both states, given the
openness of the borders between them, is their common cause, and will be
conducted in accordance with the collective security interests of the
Commonwealth of Independent States".[193] These provisions represented both
the Kazakhs' desperation at their inability to create adequate army and border
guard services of their own, and the Russian Defence Ministry's long-sought
objective of stationing Russian combat units in Russian-controlled bases in
Kazakhstan, as well as ensuring the protection of external borders which had
been left open by Russia's withdrawal.

A series of documents signed at ministerial level substantiated the above
provisions. An agreement, On the Status of Russian Federation Military
Formations Temporarily Stationed on the Territory of the Republic of
Kazakhstan, resolved what had probably been the most irritating question in
bilateral military relations. It placed Russian military units in their deployment

areas in Kazakhstan under Russian legislation and Russian military procedures, provided they did not contravene international law, and put supervision over their compliance with Russian legislation into the hands of the appropriate Russian authorities. Russian units could employ citizens of Kazakhstan (Article 2), but should respect Kazakhstan's sovereignty and legislation, not interfere in its internal affairs, nor take part in its domestic political life, including internal conflicts (Article 3). Russian military units could leave their bases or enter or leave Kazakhstan only after consultation with Kazakhstan's Defence Ministry; and the same restriction applied to flights by Russian military aircraft in Kazakhstan's airspace (Article 6). Counterintelligence protection of Russian military units, and operations relating to Russian personnel or members of their families, would be conducted by Russia's counterintelligence services (Article 11). Each country undertook to compensate the other for material damage resulting from Russian military activities or actions by Kazakh authorities, citizens or organisations affecting Russian units (Article 22). The agreement would be in force for ten years and would be extended automatically for another ten, unless either side gave six months' notice of intent to terminate it.[194]

The prime ministers also signed an agreement, On Organisation of Military Inter-State Transport on Behalf of the Russian Defence Ministry. It covered rail, road and air transportation, but dealt mainly with rail transport, the mode of most importance for Russia. It placed responsibility for administering such transportation on the Central Military Communications Directorate of the Russian Defence Ministry, and the Military Communications Service of Kazakhstan's General Staff, which were to resolve all rail transport questions cooperatively. The Russian side would prepare an annual schedule for military trains, and notify its Kazakh counterpart before 1 November of the preceding year. Applications to dispatch military trains were to be sent "to the military-transport institutions after these transportations (supplies) have been endorsed by the relevant authorities of both sides" (Article 7). The Russian and Kazakh transport organisations would allocate rolling stock, locomotives, materials for securing weapons and equipment, train crews, loading and unloading equipment, and ensure scheduled movement and security of the troops and equipment through their territory (Article 9). Overflights by military aircraft would also take place only after consultations with the appropriate authorities, responsible for air transportation and controlled by territorial air transport authorities (Article 12). Transport by road could be conducted "either singly or in column, on the basis of plans and applications, and after obtaining agreement from the appropriate authorities" (Article 13). The agreement was to be valid for five years and would be automatically extended for subsequent five year periods, unless either side declared intent to terminate it six months before the expiary of each five-year period.[195]

This agreement, together with the earlier one on transporting border guard troops, finally resolved one of Russia's most acute strategic problems, stability of lines of communication to the CIS southern border. Its only disadvantage for

Russia was the procedure for obtaining permission to transport, which could become victim to bureaucratic inefficiency and hamper the prompt movement of troops in crisis situations. But generally the agreement served mostly Russian interests, since it is difficult to see what need Kazakhstan might have to transport troops through Russia.

The Agreement on Contract Military Service and the Status of Russian Federation Citizens in the Armed Forces of the Republic of Kazakhstan opened the way for Kazakhstan to recruit experienced Russian military personnel. It gave Russian servicemen the right "to conclude contracts with the Defence Ministry of the Republic of Kazakhstan to conduct military service in its Armed Forces on a voluntary basis". They need not take an oath of allegiance to Kazakhstan, but each contract must include a pledge to perform their duties in good faith (Article 2). Article 5 banned the use of Russian Federation citizens in Kazakhstan's armed forces for participation in domestic and inter-ethnic conflicts. Any violation of this condition by Kazakhstan entitled Russian servicemen to abrogate their contracts;[196] so this provision enabled them legally to reject orders to participate in any action directed against ethnic Russians living in the republic. Other provisions dealt mostly with issues regulating the social rights of Russian contract servicemen in Kazakhstan. It was valid until 31 December 1999 and could be extended if both sides so desired. In general the agreement primarily benefited Kazakhstan, because it helped at least partially to fill the gap caused by the mass exodus of experienced Russian military personnel. However, its long-term effects are difficult to evaluate. Some Russian experts question the benefits of such arrangements, claiming that ethnocratic regimes in Central Asia will have difficulties ensuring the loyalty of Russian officers even on a mercenary basis.[197]

Of great importance to Russia were also four agreements dealing with the use of test ranges: Emba (tactical anti-aircraft defence systems), Sary Shagan (strategic antiaircraft and antimissile defence systems, including laser weapons), 929 GLIC (tests of military aircraft) and 4GSP (State Central Test Range). Kazakhstan undertook to lease these ranges to Russia.[198] Each agreement had appendices defining the limits of the range's land area. It was agreed to conclude special lease treaties specifying the procedure for transfer of the land, the inventory and composition of movable property and real estate, duration of the lease, and the rent and dates for payments. The ranges would be used and administered by the Russian military, and range commanders appointed by the president of Russia after consulting the president of Kazakhstan. Counterintelligence protection of the ranges would be covered by a separate agreement on cooperation for providing for the security of Russian military units in Kazakhstan. Russia undertook to restore and maintain the ranges' infrastructure; to conduct tests within the ranges' limits, to ensure security of works and missile launches; allow Kazakhstan's armed forces to use the ranges after consulting with the Russian side; and improve the ecological situation at the ranges, by providing for timely cleansing of them, removal of hazards caused by accidents, and compensating for damage resulting from such accidents. The land areas were to be used only for their specific purpose: geological surveys, exploitation of natural resources and other similar activities were prohibited. The agreements were for ten years with automatic extension for another ten years, if neither side declared intent to terminate them six month before the end of each ten-year period. The agreements could be suspended in case the sides failed to agree on, or subsequently breached, the conditions of lease.[199]

Thus, despite mutual objurgation, scolding and scuffling, Russia and Kazakhstan in 1995 moved substantially closer in their bilateral military ties. By 1995 the process of building a solid legal base for bilateral military cooperation was generally complete. By October 1997 they had signed 46 treaties and agreements, covering almost every possible sphere of military relations.[200] These agreements formalised a deep Russian involvement in ensuring Kazakhstan's defences, and in return bound Kazakhstan tightly to Russia in the military field. Their conclusion helped Moscow to solve some important military and strategic problems related to its interests in Central Asia. In the event of an international crisis, Russia could rely on using Kazakhstan's territory for forward defence, power projection, logistical support and mobilisation of extra personnel into the Russian army. It ensured stability of troops and armaments transportation to the CIS southern border, facilitating a rapid buildup of military power there. Finally, the Russian military presence in Kazakhstan was legally validated, retaining Kazakhstan in Russia's sphere of military influence and ensuring protection of the ethnic Russian population in the event of interethnic violence.

These developments made for a fairly optimistic forecast by the Russian Defence Ministry with regard to military cooperation with Kazakhstan. The analytical report it prepared concluded:

It is advisable to pursue the following directions of Russia's military cooperation with Kazakhstan:
1. To implement understandings reached in the agreements signed in the fields of military and military-technological cooperation.
2. To develop integrationist processes both between Russia and Kazakhstan, and within the CIS in economic, financial, customs, political, military and humanitarian spheres, in the interests of forming a union (confederative) state, primarily on the basis of the Collective Security Treaty and the Declaration of 20 January 1995.
3. To consult on military and technological policy (production, purchase, supplies of military equipment to national armed forces) and interests of defence ministries in the field of training of military specialists for national armed forces of both states. To create conditions and fulfill potential for unifying the existing military and technological base of both states.
4. To develop a common military doctrine and joint concept for construction, maintenance and logistics for national and joint armed forces and command over them.
5. To plan and later implement measures for joint (common) protection of state borders, formation and use of joint (coalition) groups of forces in extraordinary circumstances (time of war).

6. To work out normative and legal bases for creation and functioning of a union (confederative) state within the CIS collective security system, hereby specifying the conditions on which other CIS member-states can be admitted to the planned union (confederation).[201]

Kazakh official experts generally regard Russian-Kazakh military relations as an alliance. Bakaev, head of the Directorate of International Security and Arms Control of Kazakhstan's Foreign Ministry, unhesitatingly called Russia Kazakhstan's strategic ally.[202] At a press conference in Moscow on 16 May 1997, Nazarbayev confirmed the alliance nature of relations with Russia by referring to the Treaty on Friendship, Cooperation and Mutual Assistance, and specifically stating that in case of an attack against Russia or Kazakhstan, both countries would defend each other by all available means, including armed forces.[203]

Nevertheless, some Russian foreign policy analysts expressed scepticism about Kazakhstan's reliability as a military ally. S. Solodovnikov, a senior fellow at the Centre for Strategic Studies at the Moscow State Institute of International Relations, stated at the Duma hearings on Russian-Kazakh relations that none of the treaties and agreements with Kazakhstan was working, and "[t]here can be 100, 200 and 300 agreements but they remain on paper".[204] Experts at the Russian Institute of Strategic Studies noted that during his visits to the United States and Western Europe in 1994–1995, Nazarbayev "more than once spoke on issues involving, among other things, Russia's security interests, in a way somewhat contrary to an allied approach". This was interpreted as "an element of pressure on Russia to make it more conciliatory over a whole range of issues, including the military sphere".[205] These judgments are not unfounded and reflect elements of instability in the military and strategic relationships between Russia and Kazakhstan.

It is obvious that certain undercurrents of uneasiness, suspicion and mistrust continue to plague Russian-Kazakh military relationships. Thus after the agreements on the test ranges had been signed, the talks on the lease treaties dragged on. Most of the differences revolved around procedures for and amounts of rent payments. A Russian Defence Ministry report said that some substantial differences emerged over determining the cost of individual facilities, characteristics of weapons to be tested and the amount of land tax to be levied. The Russian Defence Ministry representative at the Duma hearings on Russian-Kazakh relations, Lieutenant-General Merkulov, publicly described the Kazakh negotiators' approach as unconstructive.[206] On 18 October 1996 Chernomyrdin and Kazhegeldin finally signed treaties on leasing the ranges.[207]

But immediately afterwards, the Kazakh leadership initiated a public campaign against Russian use of the ranges. From December 1996 *Kazakhstanskaya Pravda* began to publish regular articles under the rubric "Military Ranges – Bleeding Wounds on the Body of Kazakhstan". In one such article, E. Gabbasov, a member of Kazakhstan's Senate Committee for International Relations, Defence and Security, called for the ranges to be closed down and complained that the proposed rent for their use was ridiculously low at $26.5 million dollars, and should be around $1.5 billion.[208] Following the article a group of members of the Senate and Majilis sent a collective letter demanding closure of the ranges to Nazarbayev.[209] It is likely the campaign was sanctioned by Nazarbayev himself, to secure either a higher rent for the ranges or new concessions from Russia in other matters. Naturally, the campaign caused strong displeasure in Moscow.[210]

In November 1996 in Bishkek, defence officials from Kazakhstan, Kyrgyzstan and Uzbekistan decided to hold the first international military exercises in Central Asia under the Partnership for Peace program.[211] The Russians could do nothing to stop it, so decided to take part, if only to validate their regional presence. On 15 September the exercise, termed Centrazbat-97, was held in the Sayram district of South Kazakhstan province. Besides the Central Asian battalion, 500 American, 40 Turkish and 40 Russian troops took part. The exercises proved the ability of the United States, Turkey and Russia to deliver and deploy airborne troops in Kazakhstan. The scenario of the exercise assumed that a military conflict between the government and separatists had erupted, and UN collective peacekeeping troops had been sent to prevent the separatists' capturing Sayram airport, where they intended to receive weapons and ammunition flown in from an unidentified neighbouring state.[212] In principle such a scenario could be directed at Islamic militants wanting to break away from secular Kazakh state to form their own Islamic republic, with support from the territory of Afghanistan. The scenario could be equally directed against potential Russian separatists, for example, in Semirechye, where there is large Russian population, but also in other areas. Kazakh leadership could not afford to stage such an exercise in the northern provinces, simply because it would have been clearly directed against ethnic Russians and would have caused political complications.

According to some Russian experts Kazakhstan spies on some Russian military installations on its territory.[213] Russia also expressed concern over the US-Kazakh remote sensing experiment in Kazakhstan near the Russian border, involving U.S. Orion P-3 aircraft. On 24 June 1997 Russian Foreign Ministry spokesman Gennadiy Tarasov said Russia had repeatedly stated that the experiment "touches upon Russian security interests" and created "a dangerous precedent of using the CIS's airspace for conducting intelligence activity against other countries".[214] Primakov raised this question during his negotiations with Tokayev at their meeting in Moscow on 26 June 1997. Tokayev replied that Kazakhstan had informed Russia about the experiment, and emphasised that as an independent country Kazakhstan has a right to conduct any "scientific experiments" on its territory.[215]

On 28 October 1997 Russian Defence Minister Sergeyev arrived in Almaty on a three-day visit. His negotiations with the Kazakh side concentrated on sorting out outstanding military issues. During the meeting with Nazarbayev on 29 October, Sergeyev promised to hand over four more Su-27 aircraft by the end of 1997 as compensation for strategic bombers withdrawn from

Kazakhstan. They also discussed creation of a joint security system in Central Asia, with Russian participation.[216] The negotiations resulted in several signed documents. One was an agreement between the Defence Ministries on joint planning of operational activities and training of Russian and Kazakh military personnel. Joint command staff exercises were scheduled to be held in 1998. Russian and Kazakh armed forces' chiefs of general staff were to plan them jointly.

Sergeyev and Kazakh Defence Minister Altynbayev initialled an agreement on Russian payments for leasing the test ranges. According to reports, the Russian Defence Ministry is to pay $US 28 million a year. $3 million of this will be in cash, another $4 million will cover training of 1,000 Kazakh personnel a year at Russian higher military schools, and the rest will comprise supplies of weapons and materiel. Another agreement set out conditions for storing and transporting highly toxic missile fuel and other compounds from the Sary Shagan test site. The latter two agreements were to be submitted for review at the governmental level in both states. Sergeyev claimed that the visit had accomplished everything it was meant to, but this appears to be an overstatement, given the real results of the negotiations. Even where agreements were reached, progress was very qualified. Four more aircraft (in addition to forty one already supplied) fell far short of the seventy three that Russia had promised to Kazakhstan. No firm agreement was reached on the transfer of two minesweepers and two gunboats, which Altynbayev said might take part in joint patrols of the two states' national sectors in the Caspian Sea, adding that "this is in the interests of both Russia and Kazakhstan". But Sergeyev confined himself to a general statement that Russia would seek possibilities to transfer the boats. Russian reluctance to proceed with the deal was presumably due to disagreement on the status of the Caspian Sea.[217]

Fulfillment of the agreement on rent payments for the test ranges remained conditioned on the Russian Duma's attitude, which was far from positive given Russian-Kazakh disagreements on the status of ethnic Russians in Kazakhstan. The Duma is unlikely to abandon its practice of blocking allocation of funds for the test ranges and Baykonur, and the 1997 budget did not include funds for them. This may be why Sergeyev told journalists that Russia might be prepared to reduce the size of the test sites. [218] The situation around Baykonur again deteriorated when on 24 November 1997 Kazakhstan's parliamentary International Affairs, Defence and Security Committee rejected the draft law on the status of the cosmodrome on the grounds that it discriminated against Kazakhstan. The head of the Customs Service, G. Kasymov, strongly objected to the draft law, saying that it did not specify whether Kazakh law was effective on the site. Senator Engels Gabbasov said Russia had launched foreign commercial satellites from Baykonur, in breach of the agreement. A. Kalybayev, head of the Kazakh National Aerospace Agency, said Russia had paid none of the $US 115 million fee for the lease. The committee also protested that the draft law said nothing about ecology, law enforcement or customs services.[219]

The new difficulties over Baykonur's status prompted Russia to speed up its military disengagement from there. On 17 December 1997 Yeltsin issued a decree instructing the government "to approve, within two months, plans for handing over facilities of the Baykonur cosmodrome from the Defence Ministry to the Russian Space Agency". The decree provided for setting up a state enterprise, Baykonur Federal Space Centre, to take over and operate the cosmodrome's facilities. The Defence Ministry would gradually reduce its personnel there and hand over the facilities in 1998; 755 Russian military officers would stay, but would be seconded to and paid by the RSA.[220]

Kazakhstan continued expanding its military ties with the United States. During Nazarbayev's visit to Washington on 17–18 November 1997, he concluded a number of agreements on military matters. They included a Defence Cooperation Agreement which outlined plans for high level visits, additional progress on cooperative threat reduction and defence conversion, and U.S. assistance in professionalising the Kazakh military, with particular emphasis on English-language instruction and training for a noncommissioned officer corps. The sides also signed a Program of Military Contacts for 1998 which called for more than forty events and exchanges. As Secretary of Defence Cohen noted at the signing ceremony, United States and Kazakhstan were "currently working both bilaterally and through the Partnership for Peace program to build new structures for regional stability in Central Asia".[221] This was clearly a challenge to the Russian-sponsored Tashkent Treaty security system.

Thus despite all the military agreements concluded between Russia and Kazakhstan, they failed to resolve the major problems in their military relations. Differences over cooperation with NATO, on the principles of a collective security system for Central Asia, the scale of the Russian military presence in Kazakhstan, and unresolved military-related financial matters remain significant stumbling blocks to military cooperation. These problems will remain high on the agenda of bilateral relations and will to a large degree affect those relations for some years to come.

NOTES

1.   Gosudarstvennaya Duma Federal'nogo Sobraniya Rossiyskoy Federatsii, Stenogramma parlamentskikh slushaniy Komiteta po delam Sodruzhestva Nezavisimykh Gosudarstv i svyazyam s sootechestvennikami "O rossiysko-kazakhstanskikh otnosheniyakh", Moscow [No publisher], 18.04.95, pp. 9–10.

2.   Bakaev, L., "Voennoe sotrudnichestvo Rossii i Kazakhstana: sostoyanie, problemy i perspektivy", *Kazakhstan i mirovoe soobshchestvo*, No. 2(3), 1995, p. 47.

3.   Ibid., pp. 49–50.

4.   "Armed Forces of Kazakhstan: Problems and Prospects", *BBC Monitoring Service: Former USSR*, 01.12.92.

5.   Kozhokin, E. M., ed., *Kazakhstan: realii i perspektivy nezavisimogo razvitiya*, Moscow: RISI, 1995, pp. 138, 146.

6.   "Russia and Kazakhstan Conclude Military Agreements", *BBC Monitoring Service: Former USSR*, 22.08.92; "Kazakh Official Hails Mutually Beneficial Defence Agreements with Russia", *BBC Monitoring Service: Former USSR*, 16.09.92.

7.   Khitrin, U. A., ed., "Soglashenie mezhdu Ministerstvom Oborony Respubliki Kazakhstan i Ministerstvom Oborony Rossiyskoy Federatsii o poryadke prokhozhdeniya voennoy sluzhby litsami ofitserskogo sostava, praporschikami i michmanami ot 19 avgusta 1992 g.", *Zakonodatel'stvo Respubliki Kazakhstan ob organakh oborony, pravosudiya, bezopasnosti i pravoporyadka*, Chast 1, Almaty: Zheti Zhargi, 1996, p. 223.

8.   "Russia and Kazakhstan Agree on Closer Economic and Military Cooperation", *BBC Monitoring Service: Former USSR*, 03.03.93.

9.   *Nezavisimaya gazeta*, 29.04.93.

10.   *Izvestiya*, 07.07.92.

11.   Reuters News Service, 08.10.92.

12.   *Radio Free Europe / Radio Liberty (RFE/RL) Daily Report*, No. 195, 09.10.92.

13.   "Concerned about Nuclear Weapons in Ukraine and Kazakhstan", *BBC Monitoring Service: Former USSR*, 09.10.92.

14.   "Comments on Military Issues; Nazarbayev Evasive about Nuclear Withdrawl", *BBC Monitoring Service: Former USSR*, 10.02.92.

15.   "Shaposhnikov Says It is Time to Decide on Nuclear Weapons Outside Russia", *BBC Monitoring Service: Former USSR*, 13.01.93.

16.   "Shaposhnikov on Future of CIS Nuclear Forces", *BBC Monitoring Service: Former USSR*, 23.01.93.

17.   "Grachev Says Finding Compromise on CIS Strategic Forces Will Be Difficult", *BBC Monitoring Service: Former USSR*, 23.01.93.

18.   Reuters News Service, 21.02.93.

19.   Foye, S., "End of CIS Command Heralds New Russian Defense Policy?", *RFE/RL Research Report*, Vol. 2, No. 27, 2 July 1993, p. 47.

20.   Kasenov, U., Eleukenov, D., Laumulin, M., *Kazakhstan i dogovor o nerasprostranenii yadernogo oruzhiya*, Almaty: KISI, 1994, pp. 7–8.

21.   *RFE/RL Daily Report*, No. 110, 14.06.93.

22.   Bakaev, L., "Voennoe Stroitel'stvo v Kazakhstane", *Kazakhstan i mirovoe soobshchestvo*, No. 1, 1994, p. 109.

23.   Foye, S., "End of CIS Command Heralds New Russian Defense Policy?", *RFE/RL Research Report*, Vol. 2, No. 27, 2 July 1993, p. 48.

24.   *RFE/RL Daily Report*, No. 192, 06.10.93.

25.   *Nezavisimaya gazeta*, 16.12.93.

26.   *Segodnya*, 16.02.94.

27.   *RFE/RL Daily Report*, No. 55, 21.03.94.

28.   "Memorandum po itogam vstrechi v Almaty 25 dekabrya 1993 goda Premier Ministra Respubliki Kazakhstan S.A.Tereshchenko i Predsedatelya Soveta Ministrov - Pravitelstva Rossiyskoy Federatsii V.S. Chernomyrdina", *Kazakhstansko-rossiyskie otnosheniya, 1991–1995 gody, Sbornik dokumentov i materialov*, Moscow: Posol'stvo Respubliki Kazakhstan v Rossiyskoy Federatsii, 1995, p. 138.

29.   "New Data on the Strategic Arsenal of the Former Soviet Union", *Jane's Intelligence Review*, June 1995, p. 246.

30.   "Dogovor mezhdu Respublikoy Kazakhstan i Rossiyskoy Federatsiey o voennom sotrudnichestve", *Kazakhstansko-rossiyskie otnosheniya, 1991–1995 gody*, pp. 168–169, 178.

31. "Soglashenie mezhdu Respublikoy Kazakhstan i Rossiyskoy Federatsiey o Strategicheskikh yadernikh silakh, vremenno raspolozhennikh na territorii Respubliki Kazakhstan", *Kazakhstansko-rossiyskie otnosheniya, 1991–1995 godi*, pp. 163–166.

32. *RFE/RL Daily Report*, No. 37, 23.02.94.

33. Gosudarstvennaya Duma Federal'nogo Sobraniya Rossiyskoy Federatsii, Stenogramma parlamentskikh slushaniy Komiteta po delam Sodruzhestva Nezavisimykh Gosudarstv i svyazyam s sootechestvennikami "O rossiysko-kazakhstanskikh otnosheniyakh", Moscow [No publisher], 18.04.95, p. 119.

34. "New Data on the Strategic Arsenal of the Former Soviet Union", *Jane's Intelligence Review*, June 1995, p. 246.

35. "Soglashenie mezhdu Pravitelstvom Rossiyskoy Federatsii i Respubliki Kazakhstan o sotrudnichestve i vzaimnikh rasschetakh pri utilizatsii yadernikh boepripasov", *Bulleten mezhdunarodnikh dogovorov*, No. 10, 1995, pp. 37–39.

36. Gosudarstvennaya Duma Federal'nogo Sobraniya Rossiyskoy Federatsii, Stenogramma parlamentskikh slushaniy Komiteta po delam Sodruzhestva Nezavisimykh Gosudarstv i svyazyam s sootechestvennikami "O rossiysko-kazakhstanskikh otnosheniyakh", Moscow [No publisher], 18.04.95, p. 106.

37. Ministerstvo Oborony Rossiyskoy Federatsii, Analiticheskiy material o khode razvitiya voennogo sotrudnichestva Rossiyskoy Federatsii s Respublikoy Kazakhstan, No. 335/5/2/244, Moscow [No publisher], 15.04.95, pp. 2–3.

38. "Kazakh-Russian 'Breakthrough' Agreement on Military Aircraft", *BBC Monitoring Service: Former USSR*, 13.11.95; "Russia Transfers Fighter Planes to Kazakhstan", *BBC Monitoring Service: Former USSR*, 08.04.96.

39. "Russia's Sergeyev to Discuss Cooperation With Kazakhstan", *ITAR-TASS World Service*, 28.10.97.

40. ITAR-TASS, 25.04.95.

41. Nazarbayev, N., *Na poroge XXI veka*, Almaty: Oner, 1996, p. 76.

42. Ibid., p. 69, 76.

43. "Memorandum o garantiyakh bezopasnosti", *Kazakhstan i mirovoe soobshchestvo*, No. 1, 1995, p. 107.

44. On 8 February 1995 China provided Kazakhstan with similar guarantees to those envisaged in the Budapest memorandum ("Zayavlenie Kitayskogo pravitel'stva o predostavlenii Kazakhstanu garantiy bezopasnosti", *Kazakhstan i mirovoe soobshchestvo*, No. 1(2), 1995, p. 113).

45. Reuters News Service, 19.03.94.

46. Abenov, E., "Vneshnepoliticheskie interesy Respubliki Kazakhstan", *Politika*, No. 6, 1995, p. 66.

47. "Soglashenie mezhdu Respublikoy Kazakhstan i Rossiyskoy Federatsiey o poryadke ispol'zovaniya kosmodroma Baykonur", *Kazakhstansko-rossiyskie otnosheniya, 1991–1995 gody*, p. 100.

48. *Kazakhstansko-rossiyskie otnosheniya, 1991–1995 gody, Sbornik dokumentov i materialov*, Moscow: Posol'stvo Respubliki Kazakhstan v Rossiyskoy Federatsii, 1995, p. 45.

49. Reuters News Service, 01.07.93.

50. Gosudarstvennaya Duma Federal'nogo Sobraniya Rossiyskoy Federatsii, Stenogramma parlamentskikh slushaniy Komiteta po delam Sodruzhestva Nezavisimykh Gosudarstv i svyazyam s sootechestvennikami "O rossiysko-kazakhstanskikh otnosheniyakh", Moscow [No publisher], 18.04.95, p. 99.

51. "Shortage of Funds and Lack of Social Security Threatening Baikonur's Future", *BBC Monitoring Service: Former USSR*, 31.05.93.

52. ITAR-TASS, 09.04.93.

53. *Izvestiya*, 02.07.93.

54. "Russian-Kazakh Talks on Baykonur End With no Real Result", *BBC Monitoring Service: Former USSR*, 05.07.93.

55. "Kazakhstan Puts Baikonur Cosmodrome under Special Guard to Prevent Thefts", *BBC Monitorin Service: Former USSR*, 31.05.93.

56. Reuters News Service, 07.06.93.

57. "Nazarbayev and Yeltsin to Meet at Baykonur Cosmodrome", *BBC Monitorin Service: Former USSR*, 15.06.93.

58. "Russian-Kazakh Talks on Baykonur End with No Real Result", *BBC Monitoring Service: Former USSR*, 05.07.93.

59. "Russian-Kazakh 'Public Showdown' at Press Conference on Baykonur", *BBC Monitoring Service: Former USSR*, 06.12.93.

60. Reuters News Service, 20.07.93.

61. "Kazakhstan to Train Its Own Experts for Baykonur Cosmodrome", *BBC Monitoring Service: Former USSR*, 26.07.93.

62. "Statement on Cooperation Made by Presidents of Russia and Kazakhstan", *BBC Monitoring Service: Former USSR*, 09.08.93.

63. Reuters News Service, 09.08.93.

64. Ibid.

65. "Kazakhstan Seeks US Assistance to Turn Baykonur into International Space Centre", *BBC Monitoring Service: Former USSR*, 23.08.93.

66. "Further Questions on the Future of Baykonur", *BBC Monitoring Service: Former USSR*, 13.09.93.

67. "Germany's Daimler-Benz Shows Interest in Using Baykonur Cosmodrome", *BBC Monitoring Service: Former USSR*, 04.10.93.

68. "Kazakh President Tells US Congressmen Baykonur Is Kazakh Property", *BBC Monitoring Service: Former USSR*, 06.12.93.

69. "Kazakh President Nazarbayev Meets US Delegation to Discuss Baykonur's Future", *BBC Monitoring Service: Former USSR*, 20.12.93.

70. "Denial of Russia's Reported Decision to Pull Out of Baykonur", *BBC Monitoring Service: Former USSR*, 06.09.93.

71. "Further Questions on the Future of Baykonur", *BBC Monitoring Service: Former USSR*, 13.09.93.

72. Kozhokin, E. M., ed., *Kazakhstan: realii i perspektivy nezavisimogo razvitiya*, p. 151.

73. Gosudarstvennaya Duma Federal'nogo Sobraniya Rossiyskoy Federatsii, Stenogramma parlamentskikh slushaniy Komiteta po delam Sodruzhestva Nezavisimykh Gosudarstv i svyazyam s sootechestvennikami "O rossiysko-kazakhstanskikh otnosheniyakh", Moscow [No publisher], 18.04.95, p. 98.

74. "Russian Missile Troops to Be Transferred to Plesetsk", *BBC Monitoring Service: Former USSR*, 03.10.94.

75. "Further Questions on the Future of Baykonur", *BBC Monitoring Service: Former USSR*, 13.09.93.

76. "Russian Space Chief Visits Svobodnyy", *BBC Monitoring Service: Former USSR*, 21.03.94.

77. Reuters News Service, 10.11.93.

78. Reuters News Service, 04.08.94.

79. "Memorandum po itogam vstrechi v Almaty 25 dekabrya 1993 goda Premier Ministra Respubliki Kazakhstan S.A.Tereshchenko i Predsedatelya Soveta Ministrov -

Pravitelstva Rossiyskoy Federatsii V.S. Chernomyrdina", *Kazakhstansko-rossiyskie otnosheniya, 1991–1995 gody*, p. 138.

80. For example, see *Izvestiya*, 28.12.93, or Koptev's remarks on Baykonur (Reuters News Service, 29.12.93).

81. *Izvestiya*, 14.01.94.

82. Kozhokin, E. M., ed., *Kazakhstan: realii i perspektivy nezavisimogo razvitiya*, p. 159.

83. "Kazakh-Ukrainian Joint Communique Following Nazarbayev's Visit", *BBC Monitoring Service: Former USSR*, 26.01.94.

84. "Russian Foreign Minister Visits Kazakhstan", *BBC Monitoring Service: Former USSR*, 17.02.94.

85. *RFE/RL Daily Report*, No. 39, 25.02.94.

86. "Kazakhstan Calls on Russia to Compensate Ecological Consequences of Baykonur", *BBC Monitoring Service: Former USSR*, 28.02.94.

87. *RFE/RL Daily Report*, No. 27, 09.02.94.

88. Reuters News Service, 09.02.94.

89. Ivanov was clearly counting on Kazakh ignorance of the technology in general and on no Kazakh ever having been allowed to see what was at Svobodnyy in particular. The need to install new and costly equipment for surface launching of large missiles accounted for its being expected to be five years or more before Svobodnyy could launch large boosters.

90. Reuters News Service, 10.03.94.

91. "Russian Space Chief Visits Svobodnyy", *BBC Monitoring Service: Former USSR*, 21.03.94.

92. "Kazakh Government Delegation in Moscow to Prepare Summit; Premiers Meet", *BBC Monitoring Service: Former USSR*, 19.03.94.

93. "Russia and Kazakhstan Make Progress in Talks on Baykonur", *BBC Monitoring Service: Former USSR*, 21.03.94.

94. "Soglashenie mezhdu Respublikoy Kazakhstan i Rossiyskoy Federatsiey ob osnovnykh printsipakh i usloviyakh ispolzovaniya kosmodroma Baykonur", *Kazakhstansko-rossiyskie otnosheniya, 1991–1995 gody*, pp. 156–159.

95. Kozhokin, E. M., ed., *Kazakhstan: realii i perspektivy nezavisimogo razvitiya*, p. 155.

96. Dogovor arendy kompleksa "Baykonur" mezhdu Pravitel'stvom Rossiyskoy Federatsii i Pravitel'stvom Respubliki Kazakhstan, Moscow [No publisher], 1995.

97. *Segodnya*, 05.08.94.

98. *Rossiyskaya gazeta*, 07.09.94.

99. See: *Gorizont*, 21.07.95.

100. *Commersant-Daly*, 17.06.95.

101. "Kazakh Town Renamed after Baykonur Space Centre", *BBC Monitoring Service: Former USSR*, 11.12.95.

102. Kozhokin, E. M., ed., *Kazakhstan: realii i perspektivy nezavisimogo razvitiya*, pp. 155–156.

103. *Moskovskie novosti*, 01.03.95.

104. "Accident at Baykonur Said to Threaten Launch of Progress Spacecraft", *BBC Monitoring Service: Former USSR*, 02.10.95.

105. Reuters News Service, 18.09.96.

106. *OMRI Daily Digest*, No. 81, Part I, 25.04.95.

107. "Baykonur Space Centre Beset By Social and Financial Problems", *BBC Monitoring Service: Former USSR*, 16.04.96.

108. In a statement on 20 May 1997 Tuleyev said, that Kazakhstan's debt to Russia stood at $US2.3 billion ("Russian Minister Responds to President Nazarbayev's Remarks", *BBC Monitoring Service: Former USSR*, 22.05.97).

109. Gosudarstvennaya Duma Federal'nogo Sobraniya Rossiyskoy Federatsii, Stenogramma parlamentskikh slushaniy Komiteta po delam Sodruzhestva Nezavisimykh Gosudarstv i svyazyam s sootechestvennikami "O rossiysko-kazakhstanskikh otnosheniyakh", Moscow [No publisher], 18.04.95, pp. 96, 109–110.

110. Protokol ob uregulirovanii vzaimnykh finansovykh pretenziy mezhdu Rossiyskoy Federatsiey i Respublikoy Kazakhstan, Moscow [No publisher], 1995.

111. Gosudarstvennaya Duma Federal'nogo Sobraniya Rossiyskoy Federatsii, Stenogramma parlamentskikh slushaniy Komiteta po delam Sodruzhestva Nezavisimykh Gosudarstv i svyazyam s sootechestvennikami "O rossiysko-kazakhstanskikh otnosheniyakh", Moscow [No publisher], 18.04.95, pp. 89–90, 110–111.

112. *Kazakhstanskaya pravda*, 07.10.97.

113. Gosudarstvennaya Duma Federal'nogo Sobraniya Rossiyskoy Federatsii, Stenogramma parlamentskikh slushaniy Komiteta po delam Sodruzhestva Nezavisimykh Gosudarstv i svyazyam s sootechestvennikami "O rossiysko-kazakhstanskikh otnosheniyakh", Moscow [No publisher], 18.04.95, p. 138.

114. Kozhokin, E. M., ed., *Kazakhstan: realii i perspektivy nezavisimogo razvitiya*, pp. 153, 155.

115. Gosudarstvennaya Duma Federal'nogo Sobraniya Rossiyskoy Federatsii, Stenogramma parlamentskikh slushaniy Komiteta po delam Sodruzhestva Nezavisimykh Gosudarstv i svyazyam s sootechestvennikami "O rossiysko-kazakhstanskikh otnosheniyakh", Moscow [No publisher], 18.04.95, p. 102.

116. "Russian Government Approves Presidential Decree on Baykonur Cosmodrome", *BBC Monitoring Service: Former USSR*, 08.08.94.

117. *Segodnya*, 03.12.94.

118. "Russia to Phase out Defence Satellite Launches from Baykonur in 2003", *BBC Monitoring Service: Former USSR*, 06.02.95.

119. The agreement in question was, probably, "Inmarsat Technology Safeguards Agreement".

120. "Nazarbayev on Results of His Official US Visit", *BBC Monitoring Service: Former USSR*, 03.03.94.

121. Kozhokin, E. M., ed., *Kazakhstan: realii i perspektivy nezavisimogo razvitiya*, p. 157.

122. "Russian Missile Troops to Be Transferred to Plesetsk", *BBC Monitoring Service: Former USSR*, 03.10.94.

123. "Plesetsk Space Centre Being Refitted to Receive Workload From Baykonur", *BBC Monitoring Service: Former USSR*, 25.03.96.

124. "Russian Parliament Committee Rejects New Far East Launch Site Plan", *BBC Monitoring Service: Former USSR*, 31.10.94.

125. *Segodnya*, 03.12.94.

126. "Russia to Phase out Defence Satellite Launches from Baykonur in 2003", *BBC Monitoring Service: Former USSR* 06.02.95.

127. Reuters News Service, 12.05.95.

128. Pravitel'stvo Rossiyskoy Federatsii, Programma razvitiya nazemnoy kosmicheskoy infrastruktury Rossiyskoy Federatsii (na period do 2014 goda), Moscow [No publisher], 24.01.95, p. 3.

129. Ibid.

130. "Yeltsin Issues Decree Approving Creation of Svobodnyy Cosmodrome", *BBC Monitoring Service: Former USSR*, 04.03.96.

131. *OMRI Daily Digest*, No. 44, Part I, 04.03.97.

132. *Nezavisimaya gazeta*, 29.04.93.

133. *Izvestiya*, 16.05.96; *Informatsionniy bulleten' Mezhparlamentskoy Assamblei Sodruzhestva Nezavisimikh Gosudarstv*, No. 8, 1995, p. 114.

134. *Literaturnaya gazeta*, 19.08.92.

135. "Armed Forces of Kazakhstan: Problems and Prospects", *BBC Monitoring Service: Former USSR*, 01.12.92.

136. "Nazarbayev Telegram to Yeltsin with Proposals for Strengthening CIS", *BBC Monitoring Service: Former USSR*, 26.03.93.

137. "Proekt o formirovanii Evraziyskogo Soyuza Gosudarstv", *Kazakhstansko-rossiyskie otnosheniya, 1991–1995 gody*, p. 375.

138. Khroustalev, M., *Tsentral'naya Aziya vo vneshney politike Rossii*, Moscow: MGIMO, 1994, pp. 28–29.

139. Bakaev, L., "Voennoe sotrudnichestvo Rossii i Kazakhstana: sostoyanie, problemy i perspektivy", *Kazakhstan i mirovoe soobshchestvo*, No. 2(3), 1995, p. 109.

140. Kusmanuli, A., "Voennaya bezopasnost' Kazakhstana: realii, problemy, protivorechiya i perspektivy", *Evrasiyskoe Soobschestvo: ekonomika, politika, bezopasnost'*, No. 11–12, 1995, p. 44.

141. *RFE/RL Daily Report*, No. 214, 05.11.92.

142. Nazarbayev, N., "Kazakhstan: vzglyad na mirovoy poryadok, razvitie i demokratiyu, vystuplenie v Kolumbiyskom universitete", *Kazakhstan i mirovoe soobshchestvo*, No. 1, 1994, p. 7.

143. *RFE/RL Daily Report*, No. 230, 01.12.92. This decision was endorsed by the leaders of the five states at the CIS summit in Minsk on 22 January 1993 (Reuters News Service, 22.01.93).

144. "Kazakh Supreme Soviet Discusses General Bill on CIS Peace-Keeping Troops", *BBC Monitoring Service: Former USSR*, 24.12.92.

145. "Kazakh Supreme Soviet Refuses to Send Peace-Keeping Troops to Tajikistan", *BBC Monitoring Service: Former USSR*, 30.12.92.

146. "Shaposhnikov Says It Is Time to Decide on Nuclear Weapons Outside Russia", *BBC Monitoring Service: Former USSR*, 13.01.93.

147. "Shaposhnikov on Future of CIS Nuclear Forces", *BBC Monitoring Service: Former USSR*, 23.01.93; "Yeltsin Arrives in Minsk", *BBC Monitoring Service: Former USSR*, 23.01.93.

148. "Ustav Sodruzhestva Nezavisimykh Gosudarstv", *Kazakhstansko-rossiyskie otnosheniya, 1991–1995 gody*, pp. 267–269.

149. *Nezavisimaya gazeta*, 23.04.93.

150. *Nezavisimaya gazeta*, 29.06.93.

151. *Nezavisimaya gazeta*, 10.08.93.

152. "Five CIS Countries Agree on Peacekeeping Force for Tajik-Afghan Border", *BBC Monitoring Service: Former USSR* 26.08.93.

153. "Tajikistan Peacekeepers Say Uzbekistan and Kazakhstan Slow in Upkeep Payments", *BBC Monitoring Service: Former USSR*, 13.07.95.

154. *Kazakhstansko-rossiyskie otnosheniya, 1991–1995 gody, Sbornik dokumentov i materialov*, p. 303.

155. *Kazakhstanskie novosti*, 24.02.96.

156. Ministerstvo Oborony Rossiyskoy Federatsii, Analiticheskiy material o khode razvitiya voennogo sotrudnichestva Rossiyskoy Federatsii s Respublikoy Kazakhstan, No. 335/5/2/244, Moscow [No publisher], 15.04.95, p. 4.

157. Kozhokin, E. M., ed., *Kazakhstan: realii i perspektivy nezavisimogo razvitiya*, p. 118.

158. *Krasnaya zvezda*, 24.12.93.

159. Kasenov, U., *Tsentral'naya Aziya i Rossia: ternistiy put' k ravnopravnym vzaimootnosheniyam*, Almaty: KISI, 1994, p. 12.

160. "Kazakhs Refuse Russia Gas and Oil Equity Stakes", *Financial Times*, 23.03.94.

161. Nurgaliev, B., "Preventivnaya diplomatiya v Azii - problemy i perspektivy", *Vneshnyaya politika Kazakhstana, Sbornik statey*, Almaty: MID Respubliki Kazakhstan, 1995, p. 202.

162. Abenov., E., "Vneshnepoliticheskie interesy Respubliki Kazakhstan", pp. 66–67.

163. Members included Afghanistan, Azerbaijan, China, India, Iran, Israel, Kazakhstan, Kyrgyzstan, Mongolia, Pakistan, Palestine, Russia, Tajikistan, Turkey, Uzbekistan.

164. 'Soveshchanie po vzaimodeystviyu i meram doveriya v Azii na urovne zamestiteley ministrov inostrannykh del (7–8 fevralya 1996 g., Almaty)", *Diplomaticheskiy kurier*, No. 2, 1996, p. 50.

165. "16 Asian Ministers Discuss Regional, International Issues", *ITAR-TASS World Service*, 03.12.97.

166. Nazarbayev, N., "Kazakhstan - 2030: protsvetanie, bezopasnost' i uluchshenie blagosostoyaniya kazakhstantsev, Poslanie Presidenta strany narodu Kazakhstana", *Kazakhstanskaya pravda*, 11.10.97, p. 29.

167. Bakaev, L., "Voennoe Stroitel'stvo v Kazakhstane", *Kazakhstan i mirovoe soobshchestvo*, No. 1, 1994, pp. 111–112.

168. Kusmanuli, A., "Voennaya bezopasnost' Kazakhstana: realii, problemy, protivorechiya i perspektivy", *Evrasiyskoe Soobschestvo: ekonomika, politika, bezopasnost'*, No. 11–12, 1995, p. 51.

169. Bakaev, L., "Voennaya doktrina Respubliki Kazakhstan", *Evrasiyskoe Soobschestvo: ekonomika, politika, bezopasnost'*, No. 4–5, 1995, p. 46; Kusmanuli, A., "Voennaya bezopasnost' Kazakhstana: realii, problemy, protivorechiya i perspektivy", pp. 54–55.

170. "Nazarbayev's Strategy for Kazakhstan's Future", *BBC Monitoring Service: Former USSR*, 21.05.92.

171. Nazarbayev, N., "Kazakhstan: vzglyad na mirovoy poryadok, razvitie i demokratiyu, vystuplenie v Kolumbiyskom universitete", *Kazakhstan i mirovoe soobshchestvo*, No. 1, 1994, p. 7.

172. Gosudarstvennaya Duma Federal'nogo Sobraniya Rossiyskoy Federatsii, Komitet po delam Sodruzhestva Nezavisimykh Gosudarstv i svyazyam s sootechestvennikami, Vyvody i rekomendatsii po itogam parlamentskikh slushaniy "Programma 'Partnerstvo vo imya mira' i buduschee SNG", Moscow [No publisher], 1994, pp. 2–3.

173. "Nazarbayev Says Military Ties with Russia No Threat to NATO Cooperation", *BBC Monitoring Service: Former USSR*, 03.02.95.

174. Tokaev, K., "Vneshnyaya politika Kazakhstana: podkhody, prioritety i zadachi", *Vneshnyaya politika Kazakhstana, Sbornik statey*, Almaty: MID Respubliki Kazakhstan, 1995, pp. 36–37.

175. "Central Asian Leaders Seek Creation of New Peacekeeping Force", *BBC Monitoring Service: Former USSR*, 19.12.95.

176. "NATO Envoy in Kazakhstan to Discuss Security and Cooperation Issues", *BBC Monitoring Service: Former USSR*, 09.04.96.

177. Reuters News Service, 06.05.96.

178. Ibid.

179. "Central Asian Battalion to Take Part in NATO Military Exercises", *BBC Monitoring Service: Former USSR*, 09.08.96.

180. Ministerstvo Oborony Rossiyskoy Federatsii, Analiticheskiy material o khode razvitiya voennogo sotrudnichestva Rossiyskoy Federatsii s Respublikoy Kazakhstan, No. 335/5/2/244, Moscow [No publisher], 15.04.95, p. 2.

181. "Dogovor mezhdu Respublikoy Kazakhstan i Rossiyskoy Federatsiey o voennom sotrudnichestve", *Kazakhstansko-rossiyskie otnosheniya, 1991–1995 gody*, pp. 170–174.

182. "Soglashenie mezhdu Pravitel'stvom Respubliki Kazakhstan i Pravitel'stvom Rossiyskoy Federatsii o voenno-tekhnicheskom sotrudnichestve", *Kazakhstansko-rossiyskie otnosheniya, 1991–1995 gody*, pp. 179–280.

183. Kozhokin, E. M., ed., *Kazakhstan: realii i perspektivy nezavisimogo razvitiya*, pp. 138, 146.

184. Spanov, M., "Konversiya v Kazakhstane: realii i perspektivy", *Evrasiyskoe Soobschestvo: ekonomika, politika, bezopasnost'*, No. 2, 1995, p. 65.

185. Kozhokin, E. M., ed., *Kazakhstan: realii i perspektivy nezavisimogo razvitiya*, pp. 139.

186. Ibid., p. 146.

187. Bakaev, L., "Voennoe sotrudnichestvo Rossii i Kazakhstana: sostoyanie, problemy i perspektivy", *Kazakhstan i mirovoe soobshchestvo*, No. 2(3), 1995, p. 50.

188. Ibid., p. 50–51.

189. Ibid., p. 50.

190. Federal'naya pogranichnaya sluzhba Rossiyskoy Federatsii, Spravka o sostoyanii i perspektivakh razvitiya sotrudnichestva s respublikoy Kazakhstan po pogranichnym voprosam, Moscow [No publisher], 15.04.95.

191. Ibid.

192. "Deklaratsiya o rasshirenii i uglublenii kazakhstansko-rossiyskogo sotrudnichestva", *Kazakhstansko-rossiyskie otnosheniya, 1991–1995 gody*, p. 215.

193. Ibid.

194. Soglashenie mezhdu Rossiyskoy Federatsiey i Respublikoy Kazakhstan o statuse voinskikh formirovaniy Rossiyskoy Federatsii vremenno nakhodyashchikhsya na territorii Respubliki Kazakhstan, Moscow [No publisher], 1995.

195. Soglashenie mezhdu Pravitel'stvom Rossiyskoy Federatsii i Pravitel'stvom Respubliki Kazakhstan ob organizatsii voinskikh mezhgosudarstvennykh perevozok v interesakh Ministerstva oborony Rossiyskoy Federatsii i rasschetakh za nikh, Moscow [No publisher], 1995.

196. Soglashenie mezhdu Rossiyskoy Federatsiey i Respublikoy Kazakhstan o voennoy sluzhbe grazhdan Rossiyskoy Federatsii v Vooruzhennykh silakh Respubliki · Kazakhstan po kontraktu i ikh statuse, Moscow [No publisher], 1995.

197. Khroustalev, M., *Tsentral'naya Aziya vo vneshney politike Rossii*, Moscow: MGIMO, 1994, p. 29.

198. For the location of the test ranges, *see* the Map A.5 in Appendix.

199. Soglashenie mezhdu Rossiyskoy Federatsiey i Respublikoy Kazakhstan ob usloviyakh ispolzovaniya i arendy poligona Emba, Moscow [No publisher], 1995;

Soglashenie mezhdu Rossiyskoy Federatsiey i Respublikoy Kazakhstan ob usloviyakh ispolzovaniya i arendy ispitatel'nogo poligona Sary Shagan i obespechenii zhiznedeyatelnosti g. Priozerska, Moscow [No publisher], 1995; Soglashenie mezhdu Rossiyskoy Federatsiey i Respublikoy Kazakhstan o poryadke ispolzovaniya 929 Gosudarstvennogo letno-ispitatel'nogo tsentra (ob'iekty i boevyye polya, razmeshchennie na territorii Respubliki Kazakhstan) Ministerstva oborony Rossiyskoy Federatsii, Moscow [No publisher], 1995; Soglashenie mezhdu Rossiyskoy Federatsiey i Respublikoy Kazakhstan o poryadke ispolzovaniya 4 Gosudarstvennogo tsentral'nogo poligona (ob'iekt i boevyye polya, razmeshchennie na territorii Respubliki Kazakhstan) Ministerstva oborony Rossiyskoy Federatsii, Moscow [No publisher], 1995.

200. "Russia's Sergeyev to Discuss Cooperation with Kazakhstan", *ITAR-TASS World Service*, 28.10.97.

201. Ministerstvo Oborony Rossiyskoy Federatsii, Analiticheskiy material o khode razvitiya voennogo sotrudnichestva Rossiyskoy Federatsii s Respublikoy Kazakhstan, No. 335/5/2/244, Moscow [No publisher], 15.04.95, pp. 5–6.

202. Bakaev, L., "Voennaya doktrina Respubliki Kazakhstan", p. 48.

203. *Kazakhstanskaya pravda*, 28.05.97.

204. Gosudarstvennaya Duma Federal'nogo Sobraniya Rossiyskoy Federatsii, Stenogramma parlamentskikh slushaniy Komiteta po delam Sodruzhestva Nezavisimykh Gosudarstv i svyazyam s sootechestvennikami "O rossiysko-kazakhstanskikh otnosheniyakh", Moscow [No publisher], 18.04.95, p. 142.

205. Kozhokin, E. M., ed., *Kazakhstan: realii i perspektivy nezavisimogo razvitiya*, p. 119.

206. Gosudarstvennaya Duma Federal'nogo Sobraniya Rossiyskoy Federatsii, Stenogramma parlamentskikh slushaniy Komiteta po delam Sodruzhestva Nezavisimykh Gosudarstv i svyazyam s sootechestvennikami "O rossiysko-kazakhstanskikh otnosheniyakh", Moscow [No publisher], 18.04.95, p. 121.

207. "Kazakhstan and Russia Sign Cooperation Agreements", *BBC Monitoring Service: Former USSR*, 23.10.96.

208. *Kazakhstanskaya pravda*, 11.12.97.

209. *Kazakhstanskaya pravda*, 24.12.96.

210. "Russian Minister Responds to President Nazarbayev's Remarks", *BBC Monitoring Service: Former USSR*, 22.05.97.

211. "Meeting on Central Asian Military Exercises Ends in Kyrgyzstan", *BBC Monitoring Service: Former USSR*, 09.11.96.

212. *Kazakhstanskaya pravda*, 19.09.97.

213. Kozhokin, E. M., ed., *Kazakhstan: realii i perspektivy nezavisimogo razvitiya*, p. 120.

214. "Russia Denounces Plans for US-Kazakh Reconnaissance Mission", *BBC Monitoring Service: Former USSR*, 28.06.97.

215. *Kazakhstanskaya pravda*, 28.06.97.

216. "President Nazarbayev, Russian Defence Minister Discuss Military Cooperation", *BBC Monitoring Service: Former USSR*, 30.10.97.

217. Analysis of Russian-Kazakh disagreements on the status of the Caspian Sea is given in Chapter 6.

218. "Russia's Sergeyev to Discuss Cooperation with Kazakhstan", *ITAR-TASS World Service*, 28.10.97; "Russia, Kazakhstan Sign Military Cooperation Accords", *ITAR-TASS World Service*, 30.10.97; Reuters News Service, 30.10.97; *Kazakhstanskaya pravda*, 31.10.97.

219. "Parliament Committee Questions Space Site Lease", *BBC Monitoring Service: Former USSR*, 27.11.97.

220. "Baikonur Cosmodrome to Be Run by Civilian Authorities", *ITAR-TASS World Service*, 18.12.97.

221. Transcript: Cohen, Nazarbayev at Signing Ceremony, File ID:97111809.GWE, USIA Database, 18.11.97.

6

Russia and International Competition for Kazakhstan's Energy Resources

After the collapse of the USSR Kazakhstan's energy resources became an area of vigorous diplomatic struggle between major world powers, including Russia. In the new geostrategic situation both the economic and the political importance of these resources in Russia's CIS strategy increased substantially. Initially, immediate economic concerns motivated Russian policy, but later, the identification of new national interests, moved geopolitical considerations to the fore. At first glance Russian economic interest in Kazakhstan's energy resources seemed unnecessary. Russia's own energy reserves were several times those of Kazakhstan. According to 1991 assessments, Russia possessed 86% of the former USSR's proven oil , 86% of its gas and 70% of its coal reserves, versus Kazakhstan's 14%, 2% and 12% respectively.[1] In 1992 Kazakhstan's oil output was only 5.56% of Russia's.

However, the Russian oil industry had been experiencing difficulties for some time, due to lack of investment and deteriorating infrastructure. Russian crude oil output had been shrinking steadily for years, but the most dramatic fall occurred in 1992. The Russian Ministry for Fuel and Power Engineering spotted the unfavourable trend as early as April and warned that oil production in 1992 would be 360 million tonnes, 90 million tonnes less than in 1991.[2] The gravity of the problem was revealed at a government conference devoted to improving the performance of the Russian oil and gas complex, held in the Kremlin on 30 May 1992. Yeltsin, who chaired the meeting, expressed serious concern over the unprecedented fall in oil and gas production. The conference promulgated a set of measures to revitalise the industry, including developing new oil and gas fields and encouraging foreign investments.[3] Thus in 1992 Russia's immediate concern was to stabilise its own oil and gas production.

Russia's enormous gas reserves ensured that it could supply its domestic and foreign markets for many years to come.[4] The situation regarding proven oil reserves was not as good, but it would be a long time before they fell too low to meet domestic demand. A 1993 estimate by the Minister for Fuel and Power Engineering indicated that domestic demand, at 240 million tonnes per year,[5] was well below annual output. But Moscow had had an interest since Brezhnev's time in maintaining high levels of oil and gas exports, as an easy way of earning much needed foreign currency and postponing the urgent task of technological modernisation. The new Yeltsin regime looked at the oil and gas industry from the same perspective, but now required oil and gas exports to finance the costly social and economic transformation of Russian society towards capitalism. Maintaining production and exports became especially important for the regime's political survival. For Russia the problem was the lack not of energy resources, but of capital for extracting and exporting them.

Nazarbayev's regime had a similar agenda. In his strategy of nation-state building, independence had the highest priority. After the collapse of the USSR, the Kazakh leadership had no illusions about the level of independence it had achieved. In an interview with Kazakh television on the first anniversary of independence, Nazarbayev was quite frank about this: "So far we have not reached real independence. . . . To achieve independence, the economy must be independent. To have an independent economy, we will have to face many future problems, because we will have to change the economic structure itself".[6] Nazarbayev and his government turned to the energy sector as the major lever for economic restructuring, industrial modernisation and political survival. Kazakhstan's known oil and gas reserves, though smaller than Russia's, were quite large relative to its population, and Kazakhstan had regularly held second place in oil and gas production in the former USSR. At the beginning of 1993 its proven energy reserves were 2.21 billion tons of oil, 0.69 billion tons of gas condensate and 2.49 trillion cubic meters (m^3) of natural gas, or 2% of the world's proven oil and gas deposits. Estimated reserves looked even more substantial — 8 billion tons of oil, and 5 trillion m^3 of gas.[7]

Almaty based its strategy on the premise that achievement of full economic independence should start with energy independence. A report on Kazakhstan's economic security, prepared in 1994 by Sh. Zhaksibekova, a research fellow at the Kazakhstan Institute of Strategic Studies, identified formation of the policy of economic independence as the major objective, identified Kazakhstan's vast energy resources as the basis for securing its economic independence, by "providing sufficient financial means for reorientation of the entire economy", said that "expansion of oil production and growing revenue from exports open great possibilities for financing requirements for imported products and technologies, and for sustaining new investments", and concluded that "[i]f Kazakhstan cannot acquire appropriate power and potential in the immediate future, it will risk being drawn into the gravitational orbit of its stronger neighbours (China and Russia), becoming a satellite of their economies, and losing real economic and political independence".[8]

The Kazakh leadership shared this view. Deputy Prime Minister Isingarin explained in an interview that Almaty "gives priority to development of pipeline transport, primarily directed towards export, because this will determine the future flow of investments and credits into Kazakhstan's oil and gas industry, and that will predetermine economic development. . . . The objective is to abolish the economy's current excessive dependence on supplies of energy resources from neighbouring states".[9] Official pronouncements to this effect had been voiced much earlier. In late September 1992, during a working tour of East Kazakhstan, Prime Minister Tereshchenko said, "We extract our own oil, but are forced to import petrol from Russia. This dependence must end".[10]

Speaking of Kazakhstan's energy dependence seemed strange, given its large oil and gas deposits. Nevertheless, Kazakhstan's energy dependence on Russia was a fact of life, mainly because of the structure of the oil and gas complex which it inherited from Soviet times. The distribution of major industrial enterprises in the USSR was based on a single economic space and ignored inter-republican borders. As a result Kazakhstan's two major refineries, Pavlodar in the northeast and Shymkent in the southeast were located far from the main oil and gas deposits in Kazakhstan. They processed West Siberian crude, delivered via the Omsk-Pavlodar-Shymkent pipeline, and had no pipeline connection to the West Kazakhstan fields.

Western Kazakhstan had only one refinery, in Atirau (Guryev) with capacity for processing just over 4 million tonnes of crude per year,[11] only a fraction of Kazakhstan's annual oil production of more than 20 million tonnes, 15 million of it from West Kazakhstan.[12] The rest was pumped via the Uzen-Samara pipeline to refineries in Russia's Volga region. Before the USSR's collapse, Kazakhstan's three refineries processed about 18 million tonnes of crude a year, almost equal to its domestic demand of 20 million tonnes. But locally produced crude provided less than 30% of the feedstock.[13] As a result Kazakhstan found itself very unfavourably placed after independence.

For example, in 1994 Kazakhstan exported 8.14 million tonnes of oil to and imported 8.87 million tonnes from Russia. But the price correlation was very unfavourable. Russia charged Kazakhstan $US382.49 million, an average of $43.12 a tonne for its oil, but paid only $239.04 million, an average of $29.37 a tonne, for Kazakhstan's oil.[14] Kazakhstan could do nothing about this very disadvantageous situation, as it was dependent on Russian oil, whereas Russia was not dependent on Kazakhstan oil, and could buy or not buy, as it saw fit. From 1991 to 1994 there was a decline in the volume of oil processed annually of 56% at Pavlodar and 41% at Shymkent, while Atirau's output remained at the 1991 level.[15]

A similar situation existed with Kazakhstan's gas production, also concentrated in Western Kazakhstan and oriented towards exports to Russia. Russia had no dependence on Kazakhstan's gas, while Kazakhstan could meet its domestic demand of 15 billion m^3 a year only by importing gas from Russia, Turkmenistan and Uzbekistan.[16] E. Azerbaev, president of the state gas company, Kazakhgas, complained that Orenburg gas processing plant would pay only "a lower than dumping price" for gas and condensate from the

Karachaganak field.[17] From 1992 to 1994 Kazakhstan's gas production fell from 7.56 billion m³ to 4.05 billion m³, and gas exports from 5.1 billion m³ to 1.49 billion m³.[18]

The Kazakh leadership, uncomfortably aware of its weak energy position, devised various plans to eliminate its dependence. One such provided for building a pipeline from Atirau via the Kenkiyak and Kumkol oilfields to join the Pavlodar-Shymkent line. Technical and economic survey assessed the pipeline's length as 1195 km, its annual capacity as 23 million tonnes, and its cost as $1.1 billion.[19] In gas transportation, the Kazakh leadership envisaged building a pipeline from the Karachaganak oil and gas field via Aksay and Aktyubinsk to Krasnyy Oktyabr', with subsequent northeastward extension via Kustanay and Kokshetau to Akmola.[20] In addition, a small (400,000 tonnes per year) refining unit was planned for the Karachaganak gas and condensate deposit.[21] Kazakhstan had only two potential sources of capital for building these internal pipelines, its own oil and gas exports and foreign investment.

Kazakhstan began actively seeking foreign investment in its oil and gas industry very soon after independence. In April 1992 the French state-controlled oil company, Elf Aquitaine, concluded a deal to explore for oil in Atirau province. In May 1992, during Nazarbayev's visit to the United States, a contract was signed with Chevron Oil to develop the Tengiz oil field. In July 1992 British Gas and the Italian state oil company, Agip, bid successfully to exploit the Karachaganak oil and gas field.[22] The Kazakh leadership was evidently heartened by these developments, because in November 1992 First Deputy Energy Minister N. Bekbosynov announced a long-term program to increase oil and gas output to 33.5 million tonnes and 16.1 billion m³ by 1995, and 42 million tonnes and 22 billion m³ by year 2000. He stressed that Karachaganak and other deposits being developed should increase Kazakhstan's natural gas resources by 2.4 times by the 2000, enabling gas imports to be reduced by a similar proportion.[23] Addressing a conference on Kazakhstan's energy resources in Almaty on 6 October 1993, Minister of Power Engineering and Fuel Baikenov said that the national program for developing the oil and gas industry would make Kazakhstan self-sufficient in energy within three to four years.[24]

Kazakhstan's energy policy rested on maximising the involvement of Western companies in its oil and gas sector. In his address to the nation in October 1997 Nazarbayev justified it as follows: "Major companies and money from the USA, Russia, China, Britain and other leading states will be involved in development of the Caspian shelf and the Karachaganak field. This will increase the leading powers' interest in our independence".[25] The mention of Russia as only one among several equals was meant to stress that it would not have predominant influence in its former domain. Thus besides raising funds to modernise Kazakhstan's energy infrastructure and production base, Nazarbayev had a political objective to involve the major powers in competition for access to Kazakhstan's energy resources, thereby achieving de facto independence from Russia without falling into dependency on any other country.

Nazarbayev's plans definitely conflicted with Russia's strategic line of stabilising its own oil industry. Competition with Kazakhstan for foreign investment in the energy sector weakened Moscow's bargaining position vis-à-vis Western companies, limited its choice of potential investors and potentially threatened prices in traditional markets and in the new markets the Russian oil and gas industry sought to penetrate. Moscow began searching for ways to put the brakes on Kazakhstan's unrestrained cooperation with foreign investors. It found its biggest lever in the fact that all the pipelines between Kazakhstan and its potential foreign markets ran through Russian territory, and Moscow was prepared to use its control to enforce its own energy policy within the CIS.

The Kazakh leadership well understood their geographical disadvantage and made every effort to secure Moscow's cooperation in ensuring transit for its oil and gas exports through Russia's pipelines. Moscow could not openly reject Kazakhstan's approaches, because to do so could harm relations not only with Almaty but with major Western oil companies which were actual or potential investors in Russia and had the ear of their respective governments. Thus in enforcing its energy policy towards Kazakhstan, Russia had to tread lightly.

The above considerations may be the clue to the essence of the game started by Moscow with the Caspian Pipeline Consortium (CPC), which has become the major mystery in the web of intrigues surrounding the pipeline issue. At the centre of the controversy was the Oman Oil Company (OOC) owned by the government of Oman but managed by Transworld Oil Ltd., based in Houston, Texas.[26] The intrigue began to unfold in May 1992, immediately after the signing of the deal with Chevron. Tereshchenko, then Kazakhstan's prime minister, and Chernomyrdin, then Russia's minister of the oil and gas industry, went to Bermuda. Their visit resulted in a deal with the OOC to form what is now known as the CPC.[27] Everything in this deal looked suspicious, the place where it was concluded, the choice of partner, and the personality of John Deuss, president of Transworld Oil Ltd.

John Deuss, a Dutch oil trader, was rumoured to be the originator of the CPC project. He allegedly promised the Kazakhs much investment and political support from Washington, and in return demanded many things almost free of charge, including a one-third share in the CPC project.[28] His business reputation was far from perfect. In the 1970s and 1980s he was allegedly involved in shipping oil to South Africa in contravention of UN sanctions.[29] He was well and unfavourably known to Russian oil exporters. In 1978 the Soviet oil export agency Soyuznefteexport filed a complaint against Deuss and his company JOC Oil, alleging he had defrauded it of more than $100 million by not paying for oil delivered in 1976 and 1977. A protracted legal battle ensued. The contract between the two companies was ruled invalid on the technicality that only one official of Soyuznefteexport had signed it, whereas Soviet law mandated two official signatories for contracts with foreign firms. The contract did, however, contain an arbitration clause which stated disputes would be settled by a Moscow tribunal. The tribunal subsequently ordered JOC to pay approximately $100 million for the oil, and a further $100 million in costs and profits of its sales of the oil. In 1989, a Bermuda appeal court upheld the ruling.[30] Some later publications in the Russian press termed Deuss "an international swindler with a scandalous reputation", who "would hardly promote the success of the undertaking".[31] The Russian decision to deal with Deuss again seemed strange, unless they were planning something tricky; then Deuss might be the right person for them.

On 15 June 1992 Tereshchenko left for Oman for talks on cooperation in joint prospecting, extracting and transporting oil in Western Kazakhstan.[32] What exactly Tereshchenko discussed in Oman is unknown, but the likelihood that CPC was the main issue is very high, because two days after the visit the CPC was formally launched, initially by Kazakhstan and the OOC. Within three months, Oman extended to Kazakhstan a credit of $US 100 million, allegedly to be used for improvement of oil and gas extraction.[33] In practice no noticeable upgrading Kazakhstan's energy sector took place; in fact the situation continued to deteriorate.

On 22 June CPC signed a memorandum of understanding with Chevron, detailing Chevron's desire for preferential access to the pipeline to transport oil from Tengiz. The memorandum did not impose any formal obligations on Chevron, but gave CPC the aura of beingthe only pipeline partner that Chevron would have to deal with in the future. Russia joined the consortium, after some token delay, on 24 July 1992, obviously to prevent possible future accusations that it had drawn Kazakhstan into the venture. Each CPC member had an equal interest in the consortium, which was to be registered as a limited liability company incorporated in Bermuda. The original plan envisaged that the pipeline would take three years to build and cost between $700 million and $1.5 billion, depending on the route chosen.[34]

On 24 October 1992 CPC announced its plans to build an oil pipeline to link Tengiz and Baku (in Azerbaijan) with the Russian deep water port of Novorossiysk. Other options, including routes through Azerbaijan and Iran to the Persian Gulf, and through Turkey to the Mediterranean, had been discarded. The cost of the project was given as approximately $850 million. The existing pipeline from Atirau via Astrakhan to the refinery at Grozny (Chechnya) was to serve as basis for the new pipeline. This involved building a new 750-kilometre, 42-inch pipeline, and expanding Novorossiysk port with new terminal and storage facilities. The capacity of the pipeline would initially be 300,000 barrels a day, but with a capacity for 1.5 million barrels a day. The project also envisaged modernising the existing Grozny-Baku oil pipeline. It was reported that the OOC would provide all the foreign currency financing for the project, while Kazakhstan and Russia were responsible for ensuring allocation of land for the pipeline, granting tax concessions, and providing workers, materials and equipment.[35]

In December 1992 Chernomyrdin was appointed prime minister, which substantially strengthened the oil and gas lobby's position with the Russian government. In exchange for cooperation in CPC, Moscow demanded a share in the exploitation of Kazakhstan's energy resources. Immediately after his appointment Chernomyrdin went to Almaty, where he and Tereshchenko signed an agreement, On Cooperation in the Industries of the Fuel and Energy Complexes, on 24 December 1992. It was designed to secure Russian involvement in prospecting of Kazakhstan's energy resources, and said that the sides would "maintain existing business ties in conducting survey, exploration and prospecting drilling for oil and gas". Kazakhstan gave the right to drill on its territory to the Russian company Pricaspiyburneft. The signatories promised to assist in concluding contracts between each other's firms to drill on their territories (Article 6), thereby preserving Russian access to Kazakhstan's oil and gas deposits. Other similar provisions contained in Articles 7 and 13 stipulated that the sides would continue to cooperate and maintain existing business ties in constructing main pipelines for transporting oil, gas and oil products as well as in preparing oil and gas fields for commercial production. While this last point mainly suited Russia's, interest in maintaining its access to Kazakhstan's energy resources, the first obviously favoured Kazakhstan, since Almaty knew that it would need use of Russian territory for connecting its oil and gas fields to world markets.

Kazakhstan received other concessions from Moscow. Article 3 of the agreement provided that the sides would "secure mutual deliveries of the most important fuel and energy resources in 1993". Such deliveries were to be made on the basis of contracts between each other's companies and Russian domestic market prices. This guaranteed deliveries of Russian energy resources to Kazakhstan at less than world market prices. On the other hand, Russia avoided specifying either the volume of energy resources it would purchase from Kazakhstan or the price it would pay for them. The signatories also promised to ensure unhampered transportation of each other's fuel and energy products through each other's territory, including those destined for export "in volumes, established by Russian-Kazakh agreements, as well as agreements with the third countries". Here Moscow met Kazakhstan halfway, retaining for itself the right to decide how much oil Kazakhstan would be allowed to sell on foreign markets.

Article 16 stipulated that the sides would establish a working group on "creating a coordinating body for interaction of the oil and gas extracting industries".[36] Behind this was Moscow's desire to draw Kazakhstan into a multilateral arrangement within the CIS, which would limit Almaty's freedom to manoeuvre in attracting foreign investors into its energy sector and exporting its oil and gas. This clearly ran contrary to the Kazakh leadership's strategic plans, but with the launching of CPC Almaty had every reason to feel optimistic and did not want to disappoint Moscow by refusing to cooperate. Consequently, Nazarbayev initially endorsed the Russian proposal. At the International Congress of Industrialists and Entrepreneurs on 26 January 1993, he mentioned that a conference of the ministries of CIS states responsible for oil and gas, was scheduled to take place in Tyumen province, a major Russian oil-producing region, and that a mini-OPEC would be formed in the immediate future within CIS.[37] He said, "Kazakhstan is ready to take part in such a 'mini-

OPEC'," and expressed the hope that other oil and gas producers in the former Soviet Union — Uzbekistan, Turkmenistan, Transcaucasian Azerbaijan — could join this body in the future.[38]

On 22 January 1993, at the CIS summit in Minsk, Chernomyrdin urged CIS members to work together to halt the catastrophic decline in oil production. He said that efforts should be concentrated on the major West Siberian producing areas, to which he proposed sending groups of experts, and that "[c]ommonwealth states are capable of agreeing on measures, including finance . . . for speediest revival of oil output in the interests of the entire CIS". The initial reaction to Chernomyrdin's proposal was allegedly positive and supported by virtually all CIS heads of government, with the notable exception of Turkmenistan, a major natural gas producer.[39]

The meeting in Surgut, Tyumen province, took place on 2 March and was attended by the heads of government of all former Soviet republics except Latvia, Estonia and Turkmenistan. The participants signed an agreement to create new mechanisms to halt Russia's collapsing oil production and ensure adequate fuel supplies to areas suffering shortages. It provided for setting up an intergovernmental council on oil and gas, which would be called upon to unite the republics' forces in the areas of investment, scientific, technological and other forms of cooperation, and would devise a common policy to promote stability and development in the oil and gas sectors. The highest body of the intergovernmental council would be the conference of heads of state, to be held at least twice a year. The council's executive body would be the council of ministers and heads of national fuel and energy administrations. The council of ministers would meet at least once per quarter. Tyumen, Siberia's oil capital, was chosen as the council secretariat's headquarters.

Shafranik, Russia's minister for fuel and power engineering, reportedly said the agreement would lay the foundation for restoring Russia's coordinating role in the fuel and energy complex, and said in an interview that Russia would like to receive shares in the property of the oil extracting and processing enterprises in other member-states, and was ready to offer its partners shares in its own enterprises. Kazakhstan also welcomed the agreement. According to Tereshchenko, in Surgut "at least everybody finally understood that the oil problem should be resolved together. . . . The agreement is a good one, and should benefit our entire community," he told reporters after the signing ceremony, "This is just the beginning. It will lead later to the creation of a mini-OPEC".[40] However, later events showed that the agreement remained on paper; Kazakhstan had no intention of fulfilling it.

On 13 February 1993 the Kazakhstankaspiyshelf State Company was formed for the purpose of exploring for oil and gas in the Kazakh zone of the Caspian shelf. On 22 April, while in Washington, K. Baikenov, Kazakhstan's minister of energy and fuel resources, told reporters that by September the country planned to form a consortium with up to ten Western oil companies to study development of oil and gas deposits under the Caspian Sea. He said the study should take about three years and that the companies joining the consortium would be given priority in obtaining licenses to extract the oil.[41] Since Russian companies were not invited to participate in the project, this meant that they would not enjoy this priority.

On 6 April 1993 Almaty signed an agreement with Chevron, establishing a joint company, Tengizchevroil.[42] Initial plans for Tengiz development assumed production and export of 3 million tonnes of crude in 1993–1994, to double by 1995 and reach maximum capacity of 30 million tonnes per year by 2010. The cost of the project was assessed at $20 billion and its duration at forty years. Kazakhstan and Chevron each held a 50% share in the company, but 80.4% of the profits would go to Kazakhstan and 19.6% to Chevron.[43] Russia was neither consulted nor invited to participate.

The first signs of Russian dissatisfaction with Kazakhstan's behaviour appeared in early February 1993, when the Russian pipeline monopoly, Transneft, demanded that Kazakhstan lower the level of mercaptan[44] in oil from Tengiz exported through Russian pipelines. Vinnichenko, director of Transneft, warned that the Tengiz project's future would be in doubt if the mercaptan problem was not solved.[45] Meanwhile, the Uzen-Samara pipeline, linked to the Druzhba export pipeline, was the only one Chevron could use for taking its oil out of Tengiz. The section which led to Samara had a capacity of around 10 million tonnes per year, more than enough to meet Chevron's initial demands. Tengizchevroil agreed with Russia on an export quota of 3 million tonnes for 1993. But problems soon earose. First, some mechanical constraints affected output and exports. Then the Russians simply refused to let Chevron put as much crude as it wished through the pipeline. Chevron consequently managed to export only 0.98 million tonnes from Tengiz in 1993.[46] It was also faced with the prospect of building an expensive refinery complex at Tengiz. The situation naturally affected Kazakhstan's total oil exports, which fell substantially instead of growing as predicted. In September 1993, Baikenov, energy and fuel resources minister, complained in an interview that Kazakhstan's oil production and exports were being hampered, because Russia was limiting access to its pipelines. He said that oil exports in 1993 would be one million tonnes less than in 1992 due to the mercaptan problem.[47] In fact, Kazakhstan exported 6.2 million tonnes of crude through Russia in 1993, only slightly down from 6.5 million in 1992.[48] But this was little consolation for Chevron, the major loser.

The mercaptan situation was anything but straightforward. According to Auvermann, Tengizchevroil's federal relations manager, Russian mercaptan readings at Samara were often higher than those at Tengiz, which indicated that "they may have quality problems of their own". [49] On another occasion, Auvermann called Russian restrictions on oil transportations a political issue. He said, "The Russians were accepting 330,000 tonnes a month of mercaptan crude in the old days, and now all of a sudden they have become environmentally conscious. . . . Let's suppose we solve the mercaptan problem. . . . If the Russians do not want the oil they will come up with another excuse".[50] Chevron's officials saw the mercaptan problem as only a pretext, but they did not seek an accommodation with the Russians. Instead, Chevron decided to play from a position of strength. Various projects for possible alternative pipeline routes from Kazakhstan, bypassing Russian territory, began to be actively discussed, and the pipeline issue soon became the major element in a diplomatic struggle involving leading world powers.

The decision to form CPC worried Turkey. After the USSR's collapse Ankara was making vigorous efforts to strengthen its position among the Turkic nations of Central Asia, including Kazakhstan. A major pipeline through Russia would perpetuate Kazakhstan's economic dependence on its northern neighbour and deprive Turkey of an opportunity to exercise economic leverage on Central Asian politics. For Ankara the prospective route of an oil pipeline from Kazakhstan acquired not only economic but geopolitical importance. Turkey openly showed its dissatisfaction with the CPC decision at the summit of leaders of Turkic nations in Ankara on 31 October 1992. Opening the meeting, President Ozal suggested that pipelines be built to carry Azeri, Kazakh, Turkmen and Uzbek crude and gas to Turkey's Mediterranean coast for export to the West.[51]

In late February 1993 Turkey began a campaign to prevent any increase in the number of tankers passing through the straits. It told the International Maritime Organisation that the risks of pollution and accidents were unacceptable, that it was not yet contemplating unilateral action, but that while traffic separation measures and traffic services might reduce congestion in the Bosporus, they could in no way solve the problems which would follow a traffic increase.[52] The main thrust of the Turkish argument was clearly oil and gas exports from Novorossiysk. Another Turkish move came on 9 March 1993, when it signed an agreement to build an oil pipeline from Azerbaijan to a Mediterranean terminal at Yumurtalik.[53] This was the first bid for an alternative to CPC, to which Kazakhstan could later be attached.

Turkey's actions played into the hands of Chevron, which had met with Russian obstructionism in exporting Tengiz oil. Chevron had a definite interest in the outcome of the growing Turkish-Russian dispute over oil transportation through the Bosporus. Limitations on tanker traffic would make the economics of oil transportation from Novorossiysk less attractive, and thereby invalidate the economic rationale behind the Tengiz-Novorossiysk pipeline project, making alternative pipeline routes (including one through Turkey) more viable. After experiencing Russian pipeline obstructionism, Chevron would probably prefer a pipeline from Tengiz runing through some other country, desirably a U.S. ally. Of course, when pushing for a pipeline through its territory Turkey was acting in its own interests, which happened to coincide with Chevron's.

On 23 April 1993 Chevron announced that the arrangements within the CPC were unsatisfactory. Chevron Overseas Petroleum President Richard Matzke said after a joint press conference with Kazakhstan's Energy Minister Baikenov that plans to split the equity in the CPC among Russia, Kazakhstan and Oman, while giving oil companies no real equity stake in return for their investment were unacceptable. He added that Chevron was interested in pipeline projects besides the CPC.[54] On 25 May, Espy Price, vice-president of Chevron Overseas Petroleum, told an oil conference in London that three pipeline projects were being considered, but none yet met Chevron's five investment criteria, and that there was "a great deal of uncertainty about how and where a pipeline would be constructed". The five criteria comprised: ownership equitable and in proportion to the cash contribution of each participant; risks and rewards shared in proportion to capital contribution; nondiscriminatory access and tariffs for shippers; fair tariffs; and protection from political risks.[55] Turkey also used the London conference to issue a warning about the viability of channelling Kazakh crude to the Black Sea. Transport Minister Yasar Topcu said that an increase in tanker traffic through the Bosporus would not be possible for environmental and strategic reasons. Outside the conference hall, Russian and Kazakh energy officials said the minister was just trying to put pressure on Kazakhstan to join the project to build a pipeline from Azerbaijan to the Turkish Mediterranean coast.[56]

Evidently, Turkey's actions prompted Russia to reconsider its priorities with regard to Caspian energy resources. At that moment geopolitical considerations pushed economic ones into the background. Russia could not accept removal of former Soviet republics from its sphere of influence into that of Turkey, a traditional geopolitical rival. In April 1993 Yeltsin decreed formation of a large partially state-owned oil company, LUKoil, through the merger of three oil production associations.[57] It was assigned the task of coordinating Russian oil projects in the Caspian Sea basin,[58] which in practice meant penetrating the various energy projects conducted by Western companies. In October 1993 LUKoil managed to obtain a 10% stake in the consortium led by British Petroleum to develop Azerbaijan's oil fields.[59] Entry into such projects by a Russian state-controlled company was clearly designed as an instrument for preserving Moscow's economic and political influence in the region: (1) Russia would receive access to internal information in the joint ventures, and would be aware of what was going on there; (2) it would benefit from profits made by the project; and (3) it would participate in decision making, theoretically with no decisive voice, but with the substantial weight of Moscow's backing.

At this time implementation of the CPC project stalled for lack of funds. Kazakhstan counted on securing finance for the pipeline from international financial institutions. K. Baikenov, Kazakhstan's minister for energy and fuel resources, told reporters in Washington on 22 April 1993 that Kazakhstan would seek funding and assistance for the pipeline from the World Bank and Western official export credit agencies and oil companies.[60] According to some reports, CPC approached the World Bank for a loan. Publicly, the bank said it hoped to process loans to Kazakhstan by 1995, but privately, bank sources said it was not prepared to lend to the project, probably because of Deuss's involvement.[61] The bank's report of 8 April 1994 said its decision not to help fund the pipeline had put the consortium in crisis.[62] Thus Deuss' personality started to have a direct negative effect on implementation of the project, an outcome expected and welcomed by Russia. The chosen tactic was simple. Kazakhstan was drawn into a venture, implementation of which was constantly delayed for technical or financial reasons, thus hindering Kazakhstan's exports to Western markets. At the same time, involvement into the venture distracted Kazakhstan from developing alternative projects. Oman's role in the undertaking might be unclear at first, but is quite explicable. The West was interested in diversifying sources of oil imports to reduce its dependence on the Persian Gulf region. If it succeeded, the economic and political influence of the Persian Gulf states would be diminished. Oman's involvement was probably encouraged by other major oil exporters to prevent such an outcome. In this Russia's and Oman's interests coincided.

Time was playing into Russia's hands. Kazakhstan was failing to accumulate funds to restructure its energy complex, and Chevron was losing money. By April 1995 Tengizchevroil's reported losses totalled $10 million.[63] However, one unfavourable development interfered with Russia's plans, namely Turkey with its alternative pipeline projects. Turkey's entry into the game substantially raised the stakes in the diplomatic struggle around the pipeline issue. Russia undoubtedly had an advantage over Turkey, because a pipeline through Russian territory would be shorter, could utilise the existing pipeline network, would transit the territory of only one country (and that quite stable compared to others in the region), and hence would be more economically viable. But this was the case only if the pipeline's construction was making progress. If Kazakhstan saw nothing emerging from the CPC it could turn to alternative projects, perhaps through Turkey. For example, speaking to financial analysts and industry executives on 17 February 1994, Nazarbayev said the republic was still considering various options for new export pipelines, but no decisions had as yet been taken. Besides the pipeline to Novorossiysk, other options included a line via the Caspian, Baku and Turkey to the Mediterranean although he said it was a very complicated route, or through Turkmenistan and Iran to Turkey, or through Iran to the Persian Gulf.[64]

Ankara had one strong trump card, its control over the exit from the Black Sea, and intended to use it to the full. In early August 1993 Tevfik Okyayuz, a senior Turkish foreign ministry official, stated that Turkey would be forced to introduce some kind of quota system for the congested shipping lane if supertankers became common. "It is not possible for large amounts of oil to pass. . . . We don't want to raise Montreux. But we are not afraid to challenge it". Moscow's reaction was at once voiced by its ambassador to Turkey, Chernyshev, who pointed out that the pipeline route favoured by Ankara was plagued by fighting in Azerbaijan, Georgia and Turkey's Kurdish southeast. Talk of pipelines was all very well, he said, but the Montreux Convention was vital to Russia, small tankers provided the best interim solution, and "[w]e should not allow any one country to have a monopoly on the region . . . control of the pipe valve".[65]

But Turkey was undeterred. In January 1994 it announced new navigation rules for the straits, effective 1 July 1994. Under them oil tankers must give 24-hour's notice before entering to sail the straits; must transit only one at a time; if over 150-metres long would be subject to new, more stringent, minimum visibility rules; and fined if they moved without permission. The potential effects of the new rules were clear — more time-consuming and perhaps more costly tanker traffic through the straits. In February Russia warned Turkey that the new rules could create tension.[66] But Turkey's position was strengthened by an accident in the Bosphorus on 14 March, when the Cypriot tanker *Nassia* and Cypriot cargo ship *Ship Broker* collided in clear weather just before midnight. Flames engulfed both ships, leaving at least twenty four dead. The collision occurred when the northbound cargo ship had just dropped its pilot, and the southbound tanker was about to embark one. The accident's convenience for Turkey's diplomatic efforts immediately prompted speculation that it had been arranged. Interestingly, the oil aboard the stricken tanker was from Novorossiysk. Turkish diplomacy capitalised on the accident to the utmost. "It's like having atom bombs passing every day through Istanbul, a city of 10 million people," said Environment Minister Rize Akcali, and vowed that Turkey would not flinch from implementing the new navigation rules.[67]

Due to Turkish pressure a special session of the International Maritime Organisation (IMO) was convened in London on 25 May 1994 to draw up rules to improve the safety of ships passing through the Bosporus, Sea of Marmara and Dardanelles. Russia had to endure a fierce diplomatic battle with Turkey, but by mobilising the support of other nations dependent on trade through the straits managed to block the most radical Turkish proposals. The adopted measures fell short of Turkey's initial demands. They included recommendations that all vessels entering the straits comply with the Turkish reporting system, use qualified pilots, and if over 200-metres long pass through only in daylight. It also required ships to observe traffic separation schemes. The new rules would take effect on 24 November 1994.[68] The recommendations could help avoid the delays arising from Turkey's original plans, but over the long term, the problem of transiting the Bosphorus would continue. The Turkish authorities could suspend two-way traffic if a vessel was deemed unable to comply with the traffic separation scheme. There was little mention of criteria for judging this inability, which could result in arbitrary bans on vessels.

Despite the IMO's recommendations, on 1 July 1994 Turkey went ahead with implementing the new rules. Moscow, naturally, protested in a memorandum which said the new regulations went beyond ensuring safe navigation "by imposing unwarranted restrictions, up to and including the complete halting of navigation". This was interpreted as direct violation of the Montreux Convention and "other generally accepted norms of maritime law", and went on to say that Russia "cannot recognise as lawful" the introduction, in effect, of a procedure, requiring permission for passage through the straits, and imposing unilateral restrictions up to and including de facto prohibition of such passage for certain classes of ships. Application of the regulations in their current form would cause, among other things, the massing of ships at the entrance to the straits, which would only create additional navigation hazards. In conclusion the memorandum expressed serious concern over the new regulations, asked Turkey to refrain from implementing them, and warned that Russian vessels passing through the straits would comply with only those provisions of the Turkish regulations that did not conflict with the international legal norms and decisions of international organisations mentioned in the memorandum.[69]

This protest and Russia's declared refusal to comply with the new Turkish rules could not, however, remove the business uncertainty caused by the dispute over the straits. Russia needed an effective measure to alleviate concern and found it in a draft project for a pipeline from the Bulgarian Black Sea port of Bourgas to the Greek Mediterranean port of Alexandropoulis, bypassing the straits. The first reports about this plan appeared in June 1994. During negotiations in Moscow in late August 1994, Russia officially invited Bulgaria to take part in the new project and received a positive response. Bulgarian Deputy Prime Minister K. Tzochev said, "If our government agrees, we will take part in the project," and added that Greece had already confirmed its readiness.[70] In September 1994 Russia's Gazprom signed a protocol with a consortium of Greek companies to build an oil pipeline through Bulgaria and Greece. Its cost was estimated at $600 million, it was to be completed in three years and able to pump 20–40 million tonnes of oil a year.[71] The agreement was most likely a ploy, at least from the Russian side, but it effectively neutralised Turkey's claims for a pipeline through its own territory and re-established the validity of the CPC.

Russia's diplomatic duel with Turkey developed in the background of Moscow's push to penetrate the Tengiz project. On 25 December 1993, during Chernomyrdin's visit to Almaty, he and Tereshchenko signed an agreement, On Cooperation and Development of the Fuel and Energy Complexes, which to a large extent repeated the previous one but also contained a number of new elements. Chernomyrdin used Kazakhstan's dependence on Russian energy supplies to extract a number of concessions. The agreement contained an obligation "to facilitate creation of joint ventures" between each other's companies. The task of "conducting the transfer of respective packages of shares" was assigned to Kazakhstan's Ministry of Energy and Fuel Resources and Russia's Ministry of Fuel and Power Engineering. The signatories agreed to consult each other "when developing energy programs" and "bearing in mind strengthening integrative ties".[72]

In principle the agreement gave Russia legal grounds to demand an interest in Tengiz and other energy projects under way in Kazakhstan, and to request consultations with Almaty on future projects that might be launched. Not surprisingly, in January 1994 LUKoil started to press for a share of the Tengiz and Karachaganak oil and gas fields.[73] In March this pressure intensified.[74] LUKoil received unequivocal backing from Fuel and Energy Minister Shafranik, who in early 1994 demanded that Russia receive a 10% stake in major oil and gas projects initially developed by the Soviet Union outside Russia's boundaries.[75] But the Kazakhs obviously did not see things his way. On 22 March 1994, shortly before his official visit to Moscow, Nazarbayev said Kazakhstan would not give Russia any equity in Tengiz or Karachaganak.[76] During his negotiations with Yeltsin and Chernomyrdin, he refused to meet Russia's demands, and despite numerous declarations favouring increased integration, the documents agreed during this visit mentioned neither Tengiz nor Karachaganak.

This outcome was hardly conducive to implementation of the CPC project, nor a strong move on Nazarbayev's part. At least that is how Kazakhstan's position was assessed in a World Bank report of 8 April 1994. It concluded that Kazakhstan "has little choice" but to surrender some equity shares to Russia, and "[w]ithout Russian cooperation on pipelines, Kazakhstan cannot attract the high levels of foreign investment needed to develop its oil and gas sector".[77] Probably encouraged by the World Bank findings, LUKoil's President Alekperov arrived unexpectedly in Almaty in May 1994 and demanded unsuccessfully that LUKoil be given the equivalent of $1 billion in free equity in oil projects under way in Kazakhstan. Later LUKoil denied that it had asked for free equity, but Alekperov reiterated in an interview that LUKoil "is in a position to demand participation in all oil and gas projects in the region".[78] Meanwhile Chevron expressed grave concern at Almaty's and Moscow's inability to agree the terms of the CPC project, and said that until all the pipeline issues were resolved, it "will be unable to finance development of the Tengiz deposit, because it is already making significant losses".[79]

As a result the Kazakhs' irritation with the CPC and Deuss increased. In late October 1994 Nazarbayev commented that Kazakhstan might support a plan for Chevron to take OOC's place in the consortium. But this trial balloon immediately met determined opposition from Russia. On 31 October 1994 a spokesman for the Russian Fuel and Power Engineering Ministry said that Russia "joined the Caspian Pipeline Consortium which was initiated by agreement between Kazakhstan and Oman", and "any drastic changes in the consortium are undesirable for successful implementation of the project". He said that Russia supported an option whereby Chevron could join the consortium, provided it paid $400 million to cover the initial expenditure.[80] Moscow was well aware that this proposal was intrinsically unacceptable to Chevron, which had already rejected it as "unfair and inequitable".[81] Talks in Moscow on 10 November 1994 between Chevron's Chairman Kenneth Derr and Chernomyrdin failed to resolve the controversy. Moscow also rejected Chevron's request to reduce tariffs for transporting oil across Russian territory.[82]

Given Kazakhstan's dissatisfaction, CPC could not just sit idle. Some ostensible progress over the pipeline was necessary. This led to announcement of new initiatives. On 19 January 1995 CPC said it would proceed with construction of the first phase of the project, costing about $300 million, by constructing a 250-kilometers pipeline from the city of Kropotkin to a newly constructed marine terminal on the Black Sea coast north of Novorossiysk. Construction would begin by January 1996, and the pipeline would become operational by January 1997. Completion of phase one would facilitate export of up to 15 million tonnes of crude annually from Russia and Kazakhstan, via existing lines to Kropotkin from fields in Russia and West Kazakhstan. The OOC agreed to provide all the equity and guarantee financing for this stage.[83]

But the Kazakhs clearly suspected that they were being duped. Under the agreement signed in January, Kazakhstan's pipeline infrastructure at Tengiz (worth $250 million) was to be handed over to the consortium by 1 March.[84] But on 5 March 1995 the Kazakh government suspended the transfer of assets, even though Russia had already transferred pipelines in Kalmykia and other southern regions. Kazakhstan's Oil and Gas Minister Nurlan Balgymbayev told reporters Kazakhstan would only transfer the assets "if Oman opens financing for phase two".[85]

In an attempt to alleviate Kazakhstan's concerns, the Russians invited Qays Abd al-Mun'im Zawawi, Omani deputy prime minister responsible for financial and economic affairs, to Moscow. On 11 March he and Shafranik signed an agreement on the beginning of the first phase of pipeline construction in the absence of Kazakh representatives, though they had originally planned to attend the talks.[86] Kazakhstan joined the agreement only on 14 March, only after the Omani government was reported to have confirmed its commitment to invest $250–300 million in the first phase of the project, and guaranteed to make a loan if international financial organisations refused to do so. "Alma-Ata has taken a brave and wise decision", a Russian official was quoted as saying. He claimed that Kazakhstan could not afford to jeopardise a major export project "even if very influential circles asked them to do so".[87] In mid-April the Kazakh government confirmed that it would go ahead with the transfer of assets to the CPC, reportedly after assurances by Shafranik that the CPC project was a priority for Russia, which would "support its speedy launching", and that work on the first phase of the pipeline would start "on 1 January 1996 at the latest".[88]

This upsurge in activity around CPC was the direct result of a U.S. decision to play a more active role in Caspian energy policy. The new U.S. line became clear when on 3 February 1995 the State Department announced that the United States had notified several governments in the region that it would endorse construction of a pipeline through Turkey to carry oil from the Caspian region of Azerbaijan.[89] Thus for the first time the United States openly challenged Russia's role in the business of transporting energy resources from the Caspian, and this had direct repercussions on Kazakhstan, which could now count on more solid U.S. support. In April 1995 U.S. Ambassador to Kazakhstan William Courtney said at a ceremony marking Tengizchevroil's second anniversary: "In the decades to come, we believe Kazakhstan and the Caspian region will be one of the world's main sources of oil. We believe several pipelines will promote healthy competition in transport of oil".[90]

In late April 1995 U.S. Energy Department Deputy Secretary William White made a ten-day tour of Turkey, Kazakhstan, Turkmenistan, Azerbaijan, Georgia, Armenia and Russia, where he discussed the possibility of alternative pipelines from the Caspian region. After the trip, White told a news conference that there were sufficient oil reserves to warrant two pipelines, one to the Mediterranean Sea and the other to the Black Sea, and said, "I think the most significant thing was that every country — Kazakhstan, Turkmenistan, Azerbaijan, Georgia, Armenia, Turkey — expressed support for a southern pipeline route that would give them access to the Mediterranean".[91] Only Russian First Deputy Minister of Fuel and Power Engineering Anatoliy Fomin had expressed doubts, telling White that "construction of two pipelines would be unwise for this area, because its oil resources are not large enough".[92]

It was not clear whether at that stage U.S. actions were motivated simply by an attempt to help their major oil company in negotiations with the recalcitrant CPC, or already reflected the emerging U.S. strategy in the Caspian region. The former seems more likely, given the substance of White's talks in Moscow. Discussing the oil transportation issue with top Russian pipeline and government officials, White suggested that pumping capacity on the existing pipeline from Kazakhstan through Russia be increased to as much as 260,000 barrels per day by January 1997. He said the United States was waiting for Russia's response.[93]

Active U.S. support for multiple pipelines encouraged Kazakhstan to put pressure on CPC. On 6 April 1995 Prime Minister Kazhegeldin told a news conference in Almaty that he was not sure the CPC pipeline project alone would be sufficient, and that Kazakhstan could in future be forced to look for other pipeline options.[94] In May 1995 Kazakhstan signed a protocol of intent with Iran on building a pipeline from Tengiz to Aktau, for onward transportation by tankers to the Iranian Caspian Sea port of Anzali. The plan envisaged supplying up to 2 million tonnes of Kazakh oil annually to Iranian refineries in Tehran, Tabriz, Arak and Isfahan, while Iran would release an equivalent amount of oil at its Persian Gulf terminals for export to world markets.[95] On 13 June 1996 Nazarbayev and Demirel signed an agreement to push ahead with a pipeline project through Turkey. Nazarbayev told a joint news conference that a consortium would have to be formed to implement the plan, and partial financing could come from international lending agencies.[96] This was followed by the signing on 15 August 1995 of a letter of intent between the heads of the Kazakh Oil and Gas Ministry and the Turkish Energy Ministry, providing for establishment of an international corporation to build the pipeline, and of a joint venture company to make feasibility studies.[97] The stakes in the oil gamble were apparently rising.

At this time Kasenov, director of the Kazakhstan Institute of Strategic Studies, published an explicit article on oil, pipelines and geopolitics, which openly attacked Russia's policies with regard to the Central Asian republics' energy resources:

Analysis of Russia's role shows that a major determining factor of Russian policy in the region is an attempt to prevent the flow of foreign investments thither, and primarily into the oil and gas industry and construction of southward-directed oil and gas pipelines. . . . Export of oil and gas is a major source of foreign currency revenue for Russia, and supports a significant part of Russia's economy. Why should it assist competitors to enter the world oil market? Taking this into account, Kazakhstan is objectively forced to seek alternative ways of transporting its oil. . . . Efforts to construct southward-heading oil and gas pipelines, alternative to Russia's, will inevitably have serious geoeconomic and geopolitical consequences. The most important among them is that the Central Asian states' economic, energy and transport dependence on Russia will diminish or disappear altogether. Russia will have new competitors in oil and gas exports to the world market, in the shape of Kazakhstan and Turkmenistan. There will be a substantial increase in Central Asia of the role of the U.S., Britain and France and some other states, whose oil and gas companies are the main investors in the region, as well as Turkey and Iran, through which oil and gas pipelines will go.[98]

Thus the article contained an already standard set of threats, which would allegedly undermine Russia's geopolitical position if it did not meet Kazakhstan's demands. But Kasenov and other Kazakh officials who applied that sort of diplomatic pressure obviously overplayed their hand. Moscow was well aware of the problems alternative oil and gas routes would incur. The pipeline through Turkey would be much longer than the Russian one and require much more capital investment, and would pass through several states, each charging for the transit. There was no guarantee that the total amount charged would be less than a tariff to be levied by Russia. Of course, small states such as Georgia, Armenia and Azerbaijan could be more easily coerced into lowering tariffs. But they would be hard put to provide for the pipeline's security, especially given the political instability and ethnic conflicts in Azerbaijan, Georgia and Turkish Kurdistan. The Iranian route had its advantages but was politically unacceptable for U.S. oil companies, given the enmity in U.S.-Iranian relations and the U.S.-government-imposed trade embargo on Iran.[99] Besides, Iran, like Russia, was a major oil producer, with no interest in increasing competition on the world oil market. There could be no guarantee that Iranian tariffs on oil transportation would be less than Russian tariffs. Hence, all plans for alternative pipelines looked more like bluffs designed to make Russia more conciliatory.

On 4 October 1995 Kazakhstan's Foreign Minister Tokayev indicated that plans with the CPC had come to a standstill since the European Bank for Reconstruction and Development said the proposed pipeline through Russia was not financible.[100] Meanwhile, the OOC had managed to attract only the $35 million needed to prepare a feasibility study, against an estimated total requirement of $1.5 billion.[101] Also in October, Kazakhstan's Oil and Gas Minister Balgymbayev sent a letter to Shafranik, calling for a meeting in Almaty on 6 November to discuss a new pipeline from Tengiz excluding the OOC, which had failed to meet the 1 October deadline for attracting finance to the CPC project. Balgymbayev said Chevron, other Western oil companies and LUKoil had already started work on an alternative export project.[102]

As revealed on 19 October by a LUKoil spokesman, all this time the company had been negotiating secretly with the Kazakh authorities for permission to participate in the Tengiz project.[103] Thus the struggle over the pipeline routes and LUKoil's participation in the Tengizchevroil joint venture were closely interlinked.[104] The first breakthrough came on 31 October 1995, when Kazakhstan's Oil and Gas Ministry and LUKoil signed a protocol giving LU-Koil a stake in Tengizchevroil.[105] Though the size of LUKoil's share had not yet been fixed, the decision in principle to involve it in the joint venture cleared the way for sorting out the situation within the CPC. On the day the protocol was signed, Balgymbayev announced that Kazakhstan was seeking agreement with Russian and U.S. oil companies to set up a new pipeline consortium. He said that Russia and Kazakhstan would each have a 25% stake in the new consortium, while the remaining 50% would be distributed among Chevron, Mobil Oil, LUKoil, British Gas and Agip "in exchange for 100% financing of the pipeline's construction". The minister added that the OOC "can also participate in the new international company on equal terms; it will receive as much as it invests".[106] Balgymbayev also confirmed that Kazakhstan was prepared to sell part of its share in Tengizchevroil to the U.S. Mobil Oil company.[107]

Subsequent Russian steps were not difficult to predict. Naturally, CPC did not begin construction of the first phase of the pipeline which had been scheduled for 1 January 1996, because of the time taken by the structural overhaul of the consortium. John Deuss had played his part, and now he had to go. The first rumours about his intention to leave the OOC presidency and the CPC began to circulate in January 1996,[108] and his resignation followed in late February.[109] Deuss and Omani Petroleum and Minerals Minister Said Bin Shanfari then resigned from the CPC board and were replaced by Omani Commerce and Industry Minister Maqbool Bin Sultan and OOC Deputy Chairman Mohammed Bin Nasir Al Ghusaibi.[110] A period of tough and prolonged bargaining on the issue of redistribution of shares within the CPC then followed. Progress on this was hindered by lack of success in the parallel negotiations on LUKoil's stake in Tengizchevroil.

Only on 16 April 1996 did LUKoil's President Alekperov announce that Chevron had agreed to transfer one-tenth of its 50% stake in Tengizchevroil to LUKoil, in return for a $30 million bonus payment.[111] As a reciprocal goodwill gesture, Russia agreed on 17 April to increase Tengizchevroil's quota of oil to be pumped through the existing pipeline 4.5 times over the previous quota of one million tonnes per year. this was due to bring Kazakhstan an estimated $450 million of extra revenue from oil exports in 1996.[112] Simultaneously, Mobil reached agreement with the Kazakhstan government to buy Kazakhstan's 50% share in Tengizchevroil for an undisclosed sum.[113] Finally, on 23 April Nazarbayev announced that all problems had been resolved, and all documents were ready for signing during Yeltsin's forthcoming visit to Almaty.[114] The signing ceremony took place on 27 April 1996. Under the protocol on CPC reorganisation Russia received 24% of the shares, Kazakhstan 19%, Oman 7%, Chevron 15%, LUKoil 12.5%, Mobil and Rosneft 7.5% each, AGIP and British Gas 2% each, and Kazakhstan's Manaigas and Oryx 1.75%

each.[115] This was a significant success for Moscow's oil diplomacy. the combined Russian share was 44%, and in cooperation with Oman it could control all decision-making in the consortium.

The final batch of documents establishing the CPC's new structure was signed in Moscow on 6 December 1996. The distribution of shares remained unchanged. The consortium was split into two parts, CPC Russia and CPC Kazakhstan, reportedly for tax reasons. Each branch would have a different revenue stream, based on whether the oil was running through Kazakhstan or through Russia. The group would negotiate an operating agreement with Russia's Transneft, which was nominated as operator. Officials estimated the pipeline's cost at $2 billion, up from previous estimates of $1.2–1.5 billion.[116] Later it was decided that the CPC management team would be headed by a general director from LUKoil, and composed of representatives from the other parties involved.[117] Construction of the first phase of the project was to be completed in 1999, and it was to become operational at the end of 2000. In the first stage 28 million tonnes of Kazakh oil was to be exported annually via the pipeline, and this was expected to increase later to 67 million tonnes. It was estimated that over the project's forty-year life Russian central and local government bodies would collect over $20 billion in taxes and transit charges. In addition, much of the pipeline capacity would be used for Russian exports, stimulating the development of Russian oilfields.[118] Russian Deputy Prime Minister Serov told a news conference after the signing ceremony that the agreements were "an enormous step promoting the integration of Russia and Kazakhstan".[119]

On 16 January 1997 LUKoil and Chevron agreed on all the main terms for transferring one-tenth of Chevron's stake in Tengizchevroil to LUKoil. "The price of LUKoil's stake has been agreed, and talks are now focusing on when and how much LUKoil will pay," Alekperov said.[120] He added that LUKoil's next step would be to buy into Kazakhstan's stake, and an official proposal to that effect had already been made to Kazakhstan.[121] On 25 April Yeltsin endorsed the agreement on division of equity in the CPC. His decree contained measures for implementing the final CPC restructuring agreement and rules governing the company, CPC-Russia, set up to represent the Russian government. The decree exempted the company from mandatory sale of a proportion of its hard-currency revenue until the year 2013, provided that it used the money to build and operate the pipeline, repay principal and interest on any loans, create reserves, and make payments under contracts to service the pipeline.[122]

The situation with Karachaganak oil and gas field developed along similar lines. Initially, the Karachaganak project looked very promising for the new investors, British Gas and Agip, doubling British Gas's oil and gas reserves and pushing it into the big league in the world energy industry. The reserves were expected to last for seventy years, yielding four times as much gas as the British Gas Morecombe field, and as much oil as the North Sea's giant Forties field. After an initial investment of $20 million, British Gas and Agip would spend up to $6 billion in the next decade to develop the field. British Gas said that once it had worked out a profit-sharing deal with Kazakhstan, oil and gas could be piped to Europe within months.[123] Unlike Tengiz, Karachaganak was an active field, which in ten years of Soviet-period exploitation had produced 28 million tonnes of oil and 32 billion m³ of gas, including an annual maximum in 1991 of 4.2 million tonnes and 4.5 billion m³, respectively.[124] It was linked by pipeline to the Orenburg gas processing plant in Russia, from which the gas could be exported by the main pipeline to Western Europe.

The major problem for the investors was securing guaranteed access to the Russian pipeline to Western Europe. They pressed the Kazakh government to obtain guarantees, and refused to make major investments in the project until an agreement on transportation was reached. The Russians, because of the substantial amount already invested in Karachaganak in Soviet times, naturally wanted a share in it, but were not invited. When Chernomyrdin visited Almaty in December 1992, he and Tereshchenko signed an agreement, On Cooperation in the Industries of Fuel and Energy Complexes, which said the two countries would continue cooperation "in exploitation of gas fields, and primarily the Karachaganak field", and Russia undertook to accept deliveries of Karachaganak gas to the Orenburg processing plant. Kazakhstan needed the agreement to convince its Western partners that they would have no problems with gas transit through Russia. The agreement did not oblige Kazakhstan to give Russia a stake in Karachaganak, but neither did it specify the quantity of gas Russia would accept, or the price it would pay. Russia refused to include them in the agreement; they were to be determined by a contract to be concluded between Russia's gas monopoly Gazprom and Kazakhstan's state company Kazakhgas.[125] Unless and until that contract was concluded, the agreement was valueless, because Russia could price its services high enough to make the project uneconomic.

Not surprisingly, the agreement failed to convince Kazakhstan's Western partners that they had valid guarantees for gas transportation, and the negotiations on a production-sharing agreement with Kazakhstan stalled. Originally scheduled for 1 October 1993, signing of the agreement was postponed several times. An Agip executive in Almaty said that there were "no problems left to deal with in Kazakhstan, but we are concerned about the state of relations with Russia. . . . The question of transportation of course must be resolved, and that is the subject of governmental talks between Russia and Kazakhstan. We don't know how long those negotiations may drag on for, but we are hoping for an agreement in the next few months".[126] Oleg Kireyev, head of the foreign-trade association handling the deal for Kazakhstan, explained that the sides were "unable to agree the terms of the deal without Russia's participation".[127]

On 6 December 1993 Kazakh Energy and Fuel Resources Minister Kadyr Baikenov announced that the deal could be signed in the "first quarter of next year".[128] As in the case of CPC, Kazakhstan tried to put pressure on Russia by advancing proposals for an alternative gas pipeline, bypassing Russian territory. For example, in March 1994 Nazarbayev suddenly revealed a hitherto "secret" project to build a pipeline from Karachaganak to the West via Turkey. "The pipeline through Turkey is a long-term project, but definitely one to which we will give the highest priority," he said just before his official visit to Russia.[129] But no agreements on Karachaganak were reached, and the project was not even mentioned in the associated documents. The topic was raised again during a meeting between Chernomyrdin and Tereshchenko in Uralsk on 28 August 1994, but they again failed to reach agreement.[130] Meanwhile, the situation at Karachaganak continued to deteriorate. In 1993 gas production shrank to 3.6 billion m^3, and in 1994 was expected to fall to 50% of the 1991 level. Only 15 of 130 oil and gas wells and only one of 32 drilling machines were functioning.[131] According to Azerbaev, president of Kazakhgas, workers and engineers at Karachaganak had not been paid for several months, and this had led to an exodus of highly qualified personnel.[132]

These critical conditions precipitated a change in the Kazakh position. On 4 October 1994 Deputy Oil and Gas Minister Lobayev revealed to the press that British Gas and Agip had agreed to give 15% of their 20% share in the Karachaganak deal to Gazprom. "There is already a preliminary agreement", Lobayev said. He added that agreement with Gazprom was necessary to gain access to the Russian gas pipeline network, "to avoid any repetition of the sad experience of Tengizchevroil". Kazakh Oil and Gas Minister Ravil Cherdabayev told Reuters that a final contract could be signed by the end of 1994, but Lobayev was more cautious, saying only "within the next year," and that the final contract would be for twenty years, with the right to extend it automatically for another ten.[133] However commenting on these proposals Gazprom Deputy Chairman V. Remizov said, that Gazprom "was not so poor ... if there are three partners and Gazprom is invited to become the fourth, there must be equal conditions for all".[134] Some reports indicated that Gazprom was pressing for a 26% share.[135]

The problem of gas transportation from Karachaganak was on the agenda of negotiations between the Russian government and Italian Prime Minister Berlusconi, during his visit to Moscow on 14–15 October.[136] Finally on 14 November 1994 formal talks began between British Gas and Gazprom. A British Gas official said, "[i]t is normal for Russia to join this project, and even a logical step, since from the very beginning there were plans that gas will be transported through a Russian pipeline and processed inside Russian territory in Orenburg. ... In any case we have no intention of erecting any obstacles to involvement of the Russian side in this project, and we hope that gas extraction will begin as soon as possible".[137] British Gas Project Director Peter Dranfield pledged that "since mid-1992 it has become evident that involvement of Gazprom in the project would greatly assist in achieving full development of the field" and "as a result, Gazprom has been invited to participate alongside British Gas and Agip as a member of the Contractor group".[138] These statements indicated that participants in the project thought that by drawing Gazprom into it they would secure guaranteed gas transits from Kazakhstan to Western Europe, but they were mistaken.

Initially everything went as planned. On 8 December 1994 Kazakhstan's Ministry of Oil and Gas Industry and Gazprom signed an agreement, On Joint Activity in Exploitation and Development of the Karachaganak Field. The document said Gazprom would participate on equal terms with Kazakhgas, British Gas and Agip. Kazakh Prime Minister Kazhegeldin, who attended the signing ceremony in Moscow, was quoted in an official press release as saying, Russia and Kazakhstan "were together again".[139] This agreement was backed up by one at the governmental level, signed on 10 February 1995 by Chernomyrdin and Kazhegeldin. The agreement said both sides recognised the desirability of Russian participation in exploiting and developing the Karachaganak field and endorsed the agreement of 8 December 1994. They undertook to facilitate "fulfilment of measures providing for legal organisational, technical and commerce conditions in exploitation and development of the Karachaganak oil and gas condensate field".[140]

These documents opened the way for concluding a production-sharing agreement. this was signed by British Gas, Agip and Gazprom on 2 March 1995 and was termed an "interim production-sharing agreement". The accord envisaged investment estimated at around $320 million over an initial development period of up to four years. During this first phase annual output was expected to be 4–4.5 million tonnes of oil and up to 4 billion m^3 of gas. Kazakhstan was allocated 85% of the profit, with the remaining 15% to be shared among the three contractors in the proportions of 42.5% each to British Gas and Agip and 15% to Gazprom. In addition, Kazakhstan was to cover contractors' production costs estimated at $70–80 million per year. If phase one was successful, the contractors would commit themselves to a far more extensive project, involving a forty-year investment worth $10 billion to develop the field to its full potential.[141]

Gazprom later failed to pay its share of the costs, and in summer 1996 withdrew from the project,[142] ostensibly because of the other partners' refusal to recognise Russia's previous investment in Karachaganak as a contribution towards Gazprom's share in the project. But the real reason was different. From the outset Gazprom had not intended to help Kazakhstan export its gas. As the major supplier of gas to Europe (60% of all European gas imports),[143] Gazprom had no intention of creating competitors against itself in this lucrative market, especially since Russia had its own huge gas reserves and did not need Kazakhstan gas for re-export. This was made very clear by Gazprom's Chairman Rem Vyakhirev, who said at a news conference in Moscow on 7 August 1997 that his company would under no circumstances agree to give Kazakh gas an outlet through Russia to world markets. "Surrendering one's market when there is a lack of sufficient capacity is, I believe, nothing less than a crime against Russia," he said. However, Vyakhirev promised that some Kazakh gas could be accepted for processing at the Orenburg plant.[144]

After Gazprom's withdrawal, the participants in the Karachaganak project started to look for new partners to help them take the venture out of deadlock. In October 1996 Kazakh Oil and Gas Minister Balgymbayev announced that the project would have two new partners, U.S. Texaco and LUKoil.[145] Gazprom's replacement by LUKoil looked like a logical step for Russia, since LUKoil, not Gazprom, was responsible for "coordination" of Russian energy projects in the CIS. Since LUKoil is an oil, not a gas company, the change denoted a shift in Russian perception of Karachaganak as primarily an oil rather than a gas field. This combination also indicated establishment of a closer link between Karachaganak and the CPC, where LUKoil plays a major role and British Gas and Agip have a mere 2% share each.

On 18 November 1997, a forty-year production-sharing agreement with the Kazakhstan government to develop the Karachaganak field was signed in Washington in a ceremony attended by Nazarbayev and U.S. vice-president Gore. Agip and British Gas Exploration and Production will continue as joint operators, each owning a 32.5% share. Texaco received 20% and LUKoil acquired Gazprom's 15% stake. Initial production is projected at 3.6 million tonnes of oil and gas condensate annually, to be increased to 8 million tonnes and to peak from the year 2002 at 12 million tonnes per annum. Around 6.0 million tonnes of hydrocarbons annually would be transported along the new pipeline developed by CPC.[146] The agreement, however, failed to tackle the issue of what to do with the natural gas. It is highly unlikely that Gazprom will change its position and agree to export gas to Europe through its pipeline system. Some of the gas will be used for Kazakhstan's own needs and transported to other parts of the republic either through Russia or by means of swap arrangements. Another alternative is to sell the gas to Gazprom at the Russia-Kazakhstan border, but, naturally, Gazprom will pay only a very low price. Gas can also be injected back into the field to improve oil output, but the economic rationale behind this option is yet to be seen. Of course, there is always the option of building an alternative pipeline eastwards to northeast China or the power generation markets of India and Pakistan. But the cost of such a pipeline will be high and will require investors ready to take unreasonable economic risks.

The diplomatic struggle over the pipeline issue was closely interlinked with the one on the legal status of the Caspian Sea. Caspian shelf energy resources are without doubt of great importance for Russia's energy strategy in CIS. Earlier estimates, based on satellite photography and some preliminary ground research, indicated that the part of the Caspian shelf bordering Kazakhstan could contain 3–3.5 billion tonnes of oil and 2–2.5 trillion m^3 of gas.[147] In a recent statement U.S. Secretary of Energy Federico Pena estimated proven oil reserves in the Caspian region as standing between 2.1 and 4.1 billion tonnes, comparable to those in the North Sea. The Caspian region's possible reserves could yield another 23 billion tonnes, roughly equivalent to a quarter of Middle East reserves. Proven gas reserves are estimated at 6.7–9.5 trillion m^3, comparable to North America reserves. Possible gas reserves could yield another 9.3 trillion m^3.[148] Before the collapse of the USSR, Kazakhstan objected to oil and gas prospecting in the northern Caspian, on the basis of ecological concerns. But at the end of 1992, Kazakh Minister for Energy Baikenov, when in the United States, officially stated that Kazakhstan was prepared to start work in the area.[149] These plans encountered opposition from Moscow.

The controversy started to develop when, on 3 December 1993, a consortium of Western companies signed an agreement with Kazakhstan to explore the geological, geophysical and ecological features of the Kazakh region of the Caspian shelf. The consortium, formed in June 1993, included seven companies—AGIP (Italy), British Gas, the joint British Petroleum and Statoil (Norway), Mobil Oil (United States), Shell (Holland-United Kingdom) and Total (France). Kazakhstan's contribution consisted solely in granting authorisation. The project was to be coordinated by the Kazakhstankaspiyshelf State Company, formed in February 1993. The cost of the project was estimated at $500 million, and its duration three years, after which the consortium would be dissolved and the firms to undertake extraction determined by auction. Consortium members were promised preferential terms. Kazakhstan reserved the right to all the geophysical information.[150] Russia was not invited to participate.

The contract was concluded even though after the collapse of the USSR the Caspian Sea's legal status was indeterminate. Previous Russian-Iranian and Soviet-Iranian agreements were inapplicable to the new situation manifested by the emergence of three more littoral states. Moscow's first serious attempt to tackle the issue was made on 15 October 1993, when the prime ministers of Azerbaijan, Kazakhstan, Russia and Turkmenistan met in Astrakhan to discuss the Caspian's status. At the meeting Russia outlined its position, to the effect that all questions related to the use of natural resources should be settled jointly by all the Caspian states. The participants agreed to set up a council to coordinate economic cooperation in the Caspian region. At the press conference after the meeting Chernomyrdin announced that they had decided to formulate a common view on the Caspian problem, and that ways of protecting its natural wealth would be discussed at the next conference of CIS heads of government. Tereshchenko told reporters that his cabinet had not yet prepared a plan to develop oil and gas deposits on the Caspian shelf. He pledged that exploration of the shelf would be examined and supervised by an intergovernmental council on oil and gas, to be formed under CIS auspices.[151] Despite these assurances, less than two months later Kazakhstan took a unilateral decision on exploration of the shelf by Western companies.

Not surprisingly, Kazakhstan's move caused irritation in Moscow, aggravated by the fact that Azerbaijan was negotiating with a British Petroleum-led consortium over a deal to prospect for oil on Azerbaijan's Caspian shelf. If both projects went ahead unhindered, Russia would have lost control over a large part of Caspian energy resources and consequently a large share of its influence over the policies of the CIS members with Caspian coastlines. The Russians raised the issue of the Caspian Sea's status at negotiations during Nazarbayev's visit to Moscow in March 1994, but with little result. The joint protocol of the meeting between Tereshchenko and Chernomyrdin was limited to instructing their Foreign Ministries "to draft initial proposals within one month on the whole range of problems connected with the use of the Caspian

Sea basin, for the purpose of submitting them for consideration by the Caspian Sea states".[152]

With the issue of the Caspian's legal status heating up, Kazakhstan sought to establish at least a semblance of a naval presence there and requested U.S. assistance in forming a coast guard, ostensibly to prevent infiltration by Islamic fundamentalist movements. The request was directed to U.S. Secretary of Defence Perry during his visit to Almaty on 19–20 March 1994. Perry promised to help, and before the end of February 1996 U.S. patrol boats were delivered. [153] Almaty made similar approaches to Russia, but Moscow, having no interest in sponsoring Kazakhstan's naval presence in the Caspian, was unresponsive.

On 28 April 1994 the Russian government notified the British Embassy that Caspian projects "cannot be recognised" without its approval. Its note said, "[T]he Caspian Sea is an enclosed water reservoir with a single ecosystem, and represents an object of joint use within whose boundaries all issues or activities including resource development have to be resolved with participation of all the Caspian countries", and concluded that "no steps by any Caspian state aimed at acquiring any kind of advantage with regard to the areas and resources can be recognised. . . . [A]ny unilateral actions are devoid of a legal basis".[154] The note was directed to the British Embassy because of British Petroleum's leading role in the Azerbaijan project, but it had very direct repercussions for Kazakhstan. On 2 June 1994 Russian Foreign Ministry spokesman Karasin said, "[T]he Caspian Sea should not be divided into sectors" and "all questions related to the use of natural resources should be settled by all the Caspian states".[155]

Initially, Kazakhstan's reaction to these Russian demarches was passive. After all, Kazakhstankaspiyshelf's project was only at the preliminary exploration stage, not developmental as was Azerbaijan's. But some experts and officials in Nazarbayev's entourage obviously decided that Kazakhstan should take a more active stance as a preventive measure. In a report on Kazakhstan's foreign policy objectives, published in June 1994, U. Kasenov suggested that Kazakh diplomacy should pay greater attention to the problem of the Caspian's legal status, because "it could turn out to be explosive for the relationships between all five Caspian littoral states".[156] On 12 July B. Kuandykov, president of Kazakhstankaspiyshelf, said in an interview that foreign oil companies exploring the Caspian shelf off Kazakhstan were perturbed by Russian statements on the sea's legal status. "Of course Russia's position worries participants in the consortium, but I must say that our position is in accordance with world standards on demarcation of sea territories". Asked if he thought Russia would claim a share in any development of the portion of the sea claimed by Kazakhstan, Kuandykov said Russia had as yet made no official demands, and added, "We believe that we will find a solution to this problem. We are supported by Azerbaijan and Turkmenistan".[157]

Thus Kazakhstan's position on the Caspian contradicted that of Russia. Moreover, Almaty immediately began to form a coalition with Azerbaijan and

Turkmenistan to counter the Russian demands. On 19 July 1994 Kazakhstan sent a draft Convention on the Legal Status of the Caspian Sea to the other Caspian states. The draft was based on the concept of a landlocked sea, and attempted to apply the provisions of the UN Convention on Law of the Sea to the Caspian. It envisaged delimiting the coastal states' borders on the Caspian, including internal waters, territorial waters and exclusive economic zones, as well as determining each state's continental shelf. Coastal states were to possess national jurisdiction and exclusive rights to explore and exploit the mineral resources in their sector of the seabed.[158] The draft contained some provisions favouring the Russian position. It recognised the need for unhampered navigation and fishing, each state's ecological responsibility, and need for a coordinating body, which would ensure a balance between the interests of all the littoral states.[159] But all these were token concessions.

An important element of Kazakhstan's diplomatic tactics was internationalisation of the Caspian Sea dispute, involvement of powerful players who were likely to support Kazakhstan against Moscow. This was hinted at in a report by Kazakhstan's Deputy Foreign Minister Gizzatov at a conference on foreign policy issues held in Almaty in February 1995. He said that "the Caspian problem has transcended regional boundaries, and even more clearly is becoming a factor in world politics". Among those whose interests were involved, Gizzatov named Turkey, Georgia, the United States and Western Europe.[160] However, among them only the United States had real power to exert pressure on Russia. U.S. policy towards the Caspian was just being developed at that time, but its basis was already recognition of the area's importance for U.S. economic interests.

On 27–28 September 1994 during Yeltsin's visit, U.S. President Clinton raised the issue of the Caspian Sea and urged Yeltsin to disavow his Foreign Ministry's statements that Moscow would not recognise contracts to exploit the Caspian fields. Yeltsin replied that the issue should be discussed bilaterally at the level of experts.[161] This was the result of pressure on Yeltsin by the powerful oil and gas lobby, which was not prepared to forgo its interests in the Caspian without a fight. On 5 October 1994 the Russian mission to the UN distributed a document entitled The Russian Federation's Position on the legal regime of the Caspian Sea, which reiterated that unilateral action by any single state there was unlawful and would be resisted.[162] It asserted that the International Law of the Sea could not be applied to the Caspian Sea, which has no natural connection to the oceans. In Russia's opinion the legal regime determined by the Russian-Iranian Treaty of 1921 and Soviet-Iranian Treaty of 1940 was still in force. Therefore exploration and exploitation, conservation and management of the Caspian seabed should be subject to agreement by all the littoral states. The document stated that the existing legal regime could be improved by concluding new agreements between the Caspian states, but must not be replaced by a totally new regime. Finally, the document warned that Russia did not exclude undertaking such measures as it considered necessary to make other Caspian Sea states comply with the existing legal regime.[163]

Release of the document preceded the opening on 11 October of a two-day conference in Moscow of the five Caspian littoral states, called to discuss the establishment of a joint legal body on the Caspian Sea. Its purpose would be to regulate all aspects of use of the sea and its resources. It was an Iranian initiative, first put forward in October 1992. Iran was concerned about the growing Western, especially U.S., presence in the Caspian, and was looking to check it by drawing the former USSR republics into a regional organisation.[164] Iran followed Russia in condemning the agreement between Azerbaijan and the Western consortium signed on 20 September 1994 as illegal. Thus an obvious coincidence of interests emerged between Russia and Iran positions, and Moscow took advantage of it.

On 10 October 1994, the day before the conference opened, consultations took place between a Russian team led by Deputy Foreign Minister Albert Chernyshev, and an Iranian delegation led by Deputy Foreign Minister Makhmud Vayezi. According to a senior Russian diplomat, their purpose was to examine all aspects of bilateral relations, focusing on the use of Caspian natural resources. He said that the issue was particularly urgent following Azerbaijan's recent signing of an agreement with an international consortium to tap three oil deposits in the Caspian Sea, and added, "In our view, this accord holds no water, as it undermines the 1921 and 1940 Soviet-Iranian agreements".[165]

At the conference, the Iranian delegation expressed concern about the "irreparable damage that uncoordinated exploitation was likely to cause to the fragile marine environment".[166] Initially it seemed that combined Russian-Iranian pressure would make the other Caspian states agree to create a joint body to monitor the Caspian. During a break in the conference, Kozyrev told journalists that "certain progress has been made towards an agreement on regional cooperation around the Caspian Sea."[167] But in the end, Kazakhstan's and Azerbaijan's desire to revise the legal status and their insistence that further cooperation in the Caspian region be conditional upon such revision prevented conclusion of this agreement.[168] The most the five nations tentatively agreed to was "to coordinate approaches to various aspects of their activity in the Caspian Sea in order to make the region a zone of stability, good neighbourliness, peace and security".[169]

According to Kazakhstan's Deputy Foreign Minister Gizzatov: "Resolving other questions of cooperation in the Caspian without settling its legal status runs and will run into the undecidedness of the main issue. Any attempts to confirm elements of the legal regime of the Caspian in separate agreements . . . before defining it in a special Convention or a Treaty are counterproductive".[170] On another occasion Gizzatov said that Kazakhstan wanted "a single conceptual document" to define the sea's legal status and would not sign "a single decision on any aspect of the Caspian Sea's use which contains aspects of a definition of its legal status".[171] Speeding up the process of clarifying the Caspian's legal status was essential for Kazakhstan, because the lack of clarification presented a serious obstacle to foreign investment in exploitation of the Kazakhstan shelf.

Kazakh diplomatic tactics at the subsequent negotiations consisted in trying to undermine the existing legal regime of the sea and replace it with a new regime, based on international Law of the Sea. To do so Kazakh diplomacy needed to remove legal obstacles embodied in the Russian-Iranian and Soviet-Iranian treaties. Initially Kazakhstan simply claimed that in the new international situation previous agreements on the Caspian had become invalid, and a new legal status for the sea should be defined. This line was reflected in Gizzatov's speech at a conference on foreign policy issues held in Almaty in February 1995. Gizzatov claimed that "the Caspian Sea regime in the form defined in the Russian-Persian Treaty of 1921 and the Soviet-Iranian Treaty of 1940 does not correspond to the changed political situation and new realities, that is why all the five Caspian states need jointly to work out a new legal status for the Caspian Sea".[172] Trying to prove his point he alleged that neither treaty contained "any reference whatsoever to the most important components of the legal status of international water reservoirs, i.e., regimes for exploitation of the seabed and what lies beneath it, for ecology, for use of air space over the sea, not to mention such basic questions as the territorial sea and the adjacent exclusive economic zone, continental shelf, etc".[173]

Kazakhstan advanced several arguments to justify its position. One was that the jurisdiction of the Law of the Sea Convention spreads to the Caspian Sea because the convention does not contain a list of the seas to which its provisions could be applied. But this claim may be true only if the Caspian is officially recognised as a sea, and there was no consensus on that between the members of the convention. The Kazakh side tried to prove that the Caspian should be qualified as a sea because it is connected to the high seas through the Volga-Don river system. Following this logic, the Law of the Sea Convention would be applicable to, say, Kazakhstan's Lake Balkhash, because it is connected to the high seas through the Ob-Irtysh river system, or to the Great Lakes between the United States and Canada. But nobody has ever seriously tried to apply the Law of the Sea in this overextended way.

Russia's position on the Caspian issue was based on two main postulates. First, that the Caspian Sea, as a landlocked water reservoir with no connection to any ocean, could be regarded only as a lake. Second, there were international obligations assumed under the principle of continuity by the former USSR's legal successor-states. These were contained in the Alma-Ata declaration, signed by all former Soviet republics on 21 December 1991, and more specifically in the memorandum On the Question of Legal Succession in Relation to the Treaties of the Former USSR, Constituting a Common Interest, signed by Nazarbayev at the CIS summit in Moscow on 6 July 1992. The memorandum singled out international agreements concluded by the former USSR which touched upon the interests of several CIS members, and described as requiring "decisions or actions on the part of those CIS states to

whom they were applicable".[174] The Russian-Iranian and Soviet-Iranian treaties on the Caspian fell into that category.

Speaking at an international oil conference on the Caspian Sea in London in
late February 1995, director-general Khodakov of the Russian Foreign Ministry Legal Department explained that treaties between the former Soviet Union
and Iran had established the Caspian Sea as an "object of common use by the
Caspian countries, open for utilisation by them on an equal basis". He claimed
that the right of any one state to use the sea for its own purposes "can only be
acquired on the basis of an international agreement", and that "[u]nilateral
moves by Kazakhstan and Azerbaijan to declare they owned sectors of the sea
and sign deals with Western oil companies would be contested by Russia".[175]
On another occasion Khodakov stated that unilateral actions in the Caspian
"cannot change the Caspian Sea's legal status in a legitimate way" and that
Russia "reserved the right to undertake such measures as may be appropriate to
protect its rights and interests".[176]

Khodakov argued that the principle of common use was introduced by Article 2 of the 1921 treaty, which said that Russia and Iran "both have the right of
free navigation on the Caspian Sea under their own flags", and was further developed in the 1940 Soviet-Iranian Treaty on Trade and Shipping, Article 12
of which stipulated that "trading vessels carrying the flag of one of the Contracting parties in the Caspian Sea will be treated in the ports of the other
party . . . on a totally equal footing with national vessels". At the same time,
paragraph 4 of the article reserved fishing rights up to ten nautical miles from
the coast to vessels of the littoral states. In Khodakov's interpretation, combination of these provisions established the Caspian "as an object of common
use by the Caspian countries, open for utilisation by them on an equal basis
across its entire area". Khodakov pointed out that the clearest indication of the
Caspian Sea as an object of common use was contained in the exchange of
letters which accompanied conclusion of the 1940 treaty. The letters noted that
the Caspian Sea was considered by both countries as a Soviet and Iranian sea.
Khodakov stressed that "neither the USSR nor Iran ever displayed any intention of applying norms of international Law of the Sea to the Caspian. . . . Enlargement of the 'Caspian Club' does not *per se* imply any change
in the Caspian's legal status . . . its legal regime as an object of common use by
all Caspian countries, remains the same until such time as they conclude a new
agreement altering this status".[177]

Russian adherence to the common use principle was economically and geopolitically quite logical. Semiofficial Russian geological estimates showed that
if the Caspian were divided into sectors, firstly, the potential recoverable resources in the Russian sector (2 billion tonnes of oil equivalent) would come
below Kazakhstan's (4.5 billion) and Azerbaijan's (4 billion), and not far
above Turkmenistan's (1.5 billion).[178] Secondly, all former Soviet republics
would have sovereign rights in their respective sectors, and Russia would be
unable to influence with whom and to what extent they would cooperate in the
future. On the other hand, a common use regime would necessitate some mul-

tilateral body to govern exploitation of Caspian resources, and as the major power, Russia would have a decisive voice.

Not surprisingly, at the London conference Russia's position met with objections not only from Kazakhstan, but also from the United States. G. Rose, director of international energy policy at the State Department openly sided with Almaty. Rose said Russia could not impose its proposals on other states: "[D]ifferences of opinion should be settled quickly in international courts, and through direct talks among the parties". He also argued that old treaties on the Caspian Sea had not meant cooperation, even before the breakup of the Soviet Union: "At no time did the former Soviet Union offer to share development of the Caspian with Iran, nor did it seek Iran's approval of Caspian region developments that might have environmental impacts".[179] Interestingly, U.S. diplomacy, more experienced than Kazakh, chose not to challenge the validity of the Caspian Sea legal regime established by the Russian- and Soviet-Iranian treaties, but to question Moscow's interpretation of it. The United States also tried to internationalise the dispute by bringing it to world legal forums, where they expected to muster necessary support against Russia.

U.S. intervention in the Caspian Sea dispute irritated Moscow. On 22 July 1995 an unidentified high-ranking foreign ministry official said that Azerbaijan and Kazakhstan were acting under U.S. influence. He was quoted as saying that "Americans who are interested in Caspian oil absolutely overtly exert pressure on Baku and Almaty, appealing for division of the Caspian Sea and promising beneficial cooperation and large investments," that dividing the sea into national zones not only posed a threat to its ecological system, but would also leave Russia with a very small area, and "[i]f national borders are drawn on the Caspian Sea, Russia will have nothing but Astrakhan and the delta of the Volga river".[180] Kazakhstan's reaction followed without delay. On 26 July Gizzatov publicly denied that the United States was exerting pressure on Almaty. "We determine our position proceeding from our own national interests", he said.[181]

A major shift in Kazakhstan's position occurred at the conference of heads of legal departments of the Caspian states' foreign ministries, except Russia's, held in Almaty on 26–27 September 1995. Probably, realising that their initial position was untenable, the Kazakhs dropped their insistence on application of Law of the Sea to the Caspian and agreed to regard it as a lake. During the negotiations they submitted a new version of a draft Convention on the Caspian Sea's legal status.[182] Gizzatov explained that despite the change in Kazakhstan's position, Almaty still insisted that territorial waters, subsea resource rights and fishing zones should be awarded to coastal states, on the grounds that "[t]he idea of general ownership of the Caspian would not appeal to foreign investors who have already signed contracts with one of the five coastal states".[183]

To prove its point Kazakhstan tried to appeal both to international legal practice with regard to frontier lakes, and to the particular practice that had developed in the USSR and Iran. Recent statements and publications by Gizzatov centred on the argument that the Caspian legal regime provided for the de facto division of the sea. In an article he asserted that "the coastal states' practice proves the de facto division of the Caspian between Russia and Iran". To substantiate his point Gizzatov noted that neither the USSR nor Iran had consulted each other when they started prospecting for oil on the Caspian shelf. "If there was a condominium, one could have expected consultations with co-owner Iran, but such consultations did not take place. . . . This practice unambiguously proves that neither the Soviet Union nor Iran regarded the Caspian's mineral resources as an object of common ownership".[184] The force of this argument is, however, undermined by the fact that the Russian position was based on the principle of common use, not common ownership. Russian interpretation of common use from the outset rejected the notion of condominium, despite Gizzatov's attempts to prove otherwise. As explained by Khodakov, the 1921 and 1940 treaties "contained no provision establishing any joint ownership, or extending national jurisdiction of the USSR and Iran, separately, or jointly, over the Caspian. For both states the Caspian, apart from the 10-mile exclusive fishing zone, was, in legal terms, territory beyond their national jurisdiction, where they had equal rights to its utilisation".[185]

Another argument used by Gizzatov entailed citing various internal documents of Soviet ministries which he contended established de facto division of the sea. One such document was the 1970 decision of the USSR Ministry of Oil Industry to divide the Soviet part of the Caspian between Azerbaijan, Kazakhstan, Russia and Turkmenistan on the centre line basis accepted in international practice. As if anticipating possible objections Gizzatov wrote: "Some people claim that this division was conducted on the basis of an administrative decision, and cannot be regarded as having international-legal consequences. I would like to object that in the former Soviet Union there were no state borders as understood in international law. The borders had an administrative and territorial character and later, after the USSR's collapse, were mutually recognised by the new independent states as inter-state borders".[186] This position became government policy in Kazakhstan, and Nazarbayev referred to it at a press conference after the CIS summit in Moscow in March 1997. He said that, when signing the documents creating the CIS, "we recognised the administrative division within the former Soviet Union, the existence of a maritime sector belonging to the Caspian states".[187]

In practice, allusion in the Caspian Sea dispute to the administrative nature of the former USSR borders is no more than verbal acrobatics, linking two disparate notions, "administrative borders" and "administrative decision". Administrative borders between republics in the former USSR could not be established by administrative decision. They were established or changed only by the highest legislative authority, the USSR Supreme Soviet. And it never passed any law dividing the Caspian into republican sectors. USSR ministries could make internal administrative orders, for example for economic purposes, but these were binding only within a ministry's sphere of competence and could not have international legal consequences.

Gizzatov's reference to an NKVD (People's Committee of Internal Affairs) internal order, issued in 1934, which instructed Soviet border guards not to allow Iranian ships north of the Astara-Gassan-Kuly line appears juridically even stranger.[188] The NKVD was hardly renowned for adherence to any principles of legality in either its domestic or its international activities, a fact later recognised and condemned by the Soviet authorities themselves. Overall, Kazakh diplomacy failed to establish a position from which it could force Russia into making substantial concessions. This, and the likelihood that time is on Russia's side, continues to slow the pace of Kazakhstan's program for energy sector development.

Meanwhile, Russian diplomacy proceeded to strengthen its de facto alliance with Iran on the Caspian issue. On 24 October 1995 Iranian Foreign Minister Velayati met Russian Deputy Prime Minister Bolshakov in Teheran to discuss a Caspian Sea mineral agreement. Both were to review a draft Caspian convention and three corollary agreements, in which Russia proposed a 15 km offshore zone for seabed mineral exploration, and another 30 km for fishing, with a board representing the five nations responsible for issuing permits for fishery, mineral exploration and oil drilling in the sea.[189] The sides signed a joint communique calling for the five littoral states to discuss all matters related to the Caspian Sea and its resources on a basis of equal rights and common interests and emphasised their readiness to cooperate in oil exploration and exploitation in the Caspian.[190]

In early 1996 the Kazakh leadership tried to exploit Yeltsin's interest in securing Almaty's support in the Russian presidential race for extracting concessions from Moscow on the Caspian issue. The topic was raised during Yeltsin's visit to Almaty on 27 April 1996, and a joint Russian-Kazakh statement signed after the visit said that completing a Caspian Sea convention was "top priority and an urgent task". The statement allowed for each to carry out exploration in its own waters, and called for the signing of a consensus-based convention respecting "sovereignty, territorial integrity and political independence".[191] Though it was obvious from the text that Yeltsin did not yield on any questions of principle, the Kazakhs hastened to turn the document's wording in their favour. At a news conference in Almaty on 30 April, Gizzatov said that Russia had opposed offshore seismic work carried out by Kazakhstan and Western oil companies in Kazakhstan's waters as illegal and unilateral, but that both parties now recognised it as legal and were ready to cooperate. Gizzatov said the statement emphasised the principle of "respect for sovereignty, territorial integrity and political independence", and that "Almaty is satisfied with the fact that these provisions have been fixed in this document".[192] In the interest of political expediency, Russia for the time being refrained from refuting these assertions.

But after winning re-election, Yeltsin lost interest in courting Nazarbayev, and toughness returned to Russia's position. Two meetings of the five Caspian states, in Teheran on 24 October 1996 and in Ashgabat on 12 November 1996, produced no significant results. The joint communique of the Ashgabat meeting barely went beyond repeating that a convention on the Caspian Sea's legal status was priority and an urgent task, but did establish a working group to meet regularly to speed up the negotiating process. Russian Foreign Minister Primakov proposed as a compromise to recognise a forty-five-nautical mile Exclusive Economic Zone, much larger than initially envisaged by Moscow, and indicated Russia's willingness to accept other coastal states' jurisdiction over oil sites outside the forty-five-mile zone, under certain criteria to be defined by experts, and provided they were already being or were about to be developed.[193] Obviously, the major criteria would be whether or not Russian companies were involved in the development of these oil sites.

Shortly before the meeting Russia scored an important diplomatic victory by attracting Turkmenistan into its camp. At separate meeting, the foreign ministers of Russia, Iran and Turkmenistan signed a memorandum agreeing to cooperate in development of mineral resources around the Caspian, and to sign documents establishing a tripartite joint company to exploit the resources before the end of 1996. After the signing Primakov said, "We intend to create a joint company to explore and exploit hydrocarbon materials in the coastal zones of the three states", and added that the agreement was open to other Caspian states and international investors.[194] Turkmenistan's Foreign Minister Shikhmuradov said that Russia, Iran and Turkmenistan had agreed on a forty-five-mile national limit, inside which they would have exclusive rights to oil or gas, and the remaining area in the middle of the Caspian would be common territory. Explaining Turkmenistan's position, Shikhmuradov said suggestions that the former Soviet republics could go it alone without Russian and Iranian agreement were unrealistic, as Moscow could simply block the Volga-Don Canal, the main route by which Western oil companies shipped heavy equipment into the region, and "[i]t's childish to think that Azerbaijan, Kazakhstan and Turkmenistan could join hands and exclude the Russians and Iranians".[195]

The emerging coalition of Russia, Iran and Turkmenistan showed that the political tide in the Caspian had begun to turn against Kazakhstan. Nevertheless, Almaty adhered to its position, and declined to accept Russia's compromise offer. Addressing a news conference after the Ashgabat meeting, Gizzatov said that fundamental differences over the legal status of the Caspian Sea still remained; that Primakov's proposals were unpolished, but his government would study them carefully; and that "Almaty does not reject them, but this does not mean that it will accept them either".[196]

Russia's proposals were unacceptable to Kazakhstan, because the just-completed seismic survey of its Caspian shelf indicated estimated reserves of 10 billion tonnes of oil and 2 trillion m^3 of gas.[197] These were great deposits, but not in the category of "being or about to be developed". Gizzatov made it clear that "differences between the Caspian states and lack of a convention on the Caspian Sea's legal status will not deter Kazakhstan from exploring its resources, because the existing legal status allows for drilling, prospecting for and production of oil".[198] He also criticised the tripartite memorandum and announced that Kazakhstan opposed the creation of the company and had no intention of joining it. He disclosed that the memorandum was "initially formulated to extend the company's activities all over the sea", and that this "aroused sharp criticism from Almaty and Baku. . . . As a result of talks, we managed to limit this area to the coastal zone of the three countries signing the memorandum. . . . The company will not operate where Azerbaijan's and Kazakhstan's own work is under way".[199] However, Russia's real intentions regarding the company are not known. It is quite likely that the idea of a tripartite company intending to operate throughout the Caspian was generated simply to pressure Kazakhstan and Azerbaijan.

On 18 December 1996 at a meeting in Moscow, delegations from Russia, Iran and Turkmenistan resolved to form a special committee to accelerate the establishment of a joint company to prospect for and develop oil and gas reserves in the Caspian Sea countries.[200] After that, obviously with Russian support, Turkmenistan laid claim to part of the Kyapaz-Serdar Caspian oilfield, which the Azerbaijan State Oil Company SOCAR intended to develop.[201] Baku had decided to develop it several years previously, but until then Ashgabat had never contested its right to do so. Though the claim was aimed at Baku, it had direct repercussions for Kazakhstan, because it introduced an element of instability into the whole Caspian basin, undermining business confidence.

Almaty saw all the disadvantages that Turkmenistan's changed position brought to Kazakhstan's diplomatic stance on the Caspian issue. Nazarbayev invited President Niyazov to Almaty for confidential talks that took place on 27 February 1997. The Caspian Sea issue was the centrepiece of the discussion. But Nazarbayev failed to persuade Niyazov to reverse his stance. The most he managed to extract was a pledge in a joint declaration that "the sides recognise each other's right and the right of each of the coastal states to prospect for mineral resources on the Caspian seabed".[202] This provision did not add anything new to the existing situation, because clearly every coastal state had rights for exploitation of the seabed.

The declaration did not address the major controversy concerning the geographical limits within which such unilateral exploitation was permissible. Niyazov therefore neither abandoned his commitment to the Russian proposal, nor withdrew his claim to the disputed part of the Kyapaz-Serdar oilfield. Yeltsin rewarded Turkmenistan for its cooperation by cancelling Rosneft's and LUKoil's deal with SOCAR for joint exploitation of the Kyapaz-Serdar field.[203] On 22 May 1997 the working group on defining the Caspian's legal status met in Almaty. All littoral states attended, but no tangible results were expected, and none were achieved.[204]

Despite failing to push through its version of the Caspian Sea settlement, Moscow could be at least satisfied that its policy effectively prevented Kazakhstan from acquiring energy independence. In fact, Kazakh leadership failed to reach any of the proclaimed targets in its energy policy. Table 6.1 shows the dynamics of Kazakhstan's gas production in 1991–1996.

Table 6.1
Gas Production in Kazakhstan (1991–1996) (millions m³)

1991	1992	1993	1994	1995	1996
7,885	8,113	6,685	4,490	5,900	6,400

Sources: *Kazakstan: Transition of the State, A World Bank Country Study*, Washington: World Bank, 1997, p. 228; *Sodruzhestvo Nezavisimikh Gosudarstv v 1996 godu; Statisticheskiy ezhegodnik*, Moscow, 1997, pp. 47–48.

Gas production in Kazakhstan not only fell far short of the domestic demand of 16.1 billion m³ but remained lower than the levels achieved in the last years of the USSR. Kazakhstan continues to import gas in large quantities. In 1994 gas imports were 7.56 billion m³,[205] but fell to 4.27 billion m³ in 1995, because of an inability to pay. As a result gas consumption in 1995 reached a record low of 7.5 billion m³, little more than half the normal domestic demand.[206] Consequent gas shortages had negative effects on industrial production and households. Yet Kazakhstan cannot cut its gas imports to zero until the projected Karachaganak-Akmola gas pipeline is built.

Kazakhstan is still forced to export its gas from Karachaganak to Orenburg at exceptionally low prices. For example, in 1995 Gazprom took 3 billion m³ of Karachaganak gas but paid only ten months later at less than the Russian domestic price.[207] N. Balgymbayev, when still in charge of the Kazakh State Oil company, complained that Kazakhstan received a mere seventeen cents "change" on each dollar equivalent in the course of such operations. The rest is eaten up by exorbitant tariffs, product regrading, and soon. In other words, Kazakhstan is forced to sell Karachaganak's products at well below their true value. Balgymbayev said that Kazakhstan had decided to build its own gas refinery near Karachaganak.[208] But given Kazakhstan's previous experience with its energy projects, there is no telling when this refinery could be completed.

Thus despite its substantial gas reserves, Kazakhstan has not only failed to become a significant exporter of natural gas, but remains dependent on gas imports from Russia. The Duma's Committee on Property, Privatisation and Economic Activity estimated that "Kazakhstan's dependence on Russia will remain not only in immediate but in middle-term perspective, because with its vast but still unused gas deposits it will import 17 billion cubic metres of gas per year from Russia, at least until the year 2000".[209] The latest manifestation of this dependence was the conclusion of an agreement with Gazprom to supply Almaty and southern regions of Kazakhstan with Russian gas. Kazakhstan had to turn to Russia because Turkmenistan terminated gas supplies in late September, and Kazakhstan cannot transport its own gas to the south of the country.[210]

The situation was only slightly better in Kazakhstan's oil industry. Table 6.2 shows dynamics of Kazakhstan's oil production in 1991–1996.

Table 6.2
Oil Production in Kazakhstan (1991–1996) (millions tonnes)

1991	1992	1993	1994	1995	1996
26.6	25.8	23.0	20.3	20.5	23.0

Sources: Kazakstan: Transition of the State, A World Bank Country Study, Washington: World Bank, 1997, p. 228; *Sodruzhestvo Nezavisimikh Gosudarstv v 1996 godu; Statisticheskiy ezhegodnik*, Moscow: 1997, pp. 47–48.

Thus, despite the fact that Kazakhstan managed to reverse the negative trend of decreasing oil production, the republic still produces less oil than in the last years of the USSR.[211] Moreover, it fell far short of the 33.5 million tons planned by the Kazakh government for 1995.[212] The Atirau-Kumkol internal oil pipeline project has still not eventuated. Kazakhstan's domestic market therefore remains heavily dependent on Russia for imports either of crude for the Pavlodar and Shymkent refineries, and of processed oil products. Unfortunately, figures for imports of the latter are unavailable, but of 1 March 1995 Kazakhstan's debt to Russia for oil supplies amounted to 136.8 billion roubles.[213]

In 1995 Kazakhstan's oil export amounted to 11.2 million tons.[214] In 1996 it increased slightly to 12.3 million, but this too was far less than the 21.1 million tons exported in 1990.[215] Moreover, the bulk of it remains dependent on Russia's good will. Russia thwarted the possibility of alternative pipeline routes from Kazakhstan, thus perpetuating Russian control over the flow of oil from the republic. In 1997 Kazakhstan planned to export 7 million tons of oil through a pipeline across Russia, 1 million by tankers across the Caspian to Baku, 1 million through swaps with Iran, and 1 million by rail through Russia to Europe.[216] This means that 80% of Kazakhstan's oil exports continue to transit Russian territory, and this dependency on Russia is unlikely to disappear in the foreseeable future. Currently, the CPC remains the only projected new export pipeline, yet it has not entered the phase of practical implementation because of intractable problems regarding setting transit fees with local authorities in Russian provinces through which the pipeline will pass.

Of course Kazakhstan has not forsaken its efforts to find alternative energy transportation routes. Nazarbayev clearly reaffirmed this in his address to the nation in October 1997, when he said, "The second element of our strategy is creation of a pipeline system for export of oil and gas. Only a large number of independent export routes can prevent our dependence on any one neighbour and monopoly price dependence on any one consumer".[217] But so far Almaty is still unable to find a viable solution to this problem.

On 11 August 1996 representatives from the National Iranian Oil Company (NIOC) and the Kazakh government signed a 2 million-tonne annual oil swap deal.[218] The first trial shipment of 70,000 tonnes of Kazakh oil to Iran took place in March 1997. It went badly because the Tehran refinery proved unable to process it, even after removing its high mercaptan content, primarily because it was of a type unsuitable for the refinery's elderly technology.[219] Shipments to Iran had to be interrupted. Only on 17 November 1997 did Iran Deputy Oil Minister for Caspian Sea Oil and Gas Ali Majedi announce that Iran was prepared to resume oil swaps with Kazakhstan, after reduction of the high level of impurities in Kazakh crude.[220] Even if the swaps are renewed, their actual volume will be insignificant and dependent both on northern Iran's refinery capacity and on Iran's domestic demand.

Another route, called the Caucasian corridor, entails trans-Caspian transit in tankers, and rail transport through Azerbaijan and Georgia to the Black Sea ports of Batumi and Poti. Under a contract with Chevron it was planned to transport 1.2 million tonnes of oil by this route in 1997. In March 1997 the first two trainloads, carrying 5,000 tonnes of Kazakh oil, were loaded into a tanker and sent to Europe from Georgia.[221] Nazarbayev claims that after modernisation of the Caspian port of Aktau is completed Kazakhstan will export 5–6 million tonnes of oil annually by this route.[222] Two factors, however, militate against the economic validity of the Caucasian corridor. First, transhipments from tanker to rail and vice versa are time-consuming and costly. Second, capacity of the Georgian rail network is limited, which may prove unable to handle a large regular oil traffic, and could certainly not cope with output which, according to Kazakh official predictions, will reach 170 million tonnes by 2010.[223]

Not surprisingly, during Azerbaijan's President Aliyev's visit to Almaty on 10 June 1997 he and Nazarbayev proposed a plan for a trans-Caspian pipeline to Azerbaijan, which would enable Kazakhstan to increase its oil deliveries to 10 million tonnes a year. The presidents signed a memorandum on cooperation in oil deliveries to international markets.[224] Nazarbayev discussed the same plan with Georgia's President Shevaradnadze when he visited Almaty on 11 November 1997.[225] However, the economic and political viability of the pipeline remains to be seen, primarily because of failure to define the Caspian Sea's legal status.

In the second half of 1997 three factors substantially intensified the diplomatic struggle around Kazakhstan's energy resources. The first was China's entry into the game. On 4 June 1997 the China National Petroleum Corporation (CNPC) beat off rival bids from the United States and Russia in the auctioning of a 60% share of Aktobemunaigaz.[226] On 24 September Nazarbayev and Chinese Prime Minister Li Peng signed an intergovernmental agreement on cooperation in the oil and gas sector, and an agreement between the Kazakh Ministry of Energy and Natural Resources and CNPC. China obtained concessions to three hydrocarbon deposits in Aktyubinsk region and the Uzen oilfield on the Mangyshlak peninsula, second only to the Tengiz oilfield. Implementation of the Aktyubinsk project will require construction of a 3,000-km pipeline to Xinjiang, China's most westerly province. Under the Uzen project, a 250-km pipeline will be built to the northern border of Iran. The Uzen project and construction of the pipelines are estimated to cost $US 9.5 billion.[227]

It was no accident that provisions for pipeline construction found their way into the Kazakh-Chinese agreements. Almaty counted on solving its oil and gas transportation problems in this way, both to refineries in the East and for exports to international markets, bypassing Russia. This move also corresponded with Nazarbayev's strategy of balancing between the various poles of power, and manifested his intention to avoid slipping into a new foreign policy dependence, this time on the West. However, from the point of view of diversification of Kazakhstan's oil exports this can be regarded only as a limited success. The 3,000-km pipeline to Xinjiang will require time to build and how long remains unclear. The other point is that China will be building the above pipeline for its own oil consumption. To turn it into an export pipeline to world markets will require building another section to Chinese ports. It will have to be even longer than the section through Kazakhstan. To what extent China may be interested in committing its resources to such an enterprise remains to be seen. Nothing in recent Chinese statements on the issue has indicated that at this stage it is contemplating such a possibility.

A pipeline through Iran might be a viable alternative for diversification of Kazakh oil exports if it was not for the status of U.S.-Iranian relations. In the present situation, reliable export through such a pipeline cannot be guaranteed. First, the United States can oblige its oil companies not to buy oil supplied through the Iranian pipeline, which will diminish its competitiveness. Moreover, even the beginning of building of such a pipeline can damage Kazakhstan's relations with the United States and result in the withdrawal of U.S. political support for Nazarbayev and blocking of U.S. and international financial organisations' aid to Kazakhstan. On the other hand, Iran, in the same manner as Russia, can use its control over the pipeline to apply political pressure on Kazakhstan, forcing it to take an anti-American position in international relations.

The second factor was growing American involvement in Caspian Sea politics. A State Department report released in April 1997 recommended increased support for U.S. energy companies' activities in the Caspian Basin. Emphasising the region's rich oil and gas reserves, the report said the U.S. government "needs to enhance its efforts throughout the region to support American companies . . . and continue to bring U.S. companies to this market". To try to develop alternative routes to the Bosporus, the report called for encouraging market development in the Black Sea region to develop the infrastructure to transport Caspian energy to other markets.[228]

Washington redoubled its efforts to push through the concept of the so-called Eurasian Transportation Corridor, a major oil export pipeline running from Kazakhstan to Azerbaijan on the Caspian seabed, then through Georgia to Turkey. In early November 1997, U.S. Secretary of Energy Pena led a five-day presidential mission to the countries in the Caspian region. The mission included the Departments of Energy, State, and Commerce, and met the leaders of Turkey, Armenia, Azerbaijan, Turkmenistan, and Georgia. During the visit Pena actively propagated a plan for an East-West pipeline route from Baku to Ceyhan in Turkey. After the visit he stated that the leaders of Turkey, Azerbaijan, Georgia and Turkmenistan had endorsed this proposal.[229] This was a direct challenge to Russian influence and strategy in the Caspian Sea basin.

During Nazarbayev's visit to Washington on 17–18 November 1997, the issue of Caspian energy development was discussed extensively in several meetings, including President Clinton, Vice-President Gore, Energy Secretary Pena and Acting Secretary of State Talbott. During these meetings, both sides agreed on the importance of giving priority to developing a secure Eurasian Transportation Corridor with trans-Caspian segments as one of multiple pipelines to deliver Kazakhstan energy resources to world markets. Nazarbayev agreed to establishment of a working group on the issue and Gore, who led the U.S. side in the talks, told a press conference that he was satisfied that Nazarbayev had made his support for the transport corridor clear during their meetings.[230] Nazarbayev's endorsement was important for Washington, because it was aimed not only at undermining Russian influence, but also at isolating Iran. On every occasion U.S. officials stressed that Iran must be excluded from pipeline projects in Central Asia and the Caspian basin.

In turn, Washington fully supported Kazakhstan's position on dividing the Caspian Sea into national sectors as a counter to Russian-Iranian advocacy of the common use principle. The joint statement by Clinton and Nazarbayev especially emphasised the "need to adopt a Caspian Sea legal regime that establishes a clear division of property rights based on the division of seabed resources".[231] Gore was conspicuously present at the signing of an agreement between Kazakhstankaspiyshelf and Agip, British Gas, British Petroleum, Mobil, Shell, Statoil and Total on prospecting and drilling in an area of the Caspian shelf covering some 6,000 square km in the northeast Caspian, part of which had been claimed by Russia.[232] Gore's presence meant to demonstrate strong U.S. support not only for the deal, but also for Kazakhstan's position on dividing the Caspian into national sectors. Undoubtedly, U.S. support substantially strengthened Kazakhstan's position vis-à-vis Russia in the Caspian dispute. However, it remains to be seen to what extent this support can change the balance of forces in the region. Kazakhstan's reliance on the United States will alienate Almaty from Teheran and also put it at odds with a new powerful player, China, which has already committed itself to building a pipeline through Iranian territory.

Thus having initially planned to create an equilibrium of forces Nazarbayev is now running a risk of getting caught in the cross fire. There have been signs that he is retracting promises he made during his visit to Washington about the Eurasian Transportation Corridor and relations with Iran.[233] On the other hand,

China's entry into the game improved Russia's diplomatic position in the Caspian. Until recently, Russia could rely only on the support of Iran among the larger players. Now it can forge ad hoc alliances with Beijing to counter U.S. pressure. It is already clear that China's interests in the Caspian contradict those of the United States, primarily with regard to oil shipments through Iran. Kazakhstan may try to exploit Russian-Chinese rivalry for access to resources if it develops in the future, but for the time being the interests of both countries do not seem to clash in any significant way.

The third factor was that in the second half of 1997 Russia sharply raised the stakes in the struggle for control of the Caspian. In August, Russia's Natural Resources Ministry announced a tender for the right to explore a vast area in the northern Caspian estimated to hold 150–600 million tonnes of recoverable oil reserves. A part of the area put for the tender overlapped with the sector of the Caspian which Kazakhstan considers its own. Almaty reacted harshly. The Foreign Ministry expressed strong disagreement with Russia's plans, pointed out the "inadmissibility of unilateral actions, uncoordinated with Kazakhstan but taken on its territory and the necessity to reconsider the decision", and stated "[f]rom the location of the blocks put up in the tender it is clear that some of them are in Kazakhstan's sector of the Caspian Sea".[234]

During Chernomyrdin's visit to Almaty on 4 October, disagreements on the Caspian were a major topic in his discussions with Nazarbayev, but neither convinced the other. Soon after Chernomyrdin's return to Moscow, a senior Russian Foreign Ministry official said Kazakhstan's position "is, to say the least, inaccurate. . . . There have never been any borders in the Caspian Sea legalised via treaties," and "the tender conditions will include terms requiring the winner to adhere to any agreements that may be reached thereafter, including adjustments to sector boundaries".[235] However, he gave no further details of the tender. The only result that Nazarbayev and Chernomyrdin achieved was an agreement to hold bilateral consultations on the Caspian issue. These took place on 29–30 October in Moscow, at Deputy Foreign Minister level, with no tangible results.[236] On 10 December LUKoil was named winner of the tender.[237]

Interestingly, the Russian tender coincided with one called by Turkmenistan. But if the Russian tender targeted Kazakhstan, Turkmenistan's targeted Azerbaijan. Both tenders were presumably a coordinated action designed to weaken the Azeri-Kazakh axis. A few days after meeting Yeltsin, who described the Russian and Turkmen positions as "quite close", Niyazov suddenly invited tenders for oil and gas fields on Turkmenistan's Caspian shelf. Ashgabat's plans envisaged exploiting the disputed Kyapaz-Serdar field together with the National Iranian Oil Company and an unnamed Russian company.[238] The first two rounds of the tender were held on 10–11 September and Turkmen sources claimed that they attracted more than fifty-seven major foreign companies. This caused an angry reaction in Azerbaijan, SOCAR even issued a statement threatening unspecified reprisals against any Western oil companies that tendered for the disputed Kyapaz-Serdar field. Moreover, Turkmenistan reaffirmed its claims on the Chirag and Azeri fields, developed by a British Petroleum–led consortium, insisting that the Azerbaijani government give it a share of the profits.[239] On 19 November 1997 Turkmenistan appealed to the UN for assistance in settling its dispute with Azerbaijan over ownership of the Kyapaz-Serdar oilfield.[240]

Up to now the Russian government has demonstrated no intention of retreating from its initial stance. Quite the opposite, there are signs that Moscow intends to be a more active player. On 21 November 1997 Russian Deputy Prime Minister B. Nemtsov, speaking at the presentation of then Minister for Oil and Gas Industry S. Kiriyenko, said that Russia "must in no way allow our influence in the Caspian region to weaken".[241] Given the present correlation of forces in the Caspian Basin, it is unlikely that Kazakhstan will have its way in the sea's legal regime settlement. Minor recent modifications in the Russian position do not alter the situation. The proposal to divide the seabed, but not the water, can be regarded as nothing but a diplomatic manoeuvre aiming at the same goal: establishing a mechanism of common control of the Caspian with Russia as the major player. In practice exploitation of the seabed resources can not proceed without involving water sectors of the sea. This is especially true for the transportation of energy resources, which can not proceed under the seabed. Thus common control over the water area will give Russia approximately the same sort of influence over energy policy in the Caspian as if the whole sea was in the common property of the littoral states. The most probable scenario is that negotiations will drag on indefinitely, a prospect quite suitable to Moscow. Unlike Kazakhstan, Russia is not interested in speedy clarification of the Caspian's legal status. Unclarity in no way obligates Russia, nor deprives it of freedom of diplomatic manoeuvre, nor does it prevent Russian participation in various profitable projects exploiting Caspian energy resources.

NOTES

1.   Kozhokin, E. M., ed., *Kazakhstan: realii i perspektivy nezavisimogo razvitiya*, Moscow: RISI, 1995, pp. 10, 13.

2.   "Russian Oil Production Set to Fall by 90 Million Tonnes in 1992", *BBC Monitoring Service: Former USSR*, 01.05.92. Actual drop in oil production in 1992 was a bit less than predicted. It fell from 460 to 395 million tonnes (Reuters News Service, 22.01.93). Obviously, active measures undertaken by the Russian government played its role in reducing the damage.

3.   "Yeltsin and Government Discuss Oil and Gas: Deputy Premier Replaced", *BBC Monitoring Service: Former USSR*, 01.06.92.

4.   Russia accounts for 34.5% of the world's gas reserves.

5.   "Intergovernmental Council on Oil and Gas Established", *BBC Monitoring Service: Former USSR*, 05.03.93.

6.   "Nazarbayev on Kazakh TV: Talks about Economy, Religion, Nationality Mix", *BBC Monitoring Service: Former USSR*, 18.12.92.

7.   Kozhokin, E. M., ed., *Kazakhstan: realii i perspektivy nezavisimogo razvitiya*, pp. 73–74.

8.   Zhaksibekova, Sh., *Faktory povysheniya economicheskoy bezopasnost'i Kazakhstana (analiticheskiy doklad)*, Almaty: KISI, 1994, pp. 5, 10–12.

9.   "Kazakhstan budet rasshiryat' svoe prisutstvie na mirovom rynke (intervyu s pervym zamestitelem Premier Ministra Respubliki Kazakhstan Isingarinom N. K.)", *Politika*, No. 4, 1996, pp. 15–16.

10.   *Izvestiya*, 23.09.92.

11.   Auken, B., Julamanov, R., *Neft' i gaz Kazakhstana (ekonomicheskiy obzor)*, Almaty: IRK, 1995, pp. 4–5.

12.   *Kazakhstanskaya Pravda*, 17.10.96.

13.   *Petroleum Economist*, July 1995, p. 3.

14.   Ministerstvo Ekonomiki Rossiyskoy Federatsii, Spravka o postavkakh vazhneyshikh vidov produktsii mezhdu Rossiyskoy Federatsiey i Respublikoy Kazakhstan v 1994 godu, Moscow [No publisher], 04.04.95.

15.   *Petroleum Economist*, July 1995, p. 3.

16.   Reuters News Service, 02.11.92.

17.   Azerbaev, E., "V edinstve nasha sila", *Evraziya: narody, kultury, religii*, No. 1(3), 1995, p. 25.

18.   *Petroleum Economist*, January 1996, p. 6.

19.   Kabildin, K., Lobaev, A., Rakhmetova, K., "Neft' Kazakhstana v tsentral'noaziatskom, rossiyskom i mirovom kontekste", *Kazakhstan i mirovoe soobshchestvo*, No. 3(4), 1995, p. 14.

20.   "Kazakhstan budet rasshiryat' svoe prisutstvie na mirovom rynke", *Politika*, No. 4, 1996, p. 16.

21.   *Petroleum Economist*, July 1995, p. 3.

22.   Tengiz oil field is situated in the very northwest of the Mangistau province at the Caspian Sea coast. Discovered in 1970. It is one of the five biggest fields in the world. Its oil reserves are estimated to be 500–800 million tonnes. Karachaganak oil and gaz field is situated in the northeast of Western Kazakhstan province. Discovered in 1979, its reserves are estimated in 200 million tonnes of oil, 650 million tonnes of gas condensate and 1.3 trillion cubic meters of natural gas. Both fields are difficult given the depth of oil and gas bedding — 4–5.5 km (Kozhokin, E. M., ed., *Kazakhstan: realii i perspektivy nezavisimogo razvitiya*, pp. 75–76).

23.   Reuters News Service, 02.11.92.

24.   "International Oil and Gas Conference Opens in Alma-Ata", *BBC Monitoring Service: Former USSR*, 15.10.93.

25.   Nazarbayev, N., "Kazakhstan - 2030: protsvetanie, bezopasnost' i uluchshenie blagosostoyaniya kazakhstantsev, Poslanie Presidenta strany narodu Kazakhstana", *Kazakhstanskaya Pravda*, 11.10.97, p. 29.

26.   In 1991, when Kazakhstan was still a part of the USSR, OOC assisted the republic's government in working out the Tengiz agreement (*Kazakhstanskaya Pravda*, 11.07.97).

27.   *Nezavisimaya gazeta*, 30.11.95.

28.   *APS Review Gas Market Trends*, 15.07.96.

29.   *Times*, 28.04.96.

30.   *Euromoney*, January 1994, p. 89.

31.   *Nezavisimaya gazeta*, 30.11.95.

32.   "Kazakh Premier Leaves for Oman", *BBC Monitoring Service: Former USSR*, 18.06.92.

33. *Kazakhstanskaya Pravda*, 05.09.97.

34. Reuters News Service, 24.07.92.

35. "Caspian Oil Consortium Announces Pipeline Construction Plans", *BBC Monitoring Service: Former USSR*, 30.10.92.

36. "Soglashenie mezhdu Pravitel'stvom Respubliki Kazakhstan i Pravitel'stvom Rossiyskoy Federatsii o sotrudnichestve v otraslyakh toplivno-energeticheskikh kompleksov", *Kazakhstansko-rossiyskie otnosheniya, 1991–1995 gody, Sbornik dokumentov i materialov*, Moscow: Posol'stvo Respubliki Kazakhstan v Rossiyskoy Federatsii, 1995, pp. 122–126.

37. *"Izvestiya* and *Pravda* comment on Alma-Ata Industrialists Congress", *BBC Monitoring Service: Former USSR*, 30.01.93.

38. Reuters News Service, 19.12.92.

39. Reuters News Service, 22.01.93.

40. Reuters News Service, 02.03.93; "Intergovernmental Council on Oil and Gas Established", *BBC Monitoring Service: Former USSR*, 05.03.93.

41. "Kazakhstan Seeks Western Investment to Produce Energy", USIA Database, File ID: ECO404, 22.04.93.

42. Reuters News Service, 06.04.93.

43. Kozhokin, E. M., ed., *Kazakhstan: realii i perspektivy nezavisimogo razvitiya*, pp. 75–76.

44. A highly corrosive sulphur derivative, which in high concentrations in oil can destroy pipelines and storage tanks.

45. *Business Times (Singapore)*, 08.02.93.

46. *Petroleum Economist*, February 1994, p. 22.

47. Reuters News Service, 17.09.93.

48. Reuters News Service, 04.08.94.

49. *Petroleum Economist*, February 1994, p. 22.

50. *Lloyd's List*, 15.07.94.

51. *Middle East Economic Digest*, 13.11.92.

52. *Lloyd's List*, 24.02.93.

53. Reuters News Service, 09.03.93.

54. Reuters News Service, 23.04.93.

55. Reuters News Service, 25.05.93.

56. *Petroleum Economist*, July 1993, p. 38.

57. *Izvestiya*, 06.06.95.

58. *Economist*, 16.07.94.

59. Ibid.

60. "Kazakhstan Seeks Western Investment to Produce Energy", USIA Database, File ID: ECO404, 22.04.93

61. *Euromoney*, January 1994, p. 89.

62. *Financial Times*, 17.05.94.

63. *Euromoney*, May 1995, p. 16.

64. Reuters News Service, 17.02.94.

65. *Independent*, 10.08.93.

66. Reuters News Service, 14.03.94, Reuters News Service, 07.07.94.

67. *Independent*, 15.03.94.

68. Reuters News Service, 25.05.94.

69. *Nezavisimaya gazeta*, 01.07.94.

70. Reuters News Service, 27.08.94.

71. Reuters News Service, 15.09.94.

72.   "Soglashenie mezhdu Pravitel'stvom Respubliki Kazakhstan i Pravitel'stvom Rossiyskoy Federatsii o sotrudnichestve i razvitii toplivno-energeticheskikh kompleksov', *Kazakhstansko-rossiyskie otnosheniya, 1991–1995 gody*, p. 135.

73.   *Financial Times*, 21.01.94.

74.   *Financial Times*, 18.03.94.

75.   *East European Markets*, 18.08.95.

76.   *Financial Times*, 23.03.94.

77.   *Financial Times*, 17.05.94.

78.   *Economist*, 16.07.94.

79.   *Segodnya*, 01.04.94.

80.   "Russia Against Changes to Kazakh Pipeline Deal - Fuel Ministry", *BBC Monitoring Service: Former USSR*, 11.11.94.

81.   Reuters News Service, 03.10.94.

82.   Reuters News Service, 10.11.94.

83.   Reuters News Service, 19.01.95.

84.   "Kazakhstan Has Second Thoughts about Caspian Pipeline Deal", *BBC Monitoring Service: Former USSR*, 10.03.95.

85.   Reuters News Service, 10.03.95.

86.   "Russia and Oman Sign Caspian Pipeline Agreement", *BBC Monitoring Service: Former USSR*, 14.03.95.

87.   "Kazakhstan Joins Caspian Oil Pipeline Accord", *BBC Monitoring Service: Former USSR*, 24.03.95.

88.   "Kazakhstan Overcomes Reservations about Pipeline Project", *BBC Monitoring Service: Former USSR*, 21.04.95.

89.   State Department Report, Friday, February 3, File ID:POL504, USIA Database, 03.02.97.

90.   Reuters News Service, 10.04.95.

91.   Reuters News Service, 26.04.93.

92.   "USA Does Not Rule out Two Pipelines to Carry Caspian Oil", *BBC Monitoring Service: Former USSR*, 28.04.95.

93.   Reuters News Service, 26.04.93.

94.   "Kazakhstan Overcomes Reservations about Pipeline Project', *BBC Monitoring Service: Former USSR*, 21.04.95.

95.   Reuters News Service,10.05.95.

96.   Reuters News Service, 13.06.95

97.   'Kazakhstan and Turkey Agree on Oil Pipeline to Mediterranean", *BBC Monitoring Service: Former USSR*, 17.08.95.

98.   Kasenov, U., "Rossiya, Zakavkaz'ie i Tsentral'naya Aziya: neft', truboprovody i geopolitika", *Kazakhstan i mirovoe soobshchestvo*, No. 2(3), 1995, pp. 27, 29–30.

99.   On 7 May 1995 U.S. President Clinton issued the executive order prohibiting U.S. trade and investment with Iran.

100.   Reuters News Service, 06.10.95.

101.   *Segodnya*, 19.09.95.

102.   Reuters News Service, 19.10.95.

103.   Reuters News Service, 19.10.95.

104.   Russia applied similar tactics with regard to other Kazakhstan's projects. For example, on 14 February 1995 M. Alimov, an aide to Rosneft Chairman A. Putilov, said the company was considering plans to take part in the consortium exploring Kazakhstan's Caspian shelf. On 18 August 1995 during his visit to Kazakhstan LUKoil's President Alekperov said his company wants to take part in the Kazakhstankaspiyshelf

project (Reuters News Service, 14.02.95; *Segodnya*, 21.02.95; Reuters News Service, 18.08.95).

105. "Kazakhs Ready to Give Russian Firm Stake in Tengiz Oil Deal", *BBC Monitoring Service: Former USSR*, 07.11.95.

106. "Kazakhs Set up Alternative Pipeline Consortium", *BBC Monitoring Service: Former USSR*, 10.11.95.

107. Reuters News Service, 31.10.95.

108. Reuters News Service, 19.01.96.

109. *Jane's Intelligence Review*, March 1996, p. 7.

110. *APS Review Downstream Trends*, 18.03.96.

111. "Russian Oil Company Gets 10-Per-Cent Share in Kazakh Project", *BBC Monitoring Service: Former USSR*, 19.04.96.

112. "Kazakhstan Permitted to Pump More Oil across Russia", *BBC Monitoring Service: Former USSR*, 20.04.96.

113. *Lloyd's List*, 20.04.96.

114. Reuters News Service, 23.04.96.

115. Reuters News Service, 27.04.96.

116. Reuters News Service, 06.12.96.

117. Reuters News Service, 14.03.97.

118. "Caspian Pipeline Deal Signed in Moscow", *BBC Monitoring Service: Former USSR*, 09.12.96; Reuters News Service, 19.11.97.

119. "Caspian Pipeline Deal Signed in Moscow", *BBC Monitoring Service: Former USSR*, 09.12.96.

120. "Talks on LUKoil Stake in Kazakh-US Oil Venture Complete", *BBC Monitoring Service: Former USSR*, 24.01.97.

121. Reuters News Service, 16.01.97.

122. Interfax, 25.04.96.

123. *Guardian*, 02.07.92.

124. Kozhokin, E. M., ed., *Kazakhstan: realii i perspektivy nezavisimogo razvitiya*, p. 76.

125. "Soglashenie mezhdu Pravitel'stvom Respubliki Kazakhstan i Pravitel'stvom Rossiyskoy Federatsii o sotrudnichestve v otraslyakh toplivno-energeticheskikh kompleksov", *Kazakhstansko-rossiyskie otnosheniya, 1991–1995 gody*, pp. 122–126.

126. *Petroleum Economist*, February 1994, p. 22.

127. "Gazprom Claims Cut of Kazakhstan Gas Field Deal", *BBC Monitoring Service: Former USSR*, 21.10.94.

128. Reuters News Service, 06.12.93.

129. *Financial Times*, 25.03.94.

130. Reuters News Service, 28.08.94.

131. Kozhokin, E. M., ed., *Kazakhstan: realii i perspektivy nezavisimogo razvitiya*, p. 77; Reuters News Service, 04.10.94.

132. Azerbaev, E., "V edinstve nasha sila", p. 25.

133. Reuters News Service, 04.10.94.

134. Reuters News Service, 14.10.94.

135. "Gazprom Claims Cut of Kazakhstan Gas Field Deal", *BBC Monitoring Service: Former USSR*, 21.10.94.

136. Reuters News Service, 10.10.94.

137. "British Gas in Talks with Russia on Kazakh Gas Deposit", *BBC Monitoring Service: Former USSR*, 18.11.94.

138. *Lloyd's List*, 28.11.96.

139. Reuters News Service, 09.12.94.

140. "Soglashenie mezhdu Pravitel'stvom Respubliki Kazakhstan i Pravitel'stvom Rossiyskoy Federatsii o sotrudnichestve v razrabotke i razvitii Karachaganakskogo neftegazokondensatnogo mestorozhdeniya", *Kazakhstansko-rossiyskie otnosheniya, 1991–1995 gody*, p. 245.

141. Auken, B., Julamanov, R., *Neft' i gaz Kazakhstana*, p. 6.

142. *APS Review Gas Market Trends*, 15.07.96.

143. Reuters news service, 07.08.97.

144. "Russian Company Declines Kazakh Gas Outlet to World Markets", *BBC Monitoring Service: Former USSR*, 15.08.97.

145. *Financial Times*, 07.10.96.

146. Reuters News Service, 19.11.97; *Commersant-Daily*, 21.11.97.

147. Auken, B., Julamanov, R., *Neft i gaz Kazakhstana*, p. 10.

148. "Pena Wins Support for Oil Transport Corridor", File ID:97111808.GWE, USIA Database, 18.11.97.

149. Auken, B., Julamanov, R., *Neft' i gaz Kazakhstana*, p. 10.

150. *Nezavisimaya gazeta*, 04.12.93.

151. "Premiers Agree to Set up Council for Cooperation in Caspian Region", *BBC Monitoring Service: Former USSR*, 19.10.93, Reuters News Service, 02.06.94.

152. "Protokol vstrechi Glav Pravitelstv Respubliki Kazakhstan i Rossiyskoy Federatsii", *Kazakhstansko-rossiyskie otnosheniya, 1991–1995 gody*, p. 177.

153. "Perry Calls Dismantlement 'Defense by Other Means'", File ID: EUR410, USIA Database, 07.04.94; "Joint Statement on US-Kazakstan Defense Relations", File ID:96022601.WWE, USIA Database, 26.02.96.

154. *Financial Times*, 31.05.94.

155. Reuters News Service, 02.06.94.

156. Kasenov, U., *Osnovnyye itogi vneshnepoliticheskoy deyatelnosti Respubliki Kazakhstan i ee prioritetnyye zadachi*, Almaty: KISI, 1994, p. 25.

157. Reuters News Service, 12.07.94.

158. Gizzatov, V., "Pravovoy status Kaspiyskogo morya: kondominium ili delimitatsiya", *Kazakhstan i mirovoe soobshchestvo*, No. 1, 1996, p. 46.

159. Kozhokin, E. M., ed., *Kazakhstan: realii i perspektivy nezavisimogo razvitiya*, p. 80.

160. Gizzatov, V., "Kaspiy dolzhen stat' morem mira, dobrososedstva i sotrudnichestva", *Vneshnyaya politika Kazakhstana, Sbornik statey*, Almaty: MID Respubliki Kazakhstan, 1995, p. 183.

161. *Nezavisimaya gazeta*, 05.10.94.

162. *Independent*, 03.11.94

163. Gizzatov, V., "The Legal Status of the Caspian Sea", *Central Asian Quarterly*, Vol. 2, No. 3, 1995, p. 34.

164. Khodakov, A., "The Legal Framework for Regional Cooperation in the Caspian Sea Region", *Central Asian Quarterly*, Vol. 2, No. 3, 1995, p. 32.

165. "Russia and Iran Discuss Use of Caspian Resources", *BBC Monitoring Service: Former USSR*, 12.10.94.

166. Granmayeh, A., "The Caspian Sea in Iranian History and Politics", *Central Asian Quarterly*, Vol. 2, No. 3, 1995, p. 39.

167. Reuters News Service, 12.10.94.

168. Granmayeh, A., "The Caspian Sea in Iranian History and Politics", *Central Asian Quarterly*, Vol. 2, No. 3, 1995, p. 39.

169. *Lloyd's List*, 15.10.94, Reuters News Service, 24.10.94.

170. Gizzatov, V., "Pravovoy status Kaspiyskogo morya, problemy i perspektivy sotrudnichestva prikaspiyskikh gosudarstv", *Politika*, No. 3, 1995, p. 50.

171. "Kazakhstan Denies US Pressure Over Caspian's Legal Status", *BBC Monitoring Service: Former USSR*, 28.07.95.

172. Gizzatov, V., "Kaspiy dolzhen stat' morem mira, dobrososedstva i sotrudnichestva", *Vneshnyaya politika Kazakhstana, Sbornik statey*, Almaty: MID Respubliki Kazakhstan, 1995, p. 184.

173. Ibid.

174. Tsibukov, V., *Problemy pravopriemstva v Sodruzhestve Nezavisimykh Gosudarstv*, Moscow: MGIMO, 1994 p. 52.

175. *Lloyd's List*, 28.02.95.

176. Khodakov, A., "The Legal Framework for Regional Cooperation in the Caspian Sea Region", p. 31.

177. Ibid.

178. *Australian Financial Review*, 16.12.97.

179. *Lloyd's List*, 28.02.95.

180. "Russia Ready to Get Tough over Legal Status of Caspian Sea", *BBC Monitoring Service: Former USSR*, 25.07.95.

181. "Kazakhstan Denies US Pressure over Caspian's Legal Status", *BBC Monitoring Service: Former USSR*, 28.07.95.

182. "Itogi vtorogo soveschaniya rukovoditeley pravovykh sluzhb MID prikaspiyskikh gosudarstv po voprosam pravovogo statusa Kaspiyskogo morya", *Diplomaticheskiy kurier,* No. 1, 1996, p. 93.

183. Reuters News Service, 26.09.95.

184. Gizzatov, V., "Pravovoy status Kaspiyskogo morya: kondominium ili delimitatsiya", p. 44.

185. Khodakov, A., "The Legal Framework for Regional Cooperation in the Caspian Sea Region", p. 31.

186. Gizzatov, V., "Pravovoy status Kaspiyskogo morya: kondominium ili delimitatsiya", p. 44.

187. *Kazakhstanskaya Pravda*, 01.04.97.

188. Gizzatov, V., "Pravovoy status Kaspiyskogo morya: kondominium ili delimitatsiya", pp. 45–46.

189. Reuters News Service, 24.10.95.

190. "Russian Deputy Premier Begins Visit to Iran", *BBC Monitoring Service: Former USSR*, 31.10.95; Reuters News Service, 30.10.95.

191. Reuters News Service, 30.04.96.

192. "Kazakhstan Seeks Cooperation with Russia in Caspian Development", *BBC Monitoring Service: Former USSR*, 03.05.96.

193. "Foreign Ministers of Caspian States Sign Communique", *BBC Monitoring Service: Former USSR*, 14.11.96.

194. Reuters News Service, 13.11.96.

195. *Financial Times*, 23.01.97.

196. "Kazakhstan Says 'Fundamental Differences' Remain over Caspian Status", *BBC Monitoring Service: Former USSR*, 16.11.96.

197. *Lloyd's List*, 09.09.96.

198. "Kazakhstan Says 'Fundamental Differences' Remain over Caspian Status", *BBC Monitoring Service: Former USSR*, 16.11.96.

199. Reuters News Service, 14.11.96; "Kazakhstan Says 'Fundamental Differences' Remain over Caspian Status", *BBC Monitoring Service: Former USSR*, 16.11.96.

200. "Russia, Turkmenistan and Iran Take Steps to Set up Joint Oil Company", *BBC Monitoring Service: Former USSR*, 21.12.96.

201. *Financial Times*, 23.01.97.

202. *Kazakhstanskaya Pravda*, 28.02.97.

203. *Radio Free Europe / Radio Liberty (RFE/RL) Newsline*, Vol. 1, No. 89, Part I, 06.08.97.

204. "Working Group to Determine Legal Status of the Caspian", *ITAR-TASS World Service*, 22.05.97.

205. *Petroleum Economist*, January 1996, P. 6.

206. *Kazakstan: Transition of the State, A World Bank Country Study*, Washington: World Bank, 1997, p. 230.

207. *APS Review Gas Market Trends*, 15.07.96.

208. *Izvestiya*, 05.05.97.

209. Gosudarstvennaya Duma Federal'nogo Sobraniya Rossiyskoy Federatsii, Komitet po sobstvennosti, privatizatsii i khozyaystvennoy deyatelnosti, Zaklyuchenie po proektu Federal'nogo zakona "O ratifikatsii Dogovora o dalneyshem uglublenii ekonomicheskogo sotrudnichestva i integratsii Rossiyskoy Federatsii i Respubliki Kazakhstan", Moscow [No publisher], 19.04.95.

210. "Russia Starts Gas Supplies to South Kazakhstan", *ITAR-TASS World Service*, 15.11.97; "Russian Gas 'Slap in Face' for Kazakhs, Paper Says", *BBC Monitoring Service: Former USSR*, 21.11.97.

211. *Kazakstan: Transition of the State*, p. 228; *Kazakhstanskaya Pravda*, 14.08.97.

212. Reuters News Service, 02.11.92.

213. Ministerstvo Finansov Rossiyskoy Federatsii, Po voprosu finansovo-kreditnykh otnosheniy s Respublikoy Kazakhstan, Doc. No. 1-10/2-1229, Moscow [No publisher], 1995.

214. *Kazakstan: Transition of the State*, p. 230.

215. *Kazakhstanskaya Pravda*, 14.08.97.

216. Reuters News Service, 03.04.97.

217. Nazarbayev, N., "Kazakhstan - 2030: protsvetanie, bezopasnost' i uluchshenie blagosostoyaniya kazakhstantsev", p. 24.

218. Reuters News Service, 12.08.96.

219. *New Europe*, 27 April–3 May 1997, p. 42.

220. "Iran Renews Call for Caspian Sea Legal Regime", *Compass Middle East Wire*, 17.11.97.

221. Interfax, 13.03.97.

222. Reuters News Service, 11.11.97.

223. Reuters News Service, 10.08.97.

224. "Kazakhstan, Azerbaijan Sign 15 Cooperation Agreements", *ITAR-TASS World Service*, 10.06.97; *Kazakhstanskaya Pravda*, 12.06.98.

225. *Kazakhstanskaya Pravda*, 12.11.98.

226. Aktobemunajgaz, based in western Kazakhstan controls two fields with reserves of 590 million tons of petroleum and 220 billion cubic meters of gas. In 1996 its oil output was 2.6 million tonnes. In the assessment of Chinese experts this output can be doubled following projected $US 300 million of Chinese investments (China's National Oil Corporation Wins Deal to Develop Kazakh Oil Field, BBC Monitoring Service: Asia-Pacific, 06.6.97).

227. "Kazakhstan and China Sign 'Deal of the Century'", *ITAR-TASS World Service*, 24.09.97.

228. Reuters News Service, 02.05.97.

229. "Pena Wins Support for Oil Transport Corridor", File ID:97111808.GWE, 18.11.97.

230. "U.S.-Kazakhstan Joint Statement on Caspian Energy", File ID:97111903.GWE, USIA Database, 19.11.97; "Gore, Nazerbayev Expand U.S.-Kazakh Nuclear and Defense Cooperation", File ID:97111811.GWE, 18.11.97.

231. "Joint Statement on US-Kazakhstan Relations, November 18", File ID:97111807.GWE, USIA Database, 18.11.97.

232. *Nezavisimaya gazeta*, 20.11.97.

233. *Journal of Commerce*, 01.12.97.

234. Reuters News Service, 30.08.97; Reuters News Service, 24.01.98.

235. Reuters News Service, 18.10.97.

236. *Kazakhstanskaya Pravda*, 04.11.97.

237. *RFE/RL Newsline,* Vol. 1, No. 177, Part I, 11.12.97.

238. *RFE/RL Newsline,* Vol. 1, No. 98, Part I, 19.08.97; *RFE/RL Newsline,* Vol. 1, No. 103, Part I, 26.08.97.

239. *RFE/RL Newsline,* Vol. 1, No. 111, Part I, 05.09.97; *RFE/RL Newsline,* Vol. 1, No. 115, Part I, 11.09.97; *RFE/RL Newsline,* Vol. 1, No. 118, Part I, 16.09.97; *RFE/RL Newsline,* Vol. 1, No. 120, Part I, 18.09.97.

240. *RFE/RL Newsline,* Vol. 1, No. 164, Part I, 20.11.97.

241. Reuters News Service, 21.11.98.

Appendix

Table A.1
Population of Kazakhstan by Nationality (1897–1989)

Nationality	1897		1911		1926		1939		1959		1979		1989	
Kazakh	3,644,911	73.9%	4,168,918	60.8%	3,918,000	59.5%	2,315,532	38.0%	2,794,966	30.0%	5,289,349	36.0%	6,534,600	39.7%
Russian	633,311[1]	12.8%	1,851,312	27.0%	1,188,000	18.0%	2,449,590	40.2%	3,974,229	42.7%	5,991,205	40.8%	6,227,500	37.8%
Ukrainian	-	-	-	-	818,000	12.4%	658,099	10.8%	762,131	8.2%	897,964	6.1%	896,200	5.4%
Belorussian	-	-	-	-	-	-	30,467	0.5%	107,463	2.1%	181,491	1.2%	182,600	1.1%
Tatar	55,252	1.1%	77,425	1.1%	48,000	0.7%	97,496	1.6%	191,125	1.5%	313,460	2.1%	328,000	2.0%
Uzbek	64,235	1.3%	76,784	1.1%	210,000	3.2%	103,590	1.7%	36,570	1.1%	263,295	1.8%	332,000	2.0%
German	-	-	-	-	46,000	0.7%	914,040	1.5%	659,751	7.1%	900,207	6.1%	957,500	5.8%
Karakalpak	93,215	1.9%	111,425	1.6%	115,000	1.8%	-	-	-	-	-	-	-	-
Other	441,072	9.0%	602,540	8.4%	236,000	3.7%	347,330	5.7	683,865	7.3%	847,312	5.9%	840,700	6.2%
Total	4,931,966		6,852,431		6,579,000		6,093,507		9,309,847		14,684,283		16,484,400	

Sources: Aziatskaya Rossiya, t.1, St Peterburg: Izdanie Pereselencheskogo upravleniya Glavnogo upravleniya zemleustroystva i zemledeliya, 1914, pp. 82–85; Kenjenbayev, S. M., *Sovety v borbe za postroenie sotsializma (Istoriya sovetskogo stroitelstva v Kazakhstane 1917–1937)*, Alma-Ata: Kazakhstan, 1969, pp. 250–251; Bakayev, L., "Mezhetnicheskie otnosheniya v Kazakhstane", *Evraziyskoe Soobschestvo*, No. 2, 1995, p. 7; *Itogi vsesoyuznoy perepisi naseleniya 1959 goda, Kazakhskaya SSR*, Moscow: Gosstatizdat, 1962, p. 162; *Naselenie SSSR v 1987 godu, Statisticheskiy sbornik*, Moscow: Finansy i statistika, 1988, p. 103; Brown, B., "Kazakhs Now Largest National Group in Kazakhstan", *Radio Liberty, Report on the USSR*, Vol. 2, No. 18, May 4, 1990, pp. 18–19.

[1] For 1897 and 1911 this includes all Slavs.

Table A.2
Agricultural Development of Kazakhstan (1906–1985)

Category	1906	1916	1920	1928	1940	1954	1965	1985
Sown land area (thousands of hectars)	1753.8	4466.3	3300.1	4200.0	6808.6	11 521.2	30 532.8	35 796.1
Grain output (thousands of tons)[1]	599.1	2014.1	678.0	2665.0	2516.0	3942.0	17 042.8	24 408.8
Tractors employed in agriculture	-	-	-	500.0[2]	30 834.0	60 875.0	194 800.0	248 700.0
Harversters employed in agriculture	-	-	-	-	11 759.0	33 260.0	98 800.0	118 700.0
Cattle (thousands of head)	3617.0	5062.1	4200.0	6534.3	3324.8	4638.6	6833.3	9027.6
Sheep and goats (thousands of head)	11 558.0	18 364.1	13 300.0	19 169.0	6992.0	20 550.9	30 120.9	36 056.6
Horses (thousands of head)	3538.0	4340.0	.....	3544.8	815.7	1646.7	1070.3	1449.3
Meat production (thousands tons)	.....	440.0[3]	450.0	.....	226.0	325.0	768.3	1131.3
Milk production (thousands of tons)	.....	857.0[3]	900.0	.....	1099.0	1562.0	3327.8	4738.6
Wool production (thousands of tons)	.....	42.7[3]	.....	.....	13.7	38.0	80.0	97.7
Vegetable oil (thousands of tons)	.....	.....	0.3	0.4	4.7	39.3	58.2	74.1

Sources: Demko, G. J., *The Russian Colonization of Kazkhstan 1896–1916*, Bloomington: Indiana University, 1969, p.160; 171; 217–223; *Aziatskaya Rossiya*, t.1, St. Peterburg, 1914, pp. 272–273, 318; *Istoriya Kazakhskoy SSR s drevneyshikh vremen do nashikh dney*, t.4, Alma-Ata: Nauka, 1977, pp. 248–249; Kiykbaev, N., *Torzhestvo leninskoy nasionalnoy politiki v Kazakhstane*, Alma-Ata: Kazakhstan, 1968, p. 63; *SSSR –strana sotsializma, Statisticheskiy sbornik*, Moscow: CUNXU Gosplana SSSR i V/O Soyuzorguchet, 1936, p. 158; *Narodnoe khozyaistvo Kazakhskoy SSR, Statisticheskiy sbornik*, Alma-Ata: Kazakhgosizdat, 1957, pp. 56, 68–73, 141; *Narodnoe khozyaistvo SSSR v 1961 g., Statisticheskiy ezhegodnik*, Moscow: Gosstatizdat, 1962, pp. 346–347, 393–396; *Narodnoe khozyaistvo SSSR v 1989 gody*, Moscow: Finansi i statistika, 1990, pp. 435–436, 463–469, 495; *Narodnoe khozyaistvo Kazakhstana v 1976 gody*, Alma-Ata: Kazakhstan, 1977, pp. 74, 93, 100; *Narodnoe khozyaistvo Kazakhstana v 1977 gody*, 1978, pp. 53–54, 58, 62, 81–85; *Narodnoe khozyaistvo SSSR v 1979 gody*, Moscow: Statistika, 1980, pp. 214, 276–278; *Narodnoe khozyaistvo Kazakhstana v 1985 gody*, 1986, pp. 54, 77, 81, 105–110; Davis, R. W., *Industrialisation of Soviet Russia 1: The Socialist Offensive, 1929-1930*, Cambridge (Mass.): Harvard University Press, 1980, p.428–429.

[1] For the following years average output for several years is given: 1928 (1928–30); 1954 (1950–54); 1965 (1965–75); 1985 (1976–85); 1989 (1986–89).
[2] Estimate.
[3] Data for 1913.

Table A.3

Production of Some Industrial Commodities in Kazakhstan (1913–1985)

Commodity	1913	1928	1940	1954	1965	1985
Electricity (millions of kwh)	1.3	7.0	632.0	4795.3	19,237	81,263
Coal (millions of tons)	0.09	0.037	7.0	23.7	45.8	131.0
Crude steel (thousands of tons)	-	-	-	221.7	1123.4	6155.0
Rolled ferrous metall (thousands of tons)	-	-	-	208.0	391.0	4200.0
Crude petroleum (thousands of tons)	118.0	251.0	697.0	1384.0	2000.0	22,800
Cement (thousands of tons)	-	-	-	330.6	4036.9	7549.0
Construction bricks (millions)	-	6.3	220.2	587.4	1548	1940.4
Fertilisers (thousands of tons)	-	-	-	322.5	776.5	7440.3
Sulphuric acid (thousands of tons)	-	-	49.0	58.0[1]	863.6	1670.8
Metal processing machines	-	-	-	501.0[2]	1915.0	4143.0
Metallurgic equipment	-	-	-	2857.0[1]	9005.0	11,210
Leather shoes (thousands of pairs)	....	470.0[3]	1189.0	5980.0	14,995	32,260
Cotton fibre (thousands of tons)	1.9	5.8	35.0	72.1	70.4	91.9
Fabric of all types (thousands of meters)	139.0[4]	129.0[4]	472.0[5]	17,498[5]	31,300	227,800

Sources: SSSR —strana sotsializma, Statisticheskiy sbornik, Moscow: CUNXU Gosplana SSSR i V/O Soyuzorguchet, 1936, p. 157; *Narodnoe khozyaistvo Kazakhskoy SSR, Statisticheskiy sbornik*, Alma-Ata: Kazakhgosizdat, 1957, pp. 35–44; *Narodnoe khozyaistvo SSSR v 1958 g., Statisticheskiy ezhegodnik*, Moscow: Gosstatizdat, 1959, p. 234; *Narodnoe khozyaistvo SSSR v 1961 g., Statisticheskiy ezhegodnik*, Moscow: Gosstatizdat, 1962, p. 197, 240; *Narodnoe khozyaistvo SSSR v 1965 g., Statisticheskiy ezhegodnik*, Moscow: Gosstatizdat, 1966, pp. 182, 215; *Narodnoe khozyaistvo Kazakhstana v 1976 g., Statisticheskiy ezhegodnik*, Alma-Ata: Kazakhstan, 1977, p. 33; *Narodnoe khozyaistvo Kazakhstana v 1977 g., Statisticheskiy ezhegodnik*, Alma-Ata: Kazakhstan, 1978, pp 36–42; *Narodnoe khozyaistvo Kazakhstana v 1980 g., Statisticheskiy ezhegodnik*, Alma-Ata: Kazakhstan, 1981, p. 40; *Narodnoe khozyaistvo Kazakhstana v 1982 g., Statisticheskiy ezhegodnik*, Alma-Ata: Kazakhstan, 1983, pp. 41, 45; *Narodnoe khozyaistvo Kazakhstana v 1985 g., Statisticheskiy ezhegodnik*, Alma-Ata: Kazakhstan, 1986, pp. 42–52.

[1] Data for 1950.
[2] Data for 1955.
[3] Data for 1932.
[4] Wool fabric only.
[5] Wool and cotton fabric.

Table A.4
Education in Kazakhstan (1914–1985)

Category	1914	1928	1940	1954	1965	1985
Literacy of population in Kazakhstan (%)	15.7[1]	25.2	83.6	96.9	100	100
Number of schools of all types	2006	3927	7790	9043	10,728	8728
Number of pupils in schools	105,059	273,584	1,138,187	1,290,634	2,852,000	3,348,000
Number of teachers in schools	3319	7883	44,381	70,128	124,044	237,000
Specialised secondary educational institutions	7	24	118	130	169	246
Students in specialised secondary education	302	3620	30,276	61,729	171,000	277,600
Number of tertiary educational institutions	-	1	20	26	39	55
Number of students in tertiary educational institutions	-	75	10 419	45,430	144,700	273,300

Sources: Narodnoe khozyaistvo Kazakhskoy SSR, Statisticheskiy sbornik, Alma-Ata: Kazakhgosizdat, 1957, pp. 284–285, 322–327, 338–339; *Itogi vsesoiuznoy perepisi naseleniia 1959 goda, Kazakhskaia SSR*, Moscow: Gosstatizdat, 1962, p. 59; *Narodnoe khozyaistvo Kazakhstana v 1977 g., Statisticheskiy ezhegodnik*, Alma-Ata, Kazakhstan, 1978, pp. 188, 191, 195, 220. *Narodnoe khozyastvo Kazakhstana v 1985 g., Statisticheskiy ezhegodnik*, Alma-Ata: Kazakhstan, 1986, pp. 280, 253, 260.

[1] Estimate.

Table A.5
Medical Care in Kazakhstan (1914–1985)

Category	1914	1928	1940	1954	1965	1985
Number of doctors of all specialisations	244	807	2747	9153	22,494	59,400
Number of trained nurses	393	1308	11,953	27,952	76,443	180,500
Medical institutions of all types (hospitals, clinics, surgeries, obstetric stations, etc.)	257	724	3499	5347	4934	6239

Sources: Narodnoe khozyaistvo Kazakhskoy SSR, Statisticheskiy sbornik, Alma-Ata: Kazakhgosizdat, 1957, pp. 284–285, 322–327, 338–339; *Itogi vsesoiuznoy perepisi naseleniia 1959 goda, Kazakhskaia SSR*, Moskva: Gosstatizdat, 1962, p. 59; *Narodnoe khozyaistvo Kazakhstana v 1977 g., Statisticheskiy ezhegodnik*, Alma-Ata, Kazakhstan, 1978, pp. 188, 191, 195, 220. *Narodnoe khozyastvo Kazakhstana v 1985 g., Statisticheskiy ezhegodnik*, Alma-Ata: Kazakhstan, 1986, pp. 280, 253, 260.

Table A.6
Agricultural Development of Kazakhstan (1985–1995)

Category	1985	1986	1987	1988	1989	1990	1991	1992	1993	1994	1995
Sown land area (thousands of hectares)	35,796	35,618	35,591	35,658	35,229	35,182	34,936	34,840	34,060	31,672	28,659
Grain output (thousands of tons)	22,694	26,562	25,721	20,970	8797	28,488	11,992	29,772	21,631	16,454	9505
Cattle (millions of head)	9.2	9.5	9.7	9.8	9.8	9.8	9.6	9.6	9.3	8.1	6.9
Sheep and goats (millions of head)	35.5	36.4	36.4	36.5	36.2	35.7	34.6	34.4	34.2	25.1	19.6
Pigs (millions of head)	3.0	3.2	3.2	3.2	3.2	3.2	3.0	2.6	2.4	2.0	1.7
Meat in slaughter weight (thousands of tons)	1133	1300	1399	1493	1573	1560	1524	1258	1312	1207	985
Milk production (thousands of tons)	4763	5040	5185	5321	5563	5642	5555	5265	5576	5296	4619
Wool production (thousands of tons)	97.6	106.0	106.4	108.4	109.9	107.9	104.4	96.5	94.6	75.3	58.3
Vegetable oil (thousands of tons)	74.1	75.5	80.0	85.4	92.2	95.0	101.0	59.5	49.0	44.5	43.2

Sources: Strani-chleni SNG, Statisticheskiy ezhegodnik 1992, Moscow, 1992, pp. 214–224; Ekonomika SNG v 1994 godu, Kratkiy spravochnik, Moscow, 1992, pp. 87–104, 210–211; Statisticheskiy bulleten Statkoma SNG, No. 8 (96), February 1995, pp. 37–89; Statistika: Baza dannykh Statkoma SNG, Moscow; Sodruzhestvo Nezavisimikh Gosudarstv v 1995 godu, Statisticheskiy ezhegodnik, Moscow, 1996, pp. 55, 255–258.

Table A.7
Production of Major Industrial Commodities in Kazakhstan (1985–1995)

Commodity	1985	1986	1987	1988	1989	1990	1991	1992	1993	1994	1995
Electricity (billions of kwh)	81.3	85.1	88.5	88.4	89.7	87.4	86.0	82.7	77.4	66.4	66.7
Coal (millions of tons)	131.0	138.0	142.0	143.0	138.0	131.0	130.0	127.0	112.0	105.0	83.3
Crude steel (millions of tons)	6.2	6.5	6.6	6.8	6.8	6.8	6.4	6.1	4.6	3.0	66.4
Rolled ferrous metals (millions of tons)	4.4	4.6	4.7	4.9	5.1	4.9	4.7	4.3	3.4	2.3	2.1
Crude petroleum (millions of tons)	22.8	23.7	24.5	25.5	25.4	25.8	26.6	25.8	23.0	20.3	20.5
Cement (millions of tons)	7.5	8.1	8.3	8.4	8.6	8.3	7.6	6.4	4.0	2.0	1.8
Construction bricks (billions)	1.9	2.1	2.3	2.4	2.5	2.3	2.1	2.0	1.3	0.8	0.4
Fertilisers (thousands of tons)	1.4	1.5	1.6	1.7	1.7	1.7	1.5	0.9	0.3	0.1	0.2
Sulphuric acid (thousands of tons)	1.7	1.9	2.0	2.1	1.9	3.2	2.8	2.3	1.2	0.7	0.7
Metal-cutting machines (thousands)	2.8	2.6	2.2	2.2	2.3	2.6	2.4	1.6	1.2	0.4	0.06
Metallurgic equipment (thousands)	1.3	1.2	1.1	1.2	1.2	1.2	1.2	0.8	0.8	0.4	0.3
Footwear (millions of pairs)	32.3	32.5	32.7	34.1	35.2	36.5	34.1	20.2	13.5	7.8	2.1
Raw cotton (thousands of tons)	305.0	333.0	312.0	325.0	315.0	324.0	290.0	246.0	198.0	206.0	180.0
Fabric of all types (millions sq. meters)	289.0	300.0	288.0	324.0	330.0	325.0	249.0	228.0	188.0	107.0	31.1

Sources: Strani —chleni SNG, Statisticheskiy ezhegodnik 1992, Moscow, 1992, pp. 214–224; Ekonomika SNG v 1994 godu, Kratkiy spravochnik, Moscow, 1992, pp. 87–104, 210–211; Statisticheskiy bulleten Statkoma SNG, No. 8 (96), February 1995, pp. 37–89; Statistika: Baza dannykh Statkoma SNG, Moscow; Sodruzhestvo Nezavisimykh Gosudarstv v 1996 godu, Statisticheskiy ezhegodnik, Moscow, 1997, pp. 47–58; Sodruzhestvo Nezavisimykh Gosudarstv v 1995 godu, Statisticheskii ezhegodnik, Moscow, 1996, p. 49; Statisticheskiy bulleten Statkoma SNG, No. 2 (138), January 1996, pp. 100–105; Statisticheskiy bulleten Statkoma SNG, No. 8 (144), April 1996, p. 115.

Map A.1
Kazakhstan on the Verge of Accession to the Russian State

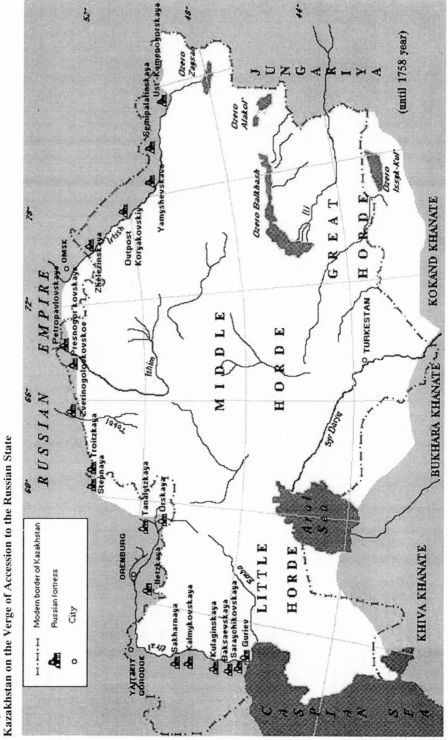

Map A.2
Administrative Borders of Kazakhstan at the End of the Nineteenth Century

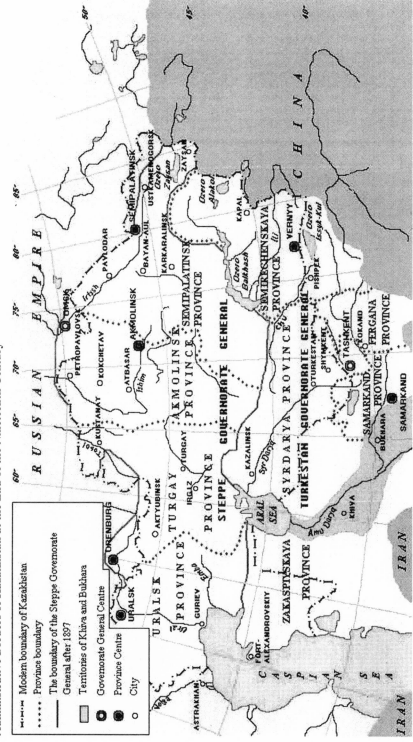

Map A.3
Kazakhstan: Ethnic-Geographical Division

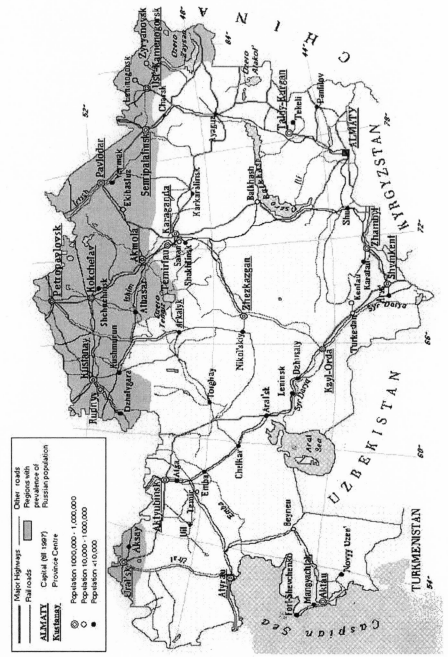

Map A.4
Cosmodrome Baykonur

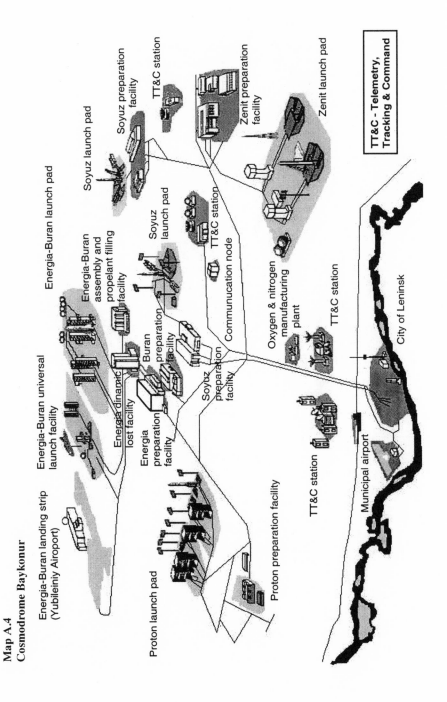

Energia-Buran landing strip
(Yubileiniy Airoport)

Energia-Buran universal
launch facility

Energia-Buran launch pad

Energia-Buran
assembly and
propelant filling
facility

Soyuz preparation
facility

Soyuz launch pad

TT&C station

Zenit preparation
facility

Zenit launch pad

Energia dinamic
lost facility

Energia
preparation
facility

Buran
preparation
facility

Soyuz
preparation
facility

Soyuz
launch pad

TT&C station

Communcation node

Oxygen & nitrogen
manufacturing
plant

TT&C station

City of Leninsk

Proton launch pad

Proton preparation facility

TT&C station

Municipal airport

TT&C station

TT&C - Telemetry,
Tracking & Command

319

Map A.5
Kazakhstan: Major Military Objects Rented by Russia

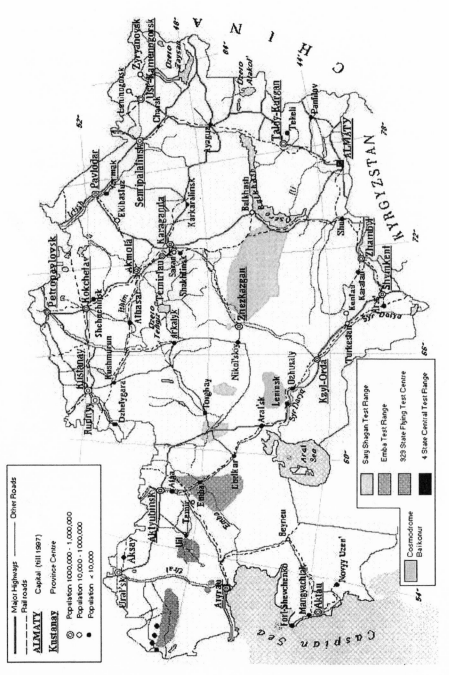

Index

Abdildin, Serikbolsyn, 120
Afghanistan, 61, 62, 228, 230, 245
Agip, 262, 277–283, 298
Akayev, Askar, 34, 179
Alash Orda, 21, 25
Alash, 24, 89, 110
Alekperov, Vagit, 273, 277, 304
Aliyev, Geydar, 10, 296
Alma-Ata riots, 10–13; assessment of, 13–18, 20, 22–24, 46
Armed Forces of Kazakhstan, 43, 70–71, 125, 130, 204, 229–230, 240
Armenia, 78, 170, 275–276, 298
Assembly of Peoples of Kazakhstan, 113, 133–134, 192
Azamat, 89
Azat, 25–26, 89, 111
Azerbaijan, 22, 24, 181, 254, 264, 266, 268–270, 274–276, 283–286, 288–290, 292–293, 296, 298, 300

Baikenov, Kadyr, 262, 266, 267, 268, 279, 282
Baker, James, 72–74, 77
Balgymbayev, Nurlan, 274, 277, 282, 294
Banking union, 67, 156–157, 159, 161, 191
Baykonur, 32, 41, 43–44, 81–84, 211–227, 246–247
Belarus (Belorussia), 28, 33, 35, 40, 45–46, 60–61, 71, 73–74, 76–77, 79, 112, 157, 159, 162–163, 167–168, 170, 180–182, 187, 190, 192–193, 204, 206, 229
Belovezhskaya agreement, 35, 46, 72, 168, 190–191
Boldin, Valeriy, 3–4
Bosporus navigation issues, 268–269, 271
Brezhnev, Leonid, 1, 3–5, 47, 260
British Gas, 262, 277–283, 298
Budapest memorandum, 210–211, 249
Bulgaria, 272
Bush, George, 75, 77, 79, 210

Caspian Pipeline Consortium (CPC), 263–265, 268–270, 272–278, 280, 282, 296
Caspian Sea, 122, 229, 237, 246, 267, 269, 275, 282–294, 296–299; and Law of the Sea, 285–289; negotiations on the status, 282–289, 292–293, 297, 300; Russian (Soviet)-Iranian agreements on, 283, 286–289; shelf of, 262, 282, 285, 293
Central Asian battalion, 235–236, 245
Central Asian states, 2, 14, 19, 99–100, 105, 122–124, 167–168, 174, 179–180, 214, 231, 236, 268; summits of, 33, 88, 157, 161; in Russian foreign policy debate, 57–

64, 242; in Russian military strategy, 78, 228–229, 233, 276

Central Bank: of Kazakhstan, 160, 169–170; of Russia, 156, 158–160, 162, 165–166, 169–170, 172

Cheney, Richard, 77

Chernomyrdin, Victor, 124, 143, 160, 162, 169, 173, 188, 207–208, 217, 219, 221, 224, 237, 240, 244, 263, 265–266, 272–273, 279–281, 283–284, 299

Chevron, 32, 79, 262–294, 267–270, 273, 277–278, 296

China, 34, 61, 76–78, 100, 122, 210, 218, 228, 249, 260, 262, 282, 297, 299, 308; Xinjiang region of, 79–80, 297

China National Petroleum Corporation (CNPC), 296

Citizenship, 24, 32, 89–91, 100–101, 103, 109, 117, 123, 125–136, 177, 185, 241

Cohen, William, 247

Collective security, 41–42, 70, 73, 78, 228–229, 232–233, 235–236, 240, 243–244, 247

Commonwealth of Independent States (CIS), 46, 57, 107, 112, 117–118, 120, 126, 142, 205–206, 213–214, 229–230, 266, 283; Charter of, 67, 163–164, 180, 231; common border of, 61–62, 143, 228, 232, 239–241, 243; Coordination and Consultative Committee (CCC), 161, 163, 165; Economic Council, 159–160; Interparliamentary Assembly, 177, 187; Interstate Bank, 159, 163, 165, 187; Interstate Council, 179, 191, 194–196; Interstate Economic Committee of the Economic Union (IECEU), 186, 187; joint armed forces of, 69–71, 76, 205–206, 211–212, 236; reform of, 127, 175; summits of, 65, 67, 69–70, 74, 76, 81, 83, 94, 156, 158–165, 167–168, 171, 175, 179–181, 186–187, 192, 194, 203–204, 266, 288, 290

Communist Party of Kazakhstan (CPK), 9, 14, 16, 18–21, 26; 16th Congress of, 6, 7; 17th Congress of, 25; plenums of the Central Committee, 8, 10–11, 16–17, 21–23

Communist Party of the Russian Federation (CPRF), 190, 192

Communist Party of the Soviet Union (CPSU), 8–11, 14, 16, 17, 21, 30, 34, 55; 19th Conference of, 13, 21; 27th Congress of, 4, 7–8; plenums of the Central Committee, 4, 8, 11, 13, 14, 16, 30; Politburo of, 1–2, 5, 6, 9–10, 13, 17, 25, 27, 46

Conference on Interaction and Confidence Measures in Asia (CICMA), 233–234

Conference on Security and Cooperation in Europe (CSCE), 210. See also Organisation for Security and Cooperation in Europe (OSCE)

Constitution of Kazakhstan, 31, 99–102, 105, 107, 117, 128, 132, 134–135, 137, 192, 213

Corruption in Kazakhstan, 5–8, 47, 107

Cossacks, 25–27, 38–39, 86–88, 90–91, 100, 116–123, 126, 131–132, 136–137, 140–143, 191, 193, 233

Courtney, William, 274

Customs policy, 67, 84, 127, 156–157, 161, 163, 170, 173, 175, 178, 243, 246

Customs union, 67, 164–165, 168, 171, 179, 182, 187–190, 193–196

Datov, Syrym, 101

Defence alliance, 80, 159–160, 229

Dependence on Russia, 59, 66, 155, 167, 182, 193, 234, 236, 261–262, 268, 272, 276, 295–297

Derr, Kenneth, 273

De-russification, 85, 101, 105, 108, 110–111, 117

Deuss, John, 264–265, 269–270, 273, 277

Dniester Republic, 85, 117

Dokuchaeva, Alexandra, 24, 117, 131

Dolgopolov, Anatoliy, 87, 118, 121, 132

Dungans, 100

Economic treaty, 35, 42, 44–45

Economic union, 155, 160, 163–165, 167–168, 171, 175, 179, 182, 186–188

Economy of Kazakhstan, 5–9, 20, 34, 38, 65–67, 105, 107, 155, 157, 172, 260–261

Edinstvo, 25

Education policy in Kazakhstan, 15, 18–19, 102–105, 113, 116, 123, 133, 139

Elections to Kazakhstan's parliament, 109, 120, 125–126, 133–136

Elf Aquitaine, 262

Emigration from Kazakhstan, 69, 111–116, 129, 139, 222, 229

Energy policy, 32, 66, 262–263, 274, 289, 294, 300. *See also* Oil and gas

Ethnic discrimination, 85–86, 89–90, 113–115, 120, 123

Eurasian Transportation Corridor, 298–299

Eurasian Union (EAU), 127, 175–187, 194, 229

Eurasianism (neo-Eurasianism), 29–30, 184–185

Eurasianists, 29, 52, 60–62, 73, 85–86, 158, 172, 174, 184–185

Fyodorov, Boris, 172, 191

Gabbasov, Engels, 244, 246

Gaidar, Egor, 158, 160

Gas production. *See* Oil and gas

Gazprom, 272, 279–282, 294–295

Georgia, 40, 181, 270, 275–276, 285, 296, 298

Gerashchenko, Sergey, 169–170

Gizzatov, Vyacheslav, 285, 287, 289, 293

Gorbachev, Mikhail, 62, 85; and Kunayev, 5–11, 13–17; nationalities policy, 3–5, 7, 10–17, 20–23, 30; and Nazarbayev, 6–11, 17, 22, 27, 34–40, 42, 46; new political thinking, 4; personnel policy, 1–3, 6, 10, 13–15, 17–20; reforms of, 1, 13, 22, 23; resignation of, 46; and union

treaty, 34, 35, 37–40, 42; and Yeltsin, 26–27, 29, 34–40, 42, 46

Gore, Albert, 207, 287, 298

Grachev, Pavel, 205, 212

Greece, 272

Gunkin, Nikolay, 26, 120, 131, 136, 140, 153

Human rights in Kazakhstan, 25, 41, 110, 115, 117, 119–120, 123, 127–129, 131–132, 137–138, 143, 181, 184

Immigration legislation in Kazakhstan, 24, 100

Independence, 18, 25, 30–31, 34–36, 39–41, 43, 45–46, 100–101, 105, 112, 116, 136, 139–140, 142, 155, 174, 177, 190, 192, 227, 233, 260–263, 291–292, 294

Integration, 59–61, 64, 67, 117, 119, 126, 156, 158–165, 167, 171–172, 174–181, 183, 185–196, 228, 243, 273, 278

Interethnic relations, 3, 5, 21, 23, 25–27, 41, 48, 91, 102, 110, 114–115, 124, 126, 128, 135, 138,–139, 184, 230, 243

International law, 42, 46, 90, 119, 241, 286–288, 290

International Maritime Organisation (IMO), 268, 271

International Monetary Fund (IMF), 66

Internationalism, 4, 14–16, 120

Iran, 61–64, 75, 122, 161, 167, 254, 264, 275–276, 283, 286, 288–293, 295–300

Isingarin, Nigmatzhan, 188–189, 222–223, 261

Islam, 16, 58–60, 63–64, 73, 124, 245, 284

Karimov, Islam, 168, 170, 179

Kasenov, Umirserik, 58, 233, 275–276, 284

Kazakh National University, 13, 19, 49, 102, 104, 110, 140

Kazakhstan Institute of Strategic Studies (KISI), 66, 109, 183, 260, 275

Kazakhstankaspiyshelf State Company, 266, 283–285, 298, 304

Kazhegeldin, Akezhan, 178, 188, 220, 240, 244, 275, 281

Khodakov, Alexander, 288, 230

Kolbin, Gennadiy, 10–13, 17–20, 22, 48

Kolomets, Petr, 137

Koptev, Yuri, 211, 215, 219, 224, 226

Kozyrev, Andrey, 57–58, 62–63, 75–77, 85–86, 123, 163, 181, 218, 230, 286

Kunayev, Dinmukhamed, 5–11, 13–20, 47, 108

Kyrgyzstan (Kyrgysia), 2, 32, 34, 55, 59, 64, 100, 157, 181–182, 189–190, 194, 230–232, 235–236, 239, 245, 254

Lad, 116–117, 123, 131–133

Land ownership in Kazakhstan, 99, 107–108, 121, 134, 136

Language policy in Kazakhstan, 20, 23–25, 31, 90–91, 99, 101–104, 113–114, 116–117, 123, 125–126, 133–135, 1137–139, 141–142

Liberal Democratic Party of Russia (LDPR), 29, 123–124. See also Zhirinovskiy, Vladimir

Lukashenko, Alexander, 180

LUKoil, 269, 272–273, 277–278, 282, 293, 299, 304

Majilis, 135, 153, 245. See also Parliament of Kazakhstan; Supreme Soviet of Kazakhstan

Mansurov, Tair, 92, 109, 112–113, 133, 174, 183

Marxist theory, 3–4, 15–16, 20

Matzke, Richard, 268

Migranyan, Andranik, 117–118

Mikitayev, Abdulakh, 100, 103, 109, 119, 127, 129, 132

Military doctrine, 70, 86, 216, 234, 243

Military exercises, 232, 245–246

Military Space Forces (MSF), 211–212, 215, 218–219, 221–222, 224–227

Military test ranges, 80, 204, 236–237, 239, 242, 244, 246

Mobil Oil, 277, 283

Moldova (Moldavia), 40, 52, 69, 85–86, 111, 117, 157

Monetary policy, 67, 157–158, 162, 166, 191

Monetary union, 164, 171–172

Montreux Convention, 270–271

Moscow State Institute of International Relations (MGIMO) Centre for International Studies 59, 174, 181–182

Multinational state, 24, 99 117, 133, 192

National currency: introduction of, 43, 45, 157–58, 167, 172–173; of Kazakhstan, 67, 139, 169; of Russia, 118, 122, 124, 160, 166, 170

National elites, 3–5, 35, 37, 183; Kazakh, 6, 14, 16–18, 20–22, 27, 29, 30, 105, 108, 124, 191; Russian, 27

National security: of Kazakhstan, 78, 206, 209–210, 229, 233–234, 260; of Russia, 58–59, 67, 78, 164, 244–245

Nationalism, 4, 15, 29, 184–185; Kazakh, 13, 14–17, 25, 113; Russian, 4, 27–29, 73, 85–86

Nation-state building in Kazakhstan, 116, 129, 196, 260

NATO, 42, 63, 77, 234, 236, 247

Nazarbayev, Nursultan, 60, 65–66, 68, 70–79, 81–84, 88–89, 91–92, 99, 101, 105–107, 109–113, 117, 119–120, 123–129, 131–143, 156–195, 204–212, 214–215, 217–218, 224–225, 229–231, 233–237, 240, 244–245, 247, 260, 262–263, 265, 270, 273, 275, 278, 280, 282, 284, 288, 290, 292–293, 296–299; and August 1991 coup attempt, 39–40; confirmed as President at a referendum, 132–134; elected First

Secretary of CPK, 23; and Kazakh
nationalism, 17, 23–25; as
Kazakhstan Prime Minister, 6–11;
and Kazakhstan's independence,
30, 46; role in Alma-Ata events,
14, 18
Nevada-Semipalatinsk movement, 21,
25, 26, 41
Nikolayev, Andrey, 143
Niyazov, Saparmurat, 168, 186, 293,
300
Non-Kazakh representation in ruling
bodies in Kazakhstan, 108–110
Novy Uzen riots, 22–23
Nuclear Non-Proliferation Treaty, 73,
77, 81, 204, 206–207
Nuclear weapons in Kazakhstan, 21,
25, 65, 71–80, 204–211, 237, 239

October 1993 events, 172, 216
Oil and gas, 66–67; exports of, 69,
260–263, 265, 267–270, 277–279,
281–282, 294–298; fields of, 79,
259, 261–262, 265, 269, 273–274,
278–279, 281–282, 285, 293, 297,
300–301; industry, 32, 42, 259–
263, 276, 279, 295; oil refineries,
261, 264, 267, 275, 294–297;
production of, 259–262, 265, 267,
276, 279–280, 293–295; reserves
of, 32, 259–262, 265, 267, 275,
279, 281, 283, 286, 293–295, 297–
299
Oman, 263–264, 269, 273–274, 278
Oman Oil Company (OOC), 263–264,
273–274, 276–277, 302
Organisation for Economic
Cooperation (OEC), 167–168
Organisation for Security and
Cooperation in Europe (OSCE), 4,
134, 152, 167, 233–234
Ozal, Turgut, 268

Pamyat, 27–28
Pan-Turkism, 24–25, 64
Parliament of Kazakhstan, 12, 91,
101–102, 113, 116–117, 131–133,
135, 137, 170, 172–173, 207, 220,
230, 246

Partnership for Peace program, 235–
236, 245, 247
Payments Union, 186–187
Peacekeeping, 228–233, 235–236, 245
Pena, Federico, 282, 298
Perry, William, 207, 210, 284
Persian Gulf, 228, 264, 270, 275
Pipelines, 65, 69, 261–265, 267–270,
272–282, 294–299; Uzen-Samara,
261, 267; Pavlodar-Shymkent,
261–262; Grozny-Baku, 264;
Atirau-Grozny, 264; Tengiz-
Novorossiysk, 264, 268, 270
Plesetsk, 215, 225–227
Primakov, Evgeniy, 143, 245, 292
Privatisation in Kazakhstan, 105–108,
130, 134–136

Rahmonov, Imomali, 170, 195
Rasputin, Valentin, 28
Rehabilitations in Kazakhstan, 13, 16,
21, 24
Renaming of settlements in
Kazakhstan, 91, 101, 222
Rosneft, 278, 293, 304
Rouble zone, 65, 67, 156–166, 168–
175
RSFSR Supreme Soviet, 29, 31, 63,
85, 89, 190
Russian Centre, 117, 131, 136
Russian Federal Migration Service
(RFMS), 101, 103, 108–109, 112–
113, 119, 124, 131, 140
Russian Institute of Strategic Studies
(RISI), 244
Russian interests in Central Asia, 58–
61, 63, 67, 88, 123, 126, 128, 144,
227–229, 233, 243, 245, 259, 270,
285–286, 288–289
Russian parliament, 29, 45, 63, 91,
119, 125, 158, 164–165, 172, 216,
229
Russian Space Agency (RSA), 211,
215, 219, 221–222, 224–227, 247
Russian State Duma, 99, 100–102,
105, 108, 113, 119–120, 124, 131–
132, 134, 138, 178, 190–193, 208,
224, 246, 294; Committee for CIS
Affairs, 108, 118–119, 132–133,
135, 235; hearings on Kazakhstan,

100, 103, 109, 112–113, 119, 121,
  128, 132–133, 211, 215; ratification
  of agreements, 131–132, 220, 226,
  244
Russians in Kazakhstan, 84–86, 89–
  91, 99, 104–109, 112, 117–120,
  122, 125, 127–132, 135–136, 138–
  144, 181, 185, 204, 233, 242–243,
  245–246
Russia's Federal Border Guards
  Service (RFBGS), 141–142
Rutskoy, Alexander, 41, 45, 62–63,
  84–86, 120

Sergeyev, Igor, 245–246
Shafranik, Yuriy, 266, 273–274, 277
Shaposhnikov, Evgeniy, 69–70, 76,
  205–206, 212, 230–231
Shell, 283, 298
Shevardnadze, Eduard, 296
Shokhin, Alexander, 122–123, 163,
  166, 168, 173
Sidorova, Nina, 117, 131, 136–137
Slavs, 105, 116–117, 139
Solzhenitsyn, Alexander, 28–30, 36,
  60
Soskovets, Oleg, 38, 189, 209, 212,
  223
Sovereignty, 25, 27, 30, 33–34, 38, 42,
  91, 113, 121, 140, 156, 159, 162–
  163, 170, 174, 183, 185–186, 190,
  193, 203, 213, 222, 229–230, 233–
  234, 241, 289, 291–292;
  declarations of, 31, 33, 35, 36, 39,
  40
Space Transportation Systems (STS),
  216
Stalin, Joseph, 3
Statoil, 283, 298
Strategic Arms Reduction Treaty
  (START), 78–79
Strategic Nuclear Forces (SNF), 203,
  205–206, 208–209
Suleimenov, Olzhas, 21, 25, 125
Supreme Soviet of Kazakhstan, 16–17,
  23–24, 27, 32, 38, 43, 46, 99, 101,
  109–110, 117, 120, 126, 131, 230
Suprunyuk, Boris, 119–120
Svobodnyy, 218–219, 224, 226–227,
  251

Tajikistan, 2, 32, 55, 59, 78, 80, 85,
  170, 179, 195, 214, 228, 230–232,
  235, 239
Talbott, Strobe, 298
Tashkent Treaty, 78–79, 83, 228–229,
  231, 236, 247
Tengiz, 32, 79, 262, 264, 267–268,
  272–275, 277, 279, 297, 301–302
Tengizchevroil, 79, 267, 270, 274,
  277–278, 280
Tereshchenko, Sergey, 68, 123–124,
  161, 166, 167, 171, 173, 207–208,
  212, 217, 219, 237, 261, 263–265,
  272, 279–280, 283–284
Territorial problem between Russia
  and Kazakhstan, 21, 22, 26, 27–31,
  39 41, 87–88, 116, 118, 120–121,
  126, 140–141, 233, 236, 245
Texaco, 282
Tokayev, Kosimzhomart, 143, 245,
  276
Total, 283, 298
Transneft, 267, 278
Treaties and agreements between
  Russia and Kazakhstan: on
  citizenship, 89, 127, 129–132, 242;
  economic, 34, 65, 68, 161, 166,
  169–171, 175, 178, 186–190, 265,
  272, 279, 281; military, 79–80, 83,
  204, 206–209, 211, 217–220, 236–
  243; political, 33, 83–84, 89–92
Tselinograd, 1979 events, 16, 22
Tuleyev, Aman, 107, 137, 142, 194,
  252
Turkey, 62, 64, 161, 167–168, 228,
  245, 254, 264, 268–272, 274–276,
  280, 285, 298
Turkmenistan, 2, 8, 32, 55, 100, 166,
  171, 181, 186, 229, 231, 261, 266,
  270, 275–276, 283, 285, 289–290,
  292–293, 295, 298–300

Uigurs, 100
Ukraine, 28, 33, 35, 45–46, 55, 61,
  69–71, 74, 76–79, 112, 156–157,
  159–160, 167–168, 171, 181, 204–
  206, 213–215, 217, 229
Union of People's Unity of
  Kazakhstan (UPUK), 110, 124

United Nations (UN), 4, 42, 77, 100,
179, 207, 210, 229, 233–236, 245,
263, 285, 300
United States (U.S.), 34, 63, 72, 74–
75, 77–79, 114–116, 134, 152, 207
210, 214–215, 225, 236, 244, 245,
247, 268, 277, 282, 284–286, 289,
297–298, 304
USSR, 57–60, 62–65, 69, 74, 76–78,
81, 84–86, 89, 105, 112, 118, 123,
130, 155–156, 158, 164, 173, 177,
183, 190, 205–206, 218, 228, 259–
261, 268, 283, 286, 288, 290–291,
294–295; Congresses of Peoples'
Deputies, 22, 28, 30, 42;
disintegration of, 1, 14, 18, 28, 36,
39, 41; Supreme Soviet of, 9, 40,
41, 291
Uzbekistan, 2–3, 5, 19, 32, 38, 46, 55,
59, 123, 157, 162, 170, 179, 182,
189, 230–232, 235–236, 245, 261,
266

Vozrozhdenie, 26

White, William, 275
World Bank, 65–66, 269, 273

Yakovlev, Alexander, 2, 4, 47
Yeltsin, Boris, 35–37, 40–44, 57, 61–
63, 68, 71, 75, 81, 83, 127–128,
156, 159, 164–165, 204–206, 212,
216–217, 226–229, 231, 235, 237,
247, 259–260, 269, 278, 285, 291–
293, 300; and CIS integration, 159,
163–165, 171–172, 174–175, 178–
181, 186, 189–191, 193–194, 196;
and ethnic Russians in the CIS
states, 85–88, 118–120, 122–124;
meetings and correspondence with
Nazarbayev, 32–34, 38–39, 45–46,
71, 78, 91, 127, 141–143, 162–163,
170, 190, 194, 211, 214, 218, 240,
273; and Russian minority in
Kazakhstan, 74, 84–85, 89; and
Russian nationalism, 27–29, 38;

Zatulin, Konstantin, 108–109, 112,
125–126, 132
Zheltoksan, 24, 26, 89, 110
Zhirinovskiy, Vladimir, 29, 123, 124,
182

About the Author

MIKHAIL ALEXANDROV works as a consultant for government and business organizations in Australia. Originally from Russia, as a member of the Evaluation and Planning Division of the Ministry of Foreign Affairs, he participated in developing new approaches to foreign policy which led to the abolishment of ideological confrontation between East and West.

ISBN 0-313-30965-5

9 780313 309656

HARDCOVER BAR CODE

CROWDING
AND BEHAVIOR

ALSO BY JONATHAN L. FREEDMAN

DEVIANCY
(with Anthony N. Doob)

SOCIAL PSYCHOLOGY
(with J. Merrill Carlsmith and David O. Sears)

CROWDING

JONATHAN L. FREEDMAN